Encountering
the Old Testament

To Susan and Yvonne
with love
Proverbs 31:10

Encountering Biblical Studies
Walter A. Elwell, General and New Testament Editor
Eugene H. Merrill, Old Testament Editor

Encountering the Old Testament: A Christian Survey
Bill T. Arnold and Bryan E. Beyer

Readings from the Ancient Near East:
Primary Sources for Old Testament Study
Bill T. Arnold and Bryan E. Beyer, editors

Encountering the New Testament:
A Historical and Theological Survey
Walter A. Elwell and Robert W. Yarbrough

Readings from the First-Century World:
Primary Sources for New Testament Study
Walter A. Elwell and Robert W. Yarbrough, editors

Encountering the Old Testament

A Christian Survey

Bill T. Arnold

and Bryan E. Beyer

Baker Books

A Division of Baker Book House Co
Grand Rapids, Michigan 49516

Designed by Peter Wyart, Three's Company, and
Dan Malda, Baker Book House Company

Worldwide coedition organized and
produced by
Angus Hudson Ltd,
Concorde House, Grenville Place,
Mill Hill, London NW7 3SA, England
Tel: +44 181 959 3668
Fax +44 181 959 3678

Printed in Singapore

Picture Acknowledgements

Illustrations
Alan Parry: pp. 121, 145, 151, 227, 306, 330, 389

Photographs
Bible Scene Slide Tours: pp. 132, 135
British Museum: 25, 55, 81, 159, 163, 241, 244, 245,
246, 255, 258, 264, 284, 338, 343, 349, 371, 399, 429,
457
Tim Dowley: pp. 39, 50, 65, 95, 118, 136, 142, 162,
168, 170, 174, 189, 198, 201, 204, 211, 217, 223, 225,
232, 239, 253, 271, 295, 305, 309, 320, 328, 332, 401,
413, 419, 443, 452, 467, 469
Jamie Simson: pp. 67, 90, 252, 254, 281, 345, 433
Peter Wyart: pp. 3, 26, 27, 62, 97, 105, 155, 156, 177,
182, 183, 185, 187, 197, 203, 243, 257, 269, 279, 283,
290, 293, 294, 297, 314, 327, 337, 355, 361, 377, 387,
397, 408, 413
Zev Radovan: pp. 373, 459

For information about academic books, resources
for Christian leaders, and all new releases from
Baker Book House, visit our web site:

http://www.bakerbooks.com

Library of Congress Cataloging-in-Publication Data

Arnold, Bill T.
    Encountering the Old Testament : a Christian survey / Bill T. Arnold and Bryan E. Beyer.
        p.   cm. — (Encountering biblical studies)
    Includes bibliographical references and indexes.
    ISBN 0-8010-2176-6 (hardcover)
    1. Bible. O.T.—Introductions. I. Beyer, Bryan. II. Title. III. Series.
    BS1140.2.A75   1998
    221.6'1—dc21   98-18612

Contents in Brief

Contents

Editor's Preface

The strength of the church and the vitality of the individual Christian's life are directly related to the role Scripture plays in them. Early believers knew the importance of this and spent their time in fellowship, prayer, and the study of God's Word. The passing of two thousand years has not changed the need, but it has changed the accessibility of many of the Bible's ideas. Time has distanced us from those days, and we often need guidance back into the world of the Old and New Testaments.

To that end Baker Book House is producing two separate but related series of biblical textbooks. The design of these new series is to put us back into the world of the biblical text, so that we may understand it as those early believers did and at the same time see it from and for our own day, thus facilitating the application of its truths to our contemporary situation.

Encountering Biblical Studies consists of undergraduate-level texts, and two surveys treating the Old and New Testaments provide the foundation for this series. Accompanying these survey texts are two collateral volumes of readings, which illuminate the world surrounding the biblical text. Built on these basic survey texts are upper-level college texts covering the books of the Bible that are most frequently offered in the curriculum of Christian colleges.

A related series, entitled Engaging Biblical Studies, provides graduate-level treatments for introduction and theology courses.

Complementing both levels of textbooks is a set of standard reference books that may be consulted for answers to specific questions or more in-depth study of biblical ideas. These reference books include *The Evangelical Commentary on the Bible, Topical Analysis of the Bible, Baker Encyclopedia of the Bible, Evangelical Dictionary of Biblical Theology,* and *Evangelical Dictionary of Theology.*

Encountering and Engaging Biblical Studies series are written from an evangelical point of view, in the firm conviction that the Scripture is absolutely true and never misleads us. It is the sure foundation on which our faith and life may be built because it unerringly leads willing readers to Jesus Christ.

Walter A. Elwell
General Editor

Publisher's Preface

Bible courses must be considered the heart of the curriculum for Christian colleges and evangelical seminaries. For Christians the Bible constitutes the basis for both our spiritual and our intellectual lives—indeed for all of life. If these courses are fundamental to Christian education, then the textbooks used for these courses could not be more crucial.

Baker Book House is launching two separate but related series of volumes for college- and seminary-level Bible courses. Encountering Biblical Studies consists of undergraduate texts, while Engaging Biblical Studies represents graduate-level treatments.

In these two series, Baker will publish texts that are clearly college-level, and introductory and biblical theology texts that are explicitly seminary-level. The textbooks for the basic college survey courses and for the more advanced college courses on individual Bible books will be designed expressly for this purpose. They will not be written for laypeople or pastors and seminarians, nor will they be primarily reference books. Rather, they will be pedagogically oriented textbooks written with collegians in mind.

Texts for the seminary courses in Old Testament and New Testament introduction and biblical theology will induct the student into graduate-level study of the Testaments, even while remembering that many seminarians are preparing for ministry rather than for further graduate study and a career in academia.

Guiding Principles

Encountering the Old Testament: A Christian Survey is the second volume to be published in the college-level Encountering Biblical Studies series. As part of the process of developing this volume, the series editors, authors, and publisher established the following principles for this basic-level college text:

1. It must reflect the finest evangelical scholarship of our day.
2. It must be written at a level that most of today's college freshmen can understand. While this level should not be so low as to constitute a "dumbing down" of the text, it must be within the reach of most students.
3. It must be pedagogically sound. This extends not only to traditional concerns like study questions for each chapter, but also to the order and manner in which material is presented.
4. It must recognize that most students today are oriented more to the visual than to the verbal, and seek to take advantage of that fact with photographs, maps, charts, and graphs.
5. It must be realistic about the level of biblical literacy achieved by most incoming freshmen.
6. It must seek to draw in the student, in part by focusing on biblical teaching concerning crucial doctrinal and ethical matters.
7. It must be as flexible as possible, which means that a paperback supplement will be provided. This supplement contains primary source readings from the ancient world that some professors prefer to skip and others would not do without.

Goals

The goals for *Encountering the Old Testament* fall into two categories: intellectual and attitudinal. The intellectual goals are to (1) present the factual content of each book of the Old Testament, (2) introduce historical, geographical, and cultural backgrounds, (3) outline primary hermeneutical principles, (4) touch on critical issues (e.g., why some people read the Bible differently), and (5) substantiate the Christian faith.

The attitudinal goals are also fivefold: (1) to make the Bible a part of students' lives, (2) to instill in students a love for the Scriptures, (3) to make them better people, (4) to enhance their piety, and (5) to stimulate their love for God. In short, if this text builds a foundation for a lifetime of Bible study, the authors and publisher will be amply rewarded.

Overarching Themes

Controlling the writing of *Encountering the Old Testament* have been three essential theological themes: God, people, and the gospel as it relates to individuals. The notion that God is a person—one and three—and a transcendent and immanent Being has been woven throughout the text. Moreover, this God has created people in his image who are fallen but still the objects of his redemptive love. The gospel is the means, the active personal power that God uses to rescue people from darkness and death. But the gospel does more than rescue—it restores. It confers on otherwise hopeless sinners the resolve and strength to live lives that please God, because they walk in the love that comes from God.

Features

The publisher's aim has been to provide an exceptionally unique resource on the one hand but not merely trendy on the other. Whether or not we have been successful remains for others to judge. Nevertheless some of the distinguishing features we hope will prove helpful to the professor and inspiring to the student include the following:

- Multimedia interactive compact disc to enhance the student's learning experience.
- Numerous illustrations, photographs, figures, tables, charts—all in full color.
- Sidebars providing two types of material. Yellow-colored boxes succinctly explore ethical and theological issues of interest and concern to modern-day collegians. Blue-colored boxes provide primary source material, including biblical and extrabiblical texts.
- Chapter outline and objectives presented at the opening of each chapter.
- Study questions, annotated bibliography, and chapter summaries at the end of each chapter.

- Ancillary items: teacher's manual, test bank, transparencies, and other items.

Supplementary Materials

Three items supplement *Encountering the Old Testament*. The first item, the instructor's manual, is available on a floppy disc, the second is a compact disc attached to the back of the book, and the third is a paperback volume.

1. Instructor's Resource Manual with Test Items. In addition to including only objective-type test items, this resource includes suggestions in using the textbook, chapter outlines, chapter objectives, chapter summaries, key terms, master transparencies, lecture outlines, and media resources.

2. Student's Multimedia Interactive CD-ROM. Developed by biblical scholar Chris Miller and educational specialist Phil Bassett, this product provides

   - video clips of interviews with the authors
   - video clips of biblical lands
   - still photos of biblical lands
   - maps
   - interactive review questions
   - visual organizers

3. *Readings from the Ancient Near East: Primary Sources for Old Testament Study*. This is a collection of primary source readings related to the Old Testament. These readings are arranged in canonical order. This volume provides translations of ancient Near Eastern documents that are useful to read hand-in-hand with the Old Testament.

The publisher is also convinced that this textbook should be as pedagogically sound as possible and that it should reflect the best insights from educational psychology. Educational consultant Janet Merrill, Ed.D., brought her expertise to bear and improved this project significantly. The publisher extends heartfelt thanks to Dr. Merrill for so capably preparing the instructor's manual, test items, transparencies, chapter objectives, and chapter summaries.

The publisher believes it is essential to obtain extensive input from professors who teach Old Testament survey courses in colleges throughout the nation. So it has surveyed teachers from approximately fifty colleges. The results of these surveys have been compiled and have been referred to continually throughout the process of conceiving, writing, and producing this textbook.

Some of the professors who participated in the surveys agreed to serve as advisory board members. The publisher wishes to thank the following members for their exceptionally helpful advice in shaping *Encountering the Old Testament.*

R. Jerome Boone
Lee University

Stephen Bramer
Briercrest Bible College

Raymond W. Clark
Covenant College

Daniel Doriani
Covenant Theological
Seminary

Hobert Farrell
LeTourneau University

Michael Holmes
Bethel College

David K. Johnson
Northwestern College

George L. Klein
Criswell College

Mark D. McLean
Evangel College

Glenn Schaefer
Simpson College

Carl Schultz
Houghton College

Andrew L. Smith
Cornerstone College

Robert D. Spender
The King's College

Gerald H. Wilson
George Fox College

Marvin Wilson
Gordon College

Alan Neal Winkler
Bryan College

William J. Woodruff
Olivet Nazarene University

Chris Miller and Phil Bassett of Cedarville College in Ohio developed the multimedia interactive CD-ROM with skill and alacrity. Dr. Miller is not only a trained biblical scholar with a Ph.D. degree from Dallas Theological Seminary but also an outstanding teacher with unusual computer savvy. Dr. Bassett provided extensive educational consulting.

To the Professor

This book targets an undergraduate audience, especially freshmen. We realize that many who use it will be taking their first course on this topic, while others have come from Christian high schools where Bible was part of the curriculum. This survey has material that will satisfy both audiences. We have also provided a glossary that clarifies difficult terms with which the reader may be unfamiliar. Study questions at the end of each chapter guide the reader and bring key points of the chapter into focus. Finally, a "Further Reading" list at the end of each chapter provides suggestions for the student who wants more information on any given topic. We hope to stretch students' thinking, whatever their background.

The underlying slant of this book is broadly evangelical. We believe the Scriptures not only spoke to their original audience, but that they continue to speak to us today. At the same time, we recognize that people from many Christian denominations will use this book. Consequently, when we discuss issues on which evangelicals have agreed to disagree, we have often chosen to survey the basic interpretations and let the particular emphasis lie with the professor.

The survey follows the canonical order of the English Bible. We have found through our research that most teachers prefer this. However, the chapter divisions make it easy for one to follow either a canonical or chronological approach.

Outlines for each Old Testament book are taken (with some modification) from the *Evangelical Commentary on the Bible*, ed. Walter Elwell (Grand Rapids: Baker, 1989). Readers seeking verse-by-verse commentary not provided by this survey may be referred to this volume for further study.

Baker Books has worked with us to produce a well-illustrated survey. Illustrative material such as charts, maps, and graphs comprise approximately 20 percent of the volume. The color format makes the book more "user-friendly" to a generation that has experienced much in the way of technological improvement. We want to give students the feeling that "they are there" as much as possible, to help them see the images the Bible so carefully paints.

We have also highlighted the relevance of the Old Testament by placing strategic "sidebars" within the text. These sidebars apply the text directly to pertinent issues of today. They help the reader understand that the Bible spoke not only then, but still speaks today. To this end, we have also interwoven application material as appropriate in the body of the text.

It is our hope and prayer that this book will help you gain a deeper love and appreciation for the message that impacts every one of us—the message of the Bible.

Ethical and theological issues

Primary source material

Focus Box: key issues and relevant applications

Key terms, people, and places

Study questions

Further Reading

To the Student

Encountering the Old Testament in a systematic way for the first time is an exciting experience. It can also be overwhelming because there is so much to learn. You need to learn not only the content of the Old Testament but also a good deal about the Near Eastern world.

The purpose of this textbook is to make that encounter a little less daunting. To accomplish this a number of learning aids have been incorporated into the text. We suggest you familiarize yourself with this textbook by reading the following introductory material, which explains what learning aids have been provided.

Sidebars

Material in yellow-colored boxes isolates contemporary issues of concern and shows how the Old Testament speaks to these pressing ethical and theological issues. Some of these boxes contain quotes from various authors, whether ancient or modern, whose thoughts shed light on the Old Testament material under discussion.

Chapter Outlines

At the beginning of each chapter is a brief outline of the chapter's contents. *Study Suggestion:* Before reading the chapter, take a few minutes to read the outline. Think of it as a road map, and remember that it is easier to reach your destination if you know where you are going.

Chapter Objectives

A brief list of objectives is placed at the outset of each chapter. These present the tasks you should be able to perform after reading the chapter. *Study Suggestions:* Read the objectives carefully before beginning to read the text. As you read the text, keep these objectives in mind and take notes to help you remember what you have read. After reading the chapter, return to the objectives and see if you can perform the tasks.

Summary

A list of statements summarizing the content of each chapter can be found at the end of each chapter. *Study Suggestion:* Use this summary list to conduct an immediate review of what you have just read.

Key Terms and Glossary

Key terms have been identified throughout the text by the use of boldface type. This will alert you to important words or phrases you may not be familiar with. A definition of these words will be found in the glossary at the end of the book and on the interactive CD-ROM. *Study Suggestion:* When you encounter a key term in the text, stop and read the definition before continuing through the chapter.

Key People and Places

While studying the Old Testament you will be introduced to many names and places. Those that are particularly significant have been set in SMALL CAPS. *Study Suggestion:* Pay careful attention to the people and places as you read the text. When studying for a test, skim the text and stop at each SMALL CAPPED term to see if you know its importance to the Old Testament.

Study Questions

A few discussion questions have been provided at the end of each chapter, and these can be used to review for examinations. *Study Suggestion:* Write suitable answers to the study questions in preparation for tests.

Further Reading

A short bibliography for supplementary reading is presented at each chapter's conclusion. *Study Suggestion:* Use the suggested reading list to explore areas of special interest.

Visual Aids

A host of illustrations in the form of photographs, maps, and charts have been included in this textbook. Each illustration

Abbreviations

Old Testament

Genesis	Gn
Exodus	Ex
Leviticus	Lv
Numbers	Nm
Deuteronomy	Dt
Joshua	Jos
Judges	Jgs
Ruth	Ru
1 Samuel	1 Sm
2 Samuel	2 Sm
1 Kings	1 Kgs
2 Kings	2 Kgs
1 Chronicles	1 Chr
2 Chronicles	2 Chr
Ezra	Ezr
Nehemiah	Neh
Esther	Est
Job	Jb
Psalms	Ps(s)
Proverbs	Prv
Ecclesiastes	Eccl
Song of Songs	Song
Isaiah	Is
Jeremiah	Jer
Lamentations	Lam
Ezekiel	Ez

Daniel	Dn
Hosea	Hos
Joel	Jl
Amos	Am
Obadiah	Ob
Jonah	Jon
Micah	Mi
Nahum	Na
Habakkuk	Hb
Zephaniah	Zep
Haggai	Hg
Zechariah	Zec
Malachi	Mal

Old Testament Apocrypha

Tobit	Tb
Judith	Jdt
Wisdom	Wis
Baruch	Bar
Sirach	Sir
1 Maccabees	1 Mc
2 Maccabees	2 Mc

New Testament

Matthew	Mt
Mark	Mk
Luke	Lk
John	Jn
Acts of the Apostles	Acts
Romans	Rom
1 Corinthians	1 Cor
2 Corinthians	2 Cor
Galatians	Gal
Ephesians	Eph
Philippians	Phil
Colossians	Col
1 Thessalonians	1 Thes
2 Thessalonians	2 Thes
1 Timothy	1 Tm
2 Timothy	2 Tm
Titus	Ti
Philemon	Phlm
Hebrews	Heb
James	Jas
1 Peter	1 Pt
2 Peter	2 Pt
1 John	1 Jn
2 John	2 Jn
3 John	3 Jn
Jude	Jude
Revelation	Rv

has been carefully selected, and each is intended not only to make the text more aesthetically pleasing but also more easily mastered.

May your encounter of the Old Testament be an exciting adventure!

Acknowledgments

It may be of interest to know how the writing assignments were distributed and which author wrote individual chapters. Most chapters were assigned according to previous publications and interests of the authors. Dr. Arnold wrote the introductory chapter on history and geography (chapter 2), all the chapters on the Pentateuch (chapters 3–9) and the Historical Books except Joshua and the Books of Samuel (chapters 10, 12, and 15–18). He also is responsible for the chapters on Job, Proverbs, Ecclesiastes, Song of Songs, Daniel, and the Epilogue (chapters 20, 22–23, and 31). Dr. Beyer wrote the introductory chapter on the origin and inspiration of the Old Testament (chapter 1) and the chapters on Joshua and the Books of Samuel (chapters 11 and 13–14). In addition to the Poetical Books introduction (chapter 19), he wrote on the Psalms (chapter 21), and all the chapters on the Prophets except Daniel (chapters 24–30 and 32–34).

The people at Baker Book House have been most helpful and encouraging throughout the production of this book, and we are grateful for their professionalism and encouragement. We would especially like to thank Jim Weaver and Maria denBoer. We also would like to thank our editor, Dr. Eugene Merrill. We have appreciated his scholarly assistance.

We also owe a great debt of gratitude to many who have helped with the preparation of this manuscript. In particular, we have both benefited from student assistants or secretaries who have helped with the manuscript of this book in a variety of ways. Dr. Arnold's assistants were Joel R. Soza, Michael K. West, and Robert W. Wilcher; Dr. Beyer's were Cheryl Brannan, Chandra Briggman, and Judy Peinado.

Finally, we especially want to thank our wives, Susan Arnold and Yvonne Beyer, who have faithfully loved and supported us with each step. As the words of Proverbs 31:10–31 ring in our ears, we gratefully dedicate this book to them.

1 What Is the Old Testament and Why Study It?

Outline

- **Canon: What Is the Bible?**
  Definition of "Canon"
  Tests for Canonicity
  The Formation of the Canon
  Hebrew and English Book Order
- **Inspiration:**
  How Was the Bible Written?
  Neo-Orthodox Theory
  Dictation Theory
  Limited Inspiration Theory
  Plenary Verbal Inspiration Theory
- **Textual Transmission:**
  How Did We Get the Bible?
  Scribal Care of the Old Testament Text
  Transmission in the Original Languages
  Transmission in Other Languages
- **Hermeneutics:**
  How Do We Interpret the Bible
  Use the Grammatical-Historical Method
  Understand the Context
  Determine the Type of Literature
  Interpret Figurative Language
  Let Scripture Interpret Scripture
  Discover the Application to Modern Life

Objectives

**After reading this chapter,
you should be able to**

- Compare the tests for canonicity
- Evaluate the most common theories
  of inspiration
- Give illustrations of textual transmission
- Explain the importance of the scribe
  in textual transmission
- List the considerations that are important
  in interpreting the Old Testament

apocryphal

canon

"Get your facts straight," I remember my high school English teacher telling us. "The most important questions you can ask are who, what, when, where, why, and how."

That was good advice for writing a research paper. It's also good advice for studying the Bible. Most students would not try to write a research paper without knowing the basic facts. Neither should we begin to study the Old Testament before learning some basic facts about it.

This chapter deals with four foundational questions every student of the Old Testament should be able to answer. What is the Bible? How was the Bible written? How did we get the Bible? How do we interpret the Bible? We will focus especially on the answers to those questions for the Old Testament.

Canon: What Is the Bible?

At first, this question sounds simple. We know what the Bible is. It's a collection of sixty-six books—thirty-nine in the Old Testament, twenty-seven in the New Testament. It's Genesis all the way to the Book of Revelation.

But people have not always agreed exactly which books comprise the Bible. For example, do the **apocryphal** books—the extra books found in Roman Catholic Bibles—belong in the Bible? What if an archaeologist should discover another letter the apostle Paul wrote? Should *that* letter go in the Bible? How did Jews and Christians first decide which books belonged in the Bible? When we raise questions such as these, we raise the issue of **canon**.

Definition of "Canon"

The word "canon" comes from the Hebrew word *qāneh* and the Greek word *kanōn*. Both words originally signified a reed or measuring stick. Just as a reed could serve as a measuring standard, so the biblical canon was a measuring standard for faith and practice. People could compare their lives to what the Bible required.[1] Furthermore, the word "canon" could denote a standard to which the biblical writings themselves must conform.

Tests for Canonicity

As God revealed his word through ordinary people, it became important to know which books came from him and which books only reflected human opinion. A consensus emerged as to what constituted proper tests for canonicity. The tests focused on three factors: author, audience, and teaching.

Test #1: Written by a prophet or prophetically gifted person

A book that was part of the canon had to be written by a prophet or prophetically gifted person. Human authors could never know God's will apart from God's Spirit assisting their understanding. The Spirit of God had to have his hand on the writing process. His presence insured the finished product was God's truth and accurately communicated God's message.

Test #2: Written to all generations

A book that was part of the canon had to impact all generations. God's message could not be confined to one audience. If a book was God's word, it must be relevant to all people of all times. The author might have written the work for a particular audience, but if it was God's Word, all who read it could profitably apply its teachings to their lives.

Test #3: Written in accord with previous revelation

A book that was part of the canon could not contradict the messages of earlier writings God had revealed. For example, if a new writing claimed to be from God but contradicted the teachings of Genesis, it could not be God's Word. God's truth remained the same and would not contradict itself. New revelation could reveal further information about God's plan and purposes, but it would never run counter to the old.

The Formation of the Canon

By applying the above principles, the Hebrew people more or less determined which books belonged in the Old Testament and which books did not. Nevertheless, some confusion existed among the general population. On certain occasions, Jewish leaders met to address this and other issues. One such meeting apparently

Chart of Old Testament Book Order

Hebrew names for the books	Hebrew arrangement and classification		English arrangement and classification		Approximate dates concerned
In the beginning		Genesis	Genesis		The Beginning
These are the names		Exodus	Exodus		
And he called	Torah	Leviticus	Leviticus	Law	to
In the wilderness		Numbers	Numbers	(Pentateuch)	ca. 1400 B.C.
These are the words		Deuteronomy	Deuteronomy		
Joshua		Joshua	Joshua		1400–1380 B.C.
Judges		Judges	Judges		1380–1050 B.C.
1 Samuel	Former	1 Samuel	Ruth		1200–1150 B.C.
2 Samuel	Prophets	2 Samuel	1 Samuel		1100–1010 B.C.
1 Kings		1 Kings	2 Samuel		1010–971 B.C.
2 Kings		2 Kings	1 Kings	History	971–853 B.C.
			2 Kings		853–560 B.C.
Isaiah		Isaiah	1 Chronicles		1010–971 B.C.
Jeremiah		Jeremiah	2 Chronicles		971–539 B.C.
Ezekiel		Ezekiel	Ezra		539–450 B.C.
Hosea		Hosea	Nehemiah		445–410 B.C.
Joel		Joel	Esther		483–474 B.C.
Amos		Amos			
Obadiah		Obadiah	Job		
Jonah		Jonah	Psalms		
Micah	Latter	Micah	Proverbs	Poetry	No specific historical
Nahum	Prophets	Nahum	Ecclesiastes	and	period covered
Habakkuk		Habakkuk	Song of Solomon	Wisdom	
Zephaniah		Zephaniah			
Haggai		Haggai	Isaiah		739–530 B.C.
Zechariah		Zechariah	Jeremiah	Major	627–580 B.C.
Malachi		Malachi	Lamentations	prophets	586 B.C.
			Ezekiel		593–570 B.C.
Praises		Psalms	Daniel		605–530 B.C.
Job		Job			
Proverbs		Proverbs	Hosea		760–730 B.C.
Ruth		Ruth	Joel		500 B.C.
Song of Songs		Song of Solomon	Amos		760 B.C.
The Preacher		Ecclesiastes	Obadiah		586 B.C.
How!	The	Lamentations	Jonah	Minor	770 B.C.
Esther	writings	Esther	Micah	prophets	740–700 B.C.
Daniel	(Hagiographa)	Daniel	Nahum		650 B.C.
Ezra		Ezra	Habakkuk		605 B.C.
Nehemiah		Nehemiah	Zephaniah		627 B.C.
1 The words of the days		1 Chronicles	Haggai		520 B.C.
2 The words of the days		2 Chronicles	Zechariah		520–518 B.C.
			Malachi		470–460 B.C.

occurred in JAMNIA toward the close of the first century A.D.

The Council of Jamnia

Jamnia (modern Yavneh) is located on the southwestern coast of Israel. The city became an important center of influence in the Jewish community after Jerusalem fell to the Romans in A.D. 70.

Scholars debate exactly what took place at Jamnia, but agree the council did not determine which books belonged in the Old Testament. Rather, it appears to have officially confirmed books most had recognized for generations. In other words, the council officially endorsed certain books, but only confirmed what they believed had been true all along.[2]

Hebrew and English Book Order

Hebrew and English Old Testaments contain the same material. However, the books appear in a different order. We do not know why. The chart above provides a comparison.

The Hebrew version divides the books into three groups: the Law, the Prophets, and the Writings. The English divides the books into five groups: Law, historical books, poetical books, Major Prophets, and Minor Prophets.

Inspiration: How Was the Bible Written?

How exactly did God's Spirit work with the human authors to inspire the sacred writings? When we raise this question, we raise the issue of inspiration.

The Bible affirms its inspiration in many places. Note, for example, Paul's words in 2 Timothy 3:16 (NIV): "All Scripture is God-breathed and is useful for teaching, rebuking, correcting and training in righteousness." Clearly, this verse affirms God as the Author of all Scripture.

Unfortunately, the Bible does not describe exactly how God inspired the human writers. What role did the human authors play in the writing of Scripture? To what extent did God's Spirit give them freedom to write in their own ways? Those who have examined the Scriptures to solve this problem have proposed many theories. Four of the most common appear below.

Neo-Orthodox Theory

Summary

Neo-orthodoxy was born in the early twentieth century, partly as a reaction to liberalism's disregard for divine authority. Karl Barth and Emil Brunner are two of its leading proponents.[3]

Neo-orthodoxy holds that God is utterly **transcendent**; that is, he is absolutely different from us and far beyond our comprehension. We can only know something about him if he reveals himself to us, as he did in Jesus Christ.

One important difference between neo-orthodoxy and **evangelicalism** is that whereas evangelicalism holds that the Bible *is* the word of God, neo-orthodoxy asserts that the Bible is *a witness to* the word of God or *contains* the word of God. As people of biblical times experienced God,

they recorded their encounters as best they could. But because they were finite creatures, sometimes their reports contained paradoxes or errors. Nevertheless, their descriptions help others understand God better. And as others experience God afresh through these accounts, the accounts become God's word all over again.

Evaluation

We commend neo-orthodoxy for its high view of God. However, the Bible is more than a witness to God's word. It *is* God's word, as it testifies (2 Tm 3:16–17). The Bible claims that as God revealed himself, people inspired by the Holy Spirit recorded his message (2 Pt 1:20–21). They could do so because God accommodated himself to their limited understanding. Neo-orthodoxy thus fails to provide an adequate explanation for all the biblical evidence.

Dictation Theory

Summary

The **dictation theory**, as the term implies, suggests God simply dictated the Bible to human scribes. God chose certain individuals to record his word and gave them the exact words he wanted. The writers wrote only what God dictated to them. This view generally has not appeared in print, but is popular in certain segments of conservative Christianity.

Evaluation

Scripture does suggest that sometimes God may have communicated a precise, word-for-word message to human authors (Jer 26:2; Rv 2:1, 8). At other times, he allowed writers to express their own personalities as they wrote (Gal 1:6; 3:1; Phil 1:3, 4, 8). Still, the Holy Spirit insured the finished work accurately communicated God's intention. Thus, the dictation theory accounts for some of the biblical evidence, but not all.

Limited Inspiration Theory

Summary

The limited inspiration view holds that God inspired the thoughts of the biblical writers, but not necessarily the words they chose.[4] God guided the writers as they wrote, but gave them the freedom to ex-

Lion and lioness relief, Nineveh, ca. 645 B.C. Jesus' words in Matthew 12:41 imply the Book of Jonah is more than simply a parable.

plenary verbal inspiration

press his thoughts in their own ways. Because the writers had this freedom, the historical details they wrote may contain errors. However, the Holy Spirit protected the doctrinal portions of Scripture from any error to safeguard God's message of salvation.

Evaluation

The limited inspiration view recognizes that Scripture contains certain statements that are hard to reconcile. But is the best solution to admit error? The Bible places great emphasis on historical detail. For example, Paul's argument in Romans 5:12–21 requires belief in a historical Adam. Jesus' words in Matthew 12:41 imply the Book of Jonah is not simply a parable; rather, a real prophet named Jonah actually preached to the Ninevites. And archaeological finds have often resolved alleged problems in the biblical record. It seems best, therefore, to affirm the trustworthiness of the entire Bible as we await further evidence to clarify the difficulties.

Plenary Verbal Inspiration Theory

Summary

Like the other views, **plenary verbal inspiration** asserts the Holy Spirit interacted with human writers to produce the Bible. The words "plenary" and "verbal" de-

scribe the particular meaning this view gives to inspiration.[5]

"Plenary" means "full" or "complete." Plenary inspiration asserts that God's inspiration extends to all of Scripture, from Genesis to Revelation. God guided the writers no less when they recorded historical details than when they discussed doctrinal matters.

"Verbal" refers to the words of Scripture. Verbal inspiration means God's inspiration extends to the very words the writers chose. But it is not the same as the dictation theory. The writers could have chosen other words, and God often allowed them the freedom to express their own personalities as they wrote. But the Holy Spirit so guided the process that the words they chose accurately conveyed the meaning God intended.

Plenary verbal inspiration thus holds that God inspired the entire Bible. Inspiration extended to the very words the writers chose, but God gave the writers some freedom to write according to their distinct styles and personalities. At the same time, he guided the process in such a way that the finished product faithfully reflected his message.

Evaluation

The plenary verbal inspiration view seems to deal best with all the biblical evidence. It recognizes the human element in Scrip-

transcription

masora

ture, and allows that different writers wrote in different ways. But it also affirms the Holy Spirit as the Bible's ultimate Author. The Spirit prompted human authors to communicate God's message of love and salvation to a world that desperately needed it.

Implications of plenary verbal inspiration

The doctrine of plenary verbal inspiration has important implications for Christians today. First, it means the Bible is trustworthy. We can trust it to provide reliable information. It provides many insights into the history of God's people and also describes God's plan for the world and for our lives. It reveals life's highest meaning, and tells us how to become all God wants us to be. We may trust it in all it affirms.

Early manuscripts of Bible texts were written on scrolls like this.

Second, plenary verbal inspiration means the Bible is authoritative. Because it is God's word, it speaks with God's authority. It calls us to read it, to understand its implications, and to submit to it. And it remains God's truth whether or not we choose to submit. The Bible sets before us two choices: to obey God's will or to oppose it. God's servant Moses called God's word life itself (Dt 32:47). What will *you* choose to call it?

Textual Transmission: How Did We Get the Bible?

We can read the Bible today because of the faithful work of many individuals over several generations. These individuals, called scribes, copied God's word by hand, taking great care to maintain its accuracy.

Scribal Care of the Old Testament Text

The scribe in the ancient world

Scribes played a crucial role in the ancient world.[6] Faithful **transmission** of accurate information was an important aspect of society. Kings counted on scribes to record royal edicts. Administrative officials needed scribes to record significant business transactions. Mistakes could have serious implications—political, economic, or otherwise.

The ancient scribes who copied the biblical texts believed they were copying the very words of God. Consequently, they took great care to preserve the copies they had received. One of the most important groups of scribes was the Masoretes.

The Masoretes

The Masoretes (A.D. 500–1000) worked to preserve the Old Testament text they had received.[7] They wanted to ensure an accurate understanding of the text and its faithful transmission to subsequent generations. They received their name from the **masora**, a complex system of markings they developed to achieve their purpose.

The Masoretes took three steps to ensure textual accuracy. First, they developed a system for writing vowels. Until

A shepherd boy accidentally discovered the first of the Dead Sea Scrolls in a cave in cliffs above Qumran, near the Dead Sea, in 1947. Archaeologists subsequently explored nearby caves and found more scrolls.

Torah

Aramaic

Akkadian

Amorite

Phoenician

Ugaritic

Ammonite

Moabite

Arabic

Masoretic Text

Samaritan Pentateuch

Dead Sea Scrolls

this time, written Hebrew contained only consonants, though a few consonants were sometimes used to indicate certain vowels. The Masoretes developed this vowel system to preserve in written form the oral tradition they had received from earlier generations.

Second, the Masoretes developed a system of accents for the Hebrew text. These accents assisted the reader in pronouncing the text, but also showed the relationship of various words and phrases in a sentence to each other. Thus, they helped clarify many difficult passages.

Third, the Masoretes developed a system of detailed notes on the text. These notes provided a means to check the accuracy of a copied text. Today, we can produce identical manuscripts on a computer or copier, but the Masoretes had to produce them by hand!

The Hebrew word for "scribe" means "counter," and the Masoretes counted everything in the text. They knew, for example, that the **Torah**—the first five books of the Old Testament—contained 400,945 letters! They knew the Torah's middle word was the Hebrew word translated "searched" in Leviticus 10:16. They knew the Torah's middle letter was in the Hebrew word translated "belly" in Leviticus 11:42. While such knowledge may seem trivial to us, the Masoretes knew such in-

formation was vital to their careful preservation of God's word. We should be grateful for their diligent work.

Transmission in the Original Languages

The vast majority of the Old Testament text was originally written in Hebrew, though a few portions (Gn 31:47b; Ezr 4:8–6:18; 7:12–26; Jer 10:11b; Dn 2:4b–7:28) were written in **Aramaic**. Both Hebrew and Aramaic are Semitic languages, in the same language family as **Akkadian** (the language of the Assyrians and Babylonians), **Amorite**, **Phoenician**, **Ugaritic**, **Ammonite**, **Moabite**, and **Arabic**.

Many Hebrew copies of the Old Testament text have come down to us.[8] Three are most important to our study—the **Masoretic Text**, the **Samaritan Pentateuch**, and the **Dead Sea Scrolls**.

The Masoretic text

The Masoretic text comes from the Masoretes. The oldest copies of this text date to somewhat earlier than A.D. 1000; however, most scholars believe these copies reflect a text from about A.D. 100. The Masoretic text is the most reliable Hebrew text we have.[9]

The Samaritan Pentateuch

The Samaritan Pentateuch, as the name implies, contains only Genesis–Deuteron-

Septuagint

Pentateuch

Targums

hermeneutics

grammatical-historical method

omy and originated with the Samaritans. The Samaritans came from the intermarriage of Jews and foreigners in the territory of the northern kingdom after it fell to Assyria in 722 B.C. The Samaritan Pentateuch's oldest manuscript dates to about A.D. 1100, though many scholars believe it is based on a text from 100–200 B.C.[10]

The Jews saw the Samaritans as half-breed compromisers who had denied their faith by intermarrying with foreigners. The Samaritans, on the other hand, felt they preserved a more ancient and pure form of the faith. Sharp theological differences were thus inevitable. The Samaritan Pentateuch is slanted in such a way as to reflect these differences. Thus, the text provides an early witness to the way the Samaritans interpreted the Pentateuch. For this and other reasons, it is not as reliable for determining the text's original reading.

The Dead Sea Scrolls

A shepherd boy accidentally discovered the first of the Dead Sea Scrolls in a cave in 1947.[11] Archaeologists subsequently explored nearby caves and found more scrolls. These scrolls date to around 100–200 B.C. and contain at least parts of every Old Testament book except Esther. They also provide much information about the community at QUMRAN, the site where the scrolls were discovered. Most important for us, they confirm the reliability of the Masoretic text.

Transmission in Other Languages

The Septuagint (LXX)

The **Septuagint**, a translation of the Old Testament into Greek, dates to about 200–300 B.C. and comes from the Egyptian city of Alexandria.[12] Its name and abbreviation (LXX) come from the fact that a team of seventy-two scholars did the translation work.

The Septuagint provides an important early testimony to the Old Testament text. Sometimes scholars have been able to resolve difficult readings in the Masoretic text by comparing it to the Septuagint. But some parts of the Septuagint are more reliable than others. For example, the **Pentateuch** is more carefully translated than the rest of the Old Testament. Why these

early differences appeared remains a mystery.

The Aramaic Targums

The Targums are collections of writings based on the Old Testament text. These Aramaic writings date from the early Christian era, though parts are earlier.[13]

The **Targums** arose during a time when many Jewish people understood Aramaic better than Hebrew, and provided common interpretations to the Hebrew text. In places, the Targums reflect a fairly literal translation of the Hebrew. Elsewhere, they add commentary and stories as they elaborate on the text's meaning. Because of this, the Targums generally do not provide a reliable witness to the Old Testament text, though they help us understand early Jewish interpretations.

Hermeneutics: How Do We Interpret the Bible?

So far in this chapter, we have discussed canon, inspiration, and textual transmission. We have examined what books make up the Old Testament, how the Spirit of God worked with the human authors to produce the Old Testament, and how the books of the Old Testament were handed down to us.

But an important question remains: How do we interpret the Old Testament? Will we always understand the text if we simply start reading? Or must we follow certain rules of **hermeneutics**, or interpretation?

Not all Bible interpreters agree on the meaning of every Bible passage. However, most acknowledge that certain guidelines help us determine the meaning of each passage. We will briefly survey some of the most important guidelines.[14]

Use the Grammatical-Historical Method

The **grammatical-historical method** seeks to find the basic "plain sense" meaning of a Bible passage by applying standard rules of grammar and syntax. It seeks to determine what the text says grammatically and what it meant historically. It tries to discover the author's original intention by careful use of the rules below.

Understand the Context

The term "context" refers to the words and sentences surrounding a word or statement that help us understand the meaning of that word or statement. Suppose I said to you, "Today, I saw the biggest trunk I have ever seen in my life." What does *trunk* mean in that statement? Was I watching an elephant at the zoo? Did I see a giant redwood tree? Or was I inspecting the back end of a large car? Without a context, you cannot tell what I mean.

Context is also important for properly interpreting a Bible passage. Bible students should study three kinds of context: immediate context, remote context, and historical context.

Immediate context

Immediate context refers to the words or phrases in the verses closest to the word or statement one is trying to understand. The immediate context usually influences the meaning the most. For example, my ambiguous sentence becomes clear if I add, "When I was looking at the zoo elephants today, I saw the biggest trunk I have ever seen in my life."

Remote context

Remote context describes the biblical material in the surrounding chapters and beyond. It also may influence the meaning of the passage in question, though usually not as directly as the immediate context does. Sometimes readers will consult other biblical books or letters by the same author to see how he uses a particular word or phrase elsewhere in his writings. They

Important Early Old Testament Texts and Their Significance

Text	Significance	Date of composition	Oldest known copy of the text(s)
Masoretic Text	Most reliable Hebrew text	About A.D. 100	About A.D. 1000
Samaritan Pentateuch	Early testimony to the Pentateuch, but with decidedly Samaritan slant	200–100 B.C.	About A.D. 1100
Dead Sea (Qumran) Scrolls	Parts of every OT book except Esther; important for confirming reliability of other manuscripts such as the Masoretic Text and Septuagint	200–100 B.C.	200–100 B.C.
Septuagint (LXX)	Early Greek translation of the OT; an important early witness helpful in confirming the original text	300–200 B.C.	A.D. 300–500
Targums	An Aramaic translation/paraphrase and commentary on the OT text; not as reliable for determining the accuracy of the OT text	Most A.D. 500–1000, though parts may go back to the first few centuries B.C.	Earliest parts about A.D. 150

genres

may even trace an idea through the Old Testament or the entire Bible.

Historical context

Historical context refers to the setting in history in which the writer wrote the Bible passage. For example, we understand the Book of Lamentations better when we realize the author was describing Jerusalem's plight after its destruction in 587 B.C. We appreciate better the meaning of a psalm of David if we know the occasion on which he wrote it. The historical context thus forms the backdrop against which the biblical writer composed his text.

Determine the Type of Literature

The Bible contains many different types (or **genres**) of literature, and the interpreter must apply somewhat different principles in each case. For example, historical narrative tells a story; it is quite different from prophecy, which calls the people to trust

Hermeneutics: How Do We Interpret the Bible?

Use the Grammatical-Historical Method

Understand the Context

    Immediate Context

    Remote Context

    Historical Context

Determine the Type of Literature

Interpret Figurative Language

Let Scripture Interpret Scripture

Discover the Application to Modern Life

Key Terms

apocryphal
canon
neo-orthodox
transcendent
evangelicalism
dictation theory
plenary verbal inspiration
transmission
masora
Torah
Aramaic
Akkadian
Amorite
Phoenician
Ugaritic
Ammonite
Moabite
Arabic
Masoretic Text
Samaritan Pentateuch
Dead Sea Scrolls
Septuagint
Pentateuch
Targums
hermeneutics
grammatical-historical method
genres

Key Places

Jamnia
Assyria
Qumran

in God or describes God's future plans for the world. Poetry and parables also require special consideration. Failure to take the type of literature into account may lead to a skewed interpretation of the biblical passage.

Interpret Figurative Language

In our daily speech, we often use figurative language. We speak of the sun rising, of being so hungry we could eat a horse, or of going the extra mile for someone. We do not mean any of these things literally; rather, these "figures of speech" communicate truth in a symbolic way.

The Bible also contains figurative language. The prophet Isaiah used it when he wrote, "The trees of the field will clap their hands" (55:12). He really meant God would cause nature to flourish. The psalmist (1:1) used it when he wrote, "How blessed is the man who does not *walk* in the counsel of the wicked." To walk in the counsel of the wicked means to take the advice of wicked people. We may arrive at strange interpretations if we fail to recognize the Bible's use of figurative language.

Let Scripture Interpret Scripture

Sometimes we find a Bible passage that remains difficult to understand even after we apply the principles of hermeneutics. Perhaps the passage has two possible meanings or seems to contradict another Bible passage.

For example, how should we understand James 2:24? The verse says, "So you see, we are made right with God by what we do, not by faith alone" (NLT). But Romans 3:28 says, "So we are made right with God through faith and not by obeying the law" (NLT) Do the two verses contradict each other, or is there another explanation?

In such cases, we should let Scripture interpret Scripture. That is, we should find another biblical text that presents clear teaching on the topic, and interpret the difficult passage in light of the clear one. We can do this because God's word does not contradict itself.

By applying this principle, we find other biblical passages that clearly teach salvation comes by grace through faith alone (Gal 3:1–6; Eph 2:8–9). Consequently, we

Summary

1. Tests for canonicity of the Old Testament must focus on the author, the audience, and the teaching.

2. The Bible itself does not tell us precisely how God inspired the human authors to write the Scriptures.

3. Four of the most widely held theories of inspiration are: neo-orthodox theory, dictation theory, limited inspiration theory, and plenary verbal inspiration theory.

4. The plenary verbal inspiration theory implies that the Bible is trustworthy and is authoritative.

5. Scribes who copied the biblical texts believed they were copying the very words of God.

6. The Masoretes did three things to preserve the text they received: (1) they developed a system for writing vowels; (2) they developed a system of accents for the Hebrew text; and (3) they developed a system of detailed notes from the text.

7. The majority of the Old Testament was originally written in Hebrew, the rest in Aramaic.

8. The most important Hebrew copies of the Old Testament are the Masoretic text, the Samaritan Pentateuch, and the Dead Sea Scrolls.

9. The Septuagint is a Greek translation of the Old Testament.

10. To interpret the Old Testament, it is important to follow the rules of hermeneutics: use the grammatical-historical method; understand the context; determine the type of literature; interpret figurative language; and let Scripture interpret Scripture.

11. In understanding the context of the Old Testament, the immediate context, the remote context, and the historical context all must be considered.

12. The Old Testament is more than an ancient book. Its principles apply to our lives today.

? Study Questions

1. What do we mean by the term "canon"? How did people know or decide which books belonged in the Bible?

2. Identify the different theories of inspiration. What do evangelicals mean when they use the term "plenary verbal inspiration"? What are the implications of plenary verbal inspiration?

3. Describe the process by which those who copied the Scriptures passed them down to us. Name and briefly describe the significance of the major manuscripts we have.

4. What do Bible interpreters mean by the expression "grammatical-historical interpretation"? Why is it important to use good rules of interpretation? How many of those rules can you name?

should reexamine James' words in their context to discover if James meant something else when he used the expression "justified by works." Indeed, a careful reading shows that James meant Abraham and Rahab proved their faith was genuine by doing good works, a concept that does not contradict Paul's teaching.

Discover the Application to Modern Life

Earlier in the chapter, we explained how one of the tests of canonicity was that a biblical book had to be written to all generations. The author originally wrote for a particular audience, but if the message was truly God's Word, it would have application to all generations.

The interpreter's final task, after applying the proper hermeneutical principles to determine what the text meant to its original audience, is to determine what the text means for today. This step is sometimes the most difficult, but also the most crucial.

To do this, we must understand what issues in our modern culture parallel the

📖 Further Reading

Brotzman, Ellis R. *Old Testament Textual Criticism: A Practical Introduction.* Grand Rapids: Baker, 1994. An excellent survey of the pertinent issues of textual criticism, easily understood by the beginner.

Fee, Gordon, and Douglas Stuart. *How to Read the Bible for All Its Worth.* Rev. ed. Grand Rapids: Zondervan, 1993. A good basic tool for learning to interpret the Scriptures correctly.

Harrison, R. K. *Introduction to the Old Testament.* Grand Rapids: Eerdmans, 1969. A classic reference work.

McQuilkin, J. Robertson. *Understanding and Applying the Bible.* Rev. ed. Chicago: Moody, 1992. A college-level exposition of the principles of good Bible interpretation.

Tov, Emanuel. *Textual Criticism of the Hebrew Bible.* Minneapolis/Assen, Netherlands: Fortress/Van Gorcum, 1992.

issues in the Bible passage we are studying. Then, to the extent they are parallel, we may apply the Bible's teaching to our modern situation.

The Bible is not merely an ancient book with a message for an ancient people. It is the word of God. It spoke to Israel, and it speaks to us today. Our task as Christians is to study it, to apply it to our lives, and to share it with a world that desperately needs to hear it.

2 Where and When Did the Events of the Old Testament Take Place?

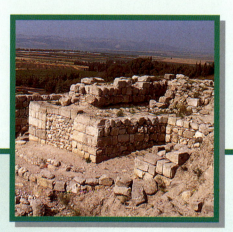

Outline

Objectives

After reading this chapter, you should be able to

- Identify on a map the three geographical regions of the ancient Near East
- Compare the development of the cultures of Mesopotamia, Egypt, and Syria–Palestine
- Discuss the key geographic features of the four subregions of Israel
- Trace the highlights of the history of Israel and the ancient Near East during the New Stone Age, Copper-Stone Age, Early Bronze Age, Middle Bronze Age, Late Bronze Age, Iron Age I, and Iron Age II
- List the different peoples who significantly influenced the history of Israel

incarnation

Fertile Crescent

We read in the New Testament that God revealed himself to humanity through the **incarnation;** that is, God took on human form in Jesus of Nazareth. This means God's revelation occurred in a specific time and place. Therefore, in order for us to understand the message of the New Testament, we must study the events of the life of Christ and the early church. The history and geography of the first-century world of Palestine provide an important background for Christians reading the New Testament.

God's revealed truth in the Old Testament is also incarnational. He revealed himself in specific times and places to a specific group of people, the Israelites. Therefore, it is important for Christians to understand the time in which ancient Israel existed. This chapter discusses the land in which God's revelation occurred and the major events of Old Testament history.

Where Did the Events of the Old Testament Take Place?

Ancient Israel was one small part of a larger area known as the ancient Near East. This term refers basically to what is known today as the Middle East. It stretches from the ZAGROS MOUNTAINS in the east to the Mediterranean Sea on the west. The northern boundaries of the ancient Near East reach to the CASPIAN and BLACK SEAS, with the CAUCASUS MOUNTAINS between them. In the south, the ancient Near East is bounded by the ARABIAN DESERT and two large bodies of water (the PERSIAN GULF and the RED SEA).

Though Israel was geographically smaller than many of her neighbors in the ancient Near East, her location made her strategically important throughout ancient history. This small piece of land forms a bridge among three continents—Asia, Africa, and Europe.[1] Israel's crossroads location had two important consequences. First, many nations and empires throughout history desired to control, or at least have access to Israel for purposes of trade

and transportation to other parts of the ancient world. Second, many foreign cultural influences poured into ancient Israel. She was exposed to great cultural interchange and commerce throughout her history.

Three Regions of the Ancient Near East

The ancient Near East contains three geographical subregions joined by an arch of rich soil known as the "**Fertile Crescent**" (notice the shaded area on the map below is shaped like a crescent). Most of the terrain of the ancient world was rugged and inhospitable to human life. The fertile lands are bordered by nearly impassable

MEDITERRANEAN SEA

EGYPT

Nile R.

mountain ranges to the north and vast deserts to the south. But within the crescent, flat lands and an abundance of water made this location the birthplace of human civilization.

The three geographical subregions of the ancient Near East were MESOPOTAMIA, Syria–Palestine, and Egypt. These three regions were all marked in early antiquity by important river cultures.

Mesopotamia

The Greek term "Mesopotamia" ("between the rivers") refers to that great stretch of land between the EUPHRATES and TIGRIS RIVERS.[2] This region extends from the mouth of the Persian Gulf northwestward along the bend in the Euphrates and reaches eastward to the Tigris at the foot of the Zagros Mountains. All of modern Iraq and parts of IRAN, SYRIA, and LEBANON make up the area known as Mesopotamia.

Mesopotamia's terrain is greatly varied—from the mountainous northern regions to the desert sands of the southwest. The weather is unpredictable and the waters of the twin rivers are capricious. Flooding posed an ever-present threat for the ancient Mesopotamians, but so did drought. Consequently, the region, especially in the south, hovered constantly between desert and swamp. Nor were there

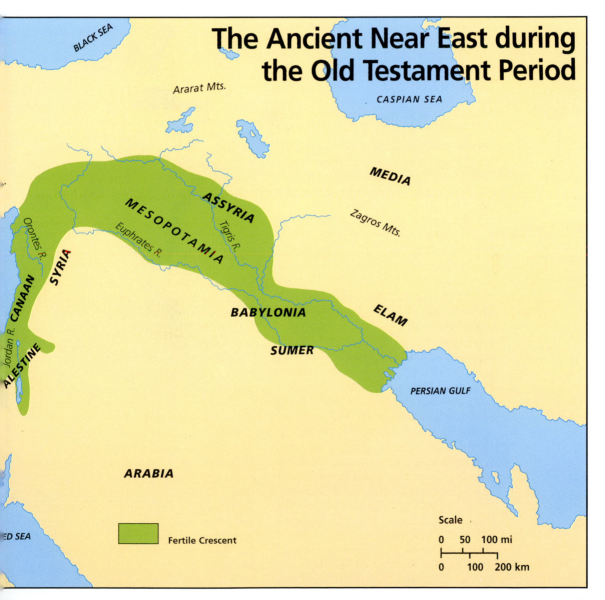

The Ancient Near East during the Old Testament Period

Neolithic Age

cuneiform

hieroglyphs

pharaoh

any natural defenses to ward off enemy invaders.

In spite of all the dangers, Mesopotamia was capable of providing the good life for those fortunate enough to live there. This was especially true in southern Mesopotamia, where the river water could be channeled to provide irrigation for crops or navigated for purposes of trade. Scholars of earliest human history believe civilization began in the foothills north of the Tigris River, when ancient Mesopotamians of the **Neolithic Age** (around 7000 B.C.) first cultivated plants, domesticated animals, and began farming. Sometime around 3100 B.C., the Sumerians invented writing in southern Mesopotamia when they discovered they could use wedgelike shapes on various materials to represent words. The wedge-shaped writing (known as **cuneiform,** from Latin *cuneus* ["wedge"] and *forma* ["form"]) was most easily incised into wet clay, a substance readily accessible in southern Mesopotamia. Often the scribe would bake the clay tablets in the sun or in an oven, producing extremely durable cuneiform tablets, thousands of which have been discovered by modern archaeologists. Cuneiform could also be inscribed on metal or stone.

The potential good life in Mesopotamia was no secret to others living in the ancient Near East. With no natural defenses, those enjoying life in Mesopotamia had to keep an eye on external threats. Throughout ancient history, Mesopotamia saw the influx of many different people groups and changes of power. The Sumerians were followed by a long succession of Semites of various nationalities. During the last quarter of the third millennium B.C., the first group of Semites, the Akkadians, rose to power and occupied southern Mesopotamia together with the Sumerians. But by the turn of the millennium, another Semitic group known as Amorites began to arrive in enormous numbers; they dominated the next thousand years of history in Mesopotamia. The Amorites eventually established major foci of power in the south at BABYLON on the Euphrates, and in the north at ASSUR and NINEVEH along the Tigris. The Babylonians in the south and the Assyrians in the north were two of the most important groups in

Mesopotamia and played a significant role in Old Testament history.

Egypt

The same geographical features that made early human civilization possible in Mesopotamia were also present on the northeastern coast of Africa along the Nile River.[3] While Mesopotamia showed a slow and gradual development from the Stone Age to the beginnings of human history, Egypt appears to have suddenly jumped overnight from the Neolithic Age into urban culture. The relative suddenness of the birth of civilization in Egypt is probably attributable to Mesopotamian influences on the Nile Valley. The development of Egyptian **hieroglyphs** (Latin *hieroglyphicus*, sacred carving) may have been influenced by Mesopotamian cuneiform, though this is far from certain.[4]

One ancient historian fittingly described Egypt as the gift of the Nile River.[5] Without question, the Nile is the dominant geographic feature of Egypt and played a major role in Egypt's history and cultural outlook on life. This great river stretches more than six hundred miles through the northeastern deserts of Africa to the Mediterranean Sea. The Nile thus created a sharp contrast between the riverside meadow and the desert on either side. The black, fertile soil of the river valley abounded with life and vitality, while the lifeless red desert sands reminded the ancient Egyptians of their mortality. The Egyptians called the rich soil of the Nile Valley "the black land" and the encroaching desert sands beyond "the red land."[6] They clearly treasured the great muddy river that brought life-giving water and soil.

Ninety percent of the ancient population lived in the fertile river valley, which was seldom more than ten miles wide. The Nile has no tributaries and the country has no rainfall except for coastal showers along the shores of the Mediterranean Sea. The Egyptians understood how dependent they were on the river to maintain life in their "black land." They gave credit to their god-king, the **pharaoh,** for the Nile's annual flood. From a source far south of Egypt, beyond their understanding, the river rose predictably every

Without question, the Nile is the dominant geographic feature of Egypt and played a major role in Egypt's history. This great river created a sharp contrast between the riverside meadow and the desert on either side.

June, peaking in September and returning to its normal level by November. This annual inundation was vitally important to continued prosperity in Egypt because its waters brought rich layers of silt and rejuvenated the soil, making Egypt's "black land" one of the richest lands in the world.[7]

But the long and narrow river valley also tended to create a severe contrast between north and south in ancient Egypt. The south included, and was distinguished by, the length of the Nile and was called Upper Egypt (since the southern region is upstream). Lower Egypt consisted of the delta created where the Nile spreads out and empties into the Mediterranean Sea. This contrast resulted in marked differences in language dialects and cultural outlooks on life. The geographically isolated Upper Egypt depended on cattle-herding, and was provincial and conservative. Lower Egypt was interested in commercial trade because of its access to European and Asian sea ports. It had an international and cosmopolitan flavor.[8] Political unification was the first task of the pharaoh, and the strategic central location of Memphis was obviously important.

Unlike Mesopotamia, Egypt enjoyed relative seclusion from the outside world. The great desert borders and the Mediterranean Sea to the north provided natural geographical boundaries and meant Egypt had fewer incidents of foreign aggression in its history. There were occasional threats from LIBYA to the west or invasions by sea. But the normal concern for Egyptian security was Asian invaders from across the body of water we now call the SUEZ CANAL. With a few exceptions, however, the Egyptians were able to contain these threats with mere police actions. Compared to Mesopotamia, Egypt was relatively free from invasion. As a result, Egypt did not encounter the large number of ethnic and cultural infiltrations dotting Mesopotamian history.

Egyptian history is, therefore, not one of constant power changes and new people groups, but rather the rise and fall of mostly native Egyptian dynasties. Some of these dynasties saw Egypt develop large empires with international significance in ancient Near Eastern history. These periods of imperial strength fall naturally into the Old Kingdom (dynasties 3–6, 2700–2200 B.C.), the Middle Kingdom (dynasties 11–13, 2000–1700 B.C.) and the New Kingdom (dynasties 18–20, 1550–1100 B.C.). Thus, the Egypt of the patriarchs was probably Middle Kingdom Egypt; that of Moses and the exodus, NEW KINGDOM Egypt. By the time of Israel's united monarchy, Egypt had lost its position as an international superpower, though it continued to wield significant cultural influence.

Syria–Palestine

Syria–Palestine is the area from the northern bend of the Euphrates along the Mediterranean coast, southward to the Sinai desert. Israel was the southernmost section of Syria–Palestine.

The great river cultures of Mesopotamia and Egypt were made possible by geographical features leading to the organization and unification of the regions. The rivers were large enough to provide accessible trade, making economic growth possible. The geographical features of Mesopotamia and Egypt made national unification possible.

By contrast, Syria–Palestine is characterized by segmentation. Smaller rivers (the Jordan and the Orontes, see map, p. 37) and vast differences of topography divided the region into subdivisions and smaller territories. Syria–Palestine was not the site of advanced civilization and national empires early in history. Instead, its primary geopolitical importance was in its role as a land bridge along the Fertile Crescent. Throughout ancient history, the empires of the great river cultures, Egypt and Mesopotamia, sought to control access to Syria–Palestine for both economic and military/political reasons.

In addition to forming a land-bridge among three continents, the area is marked by two other topographical features. First, the eastern coast of the Mediterranean Sea forms the western boundary of this area. The coast (known as the **"Levant"**) extends for four hundred miles, and became the crossroads for all trade and travel in the ancient world. The second important feature in Syria–Palestine's topography is known as the **"rift."** The Jordan Rift is a great fissure in the surface of the earth extending from north of the Sea of Galilee through the Jordan Valley and the Dead Sea to the shores of the Red Sea. To the north, this cleavage is framed by the Lebanon and Anti-Lebanon mountain ranges (see map, p. 41). The altitude descends steadily as one moves south to the Dead Sea, the surface of which is 1,275 feet below sea level, the lowest point on earth.[9]

Four Subregions of Israel

The prominent topographical feature of all of Syria–Palestine, the Jordan Rift, also plays a role in Israel's longitudinal orientation. The country is divided north-to-south into four zones: the coastal zone, the central mountain range, the Jordan Rift, and the Transjordanian Highlands.[10]

The coastal plains

These plains, as seen on map, p. 41, are narrow in the north, but gradually become broader in the south as the coastline slants westward. This region was one of the richest of ancient Israel because of its fertile soil and the accessibility of water (numerous springs and high groundwater level).

The striking characteristic of Israel's coastline compared to the rest of the Levant in the north is the lack of natural harbors. The city of Acco, in the Bay of Haifa, was the only important harbor in Israel in Old Testament times. By contrast, the coastal strip between the Mediterranean Sea and the Lebanon Mountains north of Israel had many natural harbors because of the jagged terrain rising out of the sea. The Phoenicians, who occupied this strip during most of the Old Testament period, used these harbors to good advantage, becoming expert sailors and sea-merchants. The Israelites never quite learned to trust the sea, however, and regularly had to hire Phoenician expertise whenever it was necessary to put to sea (1 Kgs 9:26–27).

This coastal zone has six subregions from north to south: the Plain of Acco, the Jezreel Valley, the Sharon Plain, the Philistine Coast, the Shephelah (or "low-hills"), and the western Negeb or southern desert (see map, p. 41). The Jezreel Valley is the only exception to Israel's longitudinal orientation, since it interrupts the central highlands and connects the coastal plains in the west with the Jordan Rift to the east. This valley's rich soil and its location as an intersection for the region's great highways (see map, p. 41) meant the major military powers of the biblical period passed through it and often attempted to control it.

The southern coastal plain was home to Israel's most bitter enemies, the Philistines, throughout most of the Old Testament period. The greatest concentration of Philistines and their five major cities occupied this plain. From the period of the judges to David's rise to the throne, the Philistines

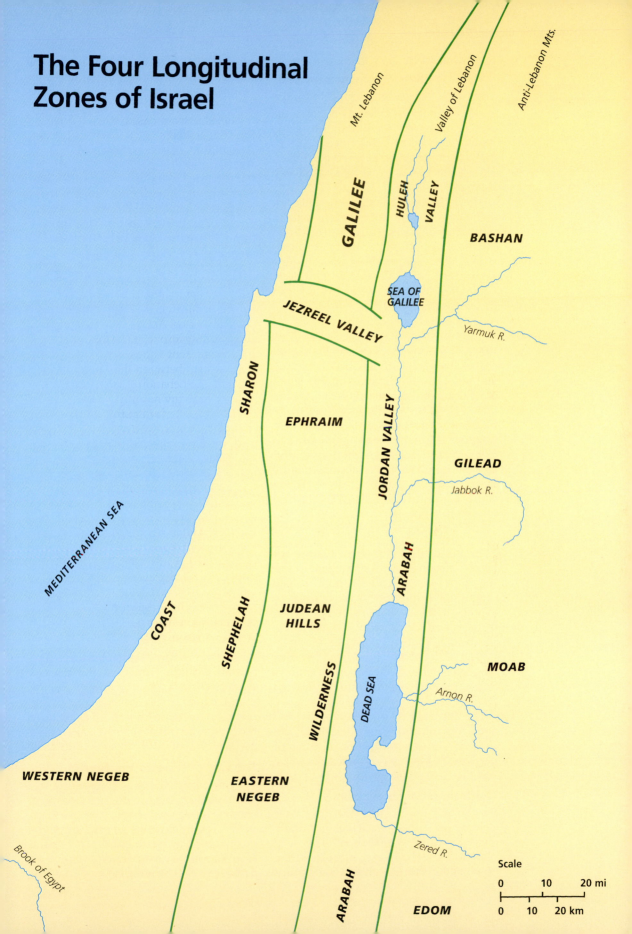

The Four Longitudinal Zones of Israel

GALILEE

Mt. Lebanon

Valley of Lebanon

Anti-Lebanon Mts.

HULEH

VALLEY

BASHAN

SEA OF
GALILEE

JEZREEL VALLEY

Yarmuk R.

SHARON

EPHRAIM

JORDAN VALLEY

GILEAD

Jabbok R.

MEDITERRANEAN SEA

JUDEAN
HILLS

ARABAH

COAST

SHEPHELAH

WILDERNESS

DEAD SEA

MOAB

Arnon R.

WESTERN NEGEB

EASTERN
NEGEB

Zered R.

Scale

0   10   20 mi

0   10   20 km

Brook of Egypt

ARABAH

EDOM

fought intermittently with the Israelites of the central highlands.

The ridge, or central mountain range

A ridge of hills rises sharply between the coastal plains and the Jordan Rift. These highlands may be subdivided into four main regions: GALILEE, EPHRAIM, JUDEAN HILL country, and the eastern Negeb (see map, p. 41).

The highest point along the Levant coast is the towering Mount Hermon, with an altitude of 9,100 feet.[11] Just south of Mount Hermon, Upper Galilee reaches elevations of over three thousand feet. A steep slope separates Upper Galilee from Lower Galilee to the south, with altitudes just below two thousand feet.

The central hills of Ephraim and the Judean hill country are quite similar. This range of mountains is protected on both slopes by deep stream beds, making east–west passage difficult. A north–south road along the eastern slope connects the hills of Ephraim with the Judean hill country. Many major cities lay along this road: MIZPAH, SHECHEM, SHILOH, and BETHEL in Ephraim, and JERUSALEM, BETHLEHEM, and HEBRON in Judah. The eastern part of the desert south of Judah (the "Negeb") has a continuation of the hills of the central mountain range.

The Jordan Rift

This main topographical feature of Syria–Palestine plays a prominent role in the shape of Israel's landscape. The deep depression in the earth's surface has an average width of 10 miles, and descends from an altitude of about 300 feet in the north to 1,275 feet below the Mediterranean at the shore of the Dead Sea.[12] In the center of the rift, the Jordan River flows down from the foot of Mount Hermon to the Dead Sea.

The Jordan Rift may be subdivided north to south into five regions: the HULEH VALLEY, CHINNERETH (that is, the Sea of Galilee), the JORDAN VALLEY, the DEAD SEA, and the ARABAH (see map, p. 41).

The Transjordanian highlands

East of the Jordan Rift, the land rises sharply into a plateau, which gradually gives way to the Arabian desert. This steep plateau reaches greater altitudes than much of the central highlands then drops precipitously down to the Jordan Valley. These Transjordanian highlands reach heights up to 5,700 feet in the south, such as in the mountains of Edom.

This mountain tableland is divided by four river canyons: YARMUK, JABBOK, ARNON, and ZERED (see map, p. 41). These rivers flow through deep gorges in the plateau into the Jordan River or the Dead Sea. Frequently in biblical history these rivers formed natural boundaries for national or political entities. The Yarmuk forms the southern border for BASHAN. The area from the Yarmuk to the Jabbok we may conveniently refer to as GILEAD. The territory between the Jabbok and the Arnon was Moabite land during most of the Old Testament period. South of the Zered was Edomite country. So the transjordanian highlands may be subdivided into four areas from north to south: Bashan, Gilead, MOAB, and EDOM. Most of the borders were fluid, changing frequently in biblical times.

The eastern extremes of the transjordanian highlands enjoy no natural border with the Arabian desert. The fate of this mountain plateau in biblical times was often tied to its relationship with the desert. Scorching winds and migratory desert nomads often made it difficult to maintain agriculture and a settled life. But the high ridges bordering on the Jordan Rift caught the last benefits of the Mediterranean storms and created enough rainfall to support sheep-herding and crops of wheat.

Highways of the Ancient Near East

Of the many important highways and communication routes of the ancient world, two international roadways require mention here.[13] Their precise courses did not vary greatly in biblical times because the broken topography of Syria–Palestine made it difficult to create new routes.

The way of the sea (Via Maris)

The title "way of the sea" comes from Isaiah 9:1 and refers to an international road running along the Levant coast (see map, p. 45). This highway was used throughout the biblical period and some of the most important cities of antiquity were located near it. The **Vulgate** rendered Isa-

Part of the western Negeb or southern desert.

iah's phrase as *Via Maris,* which was used in later times to designate the whole network of roadways from Egypt through Syria– Palestine into Mesopotamia.

On the southern coastal plain, the *Via Maris* moves northward and splits into two branches, the western continuing along the coast and the eastern passing through the Jezreel Valley to Megiddo, and from there to Hazor and Damascus and on into Mesopotamia. The various branches of this great international highway converge at Megiddo, at the entrance to the Jezreel Valley. The valley, and especially the city of Megiddo, were strategic locations for all commerce and travel in the ancient world.

The king's highway

The second important international route is the "king's highway" (taken from Nm 20:17; 21:22). This roadway extends from the GULF OF AQABAH at ELATH through the transjordanian highlands to Damascus (see map on pp. 44–45). Because of the four deep river beds in the transjordanian plateau, the highway follows a path twenty-five to thirty miles east of the Arabah on the very edge of the desert.

This was a secondary route from Damascus to Egypt, often competing with the *Via Maris*. It was most popular for nomadic caravans transporting commercial goods and for the trade of agricultural products. During the Israelite monarchy, the king's highway attained a special significance because of increased trade with Arabia.

What Events Does the Old Testament Describe?

The details of New Testament history cover only about a century. By contrast, the history of Old Testament Israel spans nearly two millennia. Over this length of time, Israelites came in contact with many different peoples and nations. The Old Testament makes frequent reference to Assyrians, Babylonians, Egyptians, Arameans, and many other important peoples. This section traces the broad outline of Israel's history, also introducing the most important people groups.[14]

Israel's Ancestry: The Patriarchs

Historians do not have enough evidence to give precise dates for many of the events we discuss in this survey text. In fact, since absolute chronology is impossible, archaeologists divide the millennia before the Christian era into periods according to the technology available at the time. So after the various stone ages (**Paleolithic, Mesolithic, Neolithic,** and **Chalcolithic**), we can refer in the broadest of terms to the **Bronze Age** and the **Iron Age.** These terms do not mean to imply that the switches from stone to bronze to iron were sudden, or that only bronze was used for tools and other utensils during the Bronze Age while only iron was used during the Iron Age. But in general, around 3300 B.C., bronze technology spread throughout the ancient Near East, and around 1200 B.C., people discovered the greater benefits of the use of iron.

The period from about 3300 to 2000 B.C. is known as the **Early Bronze Age.** This

period witnessed the invention of writing and the beginnings of human history. In Mesopotamia, the Sumerians first used cuneiform extensively for writing; in Egypt, the use of hieroglyphics during the Old Kingdom Period is well attested. In Mesopotamia and Syria–Palestine, city-states first began to grow, and with them the need for communication, travel, and trade. In Mesopotamia, a series of strong city-states gained dominance during the Sumerian Early Dynastic Periods. Toward the end of the Early Bronze Age, the first Semitic empire gained control of all of southern Mesopotamia from a power base at the city of Akkad (2334–2193 B.C.).[15] In

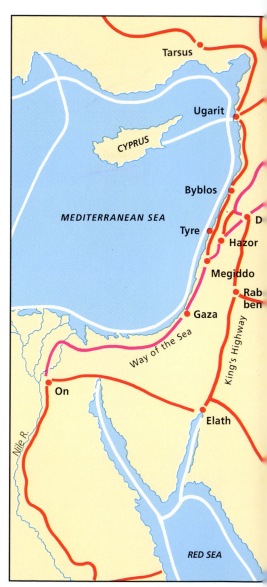

Middle Bronze Age

Egypt, the Early Bronze Age saw the flowering of the Old Kingdom Period, which was the era of the great pyramids and the apex of Egyptian culture.[16] By the close of the Early Bronze Age, all the main features of human civilization and culture had appeared in both Egypt and Mesopotamia.

Although precise dates for Israel's patriarchs (Abraham, Isaac, and Jacob) are impossible to determine, they may be generally placed in the **Middle Bronze Age** (2000–1550 B.C.).[17] This period of ancient Near Eastern history is marked by the movement of ethnic groups and new empires replacing the older powers of the Early Bronze Age. In Mesopotamia, after a brief renaissance of Sumerian culture (Ur III dynasty, 2112–2004 B.C.), the country came under the control of a new Semitic element, the Amorites. Early in the Middle Bronze Age, Amorites ruled Mesopotamia from several strong city-states in an uncertain balance of power. But then one individual from the city of Babylon was able to consolidate his strength and establish a new empire throughout Mesopotamia. HAMMURAPI rose to power in 1792 and established the Old Babylonian Empire, which endured until 1595 B.C.[18] Hammurapi is most famous for his collection of laws, many of which bear striking resemblance to the laws of Moses in the Pentateuch.

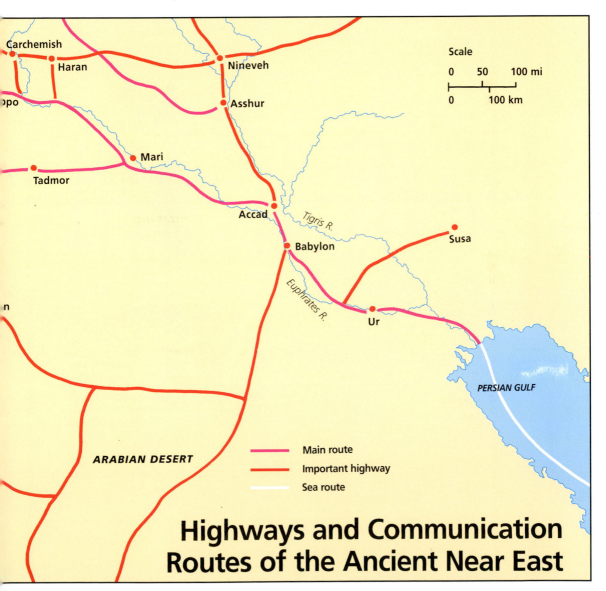

Highways and Communication Routes of the Ancient Near East

Archaeological Periods of Ancient Near Eastern History[1]

Approximate Dates (B.C.)	Archaeological Period	Israel	Ancient Near East
Before 14,000	Old Stone Age (Paleolithic)		Pre-cave culture
14,000–8000	Middle Stone Age (Mesolithic)		Cave culture
8000–4200	New Stone Age (Neolithic)		Neolithic Revolution: cultivation of crops & beginning of rain-based agriculture, domestication of animals, first permanent settlements
4200–3300	Copper-Stone Age (Chalcolithic)		Metal replaces stone in the production of tools and weapons
3300–2000	Early Bronze		Invention of writing Birth of human civilization Egyptian Old Kingdom Sumerian & Akkadian kingdoms in Mesopotamia Old Canaanite culture at Ebla
2000–1550	Middle Bronze	Israel's Patriarchs	Arrival of Amorites and other ethnic groups in Mesopotamia Old Babylonian Empire Egyptian Middle Kingdom
1550–1200	Late Bronze	Egyptian bondage Birth of Moses The exodus Wilderness wanderings Israelite conquest of Canaan	International contacts & balance of power Powerful Egyptian New Kingdom exerts influence in Syria–Palestine Rise & fall of the new Hittite Empire Kassite control in Mesopotamia
1200–930	Iron Age I	Period of the Judges United Monarchy: Saul, David, Solomon	Invasion of Sea Peoples & disruption of major powers Rise of new ethnic groups, including Arameans & Israelites. Rise of Assyria
930–539	Iron Age II	Divided Kingdom Fall of Israel in 722 Fall of Judah in 587	Weakened Egypt Assyria reaches greatest strength before fall in 612 Neo-Babylonian Empire: Nebuchadnezzar
539–332	Iron Age III	Return of Jewish exiles Ezra & Nehemiah Building of Second Temple & walls of Jerusalem	Cyrus captures Babylon in 539 Persian Empire

[1]Philip J. King, *American Archaeology in the Mideast: A History of the American Schools of Oriental Research* (Philadelphia: ASOR, 1983), 282; and Keith N. Schoville, *Biblical Archaeology in Focus* (Grand Rapids: Baker, 1978), 8–9.

covenant

**Late Bronze
Age**

New Kingdom

In Egypt, after a period of darkness and confusion called the First Intermediate Period (2200–2000 B.C.), the country once again flourished during the Middle Kingdom Period (2000–1700 B.C.). The Middle Kingdom was a time of peace and stability, and one in which Egypt engaged in trade with the Levant, resulting in the acquisition of considerable wealth. But toward the end of Middle Bronze, Egypt also succumbed to the rise of Semites, which is characteristic of the Fertile Crescent throughout this period. Native Egyptian control of the country ended when the HYKSOS, Semites probably from Syria–Palestine, took control of the Delta in the north. Whether the Hyksos invaded and took control, or whether they had been gradually growing in strength is not known. They ruled Egypt for about 150 years in what is called the Second Intermediate Period (1700–1540 B.C.). For the first time in Egypt's history, the country was conquered and dominated by foreigners.

The Middle Bronze Age world into which Abram stepped was one of peoples on the move. In Syria–Palestine, too, Semitic peoples were settling in. The Canaanites were establishing city-states in the coastal plains and valleys as early as the third millennium. These people may have been of the same Amorite stock as those who had settled Mesopotamia.[19]

Abram departed from Ur of the Chaldeans in southern Mesopotamia with his extended family and journeyed to HARAN on the Euphrates in northwestern Mesopotamia. His father, Terah, died in Haran and Abram (whose name was changed to Abraham) was called to travel on in faith to unknown lands.[20] When Abraham reached Canaan, God established a **covenant** with him and promised to give him a vast number of descendants and the land of Canaan as an inheritance. These promises were uniquely suited for a transitory, migrant Amorite looking for land to settle. After many years, Isaac was miraculously born to Abraham's wife Sarah when she was ninety years old and Abraham was one hundred years old.

Isaac's wife Rebekah had twin sons, Jacob and Esau. Although Esau was the oldest, Jacob became the child of the patriarchal promises. Jacob, whose name was changed to Israel, had twelve sons. His favorite son, Joseph, was betrayed by his brothers, sold into slavery, and taken to Egypt. While in Egypt, Joseph was blessed by God and miraculously rose to high political office in the foreign land. During a severe drought, the sons of Israel traveled to Egypt in search of food for the family back in Canaan. Much to their surprise, they were confronted by the very brother they had betrayed, and now their lives were in his hands. But Joseph provided food for them and saved their lives. Israel and all his children moved from Canaan to Goshen in the northeastern Delta of Egypt.

We can date these events no more precisely than a general time in the Middle Bronze Age (2000–1550 B.C.). The Hyksos rule of Egypt (1700–1550) may well have been the time when the children of Israel lived in Egypt and multiplied so rapidly. But once the Hyksos were expelled, a "new king arose over Egypt, who did not know about Joseph" (Ex 1:8). The "new king" probably refers to the first king of a different dynasty. For the next several hundred years, the Israelites were enslaved by the Egyptians, and forced to build their cities and drive their economy.

Israel's Beginnings: Moses and Joshua

The **Late Bronze Age** (1550–1200 B.C.) was one of international trade and balance of world powers, with Syria–Palestine caught in the middle. The Egyptians successfully ended their subjugation to the Hyksos and entered the period of their greatest political strength, the **New Kingdom** (dynasties 18–20, 1550–1100 B.C.).

Whereas Egypt was dominant throughout this period, Mesopotamia experienced a time of political weakness. After the fall of Hammurapi's Old Babylonian Empire, southern Mesopotamia was controlled by foreigners from the Zagros Mountains, the KASSITES. The long rule of the Kassite dynasty (over three hundred years) brought peace and stability to Babylonia, though not military superiority. The Kassites preferred peace treaties and other nonmilitary means of diplomacy to defend their borders. They adopted many elements of traditional Babylonian culture and raised southern Mesopotamia to a new level of international prestige during this period. The Babylonian dialect of Akkadian be-

lingua franca

Amarna Letters

came the **lingua franca,** or international language of the day.

Egypt's powerful rulers of the New Kingdom attempted to control the coastal areas of Syria–Palestine, the coastal highway to Phoenicia *(Via Maris),* and NUBIA to the south.[21] By controlling commercial trade with the Aegean and the rest of western Asia, Egypt dominated trade and acquired tremendous wealth and prosperity. At the height of this empire, AMENHOTEP IV of the 18th dynasty became pharaoh around 1353 B.C. Soon thereafter he changed his name to AKHENATEN and moved the capital about two hundred miles north of THEBES to modern EL-AMARNA. For about a decade, Akhenaten elevated Aten, the visible image of the sun, to a place of supremacy and came close to monotheistic worship. Hundreds of clay tablets written in Babylonian (the so-called **Amarna Letters**) have been found at Akhenaten's short-lived capital. These letters from Egyptian vassal-kings in Syria–Palestine and rulers in ANATOLIA and Mesopotamia reflect the politics of the mid-fourteenth century B.C. It appears that Akhenaten was no longer capable of controlling the city-states of Syria–Palestine. Whether through neglect or military weakness, Egypt began to lose its international grip in western Asia.

In Anatolia, the Hittite Empire gained control of western Asia Minor and north Syria. Under strong royal leadership, the Hittites retained control of Syria almost as far south as Damascus from about 1344 B.C. to 1239 B.C.[22] Hittite kings fought the pharaohs of Egypt's 19th dynasty for control of Syria–Palestine, eventually coming to a draw in the mid-thirteenth century. Toward the end of the Late Bronze Age, the Hittite king HATTUSHILI III and the Egyptian RAMESSES II agreed to a peace treaty, ending the hostilities between the two nations.

Sometime during the Late Bronze Age, while Israel suffered under the heavy burden of slavery in Egypt, Moses was born to the tribe of Levi. At the time of Moses' birth, the pharaoh was attempting to control the rapidly growing Israelite population by killing newborn Israelite boys. But Moses was miraculously saved by Pharaoh's own daughter and raised in the Egyptian royal court. There he was prov-

identially given the finest Egyptian education (Acts 7:22).

Moses was prepared and called by God to lead the Israelites out of their bondage in Egypt. God used a series of ten plagues to prove *he* was in control of the cosmic order, not the Egyptian god-king, pharaoh. These plagues demonstrated the superiority and majesty of Israel's God, Yahweh. God then used Moses to deliver Israel from Egypt and bring them to the Sinai Peninsula to establish a covenant with them. There he gave them the Law to maintain the new covenant relationship and protect them in the promised land they were to inherit.

The new nation, Israel, rejected God's leadership in the wilderness and refused to enter the promised land. God punished them by requiring them to wander forty years in the wilderness. During this time the rebellious generation died. Moses also died in the plains of Moab without having the privilege of entering the land promised to the patriarchs. Joshua, Moses' successor, led the nation Israel in conquest of the promised land, fulfilling the promises to the patriarchs.

Though it is impossible to give these events a precise date, it is clear that the Israelite exodus occurred sometime during the New Kingdom Period of Egyptian history. Scholars have proposed two possible dates for the exodus event, approximately 1446 or 1275 (see chapter 6). The question is whether the pharaoh of the exodus was THUTMOSE III (perhaps Amenhotep II) of the 18th dynasty or Ramesses II of the 19th dynasty. Regardless of the inability of modern scholarship to date these historical events precisely, the exodus narratives in the Bible reflect genuine Late Bronze Age customs and their factuality is certain.[22]

Israel's Statehood: David and His Dynasty

Around 1200 B.C., cataclysmic changes began to occur in the ancient Near East. The major powers (notably the Egyptians and the Hittites) suddenly declined and the political map changed dramatically. Most scholars assume the changes started with the fall of Troy (around 1250) and the subsequent fall of the Mycenaean cities on the mainland of Greece. Survivors must have fled by sea along the coasts of the

St. Catherine's Monastery, Sinai. God used Moses to deliver Israel from Egypt and bring them to the Sinai Peninsula to establish a covenant with them.

Sea Peoples

Mediterranean, disrupting all the major powers of the ancient world. These newcomers are known collectively as **"Sea Peoples."** One group of these sea peoples, known from Egyptian sources as "Peleset," settled on the southwest coastal plains of Syria–Palestine. They are known in the Old Testament as "Philistines," a term that also gave us the word "Palestine."[23]

Of the many changes brought about by the arrival of the sea peoples in the ancient Near East, two are of special significance here. First, within a century of their arrival, the political order that had existed for over three hundred years dissolved, leaving a power vacuum. Rather than military campaigns involving international powers such as the Egyptians and Hittites, local skirmishes and regionalized conflicts ensued. New ethnic groups filled the power vacuum and eventually developed smaller empires of their own, notably the

49

Arameans of Damascus and the Israelites in the highlands of Palestine.

The second result of the arrival of the sea peoples was the spread of new metalworking technology, particularly the use of iron for making weapons. Though it is not certain which group actually invented iron technology and first exploited it for weaponry, it is clear that the Philistines had the early advantage in battles with the Israelites due to a superiority in metalworking technology and monopoly of the use of iron (1 Sm 13:19–22). Gradually, iron technology replaced bronze, and archaeologists refer to the period after 1200 B.C. as the **Iron Age.**

So the period known as Iron Age I (about 1200–930 B.C.) began with the invasion of the sea peoples and the shifting of political power throughout the ancient Near East. Sometime toward the end of Late Bronze, Joshua and the children of Israel had taken Canaan and settled in the central highlands. For at least a couple centuries after the Israelite conquest, Israel governed itself as a loose confederation of twelve tribes, one for each of the sons of Jacob. During this time, leadership rose from the ranks of the common people on a temporary *ad hoc* basis. These "judges" were divinely gifted and ordained to consolidate the strength and resources of the tribes in times of national or regional crisis. Military threats arose from surrounding neighbors, particularly the Philistines to the southwest. Though a central governing body was not a necessity, the Israelites grew weary of constant military threats from surrounding enemies. They began to long for a permanent king and royal court to maintain a standing army and secure peace for the future.

The Israelite monarchy developed because of this constant threat of military invasion coupled with cultural pressure to become like other nations: "We want a king over us. Then we will be like all the other nations, with a king to lead us and to go out before us and fight our battles" (1 Sm 8:19b–20). Samuel was a prophet and judge who led Israel in the time of transition from judges to kings. With God's blessing, Samuel anointed Saul as the first king of Israel. But Saul failed to maintain his relationship with God and was eventually rejected as king of Israel. Saul's life illustrates the importance of guarding our relationship with God as the most important task we have to do. After Saul's failure, God instructed Samuel to anoint a man after God's own heart (1 Sm 13:14), the young David, as the next king of Israel.

Under David's strong leadership, Israel finally defeated the Philistines and forged

Solomon's North Palace, Megiddo. Solomon expanded Israel's borders and ruled during the only period of Israel's history that may be called an empire.

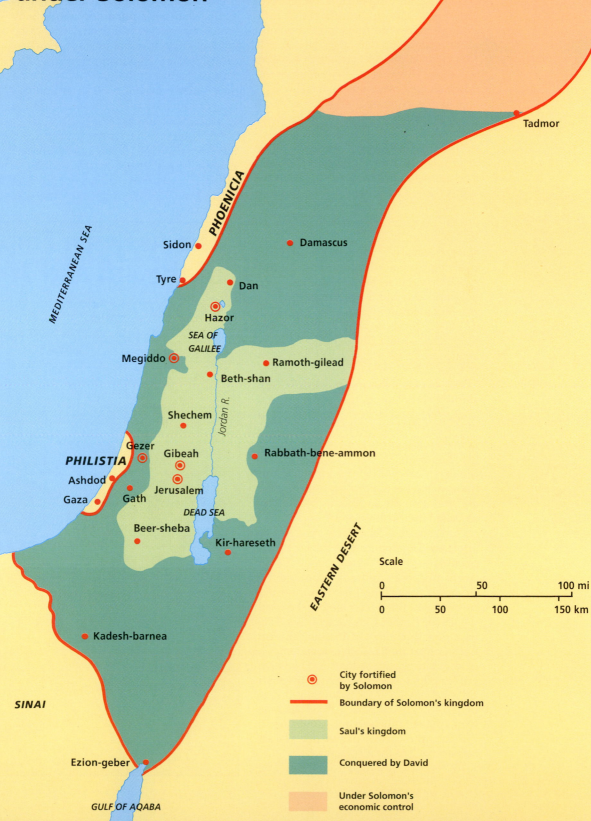

The Israelite Kingdom under Solomon

Euphrates R.

Tiphsah

Tadmor

MEDITERRANEAN SEA

PHOENICIA

Sidon

Damascus

Tyre

Dan

Hazor

SEA OF GALILEE

Megiddo

Ramoth-gilead

Beth-shan

Shechem

Jordan R.

Gezer

Gibeah

Rabbath-bene-ammon

PHILISTIA

Jerusalem

Ashdod

Gaza

Gath

DEAD SEA

Beer-sheba

Kir-hareseth

EASTERN DESERT

Scale

0   50   100 mi

0   50   100   150 km

Kadesh-barnea

SINAI

Ezion-geber

GULF OF AQABA

⊙ City fortified by Solomon

— Boundary of Solomon's kingdom

Saul's kingdom

Conquered by David

Under Solomon's economic control

Mosaic Yahwism

Canaanite Baalism

a degree of peace and security in Syria–Palestine. David's reign ushered in a period of stability that would become Israel's golden age. He unified the tribes and provided economic and political freedom. Though there continued to be much internal strife during his reign, he was able to leave a unified kingdom to his son, Solomon. This was the beginning of dynastic succession in ancient Israel.

Solomon expanded Israel's borders to the Euphrates in the north and to Egypt in the south. He ruled during the only period of Israel's history that may be called an empire. He brought great wealth and prosperity to the nation through international trade. God gave Solomon wisdom in all matters, including the ability to govern the people. The royal court grew and became more involved in the affairs of the state. Solomon's fame as an inspiring leader spread around the world, and international contact became commonplace. Solomon also had the privilege of building God's temple in Jerusalem. The reigns of David and Solomon, or the "united monarchy," would always be remembered as the ideal time of peace and prosperity (1 Kgs 4:25).

The success of the united monarchy was short-lived. Solomon, like Saul before him, allowed his heart to turn away from God: "his heart was not fully devoted to the LORD his God, as the heart of David his father had been" (1 Kgs 11:4). Shortly after the death of Solomon, the kingdom split into two weaker nations, Israel in the north and Judah in the south; this became the so-called divided monarchy.

Northern Israel fell quickly into religious apostasy. The first king of the north, Jeroboam I, attempted to use religion for political purposes and compromised the practices of ancient Yahwism inherited from Moses. But a later king of the north went even further. Omri and his son Ahab intentionally combined **Mosaic Yahwism** with **Canaanite Baalism** in an attempt to gain greater political control. The northern kingdom was also plagued by political instability. Over the two hundred years of its history (931–722 B.C.), Israel had nineteen kings in nine separate dynasties. In 722 B.C., the capital of northern Israel, Samaria, fell to the Assyrians.

By contrast, Judah, the southern king-dom, continued to have one royal family, the Davidic dynasty, for nearly 350 years (931–587 B.C.). Although Judah maintained political stability, she also fell into religious apostasy, though much more gradually than her neighbor to the north. Many of the kings of Judah were faithful to the Lord, especially early in the kingdom's history. The final century of Judah's history is marked by an interchange of good kings and bad kings. Sadly, Judah's capital, Jerusalem, fell to the Babylonians in 587 B.C.

Archaeologists refer to Iron Age II (about 930–539 B.C.), which covers Israel's divided kingdoms: northern Israel and southern Judah. Elsewhere in the ancient Near East at this time, Egypt was trying to reassert

The Assyrian Empir of the 8th and 7th Centuries B.C.

CYPRUS

MEDITERRANEAN SEA

Jerus

On

Noph

EGYPT

Nile R.

itself as a major world power. But except for a brief moment at the turn of the sixth century B.C. (26th dynasty), Egypt was never again a major player in the ancient world. The real story of Iron II is the rise and fall of new empires in Mesopotamia.

Along the banks of the Tigris River in northern Mesopotamia, a new force emerged in the Iron Age that would dominate ancient Near Eastern history for two centuries. Assyrian imperialism emerged in the mid-ninth century and began to impact the politics of Syria–Palestine. Yet Assyria went through a period of internal weakness in the first half of the eighth century. This allowed for the long and prosperous reigns of Jeroboam II in Israel

(793–753 B.C.) and Uzziah in Judah (792–740 B.C.). But success is not necessarily a sign of God's approval. While both kingdoms prospered during this half century, social injustice and moral decay began to consume the soul of Israel and Judah. This was the backdrop for the first of the classical prophets: Amos, Hosea, Isaiah, and Micah. God raised up his servants to warn the nations of impending doom and to call them to repentance.

Assyria's weakness was but a temporary lull in her rapacious drive for more power; the early eighth century was only the calm before the storm. When TIGLATH-PILESER III brought Assyria back to full strength in 745 B.C., the nation was stronger

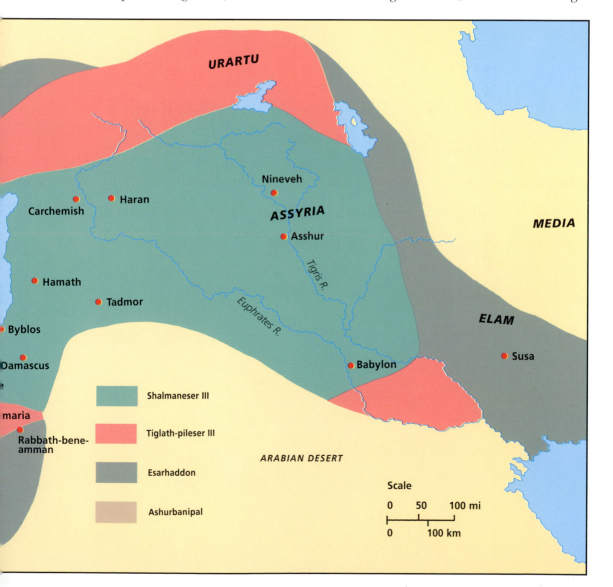

URARTU

Carchemish   Haran   Nineveh   ASSYRIA   MEDIA

Asshur

Tigris R.

Hamath

Tadmor   Euphrates R.   ELAM

Byblos

Damascus   Babylon   Susa

maria

Rabbath-bene-amman

ARABIAN DESERT

Shalmaneser III

Tiglath-pileser III

Esarhaddon

Ashurbanipal

Scale

0   50   100 mi

0   100 km

than before and ready to be used as God's instrument of destruction against the rebellious northern Israel. Over the next two decades, Israel vacillated between paying tribute to the Assyrians and rebelling against them. Finally, Tiglath-Pileser's son SHALMANESER V laid siege to Israel's capital Samaria in 725 B.C. Three years later, the northern nation fell (722 B.C.) and became a province in the enormous Assyrian Empire.

During the next century, Judah also attempted various ways of dealing with the Assyrian threat. For example, Hezekiah of Judah was anti-Assyrian, but his son Manasseh adopted a pro-Assyrian policy. During the seventh century, Assyria reached the pinnacle of its imperial power and became the first truly world empire, as well as the first in a line of such empires from a Mesopotamian base (Assyria, Baby-

lonia, and Persia) before the power shifted to the west (Greece and Rome). Under the kings of the early seventh century (SENNACHERIB, ESARHADDON, and ASHURBANIPAL), the Assyrians were able to defeat their traditional enemies to the north, the Urartians. They even captured faraway Egypt in 663. But throughout this period of international domination, Assyria had a persistent and ever-present problem closer to home. The Chaldeans of southern Babylonia were growing ever more rebellious and difficult to contain. They soon became independent and eventually replaced the Assyrians.

Under the able rulership of NABOPOLASSAR and his famous son NEBUCHADNEZZAR II, Babylonia participated in Assyria's defeat and became the next great world empire. During the 43–year rule of Nebuchadnezzar (605–562 B.C.), Babylonia

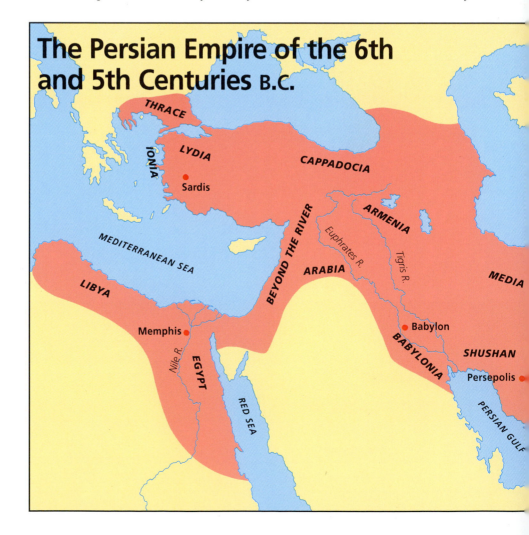

The Persian Empire of the 6th and 5th Centuries B.C.

Relief of Tiglath-Pileser III of Assyria from Calah. When Tiglath-Pileser III brought Assyria back to full strength in 745 B.C., the nation was ready to be used as God's instrument of destruction against Northern Israel.

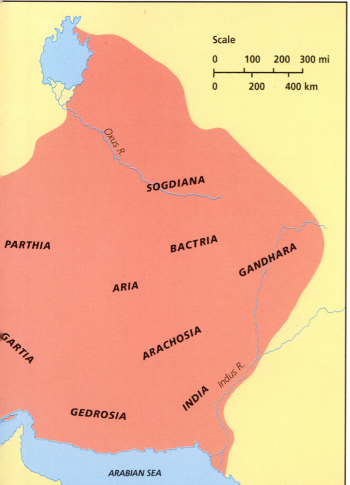

reached the apex of its wealth and political power in what is called the Neo-Babylonian Period. Judah's response to Babylonia's imperial aspirations alternated between two tactical strategies. Some favored rebellion, supported by a pathetic trust in a weakened Egypt ("that splintered reed," Is 36:6). Others, such as Jeremiah, urged Judah's submission to Babylon as a vassal state. In 597 Nebuchadnezzar attempted to end Judah's rebellious streak by capturing Jerusalem and taking King Jehoiachin into exile in Babylonia, along with many of the people of Jerusalem, including the prophet Ezekiel. Another rebellion under Zedekiah resulted in the total destruction of Jerusalem in 587.

The Babylonians not only destroyed the city and deported much of the population, but they also tore down the temple and effectively ended the Davidic dynasty. The Davidic line would barely survive through Jehoiachin during the exile. The loss of temple and kingship was a dominant and formative event in Old Testament history. It forced a rethinking of old theological assumptions and made it necessary to reformulate Israel's earlier religious convictions, especially the nature of God's covenant. All of this formed the backdrop for some of Israel's most significant prophetic figures: Jeremiah, Habakkuk, and Ezekiel.

Israel's Exile and Restoration: Ezra and Nehemiah

The final archaeological age of the Old Testament period is the Persian Age (539–332 B.C.), otherwise known as Iron Age III. The reign of the Persian king CYRUS marks the beginning of the Persian Empire. This kingdom was one of the largest in the ancient world, stretching from the isles of the Aegean Sea and the Nile across the ancient Near East to the Indus Valley.[24] The Persian Empire controlled the ancient world for two centuries. ALEXANDER THE GREAT conquered the Persians around 330 B.C.

and ended the string of world empires from a Mesopotamian base.

Cyrus established a new policy with regard to subjugated peoples and their deities. Unlike the Assyrians and Babylonians, Cyrus desired to placate as many gods as possible. He felt he could better maintain and govern his vast empire with a policy of tolerance and benevolence, rather than cruelty and brutality. The Jewish exile officially ended when Cyrus decreed that captive peoples in Babylonia were free to return to their homelands and establish a degree of self-rule. The Old Testament interprets this historical event as

Summary

1. Israel was part of the ancient Near East that is now called the Middle East.

2. The three geographical regions of the ancient Near East—Mesopotamia, Egypt, and Syria–Palestine—were joined by an arch of rich soil called the Fertile Crescent.

3. The four subregions of Israel are the coastal plains, the ridge or central mountain range, the Jordan Rift, and the transjordanian highlands.

4. Two of the important highways of the ancient Near East passed through Syria–Palestine: the Via Maris or way of the sea and the king's highway.

5. The history of the Old Testament spans a time period of about two millennia as opposed to the New Testament which covers a century.

6. The invention of writing—cuneiform in Mesopotamia and hieroglyphics in Egypt—began during the Early Bronze Age.

7. The Sea Peoples probably fled from Mycenaean cities in Greece about 1250 B.C. to the ancient Near East. This brought political changes and new metalworking technology.

8. The constant threat from military invasion from neighbors caused the Israelites to want a king.

9. The period of David's reign was a very stable time in the history of Israel.

10. Under Solomon's reign, the borders of Israel expanded northward to the Euphrates and southward to Egypt.

11. Jewish exiles returned from Babylon in three separate groups led by Zerubbabel, Ezra, and Nehemiah.

Key Terms

incarnation
Fertile Crescent
cuneiform
Neolithic Age
hieroglyphs
pharaoh
Levant
rift
Via Maris
Vulgate
Paleolithic
Mesolithic
Neolithic
Chalcolithic
Bronze Age
Iron Age
Early Bronze Age
Middle Bronze Age
covenant
Late Bronze Age
New Kingdom

lingua franca
Amarna Letters
Sea Peoples
Mosaic Yahwism
Canaanite Baalism

Key People/ Places

Hammurapi
Hyksos
Kassites
Amenhotep IV
Akhenaten
Hattushili III
Ramesses II
Thutmose III
Tiglath-Pileser III
Shalmaneser V
Sennacherib
Esarhaddon
Ashurbanipal
Nabopolassar
Nebuchadnezzar II
Cyrus
Alexander the Great
Zagros Mountains

Caspian Sea
Black Sea
Caucasus Mountains
Arabian desert
Persian Gulf
Red Sea
Mesopotamia
Euphrates River
Tigris River
Iran
Syria
Lebanon
Babylon
Assur
Nineveh
Libya
Suez Canal
Jordan Rift
Transjordanian
highlands
Acco
Bay of Haifa
Jezreel Valley
Sharon Plain
Philistine coast
Shephelah
Negeb
Galilee
Ephraim

Judean hills
Mizpah
Shechem
Shiloh
Bethel
Jerusalem
Bethehem
Hebron
Huleh Valley
Chinnereth
Jordan Valley
Dead Sea
Arabah
Yarmuk
Jabbok
Arnon
Zered
Bashan
Gilead
Moab
Edom
Gulf of Aqabah
Elath
Haran
Nubia
Thebes
El-Amarna
Anatolia

Study Questions

1. How is the Old Testament "incarnational"?

2. Why was the location of Israel strategic in ancient times?

3. Locate on a map the geographical regions of the ancient Near East and discuss their major characteristics.

4. Locate on a map the four subregions of Israel and discuss their major characteristics.

5. Discuss the international social and political climate during the patriarchal age of Israel's history.

6. Discuss the international social and political climate during the times of Moses and Joshua.

7. What was the political climate of the ancient Near East around 1200 B.C.? What effect did this have on the Israelites?

8. What political changes did Iron Age II bring to the ancient Near East? What ramifications did this have for Israel?

Further Reading

Aharoni, Yohanan. *The Land of the Bible: A Historical Geography.* 2nd ed. Trans. Anson F. Rainey. London: Burns & Oates, 1979. Best available historical geography.

Baly, Denis. *The Geography of the Bible: A Study in Historical Geography.* New York: Harper & Row, 1957.

Bright, John. *A History of Israel.* 3rd ed. Philadelphia: Westminster, 1981. A classic from a moderate perspective.

Hallo, William W., and William Kelly Simpson. *The Ancient Near East: A History.* New York: Harcourt Brace Jovanovich, 1971. Good, well-written beginning point for study of the entire ancient Near East.

Hoerth, Alfred J., Gerald L. Mattingly, and Edwin M. Yamauchi, eds. *Peoples of the Old Testament World.* Grand Rapids: Baker, 1994. Good introduction to each of the major people groups mentioned in the Old Testament.

Merrill, Eugene H. *Kingdom of Priests: A History of Old Testament Israel.* Grand Rapids: Baker, 1987. Best conservative history of Israel.

Page, Charles R., II, and Carl A. Volz. *The Land and the Book: An Introduction to the World of the Bible.* Nashville: Abingdon, 1993. A concise overview of key archaeological sites in the land of the Bible.

Roux, Georges. *Ancient Iraq.* 2nd ed. Baltimore: Penguin, 1980. Readable and informative introduction to ancient Mesopotamia.

Saggs, H. W. F. *The Greatness That Was Babylon: A Sketch of the Ancient Civilization of the Tigris-Euphrates Valley.* New York: Hawthorn, 1962. Extensive treatment by a leading scholar.

———. *The Might That Was Assyria.* London: Sidgwick & Jackson, 1984. Companion volume to The Greatness That Was Babylon.

Shanks, Hershel, ed. *Ancient Israel: A Short History from Abraham to the Roman Destruction of the Temple.* Englewood Cliffs, N.J./Washington, D.C.: Prentice Hall/Biblical Archaeology Society, 1988.

Soden, Wolfram von. *The Ancient Orient: An Introduction to the Study of the Ancient Near East.* Trans. Donald G. Schley. Grand Rapids: Eerdmans, 1994. Helpful introduction to Mesopotamia by a leading scholar of Akkadian.

Wilson, John A. *The Culture of Ancient Egypt.* Chicago: University of Chicago Press, 1951. Standard introduction.

the fulfillment of the prophecy of Jeremiah (2 Chr 36:22–23; Ezr 1:1-4).

Over the next century, three separate groups of Jewish exiles returned to Jerusalem to rebuild and start over.[25] The first group came under the political leadership of Zerubbabel and the religious leadership of the high priest Jeshua (Ezr 1–6). The returnees tried to rebuild the temple, but had to battle opposition, discouragement, and lack of resources. It was only after the ministries of the prophets Haggai and Zechariah that the second temple was finally finished in 515 B.C.

Ezra the priest and scribe led the second expedition from Babylonia in 458 B.C. (Ezr 7–10). Ezra's task was not to rebuild the country materially as the first returnees had done. He was concerned with the social and spiritual well-being of the people.

Nehemiah led the third return to Jerusalem in 445 B.C. (Neh 1–13). Nehemiah was a Jewish exile who had risen to high office in the Persian royal court. He saw his task primarily as one of rebuilding Jerusalem's city walls and providing better defense for its inhabitants. After completion of the wall, Nehemiah stayed in Jerusalem as governor of the Persian province.

The Old Testament ends with God's people restored to the land and a new temple rebuilt for proper worship of God. Yet this was clearly not a "kingdom of God," with a son of David on the throne of an empire with worldwide significance. The promises of God's sacred covenant with his people would have to wait for another time and place. The Old Testament ends in expectation and faith. God would yet fulfill his purposes in his own timing and in his own way.

Part
1

Encountering
the Pentateuch

3 Introduction to the Pentateuch

The Birth of God's People

Outline

- **What Is the Pentateuch?**
- **What Is the Pentateuch About?**
- **What Are the Overarching Themes of the Pentateuch?**
  Sovereignty of God
  History
  Fallen Condition of Humanity
  Salvation
  Holiness
- **Who Wrote the Pentateuch?**
  Authorship and Traditional Consensus
  Modern Critical Approaches

Objectives

After reading this chapter, you should be able to

- Define the term "Pentateuch"
- Draw conclusions about what the purpose of the Pentateuch was
- Identify the key message of each of the five pentateuchal books
- Compare the themes of the Pentateuch
- Apply modern critical approaches to the question of authorship of the Pentateuch
- Identify the key scholars who defined the documentary hypothesis
- Assess the contribution of evangelical scholars to the study of the Pentateuch

Pentateuch

Torah

Many people are familiar with the classic stories about Abraham, Moses, Israel's crossing through the Red Sea, and the giving of the Ten Commandments. But where do these stories come from and why are they important? How have they become so well known? In this chapter, we introduce the section of the Bible where these stories are found. These books are called the PENTATEUCH.

What Is the Pentateuch?

The term **"Pentateuch"** refers to the first five books of the Bible (from Greek *pente*, five, and *teuchos*, scroll). The biblical evidence supports the view that Genesis, Exodus, Leviticus, Numbers, and Deuteronomy belong together as a literary unit. The Old Testament probably refers to the Pentateuch when it uses phrases like the "Book of the Law of Moses" (2 Kgs 14:6) or the "Book of the Law" (Josh 1:8), while the New Testament refers to these books as "Law" in the expression "the Law and the Prophets" (Lk 16:16). Thus, we should not necessarily view the Pentateuch as five separate books. Perhaps the limited size of ancient scrolls necessitated the division into the five-book format.

The Pentateuch spans history from the beginning of time down to, but not including, Israel's conquest of the promised land. This land would later become Israel's homeland. Excluding for the moment Genesis 1–11, the story is basically one of a family that grew, by God's grace, into his people. God dramatically and miraculously saved this nation from the agony of slavery and entered into a commitment of intimacy with them. After many years of struggle, the people reached the land God had promised to their ancestors and prepared to possess it. So Genesis–Deuteronomy is a self-contained story with a clearly defined beginning, an intricate plot with many important subplots, and a decided ending.

The Jewish designation for these books is the Hebrew word **"Torah."** Though we usually translate this word "law," it means much more. It comes from a word for "teach" and is better understood as "in-struction." "Torah" is thus an appropriate tag for these first five books of the Bible, because they contain instructions for life. Together these five books establish the historical and theological foundations for the rest of the Bible, and they also teach us how to live faithfully.

What Is the Pentateuch About?

The Pentateuch is basically the story of God's people, the nation of Israel. It explains where the nation came from, how God saved her from extinction, and the struggles in her relationship with God. But the Pentateuch is not simply a "history" of Israel. It contains much that we would not expect in a national history, and omits certain details that might ordinarily be considered historically pertinent.

The Pentateuch is not just a document to provide us with important and true information, but also to strengthen our faith. It was originally meant to encourage ancient Israelites to believe and trust in God because of his faithful relationship with their ancestors. So without presenting a complete "history of Israel," it traces the actions of God and Israel *in history*. For over two millennia, believers have found important historical, religious, and theological truths in these books.

This story opens with a book of beginnings. "Genesis" comes from a Greek word meaning "origins." The first eleven chapters of Genesis describe the beginning of the universe, humanity, sin, and punishment. These opening chapters are crucial for understanding the rest of the Bible because they reveal God's nature, the role of his created universe, and the position humanity holds in that universe.

Above all else, Genesis 1–11 presents a problem. God created a universe that he evaluated as "good" (acceptable to him) at every phase of its creation. But humanity ruined what he accomplished. After Adam and Eve brought sin into the world (Gn 3), its consequences were immediately obvious. The effects of sin were evident in every aspect of God's creation, and became progressively worse. After humankind resisted other attempts to

At the conclusion of the Book of Genesis, God has miraculously delivered his people from a famine and they are living peacefully in Egypt. But many years later, the Egyptians oppressed the whole Israelite population and forced them into slavery.

covenant

stem the tide of evil, God chose a single man and his family as the solution to this awful problem.

Genesis 12–50 is the story of Abraham, his family, and their journey of faith. Their story is one of enduring value because they responded to God in faithfulness. The text presents each character honestly, with no attempt to hide shortcomings. But the point of Genesis 12–50 is that these people believed God, and he used their faith as the solution to the sin problem in the world, or at least as the beginning of the solution. So this first book of the Bible tells of the beginnings of the world and of God's people. Genesis describes the beginning of everything except God.

At the conclusion of the Book of Genesis, God has miraculously delivered his people from a famine and they are living peacefully in Egypt. But many years later, the Egyptians oppressed the whole Israelite population and forced them into slavery. The Book of Exodus opens, as does Genesis, with a problem. God's people are suffering under Egyptian bondage, and his plan to use them as the solution to sin seems impossible. But, as before, God chooses to deal with the problem by calling a faithful few individuals to serve him unconditionally.

Exodus relates the preparation and call of Moses, and his role in leading the Israelites out of Egypt ("Exodus" means "departure"). This miraculous deliverance of God's people is the formative event in Israelite history and the best example of God's power and grace. As such, the exodus is the Old Testament equivalent to the cross in the New Testament. The book also describes God's special new binding relationship **(covenant)** with his people (chapters 19–40).

The third book of the Pentateuch is Leviticus. This book seems to interrupt the historical thought flow, and impresses many modern readers as strange. But Leviticus (having to do with the sons of "Levi," or priests) is indispensable to the total message of the Pentateuch. It calls God's people to ritual and moral purity. In Exodus, God liberated captive Israel and established a unique relationship with her. Leviticus focuses on how the people can maintain that relationship. It instructs the priests in how to offer appropriate sacrifices to God. This book is thus devoted to preserving Israel's holy moral character as an aid to worship and enjoyment of the Lord and his blessings.

The Book of Numbers continues the story of Israel's journey to the promised land. The book opens with elaborate preparations for leaving Mount Sinai where the covenant has been established (including a census of the people—hence the name "Numbers"). But the book then describes a series of events in which the people chose to disobey God. Israel's disobedience cost her dearly, as God did not permit her to enter the promised land immediately. Numbers relates how God's people tragically wandered in the desert for forty years, unable to accomplish what he had in store for them.

Deuteronomy, the final book of the Pentateuch, is a series of Moses' farewell speeches. On the plains of Moab, across the Jordan River from the promised land, Moses addresses God's people and prepares them for the future. He restates the law of the covenant ("Deuteronomy" means "second law"), and warns them against turning from God to worship other deities. The book aims to reestablish the covenant between God and his people.

We may summarize the Pentateuch as follows. Genesis is a book of origins. It describes the *beginnings* of the universe and the origins of God's people. Exodus traces the *salvation* of his people, who are helpless to save themselves. Leviticus calls for *holiness* as the only natural lifestyle for the Israelites and as the only possible response to God's grace. Numbers is a book of *wanderings* in which God's people suffer the consequences of their unbelief. But the story ends on a positive note, when Deuteronomy presents a program for *renewal*.

What Are the Overarching Themes of the Pentateuch?

Several important themes run throughout the Pentateuch. The first of these is foundational for the rest.

Sovereignty of God

The Pentateuch begins by emphasizing God's **sovereignty**. The Israelite creation story (Gn 1–2) is unlike the creation stories of other ancient Near Eastern cultures. While other peoples speculated about the origins of deities, Genesis assumes the preexistence and eternality of God.

Furthermore, the Israelite God created the whole universe with no assistance from anyone (also a unique concept in ancient literature). He created it without

using preexistent matter and did so effortlessly, through the power of his spoken word. Centuries ago, the early church saw the importance of the ideas of "creation out of nothing" (*creatio ex nihilo*) and creation by divine decree (**fiat**). These have always been central doctrines of the Christian faith. So the simple style of Genesis 1 powerfully establishes God's sovereignty over his creation. The subsequent stories of the flood (Gn 6–9) and the Tower of Babel (Gn 11) also bring the point home.

The Pentateuch further demonstrates God's supreme dominion by rehearsing his dealings with individuals like Abraham, Isaac, Jacob, Joseph, and Moses. Throughout their lives, wherever they traveled across the ancient Near East, God assured them of his presence, protection, and guidance. The universal scope of his dominion stands in stark contrast to that of other deities of the ancient Near East, whose jurisdiction had definite geographical limits.

In dramatic fashion, God demonstrated his sovereign lordship over Egypt. He called Abram out of Ur of Mesopotamia, the eastern extremity of the ancient world. He protected him and guided him to Palestine, his people's future home. But could Moses and the Israelites trust God to help them against Egypt, the most advanced and sophisticated nation of the time? The plagues were spectacular demonstrations that God was lord of Egypt and, indeed, of all the earth. God's dramatic appearance at Mount Sinai (Ex 19) and his dominion over Israel during her desert wanderings further confirmed that his sovereignty knew no boundaries, geographical or otherwise.

History

A second dominant, overarching theme of the Pentateuch is the importance of history. Unlike the writings of certain religions (Confucianism, Buddhism, etc.), Old Testament religion attributed special significance to history from the beginning. Other ancient Eastern religions expressed their theology in terms of **myths**, in which important events took place beyond time and space. But in the Old Testament, God created history and worked in and through its events. This is most apparent in Israel's distinctive creation story.

Near Ur of the Chaldeans, South Iraq. God called Abram out of Ur of Mesopotamia, the eastern extremity of the ancient world, protected him, and guided him to Palestine, his people's future home.

Besides establishing God's sovereignty, the creation narratives describe the beginning of history by relating the creation of time and space (Gn 1:5, 9–10). Because history is part of God's creation, it follows that he is sovereign over human history and may alter it if he chooses. Thus, the Israelites saw their national history as an arena for divine intervention. They came to know God better by studying his acts in history. Events such as the plagues of Egypt and the giving of the Sinai covenant are more than the nation's historical heritage. They are theological truths that the Israelites recognized as unique, divine revelation.

So the Old Testament consistently presents theological truth through the medium of history. Just as the entire New Testament relates to Jesus' birth, life, death, and resurrection, so the Old Testament is inextricably tied to historical events. In the Bible, spiritual truth is always fleshed out in historical reality. Humanly speaking, faith expresses itself in works. From the divine perspective, the revelation of God's truth is always incarnational, that is, God reveals himself in time and space.

Fallen Condition of Humanity

A third important theme of the Pentateuch is its systematic appraisal of the condition of humanity. The message is painfully sim-

ple: Humankind is fallen. God created Adam and Eve as the climax of his perfect creation. They were at peace with God, having ready access to his presence and enjoying his favor. They were also at peace with his creation around them, capable of enjoying its rich and perfect fullness. This portrait of paradise is the biblical definition of shalom, "peace." Shalom means more than the absence of conflict. It refers to a life where wholeness and well-being are present. Shalom-peace is present when God is not hindered by human sin and is free to add significance and meaning to an otherwise meaningless existence.

But sin entered the Garden of Eden and immediately changed this perfect picture (Gn 3). Humanity's parents experienced separation from their gracious Creator for the first time. The loss of a peaceful relationship with God also affected the way they related to creation and to each other. These effects of sin accumulated and worsened, so that the message was clear: Humanity was incapable of righting its own wrongs. The fallenness of humanity leaves every individual with specific needs only God can address.

Salvation

The fourth principal theme of the Pentateuch is salvation. This is not just a New Testament doctrine. The Pentateuch relates the salvation of God in story form. God's love and grace moved him to take specific steps to remedy the human dilemma. The salient events in this story (the call of Abram, the call of Moses, the plagues of Egypt, the covenant, etc.) signify his love and grace, and the single thread of redemption ties these events together.

This theme is particularly striking in view of the other main points discussed above, especially God's sovereignty and humanity's fallenness. God was not forced by any third party or external circumstances to reach down to fallen humanity. His sovereignty means he has no needs, including the need for human love and worship. The only motivating factor for his redemptive actions may be found in his nature as a loving and compassionate God (Jn 3:16). This fact, combined with an awareness of the hopelessness of the human predicament, helps us understand how great his salvation is (Heb 2:1–4).

Holiness

The Pentateuch's emphasis on God's sovereign grace in redemption leads naturally to the fifth major theme. The only proper human response to God's grace and love is personal sanctity. So the Pentateuch strongly emphasizes the concept of holiness. This sovereign God is supreme in his moral character. When he draws his people to himself, he invites them to imitate his character (Lv 11:44). He brought Israel out of Egypt and made them his own people. But he expected their new relationship with him to alter their conduct forever. Holiness is the human appropriation of God's grace.

In the Pentateuch, as elsewhere in the Bible, God's grace is always followed by law. God is never content to be in relationship with his people if they are making no effort to imitate his character. So law is not intended to restrict life, but to instruct God's people in the "paths of righteousness." Law plays a dominant role in the Pentateuch, but it never serves as a fence to enslave God's people. Instead, his law protects them from their own self-destructive actions, and as a means of grace, makes them more like him.

So the Pentateuch contains the story of God's people. There is much more here than an account of his dealings with an ancient people. The church has long recognized these writings as sacred Scripture. As is true of all Scripture, God intends that this story—a story of his saving grace poured out freely on needy humans—should become our story as well. For indeed, this is the story of all who follow Christ.

For Christians, personal salvation is very similar to the story of the Pentateuch. God, the Sovereign of the universe, breaks into our personal history and provides a solution for our brokenness. Because of his love and grace, he provides salvation by his own revelation in history (incarnation). God gives us prophets and teachers to interpret his historical acts and help us maintain our relationship with him. The rest of the story is one of growth in grace, or the imitation of our Savior. So the gospel of Jesus Christ was also the gospel of the Israelites.

Who Wrote the Pentateuch?

Authorship and Traditional Consensus

The Pentateuch contains several self-claims regarding the composition of some of its parts. There are two clear references to Moses as the author of Exodus 20–23, which is known as the "Book of the Covenant" (Ex 24:4, 7). The text also claims Moses wrote the Ten Commandments at the Lord's direction (Ex 34:27). At least two other incidents are said to have been preserved in writing by Moses (Ex 17:14; Nm 33:2). There are also clear references to Moses as author of parts of the Book of Deuteronomy (Dt 31:9, 19, 22, 24).[1]

In addition to the literary activity of Moses, speeches of God are frequently introduced with such phrases as "The LORD spoke to Moses, saying" (Lv 4:1). In fact, most of the material from Exodus through Deuteronomy relates to the life and ministry of Moses in one form or another. Moses was the central historical figure during the period that Exodus–Deuteronomy describes. This fact, in conjunction with all of the internal evidence, led to a nearly uncontested tradition of Mosaic authorship for the Pentateuch.

talmud

Mishnah

source
criticism

Documentary
Hypothesis

anthropomor-
phic

monotheism

Both Jewish and early Christian tradition consistently associated the Pentateuch with Moses. The **talmud** refers to the first five books of the Bible as "the Books of Moses."[2] The **Mishnah** and the Jewish historian JOSEPHUS both accepted the Mosaic authorship of the Pentateuch.[3] The New Testament refers to the Pentateuch as the first of two sections of the Old Testament Scriptures in the expression "Moses and the prophets" (see, for example, Lk 24:27, 44).

Modern Critical Approaches

Though early tradition regarding Mosaic authorship of the Pentateuch was pervasive, it was not without early challengers.[4] But it was not until the early 1800s that the traditional consensus began to crumble, when European Old Testament scholarship seriously challenged the idea of Mosaic authorship. The combination of eighteenth-century enlightenment thinking and the evolutionary tenets of the nineteenth century resulted in a wave of speculation about the origins of the Pentateuch.

Source and redaction criticism

Toward the end of the nineteenth century, a new paradigm emerged that taught that the Pentateuch had been compiled from four separate sources. This approach is known as **source criticism**. In this section we briefly trace the basic tenets of source criticism and the various answers other modern scholars have given to the question, "Who wrote the Pentateuch?"

This theory is frequently known as the **Documentary Hypothesis** and its most pervasive protagonist was JULIUS WELLHAUSEN.[5] He formulated a theory explaining how four originally independent documents (J, E, D, and P) were combined to form the Pentateuch. By the turn of the century, leading Old Testament scholars in Germany, Britain, France, and America accepted many of Wellhausen's conclusions.

The basic components of this theory are as follows. The J document was composed around 850 B.C. in Judah and uses the divine name "Yahweh" (or Jehovah, which is "the Lord" in the English translations). In a simplistic narrative style, this document presents God in **anthropomorphic** terms (with human-like qualities). Angels appear in this document occasionally, but usually God deals directly with humans

face to face. The E document was written around 750 B.C. as a corrective to the J document. This document uses the less intimate word *Elohim* ("God"), and avoids anthropomorphic terminology. E presents the northern perspective in a prose style that is more stilted and formal than J's.

Sometime after the Assyrians conquered the northern kingdom of Israel (722 B.C.), J and E supposedly were combined into a new document, JE. This new document reflected the theological convictions after the historical crisis. Around 650 B.C., the D document was written to reinforce the cultic purity of Judah's worship. This new source stressed the importance of worshiping the Lord God (often combining "Yahweh" and "Elohim") at a central shrine, Jerusalem. The D document thus corrected and updated the less precise and older JE document. Early versions of the Wellhausen hypothesis limited D to Deuteronomy 5–26, 28. This document used a sermonic style, often expressing its theology in exhortations.

According to this hypothesis, the JE and D documents were fused into the JED source sometime after 587 B.C., when Jerusalem fell to the Babylonians. But this new document neglected the priestly concerns of the postexilic community. At some point during the middle of the fifth century B.C., the P document was written to address this deficiency. Wellhausen believed the P document contained the majority of the pentateuchal material concerning the sacrificial system. This document's legal material concerns priests, Levites, and the various types of sacrifices (e.g., Lv 1–7), and emphasizes the transcendence and awesomeness of God.

Around 400 B.C., these two final documents (JED and P) were combined into a JEDP complex of materials that comprise the Pentateuch as we know it today. Wellhausen believed that **monotheism** and cultic legislation were late developments in Israelite history. Any references to a central sanctuary with exclusive worship of God at Jerusalem had to be later than 622 B.C., when Josiah's reforms were enacted and D was composed. Religious material from the late postexilic period was read back into the ancient history of Israel. There was thus almost no historical veracity in the Pentateuch. Wellhausen's reconstruc-

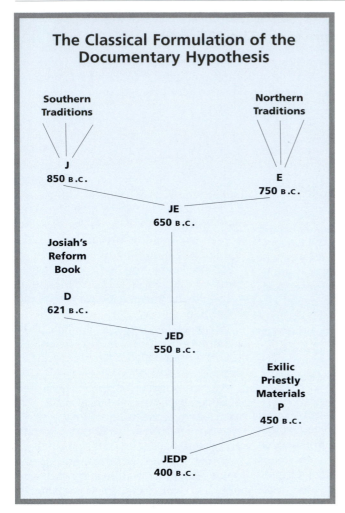

The Classical Formulation of the Documentary Hypothesis

Southern Traditions

Northern Traditions

J
850 B.C.

E
750 B.C.

JE
650 B.C.

Josiah's Reform Book

D
621 B.C.

JED
550 B.C.

Exilic Priestly Materials
P
450 B.C.

JEDP
400 B.C.

redaction criticism

form criticism

genres

Sitz im Leben

tradition criticism

tions were dominated by antisupernaturalism and philosophical evolutionary thought. The theory made no allowance for divine intervention in history, or for unique divine revelation.

The reaction of the church was clear. Early conservative scholars were vocal in their opposition to the skeptical presuppositions of the hypothesis. E. W. Hengstenberg (1802–69) was the most prolific challenger of the new and radical source theories. His criticisms were carried further by James Orr, Oswald Allis, E. J. Young, and others. These scholars claimed that the new theory violated the internal self-claims of the Pentateuch. For instance, the text claims the events described were historical and that Moses wrote sections of the Pentateuch. Conservative scholars have also maintained that the Documentary Hypothesis ignores archaeological ev-

idence from the ancient Near East, is based on evolutionary philosophies from the nineteenth century that are no longer tenable, and is too subjective. Others have protested that the hypothesis rejects the important testimony of inspired New Testament writers. On the whole, these objections have not been answered.

Form criticism

Since Wellhausen's landmark synthesis of the Documentary Hypothesis, Old Testament scholarship has taken many turns. But the road has never led far from Wellhausen's original hypothesis. **Redaction criticism** has attempted to explain scientifically how these four separate sources were edited together, but this approach has met with little agreement among scholars. **Form criticism** became a popular approach shortly after Wellhausen's development of the source theory.

The pioneering scholar of form criticism was Hermann Gunkel, who established the basic tenets of the approach around the turn of the century. He began by accepting the JEDP hypothesis. But he was not as skeptical as source critics had been about the historical value of the pentateuchal stories. Instead, form criticism analyzes the various literary types (or **genres**) found in the Bible and isolates these smaller units. By emphasizing the "situation in life" (or *Sitz im Leben*) of the smaller units, form criticism attempts to uncover the "historical kernel" for each literary genre. According to Gunkel and others, these smaller units were later joined into the four sources of the Pentateuch.

Tradition criticism

Form criticism also speculated about the oral, preliterary history of the various literary types. Were these biblical stories passed down by word of mouth over a long period of time before they were written down? A branch of form criticism thus developed in the first half of the twentieth century that devoted itself to tracing this oral tradition—**tradition criticism**. This approach, whose most celebrated exponent was Martin Noth, believed that writing came late in the development of Old Testament literary sources. The literary types reflect a long history of oral transmission, so that the pentateuchal sources

Documentary Hypothesis: The Major Players[1]

BENEDICT SPINOZA: Seventeenth-century Jewish philosopher who rejected Mosaic authorship of the Pentateuch and appeared to give Ezra credit for these books.

JEAN ASTRUC: In 1753, this French medical professor published a work on Genesis that marked the beginning of pentateuchal source criticism. Astruc believed Moses relied on sources from the patriarchal period. He used the divine names *Elohim* and *Yahweh* to divide Genesis into separate sources (later known as E and J) which he believed approximated the sources used by Moses.

J. S. VATER: In 1805, Vater argued that the Pentateuch was composed of as many as forty fragmentary sources. This became known as the fragmentary hypothesis.

W. M. L. DE WETTE: In 1807, De Wette equated the legal core at the center of Deuteronomy with "the book of the Law" discovered in the temple under the direction of King Josiah (2 Kgs 22). This became the most important criterion for dating the D document as late as 622 B.C.

H. EWALD: In 1823, Ewald proposed one basic document, the E source. This was supplemented by older J materials and a Jehovistic editor put it all together. This became known as the supplemental theory.

WILHELM VATKE: In 1835, Vatke suggested many sections of the Pentateuch were written as late as the exile, instead of early as the text claims. He anticipated Wellhausen by believing the Pentateuch was produced late in Israel's history rather than early as a religious constitution for the nation.

V. HUPFELD: In 1853, Hupfeld argued that there were actually two separate writers who had used Elohim. He also proposed Deuteronomy was a separate D document. So now there were four basic documents: J (which was the dominant of the four), E^1, E^2, and D. Hupfeld also emphasized the role of an anonymous editor as the one responsible for tying the documents together. This idea of an editor became popular with later scholars who used him conveniently to explain any inconsistencies in the documentary theory.

E. W. HENGSTENBERG: Hengstenberg was an early opponent of the source theories. In several writings during the 1830s and 1840s, he strongly challenged those who denied Mosaic authorship. Hengstenberg inspired a generation of more orthodox scholars who opposed the Documentary Hypothesis.

K. H. GRAF: In 1865, Graf agreed with Vatke about the late date of much of the Pentateuch. He argued for a foundation document that was concerned mostly with priestly interests. This he dated later than Deuteronomy, which De Wette had established at 622 B.C. He associated this so-called priestly document to the time of Ezra. At the same time, others had taken Hupfeld's E^1 source as the priestly document, and thereafter the symbol P was used. By attempting to assign dates to each of the documents, Graf went beyond source criticism and expanded the discussion to historical criticism. This paved the way for Wellhausen's formulation of the Documentary Hypothesis, which is sometimes called the Graf-Wellhausen Hypothesis.

JULIUS WELLHAUSEN: German scholars were divided over the date and sequence of the sources. Should it be PEJD or JEDP? Wellhausen published books in 1877 and 1883 in which he settled the debate and gave the Documentary Hypothesis its classical expression. He began by accepting the source analysis of previous scholars, especially Graf. His main contribution was adopting the evolutionary concepts of the nineteenth century and applying them to the history of Israel. In this way, he explained how the sources grew and how they were related to the successive stages of Israelite history. His explanation of the sources and how they were created won wide acceptance in a brief period of time.

FRANZ DELITZSCH: In his 1887 commentary on Genesis, Delitzsch attacked the hypothesis as defined by Wellhausen. He argued that all the sections attributed to Moses in the text were in fact authentic.

S. R. DRIVER: The most influential scholar of Great Britain at the time, Driver published an important *Introduction* in 1891. He modified the Wellhausen hypothesis only slightly, and established the theory as a standard approach for English-speaking scholars.

JAMES ORR: In 1906, Orr attacked the Wellhausen hypothesis on theological and philosophical grounds. He exposed the weaknesses of source and historical criticism and their attempt to reconstruct Israelite history and literature. His criticisms were never answered.

[1]Further Reading: R. K. Harrison, *Introduction to the Old Testament* (Grand Rapids: Eerdmans, 1969), 9–32.

canonical criticism

literary criticism

evolved over many centuries before people wrote them down.

Tradition criticism is more subjective than other approaches and fails to take into account evidence from elsewhere in the ancient Near East. In fact, ancient Near Eastern studies may provide control data for Old Testament scholars, no matter which method they are using. Some scholars have argued convincingly that we may avoid serious errors by making proper comparisons between the Old Testament and ancient Near Eastern literature.[6] In the case of tradition criticism, for example, studies suggest that ancient Near Eastern literary traditions were often recorded in writing soon after the events they describe, not centuries later.

Canonical and literary approaches

The second half of the twentieth century saw the rise of two new approaches to the Old Testament. The first was **canonical criticism**, with its attempt to study the received form of the Old Testament and to expose its theological message. While not totally rejecting the findings of the documentary approaches, scholars using canonical criticism seek to study the final form of the Bible since this is what has authority for the religious community.[7] They are less concerned with how the text arrived than with the internal message of the canon. This approach provides a helpful corrective to the atomizing tendencies of its critical predecessors.

A further new development is the rise of **literary criticism**. This approach also addresses the larger literary issues, but its proponents are often antagonistic to the older source and form critical approaches to the Pentateuch. A further difference is in the emphasis on text-centered, or sometimes reader-centered, analysis rather than the traditional author-centered approaches of earlier scholars.[8] Those who use this approach have produced mixed results, but the newer literary criticism seems to hold great promise for significant new insights into biblical interpretation.

Evangelical contributions

Conservative biblical scholarship has learned a great deal from these various approaches. No single approach has the definitive answer for the question of authorship of the Pentateuch. But clearly certain of these critical approaches (especially redaction, form, canonical, and literary studies) are helpful when we use them with proper ancient Near Eastern control data.[9] It is in this area that conservatives have contributed most to Old Testament scholarship—the use of ancient Near Eastern comparative materials to serve as checks and balances for proper methods of Old Testament research.

When answering the question of pentateuchal authorship, conservative scholars generally take one of three positions.[10] First, some date the Pentateuch to the Mosaic era, but allow for various degrees of post-Mosaic material. The basic structure of the Pentateuch was established by Moses, or under Moses' supervision. Later alterations and additions occurred in line with recognized ancient Near Eastern literary procedures. Minor changes, such as spelling and editorial revisions, continued

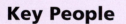

Key Terms

Pentateuch
Torah
covenant
sovereignty
creatio ex nihilo
fiat
myths
Talmud
Mishnah
source criticism
Documentary Hypothesis
anthropomorphic
monotheism
redaction criticism
form criticism
genres
Sitz im Leben
tradition criticism
canonical criticism
literary criticism

Key People

Josephus
Julius Wellhausen
Benedict Spinoza
Jean Astruc
J. S. Vater
W. M. L. De Wette
H. Ewald
Wilhelm Vatke
V. Hupfeld
E. W. Hengstenberg
K. H. Graf
Franz Delitzsch
S. R. Driver
James Orr
Oswald Allis
E. J. Young
Hermann Gunkel
Martin Noth

to occur until around Samuel's day (approximately 1050 B.C.).

Second, some conservative scholars date the final form of the Pentateuch to a period between Joshua and Solomon (as late as 930 B.C.). Most of the Pentateuch is thought to be Mosaic, but substantial amounts of post-Mosaic material were also included.

Third, other conservative scholars believe the Pentateuch acquired its current form relatively late in Israel's history (ninth to fifth centuries B.C.). These scholars recognize much that is ancient in these books. But they believe the Pentateuch grew as a result of later generations adapting Mosaic material at important crisis moments in Israel's history.

Based on the self-claims of the Pentateuch and the unity of Jewish and Chris-

tian tradition, it is prudent to assume basic Mosaic origins for most of the Pentateuch. The evidence clearly credits Moses with the substance of these books. He is its source, its originator, its authorizer. However, terms such as "author" and "authorship" are inappropriate when referring to ancient Near Eastern literary products, since they carry modern implications that were absent in antiquity.

In some cases Moses may have initiated a literary tradition that he later simply monitored. In Deuteronomy 31:9 he wrote the basic document and then entrusted its safe-keeping to the priests (see also Dt 24:8). The priests may have preserved and expanded the material, but Moses was its source. Mosaic authorship plays an important theological function in Old Testa-

Study Questions

1. What is the derivation and meaning of "Pentateuch"? What Hebrew term is used for these books and what is its meaning?

2. What is the derivation and meaning of "Genesis"? What is the problem of Genesis 1–11? What is the point of Genesis 12–50?

3. What problem is presented at the outset of Exodus? What is the meaning of "Exodus"? What role does the exodus play in Israelite history and theology? What term is used to describe the special binding relationship between God and his people?

4. What does Leviticus seek to accomplish? What portion of Israel's history is found in Numbers? What is the content of Deuteronomy?

5. What are the overarching themes of the Pentateuch?

6. What is the evidence for Mosaic authorship of the Pentateuch? What name is given to the alternative approach and who was its principal advocate?

7. What is the focus of each of the following: redaction criticism; form criticism; tradition criticism; canonical criticism; and literary criticism?

8. In what area have conservative biblical scholars contributed most to Old Testament scholarship? What three positions do these scholars take on authorship of the Pentateuch? What are their common points of agreement?

Summary

1. The Pentateuch consists of the first five books of the Old Testament: Genesis, Exodus, Leviticus, Numbers, and Deuteronomy.

2. The Pentateuch provides us with the early history of God's people and focuses on strengthening the faith of believers.

3. Genesis is known as a book of beginnings.

4. Moses is the key human figure in the Pentateuch.

5. God's sovereignty is emphasized in the Pentateuch.

6. The concept of salvation is found in the Pentateuch.

7. Questioning of Moses' authorship of the Pentateuch was begun by nineteenth-century European Old Testament scholars.

8. The primary modern forms of criticism include source criticism, redaction criticism, form criticism, tradition criticism, canonical criticism, and literary criticism.

Further Reading

Clines, David J. A. *The Theme of the Pentateuch.* Journal for the Study of the Old Testament—Supplement Series 10. Sheffield: JSOT, 1978. Important volume on the covenant theme of the pentateuchal narratives.

Dillard, Raymond B., and Tremper Longman III. *An Introduction to the Old Testament.* Grand Rapids: Zondervan, 1994. Contains a helpful survey and evaluation of the higher critical issues.

Hamilton, Victor P. *Handbook on the Pentateuch: Genesis, Exodus, Leviticus, Numbers, Deuteronomy.* Grand Rapids: Baker, 1982. Thorough introduction to the content of the Pentateuch.

Harrison, R. K. *Introduction to the Old Testament.* Grand Rapids: Eerdmans, 1969. Encyclopedic treatment by an evangelical.

Hayes, John H. *An Introduction to Old Testament Study.* Nashville: Abingdon, 1979. Survey of higher critical issues.

Livingston, G. Herbert. *The Pentateuch in Its Cultural Environment.* 2nd ed. Grand Rapids: Baker, 1987. Valuable survey of historical and cultural background.

Wolf, Herbert M. *An Introduction to the Old Testament Pentateuch.* Chicago: Moody, 1991.

ment studies, just as apostolic authority is important for New Testament books.

Though conservative scholars may differ on the date of the final form of the Pentateuch, they agree that these books of Moses are inspired, historically trustworthy and still speak with authority. Whether the final date of composition was early or late, the message began with Moses and was applicable at all periods in Israel's history. So today, the Pentateuch continues to challenge the church with God's authoritative word.

4 Genesis 1–11
The Prelude to Israel

Outline

- **Primeval History and Its Nature**
- **Contents of Genesis 1–11**
  Outline
  Creation and Its Nature (1–2)
  Sin and Its Nature (3–11)

Objectives

**After reading this chapter,
you should be able to**

- Compare the Genesis account of creation
  with the Mesopotamian account
- List the ancient Near Eastern accounts
  of creation
- Outline the major content
  of Genesis 1–11
- Identify the facts in Genesis 1
  that support the doctrine
  that God was alone at the beginning
- Chart the symmetry
  of the days of creation
- Describe the content of chapters 3–11 that
  support the major theme
  —moral failure of humankind
- Contrast the Genesis account
  of the flood with the Gilgamesh Epic

Though the primary theme of the Pentateuch is the story of God's people, this is not where Genesis begins. In order that we may fully appreciate all the actors involved in this drama, the Bible begins by telling about God and humankind as a whole. Genesis 1–11 sets the stage by describing God, his created universe, and the fallenness of humankind. So before relating the *personal* story of national Israel, the Bible first tells the sad *universal* story of all humankind. As such, these chapters are far more than mere background to the pentateuchal story. They comprise some of the most profound truths of our faith.

Primeval History and Its Nature

Israel was not alone in formulating explanations for the world's beginnings. All the great civilizations of the ancient Near East had literature that described how the universe began. Elaborate mythologies described the earliest shadowy events of prehistory, or **primeval history.** These nearly always included a **cosmogony,** or a description of how the world was made.

A comparison between Genesis and other ancient literature highlights the distinctive concerns of the ancient Israelites and illustrates the nature of Old Testament faith. The rest of the ancient Near East has nothing like Genesis 1–11. Since most modern readers already assume the oneness of the sovereign God and the significance of humanity, we usually fail to grasp the innovative contribution these chapters made as theological foundations for the rest of Scripture. As divine revelation, these chapters demolished the cherished beliefs of the day. The plurality of the gods and the insignificance of humanity were unquestioned assumptions in the ancient Near East. But God's profound truth always causes human wisdom to crumble.

Though Egyptian literature contained several parallels with Genesis, MESOPOTAMIA has proved closer to the ancient Hebrew concepts. The **Enuma Elish** (Akkadian title, meaning "When on high") is the most complete Mesopotamian account of creation and has many interesting similarities to the biblical record. The story describes a cosmic conflict between the leading deities. The young and daring Marduk kills the monstrous Tiamat, mother goddess personifying the primeval ocean. Using Tiamat's divided carcass, Marduk creates heaven and earth. From the blood of her co-conspirator, he and his father create humankind to do the hard labor of the universe, leaving the deities free from work. Out of gratitude to Marduk for rescuing them from wicked Tiamat, the gods build for him the city of Babylon, the great capital city (*ANET*, 60–72, 501–503).

But this monumental piece of literature is relatively late in Mesopotamian history (our copies come from the first millennium, though it was probably composed much earlier). Recent scholarship has found more direct parallels in an older Mesopotamian document, the **Epic of Atrahasis.** This epic is the oldest Near Eastern primeval history in nearly complete form (early second millennium). It presents in historical sequence both the creation of humanity and his near extinction in the flood in a sequence similar to that in Genesis. The Atrahasis epic confirms that the basic plot of Genesis 1–11 was well known throughout the ancient Orient.[1]

In light of the numerous ancient creation myths from the Near East, Genesis 1–11 is a relative latecomer. If we assume Moses was the source for most of the Pentateuch, the Atrahasis epic is at least five hundred years older than the Mosaic edition of Genesis. Therefore, numerous parallels with Mesopotamian literature should not surprise us.

The many comparisons between Genesis 1–11 and ancient Near Eastern literature should not give the wrong impression. There is no evidence that the Old Testament borrowed any of these parallels. Instead, the Old Testament answered the same questions other authors of the ancient world were considering—and in unique ways that expressed Israel's distinctive theology.[2] Only the Bible gives an inspired answer to these important questions of life. Although the origins of Genesis 1–11 are shrouded in mystery, God revealed to Moses the truth about creation and the nature of the world through the ancient Hebrew traditions.

The Bible is not merely a human prod-

Excerpts from the Enuma Elish

When Marduk hears the words of the gods,	I will establish a savage, 'man' shall be his name.
His heart prompts (him) to fashion artful works.	Verily, savage-man I will create.
Opening his mouth, he addresses Ea	He shall be charged with the service of the gods
To impart the plan he had conceived in his heart:	That they might be at ease!"
"Blood I will mass and cause bones to be.	–Enuma Elish VI, 1–8 (*ANET,* 68)

uct and its purpose is not just to satisfy our curiosity. Modern readers often look to Genesis to answer the wrong questions. But by comparing Genesis with other ancient literature, we learn what the fundamental concerns were. The first eleven chapters of Genesis are about the sovereign Creator, the nature of his creation, and the extent of its ruin.

Contents of Genesis 1–11

Outline

Creation and Its Nature (1–2)

The first two chapters use concise language to state succinctly what we need to know about creation. In unsurpassed literary style, the passage introduces us to the main characters of the biblical drama

(God and humanity) and describes the stage on which their relationship will be enacted (creation).

Genesis 1

Chapter 1 begins with a two-verse introduction. Interestingly, the first sentence of the Bible presents a difficult problem. The Hebrew is somewhat unique and scholars differ as to its proper interpretation. The question is one of its relationship with the rest of the chapter. Some take the sentence as subordinate to verse 2 or verse 3 (that is, as a dependent clause). In this case, verse 1 becomes a temporal clause introducing creation: "When God set about to create the heavens and the earth, the earth was a formless void . . ." (see NEB, NAB, NJPS, NRSV, and AB, though some include such a translation only in a footnote). Such a translation implies that God did not create the substance from which he made the earth. Instead, he began with preexistent matter. Scholars who hold this view often compare Genesis 1 with the *Enuma Elish,* where Marduk begins creation with Tiamat's corpse, or preexisting matter.

A more traditional interpretation of verse 1 assumes it is an independent sentence that serves as a title to the rest of the chapter. There are numerous variations of this traditional interpretation of verses 1–3.[3] The most likely is that verse 1 is a summary statement that describes the relative beginning of everything, without any reference to specifics. Verse 2 describes the nature of primeval chaos before God continued his creative work. The rest of chapter (vv. 3–31) explains *how* God created heaven and earth. This interpretation assumes an original creation that cannot be dated. Verse 2 describes the character

Table 4.1
Narrative Symmetry of the Days of Genesis One

DAY ONE/LIGHT ⟶ DAY FOUR/LUMINARIES

DAY TWO/SEA AND SKY ⟶ DAY FIVE/CREATURES FOR WATER AND AIR

DAY THREE/FERTILE EARTH ⟶ DAY SIX/CREATURES FOR THE FERTILE EARTH

DAY SEVEN/SABBATH

of this unproductive and empty matter before God spoke in verse 3.[4]

The traditional approach to verse 1 as an independent sentence is supported by all ancient versions (and most modern ones; NASB, NKJV, NIV, and JB). The grammar, vocabulary, and literary style of the passage leave it open to a wide variety of interpretations. But theologically only the traditional approach is possible. In other references to creation, the Bible is consistently clear that God created the universe from nothing and did so without taxing his powers or energy (Ps 33:6, 9; Heb 11:3).

The rest of Genesis 1 also supports the ancient Christian doctrine that God was alone at the beginning and created the universe from nothing *(creatio ex nihilo)*. He did not require some preexistent substance. By creating light and darkness (vv. 3–5) and by calling forth a land mass from the waters (vv. 9–10) God actually created time and space.

At the beginning, only God existed. He alone is the all-powerful One who is capable of speaking the universe into existence without help or assistance. This powerful truth was new to the ancient world, and represented a direct attack on doctrines such as **polytheism.** Likewise today, the opening words of Genesis, "In the beginning God . . .", give us a proper perspective on who he is and make it possible for us to accept the rest of the Bible's message. This first truth is foundational to all that follows.

Repetition and literary symmetry characterize the rest of chapter 1. Set formulas introduce each day of the creation week: "And God said, 'Let there be . . .'" Another formula concludes each day: "And there was evening and there was morning, the first [second, etc.] day." Furthermore, the

narrative symmetry means that each day corresponds with a matching day (see table 4.1).[5] The creation of light (day 1) corresponds with sun, moon, and stars to govern the use of light (day 4). The creation of the sky (day 2) prepares the reader for day 5, in which God creates the birds. This narrative structure highlights days 3 and 6 in which God makes the dry land and then creates animals and humankind to inhabit it.

The correspondence of days 3 and 6 reveals the literary climax in the passage. God evaluates each stage of creation (with the exception of day 2): "And God saw that it was good." But days 3 and 6 contain the evaluation two times. The repetition of each formula builds to the sixth day, in which God says, "Let us make people in our image, to be like ourselves" (v. 26 NLT).

It is impossible to exhaust the theological significance of being created in God's image (the *imago Dei*). The least we can say is that humanity was to have *dominion* over all creation as a result of bearing God's image. Adam and Eve were the visible representatives of God in creation. But being created as divine image-bearers also implies that humans were created specifically for relationship with God. Unlike the rest of creation, human life is not an end in itself. It comes with the privilege of relating to God.[6]

The dignity of humankind and his unique position in creation are marked by the image of God. Again, biblical truth aggressively attacked the prevailing doctrines of that day. Other ancient Near Eastern creation accounts such as the *Enuma Elish* and the Atrahasis epic portray the creation of men and women as a slave force for the gods. Humanity was more or

A flood account on Tablet XI of the Assyrian version of the Epic of Gilgamesh.

generations

less a means for the gods to avoid physical labor. But in Genesis 1, humankind is the jewel in this literary royal crown, the climax of God's creative activity.

The mandate "be fruitful and multiply" (v. 28) demonstrates that humanity was capable of communicating with God and receiving his commandments. It also implies that humanity was to continue God's creative work in the world. After the initial stage of creation, the universe was "unproductive and uninhabited."[7] But on day 3, God brought forth vegetation (v. 11). The land became inhabited when he commanded it to bring forth living creatures and when he created humanity (vv. 24, 26). So God made the earth productive and inhabited by his creative activity, and humanity is to continue the process.

If one word could summarize the essence of creation in this chapter, it would be "good" (ṭôb, pronounced "tōv"). God is pleased with all that he sees in his created order; this is especially apparent in days 3 and 6, where the evaluation is stated twice. Genesis portrays God as the divine artist who stands back to admire his handiwork. All is just as it should be, including humanity. As the climax of his creative work, humanity also pleased him and was free to serve him in complete obedience.

Genesis 2

Chapter 2 (actually, vv. 2:4–25) presents a picture of creation that complements that in chapter 1. Chapter 1 portrays in broad strokes the creation of heaven and earth, and in a general way, all the universe's contents. Chapter 2 uses finer strokes to paint in the specific features. This section describes the Garden of Eden with geographical details (note the names of the rivers). It depicts the creation of the first human couple, their ideal garden surroundings, and the intimacy of their relationship.

This unit begins with an interesting expression that is an important literary structural device in the Book of Genesis: "These are the **generations** of the heavens and the earth." The term "generations" (tôlĕdôt) means offspring or history. Elsewhere in Genesis it introduces either a genealogy or a personal history (e.g., Adam, 5:1; Noah, 6:9; etc.). The phrase occurs eleven times in the Book of Genesis. Although scholars disagree on its significance, each

occurrence probably introduces a new literary unit of the book. This is the only time the expression is not followed by a personal name and it seems in this instance to serve as a narrative hinge, introducing 2:4b–25 and summarizing 1:1–2:3.[8]

The creation of humanity is the climax of chapter 1 but the centerpiece of chapter 2. The love and tender care of God are apparent in the creation of the Garden. He meticulously prepared everything else in creation as the ideal home for humanity. His gentle, divine breath brought Adam's lifeless clay figure to life (v. 7). The relationship between God and the innocent first couple was one of great intimacy. Adam and Eve were surrounded with God's love. Yet even here, the divine command is clear ("You shall not eat . . . ," v. 17), and there is the subtle possibility of disobedience and broken relationship.

In summary, the first two chapters of Genesis introduce the main characters of the Bible's redemptive drama: God and humanity. These chapters also set the stage for the drama by describing God's creation. This introduction tells us a great deal about the character of God and the nature

What about Evolution?

Some people believe in theistic evolution (or progressive creationism), which asserts that God created humanity by using evolution. According to this understanding, human beings evolved *supernaturally* from an anthropoid (human-like) species. Christians who believe this reject the idea of a random, aimless evolutionary change, which is common among atheistic evolutionists. They deny humankind is merely the product of *natural* evolution, as though God had nothing to do with it, and use evolution only to explain the "how" of creation. Since it is a secondary law of biology, not a doctrine of creation, it does not contradict belief in a Creator God. So theistic evolutionists believe evolution was part of God's creation and completely within his sovereign work.

Though such views as theistic evolution and progressive creationism are possible, we must take seriously the biblical emphasis on the unity of human origins (Rom 5:12–19) and the historical nature of the first couple, Adam and Eve. Furthermore, Christian creationism offers the only satisfying answer to the question about life's origins. Science constantly revises and changes its theories about the beginning of the universe and human life. But because of the basic limitations of scientific investigation, it is incapable of answering these ultimate questions.

---

monotheism

of his universe. The opening chapters begin by assuming **monotheism** and the sovereign, all-powerful nature of God. These were startling concepts for ancient readers. His work in creation is beautiful and pleasing to both himself and humanity. He pronounced his work "good" *(ṭôb)* at each stage of creation. This is crucial to remember when reading the rest of the Bible.

But this section also prepares us for what happens next. Humankind's character is portrayed as perfect in chapters 1 and 2. Adam and Eve were without sin and their characters, like their bodies, were unblemished by disease and death. They were free from pain and suffering. They enjoyed unlimited access to God's wonderful presence. But this would soon change. Unlike the constant and unchanging God, humanity would fall from this blessed estate.

Sin and Its Nature (3–11)

At first glance, chapters 3-11 appear to contain an assortment of unrelated and strange stories. But in reality this unit is a carefully orchestrated symphony with a single theme: the moral failure of humankind.

Chapter 3 introduces cataclysmic changes into the ideal scene of chapters 1–2. A new character is introduced: the serpent (Satan, Rv 12:9). His seditious nature and purposes are evident in his role as the great Deceiver who challenges the goodness of God head-on. Adam and Eve are not helpless victims of some persuasive force, but collaborators in evil.

After the first sin in chapter 3, humanity changed in a number of ways. First, Adam and Eve lost their original innocence. Their opened eyes and sudden awareness of their nakedness signify their shame and guilt (v. 7). Before their sin, they knew no guilt, in either their relationship with each other or with God. Second, they lost their immediate and easy access to God's presence. Instead of meeting God in the cool of the day, they hid themselves because of a new awareness of estrangement from him (vv. 8–10). They were no longer comfortable in his holy presence. Third, they lost the peaceful paradise and freedom of the Garden of Eden when God expelled them (v. 23). Thus they lost their freedom from pain, disease, and death.

Eating fruit may appear innocent enough! But the action itself displayed something immoral below the surface: re-

On the Origin of Evil[1]

The problem of why evil exists in the world can be summarized as follows: God is either all-powerful but not all-good since he allows evil to continue, or he is all-good but unable to stop evil, in which case he is not all-powerful. There are no easy answers to this problem and ultimately only God understands why evil exists in the world. The opening chapters of Genesis shed some light on this question.

We must remember that at creation, God made Adam and Eve perfect. He did not create them as evil beings. He did, however, give them a degree of responsibility for their own behavior. They had to choose to obey or disobey God's word. To some degree, evil is inherent in free will. In this sense, humans are responsible for sin and evil, not God.

So God allows evil to continue, sometimes as judgment or punishment for sin. But not all evil is due to human sin. The fact that some people suffer unjustly is the problem of *theodicy*, which the Bible deals with in the Book of Job (see chapter 20 below). Though we cannot fully understand the problem of evil, we can know that God has solved that problem for us in Jesus Christ. Indeed, God does not require that we understand, only that we trust him as children trust their parents. The unhealthy child may not understand why he has to go to the doctor, but he must learn to trust his parents' understanding.

[1]Paul E. Little, *Know Why You Believe* (Downers Grove: InterVarsity, 1974), 80–89.

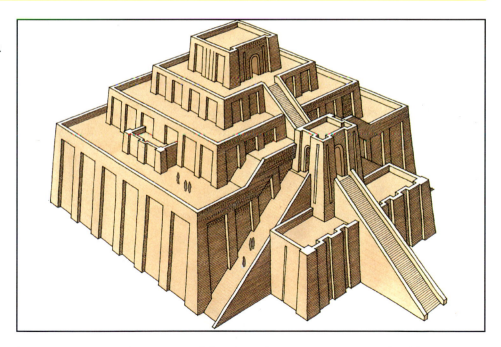

Drawing of a temple-tower or ziggurat from Ur.

bellion against God's command (2:17). Temptation always entails a challenge to God's word (3:1, 4, 5), which he speaks for our eternal good. God alone understood the full danger of disobedience. He always knows what is best for us.

Through this event, humanity unleashed an evil power in the world. In chapters 4–11 events build in a great crescendo of sin to illustrate the utter desperation of the human condition. Sin is indeed lurking at the door and "its desire is for you" (4:7, a theme verse for this passage). In chapter 4, a brother's murder illustrates how quickly sin moves from eating forbidden fruit to taking a

Human Sexuality

Sex was part of God's good and perfect creation. It was his stamp of approval on the intimate relationship between Adam and Eve before their sin (Gn 2:24–25). But just as sin has blemished the rest of creation, so sin and evil have marred our use of this gift from God (3:7).

Today, God wants Christians to enjoy sex within the confines of marriage. Sex remains part of God's good creation, a blessing for those who live in faithful, monogamous relationships. We might think of it as God's special wedding gift.

But as with any of God's gifts, sexuality becomes tainted if we misuse it. The Bible's guidelines on sex are meant to protect us from misusing God's gift and abusing each other. Premarital and extramarital sex hurt us and continue the effects of sin in our lives. God's grace can forgive and heal, but the consequences of sexual sin can last a lifetime.

Gilgamesh
Epic

human life. Humankind has now begun to reverse the creative work of God in chapters 1–2.

The genealogies of chapters 5 and 10 serve an important function in this medley of sin. Chapter 5 traces ten generations of the faithful line of Adam from Seth to Noah. The long lives of these early humans may be attributed to the slowly decaying effects of sin in the world. After the flood, the ages of Noah's descendants gradually shortened.

Chapter 6 begins with a troubling story about marriage between the sons of God and the daughters of humanity (vv. 1–8). In light of this unit's emphasis on human rebellion versus faithfulness, this is probably referring to immoral unions between the faithful line of Seth and the decadent line of Cain. However, it may also be a veiled statement on the failures of human kingship. In this interpretation, the sons of God were rulers or princes, who unjustly took the daughters of helpless commoners against their will.[9]

The point of the flood (6:9–9:29) is clear in 6:5–8. The Lord determined that sin and wickedness had grown to such an extent that creation should be destroyed. Verse 5 is most emphatic in God's evaluation of the human condition: "the wickedness of humankind was great in the earth, and . . . every inclination of the thoughts of their hearts was only evil continually."

There are many points of comparison between the story of Noah and the ancient Mesopotamian story known as the **Gilgamesh Epic** (*ANET* 72–99; 503–507). This is a touching account of how Gilgamesh, probably a historical figure who was king of Uruk around 2600 B.C., rebelled against death after he lost his friend. Gilgamesh meets Utnapishtim, who has been called the "Babylonian Noah." Utnapishtim relates how he achieved immortality when he was forewarned of a divine plan to flood the world. He survived the flood in a large reed boat, accompanied by his family and pairs of all animals. But this event was unrepeatable and gives Gilgamesh little hope for immortality. He himself fails three tests by which he could have received immortality. But in defeat he resigns himself to the inevitability of death and takes comfort in his achievements. There are obviously many similarities to as well as differences from the biblical ac-

Key Place

Mesopotamia

Key Terms

primeval history
cosmogony
Enuma Elish
Epic of Atrahasis
polytheism
imago Dei
generations
monotheism
Gilgamesh Epic
Table of Nations
ziggurat

Global or Local Flood?[1]

Christian scholars differ over the scope of the flood. Did the flood waters cover the entire globe, or just the part of the world inhabited by humans?

Geological evidence is inconclusive. Many geologists deny that global catastrophes have any role in geologic theory. Catastrophist geologists believe that some of the world's rock formations are due to a sudden universal flood that lasted about a year.

On the other hand, the language of the flood narrative seems clear. God stated his purpose as wiping every living creature "from the face of the earth" (Gn 7:4). The text reports that the waters covered "all the high mountains under the entire heavens" (7:19; and see 7:21, 23).

Some have argued these expressions are symbolic.

"The problem is one of interpretation, not inspiration."[2] Though one may wonder about the scope and nature of Noah's flood, the biblical record leaves no doubt that it was a real historical event, covering at least the inhabited world.

[1]Steven A. Austin and Donald C. Boardman,
"Did Noah's Flood Cover the Entire World?"
in *The Genesis Debate,* ed. Ronald F. Youngblood
(Nashville: Thomas Nelson, 1986), 210–29.
[2]Bernard L. Ramm, *The Christian View of Science and Scripture*
(Grand Rapids: Eerdmans, 1954), 240.

Gilgamesh Epic #1

On the seventh day the ship was completed.
The launching was very difficult,
So that they had to shift the floor planks
   above and below,
Until two-thirds of the structure had gone into
   the water.
Whatever I had I laded upon her;
Whatever I had of silver I laded upon her;
Whatever I had of gold I laded upon her;

Whatever I had of all the living beings I laded
   upon her.
All my family and kin I made go aboard the
   ship.
The beasts of the field, the wild creatures of
   the field,
All the craftsmen I made go aboard.

–Utnapishtim to Gilgamesh
–Gilgamesh Epic XI, 76–85 (*ANET*, 94)

Table of Nations

ziggurat

count, though direct literary relationship is impossible to trace.

The "**Table of Nations**" (10:1–32) classified the nations of the known world under the three sons of Noah: Shem, Ham, and Japheth. The Japhethites inhabited mostly the Mediterranean islands and Asia Minor, and were peoples most remote from Israel. Most of the Hamites were peoples with whom Israel had hostile relationships. The descendants of Shem were reserved for last because of their importance.[10] This is the line God would use to

begin to address the sin problem (see below on 11:10–32). Here finally is a glimmer of hope.

The Tower of Babel in chapter 11 highlights the pride and arrogant rebellion of humanity. Ancient Mesopotamian temple complexes often featured a stepped tower (**ziggurat**) of three to seven stages. They may have been connected to the idea that gods originally lived in mountains and the *ziggurat* served as a substitute. Near the foot of this tower stood the ancient pagan temple itself.

Summary

1. Of all the accounts of creation found in ancient Near Eastern literature, the Mesopotamian accounts are closest to the Hebrew account.

2. Chapter 1 of Genesis describes the overview of creation.

3. Chapter 2 of Genesis provides a more specific account of creation.

4. God was alone at the beginning of creation and created the universe from nothing.

5. There is inexhaustible theological significance in the fact that man was created in God's image.

6. The moral failure of humankind is the theme of Genesis 3–11.

7. The results of original sin are that humankind lost its innocence, its easy access to God, and its peaceful paradise and freedom.

8. Underlying original sin is the sin of rebellion against God.

9. Sin increased until God decided that creation should be destroyed, and he used the flood to accomplish this.

10. The Gilgamesh Epic contains similarities to the story of Noah and the flood.

11. The pride and rebellion of humankind is epitomized in the Tower of Babel.

The name of the most important city of Mesopotamia was Babylon, which, by popular etymology, came to mean "Gate of God."[11] But the Genesis account of the Tower of Babel refuted this arrogant claim. The powerful city represented humanity's unified rebellion against God and was therefore marked by confusion (Hebrew *balal*, 11:9). So Genesis turns the rebellious "gate of heaven" into confusion of speech and the dispersion of humanity. In an interesting coincidence, the wordplay still works in English, where "babble" means "to make incoherent sounds."

With a single international language and advanced building technology, humanity was unified in rebellion. But unification and peace are not the ultimate goods of society, because they can result in pride and rebellion.[12] God's response once again teaches that he who created the universe continues to govern sovereignly the affairs of humankind.

The genealogy at the end of chapter 11 (vv. 10–32) brings the primeval history to a close on a subtle note of hope. The emphasis since chapter 3 has been on the tragic avalanche of sin that has ruined God's perfect creation and humanity itself. The universal situation is nothing but despair. But here the line of Shem (cf. 10:21–32) continues and narrows to a single family, that of Terah, father of Abram.

Study Questions

1. What are the three principal subjects of Genesis 1–11?

2. How did the primeval history and cosmology of Genesis conflict with the prevailing views of the ancient Near East?

3. What are the three possible interpretations of the Hebrew in Genesis 1:1? On which interpretation is the traditional theological view based? How is this in conflict with the ancient Near Eastern views?

4. What two literary devices characterize the rest of Genesis 1?

5. What are the theological implications of being created in God's image? What word describes the essence of creation in Genesis 1?

6. What is the relationship of Genesis 2 to Genesis 1? How is the creation of humanity presented differently (from a literary standpoint)? In summary, what do these two chapters present?

7. What is the theme of Genesis 3–11? In what ways did humanity change after the first sin of Genesis 3? What challenge is always involved in temptation? What two verses depict the dangers and the spread of sin in Genesis 3–11?

8. In what way does the Table of Nations (10:1–32) hint at the way God will address the problem of sin?

9. How does the account of the Tower of Babel serve as a climax of the avalanche of sin in Genesis 3–11? How does this unit end on a note of hope?

Further Reading

Hamilton, Victor P. *The Book of Genesis: Chapters 1–17.* New International Commentary on the Old Testament. Grand Rapids: Eerdmans, 1990. Thorough exposition by an evangelical.

Kidner, Derek. *Genesis: An Introduction and Commentary.* Tyndale Old Testament Commentary. Downers Grove: InterVarsity, 1967. Theologically sensitive treatment.

Mathews, Kenneth A. *Genesis 1–11.* New American Commentary 1A. Nashville: Broadman, 1996.

Ridderbos, N. H. *Is There a Conflict between Genesis 1 and Natural Science?* Trans. John Vriend. Grand Rapids: Eerdmans, 1957. Classic work dealing particularly with the nature of "day" in Genesis 1.

Rogerson, John W. *Genesis 1–11.* Old Testament Guides. Sheffield: JSOT, 1991.

Ross, Allen P. *Creation and Blessing: A Guide to the Study and Exposition of the Book of Genesis.* Grand Rapids: Baker, 1988. Helpful evangelical study of the literary aspects of the text.

Wenham, Gordon J. *Genesis 1–15.* Word Biblical Commentary 1. Waco, Tex.: Word, 1987. Most comprehensive treatment available, including all the pertinent ancient Near Eastern materials.

Youngblood, Ronald F., ed. *The Genesis Debate.* Nashville: Thomas Nelson, 1986. Presents differing positions on the most difficult questions of Genesis.

5 Genesis 12–50
The Patriarchs: Ancestors of Israel's Faith

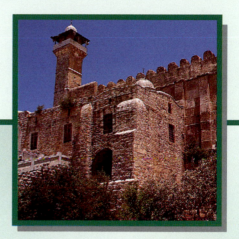

Outline

- **Background of the Patriarchal Narratives**
- **The Story of the Patriarchs**
  Abraham and Isaac (12–25)
  Jacob and His Twelve Sons (25:19–36:43)
  Joseph (37:1–50:26)
- **Theology of the Patriarchal Narratives**
  Election
  Promise
  Covenant

Objectives

After reading this chapter, you should be able to

- Contrast the focus of Genesis 1–11 with that of Genesis 12–50
- Identify the three major characters in Genesis
- Describe the covenant God made with Abram
- Explain how Abraham illustrates the Christian doctrine of conversion
- Compare the relationship of Jacob and Joseph to the patriarchal narrative
- Illustrate the theological concepts of election, promise, and covenant from Genesis

patriarch

What is a "**patriarch**"? This term refers to the individuals who stand at the fountainhead of our faith: Abraham, Isaac, and Jacob. They, their wives, and their families were pioneers of faith who paved the way for ancient Israel. They also have an honored position in the New Testament. The patriarchs are the ancestors of our faith.

Background of the Patriarchal Narratives

Genesis 12 begins a new literary unit. The differences from Genesis 1–11 are obvious. The opening section of Genesis addressed broad, universal themes in terms similar to other ancient literature. But these patriarchal accounts are narrower in scope and unique in the ancient world. They concern the members of a single family and their journey of faith in contrast to the previous section's concern with the creation of the world.

As we saw in the previous chapter, Genesis 1–11 has a twofold purpose. First, it challenged the other ancient Near Eastern belief systems by attacking them on their own turf. It borrowed themes common to all ancient Oriental cultures and adapted them to express divine revelation. Second, Genesis 1–11 painted an overwhelmingly pessimistic picture of humanity's moral failure. Once sin entered the world, it spread so rapidly it was impossible to contain.

Genesis 12–50 begins to address the sin problem. The primeval history was unmistakable in its assessment of the human condition. Though there had been a faithful line (Seth), even using a flood to destroy all of humanity except for that line could not solve the sin problem. Finally, God dispersed humankind and confused their languages. Beginning with Abram's call in Genesis 12:1–3, the Bible now introduces the solution to the world's sinful dilemma. The faithful obedience of a single individual becomes a powerful instrument in God's hands.

This unit describes events that occurred over centuries of time. Sometimes the events are separated by many years and the text leaves out intervening details. The unit also contains few references to historical events in other ancient Near Eastern nations that would give modern readers a historical anchor. Furthermore, since the patriarchs lived before Israel was a settled nation, there are no archaeological traces of their experiences. For these reasons, modern scholars do not agree on a specific date for the patriarchs. Suggested dates range from 2200 B.C. to 1200 B.C.

Some scholars even doubt these indi-

Marshlands near biblical Ur, Mesopotamia.

patriarchal
narratives

Middle Bronze
Age

viduals ever really existed. They assume later tribal groups tried to explain their own existence by conjuring up Isaac and Jacob as fictional ancestors. In the case of Abraham and Joseph, many modern scholars believe they were distant ancestors from the shadowy past who became objects of tradition and legend in later Israel. The stories about them in Genesis are not accepted as reliable, so we cannot really know the truth about Abraham and Joseph.[1]

Despite all this skepticism, none of the evidence disproves the **patriarchal narratives**, and Christians have every reason to believe they are reliable. In fact, modern archaeologists and historians have corroborated many features of the accounts we read in Genesis 12–50. So even if we are unable to date the events precisely, no evidence contravenes the trustworthiness of the patriarchal record.

Questions of date and historicity are a problem only because much of Old Testament scholarship has refused to avail itself of the growing body of knowledge on the ancient Near East brought to light by archaeology. Though we do not have the same striking *literary* parallels we saw in Genesis 1–11, the patriarchal narratives have certain *cultural* parallels that help give historical perspective. So the patriarchal accounts are a piece of Israelite "family history" that we should accept as authentic until clearly shown to be unreliable.[2]

The events of Genesis 12–50 fit well into the **Middle Bronze Age** (2000–1550 B.C.) in light of available archaeological, cultural, and literary evidence (see discussion in chapter 2 above). Even without precise dating, the patriarchal story line is clear. No more specific date is necessary when we read it in context with Genesis 1–11 and Exodus.

The Story of the Patriarchs

To this point in the biblical story, God dealt with his ruined creation on a universal scale. Despite God's redemptive aims, neither massive flooding nor dispersion of humankind stemmed the tide of evil in the world. Now the story turns to a different way. That other way is the fascinating account of one man whose exemplary faith paves the way of salvation for all. In a real sense, the human dilemma finds its solution in God's grace and the faith of Abraham. Among other important truths, this unit shows how the faithful obedience of a single individual has universal significance.

Outline

Abraham and Isaac (12–25)

As important as Abraham is in the biblical story, we know surprisingly little about the first seventy-five years of his life. Genesis 11:27–32 outlines his genealogy. But he is introduced as the leading character rather suddenly in Genesis 12:1: "Now the LORD said to Abram." He is "Abram" until Genesis 17, where his name is changed to the more familiar "Abraham." The Bible is less concerned with the history of Abram than with his obedient response to God's claim on his life.

Abram was a successful and wealthy person. But one area of his life was filled with pain and unfulfilled dreams. As God often does with us, he dealt with Abram at the point of his pain. The issue was

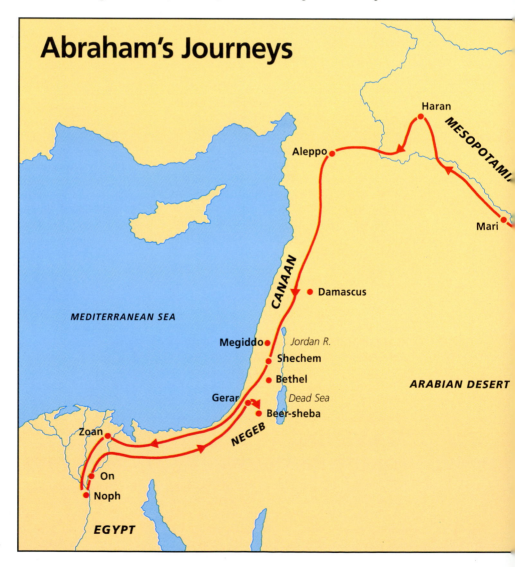

Abraham's Journeys

Haran

MESOPOTAMIA

Aleppo

Mari

CANAAN

Damascus

MEDITERRANEAN SEA

Megiddo   Jordan R.

Shechem

Bethel

Gerar   Dead Sea

Beer-sheba

ARABIAN DESERT

Zoan

NEGEB

On

Noph

EGYPT

promise

Abram's childlessness and the unique problems it presented in that ancient culture. From the beginning of the story, God's word to Abram was clear: He would make Abram's family grow into a great nation that would become a blessing for humankind. The call of Abram contained two great **promises** that were most important to an ancient man: land and descendants.

Abram's family had come originally from UR of the Chaldeans, which is probably the famous city by that name in southern Babylonia.[3] But his father Terah had settled in HARAN in modern Syria, perhaps early in Abram's life.[4] After the death of his father, Abram was left with his wife, nephew, and other members of his fam-

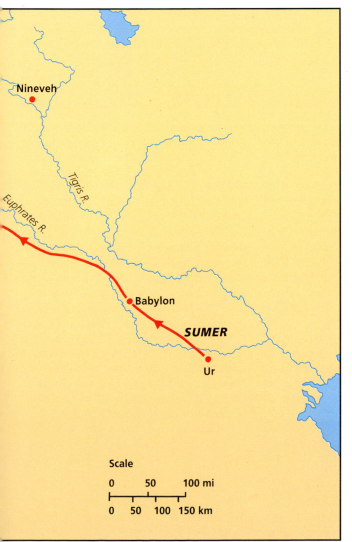

ily. But he had no children. This was a worst-case scenario for an individual of that day and age.

In the call narrative of Genesis 12, God asked Abram to leave all possible sources of security. He called on Abram to step out in faith and leave Haran to travel to an unknown land and begin life anew. Eventually, Abram traveled through MOREH, BETHEL, and the NEGEB (southern Palestine). The point of the narrative is Abram's faithfulness all along the way—from Ur to Haran to Moreh.

The rest of the unit shows how the great promises of Abram's call are worked out in his life. There are many ups and downs, and many questions about Abram's life, his resolve, and God's faithfulness. But through the suspense and drama, the message is clear: God has established a unique relationship with this man and his family. He would certainly work out his promises to Abram somehow.

For much of the story, it appears Abram would fail in the attempt. Early on, he had to survive famine and temporary exile in Egypt (Gn 12), a dispute with his nephew (Gn 13), and regional war (Gn 14). But God intervened to remind Abram of the original promises and to assure him of ultimate success (Gn 15).

In light of all these difficulties and hardships, we are not surprised that Abram questioned the future. Genesis 15 is one of those important passages in the Bible that demands our careful reading. God comforted Abram and assured him of the promises given at the time of his call (v. 1). Abram objected that he had no evidence those promises would ever become reality (v. 2). Because he remained childless during all this time, he had made other arrangements. He had adopted Eliezer of DAMASCUS, presumably a slave, to inherit his wealth. Mesopotamian examples of slave adoption suggests a man without sons could adopt his own slave.[5] But God assured Abram he would one day have a biological son who would be the child of promise. He took him outside and told him to look up and try to count the stars of heaven. So would Abram's descendants be numbered!

In one of the most important verses of the Bible (v. 6), the author states simply that Abram believed God, even though he

Scale
0 50 100 mi
0 50 100 150 km

Nineveh · Tigris R. · Euphrates R. · Babylon · SUMER · Ur

93

The Use of Slain Animals in Ancient Treaty Ceremonies

1. A LETTER FROM MARI (18th century B.C.):
I went to Ashlakka and they brought to me a young dog and a she-goat in order to conclude a covenant (lit. "kill a donkey foal") between the Haneans and the land of Idamaras. But, in deference to my lord, I did not permit the use of the young dog and the she-goat, but instead had a donkey foal, the young of a female donkey, killed, and thus established a reconciliation between the Haneans and the land of Idamaras.

–Moshe Held, "Philological Notes on the Mari Covenant Rituals,"
Bulletin of the American Schools of Oriental Research
200 (1970): 33, and see *ANET*, 482.

2. A TREATY BETWEEN ASHURNIRARI V, KING OF ASSYRIA, AND AN ARAMEAN RULER OF SYRIA, MATI'ILU OF ARPAD (8th century B.C.):
This spring lamb . . . has been brought to sanction the treaty between Ashurnirari and Mati'ilu . . . This head is not the head of a lamb, it is the head of Mati'ilu, it is the head of his sons, his officials, and the people of his land. If Mati'ilu sins against this treaty, so may, just as the head of this spring lamb is torn off . . . the head of Mati'ilu be torn off. . . . This shoulder is not the shoulder of a spring lamb, it is the shoulder of Mati'ilu, it is the shoulder of his sons, his officials, and the people of his land. If Mati'ilu sins against this treaty, so may, just as the shoulder of this spring lamb is torn out, . . . the shoulder of Mati'ilu, of his sons, his officials, and the people of his land be torn out.

–*ANET*, 532

---

covenant

was old and his wife remained barren. Somehow God would fulfill his word, even if Abram could not at the moment see how. God counted such trusting acceptance of his word as righteousness. Through such faith, Abram became the forefather of "all those who believe" (Rom 4:11).

The apostle Paul defined the doctrine of justification by faith, explaining how one becomes a Christian (Rom 3:21–31). To illustrate the doctrine, he chose Abram as the perfect example of saving faith (Rom 4). Even though Abram was advanced in age and Sarah remained barren, "no distrust made him waver concerning the promise of God" for he was "fully convinced that God was able to do what he had promised" (Rom 4:19–21). Truly this is the kind of faith God is seeking from all of us!

The remainder of Genesis 15 is likewise important for understanding biblical thought. God wanted to assure Abram of his promises and bind himself to Abram in an intimate and permanent relationship. In the eerie ceremony described here, a smoking fire pot, representing God's own presence, passed between pieces of

various animal corpses while Abram slept. The ancient custom called for COVENANT partners to walk between bleeding halves of sacrificial animals (Jer 34:18). They were, in essence, pledging not to break the new covenant, lest they become like the dead animal.[6]

Though the customs are distant and strange to us, it is clear that God was committing himself to Abram in a remarkable relationship. God was actually invoking a curse upon himself should he fail to keep his covenant with Abram. This **covenant,** or intimate and lasting relationship between God and Abram, is one of several in the Bible. We shall see this covenant with Abram modified and adapted under Moses, David, Ezra, and, eventually, Jesus Christ. Remember that the New Testament is actually a new "covenant."

In Genesis 16, Abram made alternative arrangements. Abram's wife Sarai had borne no children. Because of her advanced age, she gave her Egyptian slave-girl, Hagar, to Abram to bear children for her as a sort of surrogate mother. Again, though the custom is strange to us, the ancient Near East presents parallels illus-

The Cave of Machpelah, Hebron, by tradition the burial place of the patriarchs Abraham, Isaac, and Jacob.

trating the practice was acceptable in that culture.[7] Abram may have assumed this was God's means of providing a biological heir to fulfill his promises. Sarai and Abram were attempting to carry out God's promises in their own strength. Hagar's son Ishmael would not be the son of the promise.

God officially established the covenant with Abram in chapter 15. But the personal and life-changing consequences of relationship with God are described in Genesis 17. The opening verses make it clear: God is righteous, and he expects Abram now to live a righteous life ("walk before me, and be blameless," v. 1). In 15:6 God considered Abram as though he were a righteous man because of his strong faith. That righteousness in the Old Testament is the full love and trust of the whole person (Dt

The Gift of a Wife's Slave-girl

1. LAWS FROM THE CODE OF HAMMURAPI (18th century B.C.)

When a free man married a priestess and that priestess gave a female slave to her husband and she has then produced children, if that free man has made up his mind to marry a lay priestess, they may not allow him, since he may not marry the lay priestess.

When a free man married a priestess and she gave a female slave to her husband and she has then borne children, if later that female slave has claimed equality with her mistress because she bore children, her mistress may not sell her; she may mark her with the slave-mark and count her among the slaves.

–Laws # 144 and 146, *ANET* (adapted), 172

2. A PERSONAL ARCHIVE FROM NUZI (14th or 15th century B.C.)

Gilimninu has been given to Shennima as wife. If Gilimninu bears children, Shennima shall not take another wife. But if Gilimninu does not bear, she shall take a slave-girl from the Lullu-region as wife for Shennima. As for the concubine's offspring, Gilimninu shall not send them away.

–Adapted from E. A. Speiser, "New Kirkuk Documents Relating to Family Laws," *Annual of the American Schools of Oriental Research* 10 (1930): 32, and *ANET*, 220.

6:5), which Abram exemplified. It results in the consistent "rightness" of actions and character that God is seeking from his servants. Such living is an extension of God's own holy righteousness. Now God informs Abram: Those who live in covenant relationship with God must reflect that righteousness.

Recent literary study has isolated this unit (17:1-5) as the focal point of the Abrahamic materials.[8] It is the centerpiece in which all the important aspects of Abram's life come together. God appears to Abram when he is ninety-nine years old and changes his and Sarai's names. Henceforth in the narrative they are Abraham and Sarah—"Father of a Multitude" and "Princess." Here as elsewhere in the Bible, change of name symbolizes a new reality, a changed status before God (Saul to Paul, Simon to Peter, etc.). Furthermore, God introduces circumcision as a physical sign of the covenant. In addition, God informs Abraham that Sarah, his eighty-nine-year-old wife, would conceive and have a son within a year's time.

This is obviously a turning point in Abraham's life. The single fact that marks the turn is his covenant (*berît*) with God. The term occurs thirteen times in twenty-two verses. God often refers to "my covenant," which he has signified by name changes and the physical sign of circumcision. It is clear: God has established a unique, permanent, and binding relationship with Abraham. So Abraham, the father of our faith, illustrates the Christian doctrine of conversion. Our relationship with God through Christ marks us forever and causes radical changes in our lives.

God miraculously fulfilled his word to Abraham and Sarah. Isaac was born when Sarah was ninety years old and Abraham was 100 (17:17; 21:5). When he first left Haran for an unknown destination, Abraham must have assumed Lot would be his heir, since Abraham was already seventy-five years old. Then when Lot distanced himself from Abraham, Abraham adopted Eliezer as the next presumed heir (chapter 15). After the Lord informed Abraham that his heir would be a biological son, Abraham assumed Ishmael, son of Sarah's slave-girl, would be the heir to his estate. But God meant what he said.

The son of the covenant was not Lot, not Eliezer, not Ishmael, but Isaac!

Chapter 22 brings a surprising twist to the story. Everything in Abraham's life had centered on Isaac, the only son of his beloved Sarah. Isaac now symbolized the fulfillment of the covenant promises of land and descendants (12:1–4). Isaac was Abraham's hope for the future.

The command came from God clearly and unmistakably (22:2). The command is carefully phrased so there can be no misunderstanding. The mountaintop sacrifice will have to be Isaac, Abraham's only son by Sarah, the son whom he loves! Though this would hardly be a legitimate test of our faith, it must have struck at the core of Abraham's soul. Other deities of the ancient world required child sacrifice; perhaps this was a new aspect of God he had not yet learned.

The chapter opened with the information that this would be a test of Abraham's faith. Would he pass the test? Would Abraham obey God in carrying out this terrible requirement? Verse 3 gives us the answer. With great resolve and little hesitation, Abraham began fulfilling the command. But what struggle must have occurred! Isaac was the son of the promise; of this Abraham was sure. Yet now the God Abraham had come to trust and believe was asking for Isaac's life. If God had miraculously given Isaac life, perhaps he would bring him back from the dead (Heb 11:19).

The passage has a strange familiarity about it. The command itself and Abraham's response have direct parallels with chapter 12. Each divine directive (12:1; 22:2) calls on Abraham to take radical action that required total dependence on God. He first traveled to an unknown land; then he took his son as a sacrifice to an unknown mountain. In the first case, the command was followed immediately by a promise ("I will make of you a great nation . . ." 12:2–3). But here, there is no promise to soften the blow.

In both passages, Abraham quickly and quietly obeyed the word of God. There is no argument or debate here. We read only of obedience, of humble submission to God's will (12:4; 22:3). In chapter 12, God called on Abram to give up his past and trust in him. Now, in chapter 22, he challenges Abraham to trust him with his fu-

An oak tree marks the traditional site where Abraham pitched his tent at Mamre.

ture. As before, Abraham was up to the challenge. This event is the climax of Abraham's spiritual journey. He has proven faithful to God from Ur to Haran to Moreh and the Negeb, and now at MORIAH.

Jacob and His Twelve Sons (25:19–36:43)

Though Isaac was the son of the covenant, he soon fades as a leading character after his twin sons are born (25:24–26). Esau is the firstborn, and again, the presumed heir of the covenant promises. But birthrights have little to do with inheriting God's favor. Jacob displaced the firstborn, as is a common occurrence in the Old Testament (Ephraim and Manasseh, Moses and Aaron, David and his brothers, etc.). Privilege of position by birth has little to do with our standing before God.

The question of the Jacob stories is, "What will become of God's covenant promises?" Jacob had to run for his life after the dispute with Esau (27:41–43). So now the child of the promise is running *away* from the promised land. Furthermore, his qualities are hardly like those of Abraham. He seems more intent on seizing the moment for his own selfish purposes than on obeying the God of Abraham. His name, which means "Supplanter" or "Cheater," is justly de-

served![8] So now the story depends on this new character. What of the covenant and its promises now?

Chapter 28 provides the answer in dramatic fashion. While fleeing to the patriarchal homeland (Haran) to make a new life for himself, Jacob had a dream (vv. 10–22). In the dream, God confirmed that Jacob was the continuation of the patriarchal covenant (vv. 13–15). God reasserted his commitment to Abraham by promising to give the land to Jacob and to make him the father of a great multitude. Jacob's response was noble, if perfunctory (vv. 18–22). The reader may still not be confident of Jacob's character and intentions, but God's are now clear.

The rest of the Jacob narrative describes his marriages to Leah and Rachel in Haran, his relationship with Laban, and the births of his twelve sons. The covenant promises finally began to be fulfilled in Jacob's growing family. These twelve sons eventually became the twelve tribes of the nation Israel.

Upon Jacob's return to Palestine, he sought and found reconciliation with his estranged brother Esau. Then, in a remarkable passage (Gn 32), Jacob wrestled with God (probably meaning an angel, Hs 12:4) and God changed his name to Israel. As with his grandfather Abraham, the

Messiah

change of Jacob's name signified a change of character due to his relationship with God. Jacob was no longer the "cheater." Now he had become the one who "strives with God." As always, growth in grace means a change of lifestyle.

So now with Jacob, the patriarchal promises are partially fulfilled. The land promise will wait future fulfillment. But the descendants of Abraham are increasing in number. As one reads the Jacob narrative, one slowly realizes Jacob will eventually succeed as the heir of the covenant promises, but not without a great deal of suspense.

Joseph (37:1–50:26)

The account of Joseph is unique among the patriarchal narratives. Unlike Abraham, Isaac, and Jacob, Joseph is not in the direct line of the covenant promises. The **Messiah** came through the tribe of Judah. In that sense, Joseph is a peripheral character in the drama of redemptive history portrayed in the Bible. But the Bible is also interested in marginal characters, especially when they exemplify the kind of moral life for which God is looking.

So the Joseph narrative is included in Genesis for two basic reasons. First, Joseph's life is worthy of emulation. Under the worst of circumstances and the most extreme temptation, Joseph was faithful to God. His story demonstrates how God can use an obedient servant to accomplish his divine and benevolent purposes, even in the face of severe human persecution and opposition (Gn 50:20). Second, the Joseph narrative explains how God's people came to be in Egypt instead of in Palestine. Joseph's rise to power in Egypt and the subsequent move of Jacob and his family there meant the people of God's covenant promises were now living far from the promised land. But the book ends looking to the future ("when God comes to you," 50:25), anticipating that day when God will fulfill his promises to his people.

Theology of the Patriarchal Narratives

The patriarchal narratives contain much that is foundational for the rest of bibli-

Summary

1. The subject of Genesis 12–50 is the patriarchs.

2. Biblical scholars can find much support for the patriarchal accounts of Genesis in the work of modern historians and archaeologists.

3. The three patriarchs are Abraham, Isaac, and Jacob.

4. The Abrahamic covenant is the foundation for the other covenants of the Bible.

5. Abraham illustrates the Christian doctrine of conversion.

6. Abraham obeyed God in preparing to sacrifice Isaac, the son of the covenant.

7. Joseph was faithful to God under the worst of circumstances.

8. God elected the patriarchs not by birth or by character or by action, but because he called them.

9. Election, promise, and covenant are three theological concepts developed in Genesis 12–50.

Key Terms

patriarch
patriarchal narratives
Middle Bronze Age
promise
covenant
Messiah
election

Key People/Places

Hammurapi
Ur
Haran
Moreh
Bethel
Negeb
Damascus
Mari
Nuzi
Moriah

tained the purpose for the future nation Israel: "I will make of you a great nation . . . and in you all the families of the earth shall be blessed" (12:2–3). God brought the nation Israel into existence for a purpose: to serve as his instrument of salvation for the world. Too often, she assumed this election was only a privilege, and forgot it also brought responsibility.

The unusual circumstances surrounding the births of Isaac and Jacob illustrate further the principle of election. God's election of Isaac over Ishmael, and Jacob over Esau, was not because of their character or their actions. He elected them to continue the covenant promises before they were even born. They had not done anything good to deserve his favor. They were chosen to be in the line of the covenant promises, "not by works but by his call" (Rom 9:11).

God's election of the patriarchs focuses more on his plans for them as his instruments of salvation to the world. God chose Abraham, Isaac, and Jacob to stand in the line of the covenant. They prepared the

election

cal thought and for Christian theology in general.

Election

One of the most important ideas is that of **election**. The call of Abraham also con-

---

Study Questions

1. What is a "patriarch"?

2. What turn occurs in Genesis 12 (as compared to Gn 3–11)? What is the Bible's principal concern in presenting the story of Abram? What is the key verse on this topic?

3. How did God assure Abram with the smoking fire pot? Define a "covenant."

4. What three "other arrangements" did Abram make when Sarai remained childless?

5. What is the "turning point" in Abram and Sarai's life? What is God's requirement of them? What assurance do

they receive? What physical sign of this new relationship is introduced?

6. How did Abraham respond to the command to sacrifice Isaac? How did this command differ from the command to travel to an unknown land?

7. What question is raised by the Jacob stories? When and how does God assure the reader? What is Jacob's moment of transformation?

8. How does the Joseph story differ from those of Abraham, Isaac, and Jacob? Why is his story included in Scripture?

9. What are the major theological concepts of Genesis 12–50?

Further Reading

Baldwin, Joyce G. *The Message of Genesis 12–50.* The Bible Speaks Today. Downers Grove/Leicester: InterVarsity, 1986.

Clines, David J. A. *The Theme of the Pentateuch.* Journal for the Study of the Old Testament—Supplement Series 10. Sheffield: JSOT, 1978. Important volume on the covenant theme of the pentateuchal narratives.

Kidner, Derek. *Genesis: An Introduction and Commentary.* Tyndale Old Testament Commentary. Downers Grove: InterVarsity, 1967. Theologically sensitive treatment.

Millard, A. R., and Donald J. Wiseman, eds. *Essays on the Patriarchal Narratives.* Winona Lake, Ind.: Eisenbrauns, 1983. An excellent collection of articles by leading scholars.

Moberly, R. W. L. *Genesis 12–50.* Old Testament Guides. Sheffield: JSOT, 1992.

Ross, Allen P. *Creation and Blessing: A Guide to the Study and Exposition of the Book of Genesis.* Grand Rapids: Baker, 1988. Helpful evangelical study of the literary aspects of the text.

Wenham, Gordon J. *Genesis 16–50.* Word Biblical Commentary 2. Dallas: Word, 1994. Most comprehensive treatment available, including all the pertinent ancient Near Eastern materials.

way for the coming of Israel's Messiah, through whom salvation would be accomplished and offered to the world. Election in the patriarchal narratives is primarily to service.

Promise

A second major concept in the patriarchal narratives is that of promise. The promises of God to Abraham in Genesis 12:2–3 serve as focal points for the rest of the patriarchal account.[9] That they are only partially fulfilled in Abraham is obvious. At his death, he has acquired only a small plot of ground in the promised land (Gn 23:17–18), and Isaac hardly constitutes a multitude of descendants. Though the patriarchal family grows dramatically under Jacob, Genesis closes with their descendants living in exile in Egypt. The promises of God are sure and therefore the patriarchal narratives are forward looking. The ultimate fulfillment of these promises must await a later generation.

Covenant

A third important theological concept of the patriarchal narratives is related to promise, that is, the idea of covenant. The promises and the covenant that God established with Abraham (Gn 15 and 17), he also confirmed to Isaac (Gn 26:2–5), Jacob (Gn 28:13–15), and Joseph (Gn 48:3–4; 50:24).

God's covenant with the patriarchs is foundational to other covenants in the Bible. The covenantal relationship between God and Abraham establishes a theological framework for redemptive relationships throughout the Bible and in Christian theology. Other covenants play an important role later. The Mosaic covenant formalized the relationship between God and the nation Israel (Ex 19). The Davidic covenant made permanent the relationship between God and the royal dynasty of Israel (2 Sm 7). Jesus Christ sealed the relationship between God and his people through his redemptive life, death, and resurrection ("This cup is the new covenant in my blood, which is poured out for you," Lk 22:20). All of these covenantal relationships with God are related to the patriarchal covenant. So the covenant structure that God established with the patriarchs "underlies the program of redemption."[10]

The covenant was necessary to maintain the right kind of relationship with God. The promises were central and eternal. But the covenant taught the patriarchal believers what was expected from them in their relationship with God: "I am God Almighty; walk before me and be blameless" (Gn 17:1). We cling to the promises of God. But we must also understand that knowing and loving him means following his ways (Jn 14:15).

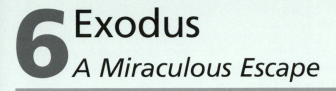

6 Exodus
A Miraculous Escape

Outline

- **Contents of the Book of Exodus**
  Outline
  The Events of the Exodus
- **Historical Problems of the Exodus**
  Historicity of the Exodus
  Date of the Exodus
  Route of the Exodus
- **Theological Significance of the Exodus**
  Deliverance
  Covenant
  Presence of God

Objectives

After reading this chapter, you should be able to

- Contrast the emphasis on beginnings in Exodus with those in Genesis
- Outline the basic content of Exodus
- Give examples of how God saved Israel
- Define casuistic law as found in Exodus
- Explain the purpose of the covenant
- Identify the three major historical problems of the exodus
- Discuss the theological significance of the exodus

The Book of Exodus is about a daring escape. Even the meaning of the word "exodus" implies a quick exit.[1] By God's grace and mercy, he rescued Israel from a life of slavery in Egypt. But the book is also about Israel's relationship with God after her departure from Egypt. Exodus describes these two main events: Israel's departure from Egypt (rescue) and her newly established alliance with God (relationship).

Contents of the Book of Exodus

Exodus is a book of beginnings, as was Genesis. The first book of the Bible related the beginning of everything. Genesis included the beginning of faith in the form of the patriarchal line. Exodus now continues that line, relating the beginning of the nation Israel.

Outline

The Events of the Exodus

The Book of Exodus describes Israel's travels under the direction of God, from Egypt through the desert to the foot of MOUNT SINAI. So the book has a geographical arrangement: Israel in Egypt (1:1–12:36),

Hebrews

Israel in the desert (12:37– 18:27), and Israel at Mount Sinai (19–40).

As the book opens, the patriarchal covenant promises are in jeopardy. The descendants of Abraham are living in Egypt, where we left them at the conclusion of Genesis. But it is now hundreds of years later. The people have grown in significant numbers, enough to become a threat to the Egyptian population (1:10). In order to control this threat, the Egyptians enslaved the **Hebrews** and attempted to control their birth rate (chapter 1).

The birth of Moses is God's answer to this terrible predicament. Exodus 2 relates how the baby was spared and raised in the Egyptian court, providing him with the best education possible (Acts 7:22). As an adult, Moses tried to take matters into his own hands in a pathetic attempt to fulfill his calling (Ex 2:11–15a). As a result, he had to flee Egypt. Moses found his way to Midian, where he started life over again. He tried to forget about the terrible plight of the Hebrews by settling into a new occupation, a new family, a new home (vv. 15b–22).

But God did not forget or forsake his people. In an important paragraph at the conclusion of chapter 2 (vv. 23–25), we are told that God knew their plight. He heard, remembered, saw, and knew of the groaning of the Israelites. God was committed to taking action to redeem his people from Egypt because of his covenant with the patriarchs (v. 24). Because of Abraham, the Israelites must be redeemed from Egypt. Moses may have forgotten, but God had not!

Moses and God were on a collision course. The Lord was determined to save the Israelites; Moses was determined to forget about them. The famous call of Moses at the burning bush (Ex 3–4) is where the two collide. The resulting debate is classic and powerful. God called Moses to go back to Egypt and lead the Israelites out of their slavery. Moses raised four objections, all of which God answered. Finally Moses simply refused to go: "please send someone else" (4:13).

God assured Moses of his presence in Egypt and of his ultimate victory. Together with the help of his brother, Aaron, Moses would become the deliverer of his people. He returned to Egypt and warned Pharaoh of impending disaster if the Egyptian ruler failed to obey God's command to let the people go. The ten plagues were intended not only to force the Egyptians into com-

Egyptian wall painting showing a scribe conducting a count of geese on an Egyptian official's estate.

Laws from Ancient Mesopotamia

1. If a citizen has accused another citizen and brought a charge of murder against him, but has not been able to prove it, his accuser shall be put to death. (Compare Ex 23:1–3)
2. If a citizen has stolen the young son of another citizen, he shall be put to death. (Compare Ex 21:16)
3. If an obligation came due against a citizen and he sold into slavery his wife, his son, or his daughter, or he himself has been bound over to service, they shall work in the house of their purchaser or obligee for three years, with their freedom reestablished in the fourth year. (Compare Ex 21:2–11)

4. If a son has struck his father, they shall cut off his hand. (Compare Ex 21:15)
5. If he has broken another citizen's bone, they shall break his bone. (Compare Ex 21:23–25)
6. If an ox, when it was walking along the street, gored a citizen to death, that case is not subject to claim. If a citizen had a goring ox and his city council warned him about it, but he did not pad its horns or tie up his ox, and that ox gored to death a member of the aristocracy, he shall give one-half mina of silver. (Compare Ex 21:28–36)

–Selected from the Law Code of Hammurapi, Laws 1, 14, 117, 195, 197, and 250–51, *ANET* (adapted), 166–76.

casuistic law

pliance, but also to teach the Egyptians and the Israelites about the sovereign character of the God of Israel. The Egyptians believed their god-king, the Pharaoh, was responsible for maintaining the life-giving Nile River and for the sun's daily rising. But the plagues demonstrated that Israel's God, Yahweh, was in control of the cosmic order.[2]

On the night of the release of the Israelites, God established a permanent memorial to commemorate the event, the Passover (chapter 12). Future generations must never forget God's great and mighty acts of salvation. Exodus 14:30–31 serves as a theological summary of the entire exodus event that became so central in future Israelite thought. The Lord saved Israel in that day and they saw the Egyptians dead on the seashore. This sight became the concrete sign that God had accomplished salvation and brought a new life for Israel.[3]

The second main unit of the book traces Israel's strange odyssey through the desert. How could Israel question God and complain about their circumstances? Had they not just witnessed the greatest miracle of history? Did they not yet understand what God had done for them? Yet sin and rebellion often fly in the face of facts. If we would only remember who God is and

what he has done for us, we would quickly obey his Word.

In chapter 19, the Israelites arrived at Mount Sinai. The rest of the book describes the events that took place there. In dramatic fashion, God met with the nation (vv. 16–25). Now he began to transform this ragtag group of former slaves into a nation devoted only to him, a "treasured possession" (v. 5). Just as he had used a covenant to establish his relationship with the patriarchs, so now he used a covenant with Israel.

The Sinai covenant was anchored in the Ten Commandments (20:1–17). The Bible actually calls these "words" instead of commandments (Dt 10:4), because they are more like ten principles for living than laws. The rest of the law is based on them. Chapters 21–23 are called the "Book of the Covenant" (Ex 24:7). These chapters list specific cases in which the principles of covenant law are applied to life. This type of law (known as **casuistic law**) was widely used in the ancient Near East. Several parallels from Mesopotamia illustrate how the Bible often used the writing styles and customs of the day to express God's revelation.

After God gave the law to Israel, Moses led the nation in a solemn and sacred covenant ceremony, binding God and nation together (24:3–8). Moses sprinkled sacrificial blood on the altar, which represented God (v. 6). Then he read the Book of the Covenant to the people and sprinkled blood on them as well (vv. 7–8). Moses called this blood "the blood of the covenant" because the ceremony was symbolic of the kind of covenant God made with Abraham in Genesis 15, using divided animals. Just as God bound himself to Abraham, he was now binding himself to Israel. This must surely be behind the words of Jesus: "This is my blood of the covenant, which is poured out for many for the forgiveness of sins" (Mt 26:28).

The purpose for the desert tabernacle was clear from the beginning (25:8). It was not like our churches, stadiums, or arenas, where large groups gather for various purposes. It was God's way of living in the midst of his people. Prior to this, God had demonstrated his presence with them in the form of pillars of fire and smoke during their desert travels (13:21–22). This large tent, however, would now be God's dwelling place. The glory of his presence, which had provided both protection and comfort, would now reside in the center of the Israelite camp. The word "tabernacle" itself (*miškān*) means "dwelling place."

The tabernacle section of the book uses repetition. Seven chapters (25–31) give detailed instructions in how to build the tabernacle with all of its furnishings. Then four chapters (35–39) relate how Moses and the Israelites obeyed in every detail. While this may be unlike the modern literature we are used to reading, the point should be clear. The people were obedient to God, down to every detail of the tabernacle's curtains, rings, and hooks.

What comes between the two sections on the tabernacle, however, is an example of rank disobedience (chapters 32–34). While Moses was on Mount Sinai receiving the law of God, the children of Israel blatantly and quickly turned from the very God who had just delivered them from their life of slavery and misery in Egypt. Apparently they wanted God to look like the familiar gods of Egypt and Canaan. So, while Yahweh was creating a nation that would reflect his moral likeness, the Israelites were trying to create God in their image.

Chapter 40 is a triumphant climax to the Book of Exodus. The recurring phrase makes the point: Moses and the Israelites performed the tasks of building God's tabernacle just "as the LORD had commanded Moses." When all was completed as required, God's wonderful glory filled the tabernacle (v. 34). The presence of God that led the Israelites in pillars of cloud and fire and that met them so dramatically on Mount Sinai would now rest on the movable tabernacle. They must leave

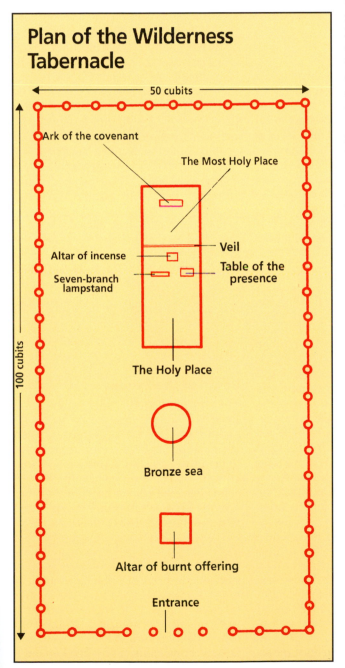

Plan of the Wilderness Tabernacle

50 cubits

100 cubits

Ark of the covenant

The Most Holy Place

Veil

Altar of incense

Table of the presence

Seven-branch lampstand

The Holy Place

Bronze sea

Altar of burnt offering

Entrance

Mount Sinai behind, but God's presence would go with them.

Historical Problems of the Exodus

Like the patriarchal narratives, the Book of Exodus gives few historical references to other times and places in the ancient Near East. Consequently, we are faced with several unanswered questions about the exodus event.

Historicity of the Exodus

The first of these is the question of its historicity. The lack of firm extrabiblical evidence leads some to deny the event actually occurred. But the exodus is so central to later Israelite thought and theology, it is inconceivable the events could have no basis in the national history. Furthermore, it seems unlikely Israel would have been so uncomplimentary about her past as to include suffering and servitude if it were not true. Those who question the historicity of the exodus ignore too many other pertinent questions.

Date of the Exodus

The second problem has to do with the precise date of the exodus. Basically there are two options, though there are many variations of these. The exodus may be dated to around 1446 B.C. or 1275 B.C.

First Kings 6:1 dates the exodus 480 years before Solomon built the temple in 966 B.C. By simple addition, we derive the fifteenth-century B.C. date, 1446, for the exodus. Judges 11:26 gives three hundred years between Jephthah's day (around 1100 B.C.) and the conquest, which would also seem to suggest the earlier date.

An Egyptian inscription known as the "Israel Stela" records the victory hymn of Pharaoh Merneptah in 1209 B.C. This inscription reports the Pharaoh's victory over several peoples in Palestine, including "the people of Israel" (*ANET*, 378). Some would argue the Israelites must have been in the land for a considerable length of time in order to be recognized by an Egyptian Pharaoh. This would also support the early date.

However, others have contended the archaeological evidence from Palestine contradicts the earlier date and suggests instead a thirteenth-century B.C. date. The 480 years of 1 Kings 6:1 must, in this case, be an ideal figure. For example, the number might be the sum total of the 12 tribes of Israel multiplied by an ideal generation of 40. The real time between the exodus and the temple would be approximately 300 years instead of 480.

Exodus 1:11 states the Israelites worked on the construction of the city of Ramesses, which is believed to have been built by Pharaoh Ramesses II (1279–1213 B.C.). Thus the exodus could not have taken place prior to 1279 B.C., when Ramesses began to rule. Also, recently published reliefs from Karnak combine with the "Israel Stela" inscription to support the later date. Since the inscription designates Israel as a "people" instead of a land or country, it may be assumed Israel had only recently arrived in the area and not yet completely settled. Thus the exodus and conquest were thirteenth-century B.C. events.

Reevaluation of the archaeological evidence shows that archaeology cannot answer this question. Archaeology can, in fact, be used to argue for the earlier date.[4] Singling out a definitive date for the exodus is currently impossible because of a lack of more complete information. Of course, we can still affirm the reality of the event, even if we do not know exactly when it occurred.

Route of the Exodus

The third problem facing those who study Exodus is identifying the route the Israelites took after leaving Egypt and then traveling through the desert from Egypt to the promised land. Ramesses and Succoth (Ex 12:37) may be identified with some degree of confidence. But the other Egyptian place-names mentioned in the narrative are not clearly identifiable.[5]

The sea that has been known as the "Red Sea" since the days of the Septuagint is actually the "Sea of Reeds" in Hebrew. Presumably the body of water Israel miraculously crossed is one of the freshwater lakes east of the Nile Delta where such reeds were found: Menzaleh, Ballah, Timsah, or the Bitter Lakes (some would add Lake Sirbonis to this list).[6] The Red Sea's

theophany

Gulf of Suez probably should be ruled out, as may the GULF OF AQABA, since these larger salt water bodies lack the reedy vegetation necessary to qualify them as the "Sea of Reeds."[7]

Once across the sea and out of Egypt, there were three basic options for the Israelite trek across the Sinai Peninsula: northern, central, or southern routes.

The northern route was along the "Way of the Sea," an international highway that stretched from Egypt to Canaan along the Mediterranean coastline. The Bible refers to this highway as the "way of the land of the Philistines" (Ex 13:17). This would have been the most direct route, though not the easiest. Archaeology has confirmed certain Egyptian inscriptions that speak of a heavy Egyptian military presence along the highway, reaching from the Nile Delta all the way to Gaza. The Israelites, with God's guidance, bypassed this dangerous northern route and took "the roundabout way of the wilderness toward the Reed Sea" (Ex 13:18). We may assume this was a more southerly direction, taken to avoid military conflict with the Egyptians. Unfortunately, we are unable to discern just what that roundabout way was. The locations of important places mentioned in the desert narratives are still uncertain—even the location of Mount Sinai.

The central route hypothesis locates Mount Sinai somewhere in northwest Saudi Arabia, beyond the Gulf of Aqaba. Some who hold this position believe the Bible's references to the **theophany** at Sinai describe an active volcano (Ex 19:18; 24:17, etc.). Geological evidence points to vol-

Dating the Exodus

Of the abundance of evidence cited in the debate, we include here only a selective list, along with the interpretation of each approach.

Evidence Approach	Fifteenth-Century Approach	Thirteenth-Century Approach
1) 1 Kings 6:1 480 years from exodus to the temple of Solomon	The numbers are taken seriously, and are literal.	The 480 years are ideal numbers and figurative.
2) Exodus 1:11 Israelites built the city of Ramesses, named for pharaoh Ramesses of the thirteenth century.	The name "Ramesses" was also used prior to the thirteenth century.	Since Ramesses came to power in 1279 B.C., the exodus could not have occurred prior to this time.
3) Judges 11:26 Jephthah refers to 300 years between his day (around 1100 B.C.) and the conquest of the Promised Land.	Jephthah was approximately correct, placing the Transjordanian conquest around 1400 B.C.	Jephthah had no historical records, and was making a broad generalization.
4) Merneptah's Stela The thirteenth-century pharaoh mentioned "the people of Israel" as inhabitants of Palestine.	Since the pharaoh mentioned them by name, the Israelites must have been there for an extended period of time. The thirteenth-century approach does not provide enough time for Israel to become recognized by Egypt.	Other groups in the inscription are designated as territorial city-states. Only Israel is referred to as a people. She must have been a relative newcomer to the area. The fifteenth-century date leaves too much time.

The view from Jebel Musa (Mount of Moses), often identified as Mount Sinai.

canically active areas in Arabia at that time, while the mountains of the Sinai Peninsula were not. Also, the land of Midian was located east of the Gulf of Aqaba. So when Moses fled Egypt, settled in Midian, and eventually met God at Mount Sinai (Ex 3:1), a region in northwestern Arabia was intended.

However, the Bible's description of God's appearance at Sinai does not require an active volcano. Many theophanies of the Old Testament describe extraordinary phenomena, and Exodus 19:18 has other more plausible explanations. Moreover, Moses' connection with the Midianites is inconclusive. The Bible relates him to a Midianite subtribe, the Kenites. This Midianite clan was not settled in a single area, but was nomadic, sometimes appearing in the Sinai Peninsula.[8] Few today would insist on the central route as the way taken by the Israelites.

Advocates of the southern route usually accept the identification of Mount Sinai with Jebel Musa (Mount of Moses), where today there is a monastery and a

basilica of St. Catherine. The identification of Jebel Musa with Mount Sinai dates to a Christian tradition from the fourth century A.D. However, the rugged granite mountains of the Sinai Peninsula offer several other possibilities for the mountain of God: Ras Safsaf, Jebel Serbal, Jebel Katarina, or Jebel Sin Bisher.

The Israelites often gave names to places in the desert as they passed through the area. But without a continuous population in the region to carry on the traditional names, we are unable to identify locations precisely. Furthermore, the Israelites lived a nomadic lifestyle during these years in the desert. Their tents, animal-skin clothing, and containers would leave behind few artifacts for modern archaeologists to discover. As a result, we have no specific information on the route, and are unlikely to acquire any soon. However, the traditional, southern route answers more questions than the others. This is our best estimate of the direction the newly freed Israelite people took on their way to God's promised land.

Theological Significance of the Exodus

The Book of Exodus and the events it describes are of paramount importance in Christian theology. God sovereignly redeemed his people from a life of bondage and bound himself to them in covenant relationship. This role of God became central for the rest of the Old Testament. The exodus as salvation event was the forma-tive beginning of the nation Israel, historically and theologically. Similarly, the life, death, and resurrection of Jesus Christ was a parallel event of salvation, which was the formative beginning for the church. Jesus spoke of his "departure" (Greek *exodos*) that he would accomplish on the cross (Lk 9:31).

Deliverance

The theme of the first section of the book is deliverance (chapters 1–18). The people of God were languishing under the heavy bondage of the Egyptians. They had no

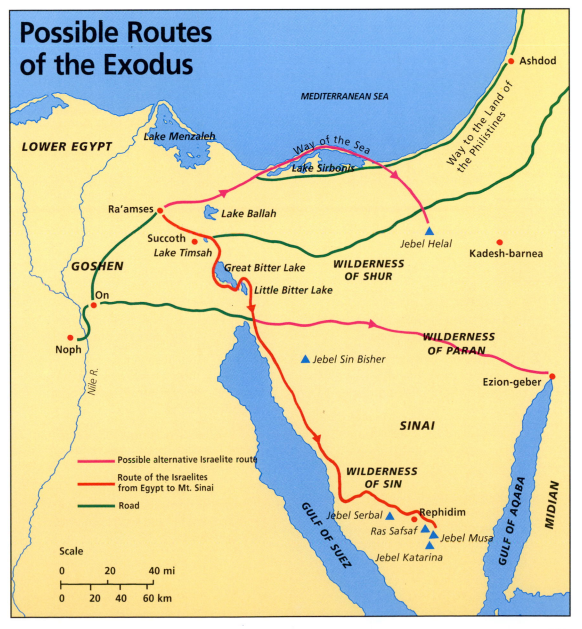

Possible Routes of the Exodus

MEDITERRANEAN SEA

Ashdod

LOWER EGYPT

Lake Menzaleh

Way of the Sea

Way to the Land of the Philistines

Lake Sirbonis

Ra'amses

Lake Ballah

Succoth

Lake Timsah

GOSHEN

Great Bitter Lake

WILDERNESS OF SHUR

Jebel Helal

Kadesh-barnea

Little Bitter Lake

On

Noph

Nile R.

Jebel Sin Bisher

WILDERNESS OF PARAN

Ezion-geber

SINAI

—— Possible alternative Israelite route

—— Route of the Israelites from Egypt to Mt. Sinai

—— Road

WILDERNESS OF SIN

GULF OF SUEZ

Jebel Serbal

Rephidim

Ras Safsaf

Jebel Musa

MIDIAN

GULF OF AQABA

Jebel Katarina

Scale

0   20   40 mi

0 20 40 60 km

covenant

Torah

leadership and no hope of escape. But God was moved by his grace and his earlier commitment to the patriarchs (2:24–25). He delivered his people by providing the necessary human leader, Moses. Through dramatic plagues, God demonstrated his sovereign control of nature and broke the Egyptian hold on Israel, freeing her to escape. The spectacular miracle at the Sea of Reeds was the ultimate act of deliverance (chapters 14–15). The helpless Israelites were now free through no merit of their own; the Lord had become their salvation (15:2).

Covenant

The theme of the second section of Exodus is **covenant** (chapters 19–40). As we have seen, the patriarchal covenant provides the foundation for the covenant at Sinai. The Abrahamic covenant (Gn 15:7–21) anticipated the covenant of blood between Yahweh and Israel (Ex 24:3–8). Just as the Abrahamic covenant involved promises of land and descendants, the Sinai covenant fulfills those promises partially and continues them (19:4–5).

However, the Sinai agreement added a new element to the covenant. Although God had demanded ethical behavior from Abraham (Gn 17:1), the details of living in relationship to God were not available to the Hebrew people in written form. The Sinai covenant was a public and specific statement of the demands of having a relationship with God, establishing clear and uplifting instruction (chapters 20–23). Though the covenantal promises are in a sense permanent and unconditional, the covenant itself requires faithful obedience to God: "You have seen what I did to the Egyptians . . . Now therefore, if you obey my voice and keep my covenant . . ." (19:4–5). The Sinai covenant placed God's **Torah** ("law"), his divine instruction, at the very center of his relationship with Israel.

The Ten Commandments and the other commands of chapters 21–23 were a natural part of the relationship between God and the Israelites. The terms of the covenant were a result of God's grace and love for his people. He issued his laws for the nation *after* he had redeemed them and established his bond of intimate relation-

Summary

1. The Book of Exodus describes how God led Israel from Egypt through the desert to Mount Sinai.

2. The Passover was God's method of commemorating the release of the Israelites from Egyptian bondage.

3. The Ten Commandments were the foundation of the Sinai covenant.

4. The tabernacle was the place where God dwelt in the midst of his people.

5. Scholars find three major historical problems with the Book of Exodus: the historicity of the exodus, the date of the exodus, and the route of the exodus.

6. The date of the Exodus is placed by some scholars in the thirteenth century B.C. and by others in the fifteenth century B.C.

7. There are three possible routes for the exodus—the northern, central, and southern routes.

8. The life, death, and resurrection of Christ is a parallel event of salvation to the exodus of Israel.

9. The Book of Exodus is important theologically in terms of the way deliverance, covenant, and God's presence are presented.

St. Catherine's Monastery, Sinai, situated close to Jebel Musa, Mount Moses.

ship with them. The law served as a seal on that relationship. Throughout the Old Testament, law is a positive expression of God's will for his people.

Laws are a part of life, whether they are natural laws of the universe or divine laws prescribed by God. We should not break any of God's laws any more than we would attempt to break the laws of nature. Trying to break the law of gravity, for example, by jumping off a high cliff only proves the law to be true and breaks instead the person who jumps! So it is with God's laws. Breaking them only hurts us and proves that God's laws are just and true (Ps 19:7–10). On the other hand, obeying his law is the right response to God's grace, not as a means of salvation, but as the response to salvation.

Presence of God

Deliverance and covenant—these are the themes of the two main sections of Exodus (chapters 1–18 and 19–40). But an emphasis on the presence of God runs throughout the whole book. The purpose of the exodus from Egypt and the covenant at Sinai, with its Law and tabernacle, can be summarized in this way: God was preparing Israel for his arrival in their midst.

The patriarchal covenant had contained the promise of descendants and a land. An element of that Genesis land-promise was living in the presence of Yahweh. When the promise was confirmed to Abraham's children, God assured them "I am [or will be] with you" (Gn 26:3 for Isaac; Gn 28:15 for Jacob). Joseph's life illustrated the principle of living in God's presence (Gn 39:2).

But at the beginning of Exodus, the land was not yet a reality and the descendants of Jacob were in danger of extinction. Even worse, the people were incapable of inheriting God's land-promise because they were unprepared to live in the land. Life in the promised land also meant life in God's presence.

The Israelites were not ready for life in God's presence because they had not yet learned of his great character. This was one of the lessons of the plagues. They

Key Places

Mount Sinai
Gulf of Aqaba

Key Terms

Hebrews
casuistic law
theophany
covenant
Torah

Study Questions

1. What are the two main events in the Book of Exodus? What "beginning" is established in the book? What is the arrangement of the book?

2. What was the point of collision between God and Moses?

3. What was the permanent commemoration of the Israelites' release from captivity?

4. What were the two intended purposes of the plagues?

5. What was the anchor of the new Sinai covenant?

6. What was the purpose of the desert tabernacle?

7. What are the possible dates of the exodus? What is the evidence for each date?

8. What is the best estimate of the route followed by the Israelites?

9. What are the theological themes of the Book of Exodus? What other emphasis runs throughout the book?

---

were unprepared to live under his lordship, as Exodus 32 demonstrates and as we shall see in the Book of Numbers. Consequently, they were also unprepared to inherit the promised land.

The book's emphasis on the presence of God is related to the important reference in Exodus 3:14. The significance of God's personal name of intimacy, Yahweh, is that he is the God who is there for Moses and the Israelites. Moses has asked God what to say if the reluctant Israelites want to know who sent him to Egypt to deliver them. Their request for a name is their way of asking, "Exactly *what kind* of God is the God of our ancestors?" (v. 13). In response, God said to tell them, "I am (the God who is there for you)." It would be a long journey. But Moses and the Israelites learned through the plagues and the exodus what kind of God Yahweh was (and is). He was a God who was present with them in their time of need and suffering. He was with them to deliver them mightily.

The exodus, in fact, marked Yahweh forever as the God who was present with Israel to deliver them. The statement that the patriarchs did not know God as Yahweh (Ex 6:3) does not mean they were completely unfamiliar with the name (see Gn 22:14, where Abraham used "Yahweh"). But after Moses and the Israelites, the name is associated with the exodus and the Sinai covenant. He is the One who was with his people to redeem them and to mark them with his holy presence.

God's desire was for a "priestly kingdom and a holy nation" that he could indwell (Ex 19:6). The purpose for the exodus from Egypt was so God could dwell in the midst of his people. The coming of God's glorious presence into the newly constructed tabernacle forms the climax of the Book of Exodus (40:34). Thus the tabernacle was the partial fulfillment of the patriarchal promise that God would be with the descendants of Abraham, Isaac, and Jacob. Eventually the temple in Jerusalem would replace the tabernacle as the habitation of God's glory. Likewise, Christ came to "tabernacle" among us (Jn 1:14; Heb 8:1–9:15). Now the Holy Spirit dwells within the church and has therefore fulfilled the ultimate purpose for both tabernacle and temple.

At the conclusion of Exodus, God's patriarchal promises are partially fulfilled. The descendants of Abraham are free and in covenant relationship with God. They are not yet living in the promised land. But they still have the promise, and at the end of the book they receive God's pres-

Further Reading

Bimson, John J. *Redating the Exodus and Conquest.* Journal for the Study of the Old Testament—Supplement Series 5. Sheffield, JSOT, 1981.

Cassuto, Umberto. *A Commentary on the Book of Exodus.* Trans. Israel Abrams. Jerusalem: Magnes, 1967. Excellent treatment from a Jewish perspective.

Cole, R. Alan. *Exodus: An Introduction and Commentary.* Tyndale Old Testament Commentary.

Downers Grove: InterVarsity, 1973. Helpful evangelical introduction to all the issues in Exodus.

Childs, Brevard S. *The Book of Exodus: A Critical, Theological Commentary.* Old Testament Library. Philadelphia: Westminster, 1974. Important literary and theological introduction to the book.

Durham, John I. *Exodus.* Word Biblical Commentary 3. Waco, Tex.: Word, 1987.

ence. Exodus is about the salvation and preparation of the Israelites for life in the land. The gift of God's presence is a pre-fulfillment reality.

The miracle at the Sea of Reeds became the primary symbol of salvation in the Old Testament. Likewise, the Sinai covenant became the principal symbol of an enduring relationship with God. Together, the exodus and Sinai covenant constitute the central act of redemption in the Old Testament. Here, the *promises* of God and the *acts* of God met to save his people from their bondage. The exodus and Sinai events are thus as central for the Old Testament as the cross is for the New.

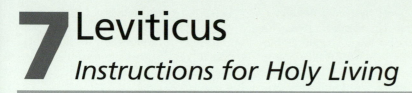

7 Leviticus
Instructions for Holy Living

Outline

Objectives

After reading this chapter, you should be able to

- Compare the uses of sacrifice in Israel with uses of sacrifice in Mesopotamian cultures
- Contrast the emphasis on worship in Leviticus with that in Exodus
- Outline the basic content of the Book of Leviticus
- List the types of Old Testament sacrifices and explain their usage
- Identify the three basic themes of the Book of Leviticus
- Describe how modern Christians relate to Old Testament law.

Leviticus is one of the most neglected books of the Bible. This is true for two main reasons. First, the book seems quite strange to modern readers. The sacrificial worship it describes is so far removed from today's believers that its very unfamiliarity prevents some from reading Leviticus. Second, Leviticus appears at first glance to interrupt the flow of events in the story of God's people. We must wait until the fourth book of the Pentateuch, the Book of Numbers, to read of Israel's journey from Mount Sinai to the edge of the promised land.

Yet Leviticus plays an essential role in God's word and makes a vital contribution to our understanding of God's relationship with humankind. We need to make the extra effort required to understand its message. We must all attempt to understand the ancient practice of sacrifice and its significance for Old Testament religion.

In a sense, Leviticus does interrupt the narrative of the Pentateuch. The story line flows naturally from the conclusion of Exodus to Numbers 10. Leviticus and Numbers 1–10 form an intermission of legal materials. But this observation illustrates the importance of the book. The Israelites would not have inserted Leviticus into their sacred literature if it were not important to their story. Its emphasis on personal, priestly, and national holiness was a necessary and integral part of that story.

Despite its strangeness and apparent awkwardness, Leviticus plays an important role in the thought flow of the Pentateuch. It was of great significance for ancient Israelites and is still pertinent for modern Christians.

Background of the Book of Leviticus

All of Israel's neighbors among the ancient Near Eastern nations practiced sacrificial worship. Animal sacrifice was common in ancient Mesopotamia and similar to that of Israel. Israel even shared many of the same terms for the different types of sacrifices with her more immediate neighbors in Canaan.[1] The sacrifices of the ancient Near East, like those of Israel, were designed to provide fellowship with the deity, to appease the gods, and to insure continuance of divine favor.

But certain differences existed between the Israelite sacrificial system and those of the ancient Near East. Superficial differences are obvious, such as a lack of burning sacrifices by fire in Mesopotamia as the Israelites did.[2] However, there are more fundamental differences that make Israel unique.

First, the Mesopotamians commonly used the sacrificial animal as a means of clairvoyance, in order to discern the future actions of the gods. Priestly special-

A round stone altar dating from around 2500 B.C. at Megiddo in the Jezreel Valley.

ists believed they could decipher the future by studying and "reading" a dead animal's entrails. Such practices were absent in Israel.

Second, the most distinctive aspect of the Israelite sacrificial system is the way it was linked to the covenantal relationship with God.[3] God gave the instructions for Israel's sacrifices during the last month and a half the people were at Mount Sinai, between the construction of the tabernacle (Ex 40:17) and the departure from the mountain (Nm 10:11). The sacrifices make up a major ingredient of the covenant bond between Israel and God. The ancient Near Eastern nations have nothing comparable.

A third unique feature of Israel's use of the sacrifices is her concept of holiness. Israel's notion of the term "holy" (Hebrew *qādôš*) was based on the elevated moral and ethical nature of God. Because this idea was so central to the covenant with Yahweh (Ex 19:6), it also impacted Israel's use of the sacrificial system for worship of Yahweh. Israel's neighbors had no such concept.

Though the sacrificial system seems strange and foreign to us, it was part and parcel of Israel's cultural environment. We should not be surprised that she was comfortable using animal sacrifices as a part of her worship of Yahweh. But we should also remember these striking differences between the way Israel and her neighbors practiced sacrifice.

Contents of Leviticus

Who were the **Levites**? Why was this book named for them? The Levites were descendants of Levi, one of the twelve sons of Jacob (Gn 29:34). Aaron and his family were chosen from this tribe to serve as priests and to offer the sacrifices. God appointed the rest of the Levites to the service of the tabernacle, to assist the priests in the worship at the sanctuary (Nm 3:5–10).

The **Septuagint** named the book for the Levites because portions of it deal with their instructions for offerings to God. These portions served as an instruction manual for the Old Testament priesthood. But the Hebrew title for the book is taken from the first word (*wayyiqrāʾ*, "and he

called"), which emphasizes that Leviticus is a continuation of the Exodus story line. The Israelites have a new covenant relationship with God, and now the Lord is sending Moses forth to the nation with instructions for proper worship (1:1–2). Since the book was intended for the whole nation Israel (as in 1:2), we should remember that it still functions as God's word for all who read it today.

Whereas Exodus ended by emphasizing *where* to worship God (i.e., the tabernacle), Leviticus deals with *how* to worship him.[4] After listing the regulations for the various types of sacrifices that may be offered to him, Leviticus deals with the priesthood and the topics of cleanness and holiness.

Outline

I. **The Offerings** (1:1–7:38)
   A. General Regulations (1:1–6:7)
   B. Priestly Regulations (6:8–7:38)

II. **The Priesthood** (8:1–10:20)
   A. Consecration (8:1–36)
   B. Installation (9:1–24)
   C. Consequences of Disobedience (10:1–20)

III. **Cleanness and Uncleanness** (11:1–16:34)
   A. Regulations (11:1–15:33)
   B. The Day of Atonement (16:1–34)

IV. **The Holiness Code** (17:1–26:46)
   A. The Sanctity of Blood (17:1–16)
   B. Moral Laws (18:1–20:27)
   C. Priestly Regulations (21:1–22:33)
   D. Worship Calendar (23:1–44)
   E. Oil, Bread, and Blasphemy (24:1–23)
   F. The Sabbath Year and Jubilee (25:1–55)
   G. Rewards and Punishments (26:1–46)
   H. Vows and Tithes (27:1–34)

Overview

The opening sections of the book deal with right forms of worship inside the tabernacle (and later the permanent temple):

the five types of acceptable sacrifices (chapters 1–7), and the conditions for representative priesthood (chapters 8–10) and for acceptable worshipers (chapters 11–16). The rest of the book (chapters 17–27, the so-called **Holiness Code**) is devoted to right living outside the tabernacle. So Leviticus is concerned with right worship and right living, with becoming holy and staying holy. The Bible consistently joins right worship inside the church to right living outside it. Any worship that tolerates and continues to permit unrighteous behavior is not Christian worship.

The first seven chapters serve as a Manual of Offerings for all Israelites (see the summary at 7:38–39). These chapters describe five different sacrifices. The first three sacrifices (burnt, cereal, and peace offerings) are the most common in the Old Testament. Each description of these offerings concludes with a variation of the expression "an offering by fire of pleasing odor to the LORD" (1:9, 13, 17; 2:2, 9, etc.). These three sacrifices stress the result of the offering from God's perspective.

The sections presenting the two other sacrifices (sin and guilt offerings) have a different arrangement and function. They are less concerned with the value of the

Types of Sacrifices

There were many types of sacrifices in the Old Testament and numerous variations of the basic ones listed here. This list includes only the prescribed sacrifices of Leviticus 1–7.

1. BURNT OFFERING,
Leviticus 1
Typical Hebrew offering, dominant throughout Old Testament history, and probably the oldest form of atonement sacrifice. The term describes an "offering of ascent," or an offering that goes up. The animal was completely burned on the altar, its smoke rising toward heaven. Leviticus required a male without blemish. Various animals were allowed according to financial ability.

2. CEREAL OFFERING,
Leviticus 2
May originally have been a present or gift, since the term simply means "gift." In levitical regulations, the cereal offering carried an expiating sense. Frequently accompanied burnt and peace offerings. Probably served as a less expensive burnt offering for those who could not afford an animal.

3. PEACE OFFERING,
Leviticus 3
The basic form of sacrifices brought on feast days. A celebrative offering, consumed by humans. Often paired

with the burnt offering, which was consumed by God. Does not appear to have been expiatory, but had to do with restoration and reconciliation. Had three subtypes: thanksgiving sacrifice, vowed sacrifice, and freewill offering.

4. SIN OFFERING,
Leviticus 4:1–5:13
Expiatory for offenses against God. Emphasized the act of purification. Involved ceremonial defilement, deception, misappropriation, and seduction. Varied across four classes of individuals: priest, congregation, ruler, and individual.

5. GUILT OFFERING,
Leviticus 5:14–6:7
A subcategory of sin offering. Expiatory, but devoted to restitution and reparation. Generally deals with profanation of sacred items and violations of a social nature.

See Gary A. Anderson, "Sacrifice and Sacrificial Offerings," in *Anchor Bible Dictionary*, ed. David Noel Freedman, 6 vols. (New York: Doubleday, 1992), 5:877–81.

An artist's impression of priests making a burnt offering on the altar in front of the tabernacle.

animals presented and more with the types of sin committed (intentional or inadvertent) and the status of the sinner. Each section dealing with these two sacrifices is marked with variations of the expression "the priest shall make atonement on his behalf for his sin, and he shall be forgiven" (4:20, 26, 31, 35; 5:6, 10, etc.). These two sacrifices, then, emphasize the result from the human perspective.

Chapters 8–10 describe the ordination and installation of the priesthood and demonstrate the consequences of improper priestly activity. We do not know the specifics about the "unholy fire" of Nadab and Abihu (10:1). But the context emphasizes the holiness of Yahweh and the necessity of approaching him *only* as he has prescribed (10:3).

Chapters 11–16 have to do with the distinction between clean and unclean. They deal with practical, everyday issues in ancient life: foods (chapter 11), childbirth (chapter 12), skin and fungus diseases (chapters 13–14), and bodily discharges (chapter 15). The food restrictions of chapter 11 build on previous injunctions regarding the eating of meat. At creation, hu-

mans were intended to be vegetarians (Gn 1:29–30). But after the flood, God granted to Noah and his family the right to eat meat as long as the blood was properly drained (Gn 9:3–4). Leviticus 11 now expands the restrictions based on the distinction between clean and unclean animals.

We do not know in every case why eating certain foods or why certain physical activities caused uncleanness. Some foods were unclean because they carried diseases. In ancient societies, where no refrigeration was possible in a hot climate, meat posed a serious threat to public health.

But there may have been theological reasons for the ban on certain foods. Perhaps some were too closely associated with pagan worship practices. Others were prohibited because of the idea that blood and life are synonymous (Lv 17:11). Israelites were required to show the highest respect for life as a gift from God, so that even edible animals must have their blood drained completely (17:13–14). The people could only eat animals that fed on various kinds of grasses, making all carnivorous predators forbidden as part of the diet.

Ultimately, we have to conclude that these chapters on the distinction between clean and unclean are object lessons teaching a hidden reality. Chapters 11–15 look forward to and prepare us for the Day of Atonement in chapter 16. They describe what is meant by uncleanness so that it may be absolved on the Day of Atonement (16:16). Just as chapters 1–7 describe the sacrifices offered at the consecration of the priesthood (chapters 8–10), so chapters 11–15 define the uncleanness that makes the Day of Atonement necessary.[5]

The Day of Atonement was one of the most sacred days in the Old Testament calendar (see also Lv 23:26–32, where it is listed in Israel's religious "feasts" or "appointed times"). Unlike many of Israel's other high holy days, it does not commemorate one of God's great and mighty acts of the past or celebrate his goodness at harvest time. On the Day of Atonement, God provided an annual time for purging all the sins and uncleannesses that were unatoned for during the year. It provided atonement for the high priest, the sanctuary, and the people, so that all might be "clean before the LORD" (16:30).

On this one day each year, the high priest was permitted to enter the Holy of Holies, the inner precinct of the tabernacle (vv. 2–3; see diagram in previous chapter). There he carried the blood of the slain offerings to make atonement for himself and the nation (vv. 14–15). For the Christian, a new High Priest has removed the need for an annual Day of Atonement. Christ entered the Most Holy Place "once for all" to make atonement, not with the blood of animals, but with his own blood (Heb 9:11–12).

The blood of the slain offerings was only part of the ceremony. Unique to this sacred occasion was the use of a scapegoat (or "Azazel," vv. 8–10, 20–22). The exact meaning of "Azazel" is unclear. Some believe it refers to a specific evil location or to a desert demon (so v. 10 may be translated, "that it may be sent away into the wilderness to Azazel," NRSV). But the Hebrew word, as understood by the ancient translations, probably refers to the goat itself ("into the desert as a scapegoat," NIV; and see NKJV). In either case, the function

of the goat in this part of the ceremony is clear. It physically symbolized the removal of the nation's sin. Aaron placed his hands on the head of the goat, confessed Israel's guilt, and then sent the goat into the desert. Significantly, the ideas of "bearing," carrying iniquities into the desert, and "forgiving," are expressed by the same Hebrew verb (*nāśā*, v. 22).

Chapters 17–27 (sometimes only chapters 18–26) are known as the Holiness Code.[6] The recurrence of the term "holy" in this section signifies its unifying principle. This term with its derivatives occurs eighty-five times in these eleven chapters. The unit prescribes the way of holiness for all Israelites. It deals with topics ranging from sexual purity to observance of sacred holidays to fair treatment of the poor. This appeal for holy living is based on God's holy character: "You shall be holy, for I the LORD your God am holy" (19:2).

Themes of Leviticus

Leviticus establishes several basic themes for the rest of biblical thought. Bible authors assumed their readers understood certain concepts, such as sacrifice, atonement, forgiveness, and holiness. Leviticus gives the fundamental definition for all of these.

Law

As we saw in the previous chapter, the Book of Exodus clarified the concept of law as it functioned in the covenant relationship between God and the Israelites. Leviticus now outlines a large body of legal material. One verse near the end of the book ties all of Leviticus to the Sinai covenant: "These are the statutes and ordinances and laws that the LORD established between himself and the people of Israel on Mount Sinai through Moses" (26:46).

But the nature of law in Leviticus is somewhat different from that of Exodus. Exodus outlined the Ten Commandments and explained how they applied to covenant life in ancient Israel. Leviticus is concerned with the laws for proper covenant worship and ritual cleansing. The question for the modern believer is,

Leviticus on Sexuality (Leviticus 18)

Israel was surrounded with sexual perversion. God warned the Israelites not to live like the Egyptians behind them or the Canaanites before them (v. 3). Their neighbors had defiled themselves with all kinds of unnatural behavior: incest (vv. 6–18), adultery (v. 20), homosexuality (v. 22), and bestiality (v. 23). Because of this, God had rejected them and expelled them from the land (vv. 24–25).

Leviticus 18 is a warning to the Israelites to guard themselves against sexual sins. Failure to listen to his warning would result in their expulsion from the promised land, just like the Canaanites (v. 28). Instead of compromise, they must listen to God's word; instead of conformity to the world's standards, they must submit to God's standards (vv. 3–5). Their relationship with God marked the Israelites as unique in the ancient world. They were to reflect his holy character, allowing him to touch every aspect of their lives. Letting God determine their standards of sexual morality also affected their definitions of family and relational faithfulness.

So Christians are marked by their relationship with God. Compromise and conformity—living like the "Canaanites" all around us—is self-destructive (vv. 25, 28). How we deal with our sexuality often reflects how seriously we have submitted every area of our lives to God's control.

---

casuistic laws

How do these laws of sacrificial rites and ritual cleansing relate to us? The same question may be asked of the **casuistic laws** of Exodus 21–23.

Many Christians distinguish among moral, civil, and ceremonial law in the Old Testament. The Ten Commandments are the moral law. Laws specific to Old Testament society are civil laws whereas laws dealing with sacrifices and ritual cleansing are ceremonial laws. Since Jesus affirmed and reestablished the Ten Commandments (Mt 5), the moral law is still applicable today. But many Christians sweep away the rest of pentateuchal law as outmoded, because it is civil and ceremonial.

But this division into moral, civil, and ceremonial law was unknown in Jesus' day. Some laws are both moral and civil, such as those against adultery, stealing, bearing false witness, and the like. Others are both moral and ceremonial, such as laws against idolatry and Sabbath-breaking. All these laws contain a moral dimension, making the lines between the categories somewhat arbitrary.[7] Furthermore, this approach to Old Testament law leads some Christians to take too lightly Paul's injunction that "all Scripture . . . is useful for teaching, for reproof, for cor-rection, and for training in righteousness" (2 Tm 3:16).

Instead of the moral, civil, and ceremonial distinction, it is better to accept some laws of the Old Testament as broad and generally intended for all societies. Others are specific applications to Israelite culture and society that cannot be applied in the same way today to our Western society and culture. On the other hand, much of the world today is closer to ancient Israel than we may think. For the majority of the world's population, the specific applications of civil law are not so far removed from ancient Israel.

Old Testament law continues to be God's word for us, though we may apply it variously in different contexts. The moral substance of all of his commands continues to speak to the church today. Jesus summed up the law as love for God and love for all humanity (Mt 22:36–40). If we ask, "Yes, but how does this or that law apply to me?" the Bible invites us to examine ancient Israel as the model and example. As we compare our situation to theirs, we accept Old Testament law as confirmed by Christ, and with the help of his Holy Spirit and lessons learned from church history, the specifics of how we

Key Terms

Levites
Septuagint
Holiness Code
casuistic laws
expiation
atonement

expiation

atonement

ought to love God and neighbor should become clear.[8]

Sacrifice

Leviticus is the primary source in the Old Testament for regulations on sacrifice and how properly to offer sacrifices to God. Yet the book seldom states explicitly what the theology behind such sacrifices is (17:11 is an exception). In general the first three sacrifices (burnt, cereal, and peace offerings) could be presented as the wor-

shiper desired. The last two (sin and guilt offerings) were used to provide **expiation** from sin. Expiation is the purging of impurity caused by sin. It results in the removal of guilt, the granting of forgiveness, and the restoration of the relationship between the sinner and God.[9]

For several of the blood offerings, the worshiper placed his hand on the head of the sacrificial animal (1:4; 3:2, 8, 13; 4:4, 15, 24, 29, 33). This action identified the animal as his substitute. This does not necessarily mean the worshiper's guilt was transferred to the animal. But the animal suffered the consequences of the worshiper's sins.

God ordained sacrificial blood as the means for cleansing sin: "I have given [blood] to you for making atonement for your lives on the altar" (17:11). Every form of life is a precious gift from God. Here God established the spiritual principle that life itself, not some lesser gift, must be returned to him for the purpose of atoning for sin. The exact meaning of the Hebrew word for **atonement** *(kipper)* is uncertain. But it somehow means the animal's sacrifice ransomed the sinner from the death

Summary

1. Sacrifice was common throughout the ancient Near East, but Israel used it in a unique manner.

2. The Levites were descendants of Levi, and they served as priests.

3. The contents of Leviticus are: the offering, the priesthood, cleanliness, uncleanliness, and the Holiness Code.

4. The basic type of sacrifices are: burnt offering, cereal offering, peace offering, sin offering, and guilt offering.

5. On the Day of Atonement the priest made a sacrifice to make atonement for himself and the nation.

6. The scapegoat symbolized the removal of the sin of the nation.

7. Leviticus established laws for proper covenant worship and for ritual cleansing.

8. Through the use of blood, God made clear that nothing less than life itself must be presented to him as an atonement for sin.

9. In Leviticus God called Israel to live a holy life, and he calls us to do the same.

Study Questions

1. Why is Leviticus one the most neglected books of the Bible?

2. What are the major differences between the Israelite sacrificial system and those of the ancient Near East?

3. Who were the Levites? Why is the book named for them?

4. What are the four main divisions of the book?

5. Distinguish the two main categories of sacrifices.

6. What was the function and ritual of the Day of Atonement?

7. What are the three major themes of Leviticus?

8. What is the basis of God's call for Israel to live a holy life?

which the sinner deserved. The animal became the worshiper's substitute and lost its life in order for the sinner to live.

The New Testament asserts that the death of Jesus Christ is now the sacrifice that makes atonement for sin (Heb 9:26; 1 Jn 2:1–2). His sacrifice was not limited to a single worshiper or nation, but is offered to the world as a means of forgiveness. It need never be repeated, for his sacrifice is sufficient for all who respond in faith (1 Pt 3:18). Christ's death on the cross has thus replaced the levitical system of sacrifices. But just as in the old system, God still invites us individually to respond in repentance and faith, so that Christ may become a substitute for us, redeeming us from our sin and guilt.

Holiness

The keynote of Leviticus is its resounding "be holy, for I am holy" (11:44–45; 19:2; 20:7, 26). God's call for Israel to live a holy life is based on his own holy character. He has not asked his people to become something he is not. The difference between his holiness and Israel's holiness is that his is intrinsic, while theirs is derived from their relationship with him.

So it is with Christians today. God summons us to live a holy lifestyle. But our holiness is derived from him, as we live in fellowship with him and learn to obey his will with the help of his Holy Spirit. Through the ancient message of Leviticus, God invites us to share in his holy character: "You shall be holy, for I the Lord

Further Reading

Harrison, R. K. *Leviticus: An Introduction and Commentary*. Tyndale Old Testament Commentary. Downers Grove: InterVarsity, 1980. Thorough introduction.

Hartley, John E. *Leviticus*. Word Biblical Commentary 4. Dallas: Word, 1992.

Ringgren, Helmer. *Religions of the Ancient Near East*. Trans. John Sturdy. Philadelphia: Westminster, 1973. Helpful background information on ancient Near Eastern religious institutions.

Wenham, Gordon J. *The Book of Leviticus*. New International Commentary on the Old Testament. Grand Rapids: Eerdmans, 1979. Most complete treatment of all the issues.

your God am holy" (19:2). This message is not time-conditioned, since the apostle Peter made it the cornerstone of his first epistle (1 Pt 1:15–16). This is indeed humankind's highest calling: to imitate God (Mt 5:48).

The Book of Leviticus is indispensable for understanding the warp and woof of ancient Israelite society and culture. Furthermore, the New Testament Epistle to the Hebrews expounds the importance of Leviticus for Christians today. It clarifies the meaning of the sacrifice and priesthood of Jesus Christ. As God's word for believers in today's world, Leviticus still speaks to us about reverence in worship, purity in lifestyle, and our need for forgiveness.

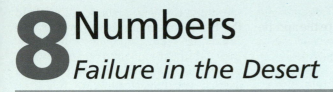

8 Numbers
Failure in the Desert

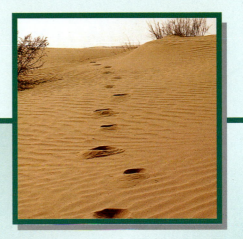

Outline

Objectives

After reading this chapter, you should be able to

- Explain the apparent disorganization of the Book of Numbers
- Outline the basic content of the Book of Numbers
- Describe the difficulties of the journey from Mount Sinai to the desert of Paran
- List Israel's acts of rebellion and the consequences of those acts
- Give examples from Numbers of humankind's lack of faith
- Describe the key events that took place in the Plains of Moab

Israel had everything going her way. God had worked a spectacular miracle in redeeming her from Egypt. Now she had a new and unique relationship with God. The Sinai covenant came complete with tabernacle, a worship program, and an elaborate legal system—Israel's new blueprint for the future. Like no other nation in history before or since, Israel had everything she needed for complete success. But Israel's is not a story of success—at least not immediate success. The Book of Numbers relates her struggles with obedience and the consequences of her disobedience.

Contents of the Book of Numbers

This book contains the census reports that Moses and the Israelites recorded while in the desert (chapters 1–4, 26). The translators of the **Septuagint** entitled the book *arithmoi*, "numbers," which our modern English Bibles follow. But the Hebrew title *běmidbar*, "in the desert," more accurately reflects the book's contents. Numbers describes events that occurred during the nearly forty years Israel wandered in the desert between Mount Sinai and the PLAINS OF MOAB.

Literary Structure

The Book of Numbers has a clear geographical and chronological arrangement in three parts. First the Israelites were encamped at Mount Sinai, then they wandered in the desert for nearly forty years, and, finally, they were on the plains of Moab.

More specifically, Numbers 1:1–10:10 contains various instructions and preparations for the journey from Sinai to the promised land. God gave these to the Israelites while they were still at Mount Sinai. Numbers 10:11–20:21 relates the failure of the Israelites to trust God while they wandered in the deserts of the Sinai Peninsula, particularly at KADESH-BARNEA in the desert of PARAN. Finally, after Israel's forty years of wandering, 20:22–36:13 describes their preparations for entering the promised land while they were on the plains of Moab.

Despite this clear geographical and chronological arrangement, the Book of Numbers presents a literary problem. The references to geography and chronology provide merely a historical framework, supporting materials of various types. Though the overarching pattern is clear, the book disperses legal sections, historical narratives, and records of censuses in a pattern that appears almost arbitrary. The combination of different types of materials (especially history and law) in an apparently random order has led some scholars to view the book as hopelessly disorganized.

But when dealing with ancient biblical books, we must not define literary artistry according to our own modern, Western criteria. A lack of such design and consistency in a book does not mean the book is confused, confusing, or without a discernible message. In fact, the materials in Numbers that seem misplaced or disorganized contribute significantly to the book's major themes. It is in the sprouting of Aaron's rod (17:1–13) and the prophecies of Balaam (chapters 22–24) that we can discern God's hand and purposes most clearly.

Moreover, it is possible to discern a consistent thematic purpose in Numbers despite its literary diversity. BREVARD CHILDS has demonstrated that the book contains a unified interpretation of God's will for his people by contrasting the holy with the profane. The Book of Numbers portrays the holy "as the presence of God, the blessing of numbers, the laws of cleanliness, the service of the Levites, the atonement of Aaron, and the inheritance of a clean land." On the other hand, "the profane consists of all sorts of uncleanliness, and results in the wrath of God, his plagues of judgment, a lost inheritance by a dying people, and the pollution of the land."[1]

The confidence with which some modern scholars have criticized the literary structure of Numbers is unwarranted. It is possible to see the book as "a travel diary," assembled by an editor sometime after the death of Moses.[2] The apparent literary disjointedness of Numbers might even be used to argue for its early date of composition. The combination of historical narrative, cultic legislation, and a variety of other materials against a backdrop

The Arrangement of the Tribes in Camp

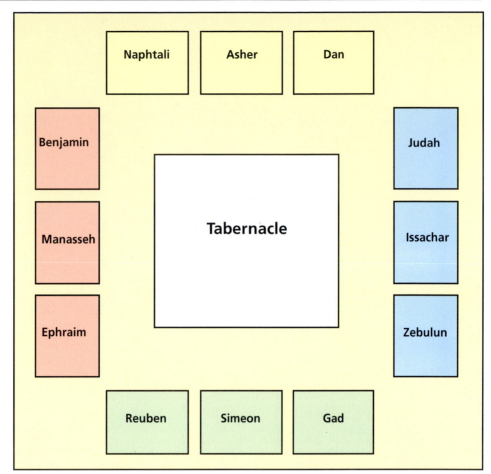

of desert life would naturally result in a more haphazard literary arrangement. In view of these circumstances, it would actually be quite surprising to find a carefully constructed and tightly composed literary whole.

The literary nature of Numbers is unique in the Pentateuch. Genesis, Exodus, and Leviticus have more unity. The written or oral sources behind Genesis, the historical nature of the Exodus materials, and the predominantly legal materials of Leviticus were unifying factors for those books.[3] Numbers is altogether unique, though the message is clear and pertinent for modern readers.

The Book's Use of Numbers

Israel's population tallies presented in the census reports have roused much debate. The two main lists (1:46 and 26:51) record over 600,000 men, which would mean Israel's total population would number 2 million or more (see also Ex 12:37). These numbers present several difficulties.

A group this size would more than fill northeastern Egypt (the land of Goshen). Such an Israelite population would have had no problem overpowering the Egyptian government. The Egyptian army numbered probably no more than 20,000 men at this time. The numbers are especially striking since the entire population of Canaan would have been well below 3 million at this time. Yet the Israelites were said to have been much smaller in number than the Canaanites—too few, in fact, to occupy the land (Dt 7:6, 7, 17). If the Israelites had been 2 million strong, they would not have feared the Egyptian army or the Canaanite population.[4]

In addition, the logistical problems of such numbers are staggering. One scholar has estimated that 2 million people marching in close order would create a line hundreds of miles long. Before the last rank had crossed the Red Sea, the first rank would have reached Kadesh-Barnea.[5]

The best solution (of several possibilities) is that the Hebrew terms used in these lists have incorrectly been limited to numerical designations. The terms "thousand" and "hundred" may originally have referred to social units (families, clans, tent groups) or to military units (captains of thousands or hundreds). For example, if we assume "hundred" designated a military contingent and "thousand" a captain, we could calculate an estimate for the total Israelite population at the time of the exodus at approximately 72,000.[6] But this solution is tentative, and a conclusive answer to this problem remains elusive.

Outline

I. **At Sinai** (1:1–10:10)
   A. The First Census (1:1–54)
   B. The Arrangement of the Camp (2:1–4:49)
   C. Legislation (5:1–8:26)
   D. Final Events at Sinai (9:1–10:10)

II. **From Sinai to Edom** (10:11–20:21)
   A. To Kadesh (10:11–12:16)
   B. At Kadesh (13:1–20:21)

III. **From Edom to the Jordan** (20:22–36:13)
   A. Aaron's Death (20:22–29)
   B. The Destruction of Arad (21:1–4)
   C. The Bronze Serpent (21:5–9)
   D. The Journey to Moab (21:10–20)
   E. Initial Victories (21:21–35)
   F. The Plains of Moab (22:1–36:13)

Overview

The Book of Numbers is about preparation. Everything in 1:1–10:10 prepares the nation to leave Mount Sinai, where they had been for almost eleven months (Ex 19:1–2; Nm 10:11). But the Israelites refused to enter the promised land in God's timing (10:11–20:21). So the rest of the book (20:22–36:13) may be viewed as another preparation to enter Canaan. This second preparation was necessary because the first did not work.

Preparations at Mount Sinai (1:1–10:10)

Mount Sinai, with its constant reminders of God's presence, was never intended to be the final destination for God's people. There comes a time to break camp, head out into the world, claim God's promises, and fulfill his calling. The first major unit of Numbers (1:1–10:10) comprises instructions for breaking camp and moving through the desert under God's direction.

Chapter 9 is the literary climax of 1:1–10:10. In the first half of the chapter, the Israelites celebrated the Passover before their departure from the mountain. Likewise, they would again celebrate the Passover before the battle of Jericho and the conquest of the promised land (Jos 5:10–12). Remembering and celebrating the mighty acts of God in the past is a good prelude for expecting his guidance and protection in the future. The rest of Numbers 9 emphasizes the role of the divine cloud over the tabernacle as an indication of God's leadership throughout the people's journeys.

The entire unit since the beginning of the book has been building to this point in chapter 9. The census mustered the strength of the nation for military preparedness and organized them around the tabernacle (chapters 1 and 2). The censuses of the Levites (chapters 3 and 4) organized them for service to the tabernacle. Their awesome responsibility is clear from the brief reminder of Aaron's two sons, Nadab and Abihu (3:4), who failed to give proper reverence to God and to take proper care with their divine service (Lv 10:1–3).

These first four chapters organized the entire nation, both laity and clergy, around the tabernacle. It was the dwelling place of God in the midst of his people, and its care and maintenance had to be done according to his instructions. Much of the preparation of chapters 1–4, then, is devoted to religious instruction. The Israelites were being prepared to maintain the awesome presence of God in their midst. They were not simply packing and moving.

The people were to maintain clean and holy lives because of God's pure and holy

The long period of desert wandering is described in Numbers 10:11–20:21.

tabernacle (7:1; 9:1, 15). The laws and instructions of chapters 1–6 are more naturally a continuation of Leviticus. But chapters 7 and 8 list important gifts and instructions that were necessary for the transportation of the tabernacle through the desert. They contribute to the literary movement toward chapter 9, preparing the Israelites for their departure from Mount Sinai.

Final preparation for departure from Mount Sinai involved instructions for two silver trumpets (10:1–10). Variations of trumpet alarms would indicate specifically how the camps of Israel would proceed in the march (vv. 5–6). The trumpets were also used to prepare for warfare (v. 9) and on various occasions of worship (v. 10). With this final bit of instruction, the people were ready for their departure.

Disobedience in the desert (10:11–20:21)

The long period of desert wandering is described in 10:11–20:21. The importance of Israel's actual departure from the mountain is underscored by the precise date in 10:11 ("on the twentieth day of the second month of the second year" since their rescue from Egypt). The divine cloud rose over the tabernacle and the people of Israel set out on their journey to the promised land (10:11–12). Moses was overjoyed at the scene and prayed that God's enemies would be scattered before them as they marched (v. 35). But unfortunately, this was only a prelude to failure. The bright optimism of chapter 10 is soon shattered by the stubborn rebellion of chapter 11.

Chapters 11 and 12 relate the difficult journey from Mount Sinai to the desert of Paran (only a few of the sites mentioned here can be positively identified, like HAZEROTH; see map). The Israelites had trouble all along the way. Numbers 11:1 sets the unfortunate tone for the next several chapters: "Now when the people complained in the hearing of the LORD about their misfortunes, the LORD heard it and his anger was kindled." They had complained from the moment they left Egypt about the lack of food in the desert. So God had miraculously provided quails and bread from heaven, called manna (Ex 16). But now their supply of quail had run out and they were weary of the manna. Once

presence in their midst. Chapter 5 describes the processes required for turning out of the camp those who defiled it. The Nazirite vow (chapter 6) emphasized the importance of dedication and faithfulness to those commitments made to God in the past. The famous Aaronic blessing (6:22–27) seems to serve as the culmination of a section on priestly activities (chapters 3–6). Note that Aaron does not actually bless the people. He is merely the instrument, the transmitter, of the Lord's blessing.

The instructions of chapters 7–10 are out of chronological sequence. The census of chapter 1 was taken on the first day of the second month during the second year after the exodus (1:2). But the instructions of chapters 7–9 were given during the previous month, when Moses erected the

The Wilderness of Paran, looking west from the modern Egypt/Israel frontier.

again God provided for them, but their rebellious attitude resulted in desert fires and plagues (11:1, 33).

There is something ironic about the Israelites complaining over their desert diet and longing for the variety of foods in Egypt. Had they forgotten they were slaves in Egypt? Is it possible they had so quickly forgotten how God had rescued them from severe pain and suffering? How could they rebuff his guidance? Their complaints were far more serious than merely whining about food. The Israelites had an inner attitude of rebellion that plays a dominant role in the Book of Numbers. They were prone to reject God's provisions and leadership for their lives, even after his miracles and deliverance from Egypt and his provision for their needs along the way.

Chapter 12 continues this theme by relating the opposition of Aaron and Miriam to the leadership of Moses, and, therefore, to God. Moses' own family was jealous of his unique position before the people as God's sole spokesman. God dramatically affirmed Moses as his chosen leader. But now the leadership, as well as the wider populace, was disagreeable and discontented. The whole nation seemed inclined to rebellion. As the Israelites left Hazeroth and moved farther into the desert of Paran (12:16), it was obvious they were not willingly following the Lord. Their destination was the promised land. But were they capable of following the promise?

Israel's ultimate failure was her refusal to enter the promised land when God offered it (chapters 13–14). Numbers 13 relates the famous story of the twelve Israelite spies, two of whom were Joshua and Caleb. When God commanded Moses to send spies into the promised land, he intended this reconnaissance mission to prepare Israel for conquering the land ("Send men to spy out the land of Canaan, which I am giving to the Israelites," 13:2). God was already in the process of "giving" the land to his people.

But the spies brought back a mixed report (13:25–33). The Canaanites were well fortified in the land and enormous in stature, making the Israelite spies look and feel like grasshoppers (13:33). So overwhelming was the task that the majority opinion was that it was impossible (apparently Joshua and Caleb were the only ones to demur, 14:6–8). When they heard the report, incredibly, the Israelites regretted ever leaving Egypt: "If only we

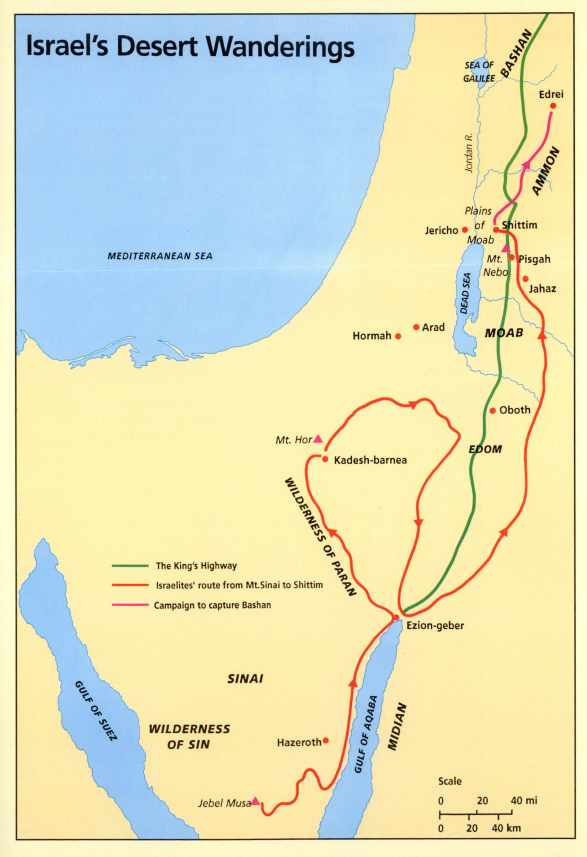

Israel's Desert Wanderings

MEDITERRANEAN SEA

SEA OF GALILEE

BASHAN

Edrei

AMMON

Jordan R.

Plains of Moab

Jericho

Shittim

Mt. Nebo

Pisgah

Jahaz

DEAD SEA

Hormah

Arad

MOAB

Oboth

EDOM

Mt. Hor

Kadesh-barnea

WILDERNESS OF PARAN

Ezion-geber

SINAI

GULF OF SUEZ

WILDERNESS OF SIN

Hazeroth

GULF OF AQABA

MIDIAN

Jebel Musa

The King's Highway

Israelites' route from Mt. Sinai to Shittim

Campaign to capture Bashan

Scale

0   20   40 mi

0   20   40 km

had died in the land of Egypt" (14:2)! They promptly decided to replace Moses with a new leader who would take them back to Egypt (14:4).

Disaster was narrowly averted when God appeared at the tabernacle in all of his glory (14:10) and Moses interceded for the people. As punishment for their distrust and disobedience, the Lord declared that everyone twenty years old and older would die in the desert. They were never to see the promised land! Only their children, after a forty-year delay, would be allowed to enter and possess it.

To make matters worse, the Israelites tried to reverse the divine judgment. Upon hearing the terrible news, the people decided they were capable of conquering the land of Canaan after all. Moses warned them it was too late and they were launching out on their own without the Lord's blessing. But they stubbornly persisted and promptly lost a major battle to the Amalekites and Canaanites at Hormah (14:39–45, see map). Chapter 14 forms a literary climax for this unit on Israel's disobedience. The Israelites persistently refused to hear the word of God through Moses, at their great peril.

Chapters 15–20 relate the subsequent wanderings of the Israelites for nearly forty years in the desert. Presumably they stayed near KADESH in the desert of Paran (13:26), though the desert of ZIN is also mentioned (20:1, and see map). But curiously, these chapters actually tell us little about the events of those years. They do not relate the course of the Israelites' travels nor any particular timetable for traveling, as the author did for the rest of the book. Instead, these chapters contain laws the Israelites were to obey once they were in Canaan and a few selected stories of failure and disobedience.

The location of the laws on offerings to be observed in Canaan is curious (chapter 15). The movement from the previous chapter to these cultic and ritualistic laws seems abrupt, and scholars have wondered why they are here instead of in Leviticus. But coming immediately after the revolt in Kadesh, these laws may be intended as a striking statement that God's purposes would continue, with or without Moses' generation of Israelites. They had refused to obey God's direction to enter and occupy the land. They were going to die in the desert. But God intended these laws for worship, and their children were to learn them in anticipation of that future day when they would live in Canaan—a day that would certainly come.[7]

The rebellion of Korah, Dathan, and Abiram (16:1) seriously threatened Israel's leadership, especially the priestly line of Aaron. But an earthquake killed the rebels and fire consumed all their followers (16:31–43). In confirmation that Aaron's family was the legitimate priestly line, Aaron successfully interceded on behalf of the people (16:44–50). As further vindication of Aaron, God caused Aaron's rod to sprout and produce ripe almonds in a test to see who was really chosen by God (chapter 17).

Chapters 18 and 19 contain more laws to protect the Israelites against uncleanness. The priests and Levites were responsible to prevent divine judgment for any uncleanness regarding the tabernacle (chapter 18). Chapter 19 is concerned specifically with ritual uncleanness caused by contamination due to any contact with the dead. Once again, these laws anticipate life in Canaan. The author has again followed a report of rebellion and failure with one of instructions for a future life in the promised land. God's plan will not be thwarted.

Moses' sin at Kadesh is a reminder that no human leader, not even Moses himself, is exempt from the consequences of unbelief (20:2–12). He spoke to the people instead of the rock (20:10–11), and thus reflected a lack of faith in God's directive. The Old Testament knows no distinction between faith and obedience. Faith is the correct response to God's word, of either promise or command.[8] So Moses' actions were comparable to the rebellion of the people when they refused to enter the promised land on God's timing. Now his fate was like theirs. He would not be permitted to enter Canaan (20:12).

The Book of Numbers is basically silent on events that occurred during the more than thirty-seven years of desert wanderings. This silence reflects the book's primary purpose. Numbers is not a history of Israel, but an essay about the consequences of disobedience. The laws of chap-

The Jordan Valley, and site of Jericho, viewed from Mount Pisgah.

ters 15–20 look to the future in the land and imply that the rebellion of a single generation cannot prevent God from fulfilling his promises to the patriarchs. The accounts of Korah's rebellion and Moses' sin at Kadesh indicate that the promises of God will be fulfilled in spite of the failure of Israel's leadership. Moses' generation was forced to mark time in the desert, but God was undeterred. He was faithful to his promises to Abraham, even when the Israelites were faithless.

Preparations in the plains of Moab (20:22–36:13)

The rest of the Book of Numbers describes events in the plains of Moab (see map 8:1). The journey to Moab was an eventful one (20:14–21:35). Moses and the Israelites faced several Amorite and Canaanite armies during this march to the promised land. The strategy was to avoid confrontation where possible, since the Israelite nation was not interested in subduing these transjordanian areas

(20:17; 21:22). They were on a mission to another place, a better place that God had promised to them.

In addition to the armies of Edom and the Amorite armies of Moab and Bashan, the journey was hampered by more complaints by the Israelites. Numbers 21:4–9 relates an episode in which "fiery" (or poisonous) serpents plagued the people because of their rebellion. When the people repented of their sin, God instructed Moses to make a bronze serpent and mount it on a high pole. Whenever one of the serpents bit an Israelite, the dying person was instructed to "look at the serpent of bronze and live" (v. 9). This event prefigured the simplicity and availability of salvation for us. Just as the ancient Israelite could be saved by looking at the bronze serpent lifted up in the desert, so may we be saved by looking in faith to Christ lifted up on the cross (Jn 3:14–15).

Numbers 22–24 presents the first of a series of events that happened to the Israelites while they camped in the plains

The Jordan Valley, Plains of Moab, and site of Jericho viewed from the west.

of Moab. Balak, the ruler of Moab, was rightly concerned about this Israelite nation encamped in his backyard. They had demonstrated a surprising ability to subjugate any enemy that tried to stand in their way. As a means of insuring military success against Israel, Balak enlisted the services of a professional magician to pronounce a curse on Israel. He enticed Balaam of northern Mesopotamia to mount his donkey and return with the official delegation from Moab for the purpose of pronouncing the curse.

The account of what happens next is both humorous and deadly serious (22:22–30).[9] Balaam's donkey proved to be more spiritually astute and sensitive than this great Mesopotamian seer, who turned out to be quite dull after all. The animal's awareness of the Lord's angel on the path saved Balaam's life (v. 33). The angel confronted Balaam and prepared him to pronounce a blessing on Israel instead of a curse.

The rest of the unit (chapters 23–24) contains the four blessings Balaam pronounced over the unsuspecting Israelite camp. Balaam articulated the exact opposite of that which Balak had commissioned him to speak, much to Balak's disappointment. But the talking donkey was not the most miraculous element of the episode. The Spirit of God came upon Balaam (24:2) and reversed the curses he had planned. This is the greatest miracle of the passage and must have surprised even the seer himself, not to mention the Moabite king. In so doing, God was fulfilling the promises of the covenant, even while Israel lay passively spread out in the valley below.

The Israelite encampment at Moab was the final stopping place before they crossed the Jordan River and entered the promised land under Joshua's leadership. In the two previous temporary camps (Mount Sinai and Kadesh), the Israelites

Key Term

Septuagint

Key Person/ Places

Brevard Childs
Plains of Moab
Paran
Hazoroth
Kadesh
Zin

had jeopardized their covenant relationship with God through apostasy. Aaron's golden calf at Mount Sinai (Ex 32) and a series of rebellions at Kadesh (Nm 11–14) threatened Israel's existence. Unfortunately, Israelite behavior in the plains of Moab was no different.

While encamped directly across the Jordan River from Jericho, the Israelites fell into the practice of Canaanite Baal worship, which would continue to plague them throughout their history (Nm 25). In Moab, the manifestation of Canaanite Baalism (Baal of Peor) included sexual immorality. Under Balaam's influence (Nm 31:16; Rv 2:14), the Israelites were quick to intermarry with the women of Moab and to worship their gods (Nm 25:1–3). God's displeasure was evidenced in a plague (25:9) that nearly brought the end of the nation.

But as in other passages where sin and punishment threaten to bring God's people to an end, the next unit presents legal material for worship in the promised land and instructions for life in the new setting in Canaan. Numbers 26 records another census taken to provide the statistical information necessary to divide up the promised land among the various tribes. So, while Israel's sin and religious apostasy seemed to imperil the covenant plan for the future, God patiently and lovingly continued to insist that they *would* enter the land.

The rest of the book (chapters 27–36) recounts the final preparations for Israel before she leaves the plains of Moab and enters the promised land. This mixture of Law and historical narrative is an implicit assurance that the covenant promises are soon to be fulfilled. Chapter 27 presents instructions for worship on special occasions in the religious calendar once the Is-

Summary

1. The Book of Numbers relates Israel's difficulty in obeying God and describes the consequences of that disobedience.

2. The Book of Numbers is arranged in three parts: the encampment at Mount Sinai, the forty years of desert wandering, and the encampment on the plains of Moab.

3. The general theme in Numbers is preparation to leave Mount Sinai and to enter Canaan.

4. The Israelites continually complained about their circumstances, forgetting that they were free and no longer enslaved in Egypt.

5. The greatest failure of the Israelites was that they refused to enter the promised land when God offered it.

6. Little is recorded about the details of the forty years of wandering in the desert.

7. God listed laws on offerings that indicated that his will would be done regardless of the Israelites' attitude.

8. Moses displayed his human nature at Kadesh, where he disobeyed God and showed his lack of faith.

9. During their stay in the plains of Moab, the Israelites had to face the armies of the Amorites and Canaanites.

10. The encampment at Moab was the final stop for the Israelites before they crossed the Jordan River.

11. The message of obedience in Numbers is used in the New Testament books of 1 Corinthians and Hebrews.

Study Questions

1. What is the English translation of the Hebrew title of this book? How does this title describe the struggle which the book depicts?

2. What are the geographical-chronological units of the book? What literary types of materials are dispersed throughout these units?

3. What problem is presented in the book's census reports?

4. Describe the major subunits of Numbers 1:1–10:10. What is the literary climax of this unit? What part is not in chronological order?

5. What time period is described in the next unit (10:11–20:21)? What inner attitude is borne out in the Israelites' complaints? How does this attitude result in the forty years of desert wanderings? What does the placement of legal materials (chapters 15, 18–19) in-

dicate about God's plan for the next generation?

6. What is the geographical location of the final unit (20:22–36:13)? What image in this unit prefigures salvation through Jesus Christ? What are the miraculous elements of Numbers 22–24? How was the covenant relationship threatened in Numbers 25? How does God's response show commitment to the covenant plan for the future?

7. How does Paul draw on Numbers in speaking to the church at Corinth?

8. What events in Numbers are mentioned in Hebrews? What point does the author of Hebrews illustrate through these events?

raelites are in their new homeland. Joshua was then designated as the replacement for Moses and the one who would lead them into the land (27:12–23). Chapters 28–36 contain instructions for land allotments, further wars with surrounding adversaries, and laws for justice and worship to be implemented in Canaan.

Use of the Book of Numbers in the New Testament

First Corinthians 10

Paul made it clear that the sins of the Corinthians were not new (vv. 1–13). As new Christians, the Corinthians must beware lest they fall back into the old ways

that once enslaved them. Paul reminded his readers that the Israelites had also begun a new life of freedom in God's grace. He used events from Exodus and Numbers to illustrate that God's people can and sometimes do fail in their new relationship with God. Even after the Israelites experienced the exodus and the miraculous bread and water in the desert, they rebelled against the very One who had delivered them.

Paul used the Israelite failure recorded in the Book of Numbers to warn the Corinthians. The Israelites fell into sexual immorality in the desert (v. 8; Nm 25:1–9), rebellious rejection of authority (v. 9; Nm 21:5) and complaining (v. 10; Nm 14:2). The result was forty years of desert wanderings and death. The Corinthian Christians were in danger of the same failures. Paul asserted that the Book of Numbers was written as a warning to them and to

Further Reading

Ashley, Timothy R. *The Book of Numbers.* New International Commentary on the Old Testament. Grand Rapids: Eerdmans, 1993. Helpful exposition and bibliographies.

Budd, Philip J. *Numbers.* Word Biblical Commentary 5. Waco, Tex.: Word, 1984.

Harrison, R. K. *Numbers: An Exegetical Commentary.* Grand Rapids: Baker, 1992 (1990).

Maarsingh, B. *Numbers: A Practical Commentary.* Trans. John Vriend. Grand Rapids: Eerdmans, 1987.

Wenham, Gordon J. *Numbers: An Introduction and Commentary.* Tyndale Old Testament Commentary. Downers Grove/Leicester: InterVarsity, 1981. Most readable and informative commentary available.

us (vv. 6, 11). He concluded: "So if you think you are standing, watch out that you do not fall" (v. 12).

Hebrews

The author of the Letter to the Hebrews refers to the account of the spies and the nation's refusal to enter the promised land as a warning to Christian readers (3:7–4:13). This letter warns the Hebrew Christians to "take care" lest they have "an evil, unbelieving heart that turns away from the living God" like the Israelites of old (3:12). Their disobedience and unbelief prevented the desert-weary Israelites from enjoying the rest and peace of the promised land. But now the Good News has come to Christians just as it did to the ancient Israelites (4:2), and there remains for us a "Sabbath rest" (4:9). Using the Israelite failure in the desert as a warning, the author encourages his readers: "Let us therefore make every effort to enter that rest, so that no one may fall through such disobedience as theirs" (4:11).

9 Deuteronomy
Restoring the Covenant

Outline

- **Contents of the Book of Deuteronomy**
  Literary Structure
  Outline
  Overview
- **Parallels from the Ancient World**
  The Hittite Parallels
  Treaty Structure in Deuteronomy
- **Significance of Deuteronomy in Biblical Thought**
  Role of Deuteronomy in the Pentateuch
  Deuteronomy and the Historical Books

Objectives

After reading this chapter, you should be able to

- Explain the chiastic structure of the speeches of Moses
- Outline the basic content of the Book of Deuteronomy
- Identify the major theme of each of the three speeches given by Moses
- Explain the purpose of Moses' speech about the law
- Demonstrate how the laws discussed in Chapters 12–26 are based on the Ten Commandments
- List the reasons why Deuteronomy is primarily a covenant document
- Compare the structural similarities between Deuteronomy and the suzerainty treaties of the ancient Near East
- Evaluate the place of Deuteronomy in the first nine books of the Old Testament

Things had not gone exactly as planned for Israel. Despite God's wonderful deliverance from Egypt and miraculous provisions in the desert, Israel had failed to obey him. She refused to enter the promised land and rebelled against God's leadership. As a result, the trip from Egypt to Canaan took nearly forty years instead of a few months. Now, a generation later, the people were finally in the plains of Moab ready to cross the Jordan River and claim the promises of God.

But Moses was not allowed to enter the land with the people. He had acted in anger at Meribah (Nm 20), and had to pass the baton of leadership to someone else. Furthermore, this generation needed to claim the covenant and its promises for themselves. It was time for the covenant of Sinai to become the covenant of Moab as well (Dt 29:1). The Book of Deuteronomy relates the reestablishment of the covenant with Israel, including the laws of the covenant. The name "Deuteronomy," from the **Septuagint** title (*Deuter-*

onomion, "second law") fails to communicate this important idea clearly, for the book is much more than a simple restatement of the law.[1]

Contents of the Book of Deuteronomy

Deuteronomy picks up the Israelites where the Book of Numbers left them, "on the plains of Moab by the Jordan across from Jericho" (Nm 36:13). The occasion for the writing of Deuteronomy was the important covenant renewal in Moab just before God's people were to enter the patriarchal land of promise. Instead of relating details of the covenant ceremony itself, the book presents Moses' farewell addresses on that occasion. The book contains three lengthy speeches of Moses intended to exhort the Israelites to keep the covenant faithfully. These addresses survey God's saving acts for the previous generation and summarize the laws of the covenant in order to prepare the new generation of Israelites for the future.

Literary Structure

The first address of Moses (1:1–4:43) recounts God's mighty acts on Israel's behalf from the time of the covenant at Sinai to this renewal ceremony in Moab. Moses wanted to teach about God's nature as savior and protector in order to motivate the Israelites to keep the covenant (4:35–40). The second speech (4:44–26:19) restates the covenant laws originally presented in Exodus 20–23. The Ten Commandments needed to be specifically applied to the people's new life in the promised land instead of their wilderness lives. The third speech (27:1–31:30) is Moses' final address to the nation. He begins with a ritual of curses and blessings dependent on covenant compliance, charges the nation to be faithful in the future, and formally commissions Joshua as his successor. The book closes with three appendixes: the "Song of Moses" (chapter 32), the "Blessing of Moses" (chapter 33), and the death and burial of Moses (chapter 34).

Recent studies have also detected a five-part concentric pattern known as **chiasm.**

The fertile oasis of Jericho lay on the opposite side of Jordan from the Plains of Moab.

The speeches of Moses may thus be described in the following fashion:

A THE OUTER FRAME:
A Look Backwards
(chapters 1–3)

B THE INNER FRAME:
The Covenant Summary
(chapters 4–11)

C THE CENTRAL CORE:
Covenant Stipulations
(chapters 12–26)

B′ THE INNER FRAME:
The Covenant Ceremony
(chapters 27–30)

A′ THE OUTER FRAME:
A Look Forwards
(chapters 31–34)

The two parts of the outer frame may be read together as a continuous whole, as is true also of the two parts of the inner frame. This type of structure emphasizes the central core, which in Deuteronomy comprises the primary body of legal instruction for ancient Israel.[2]

Outline

I. **Prologue** (1:1–5)

II. **The Great King's Faithfulness** (1:6–4:43)
   A. From Sinai to Kadeshbarnea (1:6–2:1)
   B. From Edom to the Plains of Moab (2:2–3:29)
   C. Exhortation to Obedience (4:1–40)
   D. Cities of Refuge (4:41–43)

III. **The Covenant Way of Life** (4:44–26:19)
   A. Introduction (4:44–49)
   B. The Great Commandment (5:1–11:32)
   C. Ancillary Stipulations (12:1–26:19)

IV. **Covenant Sanctions** (27:1–31:30)
   A. Ratification Ceremony (27:1–26)
   B. Blessings and Curses (28:1–68)
   C. The Covenant Oath (29:1–30:14)
   D. Call to Decision (30:15–20)
   E. Leadership and the Law (31:1–30)

V. **Appendixes** (32:1–34:12)
   A. The Song of Moses (32:1–47)
   B. The Testament of Moses (32:48–33:29)
   C. The Death of Moses (34:1–12)

Overview

The book opens with a five-verse introduction that establishes the historical and geographical basis for the rest of the book. These are speeches of Moses delivered on the plains of Moab forty years after the exodus. Verse 2 subtly reminds the reader of the consequences of sin and rebellion by stating that the trip from Mount Sinai to Kadesh-Barnea was only an eleven-day journey. But Moses begins his final addresses forty years after the exodus (v. 3).

The introduction closes with the statement that on this occasion Moses "began to expound this law" to Israel (v. 5). Deuteronomy is more than a restatement of the covenant and the laws of Exodus and Numbers, though many of those laws find new expression here. Deuteronomy is, rather, an exposition of the covenant in a new setting. The paragraph also emphasizes the speech of Moses ("Moses spoke," vv. 1 and 3). A chief claim of Deuteronomy is that Moses spoke that which Yahweh "commanded" him (v. 3). The next paragraph begins with the emphatic assertion that Yahweh our God "spoke" (the same word used for Moses's speech in vv. 1 and 3, *dibber*) to the Israelites through Moses. Let there be no mistaking this point: Deuteronomy claims to be the very words of God.

First speech: The great king's faithfulness (1:6–4:43)

The first speech presents a theology of history. By reviewing the recent past, Moses sought to prepare the nation to obey God in the future. God began with the command to leave Mount Sinai and enter Canaan, which he promised to give to Israel as the fulfillment of his promises to the patriarchs (1:6–8). Thus the covenant already ratified at Sinai was a partial ful-

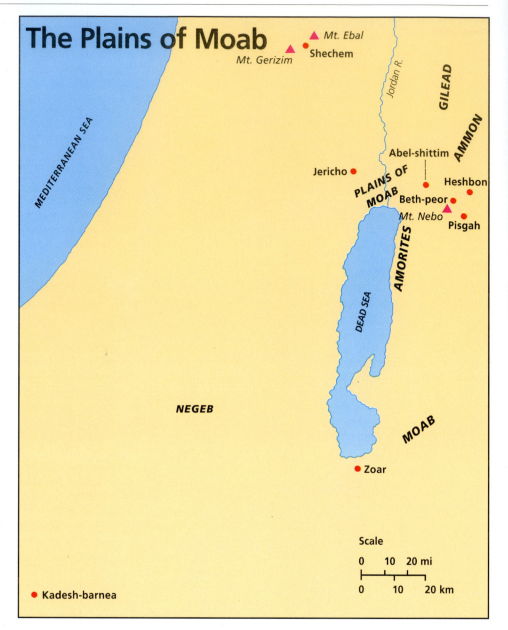

The Plains of Moab

fillment of God's promise to the patriarchs. Since that promise was as eternal as God's own character, this covenant renewal in Moab and the subsequent conquest of the promised land were certainly within God's will. Such assurances should provide the basis for obedience.

This survey of Israel's recent past illustrates the benefits of keeping covenant as well as the pitfalls of disobedience. Beginning with the command to leave Mount Sinai (1:6–7), Moses reviewed both the victories and the failures of Israel along the way. He reviewed the great rebellion at Kadesh-Barnea and its consequences in 1:26–46. But then 2:1–3:22 reminds the Israelites of their successes in the desert. They had obeyed God's command to avoid confrontation with the Edomites, Moabites, and Ammonites. Though God promised to protect the Israelites as they went around these nations (2:6–7), he warned them they were not to try to conquer their territories (2:5, 9, 19). Israel also met with success against the Amorite kings, Sihon of Heshbon and Og of Bashan (2:24–3:17). God assured Moses and the Israelites that he had given these kings

monotheism

Shema

and their lands over for defeat and charged his people to engage Sihon and Og in battle (2:24, 31; 3:2). By acting when God commanded and by strictly obeying God's directives, Israel learned that the victory is God's to grant: "The LORD our God delivered him over to us and we struck him down" (2:33; see 3:3).

After surveying such great successes, Moses reminded Israel that God's blessings are often directly related to submission to his will. Deuteronomy 3:23–29 explains that even Moses had to suffer the consequences of his sinful actions. He would not be allowed to enter the promised land with the nation because of his sin at Meribah (Nm 20). This passage provides a contrast because of its location

immediately after the description of Israel's successes. The nation succeeded by submitting to God's will, but even an individual like Moses could fail through disobedience.

Such illustrations of obedience and disobedience prepare the reader for chapter 4. Here Moses turns from reviewing the past to exhort the nation about the present and the future. He recurringly warns against "forgetting" the covenant (vv. 9, 23). Moses knows that when it comes to keeping covenant commitments, God's people have short memories.

Second speech: The covenant way of life (4:44–26:19)

Moses' sermon on the covenant in chapter 4 is a suitable preparation for the second address. Here Moses reviews the covenant stipulations and establishes them as the normative way of life for the Israelites after they enter the promised land. The unit is introduced as "the law that Moses set before the Israelites" (4:44). After an editorial introduction in 4:44–49, Moses begins his discourse by explaining that these are the "decrees and laws" of the Sinai covenant now applied to their future life in Canaan (5:1–3).

Deuteronomy 5–26 has two sections. Chapters 5–11 comprise a general statement about the covenant law. This is followed by the specific application of that law to future Israelite society and culture (chapters 12–26). The general section begins by repeating the Ten Commandments as a convenient summary of the principles of covenant living. Moses emphasizes that these covenant life-principles were not just for their ancestors at Mount Sinai. This new generation of Israelites must now accept the law as their own (5:2–3).

As we saw in the chapters on Exodus and Leviticus, law means divine instruction for righteous living. In the general presentation of this instruction, Moses gave the most important expression of the Israelite concept of **monotheism:** "Hear, O Israel: The LORD our God, the LORD is one" (6:4). This famous verse is known as the **Shema,** which is the first Hebrew word of the sentence (*šĕmaᶜ,* "hear"). The unique way in which Moses states this great truth is more than a simple philosophical expression of the idea that the Israelite God,

An artist's impression of the Israelite high priest. Moses' brother Aaron was the first high priest.

polytheism

Decalogue

Yahweh, is the only God in existence. It does mean that. But it also emphasizes the consistency of God.[3] He never changes; there is no duplicity in his character. He acts the same today as he did yesterday.

This was a new concept in the ancient Near East, since different responses from deity implied different deities, hence **polytheism.** But Yahweh is always the same, never changing or leaving any doubt about his nature. Moses' statement of monotheism answers more than the question, "How many gods are there?" It answers the question, "What type of God is our Yahweh?" It asserts that he is consistent within himself and in his dealings with humankind. He is the same for this new generation of Israelites on the plains of Moab as he was for their ancestors at Sinai, and as he is for any generation of believers. Because of this, Moses' statement of the oneness of God flows into the greatest summation of God's law: "Love the LORD your God with all your heart and with all your soul and with all your strength" (Dt 6:5; Mt 22:35–37). God *can* be and *should* be loved wholeheartedly because of his character.

The purpose of this discourse on the law is not primarily to *inform* the Israelites, but rather to *form* them spiritually. Chapters 5–11 are intended to motivate the nation to keep the covenant and obey God's covenant laws. Important concepts related to keeping covenant are the words "love" and "fear," both of which Moses uses recurringly in chapters 6–11 (ʾāhab and yārēʾ, respectively).[4] In this unit, Moses urges the Israelites to both love and fear God. These ideas are not incompatible. Rather they complement and need each other. Love without fear becomes sappy sentimentality and fails to result in obedience, the ultimate goal of chapters 5–26.[5] Likewise, fear without love becomes terror and drives people away from an intimate relationship with God. Together love and fear produce a healthy relationship with him, and result in obedience to his will. In chapters 5–11, God's commandments, statutes, and ordinances are wrapped up in the ideas of loving and fearing him.

Chapters 12–26 now present the specific applications of the covenant obligations, giving special attention to how the law relates to the new situation in Canaan. Laws pertaining to ritual worship (like those of Leviticus) are intermingled with those having to do with civil and societal issues. Those living in the promised land must exhibit obedience in all areas of life. Covenant faithfulness is not just for abstract religious observances, but for everyday life.

This unit contains a bewildering arrangement of the laws. Scholars have tended to see the arrangement of chapters 12–26 as haphazard and hopelessly beyond systematic analysis. But literary studies have recently discerned a pattern in which the laws of this unit are based on the Ten Commandments in chapter 5. STEPHEN A. KAUFMAN has described this unit as "an expanded DECALOGUE."[6] The laws of chapters 12–26 are arranged in four major issues that the **Decalogue,** or Ten Commandments, addresses.

This observation seems to have solved the structural problems in the laws of chapters 12–26, and indeed possibly for Moses' entire second speech in chapters 5–26.

Third speech: Covenant sanctions (27:1–31:30)

Moses' final discourse is actually a combination of speeches pertaining to the covenant and the transfer of leadership from Moses to Joshua. Chapters 27 and 28 could actually be taken as the conclusion to the second speech, leaving chapters 29–30 as the final speech of Moses.[8]

In chapter 27, Moses gave instructions for a covenant renewal ceremony to be performed after the Israelites had taken possession of the promised land. At the ancient city of Shechem, in the heart of the promised land, they were to build an altar and set up a stone memorial for the occasion. The city lay between MOUNT EBAL (v. 4) and MOUNT GERIZIM (v. 12). Moses gave instructions to divide the tribes, half on one mountain and half on the other. In this impressive and dramatic setting, the Israelites would recommit themselves to God's covenant. The Levites were to sing the warnings about breaking the covenant, and the people were to respond antiphonally. In one of the most moving scenes in Israel's history, this covenant renewal ceremony was held under Joshua's leadership (Jos 8:30–35).

deuteronomic
theology

The Laws of Chapters 12–26[7]

Main Issues	Regarding God	Regarding Humans
Authority	Commandment 1 chapter 12	Commandment 5 16:18–18:22
Dignity	Commandment 2 chapter 12	Commandments 6, 7, 8 19:1–24:7
Commitment	Commandment 3 13:1–14:21	Commandment 9 24:8–16
Rights & Privileges	Commandment 4 14:22–16:17	Commandment 10 24:17–26:15

Chapter 28 lists for the Israelites the blessings and curses of the covenant. In a simple doctrine of retribution (often called **deuteronomic theology**), Moses explains that faithfulness to the covenant will result in blessings in the future while disobedience will result in curses. This is the basic theology behind the historical books, as we shall see.

Though Deuteronomy's doctrine of retribution is certainly true, it is not the whole picture because it deals with the immediate future. Israel will succeed in the promised land only if she is faithful to the covenant. On the other hand, if she disobeys God, she will lose the land. The rest of biblical revelation broadens the scope by teaching that character ultimately has to do with one's *eternal* destiny. The circumstances of this life may have little to do with one's character. Someone born blind cannot be accused of being in that condition because of sin (Jn 9:1–3); people killed tragically in accidents have not met untimely death because of sin (Lk 13:4–5).

In the next part of Moses' speeches to the people (29:1–30:14), he reviews their recent victories over enemy nations and predicts their future disobedience, exile, and return to the land. Then Moses charges them to make a conscious decision to be faithful in their commitments to God (30:15–20). He has placed before them blessings and curses, a choice between life and death. Moses called on the Israelites to practice advanced decision making, to decide now what their future behavior would be. The Bible warns that we cannot afford to wait until the moment of temptation to decide what our answer will be.

In the final section of speeches, Moses makes provisions for the future of the nation (chapter 31). He begins by passing the baton to his chosen successor: "Joshua . . . will cross over ahead of you, as the Lord said" (v. 3). Later, he appears with Joshua at the tabernacle so the nation can witness the transfer of power (vv. 14–23). The whole nation could see it was the Lord who commissioned Joshua, not Moses alone (v. 23).

Chapter 31 also provides for the future of the written word. Moses wrote down "this law" (presumably the speeches of Deuteronomy) and gave the nation instructions to read it publicly every seven years (vv. 9–13). He left the copy of the written law in the hands of the Levites, who were to preserve it in the ark of the covenant (vv. 24–29).

Appendixes (32:1–34:12)

In obedience to the Lord's command to summarize the covenant in song (31:19), Moses composed a lengthy poem outlining Israel's history (32:1–32:47). In the form of a covenant lawsuit, the song surveys the nation's recent past, looks ahead to future rebellion and exile, and predicts God's covenant

forgiveness and restoration. The song was intended as a final means of motivating the nation to keep their covenant with God. The concepts expressed in the Song of Moses, and even the phrases used to express them, made a lasting impact on the nation. In fact, Deuteronomy 32 has been called the "phrase book" for the seventh- and sixth-century prophets of the Old Testament.[9] In this way, the Song of Moses served as the "Bible" for later prophets who preached about Israel's broken covenant with God.

The time for Moses' death had now arrived. After receiving instructions to go up to MOUNT NEBO where he would view the promised land from a distance (32:48–52), Moses pronounced a fatherly blessing over each tribe (33:1–29). Rather than warnings or even final exhortations, these blessings declare God's future for Israel. This places the covenant and the Mosaic law squarely within God's sovereignty. Moses has emphasized Israel's covenant obligations. But now his farewell blessings assure the nation of God's commitment to them.

The final chapter of the Pentateuch lovingly describes the death of the esteemed leader (34:1–12). The Lord identifies Canaan as the land he swore to give to the patriarchs, Abraham, Isaac, and Jacob (34:4). This new homeland is the fulfillment of that covenant promise of long ago. As Israel's representative, Moses symbolically took possession of the land by viewing it from Mount Nebo. But because of his sin at Meribah (Nm 20), Moses was not permitted to enter the land physically. Perhaps his personal tragedy is meant to warn God's servant-leaders that all forms of personal gratification run counter to God's purposes. Moses' unfulfilled promise should encourage all of us to be content in fulfilling our roles in God's great plan. Following him intimately and leading his flock faithfully is no guarantee of inheriting his promises in this life.

Moses was an unparalleled prophet in Israel's history (v. 10). From the experience and historical viewpoint of the one who added this note, God had not sent a prophet since who could compare to Moses in stature. Yet Moses prophesied of one who would come later, the Messiah who would speak for God in a way that not even Moses had done (18:15–19).

A nineteenth-century poet captured the spirit of this chapter's reverence for Moses.

By Nebo's lonely mountain,
    On this side Jordan's wave,
In a vale in the land of Moab,
    There lies a lonely grave.
But no man dug that sepulchre,
    And no man saw it e'er;
For the angels of God upturned the sod,
    And laid the dead man there.

O lonely tomb in Moab's land,
    O dark Beth-peor's hill,
Speak to these curious hearts of ours,
    And teach them to be still.
God hath his mysteries of grace—
    Ways that we cannot tell;
He hides them deep, like the secret sleep
    Of him he loved so well.[10]

Parallels from the Ancient World

As we have said, Deuteronomy contains Moses' farewell speeches. These speeches have been deliberately arranged in a document format resembling certain types of treaties common in the ancient Near East. This arrangement makes Deuteronomy first and foremost a covenant document. Its goal is to reestablish the covenant of Sinai with this new generation of Israelites, whose parents had broken the old covenant. In Deuteronomy, the Sinai covenant was being updated on the plains of Moab. As the Israelites stood in Moab, with the land of God's covenant promise just across the Jordan River, they were putting the old wilderness life behind them.

A **covenant** is a means of establishing a binding relationship that does not naturally exist otherwise. As we saw in the study of Genesis, God bound himself forever to Abraham and his family in the patriarchal covenant (chapters 12, 15, 17). In Exodus, Moses and the Israelites entered into a sacred covenant with the Lord, which carried with it life-changing obligations (24:3–8). Deuteronomy is now reaffirming that national covenant with the new generation of Israelites in the plains of Moab.

In the mid-1950s, the political and so-

Excerpts from Hittite Suzerainty Treaties

1) Preamble

These are the words of Mursilis, the great king, king of the Hittites, the valiant.

2) The historical prologue

When your father died, I did not drop you. Since your father mentioned your name to me with great praise, I sought after you. To be sure, you were sick and ailing. But I still let you replace your father and accepted your brothers, sisters, and your land in oath for you.

3) The stipulations

You shall remain loyal to me, the Hittite king, the Hittite land, and my sons and grandsons forever! The tribute imposed upon your grandfather and your father (300 shekels of high quality gold) you will also present to me! Do not turn your eyes to anyone else! Your fathers presented tribute to Egypt; but you shall never do that!

4) Provision for deposit in the temple and periodic public reading

A duplicate of this document has been deposited before the god Tessub. At regular intervals they shall read it in the presence of the king and in the presence of the sons of the country.

5) The list of gods as witnesses

The Sun-god of Heaven, the Sun-goddess of Arinna, Ishtar, the gods and goddesses of the Hittites, the gods and goddesses of the Amorites, all the olden gods, the mountains, the rivers, heaven and earth, the winds and clouds—let these be witnesses to this treaty and to the oath.

6) The curses and blessings formula

Should Duppi-Tessub fail to honor this treaty, may these gods of the oath destroy Duppi-Tessub together with his wife, his son, his grandson, his house, his land and everything that he owns. But if Duppi-Tessub honors the treaty inscribed on this tablet, may these gods protect him together with his wife, his son, his grandson, his house and his country.

Extracted and adapted from two treaties: 1) Mursilis and Duppi-Tessub (*ANET*, 203–5) and 2) Suppiluliumas and Mattiwaza (perhaps spelled Sattiwaza or Kurtiwaza, *ANET*, 205–6).

suzerainty

cial background of the Sinai covenant was discovered in treaties from the ancient Near East. Though some scholars today disagree, the consensus is that Deuteronomy shares the same structural organization as international treaties made between kings of two nations. The **suzerainty** treaties were political covenants between unequal partners. The suzerain (or overlord) agreed to a binding relationship with his vassal (or subject nation). In such an arrangement, the suzerain king offered to provide protection for the vassal, but the subject nation must faithfully pay tribute and be loyal to the suzerain exclusively. Many scholars believe the original Sinai covenant (Ex 20–24) and Joshua's covenant renewal at Shechem (Jos 24) also have this literary structure.

The Hittite Parallels

This treaty structure was used by different nations over many centuries in ancient Near Eastern history. But the best examples for our purposes are found in Hittite documents from the mid-second millennium B.C. (fourteenth and thirteenth centuries B.C.). These Hittite suzerainty covenants nearly always have the following six elements, though there is considerable variation in the order and wording of these elements.[11]

1. Preamble. This introduction usually identifies the suzerain king, giving his titles and attributes.

2. The historical prologue. A second introduction describes the historical relations between the two parties leading up to this agreement. It usually details the

benevolent acts of the suzerain on behalf of the vassal. This section is intended to make the vassal feel obligated to the suzerain for favors already received. The suzerain is hoping to exchange past benefits for future obedience to specific commands, which will be detailed in the document. This section usually uses an "I–Thou" form of address. The suzerain, as author of the document, addresses the vassal directly.

3. The stipulations. This section outlines the terms of the agreement, explaining the obligations imposed on and accepted by the vassal. It usually includes a prohibition against relationships with any other foreign nations outside the Hittite Empire. Among several other stipulations, the treaty customarily requires an annual visit to the suzerain, probably on the occasion of annual tribute, and a pledge of loyalty to the suzerain.

4. Provision for deposit in the temple and periodic public reading. The obligations of the treaty applied to the entire vassal nation, not just the king. Regular public readings ensured that the population of the vassal nation were familiar with the requirements. Also, because the treaty was protected by the deity, the document was deposited as a sacred object in the sanctuary of the vassal nation. This created the impression that any breach of the treaty would offend the local deity.

5. The list of gods as witnesses. The authors of these international treaties thought of the gods as witnesses to the treaties, like witnesses in a legal contract. The gods of the Hittites and those of the vassal country could all be appealed to as witnesses. Sometimes deified mountains, rivers, springs, sea, heaven and earth, or winds and clouds were also listed in this section (Dt 32:1; Is 1:2).

6. The curses and blessings formula. Finally, the treaty listed blessings for those who were faithful to the agreement and curses for those who were not. The Hittite king could always use military force as a threat to any vassal who broke a treaty. But the written document listed the curses and blessings of the treaty as actions of the gods. The sanctions of the treaty were religious ones, and the Hittite military machine was merely the agent of divine will.

Treaty Structure in Deuteronomy

The idea of "covenant" was important throughout the Pentateuch. The parallels between the ancient Near Eastern treaties and certain covenant passages of the Old Testament are undeniable.[12] But Deuteronomy is unique in that we have an extended portion of Scripture structured literarily according to an ancient covenant. The Hittite suzerainty treaties of the second millennium B.C. are the closest parallel to this structure.

1. Preamble. 1:1–5
2. The historical prologue. 1:6–3:29
3. The stipulations. 4–26
4. Provision for deposit of the document and periodic public reading. 31:9–13, 24–26
5. The list of witnesses. 30:19; 31:19–22
6. The curses and blessings formula. chapter 28

The structure of Deuteronomy seems to have been borrowed from the ancient treaties. But comparing God's relationship to Israel with the Hittite king's relationship to his subject nation has limitations. The parallel between Deuteronomy and the Hittite treaties has to do only with form and structure, not content.

It is not difficult to see why Israel could so easily compare her new relationship to God with the ancient Near Eastern treaties. The suzerain demanded exclusive devotion. The vassal could not form another such relationship with any other king or nation. Mosaic monotheism needed to express the exclusive nature of relationship to Yahweh. There could be no other gods involved. But the suzerain king was also under some obligation. This was a mutual commitment between two parties. So Yahweh was also committing himself to Israel. Yahweh's covenant love (*ḥesed*) is an important concept throughout the rest of the Old Testament.

Does this parallel between Deuteronomy and the second-millennium Hittite treaties help with the problem of when Deuteronomy was written (see discussion in chapter 3)? As helpful as this observation is, it only demonstrates that Deuteronomy fits well into the second millennium and could have been composed then. This

An artist's impression of a family tent from Old Testament times. During their years of wandering the Israelites lived a nomadic existence.

parallel makes it possible to date Deuteronomy to the time of Moses, though it fails to prove Mosaic authorship, since other treaties with similar outlines were used in the first millennium. It does, however, demonstrate the essential unity of the whole book. All of Deuteronomy (with the possible exception of chapters 33 and 34) were part of this treaty structure.

Significance of Deuteronomy in Biblical Thought

Deuteronomy is important for the way it ties together what precedes it to what follows. Historically, the covenant in the plains of Moab bridged the Sinai covenant with life in the promised land. So also Deuteronomy forms a literary bridge between the Pentateuch and the historical books. It looks both back in time and forward to the future. As a recrystallization

of the covenantal law, it summarizes the Pentateuch and brings this monumental first section of the Bible to a fitting close. But Deuteronomy is also forward-looking. It prepares the Israelites for their future life with God in the promised land, and lays the literary and theological foundation for the historical books.

Deuteronomy is a pivotal book in the Old Testament canon. The first nine books of the Bible (Genesis to 2 Kings) may be called the Primary History.[13] Deuteronomy is literally at the center of that history, serving as the literary and theological hinge on which all the rest swing.

Role of Deuteronomy in the Pentateuch

Deuteronomy is the culminating expression of the Mosaic covenant. As in the previous books of the Pentateuch, Deuteronomy is greatly concerned with law. Here, as nowhere else in the Pentateuch, the underlying principle of the law is *love*, which characterizes the relationship between

Deuteronomistic History

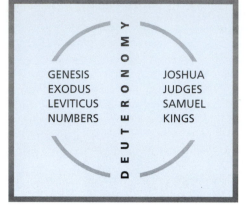

GENESIS
EXODUS
LEVITICUS
NUMBERS

DEUTERONOMY

JOSHUA
JUDGES
SAMUEL
KINGS

God and his people. The concrete imperatives of the Ten Commandments objectify this principle and then receive more specific application in the stipulations of chapters 12–26.

The basis of the nation's relationship to God flowed from his love for them and from their appropriate response of obedience. When God's people break his commandments, they break the relationship of love (Mt 22:35–40; Jn 14:15). Obedience to God's law is a byproduct of a relationship of love. Love is the essence of the relationship; law is the natural result.

Deuteronomy and the Historical Books

Deuteronomy is the foundation stone for the so-called **Deuteronomistic History.** The books of Joshua, Judges, Samuel, and Kings comprise a unit of historical books with a strong deuteronomistic influence (see next chapter). Deuteronomy sets the stage on which the drama described in the historical books takes place. The covenant's call to choose between life and death, blessings and curses, is a prelude to the story of national Israel (Dt 30:19).

God's people stand on the verge of na-

Summary

1. In the form of three addresses given by Moses, the Book of Deuteronomy presents an exhortation to the Israelites to keep the covenant.

2. The Book of Deuteronomy is organized in a five-part concentric pattern known as a chiasm.

3. The faithfulness of God is the topic of Moses' first speech.

4. The subject of Moses' second speech is a review of the covenant, which stipulates that the promised land is for the Israelites.

5. Moses presented a monotheistic approach for the Israelites as contrasted with the polytheism of the ancient Near East.

6. The arrangement of the law in chapters 12–26 follows the major topics of the Decalogue.

7. In his third speech Moses discusses the sanctions of the covenant.

8. Before his death, Moses pronounced a blessing over every tribe.

9. The organization of the Book of Deuteronomy is that of a suzerainty treaty, which was a common political agreement in the ancient Near East.

10. The six parts of a Hittite suzerainty treaty are: preamble, historical prologue, stipulations, list of gods as witnesses, curses, and blessings formula.

11. Deuteronomy is at the center of the primary history of the Old Testament.

12. Deuteronomy is the foundation for what is called Deuteronomistic history.

Study Questions

1. In what way does the title "Deuteronomy" fail to express the essence of the book? What is the geographic location in the book's opening scene? What is the occasion for its writing? What three events are depicted in detail in the book?

2. What are the subjects of the first (1:1–4:43), second (4:44–26:19), and third (27:1–31:30) literary units? Describe the book's appendixes.

3. When do the events of the book occur? How do the book's legal materials differ from the laws of Exodus and Numbers? What is the basis of Moses' authority?

4. In his first speech (1:6–4:43), what does Moses illustrate in the survey of Israel's recent past?

5. What are the two sections of Moses' second speech (4:44–26:19)? What is the function of the Ten Commandments here? What truths are contained in the Shema? What questions does it answer? How are we instructed to respond to the character of God? What is the proper balance of love and fear in our relationship with God?

How do these combine to accomplish the goal of Deuteronomy 5–26?

6. What new situation is addressed in Deuteronomy 12–26? How do the Ten Commandments provide a structure to the laws of Deuteronomy 12–26?

7. What are the two parts of Moses' third speech (27:1–31:30)? Describe the covenant renewal ceremony and the doctrine of retribution. What prediction is made and what choice is offered in the final part of Moses' speeches (29:1–30:14)? What are the two provisions for the nation's future in Deuteronomy 31?

8. How was the Song of Moses used by later prophets? What is the warning to future leaders in Moses' death outside the promised land?

9. What is a suzerainty treaty? What elements of a Hittite suzerainty treaty are seen in Deuteronomy?

10. How does Deuteronomy serve as a bridge between the Pentateuch and the historical books?

Key Terms

Septuagint
chiasm
monotheism
Shema
polytheism
Decalogue
deuteronomic theology
covenant
suzerainty
Deuteronomistic History

Key Person/ Places

Stephen A. Kaufman
Mount Ebal
Mount Gerizim
Mount Nebo

tionhood in Canaan. Deuteronomy becomes the nation's formative constitution. It is a covenant renewal document, which also prescribed their future relationship with God, with each other, and with surrounding nations. The expression of Israel's relationship to God in the form of a covenant is the most important Old Testament expression of Israelite faith. This is the distinguishing characteristic of Hebrew religion.

Further Reading

Christensen, Duane L. *Deuteronomy 1–11.* Word Biblical Commentary 6A. Dallas: Word, 1991. Unique approach, with some helpful insights.
———, ed. *A Song of Power and the Power of Song: Essays on the Book of Deuteronomy.* Sources for Biblical and Theological Study 3. Winona Lake, Ind.: Eisenbrauns, 1993. Wonderful introduction to the major issues and scholarly approaches to Deuteronomy.

Craigie, Peter C. *The Book of Deuteronomy.* New International Commentary on the Old Testament. Grand Rapids: Eerdmans, 1976. One of the best commentaries available in English.
Thompson, J. A. *Deuteronomy: An Introduction and Commentary.* Tyndale Old Testament Commentary. Downers Grove/Leicester: InterVarsity, 1974.

Part

2

Encountering the Historical Books

10 Introduction to the Historical Books

The History of Israel's Nationhood

Outline

- **Contents of the Historical Books**
- **The Role of History in the Bible**
  Herodotus, the Father of History?
  The Jewish Canon and the
    Christian Canon
  History and Theology
- **Authorship of the Historical Books**
  The Deuteronomistic History
  Chronicles and Ezra–Nehemiah
  Ruth and Esther

Objectives

After reading this chapter, you should be able to

- Identify the purpose of each of the historical books
- Explain how the Bible is more than a history book
- Discuss the role of historicity for a biblical faith
- Evaluate the Noth–Cross approach to authorship of the historical books

The Pentateuch records the birth of God's people. The account continues in the second section of the canon known as the "historical books." These books are important first of all because of their historical content. They cover a period of time at least eight-hundred years in length, from Joshua's conquest to the Persian Empire in which Esther lived.

The historical books begin by describing Israel's conquest of the promised land (Joshua). Then this section of the Bible continues by telling of the period before Israel had kings, when judges ruled the people (Judges, Ruth). They also cover the period of the monarchy. The united kingdom of Saul, David, and Solomon was eventually divided into Israel in the north and Judah in the south (1–2 Sm, 1–2 Kgs). Chronicles, Ezra, and Nehemiah retell the history from a later theological perspective and continue the narration into the postexilic restoration. Esther illustrates the role of God's people under Persian rule.

Besides their historical worth, these books are also important for what they teach theologically. They describe Israel's history, but they are more than history or a record of mere historical facts. They are God's word today for all Christian believers. The church has always affirmed the value of these books for "teaching, rebuking, correcting and training in righteousness" (2 Tm 3:16). We read these books for more than their historical value. They trace the history of God's relationship with his nation, revealing his faithfulness and steadfast love for his people even when they broke covenant. These are important events to learn *from,* not merely *about.*

Contents of the Historical Books

The Book of Joshua was written to show the surpassing value of obedience. It paints the picture of Israel's successful conquest of the promised land, highlighting the importance of absolute commitment to God's word and dependence on his power. Though there are a few examples of disobedience, in general the Book of Joshua does not contrast obedience with disobedience as do the Books of Kings.

Judges, on the other hand, relates the almost hopeless state of Israel after the conquest. The nation fell victim to religious compromise. Israel seemed incapable of sustained periods of obedience to God's will and doomed to failure. Temporary periods of obedience brought peace and success, but each time the nation fell back into sin. The Book of Judges was written to vindicate Israel's need for a king.

Ruth is inserted after the Book of Judges because the events detailed in it took place during the judges period. This little book illustrates God's sovereign care for faithful individuals who live in the midst of national religious apostasy. God used the faithfulness of a single family to work a miracle and to provide Israel's greatest king, David.

The Books of Samuel trace the early history of Israel's monarchy. Samuel was a prophet and judge who led Israel through the transition from judges to kings. The books tell the stories of Israel's first two kings: Saul and David. Second Samuel is especially devoted to describing the major events of David's kingship.

The Books of Kings detail the history of the monarchy from Solomon to the fall of Jerusalem. They contrast obedience with disobedience in order to illustrate the results of both. Things went well for Solomon initially. But his failure to remain faithful to Yahweh resulted in a divided kingdom, Israel in the north and Judah in the south. Northern Israel was religiously apostate from the start and fell to the Assyrians in 722 B.C. Judah vacillated between evil kings and a few good ones, until the wickedness of certain kings was too great. Nebuchadnezzar and his Babylonian military machine took Jerusalem in 587 B.C.

The rest of the historical books come from the postexilic period. The Books of Chronicles form the first commentary on the Scriptures. These books retell the stories of David, Solomon, and the kingdom of Judah, accounts already known from the Books of Samuel and Kings. But the Chronicler was not simply rehashing old news. He highlighted God's work among his people through David's line. He desired to follow a straight line of faith and salvation without detours into the failures

myths

of the past. His audience in the exile knew all too well the story of national moral collapse and defeat. His generation needed to be reminded of the victories of Israel's heritage as a means of providing hope for the future.

The Books of Ezra and Nehemiah, which were probably written together as one composition, present the events of the restoration in the middle of the fifth century B.C. Under Persian rule, the Jews living in Babylonia were allowed to return to their homeland to rebuild. The able leadership of Ezra and Nehemiah, along with certain prophets who were active during that time, helped the Jewish people rebuild the temple and the walls of Jerusalem. In addition to describing these physical structures, these books also relate the rebuilding of the social and religious foundations of God's people.

The fascinating little Book of Esther demonstrates how God's sovereign care and protection extend to his people, even while they are living in Persian exile. The book is a historical short story about Queen Esther and her cousin Mordecai. Unlike any other biblical book, Esther shows that even when God is silent, he is at work fulfilling his promises to his people.

The Role of History in the Bible

As we saw in the Pentateuch, Israel was unique among her ancient Near Eastern neighbors for her emphasis on history. God created time and space and is therefore sovereign over human history. It should not be surprising that a large portion of Israel's sacred writings were historical narratives.

Most religious expression in the ancient Near East was mythological. Ancient peoples generally expressed their theological convictions and worldviews through elaborate **myths,** in which important events took place outside history. Most holy books of world religions are collections of wisdom literature and religious APHORISMS. But Israel saw her own national history as an arena for divine revelation. God's word for the world is largely a narrative of his relationship with one nation, and his plan for establishing a relationship with all humankind.

Herodotus, the Father of History?

Because history was the primary means of God's revelation, Israel was the first na-

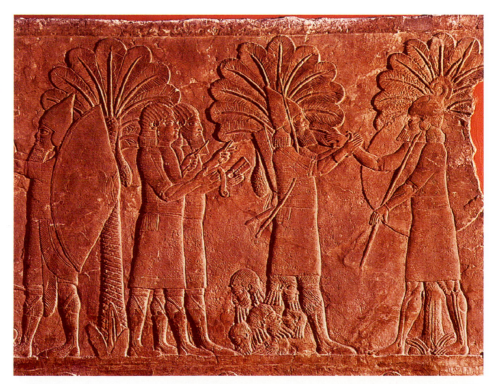

An Assyrian relief showing a scene following a battle. Northern Israel was religiously apostate and fell to the Assyrians in 722 B.C.

159

tion to give great attention to the recording of history. HERODOTUS, the fifth-century B.C. Greek historian, earned the title "Father of History" for his history of the Greek and Persian wars. But a hundred years before Herodotus, the Bible had a history of Israel containing many of the same features we now think of as history: cause-and-effect connections, continuous narration, fully developed characterization, and so on.

The Jewish Canon and the Christian Canon

History is important in both Jewish and Christian canons. As we saw in chapter 1, the Christian canon separates and groups together all the books that are predominantly historical in nature. These historical books narrate the story of Israel's history from a religious viewpoint. The Jewish canon calls Joshua, Judges, Samuel, and Kings the "**Former Prophets**." How can this be an appropriate designation for these books? What is the relationship between these books and prophecy?

The answer to this question lies in a proper understanding of both prophecy and history. Prophecy is not primarily futuristic, but concerned with obedience in time and space, in the here and now. Prophecy looks to the covenants of the past and interprets their significance for the present as well as the future. It uses history to tie the past to the present. Our historical books are appropriate in the Jewish canon as "Former Prophets" because they narrate the nation's reaction to the covenant throughout its history. These books present the history of Israel from a prophetic point of view. Jewish tradition credits prophets for the composition of some of these books (Samuel for Judges and Jeremiah for 1 Kings).[1]

Though the evidence for such conclusions is lacking, it is nonetheless logical because of the devotion to the role of prophecy in these books. They are "Former Prophets" because they relate the early history of prophecy and write the national history in light of theological and prophetical interests. Joshua, Judges, Samuel, and Kings are just as appropriate as "Former Prophets" in the Jewish canon as they are as historical books in the Christian canon.

History and Theology[2]

The Bible is more than a history book. It writes history from a decidedly religious perspective. There is no attempt at what we today might call objectivity in modern history writing. The writers are writing what scholars refer to as *Heilsgeschichte*, or **salvation history.** This designation distinguishes biblical history from general history, which usually deals with the sequence of human events in the natural sphere. The events of salvation history are supernatural divine revelations in time and space, and recorded in Scripture to promote faith.

The recording of that salvation history is important in biblical faith. The events themselves cannot be recreated and studied firsthand, only the record of the events. So faith must study the events through the written record. Biblical faith, then, assumes the historicity of the events that reveal the history of salvation. The Bible accepts as true the historical events on which the revelation is based. It also asserts the truthfulness of the interpretation of those events, which the Bible presents in written form. The written form itself then becomes an important piece of historical evidence.[3]

Biblical authors frequently appeal to events for validation of their theological points, and they assume the historical accuracy of the events they describe. The factuality of those historical events makes it possible to accept the theological assertions of the Bible as true. Historicity does not *prove* its theology is true. But historical trustworthiness is necessary in order for the theological assertions to be true because those assertions are based on the events of history.

For example, we may assert that we believe in the Lord of the Old Testament as a gracious and loving God who makes and keeps covenant with his people. That is a theological assertion. But unless Yahweh *did in fact* make and keep the covenant with the children of Israel, the theological assertion is groundless, regardless of its plausibility. If the history is not true, then the theology based on that history is mere human speculation.

The faith the Bible defines and expresses is explicitly a historical faith. It is rooted

Hexateuch

Tetrateuch

Deuteronomistic History

and grounded in the historicity of certain past events. Historicity is a necessary ingredient of biblical faith, though not an adequate basis of faith, in and of itself. Faith in the Old Testament is defined in terms of past events, no less so than New Testament faith is rooted in the resurrection (1 Cor 15:12–19).

Authorship of the Historical Books

All of the historical books are anonymous (though the personal memoirs of Ezra and Nehemiah were used to compile those books). Other biblical references to these books are of no help in determining authorship. The titles indicate subject matter of a particular book, and usually have no connection to the authors. Joshua may have been the source for much of the book bearing his name, but Samuel's death is recorded in 1 Samuel 25. It is unlikely he had much to do with composing 1–2 Samuel, despite Jewish tradition.[4] The Books of Samuel appear to be named in his honor because he is the central figure in the early sections and because of his important role in anointing Saul and David.

A central question for the authorship of the historical books is: "How do these books relate to each other and to the Pentateuch?" Many scholars have overemphasized the relationship between Deuteronomy and Joshua. Joshua is the fulfillment of the promises to the patriarchs, and much of what is assumed in the Pentateuch becomes a reality in Joshua. For example, Moses prepared the nation for the covenant renewal ceremony at Mount Ebal and Mount Gerizim, which Joshua enacted (Dt 27:5–6; Jos 8:30–35). Furthermore, many scholars have argued that the same literary sources they believe were used to compile the Pentateuch (JEDP) were used also in Joshua. Instead of a Pentateuch, these scholars have argued for a **Hexateuch,** preferring to view Genesis–Joshua as a literary unit.[5]

Other scholars have overemphasized the relationship between Deuteronomy and the four histories contained in Joshua, Judges, Samuel, and Kings. Assuming a late (seventh century) date for Deuteronomy, this theory pictures a self-contained historical work edited during the exile. Deuteronomy served as the introduction to this historical work, which extended through 2 Kings (minus Ruth). The result is a truncated Pentateuch, having only four books. These scholars refer to a **Tetrateuch** containing Genesis, Exodus, Leviticus, and Numbers, and a **Deuteronomistic History** comprised of Deuteronomy–2 Kings (excluding Ruth).

The Deuteronomistic History

The classical expression of this hypothesis was published in 1943 by MARTIN NOTH.[6] The hypothesis states that an anonymous editor (called the "Deuteronomist," and abbreviated DTR) combined several sources into a long document detailing Israel's history theologically. After Jerusalem's fall in 587 B.C., Dtr sought to interpret the tragedy as well as to explain the fall of northern Israel in 722 B.C. He traced the divine punishment of the Israelite kingdoms to their persistent sin and experiments with idolatry. His task was essentially a negative one. He attempted to answer the question, "What went wrong?"

This hypothesis has won wide scholarly approval. It has been modified in several ways, but most significant is the proposal that there were in fact two Dtr editors.

Mount Gerizim viewed from Mount Ebal. Moses prepared the Israelites for the covenant renewal ceremony at Mount Ebal and Mount Gerizim, which Joshua enacted.

FRANK MOORE CROSS has argued that the first Dtr editor (Dtr[1]) composed the initial work during the time of Josiah (640–609 B.C.).[7] According to Cross, this first edition emphasized the sins of Jeroboam I in the northern kingdom, and God's choice of David and the city of Jerusalem in the south. Since Dtr[1] lived and worked before the fall of Jerusalem, his work was more hopeful than the final edition.

The second Deuteronomist (Dtr[2]) finished the work during the exile (around 550 B.C.). This editor blamed Manasseh for Judah's collapse in an attempt to explain how Jerusalem could fall and how the royal line of David could be dethroned. Manasseh's role is parallel to that of Jeroboam I in Israel. Dtr[2] updated the history by chronicling the subsequent events from Josiah's time to the end of the southern kingdom. He used a light editor's pen, while Dtr[1] was an actual author. Thus, instead of a Hexateuch (Genesis–Joshua) Noth, Cross, and many scholars today prefer to speak of a Tetrateuch (Genesis–Numbers) followed by the Deuteronomistic History, which was compiled during the late monarchy and edited during the exile.

One of the major themes of the Deuteronomistic History, according to Noth, is its emphasis on the doctrine of retribution based on the curses and blessings of Deuteronomy 28 (see comments on **deuteronomic theology** in chapter 9). The idea of reward for obedience to the **covenant** and punishment for disobedience is foundational for the historical books. Just as Deuteronomy 32 is a "Bible," or phrase book, for the Old Testament prophets, Deuteronomy 28 may be seen as the "Bible" for the authors of the historical books.

There are several ways in which the Noth–Cross theory of a Deuteronomistic History is helpful. There can be no doubt that these historical books share a theology of retribution, which seems clearly to be based on the Book of Deuteronomy. These four historical books are all committed to the concepts of blessings and curses under the covenant. Joshua includes the Achan episode to illustrate the irreversible losses of disobedience (Josh 7). The recurring cycle of sin and punishment in Judges is clearly based on deutero-

nomic theology. The Books of Samuel demonstrate Saul and David, both under the blessing first, then both under the curse. The Books of Kings bring retribution theology to the foreground as the theological explanation for the fall of both kingdoms. Acknowledging this overarching philosophy of history brings unity to the whole.

The Noth–Cross approach also accentuates the continuity between Deuteronomy and the historical books. This is most helpful in observing, for example, the influence of Deuteronomy's "law of the king" (Dt 17:14–20) and "law of the prophet" (Dt 18:9–22) on the later historical books. These important laws stand at the center of Deuteronomy and also function as primary sources for key sections of the historical books dealing with political leadership: Joshua (Jos 23), Samuel (1 Sm 12), Elijah (1 Kgs 19), and many others.[8]

However, there are difficulties with the theory as well. Most scholars holding to this hypothesis assume a late date for the Book of Deuteronomy. They assume Dtr[1] began with a portion of Deuteronomy written during the seventh century B.C., to which he added an introduction (Dt 1:1–4:43) and various other materials. Then, using sources from the premonarchic and monarchic periods of Israel's his-

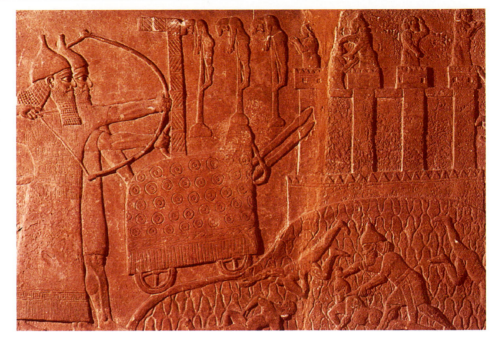

An Assyrian assault on a town, pictured in a contemporary relief. Scholars believe the historical books were written during the exile.

tory, he compiled a unified history of the period. But this rejects Deuteronomy's self-claims and ignores the parallels with ancient Near Eastern suzerain treaties, which make it clear that Deuteronomy fits well in a second-millennium context, including its introduction.

A further problem is the way many scholars dissect Deuteronomy from the Pentateuch, making it a Tetrateuch. This leaves the first four books of the Bible in an awkward literary relationship that has never been fully justified. Defined in this way, the theory forces an artificial break between Genesis–Numbers (which anticipates the conquest) and the Book of Joshua. Such a division also denies the canonical function of Deuteronomy in its authoritative reinterpretation of the first four books.[9]

In addition, the theory fails to account for the enormous amount of variety in the historical books. The Deuteronomistic History as defined by Noth exhibits less coherent overall structure than he admitted. These four historical books (Joshua, Judges, Samuel, Kings) are internally self-contained works. They are sufficiently different from each other as to require no common editor or author. Judges and Kings use a concentration of repetition to structure their contents, while Joshua and Samuel follow very different organizing principles. These four books also have considerable differences in style and overall purposes. They undoubtedly share a common worldview, a deuteronomic worldview. But they are also quite distinct in many ways.

Finally, it might be added that the entire Old Testament contains "deuteronomic" influences. It is clear that the doctrine of retribution played an especially dominant role in these historical books. But that is not to suggest the patriarchs knew no such doctrine, or that Chronicles was unaware of it. Other sections of the Old Testament have different roles to play, and the deuteronomic influence was less pertinent to that function than it was in these four books.

Thus we may refer generally to a Deuteronomistic History to signify this unified account of the history of Israel without accepting every aspect of the Noth–Cross theory. The first four historical books (excluding Ruth) are certainly related to the theology of Deuteronomy. The final edition of Kings was completed after 561 B.C., since this is the date of the last recorded event (2 Kgs 25:27–30). There is no mention of the Persians and their liberation of the Jews in 539 B.C. Therefore, we may conclude Kings was completed

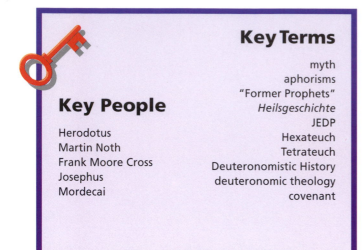

Key Terms

myth
aphorisms
"Former Prophets"
Heilsgeschichte
JEDP
Hexateuch
Tetrateuch
Deuteronomistic History
deuteronomic theology
covenant

Key People

Herodotus
Martin Noth
Frank Moore Cross
Josephus
Mordecai

of his work as a continuation and culmination of that history. To that extent, we may refer to a Deuteronomistic Historian.

Chronicles and Ezra–Nehemiah

Early Jewish tradition names Ezra as the author of 1–2 Chronicles, Ezra, and Nehemiah.[10] These last two are treated as one book in the oldest Hebrew manuscripts. Old Testament scholars have thought for many years that the author of Ezra–Nehemiah (almost certainly Ezra) was also responsible for Chronicles. But recently a new consensus has developed, which now sees Chronicles as the work of a different, anonymous author.[11] It is interesting to note that Chronicles follows Ezra–Nehemiah in the Hebrew canon rather then preceding these books as chronological order would dictate. This would support the idea that a different author produced Chronicles.

Although there is no specific claim to authorship in Ezra, the first-person ac-

during the final twenty-two years of the exile. To what extent the anonymous author of Kings had a hand in the compilation of Joshua, Judges, or Samuel is impossible to determine. But he conceived

Summary

1. The historical books also have theological importance.

2. Joshua shows the value of obedience.

3. Judges tells of the near hopelessness of Israel after the conquest.

4. Ruth illustrates God's sovereign care for individuals who are faithful in spite of national religious apostasy.

5. Samuel traces the early history of Israel's monarchy.

6. Kings tells about the history of the monarchy from Solomon to the fall of Jerusalem.

7. Chronicles is the first commentary on the Scriptures.

8. Ezra and Nehemiah present the history of the restoration in the fifth century B.C.

9. Esther demonstrates how God's sovereign care and protection extends to his people.

10. The history of Israel contrasts with the mythological approach found in the rest of the ancient Near East.

11. The authorship of all of the historical books is anonymous.

12. One popular theory of the authorship of the historical books is that an anonymous editor combined several sections into one lengthy document of Israel's history.

Study Questions

1. Approximately how much time is covered by the historical books?

2. What is the theological value of the historical books?

3. Briefly summarize the major theme of each of the historical books.

4. How did the Israelites view the concept of history?

5. What is the main concern of biblical prophecy as portrayed in the historical books?

6. Why are the historical books referred to as the "Former Prophets"?

7. From what perspective are historical events recorded in this section of the Bible?

8. How are historical facts important to the theology of the historical books?

9. Discuss the authorship of the historical books.

10. Explain the deuteronomistic history and its ramifications for the historical books.

Further Reading

Howard, David M., Jr. *An Introduction to the Old Testament Historical Books.* Chicago: Moody, 1993. Best introductory volume.

Long, V. Philips. *The Art of Biblical History.* Grand Rapids: Zondervan, 1994. Important theological discussion of all the issues.

Millard, A. R., James K. Hoffmeier, and David W. Baker, eds. *Faith, Tradition, and History: Old Testament Historiography in Its Near Eastern Context.* Winona Lake, Ind.: Eisenbrauns, 1994. Important scholarly treatment of many issues relating to the historical books.

counts in the book make him the likely candidate. Nehemiah has a similar style and worldview, and was joined to Ezra as the second part of a single composition in the Hebrew canon. It seems likely that Ezra compiled this book using the personal memoirs of Nehemiah ("the words of Nehemiah," 1:1).

Ruth and Esther

Jewish tradition credits Samuel with writing the Book of Ruth.[12] But this tradition arose probably because of the similarity of language and content in Ruth, Judges, and the Books of Samuel. The book itself contains no direct indication of authorship, and it is best to accept it as anonymous.

The Book of Esther is no more specific about authorship. Jewish tradition states that the book was written by the men of the Great Synagogue, though Josephus, the first-century Jewish historian, held that Mordecai was the author.[13] It seems likely the book was written by a Persian Jew no later than the middle of the fourth century B.C.

11 Joshua
Conquest and Division

Objectives

**After reading this chapter,
you should be able to**

- Outline the basic content
  of the Book of Joshua
- List the events God used to prepare
  Joshua for his role as leader
- Identify the three themes in Joshua
- Discuss reasons why Israel was allowed to
  conquer Canaan
- List the three challenges God
  made to Joshua after Moses died
- Explain the significant events of the
  central campaign in chapters 6–9
- Evaluate the final challenge
  Joshua gave to Israel

The Israelites stood at the edge of Canaan, on the verge of claiming the promise God had made to Abraham centuries earlier (Gn 12:7). The task ahead was both exciting and sobering. Crossing the Jordan and conquering the land posed a serious challenge. Israel would have to drive out the strong peoples who lived in Canaan's well-fortified cities (Nm 13:28–29).

The Israelites stood at the end of one era and the beginning of another. Moses, Israel's great leader, had died, and Joshua had assumed leadership. This role carried great responsibility, and many probably wondered if Joshua had the necessary skills to complete the job Moses had begun.

The Book of Joshua describes how God's people faced Canaan's challenge. They conquered the land and divided it among the tribes. They succeeded partly because of Joshua's strong leadership, but mostly because God empowered Joshua for the task. When we face great challenges, we, too, can trust the Lord to help us accomplish his purpose.

Part of the excavated site of ancient Jericho today. Jericho is one of the oldest cities in the world, and was the first city in Canaan to fall to Joshua and the Israelites.

Outline

Background of the Book of Joshua

The Book of Joshua continues the story of the Pentateuch. Deuteronomy ends with an account of Moses' death, and Joshua begins with the words, "Now after the death of Moses. . . ." God's purposes for Israel were now carried forward through Joshua.

Joshua the Man

Joshua first appears in the biblical record in Exodus 17:9–14, where the Bible records that he led Israel's army to victory over the Amalekites. We also find him at the foot of Mount Sinai as Moses received the Law (Ex 24:13) and near the tent of meeting as Moses met with God face to face (Ex 33:11). The Lord used Moses to prepare Joshua to lead Israel.

Later, Joshua was one of twelve men Moses sent into Canaan to spy out the land (Nm 13:8, 16). Joshua, along with Caleb, urged the people to take the land by faith,

Can We Practice "Holy War"?

The Book of Joshua records Israel's conquest of Canaan. God commanded his people to destroy Canaan's citizens, sparing no one. How can Christians deal with such passages of Scripture? Does the Bible encourage us to practice "holy war"?

Regarding Israel's conquest of Canaan, we need to remember the following points:

1. The people of Canaan were exceedingly wicked, and their social and religious customs angered the Lord (Lv 18:24–30).
2. God had given them time to repent, but they had not done so (Gn 15:13–16).
3. God used the Israelites as his instruments of judgment against the people of Canaan (Jos 11:18–20), just as he later used the Assyrians and Babylonians to judge Israel and Judah (2 Kgs 17:6–7; 24:20–25:7).
4. "Holy war" (or the practice of herem) occurred only at certain times during Israel's history (1 Sm 15:1-3; 2 Chr 20:15–23), and we should not view it as a pattern for future generations.

Israel's destruction of the Canaanites demonstrates how seriously God takes sin. He governs the nations, and he can and will judge those who oppose him. Christians should heed his warnings and seek to promote justice and righteousness in their nation. We dare not assume God will tolerate evil forever.

but the majority's bad report prevailed (Nm 14:1–10). God's judgment came and Israel had to wander in the wilderness until the disbelieving generation died, but the Lord spared Joshua and Caleb because of their faith. After bringing the people to the edge of the Jordan, Moses died; Joshua then led the people into the land.

Date and Authorship

The events in the Book of Joshua span approximately twenty years. If we adopt an early date for the exodus from Egypt, Joshua's ministry would cover the period from about 1405 B.C. to 1385 B.C. A thirteenth-century date for the exodus places Joshua's death a little before 1200 B.C.

Who wrote the Book of Joshua, and when? Here are the relevant pieces of evidence:[1]

- Joshua 24:26 suggests Joshua wrote at least part of the book, and Jewish tradition names Joshua as the author.
- The account of Joshua's death (24:29–31) clearly indicates another author besides Joshua, at least for this section.
- The common phrase "until this day" (4:9; 5:9; 7:26, etc.) suggests an extended amount of time has elapsed since the events described, though not necessarily an extremely long time.
- The mention of Jebusites in Jerusalem (15:63) suggests a date prior to 1000 B.C., when David conquered Jerusalem and drove out the Jebusites (2 Sm 5:6–10).
- The reference to Canaanites in Gezer (16:10) implies a date prior to about 970 B.C., when the king of Egypt conquered Gezer and gave it to Solomon (1 Kgs 3:1; 9:16).

When we look at all the evidence, it seems reasonable to conclude that much of the book comes from eyewitness accounts, perhaps from Joshua's own hand. Furthermore, the historical references suggest the book was in its present form no later than Solomon's time.

Archaeology and the Book of Joshua

Archaeologists have excavated many sites the Bible says the Israelites conquered. Evidence from Jericho, unfortunately, has proven largely inconclusive, but excavations at Lachish, Debir, and Hazor have revealed massive destruction layers from about the thirteenth century B.C. Some scholars have argued for a late date of the exodus event because of this evidence.[2]

Other scholars, however, have suggested the archaeological evidence may favor an earlier date.[3] The Bible specifically names only three cities the Israelites burned—Jericho, Ai, and Hazor. Moreover, evidence of the migration of other peoples into Palestine about 1200 B.C. suggests these people—not the Israelites—may have destroyed the many towns and villages.

Archaeology offers many benefits to Bible students, but also has many limita-

The ruins of Jericho today (Jos 6). The Lord gave Israel peculiar instructions for conquering this seemingly impregnable walled city.

ḥerem

tions. In light of the disagreement over the archaeological data, it seems wisest to await further evidence. We can still affirm the historicity of the events in the Book of Joshua, even if we do not know precisely when they occurred.

Themes of Joshua

The transition of power from Moses to Joshua

Before Moses died, he commissioned Joshua as his successor (Dt 31:3, 7–8, 14, 23). The Book of Joshua traces Joshua's development as Israel's new leader and shows God's approval of him. Joshua became, in effect, the new Moses, for the same God who worked through Moses now worked through him (Jos 1:5; 3:7).

The conquest and division of Canaan

The Book of Joshua contains two major sections. Chapters 1–12 describe Israel's conquest of the land; chapters 13–24, Israel's division and settlement of the land.

The Lord had promised the land to Abraham hundreds of years earlier (Gn 12:7). Now he commanded Israel to destroy the land's inhabitants and take possession of it for themselves. The conquest of Canaan thus serves two purposes: to bring God's judgment against the peoples of the land (Lv 18:24–25; Jos 11:21), and to bring his blessing to Israel.

The Hebrew word **ḥerem** plays an important role in our understanding of these battles. God sometimes commanded Israel to destroy completely a nation that opposed him. The *ḥerem*, or the spoil of war—be it people, animals, or goods—belonged to the Lord, and he had the right to do with it as he pleased.

After Israel had gained control of Canaan, the tribes divided the land into twelve sections. God promised to help the tribes drive out any peoples remaining in the land (Jos 13:6), but God's people lacked the faith to do so. This failure led to dire consequences, as we will see later.

God's faithfulness to his promises

The Bible stresses that Israel's conquest and division of Canaan did not happen because of Israel's great military strength. Rather, it happened because of God's faithfulness (Jos 21:43–45). The Lord kept his promise to Israel, just as he keeps all his promises to believers today (2 Cor 1:20).

Message of the Book of Joshua

Israel Conquers the Land (chapters 1–12)

Preparations for conquest (chapters 1–5)

God appeared to Joshua after thirty days of mourning for Moses had ended (Dt 34:8). The Lord challenged his new leader

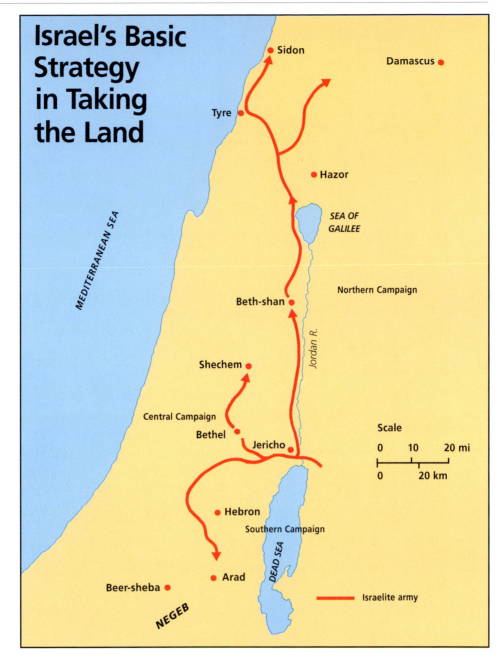

Israel's Basic Strategy in Taking the Land

Sidon

Damascus

Tyre

Hazor

SEA OF GALILEE

MEDITERRANEAN SEA

Northern Campaign

Beth-shan

Jordan R.

Shechem

Central Campaign

Bethel

Jericho

Scale

0   10   20 mi

0   20 km

Hebron

Southern Campaign

DEAD SEA

Arad

Beer-sheba

NEGEB

—— Israelite army

three times to be strong and courageous (Jos 1:6, 7, 9). First, Joshua needed to focus on the task that lay before him—to lead God's people into the land. Second, he must remember his godly heritage and meditate on God's word regularly. Third, he must remember God's presence—the Lord was with him!

Joshua approached the tribes of Reuben, Gad, and Manasseh (1:12–18). Moses had granted these tribes permission to live on the Jordan's east side, but had commanded them to help their fellow Israelites conquer Canaan (Nm 32:28–32). The tribes assured Joshua he could count on their support.

Joshua secretly dispatched two spies to Jericho (Jos 2:1–24). The spies entered the home of Rahab, a prostitute, presumably because they thought they would raise the least amount of suspicion there. When the king of Jericho heard that Israelite men had come to Rahab's home, he ordered their arrest, but Rahab hid the spies and told the soldiers the men had already left.

171

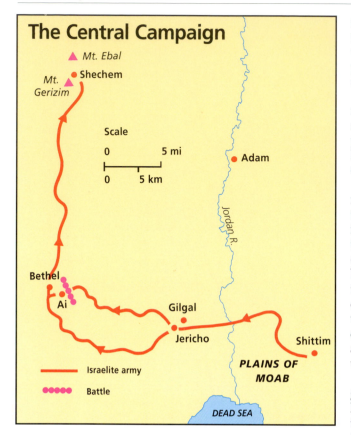

The Central Campaign

▲ Mt. Ebal

● Shechem
Mt. ▲
Gerizim

Scale

0   5 mi

● Adam

0   5 km

Jordan R.

Bethel ●

● Ai

Gilgal

Jericho

Shittim ●

——— Israelite army

●●●●● Battle

PLAINS OF
MOAB

DEAD SEA

the people could have entered Canaan from the south and completely avoided water, but God had other plans. As the people trusted the Lord's word, he worked a great miracle.

Second, we must pass the faith on to the next generation. Joshua established the stones so future generations would see the power of their God. What works of God have *you* seen him do in your life that you can pass on to others?

Joshua 5 describes two covenant memorials. The Israelites had neglected the practice of circumcision while they wandered in the wilderness, and God commanded them to perform this sign of the covenant on all their males. The people also celebrated Passover in the land for the first time, forty years after they left Egypt. The cessation of the manna from heaven, on which they had depended during their days in the wilderness (Ex 16:13–35), heralded the beginning of a new era. Israel was home at last.

Joshua's visit from a heavenly messenger (Jos 5:13–15) further linked him with Moses (Ex 3:5) and encouraged him for the battle with Jericho. God would fight for his people!

The central campaign (chapters 6–9)

Israel's strategy was to divide and conquer by taking the central portion of the land first. The central campaign included victories over Jericho, Ai, and Bethel. Of these, the battle with Jericho is by far the most famous.

The Lord gave Israel peculiar instructions for conquering Jericho, a seemingly impregnable walled city. The army was to march around the city once a day for six consecutive days, with the ark of the Lord leading the way. The priests who accompanied the ark were to carry trumpets made of rams' horns. On the seventh day, the army was to circle the city seven times, with the priests blowing the rams' horns. When the trumpet blew a long blast, the people were to shout, and God promised the walls would fall down. The people followed God's instructions and Jericho's walls fell.

The miracle at Jericho illustrates another important spiritual principle. God often chooses to act in response to his servants' faithful obedience. He sometimes

Rahab then made a covenant with the spies; she had saved their lives, now they must save hers! Rahab affirmed her faith in the Lord, as well as the fright of the people of Jericho. The men agreed that if Rahab hung a scarlet cord from her window, the Israelite army would spare all within her home. They returned to Israel's camp and reported to Joshua all that had happened.

Israel's crossing of the Jordan River demonstrated God's hand on Joshua, his new leader (3:1–5:15). The melting of the winter snow had caused the river to overflow its banks, but the Lord stopped the water and Israel crossed on dry ground, just as he had when Moses led the people through the sea. Israel camped at Gilgal, and Joshua set up a pile of stones as a memorial where Israel had crossed. Future generations could then see where God had displayed his glory.

Joshua 3–4 illustrates two important principles. First, God sometimes takes us on a route we don't expect in order to display his glory. It seemed to make little sense to lead Israel across the Jordan when

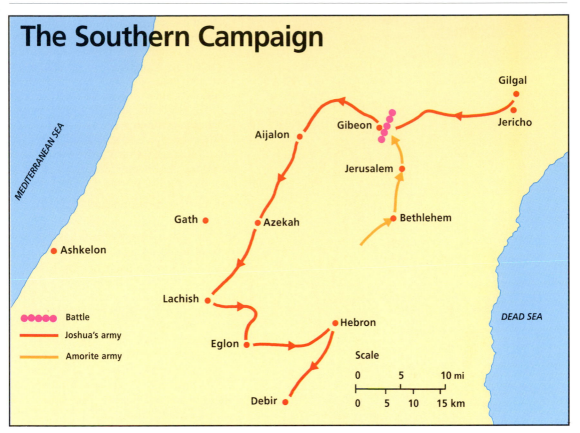

The Southern Campaign

Gilgal

Jericho

Gibeon

Aijalon

Jerusalem

Gath

Azekah

Bethlehem

Ashkelon

MEDITERRANEAN SEA

Lachish

Hebron

DEAD SEA

Eglon

Scale

Debir

●●●●● Battle

——— Joshua's army

——— Amorite army

0   5   10 mi

0   5   10   15 km

may use our talents and strengths, but most of all he wants us to submit to his plans.

The Lord commanded Joshua to destroy everything alive and give the booty to him. Only Rahab and her family survived the battle, in accordance with the spies' promise. Rahab became part of Israel, but the Gospel of Matthew tells us something even more amazing: Rahab became an ancestor of Jesus Christ (1:5)! God's grace reached out to Rahab and not only made her part of God's family, but used her to bring about the Savior of the world. Rahab's life shows how God's grace can reach all who are willing to humble themselves and put their trust in him.

With Jericho behind them, the Israelites probably assumed no one could stand in their way. Instead, Israel suffered a humbling defeat in the battle with Ai (Jos 7:1–8:35). Joshua inquired of the Lord and discovered Israel had sinned—someone had kept some of Jericho's treasure for himself! God revealed Achan, the guilty party, who died for his act of rebellion.

Achan's family also died; perhaps they had participated in his crime by helping conceal the goods.

Following the judgment of Achan's family, Israel renewed the attack against Ai. By means of an ambush group, Israel claimed victory over Ai and neighboring Bethel, who tried to come to Ai's assistance.

GIBEON, a major city of Canaan's central territory, quickly took steps to avoid a confrontation with Israel (9:1–27). Pretending to have come from a distant land, a Gibeonite delegation came to GILGAL and asked the Israelites to make a covenant with them. After agreeing to a covenant, the Israelites discovered the Gibeonites lived in Canaan. God had commanded his people to destroy the land's inhabitants, but the people had now agreed to spare the Gibeonites. Joshua and the leaders determined they would enslave the Gibeonites instead.

The southern campaign (chapter 10)

The Israelites' treaty with Gibeon meant they effectively controlled all of central Canaan. When the kings of southern

173

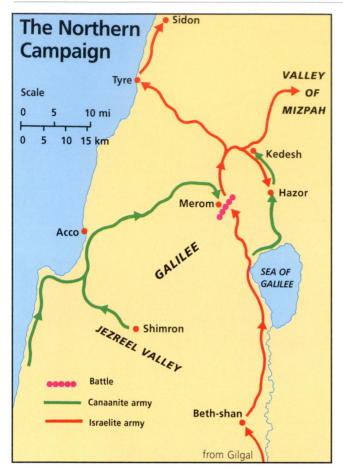

The Northern Campaign

Scale

0   5   10 mi

0   5   10   15 km

Sidon

Tyre

VALLEY OF MIZPAH

Kedesh

Merom

Hazor

Acco

GALILEE

SEA OF GALILEE

Shimron

JEZREEL VALLEY

●●●●● Battle

—— Canaanite army

—— Israelite army

Beth-shan

from Gilgal

Canaan heard about this treaty, they decided to attack Gibeon. Israel came to Gibeon's rescue, and the Lord used this occasion to rout these kings and give southern Canaan to Israel. The Lord rained large hailstones on Israel's enemies, and also prolonged the daylight to help Joshua defeat the coalition.

After the Israelites prevailed, they continued fighting other southern cities and kingdoms. Southern Canaan was soon in Israelite hands.

The northern campaign (11:1–15)

In northern Canaan, another coalition was forming. Jabin, king of Hazor, joined forces with other kings against Joshua's army. As in the southern campaign, Joshua's forces routed their foes and conquered their cities. Victory over the coalition led to continued victory over northern cities, towns, and villages.

Joshua 11:15 describes how Joshua completed the work the Lord had given Moses. God commanded Moses to take Canaan, Moses entrusted the task to Joshua, and Joshua finished the job. The same God who worked through Moses now completed his work through Joshua. This same God also will enable us to complete whatever he calls us to do.

Part of the impressive underground water system at Hazor in northern Israel. Jabin, king of Hazor, joined other kings against Joshua's army.

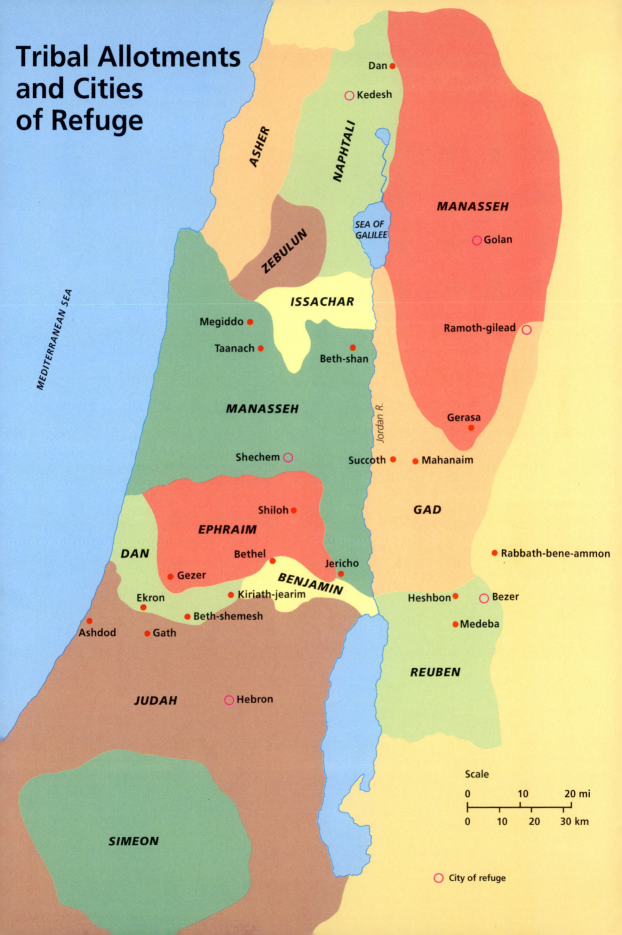

Tribal Allotments and Cities of Refuge

MEDITERRANEAN SEA

ASHER

NAPHTALI

Dan

○ Kedesh

ZEBULUN

SEA OF GALILEE

MANASSEH

○ Golan

ISSACHAR

Megiddo

Taanach

Beth-shan

Ramoth-gilead ○

MANASSEH

Jordan R.

Gerasa

Shechem ○

Succoth

Mahanaim

GAD

Shiloh

EPHRAIM

DAN

Bethel

Jericho

Rabbath-bene-ammon

Gezer

BENJAMIN

Ekron

Kiriath-jearim

Heshbon

Bezer ○

Beth-shemesh

Medeba

Ashdod

Gath

REUBEN

JUDAH

○ Hebron

Scale

0   10   20 mi

0   10   20   30 km

SIMEON

○ City of refuge

The city of Shechem is flanked by Mount Gerizim and Mount Ebal (Jos 8, 24).

Summary statement (11:16–12:24)

The Israelites had secured effective control of Canaan and the TRANSJORDAN. Although it seems these many battles practically happened overnight, Canaan's conquest actually required about six to seven years.[4] Israel's victory was really God's victory, for God used Israel as his instrument to judge Canaan's unbelieving peoples (11:20).

Israel Divides the Land (chapters 13–21)

Israel's remaining challenge (chapter 13)

The Israelites had already conquered the area east of the Jordan, but although they controlled Canaan, their task remained unfinished. Various peoples continued to inhabit Canaan's more remote areas. Israel's individual tribes received the challenge to complete the conquest by exterminating these smaller groups. As we will see, Israel did not succeed in driving out these peoples, and pagan influences soon corrupted God's people.

Israel's land inheritances (chapters 14–19)

As Joshua began to allot Judah's portion, Caleb stepped forward (14:6–15). This man of faith had accompanied Joshua forty-five years earlier when Moses sent twelve men to spy out the land (Nm 13–14). Only Caleb and Joshua had stood firm in their conviction that God would give them the

land despite the obstacles. Now, the two stood together at Gilgal, the only survivors from a generation of unbelief.

Caleb presented his own testimony. As he and the others had spied out the land, he had "followed the LORD fully" (Jos 14:8). And he was still following the Lord fully at eighty-five years of age! Caleb requested Hebron, vowing to drive out the inhabitants if God would give him victory. And God did. Caleb's life stands today as an example of faithfulness for all believers.

Joshua 15–19 describes how Joshua allotted the remaining tribes their land portions (see map). As you study the map, note the following items:

- EPHRAIM and Manasseh, the tribes that came from Joseph's sons, each received their own inheritance (Jos 16–17; Gn 48:21–22). In fact, Manasseh received territory on both sides of the Jordan.
- The text mentions several tribes that could not or did not drive out those peoples inhabiting their territory (Jos 15:63; 16:10; 17:12–13). The Israelites eventually accepted many of these people's religious practices, and this had a devastating effect on Israel's faith.
- Israel had six cities of refuge, three west of the Jordan and three east of the Jordan (Jos 20:1–9).
- The Levites received forty-eight cities among the tribes (Jos 21).

When Joshua had finished giving the tribes their land, the people gave Joshua his portion—Timnath-serah in the land of Ephraim (19:49–51). Thus, Caleb's portion was the first allotted in Canaan and Joshua's was the last. These two men of faith forever left their mark on those who inherited the land.

Israel's designated cities (chapters 20–21)

The cities of refuge (20:1–9) protected those who accidentally brought about someone's death. A person guilty of such an offense would remain at one of these cities until the high priest died. Moses had instructed the people to provide such cities (Nm 35:9–15), and Joshua now completed the task.

The Levites received no land inheritance (Jos 21). Instead, God gave them forty-eight cities among the tribes, as well as the

A market scene in Hebron, the city given by Joshua to Caleb, one of the spies sent to report on the land (Jos 14).

surrounding pasturelands on which to graze their animals. The Levites thus lived among God's people and were available to help them with spiritual matters and to arbitrate disputes.

This section closes with a testimony to God's faithfulness (21:43–45). God fulfilled all his promises to Israel, and we can count on him to do the same for us (Heb 13:8).

Israel Begins to Settle into the Land (chapters 22–24)

An early misunderstanding almost leads to civil war (chapter 22)

The tribes of Reuben, Gad, and Manasseh had helped their fellow Israelites secure the land of Canaan, thus fulfilling their promise to Joshua (Jos 1:16–18). Joshua dismissed them with his blessing, challenging them to remain faithful to the Lord and his ways.

But when the three tribes came to the Jordan, they built a large altar. The other tribes heard of it, and Phinehas, Eleazar's son and Aaron's grandson, led a delegation to investigate the matter.

At first, it appeared the eastern tribes were disobeying God's command to worship only where he said (Dt 12:13–14), and the western tribes prepared to go to war against them. But the tribe of Reuben, Gad, and Manasseh insisted they had built the altar as a testimony, a monument to remind the Israelites in Canaan that those who lived on the east side were also part of God's people. They intended the altar only to commemorate that fact.

Joshua's final challenges to God's people (23:1–24:27)

The Book of Joshua preserves two of Joshua's final challenges to God's people. No doubt he also challenged them on many other occasions to follow the Lord with all their hearts.

In his first speech (23:1–16), Joshua challenged Israel's leaders to remember the great things they had seen God do. He urged them to claim God's promise for the present and future—God would drive out the remaining peoples and establish them in the land! God's people were to demonstrate their faith by keeping the Law of Moses and not intermingling with the peoples around them. If they failed to observe these things, Joshua warned, they would surely perish.

In his second speech (24:1–28), Joshua recounted Israel's history from the days of Abraham to that day. God had shown his faithfulness every step of the way. He had acted in history to redeem his people. He had sustained his people through difficult times in the wilderness. And he had dealt with his people totally by grace.

Joshua exhorted the people to commit themselves fully to the Lord, adding his own personal testimony: "As for me and my house, we will serve the LORD" (24:15). When the people affirmed they would follow the Lord, Joshua made a covenant with them and erected a large stone as a testimony to their words. This covenant confirmed the prior covenants the people had made at Mount Sinai (Ex 24) and Moab (Dt 29–31). It also gave the people another chance to proclaim publicly their allegiance to the Lord alone, as they had done earlier (Jos 8:30–35).

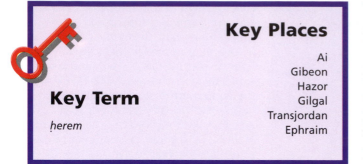

Key Term

ḥerem

Key Places

Ai
Gibeon
Hazor
Gilgal
Transjordan
Ephraim

buried Eleazar, Aaron's son. With the burial of Joshua and Eleazar, another era in Israel's history ended.

What kind of a job did Joshua do in preparing the next generation? We read the answer in Joshua 24:31: "And Israel served the LORD all the days of Joshua and all the days of the elders who survived Joshua, and had known all the deeds of the LORD that He had done for Israel." Joshua led the people by word and example, and entrusted God's message to faithful leaders who continued in it after Joshua died.

Joshua 24:31 reminds us of an important task the Lord has placed in our hands. As Christians, part of our responsibility is to place the Christian faith firmly in the hands of the next generation. Are we ready to embrace that challenge?

Three burials (24:28–33)

The Book of Joshua closes with a record of three burials. Joshua died at the age of 110, and Israel buried him in his territory. God's people also buried the bones of the patriarch Joseph, which they had brought from Egypt (Gn 50:24–25). Finally, they

Summary

1. The Israelites were successful in conquering Canaan because of the strong leadership of Joshua, who was empowered by God.

2. Joshua was most likely the author of the Book of Joshua.

3. The three themes of Joshua are: the transition of power from Moses to Joshua; the conquest and division of Canaan; and God's faithfulness to his promise.

4. God challenged Joshua to be a strong leader by focusing on the task before him, by remembering his godly heritage, and by remembering that God was always with him.

5. Israel's battle strategy was to conquer the central part of Canaan first, where a key battle was at Jericho.

6. Because Israel did not drive out smaller groups of people, their pagan influence corrupted the Israelites.

7. The land of Canaan was divided up among the twelve tribes. The Levites received forty-eight cities among the tribes.

8. Israel designated six cities of refuge to protect people who had accidentally caused the death of someone.

9. Because the tribes of Reuben, Gad, and Manasseh had built a large altar when they reached the Jordan River, the other tribes were ready to go to war, because they thought the eastern tribes had disobeyed God.

10. Before his death, Joshua challenged the Israelite leaders to remember the great things they had seen God do; he reviewed Israel's history from the days of Abraham; and he exhorted them to commit themselves fully to God.

Study Questions

1. What are the major themes of the Book of Joshua?

2. What basic plan did Israel use to conquer the land? Describe the three major waves of Joshua's military campaigns.

3. What was the significance of the cities of refuge and levitical cities?

4. Do you think Joshua was successful in fulfilling God's plan for his life? Why or why not?

Further Reading

Hess, Richard S. *Joshua: An Introduction and Commentary.* Downers Grove: InterVarsity, 1996. A solid, evangelical commentary for the serious college student.

Howard, David M., Jr. *An Introduction to the Old Testament Historical Books.* Chicago: Moody, 1993. Excellent survey of the historical books that makes good use of current scholarship.

Merrill, Eugene H. *Kingdom of Priests: A History of Old Testament Israel.* Grand Rapids: Baker, 1987. Seminary-level history of Israel that combines good scholarship and readability.

Woudstra, Marten H. *The Book of Joshua.* New International Commentary on the Old Testament. Grand Rapids: Eerdmans, 1981. For the serious student. Contains ample footnotes and references.

12 Judges and Ruth
Israel's Moral Crisis

Outline

- **The Book of Judges**
- **Contents**
  Outline
  Overview
- **Historical Problems in Judges**
  Chronology
  Political Structure
- **The Book of Ruth**
- **Contents**
  Literary Structure
  Outline
  Overview
- **The Sovereignty of God and Faithful Living**

Objectives

After reading this chapter, you should be able to

- Describe what judges are in the Book of Judges
- Outline the basic content of the Book of Judges
- Explain the reasons why Israel failed to complete the conquest
- Document the cycle used to introduce the judges
- Name the major judges and the minor judges
- Identify the central characters of the Book of Ruth
- Outline the basic content of the Book of Ruth
- Illustrate the role of a kinsman-redeemer
- Explain the law of levirate marriage
- Illustrate the sovereignty of God in the Book of Ruth

The view of Jezreel from Mount Tabor. Barak and his troops gathered on these steep slopes before charging down to attack the Canaanites under their leader Sisera.

Deuteronomistic History

The Book of Joshua was full of great success. The tribes of Israel had been unified under strong leadership and had successfully conquered the promised land. Though Joshua records momentary lapses such as Achan's sin (chapter 7), the book emphasizes Israel's success in taking and dividing the land.

But this period of great national victory was short-lived. The swift and miraculous conquest was followed by a longer period of time in which Israel seems to have lost its moral compass. During this period (approximately two centuries), Israel continually sinned against God and broke his covenant. The chosen people of God seemed determined to embrace the forbidden Canaanite religion and to depend on their own ability to defend themselves from enemy nations. Lacking strong national leadership (Jgs 17:6; 21:25) and unwilling to trust God, the nation was morally bankrupt—and seemingly unconcerned about its state of affairs.

Joshua had entered the promised land with ease. But the next period of Israel's history showed that life in God's land would be far from easy if his people persisted in their sin. Two Old Testament historical books cover this period: Judges and Ruth.

The Book of Judges

This book is part of that larger literary unit detailing the history of God's people, which continues through the Books of Samuel and Kings. Because of the theological and literary impact of Deuteronomy on this unit, we may refer to it as **Deuteronomistic History** (see discussion in chapter 10). The expression "in those days Israel had no king" (17:6; 18:1; 19:1; 21:25) suggests the author's perspective was from the later vantage point of the monarchy, looking back to the premonarchic period. The book contains no references to authorship, and we must accept it as an anonymous composition.

Contents

The central characters of this narrative are "judges" (*šōpĕtîm*), a term that gives rise to the name of the book. These "judges" were not simply legal authorities as the English word implies. They were charismatic military leaders whom God raised up and empowered for specific tasks of deliverance (2:16).[1] The office implied governing in a broad sense. These twelve judges were local or national heroes who became military rulers endowed by God's Spirit to lead the nation into victory against a particular enemy nation. After the military threat was over, the judges generally continued in leadership roles, though none of them established a royal dynasty (except for the aborted attempt by Abimelech).

Outline

I. The Incomplete Conquest (1:1–2:5)

II. Covenant Disobedience and Judgment (2:6–16:31)
  A. The Pattern of Disobedience (2:6–3:6)
  B. The Pattern Illustrated: A History of the Judges (3:7–16:31)

III. The Collapse of Society (17–21)
  A. The Breakdown of Religious Life: Micah's Idol (17–18)
  B. The Breakdown of Justice and Civil Order: Civil War (19–21)

Overview

The center of the book (2:6–16:31) is a collection of stories about the judges who ruled Israel from the death of Joshua to the rise of Samuel. An introduction is attached (1:1–2:5), along with two appen-

dixes (17:1–21:25) detailing episodes that occurred during the judges period, but which do not relate to a specific judge.

Introduction (1:1–2:5)

The book opens with the phrase "After the death of Joshua," which bears an important historical and theological function. It marks both the end of the previous period of success under Joshua and the beginning of a new era in Israel's history.[2] In contrast to the conquest and occupation of the promised land, this new period of the judges is a time of disobedience and failure.

This introductory chapter supplements the Book of Joshua and gives more details about the nature of the conquest. Joshua emphasized a unified Israel invading and conquering the promised land. This was appropriate to the purpose of that book. But Joshua also made frequent reference to the need for the individual tribes to complete what they began corporately (Jos 13:1–13; 16:10; 17:12–13, 16–18; 18:2–4). Joshua presented a picture of a great military victory, but an *incomplete* conquest.

Judges 1:1-2:5 describes the limited success of individual tribes. Judah and Simeon experienced measured success initially, but they were not able to drive out the inhabitants of the territory allotted to them (1:19). Several other tribes were also unable to gain victory over the Canaanite inhabitants of the land. This unit prepares

The site of Shiloh, the resting place of the ark of the covenant during the period of the judges.

us for the rest of Judges by informing us that the Israelites lived side by side with Canaanites, who would inevitably influence the religion and culture of God's people.

The concluding paragraph of this unit (2:1–5) confirms that Israel has been disobedient. Individual tribes compromised with the inhabitants of the land and now the conquest is incomplete. The remaining Canaanites in the land will plague them in the future (2:2–3).

Main body of stories (2:6–16:31)

Israel's failure to complete the conquest was a result of covenant disobedience and lack of faith (2:2–3). The central section of the book now goes on to demonstrate that this covenant failure was not a rare or unique occurrence. Unfortunately, covenant breaking became Israel's way of life.

This central section has its own introduction. The author prepares for the judges by introducing three basic and general facts (2:6–3:6). First, Joshua's generation was now dead, and the new generation of Israelites had rejected Yahweh (2:6–15). This new generation worshiped Canaanite gods instead of the Lord who led them out of Egypt. So the Lord became angry and allowed enemy nations to afflict Israel (2:13–14). Second, whenever the people repented, the Lord raised up judges to deliver them (2:16–23). But after the judge died, Israel lapsed back into sin and idolatry, worshiping other gods (2:19). Third, because of their failure to complete the conquest, the Israelites now lived among other nations in the promised land (3:1–6). These nations were a military threat. But more important, they were a religious threat because of Israel's tendency to accept their pagan beliefs.

The historical features of this period (described in 2:6–3:6) became the general literary pattern for the central unit of the book: Israel sins against the Lord, the Lord gives them over to an enemy nation, then the Lord sends a judge to deliver them, but the nation falls back into sin. The author of the book used the following cycle to introduce certain judges:

- *Sin:* "The Israelites did evil in the eyes of the LORD."
- *War as judgment:* "The LORD sold them into the hands of X (enemy nation) for X-years."
- *Repentance:* "But when the Israelites cried out to the LORD . . ."
- *Deliverance:* ". . . he raised up for them a deliverer, X (name of judge), who saved them."

This is usually followed by a statement that the land had peace for X-years, while the judge was alive.

Though the author uses several variations on this cycle, he repeats the pattern six times in 3:7–16:31 to highlight six particular judges: Othniel (3:7–11), Ehud (3:12–30), Deborah (4:1–5:31), Gideon (6:1–8:28), Jephthah (10:6–12:7), and Samson (13:1–15:20). In addition to these six major judges, the author gives few details about the careers of six minor judges: Shamgar (3:31), Tola (10:1–2), Jair (10:3–5), Ibzan (12:8–10), Elon (12:11–12), and Abdon (12:13–15).

The judges are by no means portrayed as exemplary and holy individuals. They were temporary leaders raised up by God to deliver his people. Some are worthy of emulation (Othniel and Deborah). But Jephthah apparently had little concept of Yahweh's requirements, and Samson's faults are renowned. As a rule, these judges illustrate God's grace and mercy for his people. They are not necessarily examples of devotion to God.

Appendixes (chapters 17–21)

The last five chapters of Judges portray an age of general anarchy and lawlessness. They narrate two horrible episodes that illustrate one of the darkest periods of Israel's national history: Micah and the migration of Dan (chapters 17–18), and the rape of the Levite's concubine and the subsequent intertribal war (chapters 19–21). Here we read of idolatry, conspiracy, senseless violence, and sexual degeneracy.

These chapters do not present a chronological history of the period. Rather, they portray what life was like during the judges period before there was a king in Israel. The repeated phrase, "in those days Israel had no king" (17:6; 18:1; 19:1; 21:25), implies the author believed the lawlessness was due to a lack of firm royal leadership. He obviously supported the monarchy and believed that it was God's

Reconstructed city gate at Dan, in northern Israel. This city was captured by the Danites when they migrated north.

instrument for providing security and peace in the land. Many scholars assume the author lived during the days of David or Solomon and was a staunch supporter of the Davidic kingdom.

Like the introduction (1:1–2:5), these chapters show Israel's failure to live in covenant relationship with God. The introduction looks back and compares the judges period to the preceding period of success under Joshua. These narratives look forward to the time of the monarchy, when the line of David would provide peace and security. The author has a monarchic perspective, regarding the chaos and moral crises of the period as the result of the absence of a king. The cry of this section, "there was no king in Israel,"

Moral Relativism in Modern Culture

The Book of Judges warns about moral relativism, or behavior based on human opinions. The Bible teaches that the standards for human behavior are God-given. Left alone, humans will always fail to live up to those standards. But with God's help and in his grace, we can learn of his will for a more righteous way (Ps 1:1–2).

In contrast to the Bible, modern culture often establishes societal standards of behavior on the basis of majority opinion. Ideals of right and wrong are determined by what the majority believes is right or wrong. But such morality is whimsical. For example, before 1973 abortion was illegal in the United States, implying that it was morally wrong and hurtful to American culture. The famous *Roe v. Wade*

decision of the U.S. Supreme Court of that year changed the societal standard.

But what really changed? Did some wrong and sinful action suddenly become acceptable, just because a powerful group decided so? Did the universal truths that previously made abortion illegal suddenly change? No. Rather, American society changed!

God's moral standards never change. Though human cultures inevitably evolve, God's requirements of righteousness and holiness never do. The specific application of those requirements have to be thought through carefully by each generation of Christians. But it is clear that God has established and revealed an absolute standard of holiness that Christians must revere more than human relativism.

amphictyony

warns that anarchy results without firm leadership.

These narratives are different from the central section of the book because the problem has a different source. In 2:6–16:31, Israel was afflicted by external enemies who oppressed them militarily. But in chapters 17–21, the problems were internal. Israel was her own worst enemy.

The author of Judges laments the fact that "all the people did what was right in their own eyes"—which was usually wrong in God's eyes! This repeated statement (17:6; 21:25) recognizes the need for absolute order in society. Morality is not relative to one's own experience. There must be an external standard that determines right and wrong in human ethics. For the author of Judges, that external standard for Israelite society was maintained by the Israelite king. For the Christian, that external absolute is still necessary, because human beings are not capable of establishing their own moral standards. Today, that external standard is still established and maintained by the heavenly King (Jn 14:15).

Historical Problems in Judges

The Book of Judges is more concerned with covenant faithfulness (or the lack of it!) than with historical details. This leaves us with a few important questions about the history of this period.

Chronology

Since the number of years each judge ruled is given, it might be possible to add up their total years and derive the precise number of years covered by this book. Such a calculation yields a period of 390 years for the judges period.[3] This assumes the judges ruled consecutively, each ruling over a unified nation of Israel.

But this assumes too much. The judges appear to have been local or regional rulers. One of Israel's problems during the judges period was a lack of central governing authority. The judges brought peace and security to a specific region for a limited period of time. Only a relatively small area was jeopardized by each military emergency. For example, Ehud stopped

the limited intrusion of Moab affecting only the areas of Benjamin and Ephraim, and Gideon's wars with the Midianites affected only the tribe of Manasseh. The book seems to suggest the judges ruled different areas of Israel concurrently.

This point is linked to the question of the date of the exodus and conquest (see chapter 6). The end of the period may be dated more precisely as the beginning of the reign of Saul (probably around 1050 B.C.). If the fifteenth-century date is correct for the exodus, then the 390 years for the judges period is possible. But the years of oppression and rest must also be added to those of the judges' reigns, raising questions about the early date.

However, the Book of Judges does not demand this length of time, since some judges ruled simultaneously instead of consecutively. We conclude, then, that the book presents only a relative chronology instead of an absolute chronology for the judges period. The shortest length of the period would be around 150 years, assuming a thirteenth-century exodus to the time of Saul (approximately 1200–1050 B.C.). The longest length would be around 350 years, assuming a fifteenth-century exodus (approximately 1400–1050 B.C.).[4]

Political Structure

What was the exact nature of the political organization of Israel during the judges period? This is another question raised by the lack of historical details in Judges.

The Israelites were a landless group of former slaves, organized in some sort of tribal society related to their family ties to Jacob. Their tribal structure served them well during their wilderness wanderings. But the Book of Judges illustrates that settled life in the land was threatened, partly due to this political arrangement.

Modern scholarship has attempted to clarify this tribal organization by drawing parallels to ancient Greece. Martin Noth suggested in 1930 that Israel's twelve-tribe system was sociologically analogous to the **amphictyony** of Delphi in Greece, dated to around 600 B.C.[5] The amphictyony was an association of twelve members centered around a central religious shrine at Delphi. The twelve members were committed to peaceful coexistence and united defense against foreign ag-

Bethlehem from the nearby hills. Naomi left her native town of Bethlehem to escape famine; when she returned, the harvest was beginning.

idyll

gression. The sanctuary was the site of yearly religious festivals and provided an important unifying center to otherwise disparate groups.

The parallels with ancient Israel seemed obvious. The tabernacle as central shrine (located first at Shechem and then at Shiloh), the periodic covenant ceremonies, and the unified military efforts all seemed to support the idea of Israel as an amphictyonic structure. This approach won wide acceptance initially.

But in more recent decades, scholars have criticized the comparisons between ancient Israel and Greece. The historical books make no mention of such a specific organizing principle. In fact, Judges seems to imply that just such a formal structure was missing in ancient Israel. Religion and ethnic ties were probably the most important unifying factors during the judges period, more so than common devotion to a central shrine. Today the term "amphictyony" can be applied to Israel only in the most general way.

What is clear is that this period was a transitional time in ancient Israel. It was the period between Joshua and the kings of the united kingdom, when judges provided leadership. The Book of Judges describes this period from the tribal nomads to the established monarchy. The transition would be critical for Israel because she came under the strong influence of Canaanite fertility religion. How she responded to that cultural pressure to compromise her faith was a defining moment for national Israel.

The Book of Ruth

Even during periods of moral crises, God is looking for faithful servants to bless. The Book of Ruth is about the sovereign work of God in the lives of unassuming, humble people during the judges period. This amazing story tells of a faithful family from Bethlehem in a period of total moral chaos and confusion. God blesses this family in a surprising way.

Contents

The Book of Ruth is a literary masterpiece. It may be categorized as an **idyll,** or a simple description of rustic life. The action centers around three main characters: Naomi, Ruth, and Boaz. Naomi and her family were forced to flee from their home in Bethlehem because of famine. During their stay in Moab, Naomi's husband and sons died, leaving her alone with her daughters-in-law. One of them, Ruth, returns to Bethlehem with Naomi to start a new life. But unless someone intervenes to help these two desperate widows, they can only expect a life of poverty and loneliness. God does, in fact, intervene to help, but in a way that neither of them could have imagined.

Literary Structure

The four chapters of Ruth are written almost like a four-act play. Each chapter (or scene) has a clear opening and concluding paragraph, and each revolves around an important dialogue. The chapters are organized according to a "problem–solution" framework. Chapter 1 portrays the problem and its severity. At the conclusion of the chapter, Naomi is without child and Ruth without husband. Together they face the realities of poverty. The following three chapters describe the slow, gradual unfolding of the solution to all of these problems. The book builds to a dramatic climax in chapter 4, which has a surprise ending.

Outline

    I. **Introduction** (1:1–5)

    II. **Return to Bethlehem** (1:6–22)

    III. **Ruth Encounters Boaz** (2:1–23)

    IV. **Ruth Visits the Threshing Floor** (3:1–18)

    V. **Boaz Redeems and Marries Ruth** (4:1–17)

    VI. **Concluding Genealogy** (4:18–22)

Overview

Though the book is named for Ruth, the story is really about Naomi and the reversal of her life's sad circumstances. The events of chapter 1 take place in Moab, or more technically on the road back from Moab. The rest of the action is set in Bethlehem and its vicinity.

Naomi and Ruth return to Bethlehem (chapter 1)

The opening paragraph (vv. 1–5) lists the cast of characters and places them in their historical and geographical contexts. Unlike the characters in the other historical books, the main characters here are not important judges, kings, or prophets. Elimelech and his family are average Israelites, negotiating their way through the everyday affairs of life.

Naomi's name is probably an abbreviation for "[God is my] delight," or "Pleas-ant[ness]." However pleasant her life may have been, Naomi's life changed forever during the decade in which famine forced the family to live in Moab. After Elimelech her husband died, her two sons married

local Moabite women. Through a series of unexplained tragedies, the two sons also died. In short order, the author has painted a dark picture. This woman, far from home, is without husband and children, and she is past her childbearing years (v. 11). She faced the most extreme and desperate circumstances possible for a woman in ancient Israel.

Having lost every source of security and comfort, Naomi prepared to return to Bethlehem to a life of loneliness and despair. Marriage was the only source of stability and security for a woman in the ancient Near East. Naomi realized the sacrifice involved for her two daughters-in-law to return with her. Moabite women living in Judah would have few chances for a new life. Naomi did what was right: She insisted both of her daughters-in-law stay in Moab to put their lives together again.

But Ruth's surpassing love and commitment to Naomi led her to refuse. She chose not to become a wife again, but to remain a daughter. Her expression of devotion to Naomi has become classic (vv. 16–17). Ruth's decision to be buried in Naomi's homeland reflects a commitment of life itself. Even in death, Ruth will never abandon Naomi.

Upon their return to Bethlehem, Naomi was hardly recognizable due to the years of hardship (v. 19). She asked that her name no longer be "Pleasant," but "Bitter," illustrating the contrast between her former life and her present circumstances. By her side stands the faithful but hardly noticeable Moabitess, Ruth. The author gives no hint that ultimately Ruth may provide the answer to Naomi's plight.

Ruth gleans in the field of Boaz (chapter 2)

The chapter opens with an important piece of information for the rest of the story (v. 1). Naomi had an in-law named Boaz, who was a man of considerable wealth and respect in the community.

Ruth nobly volunteers to go into the fields to collect what she can (v. 2). The Old Testament provides for the poor by requiring farmers to leave sheaves behind for the needy (Lv 19:9; 23:22). Verse 3 makes it clear that Ruth was unaware of the "chance" encounter described in the chap-

A woman harvesting grain in Israel today. Ruth went to the field of her husband's relative, Boaz, and picked up grain left by the workers.

ter. It just so happened (NIV's "As it turned out"!) Ruth worked in the field of Boaz that day. God was at work behind seemingly insignificant events in a way the characters could never have anticipated.

When Boaz comes from the city to inspect his laborers, he notices the industrious young woman gleaning in his field (vv. 4–17). He takes actions to provide for her safety and well-being during the work day. This act of kindness is the first cheerful thing the book records. After Ruth's widowhood and acute poverty, this must have been a turning point in her life.

Upon Ruth's return home, Naomi is pleasantly surprised by the unexpected bounty (vv. 18–23). When she learned that Boaz was responsible, she broke out in praise of Yahweh, who is consistently the great moving force behind the events of this story.

Boaz is the family's "kinsman-redeemer" (*gōʾēl*, v. 20). In Israelite society, all real property belonged ultimately to Yahweh. It was not possible legally to purchase another family's land. In hard times, one could sell the land temporarily (as a sort of lease). The kinsman-redeemer was responsible for redeeming the property and restoring it to the original family owner. Naomi may have already had hopes that Boaz was the answer to their problems ("The LORD has not stopped showing his kindness to the living and the dead," v. 20).

Ruth's request of Boaz (chapter 3)

So far, the story has been about ordinary people moving in and out of the complexities of life in an exemplary fashion. Boaz the local farmer, the bereaved Naomi, the daughter-in-law recently returned from Moab—all of these characters behave in a manner worthy of emulation. But chapter 3 is full of suspense. The question is, Will these three continue to act righteously in the midst of questionable circumstances?

This chapter contains ancient customs that seem odd to us, and their full significance is unknown. What is clear is that Boaz understood Ruth's striking actions as a proposal of marriage, and that becoming Ruth's husband would be a function of his kinsman's role (vv. 10–13).

The chapter gradually grows in suspense and anticipation. Ruth's request is an honorable one and does not constitute anything of an illicit nature. But she has placed herself in a compromising and vulnerable situation. This midnight encounter between Ruth and Boaz is dangerous. Impropriety is possible, perhaps imminent. Will the characters continue to act honorably?

The suspense and ambiguity of the narrative are soon resolved. Not only does Boaz behave nobly, but also decisively and honestly. He is genuinely honored and surprised by Ruth's request for marriage, for he assumed she would have preferred a younger man. Ruth likewise has acted

vantage of the situation and married Ruth before informing the other kinsman. Nothing forced him to delay the wedding or divulge the information to the other man. But Boaz did not consider marrying Ruth without first giving preference to the other kinsman-redeemer. His integrity is exemplary.

Ruth marries Boaz (chapter 4)

The events at the threshing floor in chapter 3 took place in the middle of the night, in darkness and seclusion. But the events of chapter 4 take place in the most public arena in any ancient Israelite city, the city gate. This was the site of important assemblies and the only proper place for conducting legal business. In the brightness of the early morning sun, in full view of all concerned, the problems of chapter 1 are quickly resolved.

We learn here for the first time of a piece

morally. She has consistently given higher priority to family obligations than to her own personal well-being (v. 10).

Boaz informed Ruth about another kinsman-redeemer who was a closer relative (vv. 12–13). He could have taken ad-

Summary

1. The history presented in the Book of Judges is part of a larger work called Deuteronomistic History.

2. The major characters in the Book of Judges are judges who served as leaders.

3. The period of the judges is one of disobedience to God.

4. God permitted enemy nations to attack Israel because Israel was worshiping other gods.

5. The cycle of events in the Book of Judges is sin, judgment, repentance, and deliverance.

6. There were twelve judges—six major judges and six minor judges.

7. The Israelites were guilty of moral relativism by doing whatever was right in their own eyes.

8. The tabernacle as a central shrine, the periodic covenant ceremony, and the unified military effort support the idea of Israel as an amphictyony.

9. The Book of Ruth is in the literary form of an idyll.

10. The contents of the Book of Ruth is basically about the sad circumstances of Naomi's life.

11. Boaz served as the family's kinsman-redeemer.

12. Boaz substituted Ruth for Naomi in a levirate marriage which was a responsibility of a kinsman-redeemer.

13. The Book of Ruth shows that God's covenant is not limited by any boundaries—national, racial, or gender.

Study Questions

Judges

1. How much time is covered by the Books of Judges and Ruth?

2. What political perspective is presented by the author of Judges/Ruth?

3. Who are the central figures of the Book of Judges? What did their duties entail?

4. To what is Israel's failure to complete the conquest attributed?

5. What is the basic literary pattern for the central unit of Judges?

6. Who were the six major judges? Who were the six minor judges?

7. What is the theme of the last five chapters of Judges?

8. According to the author of Judges, why was lawlessness so prevalent in Israel?

9. Discuss the chronological issues and problems found in Judges.

10. How is the political situation of Israel best described during this period?

Ruth

1. What is the basic theme of the Book of Ruth?

2. Who is the real central character in this story?

3. How is God's plan worked out in the events recorded?

4. What contributions does the Book of Ruth make to ethnic and racial issues?

---

levirate marriage

of agricultural land belonging to Naomi (v. 3). Old Testament law was clear that a family's real estate was inalienable (1 Kgs 21:3). Because of Naomi's poverty, the land would be sold, but a kinsman must redeem it so the property would not be lost to the family.

After the unnamed kinsman declared his intention to redeem Naomi's property, Boaz added a condition to the transaction: marriage to Ruth. Apparently, popular custom had associated **levirate marriage** as a further responsibility of the kinsman-redeemer.[6] The law of levirate marriage required the nearest relative of a deceased man to marry his widow (Dt 25:5–6). The children born to this new couple carried the name and inheritance of the first husband.

Acquiring the field would have been a significant expansion of the closer relative's own property. Marriage to Naomi would have been no problem, since she was beyond child-bearing years and the estate for his own children would not be further divided. But when Boaz substituted Ruth for Naomi, thus fulfilling the spirit of the law, the closer relative was unwilling to act as kinsman (4:6). An additional wife of child-bearing years would fragment his estate and jeopardize his own family. We may assume he was not a man of unlimited resources.

When the closer relative took himself out of the picture, the way was clear for Boaz and Ruth to marry. In one brief verse (4:13), every problem in chapter 1 meets a solution: Ruth remarries, Yahweh grants immediate conception, and a son is born. But after this verse, Boaz leaves center

Further Reading

Arnold, Bill T. "Ruth." In *Asbury Bible Commentary.* Ed. Eugene E. Carpenter and Wayne McCown. Grand Rapids: Zondervan, 1992, 347–57.

Campbell, Edward F. *Ruth: A New Translation with Introduction, Notes, and Commentary.* Anchor Bible 7. Garden City, N.Y.: Doubleday, 1975.

Cundall, Arthur E., and Leon Morris. *Judges and Ruth: An Introduction and Commentary.* Tyndale Old Testament Commentary. Downers Grove: InterVarsity, 1968.

Howard, David M., Jr. *An Introduction to the Old Testament Historical Books.* Chicago: Moody, 1993.

Hubbard, Robert L., Jr. *The Book of Ruth.* New International Commentary on the Old Testament. Grand Rapids: Eerdmans, 1988. Most thorough and complete evangelical commentary available.

Lilley, J. P. U. "A Literary Appreciation of the Book of Judges," *Tyndale Bulletin* 18 (1967): 94–102.

Sasson, Jack M. *Ruth: A New Translation with a Philological Commentary and a Formalist-Folklorist Interpretation.* 2nd ed. Sheffield: JSOT, 1989. Excellent sociological approach with a great deal of original thinking.

Webb, Barry G. *The Book of Judges: An Integrated Reading.* Journal for the Study of the Old Testament—Supplement Series 46. Sheffield: JSOT, 1987.

stage. Nor is Ruth the central figure. Suddenly Naomi comes again to the foreground. She takes into her arms the baby boy, as though she were his mother. The author has taken us from the point where Naomi was bereaved of her own two sons to this point where she now holds the new child, the son of Ruth and Boaz.

All of the problems of chapter 1 have now been resolved, and we have arrived at a happy conclusion. But before the genealogy, the story ends with a concise sentence containing a surprise ending. Naomi's friends name the child Obed, who was none other than the father of Jesse, the father of David (4:17). The son born in these unlikely circumstances to a foreign woman became the grandfather of Israel's greatest king. Of course, Matthew did not fail to see the significance of Ruth's presence in the lineage of the Messiah (1:5). The Lord's purpose was accomplished through the lives of ordinary but faithful individuals. A life committed to God meets no insignificant turns. All of life becomes sacred.

The Sovereignty of God and Faithful Living

This account of an amazing wedding and a miracle baby is really about the sovereignty of God. Though the book is named for Ruth, it is Naomi who states the problems addressed in the book (1:20–21) and who overshadows her daughter-in-law at the book's conclusion. But in another sense, neither of them is the central character. Throughout the whole narrative, it is God who watches over Naomi, Ruth, and Boaz to accomplish what is best for them in accordance with his purposes. The book is first and foremost about God and his faithful dealings in the lives of his people.

The sovereign plan of God is worked out in the book through the faithfulness of its main characters. Naomi, Ruth, and Boaz provide a striking contrast with other characters and events of the judges period. The book's placement immediately after the Book of Judges in the Christian canon, and the opening words, "In the days when the judges ruled," highlight the differences between the faithful lives of these simple people compared to the sordid affairs of the characters in Judges. During a period when many people did what was right in their own eyes, there were at least three who did what was right in God's eyes. It was through their faithfulness to God and to each other that God provided the Messiah for the world.

Finally, the Book of Ruth illustrates that the benefits of God's covenant are not limited by any boundaries, whether national, racial, or gender. Ruth is constantly referred to as the "Moabitess." Her ethnic and national background is not forgotten in the book, which teaches that even this Moabite woman can live in covenant with Yahweh and benefit from faithful relationship with him.

13 First Samuel
God Grants a King

Outline

- **Outline**
- **Background of 1 Samuel**
  Setting
  Authorship and Date
  Themes of 1 Samuel
- **The Message of 1 Samuel**
  A Period of Transition (chapters 1–15)
  David's Rise and Saul's Decline
    (chapters 16–31)

Objectives

**After reading this chapter,
you should be able to**

- Outline the content of 1 Samuel
- List the three themes of 1 Samuel
- Trace the events surrounding the ark
  of the covenant as found in 1 Samuel
- Explain the reason for Israel having
  a king
- Outline Samuel's final speech to Israel
- Identify three errors Saul made that
  revealed his heart
- Compare and contrast David with Saul
- Discuss the key events in the struggle
  David had with Saul

Have you ever asked yourself the question, "Who am I?" It's an interesting question to ponder. Who am I anyway, and where am I headed? What has God placed me here to do? Questions like these are more than interesting—they're essential. The correct answers to these questions provide the secret to living the kind of life God expects.

In 1 Samuel, we find the nation of Israel wrestling with these kinds of questions. The judges period featured much confusion and anarchy. The people longed for a leader who could pull the kingdom together and give them a sense of national pride and identity.

Outline

I. **A Period of Transition** (1–15)
   A. Samuel's Birth and Call (1:1–3:21)
   B. The Ark Narrative (4:1–7:17)
   C. Saul Becomes Israel's First King (8–12)
   D. Saul Reveals His Heart (13–15)

II. **David's Rise and Saul's Decline** (16–31)
   A. David's Anointing and Introduction to Saul's Court (16)
   B. David's Victory over Goliath (17)
   C. David's Struggles with Saul (18–27)
   D. Saul's Final Battle (28–31)

The Background of 1 Samuel

Setting

The Book of 1 Samuel begins in the judges period, a time when people did what was right in their own eyes (Jgs 21:25). The tabernacle rested at Shiloh, where Joshua had finished dividing the land (Jos 18:1). The nation lacked good political and spiritual leadership.

The major powers of the ancient Near East—Assyria, Babylon, Hatti, and Egypt—were all in decline, and posed no real threat to Israel. However, Israel's neighbors always presented a potential problem. A recent arrival was the Philistines, a people of Indo-European descent who had settled along the Judean coast.[1]

As God's people found themselves fighting the Philistines and others, they struggled with an important issue. How could they present a united front against their enemies? The Book of 1 Samuel relates how the Israelites solved the problem: They crowned a king.

Authorship and Date

The Books of 1 and 2 Samuel originally formed one united work in the Hebrew Bible.[2] Samuel's name appears in the title, but the book does not name an author. Perhaps early tradition linked Samuel's name with the work because of his great influence during this period of biblical history. We simply do not know who wrote this book.

We also do not know the exact time the Book of 1 Samuel assumed its present form. First Samuel 27:6, in referring to the city of ZIKLAG, says, "Ziklag has belonged to the kings of Judah to this day." This statement suggests some time had elapsed since the division of the kingdom around 930 B.C. We may assume the inspired author of 1 Samuel had access to good information regarding the period 1 Samuel covers. Many of the stories read like eyewitness accounts.

Themes of 1 Samuel

Samuel's ministry

The judges period featured much sin and corruption. The Israelite priesthood, under the leadership of Eli and his two sons, Hophni and Phinehas, fared no better. Eli's sons used the sacrificial system for their personal gain and also committed gross sexual sins, all the while refusing to heed their father's warnings (2:12–17, 22–25).

The Book of 1 Samuel describes how Samuel rose to prominence as a priest and judge in Israel. God judged Eli's house and established Samuel as an important leader. This man of God served the people faithfully and honestly, seeking only God's best for them.

A modern replica of the ark of the covenant based on its description in the Old Testament.

Saul's reign (the beginning of kingship in Israel)

The people became restless under Samuel's leadership. They feared external threats such as the Philistines. They observed how the nations around them had kings ruling over them, and they asked for one, too. God granted Israel's request, though the text is clear this was not God's plan for Israel at the time (8:6–7; 12:17–18).

God's selection of Saul initiated a new period in Israel's history. Whereas the judges period featured rule by many leaders from various tribes, 1 Samuel describes a time when centralized power rested in the hands of one man—the king.

The rise of the monarchy also marked the end of the theocracy. Israel had been under the direct leadership of Yahweh, their heavenly King. Now they wanted an earthly king. After this king assumed power, would the people place all their trust in him and forget the Lord? Or would they remember Yahweh was their highest King?

David's rise to prominence

Although Saul experienced some success as Israel's military leader, he showed himself unworthy of the kingship by disobeying God's commands (13:8–14; 15:1–31). The Lord subsequently instructed Samuel to go to Bethlehem to anoint the man God would choose as Israel's next king (16:1).

At God's direction, Samuel anointed David, a young Judean shepherd from Bethlehem (16:1–13). This anointing did not make David king; rather, it only affirmed him as Saul's successor. But by God's leading, David's fame began to increase. First, he became one of Saul's court musicians, who played to ease the king's troubled spirit (16:14–23). Second, David became a capable military leader, defeating the Philistine giant Goliath and leading Israel's army (17:1–18:5). This success, however, had its pitfalls. As we will see, Saul became jealous of his new leader and sought to kill him.

This church is situated at Kiriath-jearim, where the ark remained about twenty years (6:19–21).

The Message of 1 Samuel

A Period of Transition (chapters 1–15)

Samuel's birth and call (1:1–3:21)

The story of 1 Samuel begins at Shiloh, a city in the hill country of Ephraim. There, Israel had divided the land during Joshua's day (Jos 18:1–6) and established the tabernacle. The text describes two families: the family of Elkanah and the family of Eli.

Elkanah, a Levite from the hill country of Ephraim,[3] had two wives—Peninnah and Hannah. Peninnah had children while Hannah had none, and this fact proved to be the source of bitter rivalry between the two women. During a visit to Shiloh, Hannah prayed for a son, vowing to dedicate him to the Lord as a Nazirite (1:10–11; cf. Nm 6:1–21). God answered her prayer, and she conceived and bore Samuel (1:19–20). Hannah's situation illustrates how we can always take our deepest troubles to the Lord. He has asked us to pray and has promised to hear us.

After Hannah weaned Samuel, she brought him to Eli. Samuel grew up under Eli's care; soon, God would reveal his purpose for this young man.

Meanwhile, Eli's sons continued to sin. An unnamed man of God announced God's judgment on Eli's house: Both Hophni and Phinehas would die on the same day, and God would raise up a faithful priest who would obey God's commands (2:27–36).

The Lord then took steps to raise up that faithful priest. He called Samuel just as Samuel was lying down for the evening. At first, the young man thought Eli was calling him, but Eli soon discerned the call must be coming from God. Samuel's reply to the Lord—"Speak, LORD, for your servant is listening" (3:10)—provides a fine model for Christian living. We should always be ready to hear and obey God's Word to us.

All Israel soon recognized Samuel as God's prophet (3:20). Eli's failure to discipline Hophni and Phinehas had not thwarted God's purposes for Israel. At the same time God was judging Eli's house, he was raising up Eli's successor.

The ark narrative (4:1–7:17)

The Philistines had established themselves along the Judean coastline. They controlled the international coastal highway that ran through Israel and connected Mesopotamia and Syria with Egypt. The Philistines camped at Aphek, threatening to push eastward into Israel and cut the land in half. The Israelites moved quickly to stop them, gathering their army together at Ebenezer about two miles east of Aphek (4:1).

The Israelites lost the first battle, and determined a new strategy for victory: They would take the ark of the covenant into battle with them. But their plan basically amounted to treating the ark as an idol, and God did not approve. The Philistines won again, capturing the ark and killing Hophni and Phinehas (4:10–11). The battle also claimed two indirect casualties. Eli, upon hearing the results of the battle, fell off his chair, broke his neck, and died. The wife of Phinehas died in childbirth, her labor brought on prematurely by the traumatic news.

The Philistines brought their new trophy to Ashdod and set it in the temple of their god Dagon. But the ark's presence brought trouble for the Philistines. First, the Lord caused Dagon's idol to fall down and "worship" the ark (5:3–4). Second, God sent plagues of tumors and mice against the people of Ashdod and its territories (5:6; 6:4–5). God's judgment lasted seven months, the tumors and mice following the ark wherever the Philistines sent it (5:8–12).

The Philistines finally decided to return the ark to Israel. However, they first devised a plan to make it appear the plagues were merely coincidental. They put the ark on a cart and hitched to the cart two milch cows who had never pulled a cart. These two cows had calves back in the stall. If the cows proceeded straight up the road to the Israelite city of Beth-shemesh—highly unlikely under the circumstances—then the God of Israel was responsible for the calamity. If anything else happened, the Philistines would assume the evil came by chance. But God left the Philistines a clear testimony: the cows marched directly to Beth-shemesh (6:12–16), causing much celebration upon their arrival.

Unfortunately, the people of Beth-shemesh failed to show proper respect for the ark, and God sent a plague to the city. Finally the ark came to rest at Kiriath-jearim, where it remained about twenty years (6:19–21).

Samuel called the people to forsake their idols and to turn back to the Lord with all their hearts. When Israel did so, the Lord again delivered them from the Philistines and Israel recovered the territory it had lost earlier (7:7–14). Faithfulness to the Lord brought blessing, just as it does today.

Saul becomes Israel's first king (chapters 8–12)

Samuel judged Israel faithfully, but his sons did not follow his example. When Samuel grew old, the people approached him at Ramah and asked him to appoint a king (8:4–5).

Samuel hesitated to grant the people's request because he believed they should trust in the Lord rather than in an earthly king. But the Lord advised Samuel to go

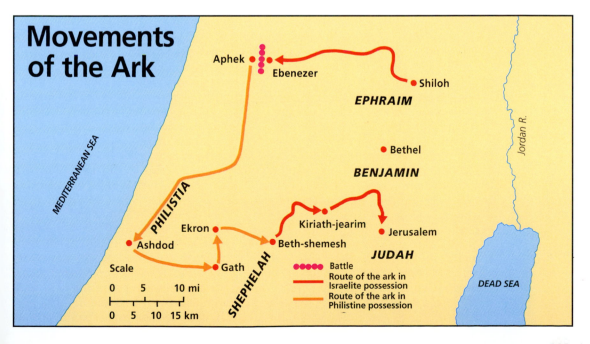

Movements of the Ark

Aphek
Ebenezer
Shiloh
EPHRAIM
MEDITERRANEAN SEA
PHILISTIA
Ekron
Ashdod
Bethel
BENJAMIN
Kiriath-jearim
Jerusalem
Beth-shemesh
JUDAH
Gath
SHEPHELAH
Jordan R.
DEAD SEA

Scale
0   5   10 mi
0   5   10 15 km

●●●●● Battle
Route of the ark in Israelite possession
Route of the ark in Philistine possession

ahead and appoint a king, assuring him, "They have not rejected you, but they have rejected me from being king over them" (8:7). Samuel solemnly warned the people of all the new burdens a monarchy would bring, but the people persisted in their desire for a king (8:10–22).

The Lord chose Saul, a man of the tribe of Benjamin, to be Israel's first king. Saul stood taller than any of the people and really looked like he would make a good king. Through circumstances God carefully guided, Samuel met Saul and anointed him king over Israel (10:1). A formal public coronation later followed at Mizpah (10:17–26).

When the Ammonites threatened Jabesh-gilead, Saul gathered an army and routed them. Some scholars have explained Saul's interest in the city by arguing his ancestors came from there.[4] At any rate, this great victory led to much celebration and praise to God, and the people affirmed Saul as king a second time at Gilgal (11:14–15). The kingdom appeared to rest in good hands.

With Saul now firmly established as king, Samuel gathered the people together. Perhaps he saw this as his final opportunity to address the nation. Clearly, now that Israel had a king, Samuel's role as judge was significantly lessened.

Samuel's speech included three parts. First, he offered to make restitution to anyone he had wronged (12:3–5). All who wished could bring their claims before the king, and Samuel would make everything right. But the people affirmed Samuel's constant faithfulness. Believers today should strive to live lives worthy of such affirmation. Our world desperately needs to see and learn again the meaning of integrity.

Second, Samuel told the people they had sinned against their God (12:8–18). God had remained absolutely faithful to the covenant, whereas Israel had failed him time and time again. Asking for a king was wrong because it was not yet God's plan for them. Furthermore, the people asked with the wrong motives, forgetting the Lord and seeking only a quick solution to their problems.[5] To show his displeasure, the Lord sent heavy rain on the land, severely damaging the wheat harvest.

Third, Samuel urged the people to follow the Lord with all their hearts (12:20–25). Yes, they had sinned, but God would forgive them if they repented, put aside their idols, and trusted in him. Samuel promised to continue to pray for them, but also issued a sober warning. If they persisted in their evil ways, not even their king could save them from God's judgment.

Saul reveals his heart (chapters 13–15)

First Samuel 13–14 records Saul's effectiveness as a military leader. He enjoyed some initial success against the Philistines (14:19–23), and secured his borders by defeating Moab, Ammon, Edom, and Syria as well (14:19–23, 47). Nevertheless, though Saul looked like a good king, his heart often betrayed him. First Samuel 13–15 reveals three such instances.

First, Saul usurped the priestly role when it served his purposes (13:8–14). Saul had gathered his army at Gilgal, where he awaited Samuel's coming to sacrifice to the Lord. Samuel had told Saul to wait seven days, but sometime during the seventh day, Saul grew impatient and offered the sacrifice himself to boost the people's morale. Samuel then arrived and told Saul God would take the kingdom from him. The Lord would choose the next king on the basis of his heart, not his stature.

Second, Saul made a rash oath and later tried to apply it in a foolish manner (14:24–46). On a day the people needed strength to fight their enemies, Saul pronounced a curse against anyone who ate before Israel had won total victory. The people's intense hunger led them to sin by eating meat with blood in it after they won the battle. And when Saul discovered that Jonathan, ignorant of his father's curse, had eaten some honey that day, he resolved Jonathan should die. Fortunately, the people prevented Saul from carrying out his decision.

Third, Saul failed to follow God's instructions concerning the Amalekites (chapter 15). Through Samuel, the Lord instructed Saul to destroy Amalekites and all they had (Hebrew *ḥerem*; see the discussion of this concept in chapter 11, including sidebar 11.1). But Saul had his own plan: He and the people spared the best

Donkeys near Samaria. Saul's search for his father's straying donkeys led him to the prophet Samuel, and to the discovery that God had chosen him to be the first king of Israel.

of the flocks and herds to sacrifice to the Lord.

Again, Samuel confronted Saul, but all the prophet received from the king were excuses:

- "The people spared the best of the sheep and oxen to sacrifice to the LORD your God; but the rest we have utterly destroyed" (15:15).
- "I did obey the voice of the LORD, . . . but the people took some of the spoil" (15:20).

Samuel's stinging reply—"Because you have rejected the word of the LORD, he has also rejected you from being king" (15:23)—finally produced half-hearted repentance (15:24–25), but it was too late. Samuel left Gilgal grieving over Saul, who had disgraced the Lord and the kingly office by his disobedience. It is vitally important for God's leaders to live lives of faithful obedience so others can learn from their example. Of course, our ultimate trust should always rest in the Lord, not in earthly leaders.

David's Rise and Saul's Decline (chapters 16–31)

In 1 Samuel 2–3, we saw how the failure of Eli and his sons to serve the people faithfully did not frustrate God's plan for the priesthood. Rather, God judged Eli's house and raised up Samuel as a faithful priest. Likewise, Saul's failure did not mean God's defeat. The Lord would seek out another man to fulfill his plan for Israel's monarchy.

David's anointing and introduction to Saul's court (chapter 16)

The Lord sent Samuel to Bethlehem, to the house of Jesse (vv. 1–13). God had chosen one of Jesse's eight sons as Israel's next king, but no one—including Samuel—knew whom God had chosen until God directed Samuel to anoint David.

Notice two important items from this account. First, the Lord looked at David's heart, not his stature. Saul looked like a king, but his heart was not right before God. David did not particularly look like a king, but his heart followed the Lord. Even today, God uses people of all kinds, but most of all, he uses people who have yielded their hearts to him.

Second, even though Samuel anointed David, David did not immediately receive the kingship. That would come later. However, David did receive something even more valuable—God's Spirit. That same Spirit is available today to empower believers to accomplish anything the Lord gives us to do.

Meanwhile, God withdrew his Spirit from Saul; the king no longer had the empowering of God to lead Israel. Furthermore, the Lord sent an evil spirit to afflict

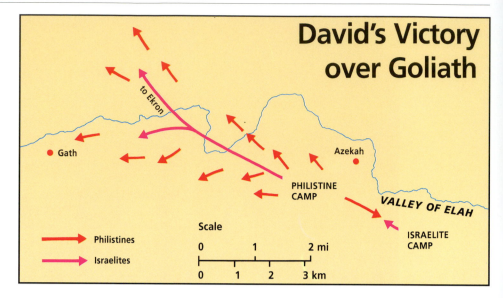

David's Victory over Goliath

him (vv. 14–23). This statement presents a theological problem: In what sense can an evil spirit come from the Lord?

Probably we should understand the expression "evil spirit from the LORD" in one of two ways. First, the Lord may have brought the evil spirit on Saul in judgment for Saul's rebellion. God does sometimes discipline his children, and this spirit may have been Saul's discipline. Second, God may have intended the evil spirit to serve a redemptive function. If the spirit caused Saul to realize his helplessness to lead Israel without God's enabling Spirit, the king might turn back to God.

At any rate, God also used the evil spirit for another purpose—to introduce David to the royal court. Saul's servants suggested the king hire a court musician to play soothing music to ease Saul's mind when the evil spirit troubled him. David had already established his reputation as a skilled musician (v. 18), and consequently received this appointment. God's purposes thus continued to move forward.

David's victory over Goliath (chapter 17)

The Philistines had pushed eastward from Ekron and Gath to an area between Azekah and Socoh, right on the border of Israelite territory. The Israelites had to stop them quickly so they would not take control of two major east–west highways in Judah's hill country. Israel's army moved westward to a mountain overlooking the Elah Valley (see map 12.1).

At this point, Goliath, a Philistine giant, issued a challenge to Israel's army. He would fight to the death anyone Israel put forward. If the Israelite won, the Philistines would serve Israel. If Goliath won, the Israelites would serve the Philistines. For forty days, Goliath continued his challenge, but no one in Israel's army dared to accept it.

One day, just as David arrived at the Israelite camp to check on his brothers, Goliath was once again issuing his challenge. David's heart burned with anger: This Philistine was taunting the armies of the living God! God's honor was at stake! David told Saul he would fight Goliath.

Saul first tried to talk David out of fighting Goliath, then suggested David wear the king's armor. But David refused, preferring his own weapon—a slingshot.

When Goliath saw David coming, he cursed him by his pagan gods, but David and his God had the last word. David brought the Philistine to the ground with a well-aimed stone, then ran to him and cut off his head. When the Philistines saw Goliath was dead, they fled in terror and the Israelites pursued them all the way to Ekron and Gath.

The story of David and Goliath illustrates three important spiritual principles:

The barren Judean wilderness. Through these hills Saul pursued the fugitive David.

- We should be more concerned about God's honor than about ourselves. David was very concerned about God's honor (vv. 26, 36, 46–47). He wasn't willing to allow Goliath to get away with taunting the armies of the living God.
- God's past faithfulness in our lives should encourage us to take more steps of faith. David had the courage to fight Goliath because the Lord had already enabled him to kill a lion and a bear (vv. 34–37).
- When we face battles that look impossible, we need to remember the battle is the Lord's. David fought Goliath, but he was merely God's instrument. The battle was really between Goliath and the Lord (v. 47).

Perhaps most important of all, the story of David and Goliath reveals David's heart. God had said he would choose Israel's next king according to his heart (13:14; 16:7). He had done so.

David's struggles with Saul (chapters 18–27)

After the victory over Goliath, David became one of Saul's leading military men. The common people loved him, as did Saul's men. Unfortunately, Saul became jealous when the people praised David more than they praised him. He began to view David more as a rival than a faithful servant (18:6–9), and these feelings of suspicion led to a dramatic struggle between Israel's king and his successor-to-be.

David's struggles with Saul include five major events. First, David and Saul's son, Jonathan, became good friends. This friendship began shortly after David killed Goliath (18:1) and lasted until Jonathan's death.

Jonathan plays a tragic role in the narrative of 1 Samuel. He loved David very much, but he also loved his father. Jonathan's constant efforts to reconcile David and Saul only brought his father's anger down on him as well (20:24–34). In the end, Jonathan died fighting the Philistines alongside Saul on Mount Gilboa (31:2).

Second, Saul became fanatical in his determination to kill David. His actions were those of a desperate man who felt his kingdom slipping away. He threw his spear at David as David sat playing the harp for him, and then sent messengers to David's house to arrest him (19:9–11). He responded quickly time and time again when people informed him of David's location (23:7–8, 19–23; 24:1–2; 26:1–2).

Saul also displayed this fanatical anger

203

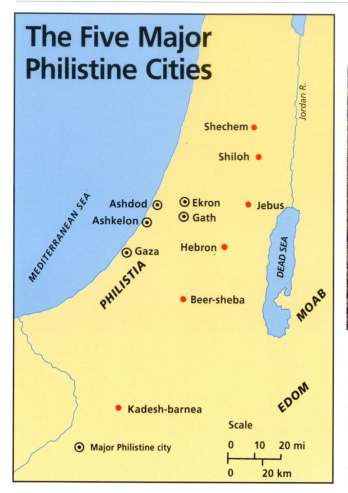

The Five Major Philistine Cities

Shechem

Shiloh

Ashdod ⊙ ⊙ Ekron   • Jebus

Ashkelon ⊙ ⊙ Gath

⊙ Gaza   Hebron •

• Beer-sheba

MEDITERRANEAN SEA

PHILISTIA

Jordan R.

DEAD SEA

MOAB

EDOM

• Kadesh-barnea

Scale

0   10   20 mi

0   20 km

⊙ Major Philistine city

against David's advocates. He hurled his spear at Jonathan when Jonathan tried to stand up for David (20:32–33). Saul also destroyed the entire city of Noʙ when he discovered its priest had given David's men provisions (21:1–9; 22:7–19).

Third, David took extreme measures to prove his loyalty to Saul. David spared Saul's life twice when the chance to kill Saul presented itself. On one occasion, Saul turned aside into a cave where David and his men were hiding, but David only cut off a piece of Saul's garment (24:3–6). David later felt remorse that he had done even this to the Lord's anointed.

On another occasion, David and his nephew Abishai sneaked into Saul's camp while the king's army lay sleeping (26:6–16). They took Saul's spear and water jug to prove they had been close enough to kill him, then retreated to a safe distance and roused the camp, displaying their evidence of loyalty.

In each of these instances, Saul expressed sorrow for his behavior toward David (24:16–22; 26:21). Nevertheless, when another opportunity to capture David presented itself, Saul would respond quickly.

Fourth, David met and married Abigail (chapter 25). Abigail's husband, Nabal, treated David and his men coldly when they asked him for provisions. David determined to destroy the men of Nabal's estate, but Abigail's intervention caused David to relent. When the Lord took Nabal's life ten days later, Abigail became David's wife.

Fifth, David, utterly frustrated with Saul, joined the Philistines (27:1–3). His action illustrates the old proverb: "The enemy of my enemy is my friend." No doubt the Philistines, aware of David's problems with Saul, assumed they might use him to their advantage.

Achish, king of Gath, gave David the city of Ziklag, and David became Achish's servant—at least formally. Secretly, David used the security of his relationship with the Philistines to further his own cause in Judah and the Neɢᴇʙ. He destroyed the foreign nomadic tribes in the area and brought the spoils to Achish, letting him think he had taken them from Judeans. Ultimately, however, the Philistine lords did not trust David, and dismissed him from their ranks before the final battle with Saul (chapter 29).

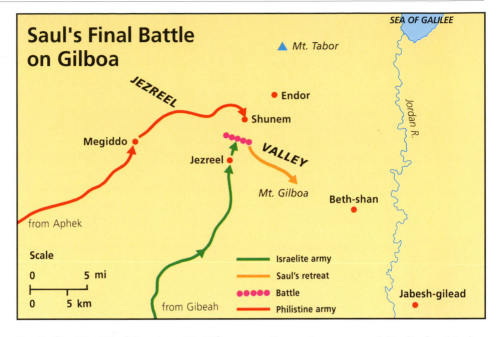

Left: Fields near the village of Endor, Israel. Saul disguised himself and visited Endor, where he heard a medium lived, asking the woman to call Samuel up from the dead.

Saul's Final Battle on Gilboa

SEA OF GALILEE

▲ Mt. Tabor

JEZREEL

● Endor

● Shunem

● Megiddo

VALLEY

Jezreel ●

Mt. Gilboa

Beth-shan ●

Jordan R.

from Aphek

Scale

0 — 5 mi

0 — 5 km

from Gibeah

— Israelite army
— Saul's retreat
●●●●● Battle
— Philistine army

Jabesh-gilead ●

Saul's final battle (chapters 28–31)

As Saul prepared for battle against the Philistines, he sought spiritual guidance (chapter 28). He inquired of the Lord, but the Lord did not answer him. Saul became desperate. He disguised himself and slipped around the Philistine camp to ENDOR, where he heard a medium lived. Saul asked the woman to call Samuel up from the dead for him.

The text seems to indicate Samuel actually did appear. The passage calls the figure Samuel, and he certainly spoke with Samuel's authority. Whether the woman had ever spoken with departed spirits before is unclear, but she did this time!

Samuel announced Saul's final judgment—Saul would die in battle with the Philistines the next day. But despite Samuel's clear warning, Saul, though terribly alarmed, proceeded with battle plans—plans that would cost him his life.

Meanwhile, the Philistine lords decided they didn't trust David to join them in battle against Saul (chapter 29). They remembered the words of the Hebrew song—"Saul has slain his thousands, and David his ten thousands"—and knew those great numbers described *Philistine* casualties! Despite David's protests of loyalty, Achish dismissed David from his service.

This dismissal certainly proved to be a blessing to David. If David had fought against Saul, many Israelites would never have forgiven him. Instead, David became an innocent bystander to the battle that claimed Saul's life.

David returned to Ziklag to find the Amalekites had looted the city and taken the women and children captive (chapter 30). At God's direction, he pursued the Amalekites, defeated them, and rescued the captives. As for the Amalekite spoils of war, he sent them as a gift to the elders of Judah, a gesture that certainly increased David's popularity among his own tribespeople.

But perhaps at the very same time David was defeating the Amalekites in Judah,

Key Places

Ziklag
Beth-shemesh
Ramah
Mizpah
Jabesh-gilead
Negeb

Nob
Endor
Elah Valley
Mount Gilboa
Shiloh

Saul was losing his battle with the Philistines on Mount Gilboa.[6] Three of Saul's sons, including Jonathan, died in battle, and the Philistine archers wounded Saul. The king, fearful his enemies would capture and torture him, fell on his own sword and died.

The Philistines found the bodies of Saul and his sons and fastened them to the gate at nearby Beth-shan.[7] But the men of Jabesh-gilead, probably because of Saul's blood ties and faithfulness to them (chapter 11), removed the bodies and gave them a proper burial.

And so the life of Israel's first king came to a tragic end. As we come to the end of 1 Samuel, the text raises a question. Saul has died, and the prophet Samuel has anointed David as Israel's next king. Saul looked like he would make a great king, but he did not. David did not look like he would make a great king. Would he? And if so, why?

Israel's struggle between theocracy and monarchy also raises another question for us. Each of us must choose to submit to some ultimate authority, whether the Lord God or another. Who's king in your life?

Summary

1. The Philistines captured the ark of the covenant and took it to Ashdod, but they suffered plagues until they returned it to Kiriath-jearim.

2. God granted Israel's request for a king, but this was not his highest will for them at the time.

3. Saul was not successful as king because he disobeyed the commands of God.

4. David became well known by serving as Saul's court musician and by being a successful military leader.

5. In his final speech as judge, Samuel offered restitution to any he had wronged, told the people they had sinned against God, and urged the Israelites to follow God with all their hearts.

6. Saul demonstrated his true heart by usurping the priestly role at Gilgal, by making a rash oath and trying to apply it, and by not following God's instruction about the Amalekites.

7. In anointing David as king, God looked at his heart rather than his physical characteristics.

8. David's defeat of Goliath illustrated important spiritual principles for contemporary leaders: we should be most concerned about God's honor, not ours; we should act on faith because of God's faithfulness in the past; and in difficult situations, we should remember that God is in control.

9. Saul became jealous of David and created many problems for David, but David continually tried to prove his loyalty to the king.

10. David joined the Philistines for a time and used this alliance to destroy foreign nomadic tribes who were harassing Judah.

11. Saul asked the woman at Endor to call up Samuel's spirit, and Samuel appeared and pronounced that Saul would die in battle with the Philistines the next day.

12. The Philistines took the bodies of Saul and his three sons and fastened them to the gate at Beth-shan.

Study Questions

1. Describe the historical setting in Israel as the Book of 1 Samuel begins. How were the people organized and who was in charge? What threats did they face?

2. What are the major themes of 1 Samuel?

3. How did Samuel's life change Israel's history?

4. Describe the reasons behind the beginning of Israel's monarchy. Why did the people want a king, and why was Saul chosen? Overall, do you think Saul was a good choice? Why or why not?

5. Describe David's rise to prominence. Why did Saul suspect him? Do you think Saul was right to be suspicious of David?

Further Reading

Baldwin, Joyce G. *1 and 2 Samuel: An Introduction and Commentary.* Tyndale Old Testament Commentary. Downers Grove/Leicester: InterVarsity, 1988. Good college-level commentary.

Brueggemann, Walter. *First and Second Samuel.* Louisville: John Knox, 1990. Rich in theological exposition and application.

Merrill, Eugene H. *Kingdom of Priests: A History of Old Testament Israel.* Grand Rapids: Baker, 1987. Seminary-level history of Israel that combines good scholarship and readability.

Wood, Leon J. *Israel's United Monarchy.* Grand Rapids: Baker, 1979. A study of the period of Saul, David, and Solomon. Contains much spiritual application.

14 Second Samuel
David's Reign

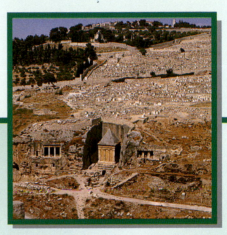

Objectives

**After reading this chapter,
you should be able to**

- Outline the basic content
  of the Book of 2 Samuel
- Recite the four themes of 2 Samuel
- Explain the different details of Saul's
  death in 1 Samuel 31 and 2 Samuel 1
- Demonstrate how David's behavior in the
  situation with Isbosheth helped him gain
  the confidence of the people
- Identify the reasons why David selected
  Jerusalem for the capital
- List the blessings of God's covenant
  with David
- Apply the results of David's sin with
  Bathsheba to contemporary life
- Relate the events of the discontent
  in David's kingdom
- Report the outcomes in Israel's history
  of the census ordered by David

Have you ever thought about what it would be like to lead a country? You would face a busy schedule every day. Many important responsibilities would rest on your shoulders. And sometimes you would have to make unpopular decisions—decisions you felt were in your country's best interest.

Second Samuel records how David became king of Israel at age thirty (5:4). The text highlights several ways the Lord used David to bless Israel. It also describes the heartache and tragedy that befell David and all Israel when God's leader failed to follow God's ways.

Outline

I. **David's Rise to Power in Judah** (1–4)
   A. David Laments over Saul (1)
   B. David Struggles against Ishbosheth (2–4)

II. **David's Reign over All Israel** (5–24)
   A. David Secures his Borders (5, 8, 10)
   B. David Captures Jerusalem (5–6)
   C. God Makes a Covenant with David (7)
   D. David Sins with Bathsheba (11–12)
   E. David Experiences Discontent within His Kingdom (13–20)
      1. *Amnon Rapes Tamar (13–14)*
      2. *Absalom Leads a Revolt (15–19)*
      3. *Sheba Leads a Revolt (20)*
   F. David Finishes His Reign (21–24)

Background of 2 Samuel

Setting

As we said in chapter 13, 1 and 2 Samuel originally formed one united work in the Hebrew Bible. As the book begins, Israel lacks a king, for Saul has died in battle with the Philistines. David, whom Samuel

anointed as Saul's successor, is in Ziklag after rescuing the city from Amalekite raiders. The Book of 2 Samuel relates how David became Israel's king and highlights certain details about his reign.

Some scholars have suggested the writer of 2 Samuel arranged his material topically rather than chronologically.[1] Second Samuel 1–10 describes how God blessed Israel when the king followed God's ways; 2 Samuel 11–24 basically describes how God judged Israel when the king strayed from God's ways.

Authorship and Date

Second Samuel is an anonymous work. As we stated in chapter 13, Samuel's ministry set the stage for Israel's monarchy. This fact may be the reason tradition attached his name to 1 and 2 Samuel.

We also do not know the exact time of the book's writing. The accounts reflect a thorough understanding of the events, sometimes relying on early written sources (1:18).

Themes of 2 Samuel

David's rise to kingship in Israel

When the people asked for a king, God gave them Saul. Saul looked like a king, but proved to be a poor one because his heart did not follow the Lord faithfully.

Early in Saul's reign, God chose David to be Israel's next king (1 Sm 16:1–13). Saul became jealous of David's popularity and sought to kill him, and David spent several years as a fugitive. But Saul's death on MOUNT GILBOA prepared the way for God's plan to proceed. David would soon occupy Israel's throne.

David's choice of Jerusalem for his capital city

The Israelites had conquered JERUSALEM during the judges period (Jgs 1:8), but the Jebusites still occupied the site. David defeated them and made Jerusalem his capital (2 Sm 5:5–9). He also brought the ark of the covenant there, making the city Israel's political and religious center (6:1–19).

Jerusalem was Israel's capital throughout Solomon's reign. After the kingdom divided, it remained Judah's capital until it fell in 587 B.C. to Nebuchadnezzar and the Babylonians.

The settlement mound at Beth-shan, Israel. The Philistines took the bodies of Saul and Jonathan here and nailed them to the walls.

God's covenant with David

David wanted to build God a temple, a "house" on which God could place his Name (chapter 7). Instead, God promised to build David a "house" of descendants! The Lord affirmed David's son would build the temple and that divine favor would not depart from David's line. God would establish David's throne forever.

This marvelous promise to David plays an important role in God's plan of redemption and salvation. It culminates in Jesus Christ, David's ultimate descendant, who one day will return to reign forever (Lk 1:32–33).

David's sin leads to serious consequences

David's inability to control his passions led to adultery with Bathsheba, and later to the murder of Bathsheba's husband Uriah (chapter 11). God forgave David when David repented, but sin's consequences haunted the king the rest of his life. Indeed, the account of David and Bathsheba forms a significant turning point in the narrative of 2 Samuel.

Message of 2 Samuel

David's Rise to Power in Judah (chapters 1–4)

David laments over Saul (chapter 1)

On the third day after David's triumphant return to Ziklag, he received word of Israel's defeat and Saul's death on Mount Gilboa. An Amalekite from Saul's camp came to Ziklag and told David the news. This man also told David he had found Saul badly wounded and, at Saul's request, had killed him to end his misery.

David's response was twofold. First, he and all his company mourned and fasted until evening. Second, he ordered the Amalekite killed for striking down Saul, the Lord's anointed. By these actions, David gave clear testimony he had neither rejoiced in Saul's death nor participated in it.

Some scholars have pointed out the discrepancy in the details of 1 Samuel 31 and 2 Samuel 1. In 1 Samuel 31, Saul falls on his own sword and dies, while in 2 Samuel 1, the Amalekite claims to have killed a badly wounded Saul. The most probable explanation is that the Amalekite was lying. He claimed he delivered Saul's death blow because he thought David might reward him in some way. But he failed to anticipate David's response and unwittingly condemned himself.[2]

David chanted a lament over Saul and Jonathan. His words revealed the depth of his love and respect for these men, and testified to his sadness and innocence regarding their deaths.

David struggles against Ishbosheth (chapters 2–4)

At God's leading, David went up to Hebron, where the men of Judah anointed him king over Judah. He also sent word commending the men of Jabesh-gilead for burying Saul's body (1 Sm 31:11–13). He informed them of his anointing and promised to show them kindness.

Meanwhile, Abner, Saul's relative and general, crowned Saul's son, Ishbosheth, king over Israel. Only the tribe of Judah followed David. The stage was set for a bitter civil war that lasted two years.

As the fighting continued, David began to gain the advantage. Abner, now Ishbosheth's general, probably sensed this, and used a dispute over his master's concubine as an excuse to defect to David's side. Abner's desertion further weakened Ishbosheth's cause.

But not everyone in David's camp was ready to trust Abner. Joab, David's nephew and general, suspected him from the beginning and eventually killed him. David denied any connection with Abner's death, and even participated in Abner's funeral procession. David's actions pleased the people and helped heal the wounds between the tribes.

News of Abner's death sent shock waves throughout all Israel. Baanah and Rechab, two of Ishbosheth's commanders, decided David had won. They killed Ishbosheth and brought his head to David at Hebron. Again, David denied any connection with the deed, and ordered Baanah and Rechab killed for their crime. Thus, only one man remained to lead Israel, and that man was David.

David's Reign over All Israel (chapters 5–24)

David had waited for God's timing, and now it had come. All Israel's tribes gathered at Hebron and anointed him king over the entire nation. The people finally had a leader who desired to follow God's purposes.

The rest of 2 Samuel recounts major events from David's reign. These events portray David's victories and failures, his righteous acts and sins. Most of all, they reveal God's grace—grace that enabled David to serve Israel well and picked David up when the results of his sin crashed down on him. The Bible offers that same grace to each of us.

David secures his borders (chapters 5, 8, 10)

Every kingdom must secure its borders. For Israel, a small nation surrounded by many hostile peoples, the task was crucial. David took steps to secure his borders and even move beyond them. His reign marked the beginning of the Israelite Empire.

The Philistines had treated David well because they viewed him as someone who could distract Saul and keep Israel weak.[3] Now that David had assumed control, they counted him an enemy and marched against him (5:17–25).

In the first battle, the Philistines camped in the VALLEY OF REPHAIM southwest of Jerusalem, while David and his men camped at Masada ("the stronghold") near the Dead Sea. David inquired of the Lord, and the Lord brought him victory at BAAL-PERAZIM.

The Philistines regrouped and gathered again in the Valley of Rephaim. This time, the Lord gave Israel victory from GEBA in the Central Benjamin Plateau all the way to GEZER at the mouth of the Aijalon Valley. This victory cleared the Philistines from Israelite territory and pushed them back to the coast. In fact, the Philistines came under David's control. They had defeated Saul, but they would not defeat David.

The Lord also gave David victories over other surrounding kingdoms—MOAB and EDOM to the southeast, AMMON to the east, and SYRIA to the north (8:1). David put garrisons in DAMASCUS and accepted **tribute**

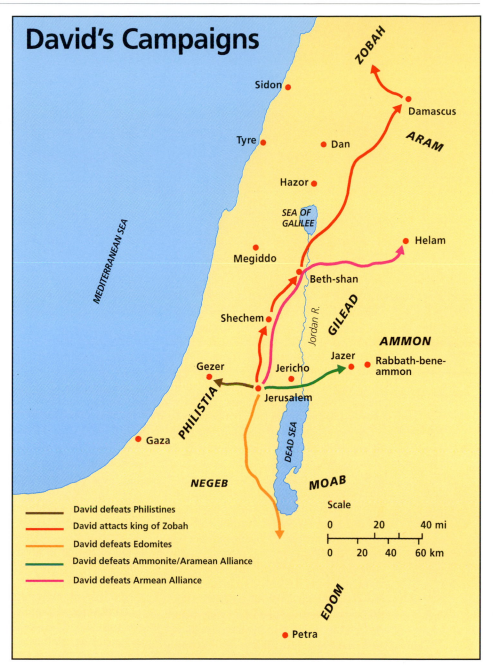

David's Campaigns

Legend:
- David defeats Philistines
- David attacts king of Zobah
- David defeats Edomites
- David defeats Ammonite/Aramean Alliance
- David defeats Armean Alliance

Scale
0 — 20 — 40 mi
0 — 20 — 40 — 60 km

Map labels: ZOBAH, Sidon, Damascus, Tyre, Dan, ARAM, Hazor, SEA OF GALILEE, Helam, MEDITERRANEAN SEA, Megiddo, Beth-shan, GILEAD, Shechem, Jordan R., AMMON, Gezer, Jericho, Jazer, Rabbath-bene-ammon, Jerusalem, PHILISTIA, Gaza, DEAD SEA, NEGEB, MOAB, EDOM, Petra

from many other Syrian city-states. He also made a covenant with Hiram, king of Tyre, who built him a palace in Jerusalem after David moved his capital there.

Conquered kingdoms sometimes joined forces against David to try to win their independence. Syria and Ammon united against Israel (chapter 10), but Joab divided Israel's army against them and defeated them. Israel's borders stood secure.

David captures Jerusalem (chapters 5–6)

For the first 7 1/2 years of his 40 1/2 year reign, David ruled from Hebron. But Hebron's location—far to the south—made the city less than ideal for a capital. David decided to move the capital about twenty miles north to Jerusalem.[4]

Jerusalem lay just within Benjaminite territory, a fact David may have considered in choosing the site. Saul, a Benjami-

The Jebusites controlled Jerusalem during David's days, but David's army entered the city through its water tunnel and conquered it (2 Sm 6:6–8).

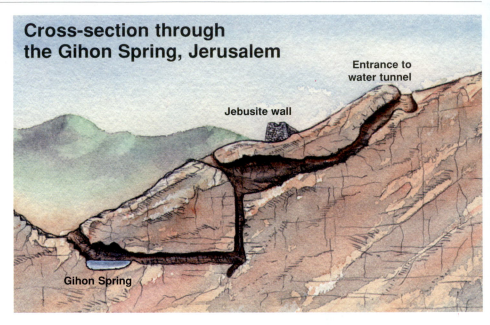

Cross-section through the Gihon Spring, Jerusalem

Entrance to water tunnel

Jebusite wall

Gihon Spring

temple

covenant

nite, had reigned from Gibeah, a few miles north of Jerusalem. Perhaps David thought restoring Israel's capital to Benjamin might ease political tensions in the land. Furthermore, the SPRING OF GIHON gave Jerusalem a plentiful water supply.

The Jebusites, part of the Canaanite population who inhabited the land during the days of Joshua (Jos 24:11), controlled Jerusalem during David's days. Their fortified city, high on a hill, made them feel invincible, but David's army entered the city through its water tunnel and conquered it (2 Sm 6:6–8). Jerusalem became the city of David.

David then brought the ark of the covenant from Baale-Judah (also known as Kiriath-jearim, 1 Sm 7:1–2). Amid much celebration, the ark entered Jerusalem, and the Levites placed it in the tent David had prepared for it. Jerusalem was becoming Israel's spiritual center as well as its political center.

God makes a covenant with David (chapter 7)

David had established himself as king over all Israel. He had defeated his enemies, and they submitted to him. His kingdom enjoyed peace and security, and his borders stood secure. David knew one thing for sure—God had *really* blessed him!

But David also realized something else. Hiram, king of Tyre, had built David an impressive palace. But where was God's palace? There wasn't one! The ark of the covenant rested in a tent while David lived in luxury. David felt the Lord deserved a better place for his Name.

Nathan the prophet assumed God would want David to build a **temple**, but God had other plans. He had not asked for a temple. Also, David was a man of war who had shed much blood; God would choose a man of peace to build the temple (1 Chr 22:8–9). David needed to submit his zeal to God's ways and timing.

Nevertheless, God rewarded David's attitude. David had wanted to build the Lord a temple out of gratitude for all God's blessings. David's attitude was commendable, even if he had the wrong solution.

David wanted to build God a house, but God told David he would build *him* one—a house of descendants. The text does not use the term **"covenant,"** but later biblical texts refer back to this event as a covenant (2 Chr 21:7; Ps 89:3). God's special covenant with David included the following blessings:

- God would provide a place for Israel to dwell securely forever (vv. 10–11).
- God would raise up David's son, who would build the temple (vv. 12–13).
- God would establish David's dynastic line forever (v. 13).
- God would establish a father–son re-

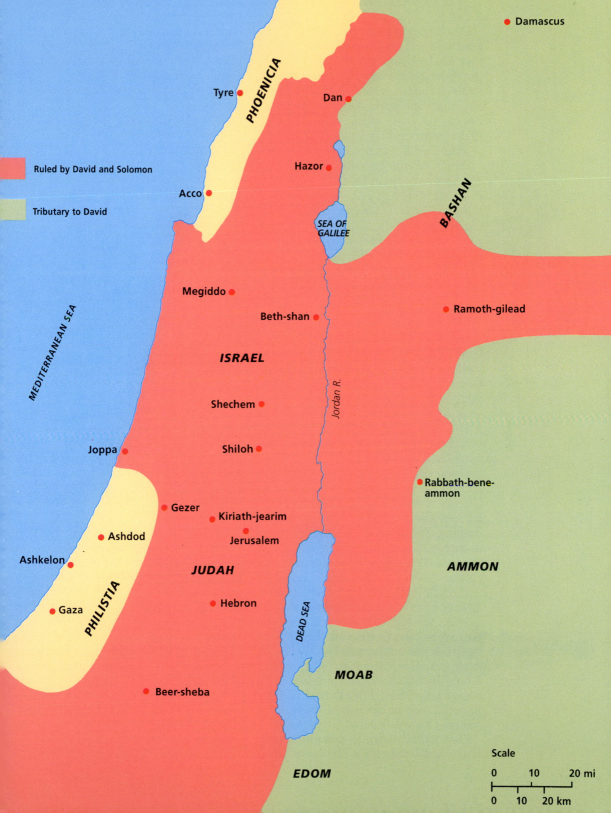

David's United Kingdom

Ruled by David and Solomon

Tributary to David

Damascus

PHOENICIA

Tyre

Dan

Hazor

BASHAN

Acco

SEA OF GALILEE

MEDITERRANEAN SEA

Megiddo

Beth-shan

Ramoth-gilead

ISRAEL

Jordan R.

Shechem

Shiloh

Joppa

Rabbath-bene-ammon

Gezer

Kiriath-jearim

Ashdod

Jerusalem

AMMON

Ashkelon

JUDAH

Gaza

PHILISTIA

Hebron

DEAD SEA

MOAB

Beer-sheba

EDOM

Scale

0   10   20 mi

0   10   20 km

lationship with David's descendants (v. 14).

- God's lovingkindness would not depart from David's dynastic line as it had from Saul (vv. 14–15).

David responded with overwhelming gratitude and amazement. Who was he that God should do this great thing through him? David's attitude serves as a model for all believers. The Bible declares an astounding truth—God has chosen to use ordinary people like us to fulfill his grand purposes! Our response should not be one of pride, but one of gratitude.

David also understood God's blessing depended partly on the faith of David's descendants (1 Kgs 2:4). But the ultimate fulfillment of God's covenant lies in Jesus Christ, the son of David (Mt 1:1). David ruled as king of Israel, but Jesus will return to rule as King of kings and Lord of lords (Rv 19:16). Until that day, we must allow him to reign freely in our hearts. As we do so, his Holy Spirit will mold us into the people he wants us to be.

David sins with Bathsheba (chapters 11–12)

David's sin with Bathsheba led to disaster. So much had gone right for him, but when he strayed from God's ways, so much went wrong. The story sounds a strong warning for today's Christians: Even forgiven sin can have lifelong consequences.

David's sin occurred after he sent Joab and the army to battle Ammon. Back in Jerusalem, while walking atop his palace, David looked down and saw a woman bathing. He desired her, and inquired about her. His servants informed him who she was—Bathsheba, the wife of Uriah the Hittite.

David's interest in Bathsheba should have stopped when he discovered she was married. Instead, he summoned her to the palace and had sex with her. When Bathsheba later informed David she was pregnant, David had a real problem. Uriah, Bathsheba's husband, had been away a long time fighting the Ammonites. It would soon be obvious he was not the father of his wife's baby!

David tried twice to make it appear Uriah had fathered the child. But when both efforts failed, he took drastic measures. He sent orders to Joab by Uriah's own hand to place Uriah in the midst of the hottest fighting, then to withdraw from him. The plan worked, and Uriah died in battle. After Bathsheba's period of mourning, David married her and she bore a son. The king thought he had gotten away with his sin, but forgot one thing: The Lord had seen the whole sinful episode!

Nathan the prophet came to David with a story. A rich man, who had plenty of flocks and herds, was entertaining a guest. Instead of taking from the abundance of his animals to feed his guest, he took a poor man's only lamb, a lamb that was really more of a family pet, and fed it to the guest.

David's anger exploded—that man should die for his lack of compassion! But Nathan's answer stopped him cold: "You are the man!" (12:7). God had blessed David abundantly. He had rescued him from Saul and given him the kingdom with all its honors and privileges. Uriah, on the other hand, had only Bathsheba, and David had taken even her from him. Now the sword would not depart from David's house—his family would experience constant turmoil and tragedy.

David felt the sting of Nathan's words and confessed his sin. Nathan assured David of God's forgiveness, but promised severe consequences. The child must die, because David's sin had caused God's enemies to blaspheme. We need to ask the Lord to protect us from temptation. Unbelievers are always watching us, and any sin they see gives them an excuse to mock God.

Amazingly, God's grace touched David's life again. David comforted Bathsheba over the child's death, and soon she conceived again. She bore another son—Solomon. He would become Israel's next king and build God's temple, just as God had promised (7:13). As we turn to the New Testament, we find God's grace extended even farther. Solomon appears in the genealogy of Jesus Christ himself (Mt 1:6)!

Before we leave this story, we want to point out two important principles for Christian living. First, all sin has consequences. David's sin brought disastrous results on him and his house. Those fac-

The Kidron Valley, outside Jerusalem. When Absalom tried to take the kingdom, his father David fled from the capital across the Kidron Valley.

coup

ing temptation should remember the high price David paid for his evil.

Second, God's grace is sufficient to cover the sins of all who call on him. David repented of his sin, and God's grace not only forgave him, but later produced a Solomon. It is important to remember this story does not condone sin in any way. We should never rationalize our actions by saying, "I'll ask forgiveness later." At the same time, God stands ready to forgive all who feel the shame of their sin and come to him in true repentance (1 Jn 1:9).

David experiences discontent within his kingdom (chapters 13–20)

Nathan the prophet had warned David the sword would not depart from the royal house. Second Samuel 13–20 describes the subsequent discontent within David's kingdom. Three events shape the narrative: Amnon's rape of Tamar (chapters 13–14), Absalom's rebellion (chapters 15–19), and Sheba's rebellion (chapter 20).

Amnon and Absalom were David's first and third sons, respectively (2 Sm 3:2).[5] Tamar was Absalom's sister; she and Absalom had Maacah, daughter of Talmai, king of Geshur, as their mother (2 Sm 3:3; 13:4). Amnon failed to control his desires for Tamar, his half sister, and these uncontrolled desires led to rape. The Scriptures warn us against allowing our passions to dominate us (Rom 13:13–14).

Absalom hated Amnon for what he had done. Two years later, when Amnon attended a party Absalom hosted, Absalom had him killed and fled to Geshur. After three years, largely through Joab's efforts, Absalom returned to Jerusalem, but another two years elapsed before David invited him to the palace.

The tension between the king and his son soon exploded into rebellion. Absalom prepared for his **coup** attempt by winning the people's hearts. He talked with them at the city gate, declaring that if *he* were king, they would receive justice. He also refused to let the people bow to him, treating them more as friends than as subjects.

When Absalom decided the time was right, he went to Hebron, the place of David's anointing (2 Sm 5:3). He also sent spies throughout the land, instructing them that when they heard the trumpet, they were to shout, "Absalom is king in Hebron!" The conspiracy quickly gained momentum, and David and his followers had to flee Jerusalem to escape Absalom's forces.

As David fled Jerusalem, he sent back Hushai, a trusted servant, to feign loyalty to Absalom and keep David informed about Absalom's plans. Hushai returned to find Absalom planning his next move. One of Absalom's counselors was

Key People/ Places

Joab
Abner
Ishbosheth
Uriah
Bathsheba
Amnon
Tamar
Absalom
Sheba
Araunah
Mount Gilboa
Jerusalem
Valley of Rephaim
Baal-perazim
Geba
Gezer
Moab
Edom
Ammon
Syria
Damascus
spring of Gihon

Key Terms

tribute
temple
covenant
coup

Ahithophel, a man whose counsel was above reproach (16:23). Ahithophel advised an immediate attack to finish David. Hushai, on the other hand, urged a carefully planned, delayed attack. He suggested if Absalom's group suffered any kind of setback, public opinion would swing quickly in David's direction. Absalom took Hushai's advice—a decision that saved David's kingdom.

Hushai relayed word to David, who crossed the Jordan to prepare for battle. The king divided his forces into three groups, and instructed them to deal gently with Absalom.

As the battle progressed, Absalom's forces suffered heavy casualties. As Absalom rode under an oak, his hair got caught in the thick branches, suspending him in midair. When Joab discovered Absalom's plight, he and his men surrounded him and killed him. Messengers brought the tragic news to David—the kingdom again lay in David's hand, but David had lost another son.

As David regained control, new seeds of discontent were already sprouting. Intertribal dissension between Judah and the rest of the tribes was clearly apparent (19:41–43), and came to a head when Sheba, a Benjaminite, initiated a rebellion. Sheba's revolt, however, lacked the level of public support Absalom's had enjoyed, and soon ended with Sheba's death.

David finishes his reign (chapters 21–24)

Second Samuel concludes with accounts of various other events from David's reign: his dealings with the Gibeonites (21:1–14), his wars with the Philistines (21:15–22), his praise to God (22:1–23:7), his mighty men (23:8–39), and his census (chapter 24).

During the days of the conquest, Israel made a treaty with the Gibeonites (Jos 9). Saul's misguided zeal against them broke Israel's covenant with Gibeon, so the Lord sent a three-year famine on the land.[6] David discovered the reason for the famine when he inquired of the Lord.

David offered to make restitution to the Gibeonites, who requested to hang seven of Saul's sons. David spared Jonathan's son Mephibosheth (2 Sm 9), but handed over seven others. The Gibeonites hanged them, and God ended the famine. Nevertheless, David's actions certainly must have hurt his relations with the tribe of Benjamin.[7]

The accounts of David's wars with the Philistines (21:15–22) further highlight the struggles Israel had with these people. The Philistines almost killed David, and some of their warriors towered over the smaller Israelites. Nevertheless, the Lord brought victory. David subdued the Philistines.

David knew the Lord had made him what he was, and expressed his praise in 2 Samuel 22. David praised God for who he was—David's rock, refuge, shield, savior, and more. God displayed his power in the heavens, yet chose someone like David to lead Israel. And the same power that enabled David to rule God's people can enable us to live the lives God intends for us today.

The stories of David's mighty men (23:8–39) portray the soldiers' dedication as they fought for David and for Israel. Stories highlight the careers of some of these men, while others appear in name only. These men demonstrated tremendous loyalty and bravery as they accomplished the things they did. Perhaps they fought so valiantly because they recognized God's hand on David. And, of course, God empowered them, too, for his purposes.

On another occasion, David determined he would conduct a census (chapter 24), an act that showed more faith in numbers than in God. Second Samuel 24:1 says the Lord was angry with Israel and enticed David to number them. First Chronicles 21:1 clarifies that God allowed Satan to entice David to make such a decision. As Joab completed the census, God brought judgment on Israel, and thousands died.

The prophet Gad gave David his choice for restitution. Would David choose famine, flight before his enemies, or pestilence? David chose to leave judgment in God's hands. He knew he could expect little compassion from his enemies, but with God, he always had hope.

The plague ceased at the threshing floor of Araunah the Jebusite, and the prophet Gad instructed David to build an altar there. Araunah offered to donate everything David needed, but David refused, saying, "I will not sacrifice to the LORD my God burnt offerings that cost me nothing" (24:24).

Again, David revealed his heart. God had abundantly blessed him, and David would not show his gratitude with an offering that cost nothing. He paid Araunah full price, offered his offerings, and called on God's Name. The Lord heard David's prayer, and ended the plague. Later, Araunah's threshing floor became the site of God's temple (2 Chr 3:1).

The Book of 2 Samuel records how God

Summary

1. The themes of 2 Samuel are about David and his rise to kingship, his selection of a capital city, God's covenant with him, and his great sin and its consequences.

2. David was anointed king by the men of Judah at Hebron, but Abner crowned Saul's son, Ishbosheth, king over Israel.

3. David's reign was the beginning of the Israelite empire.

4. David moved the capital to Jerusalem because it was better located, it would ease political problems because it was within Benjaminite territory, and it had a good water supply.

5. While Jerusalem became Israel's political center, David also made it the spiritual center by bringing the ark of the covenant from Kiriath-jearim and placing it in a tent there.

6. God made a covenant with David that included the promise that he would provide a place for Israel to dwell; that David's son would build the temple; that God would establish David's dynastic line forever; that God would establish a father–son relationship with David's descendants; and that God's lovingkindness would not depart from David's line.

7. From his sin with Bathsheba, David learned that all sin has consequences, but that God's grace is sufficient to cover all sin when the sinner calls on God in genuine repentance.

8. Three major events that aided the growing discontent with David's kingdom: Amnon's rape of Tamar, Absalom's rebellion, and Sheba's rebellion.

Study Questions

1. Identify the major themes of 2 Samuel. How is 2 Samuel different from 1 Samuel?

2. Describe the events that led to David's ultimate victory over Saul's house.

3. Why was the conquest of Jerusalem such a significant victory for David?

4. Describe God's special covenant with David.

5. How did David's sin with Bathsheba lead to serious consequences in his life and reign?

Further Reading

Baldwin, Joyce. *1 and 2 Samuel: An Introduction and Commentary.* Tyndale Old Testament Commentary. Downers Grove/Leicester: InterVarsity, 1988. Good college-level commentary.

Merrill, Eugene H. *Kingdom of Priests: A History of Old Testament Israel.* Grand Rapids: Baker, 1987.

Seminary-level history of Israel that combines good scholarship and readability.

Wood, Leon J. *Israel's United Monarchy.* Grand Rapids: Baker, 1979. A thorough survey of the period of Saul, David, and Solomon. Contains much spiritual application.

placed David on Israel's throne. David's heart was right before God, and God made a special covenant with David. David sinned greatly, but confessed it when he realized it and sought to make restitution. Deep down inside, David always wanted to make things right.

David received God's forgiveness, but his sin had terrible consequences. He saw the lives of three of his children ruined, and later, as he lay dying (1 Kgs 1), two more sons contended for his throne. David's story warns us to resist sin or live to regret it. God's power can give us victory over temptation (1 Cor 10:13) and help us live as God desires (Phil 2:13).

15 First Kings
The Glory of Solomon and the Beginning of the End

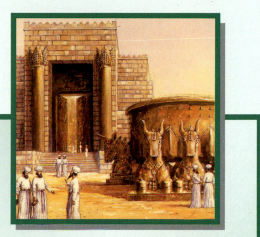

Objectives

After reading this chapter, you should be able to

- Discuss the question of the authorship of Kings
- Analyze the methods used by the author of 1 Kings
- Apply the regnal content to 1 Kings
- Outline the content of 1 Kings
- List the Kings of the divided kingdom
- Trace how the office of prophet developed

The first Book of Kings continues the religious history begun in the Book of Joshua. First Kings tells of Solomon's great kingdom and the early history of the divided monarchy. Together with 2 Kings, this narrative surveys over four centuries of history, outlining the Israelite monarchy from Solomon to the end. It traces the failure of the Israelite nation to maintain her covenant with God. The Books of Kings tell the sad story of Israel's tragic destruction because of her refusal to be faithful to God.

The Author and His Method

Who wrote the Books of Kings? How and why did the author write them? We can only give partial answers to these questions. Ancient Jewish tradition identifies Jeremiah as the author of 1 and 2 Kings.[1] The books themselves provide no direct information about the author, and it is better to view the books as anonymous (see the discussion of the Deuteronomistic History in chapter 10).

The books contain mostly **historical narrative**. It may be argued that this is the earliest genuine historiography in world literature. For the first time in human history, a nation produced a continuous narrative organizing documents in an orderly presentation with a single overarching purpose.[2]

However, these books are much more than history. The author tied the historical narratives together with grand religious convictions. He presented Israel's past from a prophetic and theological point of view. The author rehearsed the list of Israel's kings carefully and systematically, with the goal of critiquing each one's faithfulness to God's covenant. The books trace the consequences of sin as opposed to the benefits of obedience. This leads us to consider further the questions of why and how the author wrote these books.

Retribution Theology

As with the other books of the **Deuteronomistic History** (see chapter 10), the overriding concern in the Books of Kings is the **theology of retribution** based on the Sinai covenant, especially as expressed in Deuteronomy. Moses' final discourse in Deuteronomy listed the blessings and curses of the covenant (chapter 28). The author of these books is convinced of the truth of this teaching. Obedience to God's commands brings blessing while disobedience brings failure. For the author(s) of Kings, history is the foundation on which this theology is proved.

The author evaluates each king based on the monarch's loyalty to the God of Israel as worshiped in Jerusalem.[3] He wrote a history of Israel's monarchy in order to illustrate the two paths in life between which all of us must choose. The one pursues God in heart as well as in religious forms, and so pleases him. The other fails to obey God because of a lack of devotion and is ultimately self-destructive.

Regnal Formula and Sources

This overriding religious motivation answers the question, "Why did the author write the Books of Kings?" But it also helps answer the question, "How did the author compose these books?" Each king is discussed in turn by means of a set introduction and conclusion formula. This formula contains an evaluation of each king, based on his faithfulness to the covenant and his willingness to walk in the ways of King David, the ideal Israelite king. Many of the kings who failed to maintain the covenant with the Lord were compared to Jeroboam I of Israel, who epitomized rebellion and disregard for God (15:33–34; 16:25–26).

The author's primary concern is covenant faithfulness and loyalty to God, not political prowess. This means he gives little attention to the important political achievements of Omri, Jeroboam II, and Uzziah. On the other hand, he is intensely interested in the religious apostasy of Jeroboam I, Ahab, Ahaz, and Manasseh and in the religious reforms of Jehu, Hezekiah, and Josiah. The author has little to say about Omri's important reign in Israel. He devotes long narratives to Omri's son Ahab, who was less significant politically. But the ideological conflict between the Hebrew faith and **Canaanite Baalism** took place during Ahab's reign (16:29–33).

After the death of Solomon in chapter

Steps at the north gate, Megiddo. Archaeologists have excavated walls and gateways at Megiddo, Hazor, and Gezer dating from the time of Solomon.

royal annals

archives

chronicles

Example of the Regnal Formula for 1 and 2 Kings

1. Introductory sentences

a) Synchronistic statement

"In the eighteenth year of the reign of Jeroboam son of Nebat, Abijah became king of Judah." (1 Kgs 15:1)

b) Age and/or length of reign

"He [Abijah] reigned in Jerusalem three years." (1 Kgs 15:2a)

c) Matriarchal reference

"His mother's name was Maacah daughter of Abishalom." (1 Kgs 15:2b)

2. Evaluation sentence

"He committed all the sins his father had done before him; his heart was not fully devoted to the Lord his God, as the heart of David his forefather had been." (1 Kgs 15:3).

3. Chronicles reference

"As for the other events of Abijah's reign, and all he did, are they not written in the book of the annals of the kings of Judah?" (1 Kgs 15:7)

4. Death, burial, and successor accounts

"And Abijah rested with his fathers and was buried in the City of David. And Asa his son succeeded him as king." (1 Kgs 15:8)

11, the author presents the rulers of Israel and Judah in review. He dates each king by synchronizing that king's accession year with the reign of the monarch in the other kingdom. The author alternates kings of Israel and Judah, though not necessarily in chronological order, resulting in a few unusual historical sequences. For example, he discusses Baasha's border wars with Asa before formally introducing Baasha (15:16–33).

The author used three primary sources. The "book of the annals of Solomon" (11:41) appears to have contained **royal annals** typical of other kingdoms of the ancient Near East. The "book of the annals of the kings of Israel" (14:19; 15:31, etc.) and the "book of the annals of the kings of Judah" (14:29; 15:7, etc.) presumably listed each king's political activities and were official state records preserved in the royal **archives**. By comparison with numerous such documents found in royal or temple archives of ancient Near Eastern nations, these would have included king lists, annals and **chronicles**, royal inscriptions, **historical epics**, and biographical data.[4]

Comparison with other ancient Near Eastern royal archives shows that the author of Kings used contemporary sources similar to those royal inscriptions, especially the neighboring Aramean states in Syria.[5] The author of Kings appears to have had before him official royal documents from the archives of ancient Israel and Judah. The fact that these original Hebrew royal inscriptions have not yet been discovered is an accident of modern archaeology.

Historical Perspective from the Exile

The author of these books witnessed the fall of the southern kingdom and the failure of the Israelite nation to maintain its unique relationship to God. The Books of Kings were completed after 561 B.C., since this is the date of the last recorded event (2 Kgs 25:27–30). The author makes no reference to Cyrus the Persian and his liberating edict of 539, which officially brought the exile to an end (2 Chr 36:22–23). We assume the work was completed sometime during these last twenty-two years of the Babylonian exile.

From his perspective in the exile, the author was able to review the kings of both Israel and Judah. From the point of view of human history, it was a period of world empires. After Solomon's impressive kingdom, the Assyrians and Babylonians imposed their might on the ancient world. Israel increased and became strong again only when these greater Mesopotamian powers were in temporary periods of decline.

This is one possible explanation. Those same events were interpreted by the author of Kings during the exile from a different perspective, a God-given perspective. He looked back over the history of the Israelite monarchy and explained the events theologically. The world empires had been instruments in God's hands to punish his people. The Assyrians and Babylonians were able to do only what they were permitted to in God's timing, and indeed, at his bidding. The author traced the political and military failures of the Israelite kings to a lack of covenant loyalty.

Contents of 1 Kings

The narrative running through 1 and 2 Kings has three parts. The first unit covers King Solomon (1 Kings 1–11). These chapters describe his dramatic rise to power (chapters 1–2), his great accomplishments (chapters 3–10), and his tragic end (chapter 11). The second unit treats the history of the divided kingdom, and reveals the relationship of Israel and Judah to each other (1 Kgs 12–2 Kgs 17). Sometimes the relationship was peaceful, sometimes it was not. The third and final unit (2 Kgs 18–25) narrates the final years of the kingdom of Judah in the south after the northern kingdom fell to the Assyrians in 722.

Outline

I. **The United Kingdom under Solomon** (1:1–11:43)
   A. Beginning of Solomon's Reign (1:1–2:46)
   B. Glory of Solomon's Reign (3:1–10:29)
   C. Tragic End of Solomon's Reign (11:1–43)

II. **The Divided Kingdom** (12:1–22:53)
   A. Enmity between Israel and Judah (12:1–16:28)
   B. Peace and Friendship between Israel and Judah (16:29–22:53)

Overview

The glory of Solomon (chapters 1–11)

These chapters describe the height of Israel's political and military power. Only during Solomon's reign did Israel become a major player in the arena of international power politics. But Israel's brief period of strength and prestige was ruined by Solomon's religious apostasy. Solomon's unfaithfulness to the covenant erased all the great accomplishments of his reign. Shortly after his death, Israel's period of glory was over. Though it was the nation's greatest moment politically, it was remembered in the Bible as one of its most tragic. This is a story of missed opportunities.

The Dome of the Rock is built over the site where Solomon erected the temple. One of the grand moments of Israel's history was the dedication of Solomon's temple.

theophany

Solomon was neither the crown prince nor David's oldest living son. He had no legitimate claim to be David's successor. So the narrative begins by relating how Solomon became king (chapters 1–2). Adonijah, David's fourth and oldest living son, was in line to succeed his father on the throne. But like Amnon and Absalom, other sons of David who were apparent heirs to the throne, Adonijah was unwilling to wait for God's timing. He attempted to take the kingdom in his own strength and against God's will.

The next unit of 1 Kings describes the magnificent reign of King Solomon (chapters 3–11). With the exception of chapter 11, this unit recounts the glorious side of Solomon's kingdom. The unit is marked by his great building activities and two appearances of God to Solomon. The early stages of his reign were marked by love and obedience: "Solomon showed his love for the LORD by walking according to the statutes of his father David, except that he offered sacrifices and burned incense on the high places" (3:3). This single flaw could be rectified when he built the new temple in Jerusalem.

The Bible states clearly why Solomon's reign was so glorious. Israel flourished during his kingdom, not because of Solomon's ingenuity or gifts, but because of his God-given wisdom. The first appearance of God (or **theophany**) to Solomon was at GIBEON (chapter 3). God promised to grant Solomon whatever he requested (v. 5). Rather than asking for riches, long life, or victory over his enemies, Solomon asked for wisdom. God was so pleased with this request that he granted riches, long life, and victory in addition to wisdom (vv. 12–13). All of these blessings, however, were conditioned on continued obedience (v. 14). This last reminder was an ominous warning.

As soon as Solomon returned to Jerusalem, two prostitutes in legal dispute presented him with an opportunity to demonstrate his wisdom (vv. 16–28). The women lived in the same house and each had newborn sons, three days apart in age. During the night, one baby tragically died. The mother of the dead baby switched the babies before the other woman woke. Now they both claimed the living child was theirs, and there was no one to refute these claims. In a famous decision, Solomon gave the order to cut the living baby in two and give half to each woman. While the real mother pleaded to let the child live, the lying woman said to let the child die. Then Solomon proclaimed that the child should not be killed, but given to the real mother, now known clearly by her desperate plea. News of the verdict and Solomon's God-given wisdom quickly confirmed that Solomon was indeed God's chosen king for Israel (v. 28).

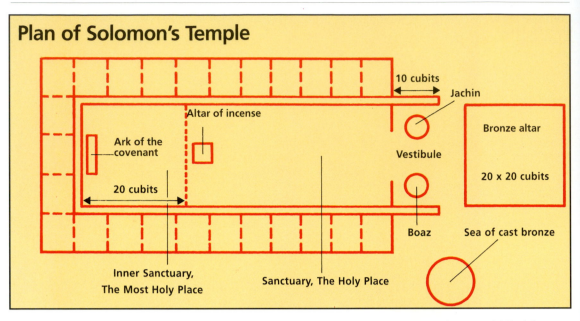

Plan of Solomon's Temple

10 cubits

Jachin

Altar of incense

Bronze altar

Ark of the covenant

Vestibule

20 x 20 cubits

20 cubits

Boaz

Sea of cast bronze

Inner Sanctuary, The Most Holy Place

Sanctuary, The Holy Place

Solomon's administrative skills reflected his great wisdom (chapter 4). The organization of his cabinet (vv. 1–6), his regional districts (vv. 7–19), and the extent of his royal rations (vv. 20–28) illustrate the splendor of his kingdom. This was one of the few times in Israel's history when all the territory promised to Abraham in the patriarchal covenant was actually under her control (v. 21; and see Gn 15:18). The combination of peace and plenty provided by Solomon for each Israelite (v. 25) became a symbol of the messianic age (Zec 3:10). Solomon's wisdom was unsurpassed (4:29–34). Just as the law came from Moses and the psalms from David, wisdom was Solomon's contribution to Israelite religion.

Solomon's extensive building activities also demonstrated his God-given wisdom (5:1–8:66). His diplomacy with Hiram king of Tyre (chapter 5) provided the necessary artisans and material for the ambitious building plans. The prosperity and peace of Solomon's kingdom made possible the construction of the temple of the Lord, the royal palace, and the temple furnishings (chapters 6–7). Though the biblical text gives many of the temple's specifications and dimensions, it is impossible for modern reconstructions to represent its exact appearance.[6]

One of the grand moments of Israel's history was the dedication of Solomon's temple (chapter 8). During the moving cer-emony, the glory of the Lord filled the new temple. God honored Solomon's obedience by bestowing his holy presence (8:10–11), just as he honored Moses' faithfulness when Moses constructed the tabernacle (Ex 40:34). In one of the great prayers of the Bible, Solomon represented the nation in his praise of God (8:23–24) and entreated God to fulfill his promises to David (vv. 25–26).

In a second theophany similar to the one at Gibeon, God appeared to Solomon and assured him he had answered the king's prayer (9:2). He consecrated ("made holy," *hiqdāš*) Solomon's temple and placed his name there forever (9:3). But God's promises did not guarantee the success of a rebellious Israel ("If you walk before me in integrity of heart . . . I will establish your royal throne," 9:4–5). His sovereign promises never abrogate human accountability.

The spectacular accomplishments of Solomon drew international attention. The queen of Sheba's visit was apparently a trade mission (10:10, 13). But the account in chapter 10 also demonstrates Solomon's wisdom and wealth as they were viewed by surrounding nations. God's promises to Solomon while he was at Gibeon (3:13) had been fulfilled (10:23). But the Bible is clear that material blessings, even spiritual blessings, are no guarantee of God's abiding favor. God requires covenant faithfulness of all his children. Chapter 11 concludes the narrative on Solomon by relat-

An artist's impression of Solomon's temple, with the great golden laver in the foreground.

monotheism

ing his personal moral failure. Though God gave him every reason to succeed and blessed him with every imaginable blessing, Solomon's personal sin eventually led to the division of his great empire into two weaker kingdoms.

Early in Solomon's reign, he entered a political alliance with Egypt, which involved a royal wedding to the daughter of Pharaoh (3:1). This hinted at future trouble. Large royal harems were not uncommon in those days. Solomon's numerous political marriages seemed an innocent way to strengthen foreign alliances (11:3). But God had specifically forbidden such intermarriages (11:2; Dt 7:4; 17:17). Now, in Solomon's old age, the religious apostasy his foreign wives brought into the royal court adversely af-

fected his faith. He slowly and gradually drifted from an exclusive **monotheism** and began incorporating the worship of other gods (11:4). Religious compromise is almost never swift and obvious, but happens gradually as one drifts slowly away from God.

Solomon's personal moral failure resulted in national tragedy. God would not permit the kingdom to remain a unified whole after Solomon's death, but would give only a small portion to Solomon's son (11:9–13). Because Solomon failed to maintain the covenant, God raised up adversaries to afflict him in the south (Hadad the Edomite, vv. 14–22), the north (Rezon of Damascus, vv. 23–25) and internally (Jeroboam the Ephraimite, vv. 26–40). Early in his reign, Solomon had been free

regnal formula

Yahwism

of military threat. Now he had trouble within and without.

Chapter 11 is a pivotal point in the Books of Kings. All had gone well for Solomon, who seemed to have fulfilled the promises to the patriarchs and accomplished all that God wanted for his people. But from this point on, the narrative of 1 and 2 Kings is a tragic tale of destruction and loss. The tragedy of Solomon's life is that he failed to remain faithful to God in spite of God's obvious provisions for his kingdom. Instead of Solomon, David is the Bible's ideal king of Israel, though he never attained the political heights reached by his son. God's word is more interested in faithfulness to the covenant than in international prestige.

Divided kingdom begun (chapters 12–22)

The second main unit of 1 Kings continues through 2 Kings 17:41. This section begins by narrating the division of Solomon's empire into two smaller kingdoms, Israel in the north and Judah in the south. At first there were hostile relations between the two (1 Kgs 12:1–16:28). This was followed by a period of peace between the two nations (1 Kgs 16:29–2 Kgs 8:29). Renewed hostilities dominated the relationship prior to the fall of the northern kingdom (2 Kgs 9–17).

The author concluded the account of Solomon's life and reign with the **regnal formula** (1 Kgs 11:41–43). Beginning with this unit, the author considered each ruler of the divided kingdom, using the regnal formula as a structuring device.

The early divided kingdom is a story of conflict between Jeroboam in the north and Rehoboam in the south (chapters 12–14). The narrative relates the political intrigue and treachery involved (chapter 12). But, as we have seen, the author is more interested in tracing the consequences of religious unfaithfulness and the role of the prophets. In Jeroboam's attempt to consolidate his new northern kingdom, he introduced religious innovations that threatened the nature of genuine **Yahwism** (12:25–33). His golden calves at Bethel and Dan may have been perceived as pedestals upon which the invisible Yahweh rode in victory. But this was still forbidden by God and came perilously close to blatant idolatry as practiced by the surrounding nations.

The author describes two prophets sent from God to renounce Jeroboam's religious apostasy. The first is an unnamed "man of God" from Judah sent by the Lord to condemn Jeroboam (13:1).[7] The king's new religious practices in the north were nothing short of rejection of the Lord's word (13:4–10). The second prophetic pronouncement was made by a prophet named Ahijah (14:1–18). The prophet announced that Jeroboam had done more evil than all who preceded him and that he had rejected God himself (v. 9). Future generations would measure evil by comparison with Jeroboam's great sin. Ahijah predicted that Jeroboam's dynasty would be short-lived, among many other horrible consequences of the king's sin (vv. 10–11).

In the next unit, the author summarizes the histories of individual reigns of Israel and Judah (14:21–16:28). In the evaluation of Rehoboam's reign, the author's concern is that Judah's sins have become more widespread than at the time of Solomon (14:22–24). As in Genesis 3–11, the author is aware that unchecked sin pervades and decays like a disease.

The consistent theme of this unit is the enmity and war between Israel and Judah during this time. Abijah of Judah and Jeroboam of Israel continued in warfare (15:7), as did Asa of Judah and Baasha of Israel (15:16). Asa and Baasha were involved in a border dispute involving districts in Benjamin (15:17–22). Under Baasha, Israel pressed south and claimed Ramah, which was only five miles north of Jerusalem. Baasha fortified Ramah because of its strategic location on a main north–south highway. From this vantage point, Baasha could safeguard the new border and prohibit northern Israelites from worshiping in Jerusalem.

Asa responded by enticing Ben-Hadad, king of Damascus, to invade Israel from the northeast, which would relieve military pressure on Jerusalem in the south. When Baasha withdrew to plan his defense against Ben-Hadad, Asa tore down the Israelite fortifications in Ramah and used the materials to fortify Geba and Mizpah closer to the northern border of Benjamin. There were no significant changes

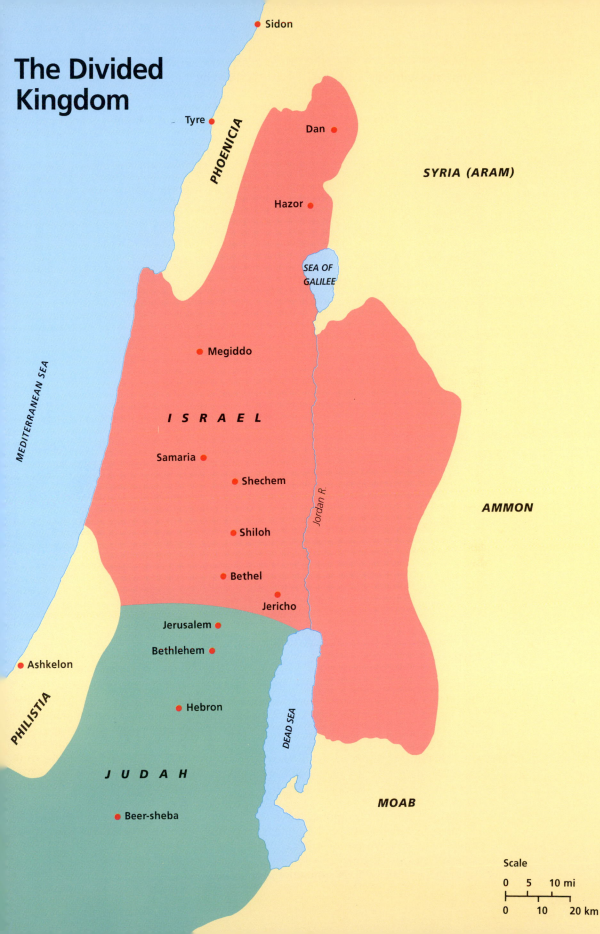

The Divided Kingdom

Sidon

Tyre

PHOENICIA

Dan

SYRIA (ARAM)

Hazor

SEA OF GALILEE

Megiddo

I S R A E L

Samaria

Shechem

Jordan R.

AMMON

Shiloh

Bethel

Jericho

MEDITERRANEAN SEA

Jerusalem

Bethlehem

Ashkelon

DEAD SEA

PHILISTIA

Hebron

J U D A H

MOAB

Beer-sheba

Scale

0   5   10 mi

0   10   20 km

Kings of the Divided Monarchy[1]

Israel		Judah	
Jeroboam I	930–909	Rehoboam	930–913
Nadab	909–908	Abijah	913–910
Baasha	908–886	Asa	910–869
Elah	886–885		
Zimri	885		
Omri	885–874		
Ahab	874–853	Jehoshaphat	872–848
Ahaziah	853–852		
Joram	852–841	Jehoram	848–841
Jehu	841–814	Ahaziah	841
		Athaliah	841–835
Jehoahaz	814–798	Joash	835–796
Jehoash	798–782	Amaziah	796–767
Jeroboam II	793–753	Uzziah	792–740
Zechariah	753		
Shallum	752		
Menahem	752–742	Jotham	750–732
Pekahiah	742–740		
Pekah	752–732	Ahaz	735–715
Hoshea	732–722	Hezekiah	729–686
		Manasseh	696–642
		Amon	642–640
		Josiah	640–60
		Jehoahaz	609
		Jehoiakim	608–598
		Jehoiachin	598–597
		Zedekiah	597–587

[1]Edwin R. Thiele, *The Mysterious Numbers of the Hebrew Kings: A Reconstruction of the Chronology of the Kingdoms of Israel and Judah,* rev ed. (Grand Rapids: Eerdmans, 1965), and Eugene H. Merrill, *Kingdom of Priests: A History of Old Testament Israel* (Grand Rapids: Baker, 1987), 320. Dates in other sources will vary widely depending on the chronological system used in those sources. For convenient summary of this complex issue, see Donald J. Wiseman, *1 and 2 Kings: An Introduction and Commentary,* (Tyndale Old Testament Commentary; Downers Grove: InterVarsity Press, 1993), 26–35.

in this border until the northern kingdom fell in 722 B.C.

This unit on the histories of individual rulers culminates in the brief treatment of Omri (16:21–28). Omri of Israel (885–874 B.C.) forged such an impressive kingdom that Assyrian documents from a century later still referred to northern Israel as "the house of Omri" (*bît ḥumrî*). He extended Israel's borders eastward into Moabite territory, as the famous **Mesha Inscription** testifies.

Though Omri was a significant political force, this terse paragraph mentions only his unusual rise to power, his acquisition of Samaria as a new capital city, and his unprecedented evil. His move of the

capital to Samaria may have been to coerce his subjects to worship other deities in addition to Yahweh.[8] This religious apostasy was of more concern to the author of 1 Kings than his significant political accomplishments. Omri's alliance with the king of Sidon resulted in the marriage of Omri's son Ahab to the princess of Sidon, Jezebel. This marriage was not unlike Solomon's many marriages, both in its motivation as a political move and in its spiritual consequences.

The final unit of 1 Kings describes a period of peace and friendship between Israel and Judah (16:29–22:53). This unit demonstrates further that the author is less concerned with political prowess (such as

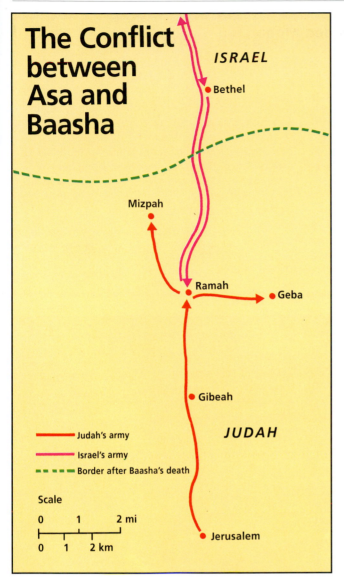

The Conflict between Asa and Baasha

ISRAEL

Bethel

Mizpah

Ramah · Geba

Gibeah

JUDAH

Jerusalem

— Judah's army
— Israel's army
- - - Border after Baasha's death

Scale

0   1   2 mi

0   1   2 km

the **office of prophecy** began to emerge based on the ministries of Elijah and Elisha. Prophets became God's instruments of warning to the king and the nation. Doom was imminent because of their sin. The author included narratives on Elijah's ministry (chapters 17-19, 21 and 2 Kgs 1) interwoven with the account of Ahab's wars with Damascus.

Elijah appears on the scene with no introduction (17:1). He reminded Ahab that Yahweh, not Baal, is God of Israel. His announcement that dew and rain would cease was a direct challenge to Baal, the Canaanite god of storm and rain—a challenge issued by Yahweh, the God of the desert!

At the end of a drought lasting three years and six months (18:1; Lk 4:25), Elijah issued a challenge to the hundreds of Baal prophets and the nation (18:19). They would all meet at Mount Carmel and determine once and for all who is the God of heaven. Mount Carmel was believed to be sacred to Baal, so Elijah challenged Baal on his own turf.[9] Because of the severe drought, Elijah was in control and able to force Ahab and the nation to make a choice. He soundly condemned their double-minded religion: "How long will you waver between two opinions? If the LORD is God, follow him; but if Baal is God, follow him" (18:21). Devotion to God requires single-hearted commitment to his truth. Any compromise is wavering "between two opinions."

The pagan prophets used all their magical arts to entice Baal to rain down fire from heaven, all to no avail. Then Elijah prayed a simple prayer, and the fire of the Lord fell (18:36–38). The Lord won a great battle through Elijah that day, but the war was far from over. Queen Jezebel threatened Elijah's life (19:2). After the jubilant victory at Mount Carmel, Elijah was not prepared physically or emotionally to continue the conflict. It was easier to run away and ask God to use some other servant to continue the battle against Baalism (19:3–4).

Self-doubt, depression, even suicidal thoughts are possible after mountaintop experiences. But God gave Elijah just what he needed: rest and food (19:5–8) and a fresh vision of God's divine majesty tailored especially for Elijah's emotional stress (19:9–18). It is not outside of God's

office of prophecy

Omri) than with covenant breaking. The author interrupted the regnal formula used to introduce and conclude the reign of Ahab (16:29–34 and 22:39–40). Using the formula as a sort of literary envelope, the author incorporated events having to do with the crucial struggle between genuine Yahwism and Canaanite Baalism. It was one thing for Jeroboam to make idols for the worship of Yahweh. But Omri and Ahab tried to forge a new religion that struck at the very heart of Hebrew faith (16:31–33). The struggle described in these chapters was over the future of Israel. Her very existence was threatened by religious compromise.

Out of this great ideological struggle,

Excerpts from the Mesha Inscription[1]

In the mid-ninth century B.C., Mesha, king of Moab, commemorated the accomplishments of his reign in a document containing thirty lines of text. The text was written in the Moabite language on a basalt block three feet high and two feet wide.

I am Mesha, king of Moab. The god Chemosh saved me from all the kings and caused me to triumph over all my adversaries. As for Omri, king of Israel, he subdued Moab many years, because Chemosh was angry at his land. And his son followed him and he also said, "I will subdue Moab." But I have triumphed over him and over his house, while Israel has perished forever! Omri occupied Medeba in Moab and dwelled there in his time and half the time of his son, forty years; but Chemosh dwelt there in my time.

[1]Extracted and adapted from the Mesha Inscription (*ANET*, 320–21).

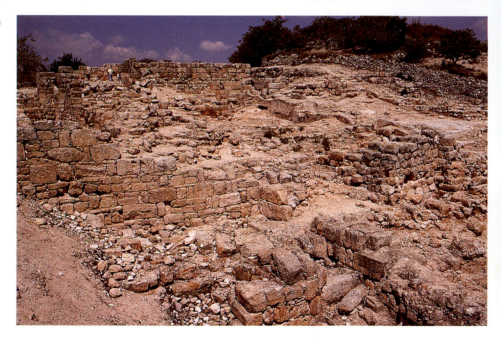

Israelite remains at Samaria, the city chosen by Omri as his capital for strategic reasons. Ahab too had his palace here.

character to appear in a strong wind, earthquake, or fire (19:11–12). But on this day, Yahweh appeared to Elijah in "a gentle whisper." After his retreat alone with God, Elijah was ready to return to the battle and anoint his successor, Elisha. God is quick to pursue his servants lovingly through whatever means necessary.

The two battles between Ahab and Ben-Hadad II of Damascus (son of the Ben-Hadad of 15:18) provided Ahab with a final opportunity to heed the words of Yahweh through the prophet (20:1–43).

Though there was a measure of success, Ahab failed to embrace the prophetic word of the Lord (20:42–43). These episodes prepare for Ahab's death recorded in the final chapter of the book.

The famous episode of Naboth's vineyard (chapter 21) illustrates the extent of Ahab's sin and seals his fate. Naboth was a citizen whose property was adjacent to the royal palace in Samaria. The king wanted to annex Naboth's vineyard to the royal holdings, but ancient Israelite law prohibited the sale of one's inheritance.

Summary

1. In the Books of Kings, we find the earliest genuine historiography in world literature.

2. The theology of retribution is the main topic of the Book of 1 Kings.

3. The method used to write the Book of 1 Kings is regnal formula, in which every king is evaluated in terms of his faithfulness to the covenant and his willingness to follow the example of King David.

4. The sources used by the author to write 1 Kings are all annals from the royal archives—annals of the kings of Israel, annals of the kings of Judah, and annals of Solomon.

5. The major topics used to organize Kings are: the history of King Solomon, the history of the divided kingdom, and the history of the final years of Judah.

6. The great political and military accomplishments of Solomon are overshadowed by his unfaithfulness to the covenant.

7. When God first appeared to Solomon, Solomon requested wisdom, and that pleased God because Solomon did not request riches or a long life or victory over enemies.

8. Solomon's great wisdom is illustrative of how he solved legal disputes, how he administered the nation, and how his building program was conducted.

9. Through the influence of his foreign wives, Solomon compromised and added the worship of other gods to monotheism.

10. Solomon's empire was divided into two smaller kingdoms—Israel in the north and Judah in the south.

11. Prophets were introduced in 1 Kings when Elijah became God's spokesman to warn the nations.

Study Questions

1. How much time is covered by 1–2 Kings?

2. What is the overall theme of this work?

3. Discuss the authorship of Kings.

4. What is the overarching concern of this historical work?

5. Define retribution theology.

6. What is the regnal formula?

7. From what historical perspective does the author of Kings write?

8. From a biblical standpoint, why is the reign of Solomon seen as a tragic event?

9. What important biblical office began to emerge during the time of 1 Kings?

10. Contrast and compare the office of the professional prophets with those of the true prophets. How do these forms of prophecy relate to 1 Kings?

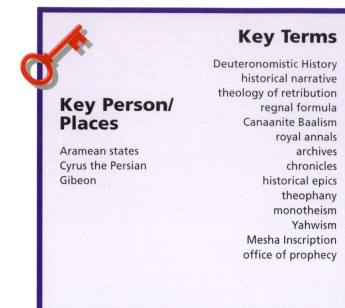

Key Terms

Deuteronomistic History
historical narrative
theology of retribution
regnal formula
Canaanite Baalism
royal annals
archives
chronicles
historical epics
theophany
monotheism
Yahwism
Mesha Inscription
office of prophecy

Key Person/Places

Aramean states
Cyrus the Persian
Gibeon

in other countries. She took matters into her own hands. Through treachery, deceit, and the murder of Naboth, she acquired the vineyard for Ahab. But once again, the prophet Elijah was there to announce judgment (vv. 17–24). Ahab had "sold himself to do evil in the eyes of the LORD" (v. 25; and see v. 20). As a result, Elijah proclaimed that Ahab and Jezebel would die violent deaths and that Ahab's dynasty would be completely destroyed.

But even an Ahab can repent! His genuine remorse postponed the fulfillment of Elijah's prophecy until the days of his wicked son Joram (2 Kgs 9:22–26, 30–37).

Chapter 22 relates Ahab's final battle with Damascus, a battle in which Ahab lost his life. Jehoshaphat of Judah was paying Ahab a visit, illustrating the congenial relationship between Israel and Judah at this time (vv. 2–4). In preparation for battle, Ahab and Jehoshaphat consulted the professional prophets to discern the outcome.

The idea seemed appalling to Naboth (v. 3). Ahab had enough respect for the law to know he was unable to reverse Naboth's decision (v. 4).

Jezebel, being the daughter of the king of Sidon, assumed the Israelite king should be above the law, an absolute monarch as

The point of the narrative is the contrast between the professional prophets and Micaiah, son of Imlah. For Ahab, prophecy was a form of magic in which the prophet manipulated God. The professional prophets merely repeated the king's de-

Further Reading

DeVries, Simon J. *1 Kings.* Word Biblical Commentary 12. Waco, Tex.: Word, 1985.

Gray, John. *I & II Kings: A Commentary.* 2nd ed. Old Testament Library. Philadelphia: Westminster, 1970. Useful, though technical and difficult reading.

Howard, David M., Jr. *An Introduction to the Old Testament Historical Books.* Chapter 6: "1 & 2 Kings," 169–204, and chapter 7: "Historical and Cultural Context for 1 & 2 Kings," 205–29. Chicago: Moody, 1993.

Long, Burke O. *1 Kings: With an Introduction to Historical Literature.* Grand Rapids: Eerdmans, 1984.

Long, V. Philips. *The Art of Biblical History.* Grand Rapids: Zondervan, 1994. Important theological discussion of all the issues.

Walton, John H. *Ancient Israelite Literature in Its Cultural Context: A Survey of Parallels between Biblical and Ancient Near Eastern Texts.* Chapter 5: "Historical Literature," 111–34. Grand Rapids: Zondervan, 1989.

Wiseman, Donald J. *1 and 2 Kings: An Introduction and Commentary.* Tyndale Old Testament Commentary. Downers Grove/Leicester: InterVarsity, 1993. Best evangelical commentary available.

sire in the form of prophecy in an attempt to ensure the desired outcome. But for Jehoshaphat, the prophet was a mouthpiece for God. The word of the prophet made the will of God known to humans, regardless of the king's desires (v. 8). Ahab's death vindicated Micaiah, the true prophet of the Lord, and proved the professional prophets wrong.

16 Second Kings
The End of National Israel

Outline

- **Contents of 2 Kings**
  Outline
  Overview
- **Themes of the Books of Kings**

Objectives

After reading this chapter, you should be able to

- Outline the basic content of the Book of 2 Kings
- Compare the ministry of Elisha with that of Elijah
- Relate at least ten episodes of Elisha's life
- Present the author's purpose for writing 2 Kings
- List the key figures in Judah and Israel
- State the cause for the fall of Israel
- Differentiate between the good and bad kings of Judah
- Demonstrate how prophecy was fulfilled in 2 Kings

Second Kings describes the miserable end of the nations Israel and Judah. After the death of Solomon, 1 Kings describes the slow unraveling of the many wonderful accomplishments of the united monarchy reported earlier in that book. Second Kings continues the story of gradual decay, with only brief interludes of hope, until both nations have finally tasted the consequences of rebellion against their covenant God.

Contents of 2 Kings

Second Kings picks up the narrative at Ahab's death and carries it through the destruction of Jerusalem and slightly beyond. This covers a period of nearly three hundred years. At the beginning of the book, both Israel and Judah are relatively secure. When it concludes, both have been subjected to divine discipline. Through it all runs the thread of growing religious apostasy, first in Israel and then in Judah. The author goes to great lengths to show how this apostasy led directly to destruction.

Outline

Overview

The book chronicles the history of first a divided Israel and Judah, and then a solitary Judah. The first 17 chapters are given to the more than 100 years from Ahaziah to the destruction of Israel in 722 B.C. (chapters 1–17). Then, eight chapters (18–25) cover the 136 years of Judah's sole existence.

As with 1 Kings, the accounts do not attempt to give a comprehensive record of all events during the years covered. Rather, they provide a theological analysis of those particular persons or events that had an effect on the eventual outcome of the nations. The basis for that analysis is obedience or disobedience to God's law (17:13–23; 21:10–16), especially as seen in Deuteronomy.

Divided kingdom continued (chapters 1–17)

In the first main unit (1:1–17:41), the author gives an account of the uneasy coexistence of Israel and Judah. This unit begins in 1 Kings 12:1 and continues until the fall of the northern kingdom (2 Kgs 17:41).

Ahaziah was guilty of continuing both the Canaanite fertility religion of Ahab and the idolatrous calf worship of Jeroboam I (1 Kgs 22:52). His reign was cut short by an injury received in a fall (2 Kgs 1). Fearful that the injury might be fatal, he sent messengers to PHILISTIA to ask BAAL-ZEBUB about his health. This deity was a form of Baal worshiped by the Philistines at Ekron.

The messenger of God intercepted the messengers of the king. Elijah asked, "Is it because there is no God in Israel that you are going off to consult Baal-Zebub, the god of Ekron?" (1:3). Elijah's message warned the king that the God of the universe, the only true God, was also the God of Ahaziah.

When Ahaziah attempted to capture Elijah, God's intervention killed one hundred men and two captains. Some may question the morality of this event, but it was wrong for Ahaziah to attempt to control God's prophet. Today's readers should not impose arbitrary modern standards on this episode, which illustrates that rebellion against God results in judgment.[1] Once Elijah was assured of his safety, he went to Ahaziah and announced that, in fact,

A stretch of the Jordan River near Galilee. Elijah parted the waters of the Jordan (2:8) as Moses had parted the sea.

the injury would be fatal, according to the word of Yahweh. Ahaziah had rejected the only One who could restore him to health.

Chapter 2 is a transitional passage. It closes the narrative on Elijah, and opens the author's presentation of the Elisha materials. Elijah is one of two Old Testament characters (see also Enoch, Gn 5:22–24) who ascended into heaven without experiencing physical death. For this reason, they were viewed as especially dear to God. This is also an Old Testament foreshadowing of the idea that being out of the body is to be with the Lord (Phil 1:21–24).

This passage portrays Elijah as a second Moses. When Elijah parted the waters of the Jordan River (2:8) as Moses had parted the sea, he initiated a new stage in Israel's history. Elijah marks the beginning of a new role for prophets in ancient Israel. The cloak he used to strike the water represented his power and personality.

Before Elijah's ascension into heaven, he granted his assistant Elisha one request (2:9). Elisha's desire for a "double portion" of Elijah's spirit refers to Old Testament inheritance laws in which the firstborn son received two shares of the estate (Dt 21:17). Elisha was asking to become Elijah's successor. After Elijah was gone, Elisha used

his predecessor's cloak to divide the Jordan River in the same way Elijah had done. Elisha had become Elijah's Joshua, continuing the work begun by the second Moses (2:13–14).

As 1 Kings ended with the ministry of Elijah, 2 Kings contains an early unit devoted to the ministry of his successor, Elisha. Chapters 2–8 contain groups of stories dealing with the prophet Elisha interwoven with the events of Jehoram, son of Ahab, king of Israel. Earlier, Elijah's ministry dealt chiefly with the king and had major political and national overtones. While Elisha's ministry also had a national scale, the events of these narratives cover a wider area of topics, affecting nation, religious groups, and individuals alike. Episodes from the life of Elisha include the following:[2]

- Elisha receives a call, 1 Kings 19:19–21
- Elisha succeeds Elijah, 2 Kings 2:1–18
- Elisha heals the water, 2 Kings 2:19–22
- Elisha judges his mockers, 2 Kings 2:23–25
- Elisha prophesies concerning Moab, 2 Kings 3:1–27
- Elisha performs a miracle for a poor widow, 2 Kings 4:1–7

- Elisha performs a miracle for the Shunammite woman, 2 Kings 4:8–37
- Elisha ministers at Gilgal, 2 Kings 4:38–44
- Elisha heals Naaman, 2 Kings 5:1–27
- Elisha makes an axhead float, 2 Kings 6:1–7
- Elisha plagues the Syrian army, 2 Kings 6:8–23
- Elisha delivers the nation, 2 Kings 6:24–7:20
- Elisha preserves the Shunammite woman's family, 2 Kings 8:1–6
- Elisha deals with affairs of state, 2 Kings 8:7–15; 9:1–13; 13:14–19
- Elisha dies and a postmortem miracle occurs, 2 Kings 13:20–21

Elisha's ministry was instrumental in the destruction of the dynasty of Omri, the father of Ahab, in Israel (9:1–10:28) and of Queen Athaliah, Ahab's daughter, in Judah (11:1–20). The events relating to Elisha receive a disproportionate amount of attention (about two-fifths of the whole book), especially since Elisha is not a king in a book devoted to the history of Israelite kings. The amount of Elisha materials is due to the author's purpose. He wanted to write not a survey of the events, but an explanation for the destruction of both kingdoms. In the Books of Kings, the greatest single cause for the failure of Israel was the policies of their kings and their lack of obedience to the prophetic word. In 2 Kings, the author praises only Hezekiah and Josiah, because of their high regard for the word of God. All the other kings were neglectful at best, and evil at worst.

The extended section on Elisha, therefore, illustrates the author's main concerns. Because of the prophet's ministry, and even the minimal cooperation of Jehu, king of Israel, the ideological conflict with Canaanite Baalism begun with Ahab and Elijah was over. The ministries of Elijah and Elisha inspired a revolution against the dynasty of Omri and his policy of friendship with the Canaanite **city-states**, such as Tyre and Sidon. Ahab his son had continued that policy, which also incorporated the worst of Canaanite religion into the official national policy.

The point of the Elijah–Elisha narratives, then, is that the kingdom succeeded when it followed the leadership of the prophets.

Failure and destruction resulted when the kings rejected the word of God offered through the prophets. These narratives about Elijah and Elisha relate many victories for the prophets of Yahweh. But the tide of religious apostasy was not easily stemmed. Sadly, the book continues the tale of ruin for both kingdoms.

Jehu's bloody purge of the royal house of Omri was the judgment of God against Canaanite Baalism (chapters 9–10). Elisha commissioned an unnamed prophet to anoint Jehu, commander of the Israelite army, to destroy Ahab's house and to avenge the blood of Yahweh's prophets killed by Jezebel. Jehu successfully terminated Ahab's dynasty (prophesied by Elijah, 1 Kgs 21:21), but he was unable to recover militarily. Hazael of Syria captured much of his territory (10:32–33). Shalmaneser III of Assyria compelled him to pay tribute, and ironically called him "Jehu, son of Omri."[3]

King Jehoram of Judah had married Athaliah, daughter of Ahab of Israel, as a seal of the political alliance between north and south (2 Kgs 8:18). Jehoram's son, Ahaziah, had been swayed by the religious policies of Ahab's dynasty, probably because of the influence of his evil mother (8:26–27; cf. 2 Chr 22:3–5). As part of his purge of the house of Ahab in the north, Jehu also killed Ahaziah of Judah due to his commitments to the religious and political policies of Ahab (9:27).

When the wicked queen mother, Athaliah realized Jehu had killed her son, she attempted to exterminate the Davidic line in Jerusalem, in revenge for Jehu's slaughter of her family in the northern kingdom (chapter 11). She nearly succeeded. But one of the king's sons, one-year-old Joash (contraction of Jehoash), was hidden by his aunt in the temple of the Lord. For six years Athaliah ruled Judah while supporters of the Davidic dynasty kept Joash in hiding. In the seventh year, Jehoiada, the chief priest, orchestrated a revolt. He killed Athaliah, placed the seven-year-old Joash on the throne, and led the nation in a covenant renewal ceremony (11:4–21).

As long as young king Joash had the powerful Jehoiada to guide and advise him, he was faithful to the covenant (12:2). Joash even decided to repair the temple of

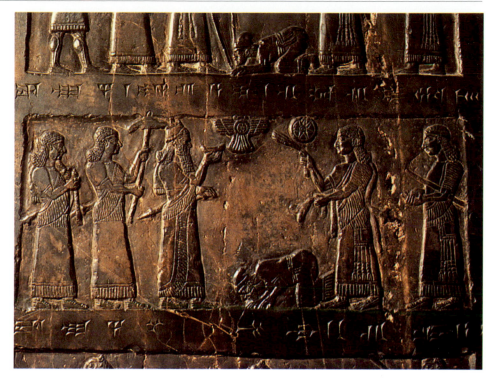

Jehu of Israel pays tribute to Shalmaneser III of Assyria; detail from the Black Obelisk.

the Lord because the people were still using the pagan shrines at the high places for worship, even after Baal worship had been purged from Jerusalem (12:3–5). Unfortunately, after Jehoiada's death, his godly influence over Joash was soon forgotten, and the nation fell into severe apostasy again (2 Chr 24:17–25).

With the rise of Jehu and his dynasty in the north (chapters 9–10), the time of peace between northern Israel and southern Judah had ended. The remaining chapters of this unit (chapters 13–17) alternate between kings of the two nations, culminating in the fall of the northern kingdom.

Chapter 13 summarizes the reigns of Jehu's immediate successors in the north: Jehoahaz and Jehoash. It also relates Elisha's final prophecy and death (vv. 14–20). In a test of Jehoash's faith, Elisha instructed the king to shoot an arrow eastward, toward Syria, and to strike the ground with the other arrows. Elisha prophesied that Israel would be successful over Syria, but not completely, because the king held back his zeal. Jehoash may have desired to maintain a weakened Syria as a buffer state against the rising power of Assyria. Elisha would have certainly opposed this policy. The use of bow and arrows was not sym-

pathetic magic, but a symbolic act like others in the Bible related to warfare (cf. Jos 8:18).

Chapter 14 continues the history with the reign of Amaziah of Judah. Though he was a relatively good king (v. 3), he provoked a war with Jehoash of Israel (vv. 8–14). Jehoash invaded Jerusalem, plundered the temple, and took many hostages.

Chapter 14 concludes with a brief summary of the reign of Jeroboam II of Israel (vv. 23–29). He was the fourth king in Jehu's dynasty and reigned an unprecedented forty years (793–753 B.C.). Because of Syria's weakness during this period and Assyria's preoccupation with other enemies to the north, Jeroboam enjoyed a long and prosperous rule. He restored Israel's borders to those of the days of David (14:25, 28).

However, prosperity and success do not always mean God is smiling on one's ethical and moral character. Jeroboam's Israel abused both power and wealth. The earliest writing prophets (Amos and Hosea) condemned the nation's oppression of the poor and the king's exploitation of royal privilege. Indeed, the growth of decadence and greed in the northern kingdom dur-

The Rise of Prophecy

Moses was the nation's premier prophet. He is called a prophet because of the directness with which the Lord spoke to him (Dt 34:10). He stands at the head of a great tradition, and the prophetic message is rooted in Mosaic revelation. Nevertheless, prophecy did not become a permanent element of Israelite society with Moses.

The role of prophecy changed with the rise of the monarchy. When the nation requested kings, Samuel became a guardian of the theocracy, to ensure that God was still the real King. The human monarch was merely his representative. Samuel defined the future role of the prophet as the messenger from God who held the king in check. From Samuel and Saul forward, many Israelite kings had their prophetic counterpart: David and Nathan, Ahab and Elijah, Hezekiah and Isaiah.

Elijah played a significant role in the development of Israelite prophecy because of his attack on Israel's apostasy. He gave definition to the future prophets as Israel's covenant prosecutors. One can use a river metaphor to describe the rise of Old Testament prophecy. Moses is like the *fountainhead,* Samuel the *rapids* of the prophetic stream, and Elijah the *course* of the classical prophets.[1]

The function of prophecy in Israel was unique among nations of the ancient Near East. Other peoples had prophets, but they were clairvoyants whose purpose was to manipulate the deities. Israel's prophets were messengers of God who confronted the king and the entire society with his holy word. Nowhere else in the world could a reigning monarch be held accountable to such a prophetic voice.

[1]Willem A. VanGemeren, *Interpreting the Prophetic Word* (Grand Rapids: Zondervan, 1990), 27–39.

---

ing the first half of the eighth century resulted in a flurry of new prophetic activity—all condemning the nation.

Chapter 15 begins with the history of Azariah of Judah (vv. 1–7). Azariah is also known as Uzziah in Kings and especially in Chronicles and the Prophets. We may assume one of these names was his birth name and the other was his throne or coronation name. Counting coregencies at both ends of his reign, Azariah/Uzziah ruled for fifty-two years. He enjoyed the peace and stability in Judah that Jeroboam II enjoyed in Israel (2 Chr 26:1–23).

After the brief overview of Azariah/Uzziah, chapter 15 switches to some of the last kings of northern Israel (Zechariah, Shallum, Menahem, Pekahiah, and Pekah, vv. 8–31), before switching back to Jotham of Israel (vv. 32–38). The instability of the northern kingdom is obvious from the quick succession of kings, the number of assassinations, and the brevity of reigns. The author sounds an ominous note about the future of the kingdom in his discussion of Menahem's reign. "PUL" (vv. 19–20) is an alternate name for TIGLATH-PILESER III of Assyria (745–727 B.C.). This energetic Assyrian revived his nation's might and extended its empire to the west. Menahem was able to hold him off only by paying enormous tribute, which he extracted from the wealthy class in Israel. But this was only a temporary respite. Under Pekah, Tiglath-Pileser began taking Israelite territories and deporting citizens (v. 29). The new Assyrian presence in Syria-Palestine would eventually lead to Israel's destruction.

Before describing Israel's fall, the author switches back to Ahaz of Judah (chapter 16). Amazingly, Ahaz took Judah's apostasy to new levels of perversion, just as Israel was facing destruction for her own sins. For the first time in Judah's history, a king in Jerusalem imitated the sins of northern Israel (v. 3).

While Ahaz was king in Jerusalem, the last king of Syria (Rezin) and Pekah of Israel tried to force him to join them in defiance of Tiglath-Pileser of Assyria. Ahaz had to choose between political alliances with these weak kings to his north or sub-

Assyrian relief showing a deportation during Tiglath-Pileser III's campaign. Ahaz chose to trust Tiglath-Pileser rather than God.

mission to the Assyrians. This led to one of the classic confrontations between prophet and king (read Is 7 along with this unit). Isaiah forced Ahaz to make an entirely different decision. His choice was really between trust in God or trust in his own ability to play the power games of international politics.

Ahaz chose to trust Tiglath-Pileser rather than God (note the expression, "I am your servant and vassal," v. 7). An Assyrian vassal could expect protection from enemy attack. But the protection came at a great price. The palace and temple resources were depleted in order to send a "bribe," which Tiglath-Pileser accepted as tribute (v. 8). From this time forward, Judah would never really be free. Mesopotamian political power would dominate the rest of her history.

Chapter 17 opens with a brief survey of the last king of Israel, Hoshea (vv. 1–6). He apparently sought an alliance with Egypt for protection against the Assyrians. But this was viewed as treason to Tiglath-Pileser's successor, Shalmaneser V (727–722 B.C.). After a three-year siege, the Assyrian king captured Israel's capital,

Samaria, and deported many of its citizens (vv. 5–6).[4]

The author's purpose for outlining Israel's tragedy comes to the surface in 17:7–23. Here the author explicitly states the causes for Israel's destruction in purely theological terms. The nation did not fall simply because it had a smaller army. Israel broke the Lord's statutes and commandments (vv. 15–16). They "followed worthless idols and themselves became worthless" (v. 15). Ultimately it was Yahweh who was responsible for Israel's fall (vv. 18, 20, 23).

The Assyrians controlled conquered nations by deporting large portions of the citizenry and replacing them with inhabitants from other conquered areas. The concluding unit of chapter 17 (vv. 24–41) describes the settlement of foreigners into the area. The combination of foreign religious beliefs with the already heretical practices of northern Israel resulted in continued apostasy in Samaria (v. 29). The mixtures of peoples produced the Samaritans, who would become future enemies of Judah. The Samaritans and their religion continued into New Testament times

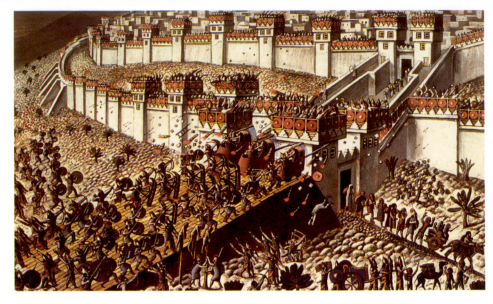

An artist's impression of Sennacherib's siege of the stronghold of Lachish, fortified by Rehoboam.

(Jn 4:9, 19–20), and still endure today among a tiny band of followers.

Judah alone (chapters 18–25)

This final unit traces Judah's fortunes after the fall of Israel. Judah's royal leadership in Jerusalem oscillated between genuine religious reform (Hezekiah and Josiah) and absolute apostasy (Manasseh and Jehoahaz). We know more about this period of Israel's history than any other because of the amount of material available, both biblical and extrabiblical. This unit should be read along with the parallel sections in 2 Chronicles 29–32 and Isaiah 36–39. Also, the Assyrian records corroborate the events and portray them from another perspective.

The Assyrian threat did not go away after the destruction of Israel in 722. SHAL-MANESER'S successors continued the aggressive military policies, and SENNACHERIB (705–681) invaded Judah in 701, during Hezekiah's reign (18:13–19:37). But by the turn of the next century, the Assyrians were replaced by another equally brutal empire: Babylon. Second Kings ends with the destruction of Jerusalem and the beginning of the Babylonian exile at the hands of Nebuchadnezzar.

The largest unit in this section is devoted to good king Hezekiah (chapters 18–20). Hezekiah led an unparalleled religious reform (18:4–6); revolted against Assyria, thus reversing the policy of Ahaz (18:7); and reconquered Philistia (18:8).

Hezekiah's commitments to the Lord's covenant meant he refused to play the power games so common in international politics of the day. His rebellion against Assyria looked like suicide. Sennacherib's threat against Jerusalem is the subject of 2 Kings 18:13–19:37. When it seemed that defeat for Judah was inevitable, Hezekiah went to the temple and prayed one of the greatest prayers found in the Bible (19:15–19). He sought the welfare of God's kingdom and asked deliverance for God's sake. The Lord promised deliverance through the prophet Isaiah (19:20–34). In three brief verses (19:35–37), the narrator relates that Sennacherib's great army was devastated by a miracle of God; Sennacherib returned to Assyria and was assassinated. The Assyrians underestimated Hezekiah's God.

Chapter 20 relates two other episodes from the life of Hezekiah. His miraculous recovery from illness portrays Hezekiah as the recipient of divine favor (vv. 1–11). But Isaiah condemned his cordial reception of the Babylonian envoys (vv. 12–19). Hezekiah normally prayed about major concerns (see 19:15 and 20:2), but here he seems to act alone, proudly displaying the trappings of power and prestige as though he had personally acquired them.

Hezekiah's son and grandson were among Judah's most wicked kings (Manasseh, 21:1–18; Amon, 21:19–26). Manasseh had the longest reign of any king of Israel or Judah (696–642). But this is not to imply

Book of the Law

Sennacherib's prism, which mentions King Hezekiah of Judah.

that Manasseh was favored by God, since his reign was the blackest period of Judah's history. The parallel account in Chronicles (2 Chr 33:1–20) confirms the picture of 2 Kings. Manasseh's Judah was more sinful than the pagan nations driven out of Canaan during the Israelite conquest (21:9). His reign contrasts with that of the good Hezekiah who preceded him and Josiah who followed him. Ultimately, the author of Kings blamed the fall of Jerusalem on Manasseh's reign (21:11–15; 24:2–4).

Josiah was the last godly king before the Babylonian exile (22:1–23:30). He was a religious reformer of the highest order. While he was still a young king, his high priest found the "**Book of the Law**" in the temple of the Lord (22:8–10). This was probably all or part of Deuteronomy, which had been deposited in the temple at Solomon's dedication (1 Kgs 8:1–4; Dt 31:26). This temple copy had been neglected during the reigns of Manasseh and Amon. The discovery of the law-book greatly affected the young king (22:19). He quickly purged pagan worship from the country, reestablished the covenant with the Lord, and reinstituted the Passover feast which had been neglected since the time of the judges (23:22). Genuine spiritual reforms, whether national or individual, are always accompanied by a reaf-

Sennacherib's Account of His Campaign in Judah (701 B.C.)

Sennacherib's military campaign into Judah in 701 is well attested in the Assyrian sources. His own account of the event, adapted here from official Assyrian annals, agrees remarkably well with the biblical account. The Assyrian record, of course, omits the miraculous defeat of its army (2 Kgs 19:35). The statement that Sennacherib imprisoned Hezekiah in Jerusalem "like a bird in a cage" is a tacit admission that the Assyrian was unable to capture Jerusalem.

As to Hezekiah, the Jew, he did not submit to my yoke. I laid siege to 46 of his strong cities, walled forts and to the countless small villages in their vicinity, and conquered them by means of well-stamped earth-ramps, and battering-rams brought near the walls combined with the attack by foot soldiers. I drove out of these cities and villages 200,150 people, young and old, male and female, horses, mules, donkeys, camels, big and small cattle beyond counting. Himself I made a prisoner in Jerusalem, his royal residence, like a bird in a cage. . . . Thus I reduced his country, but I still increased the tribute due to me as his overlord which I imposed upon him later.*

Abridged and adapted from the Prism of Sennacherib of the University of Chicago's Oriental Institute (*ANET*, 288).

A relief showing Assyrian soldiers carrying off booty from Lachish.

remnant

firmation of the importance of God's word (as in the Protestant Reformation).

Assyria's capital city, NINEVEH, fell to the Babylonians and Medes in 612 B.C. But a **remnant** of the Assyrian army was embedded near the Euphrates River to the northeast of Judah. Pharaoh Necho II of Egypt supported the Assyrians in the hopes of preventing Babylon from gaining sole control of Mesopotamia and succeeding Assyria as the next great world empire. When he went north in 609 B.C. to assist the Assyrians, Josiah met him at MEGIDDO to intervene. But Josiah lost his life in the effort, and the tragic event closed the books on Judah's last, best hope for genuine reform (23:29–30).

Josiah was followed by a succession of weak kings, none of whom was able to slow Judah's rapid march to destruction (23:31–25:21). The author concluded his sad story with brief summaries of the last four kings: Jehoahaz (23:31–35), Jehoiakim (23:36–24:7), Jehoiachin (24:8–17), and Zedekiah (24:18–25:21). The account of Zedekiah's reign includes details of Jerusalem's fall and its destruction at the hands of the Babylonians (25:1–21). The prophets, especially Jeremiah and Habakkuk, shed more light on this tragic event and its emotional consequences.

The author attached two appendixes to conclude the narrative. The history of Judah under the Babylonian puppet ruler, Gedaliah, would update readers in the exile (25:22–26). More information on this period is available in Jeremiah 40:7–41:9.

The second appendix (25:27–30) hints that even in those desperate times, God's covenant love for his people was still at work. In the spring of 561 B.C., Nebuchadnezzar's son, who followed him as king of Babylon, released Jehoiachin from captivity. The Books of Kings end on the hopeful assertion that a son of David was alive and well. Whatever the human motivation behind Jehoiachin's release, God's decree was that the family of David, though severely chastened, would not be exterminated (Mt 1:1–16). Though humans break their covenant, God keeps his.

Themes of the Books of Kings

Of the many important theological themes of Kings, we will highlight just two.[5] First, the entire Deuteronomistic History, especially the Books of Kings, presents the history of Israel from the viewpoint of the Mosaic covenant. During the exile, the author of Kings was able to reflect on what had occurred over four centuries of history. The books assume the disasters of 722 and 587

Summary

1. In the Book of 2 Kings, both Israel and Judah are secure at first, but because of their apostasy, both are destroyed.

2. The approach in 2 Kings is to present a theological analogy of the persons or events that were influential in bringing destruction on Israel.

3. Beginning with Elijah, prophets in Israel played a new role, one that represented their power and authority.

4. Elisha's ministry helped bring the destruction of the dynasty of Omri in Israel.

5. When the kingdom followed the leadership of the prophets they succeeded.

6. In 2 Kings 15, the instability of Israel is evident because there is a rapid succession of kings.

7. Shalmaneser V captured Samaria after a siege of three years.

8. Israel was destroyed because the people broke God's statutes and commandments, followed worthless idols, and became worthless themselves.

9. When Jerusalem was destroyed, Judah began a period of Babylonian exile.

10. Two important theological themes are found in the Books of Kings. First, the books present the history of Israel from the viewpoint of the Mosaic covenant. Second, prophecy has a significant role.

Torah

were due to the nation's failure to maintain the covenant that God established at Mount Sinai. This is based on the so-called retribution theology of Deuteronomy (see discussion in chapter 10).

Deuteronomy stated clearly that Israel would succeed in the promised land only if she remained faithful to the covenant. Disobedience meant the nation would lose the land. In a simple doctrine of retribution, Moses linked covenant faithfulness to blessings and disobedience to future curses (Dt 27–28). This idea became the "Bible" for the authors of the historical books. It provided the theological explanation for the nation's fall and the loss of the promised land. Northern Israel failed because of the crimes of Jeroboam I, and Judah because of the wicked reign of Manasseh (1 Kgs 14:15–16; 2 Kgs 17:22–23; 21:11–15; 24:2–4).

This retribution theology became the basis for the author's evaluation of each king of Israel as good or bad. Each king was evil like his fathers (especially Jeroboam I), or good like David. The author of Kings assumed the authority of the written **Torah** of God, which became the foundation document for his "either-or" eval-

Key Terms

Baal-Zebub
city-states
Book of the Law
remnant
Torah

Key People/Places

"Pul"
Tiglath-Pileser III
Shalmaneser V
Sennacherib
Pharaoh Necho II
Philistia
Nineveh
Megiddo

Study Questions

1. How much time is covered by the Book of 2 Kings?

2. What is the overall theme of this book?

3. What is the theological purpose of 2 Kings?

4. What is the importance of Elisha's ministry as portrayed in 2 Kings?

5. Briefly describe the ideological conflict between Baalism and the worship of God as found in 2 Kings.

6. Describe the international political situation of 2 Kings. How does this tie in with the author's purpose in writing this book?

7. What lasting effect did the Assyrian policy of deportation have on God's people?

8. Briefly list some of the positive aspects found in 2 Kings, especially in relation to the good kings.

9. What are the main theological themes of 2 Kings?

uation of each king.[6] The blessings and curses of the Mosaic law (Dt 27–28) became the authoritative framework for the author's interpretation of Israel's history. Each king was either obedient and therefore blessed, or disobedient and therefore cursed. And this approach began with the assumption that the Mosaic covenant was the authoritative word of God.

The story told in the Books of Kings is a sad one. But it emphasizes over and over again the importance of godliness and faithfulness in our commitment to God. Success in our lives is too often gauged by our external accomplishments, measured in purely human terms. The Books of Kings teach that personal covenant faithfulness and obedience to God is the *only* measure of successful living.

The second theological theme is the role

Further Reading

Cogan, Mordechai, and Hayim Tadmor. *II Kings: A New Translation with Introduction and Commentary.* Anchor Bible 11. Garden City, N.Y.: Doubleday, 1988. Most useful for cultural and historical context.

Gray, John. *I & II Kings: A Commentary.* 2nd ed. Old Testament Library. Philadelphia: Westminster, 1970. Useful, though technical and difficult reading.

Hobbs, T. R. *2 Kings.* Word Biblical Commentary 13. Waco, Tex.: Word, 1985.

Howard, David M., Jr. *An Introduction to the Old Testament Historical Books.* Chapter 6: "1 & 2 Kings," 169–204, and chapter 7: "Historical and Cultural Context for 1 & 2 Kings," 205–29. Chicago: Moody, 1993.

Walton, John H. *Ancient Israelite Literature in Its Cultural Context: A Survey of Parallels between Biblical and Ancient Near Eastern Texts.* Chapter 5: "Historical Literature," 111–34. Grand Rapids: Zondervan, 1989.

Wiseman, Donald J. *1 and 2 Kings: An Introduction and Commentary.* Tyndale Old Testament Commentary. Downers Grove/Leicester: InterVarsity, 1993. Best evangelical commentary available.

and significance of prophecy in the Books of Kings. This is truly a prophetic history, interested in how the word of Yahweh functions in history. As such, it contains a promise–fulfillment motif throughout.[7] For example, just before his death, Elisha prophesied that Israel would defeat Syria three times (2 Kgs 13:19). In the closing formula for King Jehoash of Israel, the author explicitly said Jehoash defeated Syria "three times," making the fulfillment pattern obvious (2 Kgs 13:25). This illustration could be repeated many times over.

The prophetic perspective is most apparent in the author's theological explanation for the fall of both kingdoms. Both had been justly warned by God's "servants the prophets" (2 Kgs 17:23; 24:2). But the nations persisted in sin, rejecting the prophetic message. The word of God was at work in the nations to bring them to an end, just as certainly as it also works to bring salvation. The Books of Kings teach the importance of hearing and obeying the word of God.

17 First and Second Chronicles

A Look Back

Outline

Objectives

After reading this chapter, you should be able to

- Identify the author's purpose for writing Chronicles
- Explain the position of Chronicles in the canon
- Outline the content of Chronicles
- Justify the genealogical lists in 1 Chronicles 1–9
- Explain why only Saul's sin and punishment are recorded in Chronicles
- Tell the meaning of Chronicles for contemporary Christians
- Show how the time in which Chronicles was written affected the way the author wrote
- Point out the role of the temple in Chronicles

A century or more after the Books of Kings were written, the circumstances for God's people had improved little. It is true the exile had ended and many faithful Jews had returned to Jerusalem from Babylon and other parts of the world. But the Messiah had not come as some had hoped. The small population in Jerusalem felt discouraged and lost. Had God forsaken his people? Had the promises to David failed? The author of Chronicles looked back across the centuries of Israel's history in order to trace God's covenant promises through the broken circumstances of a defeated nation all the way down to his own day. His look back is intended as a message of reassurance and hope, and is pertinent for every generation of believers.

The Author and His Purpose

Early Jewish tradition named Ezra as the author of these books.[1] Scholars have agreed for many years that the author of Ezra–Nehemiah, probably Ezra himself, also wrote the Books of Chronicles.[2] The text itself, however, makes no specific statement about authorship.

Recent scholarship has tended to view Chronicles as the work of an author other than Ezra.[3] This view is supported by Chronicles' location in the Jewish canon after Ezra–Nehemiah (see below). Chronological order would dictate Chronicles coming before Ezra–Nehemiah. We may assume a single author would have grouped the two works together in sequence. Another interesting problem is the common material tying the two works together (2 Chr 36:22–23 and Ezr 1:1–3). Some assume this means Chronicles and Ezra–Nehemiah were written together and that the decree was repeated when the two documents were separated. But the reverse may be true. The repetition of the decree could equally well reflect an intentional effort to join together two separate and originally independent documents.[4] Recent scholarship considers Chronicles the work of an anonymous author in the postexilic period, someone other than the author of Ezra–Nehemiah (see discussion in chapter 10).

On the basis of the genealogies, we may assume the author wrote these books during the second or third generation after the exile ended. Many scholars have dated Chronicles to between 450 and 400 B.C. This date is supported by Chronicles' position as the last book of the Hebrew canon.

An Arab castle at Palmyra, Syria. Solomon specially fortified this town.

The Israelite citadel at Hazor. This stronghold was also fortified by Solomon.

The chronicler produced what we may call the first commentary on the Scriptures. Some of his information comes from sources that are unknown and unavailable to us. This includes, for example, David's elaborate plans for Solomon's construction of the temple (1 Chr 22:1–5). But the majority of the author's material comes from the Books of Samuel and Kings. His purpose is apparent from his inclusion of certain episodes from these older biblical books and his omission of others. For example, when the chronicler discusses David, he discreetly chooses to omit any reference to the Bathsheba incident (2 Sm 11) and fails to mention the details of Adonijah's attempt to usurp the throne (1 Kgs 1:5–2:24).

The author's use of his sources is likewise apparent in his discussion of Solomon's magnificent reign. Often he quotes almost verbatim from 1 Kings, but omits entirely any reference to one of the most important ideas in the Kings narrative—Solomon's great apostasy in 1 Kings 11:9–13. This selectivity was due to the author's purpose, which was to trace the history of faith and salvation.

The chronicler's readers knew the Books of Samuel and Kings, and were all too familiar with the failures of the past. They did not need to be reminded of the sin and punishment of their ancestors. The author of Chronicles desired, instead, to follow a straight line of trust in God, with no detours. He avoided all avenues that might detract from his main objective, which was to remind his readers of the victories of their heritage and to assure them of triumphs in the future.

This was not an attempt to rewrite history or gloss over the failures of the past. Chronicles is a statement of faith that God's promises are true. Despite the circumstances of the postexilic period, God still had plans for Israel's future. Jerusalem appeared to be full of nothing but poverty and strife. But appearances can be deceiving. The Books of Chronicles boldly proclaimed that God's covenant and its promises were still valid. All was not lost!

So the author, in a sense, produced the first "Bible commentary." He used the biblical sources (especially Samuel and Kings) to show that God was still at work among his people. Since the author was aware of these biblical books and used them in his own composition, we will now explore the relationship between Chronicles and other books in the canon. The author's distinctive purpose means the Books of Chronicles have a direct relationship with other books in the Old Testament.

Chronicles and the Canon

Coming as they do at the close of the Old Testament period, the Books of Chronicles contain traces of nearly every theological concept expressed in the rest of the Old Testament canon. Since the author was dependent on other books of the canon, it will be helpful for us to examine the relationship between Chronicles and those other books, especially Samuel and Kings. The situation is all the more intriguing because Chronicles has a different placement in the Christian and Jewish canons.

Location in the Canon

In our English Bibles, the Books of Chronicles immediately follow the Books of Kings and precede Ezra–Nehemiah. In this location, they are chronologically placed in the Old Testament historical books, the second part of the Christian canon. This is not the case in the Hebrew Bible (see chapter 1). There, Chronicles comes at the end of the entire collection of biblical books, after Ezra–Nehemiah. This location is surprising since it reverses the natural sequence of Ezra–Nehemiah and Chronicles.

Various attempts have been made to explain the reverse order of the Hebrew canon.[5] Perhaps the Jews recognized a later date of authorship for Chronicles, or Ezra–Nehemiah was accepted as canonical earlier than Chronicles. But there may also be a theological message here. The reverse order may have been deliberate, in order to end the Old Testament on a positive note (the exile-ending edict of Cyrus, 2 Chr 36:22–23). The canonizers of the Hebrew Bible may have been encouraging the readers to experience freedom from their personal exile.

Relationship to Samuel and Kings

As we have said, the chronicler had a different purpose from his primary sources, the Books of Samuel and Kings. Samuel gave the history of the early monarchy, showing the rise and fall of Saul and the rise of David. That account legitimized Israelite kingship and showed the conditions under which God would bless the king. The Books of Kings continued and concluded the account of the monarchy. The theological purpose there was to trace the consequences of sin as opposed to the benefits of obedience.

The author of Chronicles did not contradict the earlier histories or refute their truthfulness. On the contrary, the chronicler appears to have given the biblical sources greater authority than other sources available to him. Yet he was not bound to them rigidly. He employed the earlier biblical accounts creatively to write a history of God's work in Israel that spoke to the needs of his postexilic audience. In this way, the chronicler stands early in the tradition of interpretation. The author of Chronicles was "the last example of Israel's genius for retelling her sacred history."[6]

Contents of 1 and 2 Chronicles

The fifth century B.C. was a dreary period in Israel's history. The great empire of

Bedouin near the biblical ports of Elath and Ezion-geber. Jehoshaphat built a fleet at Ezion-geber, on the Gulf of Aqaba, but the ships were wrecked before they could sail.

An Assyrian relief depicting the Israelites bringing tribute to Assyria.

David and Solomon had long since crumbled. The Assyrians had destroyed northern Israel and the Babylonians left little of Jerusalem. During the fifth century, the powerful Persian Empire reached its zenith. All that remained of national Israel was the tiny province of Judah, a small portion of Persia's vast domain. Solomon's magnificent temple had been replaced by one of much less splendor during the time of Haggai and Zechariah (516 B.C., Ezr 6:14–15). The once great Davidic monarchy had been reduced to a provincial governorship subject to Persian authority.

To make matters worse, the initial freedom of the release from exile in 539 B.C. had raised the hopes and expectations of the Jewish people. It was a time of high anticipation. Soon, many thought, the Messiah would come and usher Judah into a new age of greatness. But those hopes were quickly disappointed. Those who returned to Jerusalem found the city in shambles. The population was small and lacking in material wealth. It was soon apparent that the messianic age had not arrived. Against this gloomy backdrop, the chronicler offered profound encouragement to his readers. Despite the circumstances, God's purpose for Israel was still in effect through his promises to David (1 Chr 17:7–14).

Outline

Overview

restoration

The Books of Chronicles center around the reigns of David and Solomon. As background to those two kings, 1 Chronicles opens with several genealogical lists, with historical statements interspersed among them (1 Chr 1–9). The reign of David is the topic of the rest of 1 Chronicles (chapters 10–29). Second Chronicles begins with the reign of King Solomon (chapters 1–9). The remainder of 2 Chronicles (chapters 10–36) relates the history of the Davidic dynasty.

The genealogies (1 Chr 1–9)

The genealogical lists trace history from the first man, Adam, through the central figure of the narrative, David, to the author's own day. These chapters may appear uninteresting and unnecessary to modern readers. But they were of paramount importance to the readers of the postexilic period. By means of these genealogical lists, the author of Chronicles demonstrated a national identity reaching back across the tragedy of the exile. The lists demonstrated a continuity between generations. The first readers could believe that the promises God gave their ancestors before the exile were also for them. Similar lists provide important background for other historical books of the Bible: Genesis 5, Matthew 1:1–17, and Luke 3:23–38.

The list of the tribe and family of Saul (chapter 8) serves as a transition to the first narrative section of Chronicles: the death of Saul and the coronation of David (10:1–11:3).

The reign of King David (1 Chr 10–29)

The author was mainly interested in what he perceived to be God's chosen instruments of salvation: the Davidic line of kings, the city of Jerusalem, and the temple. Consequently, he passed over Saul's life and recorded only Saul's ignominious death as background information to David's rise to power.

On the other hand, the brief narrative on Saul presented one of the chronicler's most important theological concepts. The author repeated the terms used to describe Saul's sin and punishment in 1 Chronicles 10:13–14: Saul died because of his unfaithfulness to the Lord; he failed to keep the word of the Lord and did not inquire of the Lord, so the Lord put him to death. Saul's life and death became for the author a prototype or pattern of the exile situation. It painted a picture that kept recurring throughout Israel's history. It was a pattern with which the readers of Chronicles could identify—it was an "exilic" archetype. But the author balanced this prototype with the theme of "**restoration**" in the following chapters. For the chronicler, David fulfilled in part a savior role.[7]

The author first described how David became king, and his military exploits and successes (chapters 10–20). Then the chronicler went into great detail about David's preparations for building the temple (chapters 21–29). Since the author viewed the temple as central to God's plan of salvation, these elaborate plans for its construction revealed David's true character as Israel's leader in the faith.

The reign of King Solomon (2 Chr 1–9)

These chapters relate the grandeur of Solomon's kingdom, as did the author's sources in 1 Kings. But the chronicler is more interested in the temple's construction and dedication. His account of Solomon's reign is shorter than the parallel passages in 1 Kings 1–11. This unit includes only events that reflected the author's concern for the temple. More specifically, the chronicler focused on the religious institutions and worship connected with the temple, so he even abbreviated the 1 Kings account of the actual construction of the temple (chapters 3 and 4).

The familiar verse in 2 Chronicles 7:14

is a key verse for the work of the chronicler: "If my people, who are called by my name, will humble themselves and pray and seek my face and turn from their wicked ways, then will I hear from heaven and will forgive their sin and will heal their land." This program for repentance established the prototype of salvation from the exilic situation first described in the death of Saul (see above on 1 Chr 10:13–14).[8] Saul's life and death became the pattern of the exilic situation, which was repeated in Israel's history. But 2 Chronicles 7:14 is the pattern for restoration. The chronicler presented these two models (restoration and exile), and called his readers to assess their own situation in the light of these archetypes, or patterns.[9] The Books of Chronicles still call us to humility and repentance.

Hezekiah's tunnel, Jerusalem. When the Assyrians threatened Jerusalem, Hezekiah cut a special tunnel to channel water into his capital city.

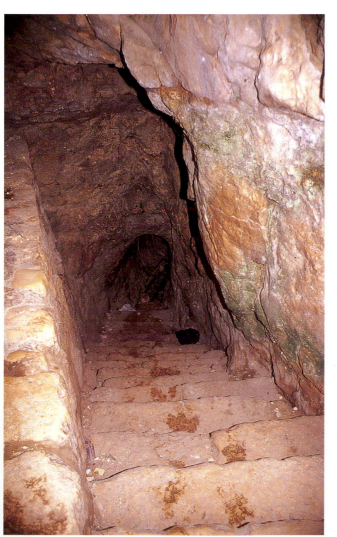

The kingdom of Judah (2 Chr 10–36)

Soon after Solomon's death, the kingdom crumbled in two, partly due to the ineptitude of his son Rehoboam. The history of the northern kingdom lay outside the scope of the author's purpose. In this section, he was interested in tracing the kings of Judah from Rehoboam to the Babylonian exile. His purpose was not to demonstrate the failure of God's promise to David (1 Chr 17). On the contrary, he wanted to show that salvation (which was certain for the future) was still linked to the Davidic dynasty and the Jerusalem temple. God had not abandoned his basic institutions of salvation.

The author of 2 Kings covered Hezekiah's religious reforms in one brief verse (18:4) and devoted three chapters to his political achievements. By contrast, the chronicler detailed the reforms in 2 Chronicles 29–31. His purpose was to illustrate that when the son of David cared for God's house and provided for genuine worship, God brought peace to the kingdom (chapter 32).

The chronicler told of Manasseh's capture, exile in Babylon, repentance, and restoration, none of which is included in the Kings' account. The author of Kings desired to highlight only the severity of Manasseh's crime. But the chronicler portrayed the mercy of God to the people in exile. Just as the king who was most responsible for the Babylonian exile (2 Kgs 23:26) could turn from his sin and find grace, so could the people.

The chronicler's work ends with the edict of Cyrus of Persia (2 Chr 36:22–23). The edict signals the end of the exile, the release of the Jews, and Cyrus's support for rebuilding the temple. By ending on this note, the author shed a ray of hope across the Books of Chronicles. The temple lay in ruins, but God had begun to "hear from heaven" and to "heal their land" (2 Chr 7:14). If the returnees would follow the good examples of David, Solomon, Asa, Jehoshaphat, Hezekiah, and Josiah, God would bless them again.

The paragraph is paralleled by Ezra 1:2–3. It serves as a tag at the conclusion, marking the beginning of the restoration period and directing the reader to continue reading in the Book of Ezra.

Deuteronomistic
History

Themes of the Books of Chronicles

The chronicler had the benefit of writing his history after many of the Old Testament books were already considered authoritative. He inherited a tradition rich in already familiar theological concepts. As a result, the chronicler felt little need to make explicit statements regarding such widely accepted truths as monotheism, the sovereignty of God, and other basic theological concepts.

On occasion, the chronicler developed a theological concept of biblical faith beyond its expression in the earlier biblical books. For example, he took the retribution theology of the **Deuteronomistic History** for granted. He only added to the concept slightly by emphasizing the immediacy of punishment or blessing (1 Chr 28:9). Each separate generation of believers is blessed for obedience or cursed for unfaithfulness. This immediacy assumes the truth of the original deuteronomistic emphasis, but goes a step beyond it.[10]

Of the Old Testament's theological heritage accepted by the chronicler, there were two themes that were particularly dear to him: (1) David and his dynasty and (2) the temple and the proper worship of God.

David and His Dynasty

The figure of David casts a long shadow across the Books of Chronicles.[11] The genealogies emphasize David and his line. The rest of 1 Chronicles is devoted to David's reign. Second Chronicles begins with nine chapters on David's son and successor. The remainder of 2 Chronicles centers on the Davidic line of kings in Jerusalem, the heirs of the covenant promises to David.

The Davidic covenant was established in 2 Samuel 7. This became one of Israel's most important theological concepts, taking a position alongside the Abrahamic and Mosaic covenants. It provided the basis for concepts regarding the Messiah, the ideal son of David. The chronicler followed 2 Samuel 7 closely in his presentation of the Davidic covenant in 1 Chronicles 17, emphasizing the eternal aspect of the divine decree. The author of Chronicles viewed David and Solomon together, establishing an eternal dynasty. This contributed to Israel's messianic expectation, since the chronicler was clearly longing for the day when a son of David would once again rule over all Israel.[12]

The chronicler's views of David related to his perception of Israelite kingship. The Israelite monarchy was meant to be representative from the beginning. God would continue to function as the true King; Saul was the human representative or agent of government. But Saul became the pattern of the exilic situation in Chronicles. The beauty of the Davidic dynasty lies in the divine promise that the transfer of royal

The Cyrus Cylinder, describing the Persian capture of the city of Babylon. The text also talks of Cyrus's policy of allowing conquered peoples to return and to rebuild their homelands (*ANET* 316). This is the decree referred to in 2 Chr 36:22–23 and Ezra 1:2–4.

Summary

1. There is some discussion about who wrote 1 and 2 Chronicles, but recent scholarship attributes it to an anonymous postexilic author.

2. Chronicles constituted what may be called the first biblical commentary, with the primary sources being the Books of Samuel and Kings.

3. The location of Chronicles is at the end of the biblical books in the Hebrew canon, but in the English Bible it follows the Books of Kings and comes before Ezra and Nehemiah.

4. The focus of the Book of Chronicles is on the reigns of David and Solomon.

5. The genealogical lists demonstrate a national identity going back before the exile and provide a continuity between generations.

6. The author of Chronicles was most interested in the Davidic list of kings, the city of Jerusalem, and the temple as God's instruments of salvation.

7. The chronicler was more interested in the construction and dedication of the temple than he was in the details of the grandeur of Solomon's kingdom.

8. The author of Chronicles calls the readers to assess their own situations in light of the two models—restoration and exile—which he presents.

9. The themes that appear to be especially important to the chronicler are: (1) David and his dynasty, and (2) the temple and the proper worship of God.

power would never be broken again (1 Chr 17:13). From the time of King David, Israelite kingship was placed forever into the hands of the sons of David.

The chronicler also believed in an equation between the kingdom of God and the kingship of Israel.[13] Though the Books of Chronicles contain many references to illustrate this, the best example is Abijah's reference to "the kingdom of the LORD, which is in the hands of David's descendants" (2 Chr 13:8).

David and Solomon are also central in the Books of Chronicles because of their roles in building the temple and establishing true and valid religious practices in Jerusalem.

The Temple and the Worship of God

The temple plays a central role in the Books of Chronicles.[14] During an age when God's people were struggling to identify themselves, the temple provided an important symbol of God's abiding presence with his chosen people. The second temple, built under Haggai and Zechariah, established a powerful link between preexilic Judah and the postexilic restoration community. As such, the temple formed a bridge for the postexilic community, reaching back to their ancestors in the faith. The Davidic dynasty was temporarily lost,

Key Terms

restoration
Deuteronomistic History

Study Questions

1. Who is traditionally viewed as the author of 1–2 Chronicles?

2. In what time period were these books composed? How do we know?

3. How are 1–2 Chronicles the "first commentary on the Scriptures"?

4. What was the author's purpose in writing 1–2 Chronicles?

5. What message of hope do these two books contain?

6. Briefly describe the relationship between Chronicles and the other books in the canon.

7. How is the location of 1–2 Chronicles in the Hebrew Bible important?

8. Why are the genealogies important to the purpose of this writing?

9. What role does the Davidic royal line play in Chronicles?

10. What are some of the major themes of Chronicles?

but the temple was in Jerusalem again. It supplied continuity to believers who felt insecure and uncertain of their future.

But the temple was more than a link to the Davidic and Solomonic period. It represented God's presence in the midst of his people in its most fundamental form. As such, the temple also provided continuity to the Mosaic period and the Pentateuch. Just as the tabernacle was God's dwelling place in the midst of the tribes in the wilderness, so God was once again dwelling with his people.

The assessment of subsequent kings in the Davidic dynasty (2 Chr 10–36) was usually based on their faithfulness and allegiance to the temple and to the proper forms of religious practice. Thus the chronicler's emphasis on the temple ties all his major themes together. The centrality of David and Solomon is related to their building of the temple and establishing

Further Reading

Braun, Roddy. *1 Chronicles.* Word Biblical Commentary 14. Waco, Tex.: Word, 1986. Discusses theological contributions of Chronicles.

Dillard, Raymond B. *2 Chronicles.* Word Biblical Commentary 15. Waco, Tex.: Word, 1987.

Howard, David M., Jr. *An Introduction to the Old Testament Historical Books.* Chapter 8: "1 and 2 Chronicles," 231–72. Chicago: Moody, 1993.

Japhet, Sara. *I and II Chronicles: A Commentary.* Old Testament Library. Louisville: Westminster/John Knox, 1993. Exhaustive and thorough treatment, though not light reading.

Selman, Martin J. *1 Chronicles: An Introduction and Commentary.* Tyndale Old Testament Commentary. Downers Grove/Leicester: InterVarsity, 1994. Helpful introduction with rich theological insights.

———. *2 Chronicles: An Introduction and Commentary.* Tyndale Old Testament Commentary. Downers Grove/Leicester: InterVarsity, 1994. Helpful introduction with rich theological insights.

Williamson, H. G. M. *1 and 2 Chronicles.* New Century Bible Commentary. Grand Rapids/London: Eerdmans/ Marshall, Morgan & Scott, 1982. Together with Japhet, builds new consensus on authorship.

the acceptable forms of Yahweh worship. The success of the Davidic dynasty was dependent on continued care and attention to the temple and right worship of God. For the chronicler, royal authority was God-given, but was conditioned on covenant faithfulness. In this way, the author of Chronicles stands squarely at the center of biblical thought.

18 Ezra, Nehemiah, and Esther

A Time to Rebuild

Outline

- **The Books of Ezra and Nehemiah**
  Contents
  Problems of Interpretation
- **The Book of Esther**
  Contents
- **Theological Themes**
  Ezra and Nehemiah
  Esther

Objectives

After reading this chapter, you should be able to

- Explain the benefits of studying Ezra, Nehemiah, and Esther together
- Outline the basic content of the Book of Ezra
- Outline the basic content of the Book of Nehemiah
- Outline the basic content of the Book of Esther
- Compare the literary styles used in Ezra, Nehemiah, and Esther
- Discuss the question of the authorship of Ezra, Nehemiah, and Esther
- Explain the chronology of Ezra and Nehemiah
- Identify the theological themes in Ezra, Nehemiah, and Esther

Ezra, Nehemiah, and Esther conclude the Old Testament section of the canon known as the historical books. They continue the history of God's people during the postexilic period. Ezra and Nehemiah recorded the events of the return from exile and the restoration of Judah. Esther illustrated how the faithfulness and courage of a single Jew made a difference in the world in which she lived. These books have a common origin in the Persian period. They share a postexilic perspective on God's relationship with his people and a hope of future blessings.

These books are different in many ways. Ezra–Nehemiah (as one volume) is anchored in historical fact. The author used lists, records, royal edicts, memoirs, and the like, to present his history of the restoration period. Esther, on the other hand, is an artfully written narrative that communicates through the skillful use of dialogue, intricate plot, and elaborate characterization. Esther is no less historical, but the author does not intend to record a documented historical treatise. Rather, the Book of Esther engages the reader in the subtlety of relationships and faithfulness to God.

In this way, these books from the Persian period complement each other.[1] Esther's secular atmosphere balances Ezra–Nehemiah's piety. Ezra–Nehemiah's historical details offset Esther's entertaining story line. Esther's view from the exile in Persia counters Ezra–Nehemiah's loyal devotion to the Jewish homeland. Though written with drastically different styles and purposes, these books share a common perspective. They are interested in God's continued blessings on the covenant community.

The Books of Ezra and Nehemiah

These books are almost always studied together for a number of reasons. First, they appear to come from a single author or editor. Second, they deal with the same general time period and are roughly sequential. Third, they are combined as one book in the Jewish canon.

Contents

The Books of Ezra and Nehemiah trace the history of the Jews from their first return from exile (538 B.C.), through a second return led by Ezra himself (458 B.C.), to their rebuilding activities and religious reforms in the mid-fifth century, led by both Ezra and Nehemiah.

Assyrian relief showing ambassadors from a foreign state.

Outline

Ezra

I. First Emigration (1:1–2:70)
- A. Cyrus's Proclamation (1:1–4)
- B. Treasures for the Temple (1:5–11)
- C. The Emigrants (2:1–70)

II. Restoration of the Temple (3:1–6:22)
- A. Rebuilding the Altar (3:1–6)
- B. Rebuilding the Temple (3:7–13)
- C. Opposition (4:1–5)
- D. Later Opposition (4:6–24)
- E. God's Encouragement (5:1–2)
- F. Official Inquiry (5:3–17)
- G. Completion and Dedication of the Temple (6:1–22)

III. Second Emigration (7:1–8:36)
- A. Ezra (7:1–10)
- B. Official Recognition (7:11–26)
- C. Ezra's Praise (7:27–28)
- D. The Emigrants (8:1–14)
- E. A Search for Levites (8:15–20)
- F. The Journey (8:21–36)

IV. Intermarriage (9:1–15)

V. Confession and Separation (10:1–44)
- The Confession (10:1–17)
- Those Guilty of Intermarriage (10:18–44)

Nehemiah

I. A Pathetic Report (1:1–11)
- A. The Report (1:1–3)
- B. Nehemiah's Prayer (1:4–11)

II. Nehemiah's Commissioning (2:1–20)

III. Jerusalem's Wall and Gates (3:1–7:3)
- A. The Builders (3:1–32)
- B. Opposition from Without (4:1–23)
- C. Opposition from Within (5:1–19)
- D. Further Opposition from Without (6:1–14)
- E. Completion of the Wall (6:15–19)

IV. The Exiles (7:1–73)

V. Spiritual Renewal (8:1–10:39)
- A. The Law (8:1–9)
- B. Celebration (8:10–18)
- C. Confession (9:1–37)
- D. Covenant Renewal (9:38–10:39)

VI. Residents, Priests, and Levites (11:1–12:26)
- A. New Residents for Jerusalem (11:1–36)
- B. Priests and Levites (12:1–26)

VII. Dedication of the Wall (12:27–47)

VIII. Final Reforms (13:1–31)

Overview

The Book of Ezra opens with six chapters detailing the first return after Cyrus's decree in 538 B.C. Zerubbabel, grandson of King Jehoiachin, provided the political leadership during this time, and the prophets Haggai and Zechariah supplied the spiritual inspiration. Ezra 7–10 describes Ezra's return to Jerusalem, his effective ministry, and his confrontation with those who had married unbelievers.

The Book of Nehemiah opens with six chapters based on Nehemiah's own memoirs. After introducing the reader to Nehemiah, this unit relates how he journeyed to Jerusalem from Persia and successfully rebuilt the walls of Jerusalem against considerable odds. The rest of Nehemiah (chapters 7–13) deals with the religious and social reforms of Ezra and Nehemiah.

First Return and the Rebuilding of the Temple (Ezr 1–6)

After King Cyrus of Persia captured Babylon, he issued a decree releasing the Jews and permitting them to return to their homeland (1:2–4, see illustration 17.1). In 538 B.C., the first group of Jews returned to Jerusalem under the leadership of Zerubbabel (2:2). The relationship of Zerubbabel to Sheshbazzar, who is also called the governor of Judah (1:8), is uncertain. While some scholars have concluded they were the same individual with two names, it is better to assume Sheshbazzar was the first Persian governor of Judah and began the work on the temple's foundation. At some later unknown date, Zerubbabel replaced him as governor and finished the work.[2]

The very presence of Zerubbabel gave hope to this first group of returning Jews. Because he was in the direct line of King David and had been placed in a position of leadership by the Persians, he was the object of messianic hopes (Hg 2:23; Zec 4:14). As such, Zerubbabel played an important role in the early restoration period. But for reasons that the biblical authors fail to explain, he simply disappeared from the record after the temple was rebuilt.

Under the leadership of Zerubbabel and Jeshua the high priest (variant spelling of Joshua), the returnees quickly began restoring Jerusalem. First, they dedicated themselves to reestablishing their God-given forms of worship (3:1–6). Next, they began rebuilding the temple, the most important element of their national identity (3:7–6:22). They were able to lay the foundation for the new temple with great pomp and ceremony (3:10–11). But many were old enough to remember the former glory of Solomon's original temple. They could see this new structure was going to be plain by comparison. Many cried in discouragement during the praise ceremony. The cries of praise and thanksgiving blended with the cries of disappointment and loss (3:12–13). God's work demands all that we have, and sometimes challenges us to go beyond what we think we are capable of doing. But ultimately, life in his service is always rewarding and fulfilling.

The Jews were unable to finish the temple. Their resources were insufficient and the work was hard. In addition, they experienced fierce opposition at every hand. The Samaritans in the north were descendants of the mixed marriages between Israelites and various groups moved into Samaria by the Assyrians after Israel fell in 722 B.C. (2 Kgs 17:24). They initially offered to assist in the rebuilding efforts. But Zerubbabel, Jeshua, and the Jews probably detected subversive motives behind the offer. They used Cyrus's decree (1:2–4) as an excuse to exclude the Samaritans from participating in the work. Snubbed by this rejection, the Samaritans proved themselves to be true "enemies of Judah and Benjamin" by opposing the work of the Jews (4:1–5).[3]

The account of Samaritan opposition to the Jews in 4:6–23 is out of chronological sequence. This section details the conflict that occurred fifty years later, when the Samaritans stopped the Jews from rebuilding the walls of Jerusalem. The mention of their opposition to rebuilding the temple reminded the author of later similar trouble. He inserted 4:6–23 parenthetically in order to present the total picture of conflict between Jews and Samaritans during this general time period. Verse 24 pulls the reader back to the difficulties of rebuilding the temple, a topic left off in 4:1–5.[4] The author has included the accounts of Samaritan opposition in chapter 4 in a literary fashion rather than a chronological one.

Chapters 5 and 6 conclude the narrative on the temple's reconstruction. After laying its foundation in 536 B.C., the Jews had failed to finish the building due to opposition and hardship. Sixteen years later, the Spirit of God moved the prophets Haggai and Zechariah to inspire the people (see chapter 34). Haggai urged the Jews to pay as much attention to God's house as they did to their own. Zechariah encouraged the people with his visions and sermons of future blessings if they would obey God's will. Their ministries motivated Zerubbabel, Jeshua, and the people to continue the work. Despite ongoing opposition from their neighbors, the Jews completed the temple in 516 B.C. and reestablished the religious personnel with joyful celebration (6:14–18).

SECOND RETURN UNDER EZRA (EZR 7–10)

The second unit of the Book of Ezra recounts Ezra's return to Jerusalem and his ministry there. The author has skipped approximately fifty-eight years from the construction of the second temple to Ezra's return in 458 B.C. We know almost nothing about the restoration community during this interval. Although this author was intensely interested in history, his main concern was not to write a thorough history of the postexilic community, but to trace the important religious and theological ideas that shaped that community.

Ezra was the towering figure of the restoration community. His genealogy traced his lineage back to Aaron, brother of Moses and first high priest (7:1–5). Such an impressive heritage validated Ezra's right to function as scribe (7:6), which meant he was a student and teacher of the law, not just a copyist. He was a guardian of the *tôrâ* of Moses, implying he continued the traditions of the Pentateuch, the law of God (see p. 62). The "gracious hand" of God was upon Ezra (7:6, 9), because he had devoted himself (literally, "fixed his heart") to the law of the Lord (7:10). He was a blessed scholar, because he sought to do more than study. Ezra strove also to *live* and *teach* God's ways (7:10). Likewise, as we grow in our understanding of God's word, we must also grow in our obedience, and, like Ezra, teach others by word and example.

In 458 B.C., Ezra led a second group of Jews back from exile in Babylon, some eighty years after Zerubbabel's first return (Ezr 7–8). Again, God's hand was upon the returnees, so that they made the trip quickly and safely (8:31–32).

The all-consuming question for the restoration community during this period was how to maintain a distinctive identity in a changing world. With the loss of

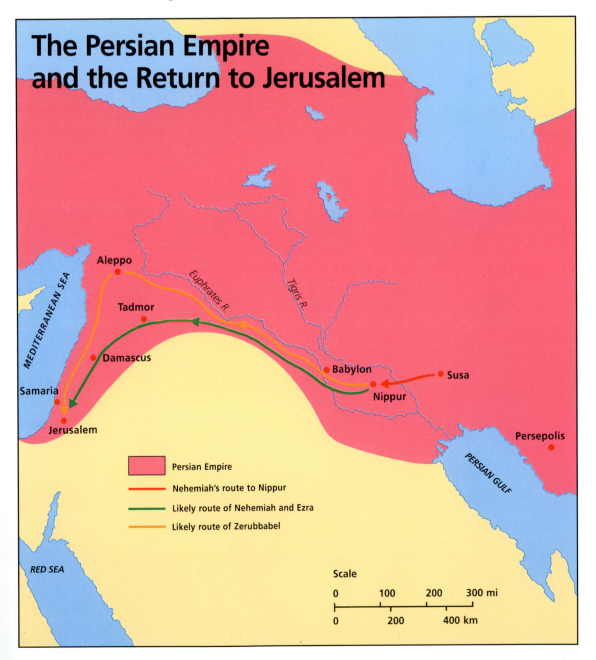

The Persian Empire and the Return to Jerusalem

MEDITERRANEAN SEA

Aleppo

Tadmor

Damascus

Samaria

Jerusalem

Euphrates R.

Tigris R.

Babylon

Nippur

Susa

Persepolis

PERSIAN GULF

RED SEA

Persian Empire

Nehemiah's route to Nippur

Likely route of Nehemiah and Ezra

Likely route of Zerubbabel

Scale

| 0 | 100 | 200 | 300 mi |

| 0 | 200 | 400 km |

Excerpts from the Cyrus Cylinder

The "Cyrus Cylinder," discovered in Babylon in 1879, illustrates the religious tolerance and pluralism of the Persian period.

I returned the divine statues from many sacred cities to their sanctuaries, which had been in ruins for a long period of time. I reestablished permanent sanctuaries for them. At the command of Marduk, Great God of Babylon, I restored the gods taken by Nabonidus. He had angered Marduk by taking captive the gods of Sumer and Akkad and placing them in Babylon. But I resettled them peacefully in their former chapels where they are happy.

May all the gods whom I have resettled in their former sanctuaries intercede daily on my behalf to Marduk and his son Nabu. May they ask for me to have a long life and may they say to Marduk, my lord, "May Cyrus the king who worships you and Cambyses his son, . . ."

[1]Edwin M. Yamauchi, *Persia and The Bible* (Grand Rapids: Baker, 1990), 87–89; and *ANET* 315–317.

---

syncretism

Davidic kingship and national independence, the Jews had lost all tangible signs of God's blessings. How could little Judah maintain a national identity as the people of God in the vast Persian Empire?

Moreover, the principal theological ideal that held sway throughout the Persian Empire was religious **syncretism,** or the merging of differing religious beliefs into one system. The whole world seemed to believe all roads led to heaven and no single group had the right to claim an exclusive handle on truth. Yet ancient Israelite Yahwism was by definition exclusivistic. And Israel's sacred Scripture claimed God had uniquely revealed himself to Israel. National Israel had in fact failed because of her unwillingness to worship Yahweh and Yahweh alone. Would it be possible for later Judah to resist the same impulses and to withstand the universal pressure to compromise her religious distinctiveness?

This is the background to Ezra's dismay at the news that many in Judah, including the leadership, had intermarried with neighboring peoples who practiced pagan religions (9:1–4). Marriage to foreigners had not been categorically forbidden in the law, nor was this simply a prescription against interracial marriage. Rather, this was consistently a religious problem.[5] Israel's history illustrated graphically how quickly Israelite religion deteriorated due to interfaith marriages (examples are Jgs 3:5–6 and the royal marriages of Solomon

and Ahab). Ezra led the people in a public prayer of repentance (9:5–15). The mixed marriages were not simply a matter of racial purity, nor was this legalism. They were "sins" that resulted in "guilt" (9:6). Ezra's prayer makes it clear that such marriages were tantamount to repeating the great sins of their ancestors. These marriages would have to end or the exile would never really be over. The Jews of the restoration community were in danger of melding into the Persian Empire. Doing nothing would have meant the end of God's people (9:14).

Moved by Ezra's deep contrition, the people consented to radical measures (10:1–4). Ezra had not exercised his legal authority to dissolve the marriages without the consent of the people, for this was more than a legal matter. These marriages jeopardized the covenant community and the revelation of God himself. Extreme and drastic measures were required to prevent Yahwism from dissolving and blending into the amalgam of religious practices of the Persian period. Over a three-month period, the mixed marriages were systematically dissolved (10:12–44).

NEHEMIAH REBUILDS JERUSALEM'S WALLS (NEH 1–6)

The opening paragraph of the book implies that some recent catastrophe had befallen the city. The inhabitants of Jerusalem were in distress and its walls lay in ruins

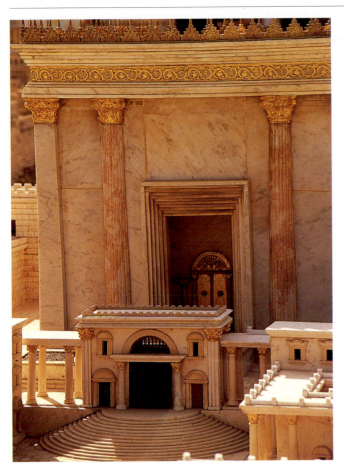

A model of the Second Temple. The first concern of Ezra and the returning Jewish exiles was to rebuild the temple.

my requests," 2:8). Though Jerusalem was surrounded by fierce opponents (2:10, 19), Nehemiah inspired the people to begin rebuilding (2:17–18).

Nehemiah 3 is a remarkable list of individuals who shared the responsibilities of the work. Priests led the way, but people from all walks of life joined in, truly making this a joint effort. Archaeological evidence has verified some of the details of this chapter, and suggests Nehemiah's Jerusalem was smaller than the preexilic city.[7]

The rest of this unit (4:1–6:19) recounts the difficulties the Jews encountered when they began rebuilding the city walls. The problems were both external and internal. The Samaritans under Sanballat and other adversaries from among the Ammonites, Arabs, and Ashdodites opposed the work (4:7). In short, Nehemiah had enemies all around him. But he constantly encouraged the people to keep working and praying. Half his crew worked construction, while the other half stayed armed and ready to defend the city (4:16). His method of dealing with opposition was prayer followed by suitable action (4:9) and he always gave God credit for successes (4:15).

Nehemiah was concerned with more than Jerusalem's physical structures. The city's social ills also threatened to undo God's work among the Jews (chapter 5). An economic crisis had led some Jews into slavery and others had mortgaged their property. Social injustice would turn the physical rebuilding into a futile activity. Nehemiah called for clemency from the leaders. Debts were forgiven and economic stability restored. Nehemiah's remarkable leadership is exemplary in chapter 5. His ability to lead the people to make hard moral decisions was undoubtedly because of his leadership by example. He refused to accept the governor's expense account, which other governors before him had used (vv. 14–19). These monies came from the taxes that had caused much of the hardship among the people in the first place. In many ways, Nehemiah provides a beautiful example of Christian stewardship. It was legal for Nehemiah to take the governor's wages, but not just. Some things are legal, but not right for the Christian. The closer we draw to God, the less we ask what is permissible ("What can I

(1:3). It seems likely that the crisis described in Ezra 4:23–24 had left the city without sufficient defenses.[6] By 445 B.C., Jerusalem's future was at risk and God's people were in danger. The first six chapters of the Book of Nehemiah narrate the events of Nehemiah's arrival in Jerusalem and his leadership in rebuilding the walls.

Nehemiah was an exiled Jew who had risen to high office in the Persian Empire (like the exiles Daniel and Esther). His title as the "cupbearer" to King Artaxerxes I of Persia does not mean Nehemiah was a royal butler, but more like a personal advisor to the emperor of the world (1:11). Upon hearing the news that his people in Jerusalem were still in disgrace, Nehemiah prayed that God would grant him success before his master (1:11). In a turn of events Nehemiah believed was miraculous, Artaxerxes permitted him to move to Jerusalem and provided the means and protection necessary to rebuild the city's defenses ("because the gracious hand of my God was upon me, the king granted

get away with and still be a Christian?") and the more we think about what pleases him.

In Nehemiah 6, the external opponents to Nehemiah's work tried one more approach. In chapter 4, they began by mocking and deriding the plans to rebuild the walls (vv. 2–3). Then they tried to intimidate the builders (vv. 7–8). Here they attack Nehemiah personally. But Nehemiah's resolve and devotion prevailed, and the walls were completed in only fifty-two days (6:15).

EZRA'S AND NEHEMIAH'S REFORMS (NEH 7–13)

After construction of the city walls, this last unit of Nehemiah details the social and religious reforms undertaken by Ezra and Nehemiah. Indeed, it is possible to view this as the second and last section of a two-part volume. Part 1 narrates three great returns led by Zerubbabel, Ezra, and Nehemiah (Ezr and Neh 1–6). Part 2 relates the renewal and reform of the congregation.[8]

Nearly a hundred years after Zerubbabel's first return, the population of Jerusalem was still small (Neh 7:4). In order to encourage them, Nehemiah felt inspired to register the people by genealogies (7:5). Though reading chapter 7 may seem tedious today, these lists of names were an important source of comfort in that day. The list elaborated on Ezra's original list (Ezr 2) and demonstrated continuity with the past. When all seemed lost and hopeless, these details proved God's blessings extended across the centuries.

With God's help, the people had rebuilt the temple and the walls of Jerusalem. The spiritual and political leaders (Ezra and Nehemiah) recognized that the time was right to renew the covenant. The unit in Nehemiah 8–10 records Ezra's ministry of the word and details one of the most vivid covenant ceremonies in the Bible. In a dramatic public reading of the law of Moses (8:1–12), the people learned of God's great love and commitment to them.

Ezra's ministry of the word of God had several profound effects on the people. They responded quickly in reverence and true worship (8:6; 9:3). They revived the ancient customs for celebrating the Feast of Tabernacles (8:13–18). The Levites led

the people in confession of their national guilt (chapter 9). And the covenant of God with Israel was reestablished, as prescribed in the Pentateuch (9:38–10:39). All genuine revivals throughout history have been rooted in a renewed interest in God's word.

The rest of the book recounts Nehemiah's other measures to strengthen the people of Jerusalem. The restored city was able to hold more population. Nehemiah 11 describes how more citizens were brought to live there and gives a list of the city's expanded population. The list of priests (12:1–26) stressed continuity with the past, which was vital for the psychological well-being of the nation. Nehemiah 12:27–47 is the climax of Nehemiah's career. With great joy and celebration, the people dedicated Jerusalem's restored walls. This great "dedication" (ḥănukkâ, 12:27) parallels the dedication of the temple in Ezra 6:17. Nehemiah 13 concludes with other social and religious reforms led by Nehemiah.

Problems of Interpretation

The Books of Ezra and Nehemiah raise several questions that have been answered in diverse ways over the years. Of these, authorship and chronology are the most pressing.

Authorship

The scholarly consensus for many years was that the same author was responsible for Chronicles and Ezra–Nehemiah, and that this single author was probably Ezra himself. But as we have said, that consensus has crumbled (chapter 10, and especially chapter 17, note 3). In recent decades, scholars have garnered impressive evidence in favor of separate authors for Chronicles and Ezra–Nehemiah.[9]

Unlike most Old Testament narratives, these books often use first-person accounts, giving insight into the ultimate origins of the material. For example, the use of first-person narration beginning in Ezra 7:28 makes it unlikely anyone but Ezra wrote Ezra 7–10. Much the same can be said about large sections of Nehemiah and his so-called memoirs. As a result, it is likely that these books developed in three stages. First, anonymous historians compiled several primary sources roughly contemporaneous with the events they relate. Second, the memoirs written by Ezra and Nehemiah themselves were compiled around 400 B.C. These make up the sections containing the first-person accounts. Finally, an editor around 300 B.C. composed Ezra 1–6 and added these chapters as an introduction to the whole composition.[10]

Chronology

The second difficulty in Ezra–Nehemiah is the sequence of the events described. According to the internal evidence of the books, the chronology seems quite straightforward.

538	Cyrus's decree
520	Work on the temple renewed
515	Completion of the temple
458	Ezra's return to Jerusalem
445	Nehemiah's journey to Jerusalem

Part of the Western Wall, Jerusalem. Some of the oldest masonry in the Temple Mount dates to the time of Zerubbabel.

But for several complex reasons, many scholars have reversed the order of Ezra's and Nehemiah's trips to Jerusalem. The date for Ezra's return is given as the seventh year of Artaxerxes in Ezra 7:7–8. Assuming this is Artaxerxes I, the date is fixed at 458 B.C., and the sequence presented in the Books of Ezra and Nehemiah is correct. But if the reference is to Artaxerxes II, Ezra's return would be 398 B.C.

Scholars who contend for this reverse sequence argue this explains why Nehemiah never mentions Ezra in his memoirs (Neh 1–7 and most of 12–13). Ezra's ministry, they believe, would not have begun until several decades later. However, the isolation of Nehemiah's memoirs from the rest of the book is a subjective matter, and Nehemiah's failure to mention Ezra by name in his first-person accounts is an argument from silence. The alternative date for Ezra's return raises more questions than it answers. The biblical evidence in favor of the traditional sequence of events is impressive, and the difficulties it raises are not insurmountable. It is far better to accept the traditional chronology as presented in the books themselves.[11]

The Book of Esther

The Old Testament historical books close with this romantic drama written as a short story, yet having all the marks of authentic

monotheism

history. The events described in the Book of Esther began in 483 B.C. (1:3). This means these things happened between the first return under Zerubbabel (538 B.C.) and the second return led by Ezra (458 B.C.). The action takes place in and around Susa, the capital of the Persian Empire (see map on p. 255).

The author nowhere refers to God in this book, nor does he mention Abraham, the covenant, prayer, or Davidic kingship. Esther is never quoted in the New Testament and is the only Old Testament book not represented in the Dead Sea Scrolls. Over the centuries, many have discounted the book as hopelessly secular and wondered how it came to be included in the canon. However, the power of the message lies partly in its subtlety. Indeed, the author seems to entice his reader into a web of subtleties too ironic and interconnected to be mere happenstance. A larger power is at work here, and in this context, it becomes clear that God is the main character of the book. The author wants to demonstrate that even where God is not apparent, he is at work on behalf of his people.

Contents

As we saw in the discussion of Ezra and Nehemiah, the question of Jewish distinctiveness and the exclusive worship of Yahweh was the critical question for God's people in Jerusalem during the rule of the Persian Empire. Those Jews who still lived in exile, like Esther and Mordecai, struggled with the same issue. The worship of Yahweh could never be one religion among many, as the Persians insisted. Exclusive **monotheism** was not compatible with Persian pluralism. To the Persians, who valued inclusiveness, the Jews seemed unreasonably intolerant, which led to hostility.

The Book of Esther demonstrates how God's people should respond to a pluralistic and multireligious society. In the worst of circumstances, God is looking for people who will trust him and him alone. The book tells the story of a beautiful woman and her uncle who risked their lives to save the Jews from destruction. The story is one of danger, intrigue, and suspense. The book also explains the historical origins of the Jewish Feast of Purim (see below).

Outline

I. **Vashti's Refusal** (1:1–22)

II. **Esther's Accession** (2:1–18)

III. **Mordecai's Service** (2:19–23)

IV. **Haman's Plot** (3:1–15)

V. **Mordecai's Request** (4:1–17)

VI. **Esther's Request** (5:1–14)

VII. **Mordecai's Reward** (6:1–14)

VIII. **Haman's Punishment** (7:1–10)

IX. **The King's Edict** (8:1–17)

X. **The Jews' Triumph** (9:1–10:3)

Overview

The author structured the Book of Esther around a problem–solution format. After a two-chapter introduction giving the necessary historical background, the problem—Haman's evil plot—is introduced in chapter 3. The rest of the book presents the solution gradually.

ESTHER BECOMES QUEEN (CHAPTERS 1–2)

The book's opening chapters introduce the reader to the main characters, Esther and Mordecai, and explain how they came to occupy such exalted positions in the Persian Empire. When Queen Vashti refused a whimsical and foolish request of King Ahasuerus (Xerxes I, 486–465 B.C.), he immediately deposed her (chapter 1). In the search to find a suitable replacement for the queen, the king's representatives searched throughout the kingdom for the most attractive young virgins from whom the king could choose a new queen (2:1–4).

Among these young women, one stood out above the rest. Esther was the niece and adopted daughter of Mordecai the Jew (her own parents were dead, Est 2:7). The lovely Esther was well liked by all who knew her at the palace. The king loved Esther more than all the other candidates, and he made her his new queen (2:17). All the while, according to Mordecai's instructions, Esther chose not to reveal her identity as a Jew, in order not to arouse suspicion of disloyalty to the empire. This last point is stated in 2:10 and again in 2:20 to arouse suspense and heighten the drama.

An artist's rendering of a griffin, from a glazed-block relief at Susa, capital of the Persian Empire.

At the end of the introduction, the author includes one last bit of background that becomes important later. Mordecai secretly learned of a plot to assassinate King Ahasuerus (2:21–23). He told Esther, who warned the king and prevented the coup from taking place. The plotters were executed and Mordecai's deed was recorded in official Persian documents.

Haman's Evil Plot to Destroy the Jews (chapter 3)

Sometime later, Mordecai's devotion as a Jew led to trouble. Palace officials of the king's prime minister, Haman, noted that Mordecai refused to bow down to Haman, as all royal officials had to do. Mordecai refused to pay to any human the adoration and worship due only to God. Enraged, Haman convinced the king to issue an official Persian edict, commanding the slaughter of the Jewish people, who were obstacles to Haman's personal ambitions. By casting *purim*, or lots, they determined that all Jews would be killed on the thirteenth day of the month Adar (3:7, 13). As an official Persian decree, the order was irrevocable (1:19; 8:8; cf. Dn 6:8, 12, 15).

Mordecai and Esther Act to Save the Jews (chapters 4–10)

Only one hope remained for saving the Jewish people. Only Esther had the personal influence with the king necessary to prevent the tragedy from becoming a reality. Mordecai urged Esther to reveal her identity as a Jew and to plead for the life of her people (chapter 4). But no one was allowed to approach the king unsummoned at the risk of execution (4:11). Esther was finally convinced to risk her life for her fellow Jews by Mordecai's penetrating question, which is the theme of the book: "Who knows but that you have come to royal position for such a time as this?" (4:14). God's favor is never meant to be squandered in selfish indulgence. Achieving God's purpose for our existence is more important than personal comfort. Esther agreed to risk her life in an attempt to intercede. But first she instructed all Jews in Susa to fast for three days. Her resolve rings in the words, "If I perish, I perish" (4:16).

Three days later, Esther approached King Ahasuerus, who fortunately received her without hesitation. Surprisingly, she requested only a private dinner with the king and Haman for that evening. At the dinner, she requested they meet again for dinner the next evening. Haman's joy at being included in these private banquets with the royal couple quickly changed to rage when he saw Mordecai again refusing to bow down to him (5:9). In anger, he ordered the construction of a seventy-five-foot gallows just outside his home, where he intended to hang Mordecai (5:14).

In a manner that can only be explained in God's sovereign providence, the king was unable to sleep that night (6:1). He asked for his journal to be read aloud, and

Summary

1. The Books of Ezra, Nehemiah, and Esther have a common origin in the Persian period of Jewish history.

2. King Cyrus of Persia captured Babylon and issued a decree that released the Jews.

3. The Jews were able to rebuild the temple in Jerusalem, but because of numerous problems, it was not completed until 516 B.C.

4. Ezra was an important scribe in the community of Jews that returned from Babylon.

5. Nehemiah was concerned that the walls of Jerusalem were in ruins, and he was the person who was able to motivate the people to rebuild them.

6. Ezra and Nehemiah led the people in the renewal of the covenant.

7. The author of Ezra and Nehemiah was unique in that he used first-person accounts.

8. The Book of Esther is a romantic novel that is written as a short story.

9. The exclusive worship of God was a critical matter for the Jews during the rule of the Persian Empire. The Book of Esther shows how God's people should respond in a pluralistic society.

10. The Jewish Feast of Purim originated because of the way God saved Mordecai from Haman.

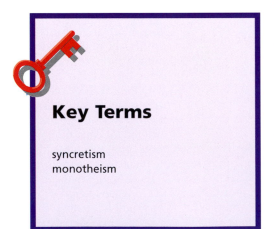

Key Terms

syncretism
monotheism

was thus reminded of how Mordecai had saved his life. When he learned that Mordecai had never been properly rewarded, he summoned Haman, who had just arrived. Without disclosing whom he had in mind, the king asked Haman what special rewards he could bestow on a man he wanted especially to honor. Haman, unable to imagine anyone more deserving than himself, assumed the king wanted to honor him. He suggested what he deemed a suitable reward. The king should give that man a royal robe and horse, and a noble prince to march before him through the city, crying, "This is what is done for the man the king delights to honor!" (6:7–9). King Ahasuerus thought that sounded fine. The reward went to Mordecai, and in an amazing twist of irony, Haman was the noble prince who escorted him through the city (6:11).

After such a humiliating experience, Haman must have hoped for better things from the dinner with the king and queen later that evening. But at dinner Esther revealed Haman's evil intentions and pleaded for mercy for her people (7:3–6).

Appalled at Haman's behavior, the king ordered that he be hanged on the very gallows he had intended for Mordecai (7:9–10). But there is even more irony. The king gave Haman's estate to Esther, who gave it to Mordecai. The king also made Mordecai the successor to Haman (8:1–2).

The matter of Haman's decree still posed a problem. It could not be revoked, but the king allowed Mordecai to issue another official decree in an effort to counter its effects. The second order allowed the Jews in every city of the Persian Empire to defend themselves from any attack on the thirteenth day of the month of Adar (8:3–17). On the dreaded day, the Jews successfully defended themselves from their enemies (9:1–19). The next day, the fourteenth, became a day of great celebration, except in Susa, where more battles occurred. The Jews of Susa celebrated their victory on the fifteenth of Adar (9:16–19).

Mordecai and Esther wrote to all the Jews of the empire, establishing the feast of Purim as an annual time of celebration on the fourteenth and fifteenth of Adar (9:20–28). The holiday was called Purim because of the *pur,* or "lot," which Haman cast to determine the date of his proposed extermination of the Jews. These two days in the month of Adar became permanent reminders of how their sorrow turned to joy and their mourning into celebration (9:22). The book closes with a brief note on

Study Questions

Ezra–Nehemiah

1. What period of time is covered in the Books of Ezra, Nehemiah, and Esther?

2. Discuss some of the important differences among these books. How do these differences make the books complement each other?

3. Why are Ezra and Nehemiah often studied as one continuous work?

4. What role did Ezra play among the returning exiles?

5. What is the all-consuming question faced by the people at this time?

6. Discuss the concept of Israelite Yahwism as exclusivistic.

7. Why were the mixed marriages found in the Book of Ezra a threat to God's people at this time?

8. With what events is the Book of Nehemiah concerned?

9. What social problems are found among the Israelites at this time?

10. Discuss the problems of authorship and chronology connected to Ezra and Nehemiah.

11. What are some of the theological themes of Ezra and Nehemiah?

Esther

1. What unusual feature does the Book of Esther have?

2. What is the theme of this book?

3. Discuss the subtleties of this book and how they affect the story being told.

4. Who is the main character of Esther?

5. What does the Book of Esther teach about life in a pluralistic and multireligious society?

Further Reading

Baldwin, Joyce G. *Esther: An Introduction and Commentary.* Tyndale Old Testament Commentary. Downers Grove: InterVarsity, 1984. Baldwin is always useful reading.

Clines, David J. A. *Ezra, Nehemiah, Esther.* New Century Bible Commentary. Grand Rapids/London: Eerdmans/Marshall, Morgan & Scott, 1984. Carefully written and containing many helpful insights.

Fensham, F. Charles. *The Books of Ezra and Nehemiah.* New International Commentary on the Old Testament. Grand Rapids: Eerdmans, 1982. Helpful and thoroughly evangelical.

Howard, David M., Jr. *An Introduction to the Old Testament Historical Books.* Chapter 9: "Ezra-Nehemiah," 273–313. Chicago: Moody, 1993.

Kidner, Derek. *Ezra and Nehemiah: An Introduction and Commentary.* Tyndale Old Testament Commentary. Downers Grove: InterVarsity, 1979.

McConville, J. Gordon. *Ezra, Nehemiah, and Esther.* Daily Study Bible. Philadelphia: Westminster, 1985.

Moore, Carey A. *Esther: Introduction, Translation, and Notes.* Anchor Bible 7B. Garden City, N.Y.: Doubleday, 1971. Excellent, though critical commentary.

Williamson, H. G. M. *Ezra, Nehemiah.* Word Biblical Commentary 16. Waco, Tex.: Word, 1985. Lucid and original, this is easily the best commentary available.

———. *Ezra and Nehemiah.* Old Testament Guides. Sheffield: JSOT, 1987.

the successes of King Ahasuerus and his second in command, Mordecai (10:1–3).

Theological Themes

Ezra and Nehemiah

The Books of Ezra and Nehemiah take for granted the truth of many elements of ancient Israel's faith. They build on the great principles of Old Testament theology instituted in earlier books, but with new emphases. For example, this author, like earlier biblical authors, gives pride of place to history in ancient Israel's religion. He describes events separated by a century or more, often with large gaps of silence between the events. The author groups stories of opposition literarily in Ezra 4, though these historical events were separated by five decades. Or he moves easily from the construction of the temple (516 B.C.) to the arrival of Ezra (458 B.C.), with no discussion of the intervening decades (Ezr 6–7).

The overarching theme tying these his-

torical events together is the author's assumption that they are "divinely related steps in what may properly be regarded as a history of salvation."[12] The direct intervention of God is less visible here than in the exodus and conquest narratives that are so commonly referred to as salvation-history. But this author has tied many diverse types of historical material together with the assumption that together they portray God's handiwork.

The way in which Ezra and Nehemiah are most obviously indebted to what preceded is the emphasis on "the law of the LORD" or "the law of Moses" (Ezr 7:10; Neh 8:1; etc.). The author refers to other sections of sacred Scripture as well, such as Jeremiah (Ezr 1:1) and the Psalms (Ezr 3:11). The Old Testament attached special significance to God's word from the beginning. But with Ezra and Nehemiah, Scripture was elevated to a new level of authority and power. This dominant role of Scripture continued in both Judaism and Christianity.

Esther

Some would suggest it is futile to speak of theological ideas in Esther, since God is nowhere mentioned in the book. But the story contains a remarkable series of "coincidences." Esther *happened* to be selected as Vashti's successor; Mordecai *happened* to uncover the plan to assassinate the king; Ahasuerus *happened* to have insomnia on the night before Haman planned to kill Mordecai; the selection of royal chronicles read to the king that night *happened* to contain the report of Mordecai's good deed. These "coincidences" are not limited to the realm of God's people. Persian kings and royal officials also move and act under the unseen hand of the great Sovereign Lord. Though God is not mentioned, he is the central character of the book, more so than Esther or Mordecai. This makes the Book of Esther extremely relevant for our day, for God is still sovereignly at work to save his people.

Part

3

Encountering the
Poetical Books

19 Introduction to the Poetical Books

The Literature of God's People

Objectives

After reading this chapter, you should be able to

- Name the poetical books of the Old Testament
- Illustrate the four common characteristics of Hebrew poetry
- Define the types of parallelism
- Give an example of chiasm
- Explain how an acrostic is used as a literary device in poetry
- Explain how the discovery of the Ugaritic language has enhanced our understanding of Hebrew poetry
- State the basic contribution made by each poetical book

meter

rhyme

parallelism

synonymous
parallelism

antithetic
parallelism

synthetic
parallelism

What Are the Poetical Books?

When we use the expression "poetical books," we are referring to the Books of Job, Psalms, Proverbs, Ecclesiastes, and Song of Songs. Poetry also occurs in many other Old Testament books, but these five books contain a large portion of it. Furthermore, in every poetical book except Ecclesiastes, poetry provides the predominant literary form. Ecclesiastes nevertheless became associated with the poetical books at some early time, probably because of its affinities with Hebrew wisdom literature.

This chapter highlights some of the basic characteristics of Hebrew poetry and also briefly compares Hebrew poetry with the poetry of its ancient Near Eastern neighbors. Doing so will help clarify the special contribution the poetical books have made to the Bible and to our Christian faith.

Common Characteristics of Hebrew Poetry

Hebrew scholars disagree over what exactly constitutes Hebrew poetry.[1] Nevertheless, they agree that Hebrew poetry typically displays certain characteristics. The most common are discussed below.

Meter

In most modern poetry, **meter** and **rhyme** play important roles. Each line follows a certain meter or accent pattern and the last words of lines often rhyme. Consider the following nursery rhyme:

Mary had a little lamb,
Its fleece was white as snow.
And everywhere that Mary went
The lamb was sure to go.

Notice the meter and rhyme of this verse. The first and third lines have four basic accents—"MA-ry HAD a LIT-tle LAMB," "And EV-ry-WHERE that MA-ry WENT." The second and fourth lines have three basic accents—"Its FLEECE was WHITE as SNOW," "The LAMB was SURE to GO." The second and fourth lines also have last words ("snow," "go") that rhyme.

Hebrew poetry relies much more on meter than on rhyme, though rhyme sometimes does occur. Some commentators have suggested ancient writers used metric patterns to convey certain moods or ideas.[2] These scholars do not agree completely, but they do concur that Hebrew poetry clearly uses a variety of metric styles.

Parallelism

Parallelism is the most important feature of Hebrew poetry.[3] When we use the term, we mean we have at least two parallel lines of verse, that is, each complements the other(s) in some way. Typically, the lines display parallelism of thought rather than parallelism of rhyme or sound. Three primary types of parallelism occur in Hebrew poetry: **synonymous parallelism, antithetic parallelism,** and **synthetic parallelism**.

Synonymous parallelism

Synonymous parallelism involves a repetition of the same thought or a similar thought. The two parts basically reflect the same idea. For example, consider Psalm 19:1:

The heavens declare the glory of God;
the skies proclaim the work of his hands.

The two lines repeat the same basic thought. "Heavens" and "skies" are parallel, as are "declare" and "proclaim." "The work of his hands" parallels "the glory of God." Another well-known example is Proverbs 9:10:

The fear of the LORD is the beginning of
    wisdom,
and knowledge of the Holy One is under-
    standing.

For other examples, see Proverbs 16:18, 28; 18:6–7.

Synonymous parallelism can also occur using questions. Note Psalm 15:1:

LORD, who may dwell in your sanctuary?
Who may live on your holy hill?

The psalms would sometimes have been accompanied by musical instruments such as these.

Again, the two lines complement each other, reflecting the same idea. Each presents a question, and "sanctuary" parallels "holy hill," the place of God's sanctuary.

Sometimes in synonymous parallelism the second line will not totally parallel the first line. In such a case we have incomplete parallelism. Psalm 24:1 provides a good example:

> The earth is the LORD's,
>   and everything in it,
> The world, and all who live in it.

The expression "is the LORD's" is missing from the second line, but the reader clearly understands the thought from the previous line. Proverbs 19:29 provides another example:

> Penalties are prepared for mockers,
> and beatings for the backs of fools.

In this verse, the verbal idea—"are prepared"—carries over from the first line into the second line.

Antithetic parallelism

Antithetic parallelism is easy to recognize. The two lines stand in sharp contrast to each other; usually the conjunction "but"

provides a clue. Psalm 1:6 gives us a good example:

> For the LORD watches over the way of the righteous,
> But the way of the wicked will perish.

The psalmist contrasted the Lord's providential care of his people with the destruction the wicked would someday experience. The parallel elements likewise contrast with each other. "Way of the righteous" contrasts with "way of the wicked." "Watches over" contrasts with "perish."

The Book of Proverbs also yields many good examples of antithetic parallelism. Note how in each example below, the first and second lines express opposite ideas:

> Ill-gotten treasures are of no value,
> but righteousness delivers from death (10:2).

> Lazy hands make a man poor,
> but diligent hands bring wealth (10:4).

> The memory of the righteous
>   will be a blessing,
> but the name of the wicked will rot (10:7).

Synthetic parallelism

In synthetic parallelism, the second line normally completes a thought the first line

An Assyrian relief showing captive musicians.

chiasm

left incomplete. The two lines stand in relationship to each other, but that relationship is not as clearly defined as in synonymous or antithetic parallelism.

Some interpreters have questioned whether synthetic parallelism is really parallelism at all. They suggest the term merely provides a catch-all category for verses that do not display characteristics of synonymous or antithetic parallelism. Look at the following examples as you consider the question:

Psalm 1:3	He is like a tree planted by streams of water, Which yields its fruit in season and whose leaf does not wither.
Psalm 2:6	I have installed my King On Zion, my holy mountain.
Ecclesiastes 11:1	Cast your bread upon the waters, for after many days you will find it again.

In Psalm 1:3, the second line adds to the thought of line 1 by further describing the tree by the water. The second line of Psalm 2:6 adds to the thought of the first line by explaining where God has installed his king—on Zion. The second line of Ecclesiastes 11:1 gives the reason for the command of the first line.

Whether we call this phenomenon syn-thetic parallelism or not, the poetical books do feature many verses of this type where the second line completes the thought begun in the first.

Chiasm

Chiasm is another literary feature of Hebrew poetry.[4] The word "chiasm" comes from the Greek letter "chi," which is written like the letter "X." Chiasm occurs when two successive lines of poetry reverse the order in which parallel themes appear, "criss-crossing" each other. Consider the example below:

> **O Lord,** *forgive me;*
> *Blot out my sin,* **O God of my salvation.**

Here we have an example of synonymous parallelism; The bold elements parallel each other and the italic elements parallel each other. But notice how the two parts reverse themselves in the second line. "O Lord" (part A) parallels "O God of my salvation" in the second line, while "forgive me" (part B) parallels "blot out my sin." We call this an A-B-B-A pattern because parts A and B switch their order in the second line. More complex arrangements also occur, such as A-B-C-C-B-A.

Sometimes an extended passage features chiastic structure. Psalm 8 provides such an example. Verses 1 and 9 describe God's majesty. Verses 2–3 describe God's

The Chiastic Structure of Psalm 8[1]

A GOD'S EXCELLENT NAME: (1a) O Lord, our Lord, how majestic is your name in all the earth!

   B GOD'S RULE: (1) You have set your glory above the heavens. (2) From the lips of children and infants you have ordained praise because of your enemies, to silence the foe and the avenger. (3) When I consider your heavens, the work of your fingers, the moon and the stars, which you have set in place,

      C HUMANITY'S SMALLNESS: (4) what is man that you are mindful of him, the son of man that you care for him?

      C' HUMANITY'S GREATNESS: (5) You made him a little lower than the heavenly beings and crowned him with glory and honor.

   B' HUMANITY'S RULE: (6) You made him ruler over the works of your hands; you put everything under his feet: (7) all flocks and herds, and the beasts of the field, (8) the birds of the air, and the fish of the sea, all that swim the paths of the seas.

A' GOD'S EXCELLENT NAME: (9) O Lord, our Lord, how majestic is your name in all the earth!

[1]Adapted from Robert L. Alden, *Psalms: Songs of Devotion* (Chicago: Moody, 1974), 24.

contains an A-B-C-C-B-A pattern. It contrasts God's rule and humanity's, humanity's smallness and greatness, and wraps all these thoughts with praise to God—"O LORD our LORD, how majestic is your name in all the earth."[5]

Acrostics

Acrostics are alphabetic poems. Imagine that you wrote a twenty-six-line hymn of praise to God. In an acrostic, the first line would begin with the letter "A." The second line would begin with the letter "B," the third with "C," the fourth with "D," and so on throughout the alphabet. Imagine trying to stay on the same topic and trying to fit it all together! (You might even want to try it if you have the time.) This technique worked the same in biblical Hebrew except the Hebrew alphabet contained twenty-two letters instead of twenty-six.

The poetical books feature many acrostics. Psalm 119 is probably one of the most famous examples. The first eight verses begin with *aleph,* the first letter of the Hebrew alphabet. Verses 9–16 begin with *beth,* the second letter, and so on throughout the psalm. And each verse emphasizes something special about the Word of God! Proverbs 31:10–31, a poem describing the virtuous woman, also employs acrostic style.

Acrostics are one of the many creative styles human authors used in the writing

acrostic

rule, whereas verses 6–8 describe humanity's rule. Verse 4 describes humanity's smallness contrasted with humanity's greatness in verse 5. Thus, the psalm

Excerpts from the Baal Cycle

The following excerpt from a Baal epic from Ugarit will help you get a better understanding of Baal and his power among the Canaanite pantheon:

"Now the gods were sitting to eat, the holy ones to dine, Baal attending upon El. As soon as the gods spy them, spy Yamm's messengers, the envoys of Judge Nahar, the gods drop their heads down on their knees and on their princely thrones.

Baal rebukes them: 'Why, O gods, have you dropped your heads down on your knees and on your princely thrones? I see the gods are cowed with terror of Yamm's messengers, the envoys of Judge Nahar. Lift up your heads, O gods, from on your knees, from on your princely thrones, and I'll answer Yamm's messengers, the envoys of Judge Nahar!'"

[1]Translation adapted from James B. Pritchard, ed., *Ancient Near Eastern Texts Relating to the Old Testament,* 3rd ed. (Princeton N. J.: Princeton University Press, 1969), 130.

Ugaritic

Akkadian

cuneiform

of God's word. The Holy Spirit inspired the writers to express themselves in ways that would challenge our creative energies today.

Ugaritic Parallels

The term "**Ugaritic**" denotes the language spoken at ancient Ugarit (modern Ras Shamra) on the Mediterranean coast of what is now modern Syria. Archaeologists began to excavate Ugarit in 1929, and the site has proven invaluable for the study of the Bible and of the ancient world from which it came.[6]

Ugarit was especially prominent in Syria from 1500 to 1200 B.C. Archaeologists discovered many texts written in the **Akkadian** language, but other **cuneiform** texts appeared alongside them. Scholars soon realized the language was alphabetic and contained thirty signs in contrast to the hundreds of signs in Akkadian. They named the language Ugaritic.

Ugaritic is very similar to biblical Hebrew even though it uses a different script. Hundreds of words appear in both languages with basically the same meaning. This fact helps us understand the biblical text better in at least three ways.

First, certain rare Hebrew words occur more commonly in Ugaritic, so we can be more certain of the meaning of the biblical words. Perhaps a rare Hebrew word occurs in a difficult context, but in Ugaritic

Summary

1. The poetical books are Job, Psalms, Proverbs, Ecclesiastes, and Song of Solomon.

2. Meter, parallelism, chiasm, and acrostics all play a role in Hebrew poetry.

3. Hebrew poetry has three types of parallelism—synonymous, antithetic, and synthetic.

4. Chiasm is a literary device in which the content of two parallel lines of poetry is reversed.

5. Acrostic Poetry is written with the first word of every line in alphabetic order.

6. The cuneiform language spoken in ancient Ugarit is called Ugaritic. This is an alphabetic language made up of thirty signs.

7. Ugaritic contributes to a better understanding of the Hebrew text in that it adds clarity to rare Hebrew words; it uses the same style of parallelism; and it provides background about the polytheism of ancient Israel's time.

8. Job is important because it looks at the question about why good people sometimes suffer.

9. The Book of Psalms has given us many songs from ancient Israel.

10. Proverbs provides us with practical guidelines for living.

11. The meaning of life is explored in Ecclesiastes.

12. Song of Solomon focuses on the joy of romantic love.

Study Questions

1. What are some of the common characteristics of Hebrew poetry? How does biblical poetry differ from much of our modern poetry?

2. How would you explain parallelism to someone who had never heard of it?

3. Describe the significance of the Ugaritic tablets to the study of the Bible, particularly to Hebrew poetry.

---

polytheistic

Baal

Asherah

the word occurs a dozen times in clear contexts. We then can try the meaning of the Ugaritic word for the Hebrew word in the biblical text to see if the Ugaritic meaning fits. In this way, Ugaritic texts have sometimes clarified the meaning of difficult Hebrew words or passages.

Second, Ugaritic poetry contains many similarities to Hebrew poetry. For example, parallelism also occurs in Ugaritic poetry. The biblical writers thus used a poetic style common to some other people of their time. However, whereas the people of Ugarit used this poetic style to write the stories of their gods and goddesses, the biblical writers used it to praise and worship the one true God of heaven.

Third, Ugaritic poetry helps us understand the **polytheistic** world that surrounded the Hebrews. The texts reveal much about **Baal** and his consort **Asherah**, whose worship the prophets thoroughly denounced. We now know from the testimony of the people who worshiped Baal and Asherah what the people believed these gods were like.

The Poetical Books Themselves

The poetical books have an important contribution to make to our Christian faith

Further Reading

Alter, Robert. *The Art of Biblical Poetry.* New York: Basic, 1985. Explores the many features biblical writers used in their poetic writings.

Berry, Donald K. *An Introduction to Wisdom and Poetry of the Old Testament.* Nashville: Broadman & Holman, 1995. A detailed discussion of biblical wisdom literature, its parallels in the biblical world, and its use by Jews and Christians over the centuries.

Bullock, C. Hassell. *An Introduction to the Old Testament Poetic Books.* Rev. ed. Chicago: Moody, 1988. An upper-level college or basic seminary-level survey. Covers the basic interpretational issues well.

Craigie, Peter C. *Ugarit and the Old Testament.* Grand Rapids: Eerdmans, 1983. A classic survey of the information from Ugarit that sheds light on the Old Testament.

Petersen, David L. and Kent Harold Richards. *Interpreting Hebrew Poetry.* Guides to Biblical Scholarship. Minneapolis: Fortress, 1992. A short, more technical discussion.

today. Job addresses the problem of why righteous people sometimes suffer terrible trials. Psalms provides many songs of Israel and invites us to join the ancient voices in singing to God. Proverbs offers us timeless principles expressed in catchy, creative ways. Ecclesiastes explores the meaning of life and concludes that only a personal relationship with God gives life real meaning. And Song of Songs celebrates the joy of love in a romantic love poem.

20 Job
One Man's Search for Justice

Outline

- **Introduction to Wisdom Literature**
  Ancient Near Eastern Wisdom Literature
  Old Testament Wisdom Literature
- **Contents of the Book of Job**
  Outline
  Overview
- **The Author and His Times**
- **Theological Themes**

Objectives

**After reading this chapter,
you should be able to**

- Identify the two major classifications
  of wisdom literature of the ancient
  Near East
- Describe the key characters of the wisdom
  literature of Egypt
- Contrast the wisdom literature of Egypt,
  Mesopotamia, and the Old Testament
- Outline the basic content
  of the Book of Job
- Give examples of the approaches used
  by Job's three friends in their attempts
  to help him
- Define theodicy
- Evaluate all of the speeches made
  before Job
- Compare Job and his speakers' view
  of retribution with God's view

wisdom
literature

sages

dialogues

monologues

retribution

The Book of Job is one of three in the Old Testament in the collection known as **wisdom literature**. After a brief discussion of the meaning of this phrase, attention will turn to the details of this fascinating book.

Introduction to Wisdom Literature

The expression "wisdom literature" does not occur in the Old Testament. This is a designation modern scholars use for three books that share "wisdom" features: Job, Proverbs, and Ecclesiastes. In addition to these three, selected Psalms are also part of the collection (Pss 1, 37, 49, 73, etc.), and Song of Songs is similar to wisdom literature in its didactic function and literary form. So all the books included in the section of the canon called "poetic" are related to wisdom literature (chapter 19 above). But wisdom ideas also reach beyond the poetical books of the Bible. Several of the prophets use wisdom sayings and parables in their sermons (Hosea, Isa-

iah, etc.), and the teachings of Jesus have many examples of wisdom concepts.

Ancient Near Eastern Wisdom Literature

Old Testament wisdom literature had an international backdrop. The author of 1 Kings compared the wisest of Israel's wise men, Solomon, to the wise men of Mesopotamia, Canaan, and Egypt, the known world of that time (1 Kgs 4:29–34). Each nation apparently had wisdom teachers who reflected their own particular nationalistic wisdom traditions. Archaeologists have discovered examples of wisdom literature from all parts of the ancient Near East.

The wisdom literature of the ancient Near East may be categorized in two general groups. First, there are brief proverbial maxims stating observations about life in general. These tend to be instructional or didactic in nature and are usually optimistic about life. Second, **sages** of the ancient Near East produced documents containing lengthy discourses or essays grappling with life's most difficult problems. These **dialogues** or **mono-**

Wisdom literature touches on all issues that explore the meaning of life.

Excerpts Adapted from the Teachings of Ptahhotep[1]

(Suggested parallels are in parentheses)

He said to his son:

Do not become arrogant because of your knowledge, nor confident because you are wise. Take advice from the simple as well as the wise. You never reach your full potential, always having more to learn. Good speech is hidden like an emerald, but may be found as women grinding grain. (Prv 2:1–5)

If you are fortunate enough to sit at table with someone greater than yourself, take graciously what is offered to you. Do not become envious and greedy, always wanting more. (Prv 23:1–3) If you become a messenger for important individuals, be completely reliable in every assignment you receive. Carry out your errand precisely. (Prv 25:13)

If you are a visitor in a house, under any circumstances—whether you visit as master, brother or friend—stay away from the women of the house! A thousand men have been distracted from their duties by pretty faces, to their disadvantage. One is easily made a fool by shapeliness and beauty. It is a dream world, and pursuing it is deadly. Avoid lust and sickness of the heart and you will prosper. (Prv 6:23–29)

[1]Extracted and adapted from the Instruction of the Vizier Ptahhotep (*ANET*, 412–14).

dent is "child," or "son" (as in Prv 1:8). This reflects the concept that the family was the most important educational unit of the ancient world, as was also true of ancient Israel (Dt 6:6–7).

The earliest of these collections claims to originate with PTAHHOTEP, VIZIER of KING IZEZI of the Fifth Dynasty (about 2450 B.C.). The *Instruction of Ptahhotep* contains thirty-seven maxims given by Ptahhotep to his son and designated successor. The collection seeks to train the son in human relations, preparing him for the actions and attitudes that will make him a successful official of the state. A much later collection, the *Instruction of Amenemope* from around 1200 B.C., contains thirty chapters of instructions for well-being, many of which closely parallel certain Old Testament proverbs.

Mesopotamian discursive wisdom

The second type of wisdom literature from the ancient Near East came primarily from Mesopotamia. These documents contain discourses, or extended speeches, about the problems of justice in the world. The discourses may be soliloquies, dialogues with the deity, or the speeches of many participants.

As was true of Egyptian instructional literature, the Mesopotamian authors had no word for wisdom that included the high morality and piety of Israelite wisdom literature. For this reason, the expression "wisdom literature" is not strictly appropriate for the Mesopotamian discoursive material. "Wisdom" and the adjectives for "wise" in the Mesopotamian documents rarely have moral content, and generally refer to skill in magical practices.[3] This is a subtle distinction from Israelite wisdom literature, where the "wise" person is one who fears the Lord.

On the other hand, the content of these documents invites comparison with Job and Ecclesiastes. The Mesopotamian dialogue material accepts the doctrine of **retribution**—goodness results in prosperity and wickedness leads to suffering. The problem arises when good people suffer. The Mesopotamian authors sought to explain the problem by asserting that the righteous person does not exist. The person who suffers does so because of crimes he has committed. Ultimately, the

logues are frequently, but not always, pessimistic.

Egyptian instructional wisdom

A few ancient Near Eastern examples of instructional wisdom have come from Mesopotamia, but most are from Egyptian literature.[1] Though Egyptian does not have a word for "wisdom" per se, the Egyptians delighted in collections of wise sayings that helped one lead a successful life. This type of literature they called "instruction."[2] In these documents the teacher is often "father" or "mother" and the stu-

Excerpts Adapted from the Babylonian Theodicy[1]

The Babylonian Theodicy is a dialogue between a sufferer and his comforting friend.

Sufferer to his friend: Your opinion is like the north-wind, a pleasant breeze for everyone. Pure and choice is your advice. But I have one problem for you: those who neglect the god prosper, while those who devoutly pray become poor and weak. (Jb 21:7–16)

Friend to the sufferer: Unless you seek the will of the god, what hope have you? Whoever serves his god faithfully never lacks food, even when food is hard to come by. So seek the calming breath of the gods, and this year's losses will be recovered in a moment.

Friend to the sufferer: O wise one, O scholar, who has mastered knowledge, your heart is wrong when you accuse the god unjustly. The mind of the gods is like the center of the heavens, far removed from you. Its knowledge is difficult and beyond human comprehension. (Jb 11:7; 15:2–4)

Sufferer to his friend: Listen carefully, my friend, to what I say. Heed the choice expression of my words. (Jb 21:2–3)

Friend to the sufferer: When the great primeval, creator gods of the universe created humankind, they gave him twisted speech. They endowed them forever with lies and not the truth. (Jb 15:5–6)

[1]W. G. Lambert, *Babylonian Wisdom Literature* (Oxford: Clarendon, 1960), 63–91; and *ANET*, 438–40, where it is called "A Dialogue About Human Misery."

Kassite period

monotheistic

of wisdom") is a lengthy monologue in which a noble Babylonian recounts how he met with every sort of disaster before the god Marduk eventually restored him to his position. This text comes from the **Kassite period** of Mesopotamian history (fourteenth to twelfth centuries B.C.). The Babylonian Theodicy is an elaborate dialogue between a sufferer and his friend. In the friend's speeches, he seeks to defend the retribution doctrine against the sufferer's complaints.[5]

Old Testament Wisdom Literature

Ancient Near Eastern literature has many obvious parallels in both form and content to the Old Testament wisdom books.[6] In fact, the Book of Proverbs contains more direct parallels with ancient Near Eastern literature than any other book of the Bible. Some points of contact with the parallels are more direct than others, such as Proverbs 22–24 and the *Instruction of Amenemope* (see discussion in chapter 22 below). Others are parallel in matters of theme and emphasis, such as Job and *Ludlul bēl nēmeqi*.

By comparing Job, Proverbs, and Ecclesiastes to the literature of the ancient Near East, we learn a great deal about how the ancient Israelites interacted with the literature and worldview of their neighbors. They were comfortable incorporating materials from other cultures, as long as they eliminated polytheistic elements. As such, the wisdom literature provides a wonderful example of cross-cultural communication of faith.[7] Sometimes the Israelites adapted ancient Near Eastern material with little or no alterations, such as Proverbs and the Egyptian wisdom materials. At other times, the Israelite authors used pagan literature in which they made theological modifications. Other parallels appear to have been so thoroughly changed by Israelite theological alterations as to be hardly recognizable.[8]

Wisdom literature touches on all issues that explore the meaning of life. In ancient Israel, that exploration was unique in the ancient world, because it had a thoroughly **monotheistic** perspective. In the Old Testament, the foundation of wisdom is the fear of the Lord expressed in genuine faith (Prv 1:7).

Mesopotamian solution to the problem of suffering is to place the blame on the sufferer, who can only accept the fate hurled upon him or her by the unfathomable gods.[4] As we shall see, the problems posed by Job and Ecclesiastes are similar, though their solutions are very different.

Of the several examples of the Mesopotamian dialogue literature, we will only mention two of the most important here. The text known by its opening phrase *Ludlul bēl nēmeqi* ("I will praise the Lord

Job was a wealthy man until he lost his donkeys, sheep, and camels.

Contents of the Book of Job

The book opens with a two-chapter prose introduction giving the reader the necessary background for what follows (chapters 1–2). The main body of the book is in poetry and contains the speeches of Job, his advisors, and, finally, God (3:1–42:6). The book closes with a brief epilogue, again in prose (42:7–17). The prose PROLOGUE and epilogue create a literary frame for the poetic speeches.

Outline

Overview

The Book of Job reads like a play, the main characters of which are introduced in the prose prologue (chapters 1–2). The author of this prologue assumes an omniscient point of view, that is, he seems to know everything. He can evaluate Job's inner thoughts, and he relates the dialogue between God and Satan.

The speeches at the center of the book

The speeches at the center of the book wrestle with some of life's most difficult questions.

theodicy

wrestle with some of life's most difficult questions. Specifically, the speakers deal with undeserved suffering and the attendant problem of **theodicy.** Theodicy is the attempt to justify God's ways in the world. If God is both all-powerful and all-loving, as the Bible everywhere claims, then how can evil exist in the world? How can the wicked prosper if God is just? Why do good people suffer, and how could God let it happen?

Ancient Israel's monotheism raised this question. Since the only true God is both all-powerful and all-good, the presence of evil in the world creates a philosophical quandary. If God were perfectly good, he would not allow evil to exist in any of its various forms (wars, famine, crime). Therefore, there must be some limit to his ability to control the circumstances of the world, and he is not all-powerful. On the other hand, if God were all-powerful, the fact that evil events and circumstances occur must mean he sees nothing wrong with them. Therefore, he is not all-loving.[9] The Book of Job is one man's search and discovery for the answer to this dilemma.

The prologue (chapters 1–2)

The opening verse of the book describes Job as a "blameless and upright" man who "feared God and shunned evil." Such integrity led God to ask Satan the terse question, "Have you considered my servant Job?" (1:8). Satan's accusatory reply (1:9–11) marked the beginning of a series of events that resulted in the loss of Job's children and his substantial wealth. But even in the wake of total ruin, Job remained faithful to God (1:22).

Satan challenged Job's credibility again by asserting that extreme physical suffering in addition to the loss of possessions and family would cause him to curse God (2:4–5). So God allowed Satan to afflict Job with painful boils all over his body. Job sat destitute and alone on a heap of ashes, scraping his diseased skin with a piece of broken pottery (2:8). Just when we feel Job's situation could not possibly get worse, his wife advises him to abandon his faith and to die cursing God (2:9). But even in these dire circumstances, Job did not sin (2:10b).

The prologue also introduces Job's three friends: Eliphaz, Bildad, and Zophar (2:11). The Hebrew term "friends" has a wide range of meanings, including "intimate counselor" and "close friend."[10] Despite their harsh rhetoric at times, these three were motivated by their love and commitment to Job. Moved by the noblest intentions, Job's friends arrived to "sympathize with him and comfort him" (2:11). His suffering was so severe they hardly recognized him. They sat silently with Job for a week, mourning his losses. Job's lament in chapter 3 breaks the silence and begins the dialogue.

Dialogue between Job and his three friends (chapters 3–31)

The second unit of the book is composed of the speeches of Job's three friends and his reaction to each.

JOB'S COMPLAINT (CHAPTER 3)

Job begins the colloquy by cursing the day of his birth and wondering why he did not die at birth. He is convinced that his has been a fate worse than death.

THE SPEECHES OF JOB'S FRIENDS AND HIS RESPONSE TO EACH (CHAPTERS 4–27)

This unit contains three cycles of six speeches each. Each cycle includes a speech by Job's three friends, answered in turn by a speech from Job. The final cycle is incomplete (chapters 22–26) since it omits the final speech by Zophar.

Each of these three individuals had his own characteristic approach to Job's problems. Eliphaz emphasized God's justice and purity, and taught that people (including Job) bring trouble on themselves. Bildad typically appealed to tradition and considered himself a defender of orthodox doctrine. He explained that an individual who pursues wickedness (like Job) should not be surprised by divine punishment. Zophar considered himself a RATIONALIST, and reasoned that Job's punishment was no less than can be reasonably expected. Though Job's friends were approaching the problem from the perspective of Israelite monotheism, their solutions failed to transcend the Mesopotamian solutions (see above). They continued to place the blame on Job.

Eliphaz began the first cycle by reminding Job of God's justice and humankind's inability to live up to God's holy standard (4:17). He encouraged Job to find comfort in the Lord's chastening (5:17) and to expect a restoration of his lost estate (5:18–27). In chapters 6 and 7, Job answered that his so-called friends were not helping his situation. He challenged his associates to be specific about his guilt (6:24, 30), implying that God's reproof was out of proportion to his sin. Death appeared to be the only resolution for his problems (7:16–21).

Bildad considered Job's answer as so much wind (8:2). He supported Eliphaz's statement that God is just (8:3) and that surely God would not reject a blameless man (8:20), implying that Job, by reason of his great suffering, *must* be guilty of sin. He suggested that Job should "look to God" and expect to be restored to his former life (8:3–7). Job admitted that a man cannot be "righteous before God" (9:2). But, after all, the issue is power rather than justice. God is the Creator, who commands the sun and the mountains and does things beyond understanding (9:10). He destroys the innocent *along with* the guilty, and who is to argue (9:22)? Life is brief and fruitless (9:25–31). Job again wondered why he was even born and longed for the peace of the grave (10:18–22).

In Zophar's speech, he rebuked Job for his theological outlook, which he termed "babble" (NRSV, 11:3). He summarized Job's attitude in the quote "My beliefs are flawless and I am pure in your [God's] sight" (11:4). But Zophar warned that, in fact, the opposite was true. God's punishment was actually less than Job's guilt

The foothills of Mount Hermon, northern Israel. Eliphaz asks: "Were you there when God made the mountains?" (15:7).

called for (11:6b). Thus Zophar concluded that Job should put his iniquity and wickedness "far away" (NKJV, 11:14) and surely his life will once again be "brighter than noonday" (11:17). Job concluded this first cycle of speeches by asserting that his understanding was not inferior to that of his three friends (12:3; 13:2). All the universe, including beasts, birds, plants, and fish, know that God is in control of all that happens (12:7–10). All Job desired was the opportunity to defend himself personally before God (13:13–19). Instead, God persisted in persecuting Job (13:24–27). Job once again longed for death (14:13).

Eliphaz began the second cycle of speeches by accusing Job of abandoning prayer and the fear of God with his windy discourses (15:2–4). He reminded Job that his three friends had great wisdom too (15:7–8), and they stood in an ancient tradition when they insisted that severe sin in Job's life had caused his suffering (15:17–35). Job answered that he had heard all this nonsense before (16:3–4). He longed instead for a witness in heaven to mediate for him with God (16:19).

Bildad resented being considered "stupid" in Job's sight and he presented a dreary picture of the wicked (18:3), implying the serious extent of Job's sin. But Job rejected such a harsh, unjust pronouncement. With a warning to his comforters, Job looked to the future when he would be vindicated before God (19:25–27).

Next, Zophar used virulent language to condemn the wealthy, who presumably acquired their possessions through greed and oppressing the poor (20:19). After vividly describing the punishment of such individuals, Zophar stated this is the portion from God for a wicked man, suggesting that greed was Job's problem (20:29). But in response, Job pointed out how the wicked continued to prosper and go to their graves fat and satisfied (21:23–26). In desperation, he concluded that the comfort of his three friends was worthless and their answers false (21:34).

Eliphaz opened the third cycle by trying to identify specific sins Job had committed, most of them sins of omission (22:4–7). He pleaded with Job to put away his unrighteousness and return to God (22:23). Job, however, was certain of his

innocence and longed again to defend himself before God (23:4, 10–12). Job's main contention was not that he was innocent of any wrongdoing, but that his punishment and suffering far exceeded his guilt.

Bildad's brief speech in chapter 25 emphasized the impossibility of living a righteous life before God. Job maintained his integrity and innocence (27:1–6), and expressed his exasperation with his friends' flawed application of the retribution principle to his situation.

Job's Summarizing Speeches (chapters 28–31)

Chapters 28–31 are various speeches of Job in which he praised the virtues of wisdom (28), reminisced about his life before the tragic events of the prologue (29), lamented his present miserable condition (30), and denied he was ever guilty of lust, greed, adultery, mistreating slaves, trusting in riches, idolatry, or unfair business practices (31). Finally, Job affixed his signature (31:35) and waited for justice to be done.

The central message of the book is implied in the hymn to wisdom (chapter 28). Wisdom belongs ultimately to God (vv. 20–28), and all human attempts to grasp it or contain it are doomed to failure. This is Job's confession and ultimately his salvation. Rather than assume false guilt and live a lie, Job waited on God's vindication.

Elihu joins the dialogue (chapters 32–37)

In the next unit of the book, a new character is introduced. Elihu was a young man who had grown angry while listening to Job justify himself rather than God (32:2). But he was also upset with Job's friends because they had found no answer and yet had condemned Job (32:3). It is true that Job's situation has not improved. God appears to have become an enemy, and without just cause. And perhaps the most perplexing aspect of the situation is God's complete silence and unresponsiveness to Job's prayers. Indeed, the comfort of Job's three counselors seems to have hindered his understanding of his relationship to God.

Elihu, hoping to rectify the situation, began with a long apology for his youth and a plea for them to pay careful atten-

Scene from the wall paintings in the tomb of the Egyptian Nebamun. Ancient Egypt created most examples of instructional wisdom.

tion since wisdom is a gift of God rather than a consequence of age. He addressed Job directly and recapitulated the problem as one of unanswered prayer (33:13). Elihu contended that God used suffering and chastisement to correct humankind (33:19). And prayer is man's method of acknowledging and submitting to God's correction (33:26–30). In chapter 34, Elihu embarked upon a second speech, in which he reproached Job for questioning God's justice. God is just, and by denying this, Job had added rebellion to his sin (v. 37).

In a third discourse, Elihu informed Job that God was unaffected by events on earth. If God has been silent, it was because he recognized insincerity in Job's requests (35:13–16). Finally, Elihu spoke on God's behalf (36:2). He informed Job and his counselors that God is just in his treatment of king and slave alike, and in any situation, repentance is the key (36:10–12). As in other cases, Job's afflictions and suffering may be the means of deliverance.

The Lord finally speaks (38:1–42:6)

All along, the book has been crying out for God to answer. Finally, the Lord broke his silence and answered all objections.

We are not told how much effect Elihu's speeches had on Job and his friends. But his emphasis on God's omnipotence and justice and humanity's ultimate need for genuine repentance, set the stage for God himself to burst on the scene. In a way that

silenced all debate (40:3–5), the Lord himself answered Job from the midst of a fierce windstorm (or whirlwind, 38:1 and 40:6). He began by rebuking Job for speaking in ignorance and reminded him of his mortality (38:3). Then he challenged Job to answer a series of questions centering on the awesome strength and power of God as Creator and Sustainer of the universe. What did Job know and understand of such things as the founding of the earth (38:4), the confining of the sea (38:8), the courses of the constellations (38:31), and more? The Lord challenged Job to answer (40:1–2), but Job was speechless (40:3–5). He simply acknowledged his inadequacy and agreed to keep silent before God.

Then the Lord challenged Job to compare his own strengths with that of God's ("Do you have an arm like God's?" 40:9). This is followed by poems about two of God's creatures, BEHEMOTH (i.e., the hippopotamus) and LEVIATHAN (probably the crocodile), in which God underscored their strength, resilience, and apparent indestructibility (40:15–41:34). Job immediately acknowledged God's omnipotence ("I know that you can do all things," 42:2) and his own ignorance ("I spoke of things I did not understand," 42:3). The Lord's speeches had stripped Job of his pride and self-sufficiency, and all that remained was a debasing need to repent. Job concluded: "My ears had heard of you but now my eyes have seen you. Therefore I despise myself and repent in dust and ashes" (42:5–6).

The epilogue (42:7–17)

The epilogue consists of two concluding events. First, the Lord reprimanded Job's three friends for not speaking rightly on his behalf. Second, he restored the fortunes of Job to the extent that Job's latter days were better than his former days (v. 12). Thus, Job's faithfulness was vindicated and God's was illustrated.

The Author and His Times

The origins of Job are shrouded in mystery. The author of the book is anonymous. Nor does the book indicate precisely when or where the events it describes took place. Job's home in the land of Uz was probably between EDOM and northern Arabia, and his friends came from the vicinity of Edom.[11] Details about when these events took place are even more vague. Many of the circumstances seem patriarchal: Job offers sacrifices without the benefit of a priest, his wealth is measured in terms of flocks and servants, and his long life-span (140 years) harkens back to Genesis. Because of these observations, many have assumed a pre-Mosaic origin for the book.

The linguistic evidence of Job is inconclusive. The book contains both very old and relatively late Hebrew terms. This indicates Job has had a long history of transmission, being copied and recopied many times. In addition, the main character of the book may not even have been Israelite. Besides the Edomite geographical references, the book contains no reference to Mosaic law or the covenant, and God is seldom identified as Yahweh. The reader is forced to accept this book as detailing events "about a famous man who lived a long time ago in a land faraway."

Scholarly debate about the time of composition ranges from the early eighth century B.C. (contemporary with Isaiah) to the third century B.C. (second-temple Judah). Recent literary comparisons between Job and Isaiah have led some to accept the eighth-century date as the most likely time for the date of Job's composition.[12]

Theological Themes

The Book of Job makes an important contribution to the Old Testament collection of theological ideas. The Sinai covenant between Yahweh and Israel established one of Israel's most lasting theological concepts—retribution theology. The curses and blessings of Deuteronomy (Dt 28, see p. 147) became the starting point for much of biblical theology. Stated simply, you reap what you sow (Gal 6:7; 1 Pt 3:12). This is how God governs the world. The very rightness of right leads to blessings, and the wrongness of wrong leads naturally to disaster.[13]

But this doctrine of retribution is a general moral principle of God's administration of justice, not a hard and fast rule to be applied to every individual case. Job's friends failed to understand this. Job's case was exceptional. He needed compassion, not advice. But Job's friends are not the only ones who failed to understand the limits to retribution theology, for Job himself was also committed to it as the orthodox approach to suffering.

The conflict in the book of Job may be illustrated by an equilateral triangle.[14] At the top corner of the triangle stands God, who turns his face to humans and is accessible to them. At another corner is Job, the blameless and upright man. The last

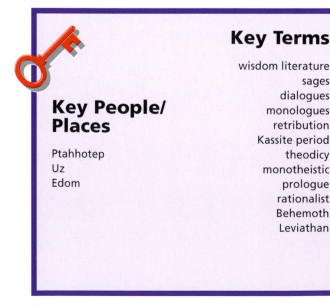

Key People/ Places

Ptahhotep
Uz
Edom

Key Terms

wisdom literature
sages
dialogues
monologues
retribution
Kassite period
theodicy
monotheistic
prologue
rationalist
Behemoth
Leviathan

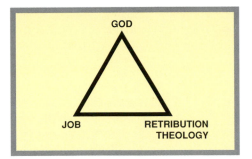

corner stands for the doctrine of retribution, held to by all speakers of the book, including Job. The Book of Job attempts to hold all three ideas simultaneously. All three are concepts held dearly by the characters of the drama. But Job is a good man who suffers intensely. His experience puts something—or someone—in jeopardy.

One of these treasured ideas must be abandoned, for they cannot all be maintained. The friends cancel out Job, maintaining God and retribution theology. Job all but gives up God, while he vigorously maintains retribution theology and his innocence. But in the end, God eliminates their understanding and application of retribution theology.

The New Testament also deals with the problem of undeserved sin. When Jesus was asked, "Who sinned, this man or his parents, that he was born blind?" his answer was surprising: "Neither this man nor his parents sinned, . . . but this happened so that the work of God might be displayed in his life" (Jn 9:2–3). In short, nobody sinned. There is a vast area of human misery and suffering that is nei-

Summary

1. Modern scholars have classified the Books of Job, Proverbs, and Ecclesiastes as "wisdom literature," but the sharing of wisdom is also found in other Old Testament books.

2. Throughout the ancient Near East, the nations had wisdom teachers. In the Old Testament, the wise men of Mesopotamia, Canaan, and Egypt were compared with Solomon.

3. Near Eastern wisdom literature can be divided into brief proverbial maxims intended to teach about life, and longer discussions dealing with the problems of life.

4. Ancient Egypt created most examples of instructional wisdom, which focused on successful living.

5. Mesopotamia produced documents containing lengthy speeches about the problems of justice in the world.

6. Mesopotamian culture accepted the doctrine of retribution.

7. The Book of Job considers some of the most difficult questions of life, foremost among which is the problem of theodicy.

8. Job's three friends tried to help him through this difficult time in his life, and each had his own methodology.

9. The general message of the Book of Job is that wisdom belongs to God and resolute faith in him will be vindicated.

10. When God finally spoke, Job acknowledged God's omnipotence as well as his own ignorance and he repented.

11. Retribution theology is the theology of Job and all of the speakers of the Book of Job, but God eliminated their understanding and application of retribution theology.

12. There is no conclusive information that identifies who the author of Job was.

Study Questions

1. What biblical books do modern scholars designate as "wisdom literature"? Differentiate between Mesopotamian discoursive material and Israelite wisdom literature. How did the Israelites interact with the literature and worldview of their ancient Near Eastern neighbors? What is the Old Testament foundation of wisdom? What topic is explored in wisdom literature?

2. What are the difficult questions of life addressed in Job? What aspects of God's character are challenged by the presence of evil in the world?

3. What is the central message of the book?

4. Describe the points of view of Eliphaz, Bildad, and Zophar. Where did they place the blame for Job's suffering? What was Job's response?

5. How does Elihu characterize Job's problem? To what does he attribute God's silence? What does he see as the key to alleviating Job's suffering?

6. How does the Lord rebuke Job in 38:1–42:6? What is Job's response?

7. How does God respond to Eliphaz, Bildad, and Zophar? What is the final outcome for Job?

8. What is known about the writing of Job and the geographical setting of the book?

9. How does Job contribute to an understanding of retribution theology? How does the book answer the problem of theodicy?

Further Reading

Andersen, Francis I. *Job: An Introduction and Commentary.* Tyndale Old Testament Commentary. Downers Grove/Leicester: InterVarsity, 1976 Insightful exposition from an evangelical perspective.

Bullock, C. Hassell. *An Introduction to the Old Testament Poetic Books.* Rev. ed. Chicago: Moody, 1988. Helpful introduction to all the poetical books.

Clines, David J. A. *Job 1–20.* Word Biblical Commentary 17. Dallas: Word, 1989.

Dhorme, Édouard. *A Commentary on The Book of Job.* Trans. Harold Knight. Nashville: Thomas Nelson, 1984.

Hartley, John E. *The Book of Job.* New International Commentary on the Old Testament. Grand Rapids: Eerdmans, 1988. One of the best recent commentaries available.

Pope, Marvin H. *Job: Introduction, Translation, and Notes.* 3rd ed. Anchor Bible 15. Garden City, N.Y.: Doubleday, 1973. Excellent background information presented by a leading Near Eastern scholar.

Rad, Gerhard von. *Wisdom in Israel.* Trans. James D. Martin. Valley Forge, Pa.: Trinity Press International, 1993 (1972). Thought-provoking introduction.

ther punitive nor redemptive. It is just meaningless. Like Job, the believer who suffers must realize that "nothing but the Voice [of God] from the tempest can meet his case."[15] With Job, we wait and long for that day, and remain faithful to the Voice.

Job provides the biblical answer to the problem of theodicy. God is able to work all things—even evil things—together for good (Rom 8:28), and those who are faithful to him to the end will benefit from the evil they must suffer. But this answer in Job is incomplete without the rest of biblical revelation. For it is in Jesus Christ that the greatest evils the world can offer—betrayal and crucifixion—meet with the ultimate good—forgiveness, and cleansing.

21 Psalms
The Songbook of Ancient Israel

Outline

Objectives

**After reading this chapter,
you should be able to**

- Define the word "psalm"
- Name the writers of the psalms
- Explain how the psalms make a unique
  contribution to the Bible
- Describe the arrangement of the five
  divisions of the Book of Psalms
- List the various types of psalms
- Suggest how the psalms can help
  the contemporary Christian

How do people praise God through music in your church? Do they sing out of songbooks or hymnals? Does the congregation read words to songs on transparencies beamed to screens at the front of the sanctuary? Perhaps you sing with piano and organ accompaniment, or maybe you have other instruments. Some congregations may sing without any instruments. One thing is certain—Christians use many different styles of music to praise the Lord!

But no matter what the worship style, you probably use the psalms as part of your worship. The Book of Psalms has contributed the words to many of our favorite hymns and choruses. Even many modern songs and choruses get their words from the psalms. As we study this songbook from ancient Israel, we will understand more about the great truths God's people believed and expressed through their worship. We also will see how much these ancient songs have shaped Christian worship today.

Background to the Psalms

The Name "Psalms"

The word "psalm" comes from the Greek word *psalmos*, which means a song or a hymn. The Hebrew word for the book is *tĕhillîm* and means "praises." The book contains a collection of 150 songs from Hebrew religious life and worship—songs dear to the people's hearts and reflective of their personal experiences. One could say the psalms represent an ancient songbook of God's people.

Authorship of the Psalms

Who wrote the psalms? Asking that question is like asking who wrote our modern hymnals today. The answer would be—lots of people! Many composers contributed to the collection of songs and poems we now know as the Book of Psalms. Sometime after the Babylonian exile, someone compiled these psalms into one volume.

David

King David exerted a major influence on the Book of Psalms. Seventy-three psalms begin with the expression a "Psalm of David." Some people have suggested David may not have written all seventy-three. Perhaps some were written to David or in honor of him; indeed, one *could* understand the Hebrew that way. In general, we probably should assume David wrote all or most of those with this title.

David wrote many different kinds of psalms—praises, laments, penitential psalms, imprecatory psalms, royal psalms, messianic psalms. (We will discuss each of these psalm types below.) First Samuel 16 recounts David's musical talent as he played before King Saul. First Chronicles 15–16 also describes David's great interest in establishing music for public worship. And as king, he would have had the leisure time to reflect and compose his music, much of which he dedicated to God.

Many of David's psalms describe specific times in his life. He wrote Psalm 3 when he fled from his son Absalom. He wrote Psalm 51 after Nathan confronted him about his sin with Bathsheba. He wrote Psalm 57 as he hid from Saul in a cave. Key moments in David's life moved him to write these psalms that have spoken to so many over the generations.

Asaph

Asaph played an important musical role in the public worship David established in Jerusalem (1 Chr 15–16). In fact, David appointed Asaph as chief musician (1 Chr 15:4–5). Psalms 50 and 73–83 are attributed to him. Like David, Asaph wrote a variety of psalm types.

The sons of Korah

The name "Korah" first appears in Numbers 16–17, where it refers to a man who contended with Aaron for the right to the priesthood. God judged Korah and his followers and put them to death and vindicated Aaron's line.

Do the psalms that mention "the sons of Korah" refer to this Korah's children? Scholars disagree.[1] The name also appears in 2 Chronicles 20:19, where it refers to a guild of temple singers. Perhaps the name "Korah" was common enough that it referred to two or more different families. Certain psalms credited to the sons of Korah reflect the time of the Babylonian

The Hebrew title of Psalm 23, probably the best-loved of all, says it is by David, the king who once looked after his father's sheep in the hills around Bethlehem.

exile or later (Pss 44, 85). Others may have come from an earlier time.

Other authors

Who else contributed to the Book of Psalms? Psalm 90 is ascribed to Moses, who led God's people from slavery in Egypt to freedom in the promised land. Psalms 72 and 127 are credited to Solomon. The Bible tells us Solomon wrote many proverbs and songs (1 Kgs 4:32), but apparently only two made their way into the Book of Psalms. About fifty psalms have no heading, and their authorship remains a mystery. Maybe some of the authors already mentioned wrote them, but we do not know for sure.

The Unique Place of the Psalms in God's Word

The psalms have a unique place in God's Word. First, they give us insight into Israelite worship. What were the songs the people sang? What was dear to their hearts? What themes commonly recurred as they praised God? We can study the Book of Psalms and begin to find answers to such questions.

The psalms describe Israel's corporate and personal worship. Certain psalms served the entire body of believers. For example, the congregation clearly used Psalm 136 as a responsive reading. The worship leader would read a line and the people would respond, "His love endures forever."

Other psalms relate an individual's personal experience. Psalm 3 describes David's intense feelings as he fled from his son Absalom. David felt as though all his friends had deserted him, but he clung to his faith in the Lord. Many other psalms also reveal individual worship experiences.

Second, the psalms have a unique place in God's word because they deal with all aspects of Hebrew life. People praised God for his mighty deeds and for special blessings. They also asked his forgiveness for their sin. Sometimes they lamented life's difficult circumstances or implored God to curse enemies of the faith. The psalms touch virtually every area of life.

Because the psalms concern almost every aspect of life, many people find them valuable for counseling. The words of this book strike a sympathetic chord with many people because they see how the writers of Scripture went through the same struggles they are going through. No matter what the situation in which we find ourselves, probably at least one psalm speaks to the issue at hand. The psalms state God's truth in a beautiful style that speaks to both our minds and our hearts.

An artist's impression of an Israelite musician playing the *nebel*, a stringed instrument with up to ten strings (Ps 71:22).

to "tie off" that part of the Book of Psalms. The one exception is Psalm 150, a grand psalm of praise that fittingly concludes the entire collection.

Theories on the Psalms' Arrangement

Apparently these five books circulated independently at one time. But how and when did someone compile them into the book we know as Psalms? And what criteria originally resulted in their division into five books?

Bible interpreters have come to no real conclusions in addressing these issues.[2] Some have suggested authorship as a possible factor, but this appears doubtful. David's psalms, for example, are scattered throughout. Others have suggested the psalms may have been grouped according to the particular name(s) of God the authors used. This view has some merit, as different books tend to prefer one name over another, but many exceptions exist. It seems the final answer regarding the arrangement of the Book of Psalms must remain a mystery.

Psalm Titles

Many psalms have titles. Some of these titles are as simple as the statement "A psalm of X," where X represents the name of a person (Ps 15). Usually that person is the psalm's author, though the possibility remains that someone else wrote the psalm in honor of that person. Sometimes titles describe the setting in which the author wrote the psalm (Ps 3) or give a dedication of some sort (Ps 4).

Psalm titles have an ancient origin and may go back as far as the original manuscripts. All ancient copies of the psalms contain these headings, so we should treat them as reliable unless further evidence reveals they were added later.

Psalm titles also sometimes feature musical notations. We do not know what many of these mean, though theories abound.[3] Some psalms have the notation "To the Choir Master," which suggests the people sang them in public worship. Other terms like *selah, miskal, shiggaion,* and *maskil* remain a mystery.

The Division of the Psalms

The Book of Psalms is divided into five books. The divisions apparently reflect an old tradition but no one really knows why the psalms are divided the way they are. The section below presents some basic thoughts on the issue.

The Basic Arrangement

The five basic divisions of the Book of Psalms are Psalms 1–41, 42–72, 73–89, 90–106, and 107–150. The closing verses of the last psalm in each collection typically contain some kind of **doxology** or ascription of praise to the Lord that serves

Classification of the Psalms

The German scholar Hermann Gunkel laid the foundation for the study of psalm classification.[4] Gunkel, a student of form criticism, noted that psalm writers commonly used certain poetic forms and styles to express similar ideas. For example, hymns of praise typically followed a certain pattern, as did community laments, psalms of thanksgiving, and more. Other scholars have built on Gunkel's foundation.[5]

Our discussion below presents various psalm types (or **genres**). Though some parallel Gunkel's classifications, others reflect basic distinctions in theme or content.

Psalm Type	Basic Characteristic(s)
HYMNS	Songs of praise and thanksgiving to God for who he is and what he has done
PENITENTIAL	Confess sorrow for sin, appeal to God for grace and forgiveness
WISDOM	General observations on life, especially God and our relationship to him.
ROYAL	Focus on the king as son of David and as God's special instrument to rule his people
MESSIANIC	Describe some aspect of the Messiah's person or ministry
IMPRECATORY	Call for God's judgment against God's enemies and/or his people's enemies
LAMENT	Lament one's condition; usually include statement of lament, statement of trust in God, and affirmation of praise to him.

Hymns

Basic characteristics of hymns

Some psalms are **hymns** of praise. Writers praised the Lord and offered him thanksgiving for who he was and what he had done. The hymns they wrote sometimes featured individual praise and at other times corporate praise.

Examples of hymns

Psalm 8 provides a good example of a hymn of praise. Perhaps David walked outside one night, looked up at the vast expanse of heaven, and wrote this psalm. He marveled at God's greatness, his own smallness, and the wonder that God should love and choose humanity to accomplish his purposes. The psalm thus reflects David's own experience with the Lord.

Psalm 136 provides another example of a hymn of praise. This psalm was used in Israel's corporate worship as a responsive reading. The worship leader or first group would read the first half of each verse, and the rest of the people would answer with the second part of each verse—"His love endures forever." The psalm calls God's people to praise him for his majesty, his creative power, his saving power, his sustaining power, and his faithfulness.

Psalm 150 is also an example of a hymn. The command to praise the Lord occurs thirteen times in six verses! The writer called worshipers to praise the Lord in his sanctuary and in the heavens, and to praise him for his power and greatness. He fur- ther called them to praise God with a number of instruments—trumpet, harp, lyre, tambourine, flute, and cymbals. Finally, he called on all flesh to praise the Lord. What a powerful way to end the Book of Psalms!

Penitential Psalms

Basic characteristics of penitential psalms

Penitential psalms express sorrow for sin. Basically, the psalmist says, "O God, I'm sorry for my sin. Please forgive me." As with hymns, penitential psalms may reflect the repentance of one person or of the community of worshipers. They confess sorrow for sin and appeal to God's grace for restoration.

Examples of penitential psalms

Psalm 38 is an example of a penitential psalm. In this psalm, David described the

wisdom psalms

royal psalms

guilt that overwhelmed him as he dealt with his sin. He suffered greatly and his friends and companions deserted him. His pain never left him. As he struggled, David asked the Lord to stay near him, and called Him his Savior.

Psalm 51 provides perhaps the most famous example of a penitential psalm. The heading provides the historical context: "A psalm of David, when the prophet Nathan came to him after David had committed adultery with Bathsheba." David committed adultery with Bathsheba; she became pregnant with his child; David arranged the death of Uriah her husband in battle; Nathan the prophet confronted him with his sin; and David poured out his repentant heart to the Lord in the words of Psalm 51.

David began by appealing to God to forgive him. David didn't deserve God's favor, for sin enveloped him. He agreed with the Lord's indictment—he needed cleansing from his evil. He needed God to purify his heart. If God would forgive him and restore him, perhaps God could again use David to further his purpose. People today often feel like God can never use them effectively because of their past, but the words of this psalm give hope. God's grace can overcome the most terrible sin!

Wisdom Psalms

Basic characteristics of wisdom psalms

Wisdom psalms represent a third psalm type. These psalms relate general observations about life. The writers typically make little effort to defend the truths they expound. Rather, they simply present them as self-evident descriptions of the way God has intended life to be. They usually describe God and our relationship with him in one or more of its facets (see chapter 20 above on wisdom literature in general).

Examples of wisdom psalms

Psalm 1 provides a good example of a wisdom psalm—direct, to-the-point observations on life. Blessed are those who avoid sin in all its forms and delight in God's word! They will become like trees planted by streams of life-giving water; they fulfill God's highest purpose for

them. But the wicked find no such favor. They pursue evil and run from God's word. Therefore, God's day of judgment will overtake them and they will perish. But God knows the way of those who truly follow him.

Psalm 14 is another example. David described the fool, who said God did not exist. Those who followed the fool also followed wickedness. They lived immoral lives because they did not believe God's judgment would ever come. But David assured his readers that one day God would restore the fortunes of the righteous. Living for the Lord was worth the effort!

Asaph, one of David's musicians, wrote Psalm 73. In it, he offered his personal testimony. Asaph felt discouraged because even though he followed the Lord faithfully, he suffered, while the wicked practiced evil and lived better than he did. In fact, Asaph testified that he almost decided serving the Lord was pointless! But one day, as he stood in God's sanctuary, he realized the priceless heritage he had. God was his portion forever, and nothing else on earth really mattered. Asaph encouraged his hearers to learn from his example.

Royal Psalms

Basic characteristics of royal psalms

Royal psalms focus on Israel's king. They usually describe him as God's special representative to rule Israel. The Lord would accomplish his purpose through his anointed servant. They also sometimes portray him as heir to God's covenant with David (2 Sm 7). His faithfulness would bring God's blessing forever.

Examples of royal psalms

Psalm 2 provides a good example of a royal psalm. It begins by describing the nations' haughty attitude toward the Lord and his anointed—Israel's king. But God would deal with them in his fury. He had installed his king on Mount Zion and established a father–son relationship with him. Many interpreters believe this psalm was a coronation psalm that Israel recited as she crowned a new king.

Psalm 45 is a second example of a royal psalm. Verse 1 mentions a dedication to the king, and verses 3–5 challenge him to

The old city of Jerusalem viewed from the summit of the Mount of Olives. Several psalms were written for pilgrims as they approached the holy city of Jerusalem.

Messiah

march victoriously in battle. Following praise to God in verse 6, verses 7–9 extol the king's love of righteousness and affirm God's anointing of him. The rest of the psalm praises the king for his splendor as he prepares for his wedding.

Psalm 110 is yet another example of a royal psalm. The word "king" does not occur until verse 5, but David referred to himself in the word "my" in verse 1—"The LORD says to *my* Lord: 'Sit at my right hand until I make your enemies a footstool for your feet.'" The Lord would shatter other kings and extend David's scepter. He also ordained David a special kind of priest. The Lord's presence with David would result in God's people winning ultimate victory. Those kings who opposed Him would fall to His fury.

Messianic Psalms

Basic characteristics of messianic psalms

MESSIANIC PSALMS, as their name implies, describe the **Messiah**, God's anointed one. The term "messiah" comes from the Hebrew word *māšîaḥ* (ma-SHE-ach), which means "anointed one." Prophets, priests, and kings all experienced God's anointing, so anyone serving in one of these three offices could be called an anointed one. But *the* Messiah, *the* anointed one, would one day restore Israel and estab-

lish everlasting salvation. The messianic psalms depict one or more aspects of his coming.

Examples of messianic psalms

We have already labeled Psalm 2 a royal psalm because it dealt with Israel's king. But Psalm 2 described the king as the Lord's anointed (messiah) and as his son. Psalm 2:7—"You are my son; today I have become your Father"—is cited several times in the New Testament in reference to Jesus Christ. Israel's king became God's "son" on the day he became king, but God proved Jesus Christ his eternal Son by raising him from the dead (Acts 13:33). Psalm 2 thus describes the Messiah as God's Son.

Psalm 16 provides another example of a messianic psalm. In the midst of his trouble, David affirmed God would never abandon him. In fact, he had great hope even beyond the grave. In Acts 2:24–34, Peter proclaimed how Jesus, David's descendant, ultimately fulfilled David's words. David's body still lay in a Jerusalem grave, but Jesus sat at the Father's right hand! Psalm 16 thus describes the Messiah as risen and glorified.

Psalm 22, another messianic psalm, is also a lament psalm. It begins with words Jesus uttered from the cross—"My God, my God, why have you forsaken me?" (cf. Mt 27:46). David originally spoke

309

these words in deep despair. He felt God had abandoned him. In fact, he described his pathetic situation in verses 14–18. But the Holy Spirit so guided his words in these verses that one thousand years later, they graphically portrayed Jesus as he hung on the cross.

By the sovereign leading of the Holy Spirit, David's psychological and emotional suffering foreshadowed Christ's physical suffering. Psalm 22 describes the Lord's agony on the cross as he died as God's perfect offering for sin.

Other psalms also fall into the category of messianic psalms. Psalm 45 describes Christ's kingship (Heb 1:8), while Psalm 110 denotes Christ's role as Lord of David and our great High Priest (Mt 22:41–46; Heb 5:6). The Book of Psalms thus graphically portrays Jesus as Son of God, sacrifice for sin, our great High Priest, risen

from the dead, King of kings and Lord of lords. And all this was written centuries before his birth!

Imprecatory Psalms

Basic characteristics of imprecatory psalms

Imprecatory psalms call for God's judgment on the psalmist's enemies. Like many other psalm types, they can be individual or corporate in nature. An individual may ask God to judge his enemies, or a psalm may describe the feelings of all Israel as the people call for God to bring his wrath against an oppressive nation. Because of their angry content, imprecatory psalms have provoked much theological discussion. How could such words have become part of Scripture?

Examples of imprecatory psalms

Psalms 35 and 69 provide two examples of imprecatory psalms from the pen of David. In them, David asked God to take his side against those who contended with him. They plotted against him, planning his downfall. David asked the Lord to intervene and judge them. He asked for God's judgment not only to rescue him, but to rescue his people. How dare God's enemies try to attack his chosen nation? They would pay a dear price if God answered David's prayer!

Psalm 137 is an emotionally stirring psalm. It comes from the days immediately following the exile to Babylon. In it, the writer, himself a captive, asked God to avenge his people. The Babylonians had mocked them, and the Edomites had turned traitor on them at the last minute. The psalmist lashed out—how blessed would be the one who destroyed Babylonian infants by dashing them against rocks!

Many Bible readers find the imprecatory psalms troubling. How could someone write such words under the inspiration of the Holy Spirit? Such psalms certainly help us see the human side of Scripture. The psalmists cried out in anger and frustration, and in their pain, they realized their own weakness. Nothing they could do could change their horrible situation.

But imprecatory psalms also leave

Study Questions

1. Name the major contributors to the Book of Psalms. What makes the book such a unique book in God's word?

2. Identify the various psalm types and describe their general characteristics. What kinds of expressions would you expect to find in each type? Try to write a psalm that fits each style.

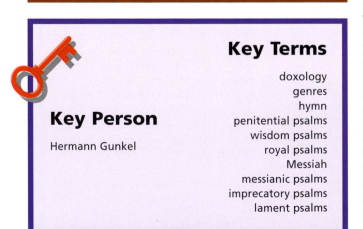

Key Terms

doxology
genres
hymn
penitential psalms
wisdom psalms
royal psalms
Messiah
messianic psalms
imprecatory psalms
lament psalms

Key Person

Hermann Gunkel

lament psalms

judgment in God's hands. The psalmist called for God's judgment, but he called for *God* to do it. Though he might not separate the sin from the sinner, he recognized that only God held absolute right to judge. And he asked that God might do it soon.

Lament Psalms

Basic characteristics of lament psalms

Lament psalms comprise the last psalm type in our study of the Book of Psalms. They typically contain three elements, though these elements do not always come in the same order.

First, they bemoan one's condition—"O Lord, what a miserable state I am in." Second, the psalmist states his trust in God. Somehow God will bring him through his trials. Third, the psalmist usually ends with some kind of praise. God has heard his prayer and will eventually intervene for him!

Examples of lament psalms

Psalm 3 is an example of a lament psalm. According to the title, David wrote it when he fled from Absalom his son. During this time of personal struggle and despair, David called out to his God.

David began by bemoaning his situation—"O LORD, how many are my foes! How many rise up against me!" Many even believed God had abandoned him! Nevertheless, David affirmed his trust in the Lord. The Lord stood as a shield around him. He had answered David's prayers before, and he would answer them again.

By the time David reached the end of

Summary

1. The Book of Psalms essentially represents an ancient songbook of Israel.

2. There are many writers who contributed to the Book of Psalms—David, Asaph, the sons of Korah, Moses, Solomon, and a number of anonymous writers.

3. The psalms make a special contribution to the Bible because they provide us with an understanding of Israelite worship, and they give information about all aspects of Hebrew life.

4. There are five basic divisions of the Book of Psalms: 1–41, 42–72, 73–89, 98–106, and 107–150.

5. The German scholar, Hermann Gunkel, laid the foundation for a classification of the psalms.

6. The basic classification of the psalms includes the following types: hymns, penitential psalms, wisdom psalms, royal psalms, messianic psalms, imprecatory psalms, lament psalms.

7. Hymns focus on individual or corporate praise to God.

8. Confession and repentance are found in psalms classified as penitential.

9. Wisdom psalms provide general observations about life.

10. The focus in royal psalms is on the king of Israel.

11. Messianic psalms describe the Messiah.

12. When a psalm calls on God to judge enemies, the psalm is classified as an imprecatory psalm.

13. Lament psalms bemoan one's condition, state trust in God, and end with praise.

Further Reading

Kidner, Derek. *Psalms 1–72: An Introduction and Commentary.* Tyndale Old Testament Commentary. Downers Grove: InterVarsity, 1973. Solid college-level commentary.

———. *Psalms 73–150: An Introduction and Commentary.* Tyndale Old Testament Commentary. Downers Grove: InterVarsity, 1975. Solid college-level commentary.

Longman, Tremper, III. *How to Read the Psalms.* Downers Grove: InterVarsity, 1988. A good college-level treatment of the various psalm types and how to interpret them.

the psalm, he was praising God—"From the Lord comes deliverance. May your blessing be on your people." Taking our deepest concerns to the Lord and trusting him with them often results in such a change of attitude. Suddenly, the troubles don't appear so big anymore!

Other lament psalms include Psalms 4 and 6. In each, David expresses his anguish to the Lord and asks how long he must wait before God delivers him. But through his distress, he places his trust squarely in the Lord. In the end, he can sleep in peace (4:8), because the Lord provides all the security he needs. God has heard David's prayer, and will deliver him from his enemies.

The Psalms and the Christian

The psalms remain a treasury of spiritual help for all believers. Their words speak to our hearts as surely as they have spoken to others since the days they were written. Whatever our mood, whatever our condition, the ancient voices call us to hear them. They, too, have experienced the joy, the sadness, the mourning, the sin, the anger, the confession, the forgiveness, and other experiences that touch our lives so deeply. They call us to learn from them as the Holy Spirit uses their words to draw us closer to the Lord.

22 Proverbs
Advice on Living in God's World

Outline

- **What Is a "Proverb"?**
- **Contents of the Book of Proverbs**
  Outline
  Overview
- **Authorship**
- **Theological Themes**

Objectives

**After reading this chapter,
you should be able to**

- Define "proverb"
- List the two types of wisdom literature
- Outline the basic content of the Book of Proverbs
- Present the purpose of Proverbs
- Identify the proverbs of each contribution of sayings
- Discuss the theological themes of the Book of Proverbs and their importance to successful living

proverb

The Book of PROVERBS is the second book in the collection known as "wisdom literature" (see introduction to wisdom literature in chapter 20). The book has something to say about nearly every aspect of faith and life. Other portions of the Bible present God's law, narrate historical events involving his people, or record hymns of praise. But the Book of Proverbs consolidates ancient Israel's truths based on experience and offers believers of every generation practical advice on holy living.

The Book of Proverbs is a collection of short sayings instructing the reader how to live well. Like the Book of Psalms, the Book of Proverbs is a collection of collections. It contains proverbs and wisdom sayings from different authors and sources compiled in a library of wisdom teachings on how to "fear the LORD and shun evil" (Prv 3:7).

What Is a "Proverb"?

Generally speaking, a **proverb** is a succinct and persuasive saying proven true by experience. The topics addressed cover everything in God's universe and how it operates. Over time, these statements were collected and related to each other. The result is a collection of timeless truths or basic values proven by previous generations. The unifying purpose of the collection is to encourage the reader to live righteously and justly before God.

We may also state what a proverb is not. First, proverbs are not promises. Christian parents would love to claim Proverbs 22:6 as a promise from God: "Train children in the right way, and when old, they will not stray" (NRSV). But unfortunately, this is not a guarantee that Christians will raise only Christian children. Sometimes young people reject the Christian training they received as children and refuse to accept the leadership of godly parents. Instead, this proverb is a general principle that godly training will stay with children, and *in most cases,* children raised in righteous families will accept the direction of their parents. Again, proverbs are statements of general truth, not hard-and-fast promises.

Second, proverbs are not commands. Many proverbs begin with imperatives, or instructions given in the second person.

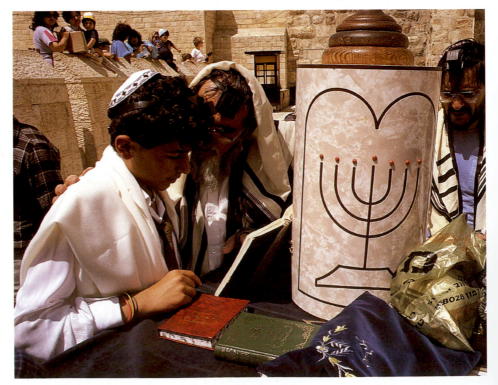

A young man at his bar mitzvah at the Western Wall, Jerusalem. Proverbs is a collection of down-to-earth sayings designed to teach practical wisdom. Much of the advice is addressed to young men.

Excerpts Adapted from the Teachings of Ahiqar[1]

Ahiqar was advisor to Sennacherib, king of Assyria (704–681 B.C.). His "teachings" were preserved in Aramaic from the fifth century B.C. on eleven sheets of palimpsest papyrus, or recycled paper. German archaeologists discovered the document in southern Egypt in 1906 and 1907.

The sayings of Ahiqar selected here were for his nephew and adopted son, Nadin, whom Ahiqar was grooming to replace him. Parallels with Old Testament proverbs are suggested in the parentheses.

Do not withhold your son from the rod, or else you will not be able to save him. (Prv 13:24)

My son, do not chatter too much so that you wind up speaking every word that comes into your mind. People's eyes and ears are always watching your mouth, so beware lest it be your downfall. More than everything else, watch your mouth. (Prv 4:23–24).

Do not take the word of a king lightly: let it be healing for your flesh. (Prv 16:24).

If a man be small, but becomes great, his words soar above him. For the opening of his mouth is a statement of the gods and if the gods love him they will put something good in his mouth to say. (Prv 16:1).

Whoever fails to take pride in the names of his father and mother, may the sun not shine on him. (Prv 20:20).

[1]James M. Lindenberger, *The Aramaic Proverbs of Ahiqar* (Baltimore: Johns Hopkins University Press, 1983), and *ANET*, 427–30.

when choosing your friends, because your friends affect your character. If you associate with quarrelsome people, you will tend to become quarrelsome. Or take, for example, the proverb in 24:27:

Finish your outdoor work and get your
fields ready;
after that, build your house.

Some well-meaning Christian might argue from this verse that one should not live in a house until learning an outdoor skill. But surely this proverb is a general statement against personal consumption before having a means of income. This is a time-honored concept about producing before consuming, or, as the apostle Paul said, "Anyone unwilling to work should not eat" (NRSV, 2 Thes 3:10).

Rather than promises or commands to be applied in every case, the proverbs are general principles of life. Here is the wisdom of the ages, tried and true, compelling in its presentation and uplifting in its ethics. Because of their terse style, proverbs are not to be skimmed or read quickly. Their condensed language makes it necessary to read them slowly and contemplatively. These time-honored truths take time to fathom.

Their general quality also means you should always be looking for the underlying principle of the statement. For example, the English proverb "Look before you leap" is memorable because of the single-syllable words and the recurrence of the letter *l*.[1] Though it means the same thing, it would be much more difficult to remember the following statement: "In advance of committing yourself to a course of action, consider your circumstances and options." The longer, more elaborate saying is certainly more precise, but it is admittedly harder to remember. The catchy and memorable "Look before you leap" is more compelling and forceful, simply because of its proverbial nature. But it could also be misunderstood. It does not say what to look for or where one should look before jumping. Nor does it say how long one should wait to jump after looking. In fact, the proverb is not really about jumping at all.

Likewise, when reading the Bible's proverbs, you should remember their

Yet they must be interpreted carefully for our day.

Make no friends with those given to anger,
and do not associate with hotheads,
or you may learn their ways
and entangle yourself in a snare.
(NRSV, Prv 22:24–25)

Someone might innocently take this proverb to mean they should not befriend anyone with a temper. But the general principle here is that you should take care

broad, general nature. Take them on their own terms, as general observations about how life works.

Contents of the Book of Proverbs

Wisdom literature in general is of two types (see chapter 20). The first is discursive wisdom, which grapples with the difficult issues of life and is usually pessimistic. The Book of Job is an example of this type of wisdom literature. The second type of wisdom literature is instructional or didactic in nature and is usually optimistic about life. The Book of Proverbs is an example of this second type. Old Testament instructional wisdom, such as Proverbs, has its closest parallels with Egyptian instructional wisdom, though Mesopotamia has examples as well.

The Book of Proverbs continues the themes of other portions of the Old Testament by contrasting two ways of living life. On the one hand, there are those who reject God's laws and refuse to keep his covenant. Proverbs designates these individuals as "fools" and their life choices as "folly." On the other hand, those who carefully maintain their relationship with God and adhere to his ways are called "wise" and their lives are characterized by "wisdom."

Outline

I. **Title and Prologue** (1:1–7)

II. **Wisdom and Some Opponents** (1:8–9:18)
   A. Criminals (1:8–19)
   B. Wisdom's Call (1:20–33)
   C. Wisdom's Rewards (2:1–4:27)
   D. Adultery (5:1–23)
   E. Business and Society (6:1–19)
   F. Adultery (6:20–7:27)
   G. Wisdom Praised (8:1–36)
   I. Human Choices (9:1–18)

III. **The Proverbs of Solomon** (10:1–22:16)

IV. **Sayings of the Wise Men** (22:17–24:34)

V. **Solomonic Proverbs from Hezekiah's Collection** (25:1–29:27)

VI. **Sayings of Agur** (30:1–33)

VII. **Sayings of Lemuel** (31:1–9)

VIII. **Postscript: The Excellent Wife** (31:10–31)

Overview

The book contains seven collections of proverbs from various authors. A seven-verse introduction (1:1–7) states the book's purpose.

Title and introduction (1:1–7)

The opening verse associates the Book of Proverbs with Solomon, Israel's greatest wiseman and the catalyst of her wisdom literature. The book's purpose is clear by the repetition of "for" in verses 2–6:[2]

> 2) *for* attaining wisdom
> and discipline;
> *for* understanding words
> of insight;
> 3) *for* acquiring a disciplined
> and prudent life,
> doing what is right and just
> and fair;
> 4) *for* giving prudence
> to the simple,
> knowledge and discretion
> to the young—
> 5) let the wise listen and add
> to their learning,
> and let the discerning get
> guidance—
> 6) *for* understanding proverbs
> and parables,
> the sayings and riddles
> of the wise.

The book's goal is instruction, particularly for the young (v. 4), but it is also helpful to those who already have wisdom (v. 5).

Much more than intellectual information or head-knowledge, the instruction found in this book is based on the reverence and worship of Yahweh: "the fear of the LORD is the beginning of knowledge" (v. 7a). As its "beginning," the fear of God is the first and controlling principle of wisdom "rather than a stage which one leaves behind."[3] So the knowledge offered here

Women and the Book of Proverbs

The material in the Book of Proverbs was probably part of the curriculum for training young men who were preparing to take positions of leadership in the Israelite monarchy. Such positions were not open to young women in that society and culture, which leads to a definite masculine inclination in the book. "My son" is the often-repeated designation for the student.

Yet the book holds womanhood in the highest regard. The instruction of the mother is on a par with that of the father (1:8; 10:1), and the joy of a good wife is valued above all else (12:4). In this light, it is interesting that the book concludes with the magnificent poem to the excellent woman (31:10-31).

Reading the Book of Proverbs in our day requires several adjustments. Politically, we do not live under a monarchy whose leadership roles are limited to men. Culturally, we are not all of the same ethnic, religious, or socioeconomic fabric as were the ancient Israelites. When we read Proverbs today, we need to remember that these excellent instructions for living, though originally intended for young men, need to be offered to women as well. As women assume their roles alongside men in the workplace, the church, and the home, they also need the benefit of these ageless truths about life in God's world.

to the father's instruction and the mother's teaching. These sayings often contrast sexual immorality with devotion to wisdom, which involves sexual purity. The total picture is one of wisdom's great value.

The unit begins with an introduction that highlights the two ways of 1:7, the way of wisdom and the way of folly. The way of wisdom follows that path laid out before the young man by his parents (1:8–9). The wise young man will adorn himself in his father's instruction and his mother's teaching, which prepare him for life. But the way of folly is the path suggested by the young man's peer group, which pressures him into a life of sin, ultimately resulting in an early grave (1:10–19).

Several paragraphs in this unit praise the virtue of wisdom and enumerate the rewards of pursuing God's knowledge.

1. 1:20–33. This is the first of several passages in which wisdom is personified as a woman. Here she pleads urgently and emotionally to all who pass by the gates (the public gathering place in ancient cities). Rejecting her advice is tantamount to hating knowledge and rejecting the fear of Yahweh. This is ultimately self-destructive (vv. 28–32). But her invitation is to life and security (v. 33).

2. 2:1–22. This paragraph assures the youth that wisdom is attainable if one searches for it "as for silver" (v. 4). Wisdom, knowledge, and understanding are gifts from the Lord, which come from his own mouth (v. 6). This is more than mere human insight, but the truths of God's eternal ways.

3. 3:1–35. Further benefits of wisdom are a lifetime of serenity and victory. The central themes of this unit are poignantly stated in two important verses that summarize the biblical approach to life:

> Trust in the LORD with all your heart
> and lean not on your own
> understanding;
> in all your ways acknowledge him,
> and he will make your paths straight.
> (vv. 5–6)

is a relationship with the covenant God and dependent on his self-revelation. The contrasting line of verse 7 ("but fools despise wisdom and discipline") warns the student that on the path to wisdom he will meet those who will oppose his journey and encourage him to join them in other pursuits.

In praise of wisdom (1:8–9:18)

The material in these chapters consists of longer, well-crafted discourses, whereas most of the other collections in the book have shorter, tightly written sayings with little obvious editorial arrangement.[4] The sayings in 1:8–9:18 are a series of "fatherly talks," in light of the recurrence of the words "my son" and the several references

4. 4:1–27. This chapter contains the urgent teachings of a father for his son in which he again offers two paths. These time-honored truths have been handed

distichs

down from generation to generation (vv. 3–4). The contrast between two ways in life culminates in "the path of the righteous," who walk in the safe light of day, and "the way of the wicked," who stumble about in deep darkness (vv. 18–19).[5]

5. 5:15–23. The joy of marital faithfulness is another benefit of wisdom. In explicit language, the paragraph explains that sexual delight is God's gift to a married couple. Faithfulness to one's wife is a source of joy and satisfaction. But breaking the marriage vows is calamitous.

6. 8:1–36. The praise of wisdom has risen in a great crescendo to this point. Proverbs 8 is the pinnacle of the Bible's view of wisdom, and strikes a remarkable contrast with preceding sections that warn against sexual infidelity, especially chapter 7. Wisdom is personified as a woman who is to be cherished, adored, and honored.[6] Thus the contrast between Lady Wisdom and the adulteress of chapter 7 is profound, and would provide the young man with clear choices between a life of wisdom and a life of sin.

Lady Wisdom was the first of the Lord's created order and stood at his side as he fashioned the universe (vv. 22–31). But by God's grace, she also takes her stand in the marketplace, in the soiled streets of everyday human commerce, to offer life and understanding to the simplest and slowest of the human race (vv. 1–21). Like the temptress of chapter 7, Lady Wisdom aggressively seeks to be found by humankind. But in contrast, those who embrace wisdom find life itself (vv. 35–36).

Proverbs 1:8–9:18 contains several sections warning against adultery and the dangers of immoral women.

1. 5:1–14. This paragraph has two discourses warning against sexual sins. No matter how alluring a seductress may be, her surface beauty only covers the decay and ruin at the heart of her motives (vv. 3–5). The second discourse lists the dire consequences of sexual impurity (vv. 7–14).

2. 6:20–35. The effects of sexual sin are so great that they destroy whoever submits to them. "Can a man scoop fire into his lap without his clothes being burned" (v. 27)?

3. 7:1–27. This is the most powerful unit on the dangers of sexual impurity. The

opening paragraph (vv. 1–5) illustrates the importance of making careful decisions. The warnings against sexual sin must take root in the heart before the moment of temptation. The best advice possible for a young person, as presented here in the wisdom of God, is to guard these words and commands as the pupil ("apple") of one's eye. The rest of the chapter describes what happens to the simple-minded young man who gives in to the temptress (vv. 6–27). His first mistake is going to the wrong place at the wrong time, where he is seemingly defenseless before her advances (vv. 8–9). When he surrenders to her, he follows her "like an ox going to the slaughter" (v. 22). The concluding paragraph begs the reader to look past her beauty to the heap of corpses who are her victims (vv. 24–27).

Proverbs of Solomon (10:1–22:16)

After the parental discourses of the first unit, the youth is now ready for the many specific proverbs of this larger section. The title ("The proverbs of Solomon," 10:1) sets the preceding collection of discourses off from this unit of individual proverbs. The unit consists largely of a collection of proverbial sayings in poetry of two lines each (**distichs**). The parallelism is almost always antithetical, as in the first aphorism: "A wise child makes a glad father, but a foolish child is a mother's grief" (NRSV 10:1).

These proverbs cover topics as diverse and wide-ranging as life itself: poverty and wealth, slander, self-discipline, speech and silence, work and laziness, rash promises, discipline in education, sickness and grief, old age, and more.[7] There does not appear to be an organizing principle or structure in this collection. The seemingly haphazard order of these proverbs reflects the random manner in which we deal with the life-issues they address.[8]

Sayings of the wise men (22:17–24:34)

This separate collection is marked by the opening paragraph (22:17–21). These are "sayings of the wise" to which the student should affix his heart and pay close attention. Careful observance of these sayings will result in trust in the Lord and a solid foundation in the truth.

Excerpts from the Teachings of Amenemope[1]

(Compare with Prv 22:17–23:11)

Give your ears, listen to the things which are spoken. See for yourself these thirty chapters. They are pleasant, they educate. Guard yourself from robbing the poor, from being violent to the weak. Do not associate with the rash man nor approach him in conversation . . . when he makes a statement to snare you and you may be released by your answer. As for the scribe who is experienced in his office, he will find himself worthy of being a courtier.

Do not eat food in the presence of a noble or cram your mouth in front of him. If you are satisfied pretend to chew. It is pleasant in your saliva. Look at the cup in front of you and let it serve your need.

Do not strain to seek excess when your possessions are secure. If riches are brought to you by robbery, they will not stay the night in your possession.

Do not covet the property of a poor man lest you hunger for his bread. As for the property of a poor man it obstructs the throat and wounds the gullet. Do not pour out your heart to everybody so that you diminish respect for yourself. Do not remove the boundary stone on the boundaries of the cultivated land nor throw down the boundary of the widow lest a dread thing carry you off.

[1]Extracted from the Instruction of Amenemope (ANET, 421–24). J. Ruffle, "The Teaching of Amenemope and Its Connection with the Book of Proverbs," Tyndale Bulletin 28 (1977): 29–68. See John H. Walton, Ancient Israelite Literature in Its Cultural Context: A Survey of Parallels between Biblical and Ancient Near Eastern Texts (Grand Rapids: Zondervan, 1989), 192–97, for complete discussion.

gued that the Egyptian text was translated from an older Hebrew version. But most agree that the Hebrew proverbs were modeled on an Egyptian original. Indeed, the Hebrew text tends to clarify its Egyptian counterpart in places.[9] Any doubt about the direction of borrowing was resolved by recent findings that require a new date of composition for the Egyptian text. It is now virtually certain that the *Instruction of Amenemope* came from around 1200 B.C., over two hundred years before Solomon.[10]

It is not surprising that biblical authors felt free to draw on material from surrounding cultures. The title of this section ("sayings of the wise") may imply foreign origins, and chapter 30 as well as part of chapter 31 were probably contributions of non-Israelites. And we have already seen that Job may have foreign origins. The idea of Israelite borrowing is especially not surprising of proverbs, which after all, are based on life-experiences and observations about the universe. Ancient Israelites recognized and respected the value and truthfulness of some of the Egyptian observations about life, though they condemned all forms of polytheism. So the borrowing here was not rigid, but creative. The author of this section felt free to adapt the material for Israel's unique worship of Yahweh.

It should also be remembered that proverbs, though based on human experiences, are not merely humankind's observations about the world. The instructions are also part of God's revelation to Israel and to modern believers. This section's dependence on an Egyptian set of proverbs does not undermine the role of God's inspiration in the composition of the Book of Proverbs.

Solomonic sayings from Hezekiah's collection (25:1–29:27)

According to the introduction of this section, scribes in Hezekiah's court copied and compiled this collection of "more proverbs of Solomon" (25:1). As in other sections of Solomon's proverbs, these are marked by their short, forceful style. But Hezekiah's scribes have organized certain proverbs into small, topical collections (as in 1:8–9:18).

Many of these proverbs would have

These "thirty sayings" (22:20) have much in common with the Egyptian document known as the *Instruction of Amenemope*, which has a prologue and thirty chapters of "instructions for well-being" (see introduction in chapter 20 above). The relationship between the Egyptian proverbs and this section of the biblical book (especially 22:17–23:14) is too close to be coincidental. Some scholars have ar-

A market trader weighs out his produce in Bethlehem. The Lord wants weights and measures to be honest (11:11).

been of great interest to Hezekiah, the religious reformer (see 2 Chr 29–31). They frequently deal with topics of leadership and those who associate with leaders. Kings are noted for their thirst for the truth (25:2–3), and they grow weary of boastful subjects who are motivated by vain pride (25:6–8).

Sayings of Agur (30:1–33)

The proverbs of Agur, son of Jakeh, and those of King Lemuel (31:1–9) appear to have existed independently before they became part of the biblical book.[11] Most commentators assume they were of Arabian descent, a theory supported by a slight textual variant (see NIV's note "of Massa" at 30:1 and 31:1). Neither Agur nor Lemuel is known outside these biblical references, and their origins remain in doubt.

Agur's collection is marked by the rep-

etition of numerical sayings, such as "There are three things that are too amazing for me, four that I do not understand" (30:18). The chapter opens with the author's candid confession that he does not have great wisdom and understanding (30:1–9). His numerical statements demonstrate his need for more learning and insight. As elsewhere in the Book of Proverbs, Agur's collection illustrates that pride is the enemy of wisdom and is therefore no friend of God.

Sayings of Lemuel (31:1–9)

King Lemuel's proverbs, learned at his mother's knee, warn about royal responsibility. Kings should take care not to indulge their appetites at the expense of their people. Specifically, Lemuel's mother warns him about drunkenness, which will lead to neglect of the law and persecution of the oppressed.

The wisdom of finding an excellent wife (31:10–31)

These verses are an **acrostic,** meaning that the first letter of each line of poetry is the next successive letter of the Hebrew alphabet. Hence, there are twenty-two lines, one for each of the twenty-two letters of the alphabet. This is a favorite technique of the talented Old Testament poets (see for example, Ps 119 and Lam 3).

It is fitting that the Book of Proverbs should end on the importance of finding a good wife. It has warned against sexual

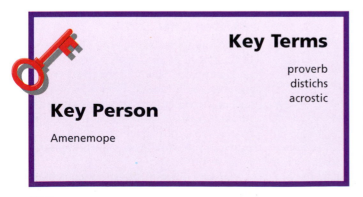

Key Terms

proverb
distichs
acrostic

Key Person

Amenemope

impurity all along the way. The book has also exalted the role of women, and even personified wisdom as a woman worthy of marriage. The young man, beginning his life of service to God, can be ruined or made successful by his decision of a life partner (31:23). His choice of a wife is the first test of his character, and his success depends partly on her character as well.

In these closing paragraphs, the book seems to be emphasizing the role of the virtuous wife and mother as the one most able to build up a character of wisdom in her family. This great woman's family will rise up and call her blessed (31:28–31).

Authorship

The book contains several references to Solomon's role in the proverb traditions of Israel. The proverbs in 10:1–22:16 are called "the proverbs of Solomon" (10:1), and those of chapters 25–29 are "more proverbs of Solomon, copied by the men of Hezekiah king of Judah" (25:1). The opening verse of the book associates the whole collection with Solomon.

Indeed, biblical testimony in general supports the idea that Solomon stood at the fountainhead of Israel's wisdom traditions (1 Kgs 4:29–34; Pss 72:1; 127:1; Song 1:1). Though many modern biblical scholars reject this possibility, a study of the formal structure of the Book of Proverbs suggests an early first millennium date for its composition, which supports the biblical witness.[12] The evidence implies that Solomon composed much of the material in the Book of Proverbs. Contributions of other wisdom teachers were attached to Solomon's collection, because he was the impetus and patron of the Israelite wisdom tradition.

Theological Themes

The Old Testament gives few details about how ancient Israelites educated their children. Apparently, education took place in the home (Dt 6:4–9; Prv 23:22–25). What

Summary

1. A proverb is a short saying about principles of living that have been proven by life experience, but a proverb is not a promise or a command.

2. There are two types of wisdom literature: discursive wisdom as found in Job and instructional literature as found in Proverbs.

3. The major objective of the Book of Proverbs is instruction for all.

4. Proverbs 1–9 are basically parental discourses to children.

5. The proverbs in chapters 10–22 are specific proverbs for youth, covering a variety of subjects.

6. The thirty sayings of Proverbs 22–28 are similar to those found in the Egyptian document, The Instruction of Amenemope.

7. The Book of Proverbs contains sayings of Solomon, Agur, and Lemuel.

8. The collection of sayings of Agur emphasizes how the enemy of wisdom is pride.

9. The acrostic is the literary device used in Proverbs 31.

10. Education is addressed in the Book of Proverbs, where the contents of Israelite education are described. This includes education for living in a proper relationship with God and his created world.

Study Questions

1. What is the focus of this book of short sayings? Define a "proverb." How does a proverb differ from a promise or a command?

2. How does the "wisdom" of Proverbs differ from that of the Book of Job? What two things are contrasted in the Book of Proverbs?

3. What is the goal of the book? Who is the target audience? What is the first and controlling principle of wisdom?

4. How is the first collection of sayings (1:8–9:18) different from most of the other collections in the book? Where does one find the pinnacle of the Bible's view of wisdom? What is the most powerful unit on the dangers of sexual impurity?

5. Which unit may have been based on an Egyptian text?

6. Why would the sayings of 25:1–29:27 have been of interest to Hezekiah?

7. What is known about the origin of the sayings of Agur (30:1–33)?

8. Why is the unit on finding an excellent wife (31:10–31) a fitting end to the Book of Proverbs?

9. What place did Proverbs hold in Israelite education? How did the Israelites view faith and knowledge? What is the underlying essence of knowledge or wisdom as presented in Proverbs?

is clear is that the Book of Proverbs presents the *contents* of Israelite education. Though the book obviously deals with knowledge and secular education, this is not the limit of its concern.

Proverbs intends to present wisdom needed for successful living. It provides instruction for living in relationship with God and his created world. Ancient Israelites did not compartmentalize their faith as moderns do. For them, there was only one world of experience, in which rational perceptions and religion were not differentiated.[13] Experiences of Yahweh were experiences of the world, and the Israelites made no attempt to separate faith from knowledge. Thus the "fear of the LORD is the beginning of knowledge/wisdom" (1:7; 9:10).

Knowledge (at least this kind of knowledge) is primarily relational, not propositional. In other words, there is much more to knowing truth than learning its propositions, its proven assertions. The brightest people in the world may acquire

tremendous insight about the world, even about God, and still not know him. The wisdom offered in the Book of Proverbs is wisdom rooted in a personal knowledge of God.

This kind of wisdom has more to do with character than intellect. Intellect is obviously important in grasping the truths of God. But his truths are ones to which we are called to commit our lives. Without such commitment, we have missed true wisdom, which has its beginning in relationship to him.

This relational knowledge has an impact on our human relationships. The Book of Proverbs has much to say about our relationships with parents, spouses, and families. A key element of wisdom in human relationships is sexuality, an important issue in this book. Proverbs acknowledges the power of sex in our relationships. That power translates into potential for the most fulfilling relationship possible, the beauty of love within marriage. On the other hand, the power of sex presents a dangerous

Further Reading

Alden, Robert L. *Proverbs: A Commentary on an Ancient Book of Timeless Advice.* Grand Rapids: Baker, 1983. Easy, commentary-like treatment of the book.

Bullock, C. Hassell. *An Introduction to the Old Testament Poetic Books.* Rev. ed. Chicago: Moody, 1988. Helpful introduction to all the poetical books.

Garrett, Duane A. *Proverbs, Ecclesiastes, Song of Songs.* New American Commentary 14. Nashville: Broadman, 1993. Best comprehensive commentary available. Contains thorough scholarly presentation, yet sensitive to theological issues as well.

Hubbard, David A. *Proverbs.* Communicator's Commentary 15A. Dallas: Word, 1989. A useful treatment that is more scholarly than most commentaries in this series.

Kidner, Derek. *The Proverbs: An Introduction and Commentary.* Tyndale Old Testament Commentary. Downers Grove/Leicester: InterVarsity, 1964. Valuable insights, though concise. Includes concise discussions of key topics: marriage, family, children, etc. Excellent for beginners.

Mouser, William E., Jr. *Walking in Wisdom: Studying the Proverbs of Solomon.* Downers Grove: InterVarsity, 1983. Introduction to the unique literary features of Proverbs. Helpful discussion of poetry.

opening for wreckage. Those who abuse this powerful and precious gift of God outside his will are on a collision course with disaster.

As we saw in chapter 20, the retribution theology of the Pentateuch has an important role to play in wisdom literature. The Book of Proverbs illustrates the retribution principle by emphasizing the two ways of living between which all of us must choose: the way of wisdom or the way of folly. The way of wisdom is a way of living in relationship with God, and seeks to learn more about his ways in the world. The way of folly lives without regard for God or his instruction. To choose the second alternative is self-destructive.

23 Ecclesiastes and Song of Songs

Israelite Faith in Everyday Life

Outline

- **The Book of Ecclesiastes**
  Contents
  Authorship
- **The Song of Songs**
  Contents
  Authorship
- **Theological Themes**
  Ecclesiastes
  Song of Songs

Objectives

After reading this chapter, you should be able to

- State the themes of Ecclesiastes and Song of Songs
- Outline the basic content of the Book of Ecclesiastes
- Discuss the themes of Ecclesiastes and Song of Songs
- Relate the key issues surrounding the authorship of Ecclesiastes
- Outline the basic content of the Song of Songs
- Find ancient Near Eastern metaphors in Song of Songs

Ecclesiastes and Song of Songs conclude the Old Testament section of the canon known as the poetical books. They depict important aspects of life in ancient Israel that relate to universal human experiences. Everyone around the world can relate to the struggle of faith in Ecclesiastes and the need for human love in Song of Songs. Ecclesiastes demonstrates how faith can triumph over doubt; Song of Songs celebrates the love shared between husband and wife.

The Book of Ecclesiastes

The book reflects a time of despair. The promises of the covenant seem far distant, the glories of national Israel forgotten, and the shining hope of the prophets lost. But even in the midst of such desperation, the poet discovers the rich truths proclaimed in the other wisdom books of the Old Testament (Job and Proverbs). The "fear of God" is the only sure foundation for building one's life (Jb 28:28; Prv 1:7). Ecclesiastes teaches that the only hope of enduring the present is to fear and obey God (12:13–14).

Contents

The term "ecclesiastes" has a long history. It came into English through the Latin and Greek translations of the Old Testament (**Vulgate** and **Septuagint**). It translates the Hebrew word *qōhelet* in 1:1: "The words of QOHELET, son of David, king in Jerusalem." The Hebrew term occurs nowhere else in the Old Testament except in this book (seven times) and its meaning is uncertain. It appears to refer to one leading an assembly, and therefore "ecclesiastes" was understood as the leader or speaker for the assembly. Some translations use "preacher" (KJV, NKJV), but the term is used as a proper noun in the book and Qohelet is more of a philosopher than a preacher.[1] Many of the newer translations use "teacher" (NIV, NLT, NRSV).

Qohelet's purpose is clear in the motto, stated at the outset and repeated at the conclusion to form a literary envelope for the whole book: "Vanity of vanities! All is vanity" (1:2; 12:8 NRSV). The Hebrew term translated "vanity" *(hebel)* has many connotations: absurdity, frustration, futility, nonsense, emptiness, and vapor. The NIV has "Meaningless! Meaningless! Everything is meaningless!" The term can refer to a passing vapor, emphasizing its insubstantial and transitory nature. Qohelet warns against a life caught in the pursuit of absurd and empty pleasures that have no lasting value.[2] Life without God at the center is meaningless.

Outline

There are many Jewish tombs on the slopes of the Mount of Olives, Jerusalem. The writer of Ecclesiastes speaks of a time to be born and a time to die (3:2).

Overview

Just as Job is a collection of speeches, Psalms a collection of songs, and Proverbs a collection of short wisdom sayings, so Ecclesiastes is a collection. This book contains a variety of literary types, all making the same point, such as poetry, narrative, proverbial sayings, and brief meditations. These types, in spite of their variety, share a common theme: Life, and our preoccupation with material and temporal things, is meaningless. The teacher believes that when all the trivial layers of life are stripped away, all we have left is to "fear God" and "enjoy life."

TITLE AND THEME (1:1–11)

The book's thesis is that everything is meaningless: "Vanity of vanities! All is vanity" (1:2; 12:8 NRSV). The Hebrew literary form "X of X" indicates the superlative and intensifies an idea. For example, the "Holy of Holies" is the most holy place, the "king of kings" is the greatest king, and the "Song of Songs" is the best of songs. The vanity and meaninglessness in this book's motto is intense and all-encompassing: "Everything is utterly meaningless."

Nor does our work produce accomplishments that make life meaningful (vv. 3–11). As the sun rises and sets, and as the wind blows around in its endless courses, so our labors are repetitive and futile (vv.

5–6). And so it has been from the beginning. The more human beings pride themselves in their achievements and development, the more things remain the same: "there is nothing new under the sun" (vv. 9–10).

WISDOM REFLECTIONS (1:12–4:16)

Using King Solomon as an example, the book teaches that even fame is no guarantee of a meaningful life. Assuming the unlimited riches and resources of the great king, the teacher searches for significance in life through Solomon's royal accomplishments. But even the accomplishments of King Solomon were disappointing: wisdom (1:13–18; 2:12–16), pleasure (2:1–3), building projects and riches (2:4–11). In despair, the great king summarizes all his pursuits as total vanity, a "chasing after the wind" (a phrase that recurs in this unit, 1:14, 17; 2:11, 17, 26). Ultimately, we mortals can do nothing better than eat, drink, and find satisfaction in our work. But even this is not of our own, but a gift of God (2:24–25).

The catalog of times (3:1–15) affirms that the variety of times and seasons of life are set by God. All our hard work can never change the way God has established these cyclic patterns of life (v. 9). All we can do is "be happy and do good" while we are alive (v. 12). It is God's gift for us to "eat and drink, and find satisfaction" in our

An elderly Orthodox Jew prays at Jerusalem's Western wall. Chapter 12 of Ecclesiastes contains a moving poem about old age (vv. 1–8).

work (v. 13). We must simply enjoy God's wonderful creation and understand that everything he has done is intended to lead us to revere and serve him (v. 14).

The prospect of death is also undeniable. In this sense, humans are no better off than the animals; all breathe the same air and all can expect one day to die (3:19–20). Again, the only consolation is enjoyment of our labor (3:22).

The teacher considered all the oppression "under the sun," and despaired of hope. He concluded that those who have already died are better off than the living. Better still are those who have not been born at all (4:2–3). Achievements, wealth, companionship, and the glory of rising from poverty to kingship—all are "meaningless, a chasing after the wind" (4:4, 6, 7, 16).

ADMONITIONS AND OBSERVATIONS (5:1–12:8)

The teacher continues his assessment of life's activities, which he views as all meaningless. Religion (5:1–7) and wealth (5:8–17) fail to add meaning to life. The best advice the teacher can offer is to eat and drink and be satisfied with work "during the few days of life God has given" (5:18). This was a theme first sounded in 2:24–25, and emerges as the teacher's philosophy of life, giving a glimpse of hope in an otherwise gloomy book. After he con-

cludes there is no justice to be had in this life, he declares there is nothing "better for people under the sun than to eat, and drink, and enjoy themselves" (8:15, NRSV).

The future holds no guarantees, and it is useless to hope for better. The stillborn child is better off than someone who lives a life of disappointment (6:3–6), and the day of death is better than the day of birth (7:1). Wisdom is helpful for the one who has it, but righteousness does not save (7:5–14). The teacher has witnessed a righteous man perishing in his righteousness, and a wicked man living long in his wickedness (7:15). Human power is arbitrary and unpredictable, so those who serve in the royal court must learn to live with the inevitable abuse of power (8:2–8).

The theme of 8:9–9:10 is summarized in 9:2: "All share a common destiny—the righteous and the wicked, the good and the bad, the clean and the unclean, those who offer sacrifices and those who do not." As elsewhere, the Teacher laments that death is inevitable and we must all face that fact. All we can do is enjoy the life God has given in spite of our unanswered questions (9:7–10).

The next unit (9:11–12:8) begins with an assertion about the uncertainties of life: "The race is not to the swift or the battle to the strong . . . but time and chance happen to them all" (9:11). Even wisdom does

Excerpts Adapted from the Epic of Gilgamesh[1]

This passage from the Epic of Gilgamesh parallels Ecclesiastes 9:7–9. The disparaging words of Siduri remind Gilgamesh that we all must face death, and that he must learn to enjoy this fleeting life as much as possible.

Gilgamesh, where do you think your roaming will
  get you?
You will not find the eternal life you are seeking.
Remember that when the gods created
  humankind,
they set death aside for us, reserving life for
  themselves.
But you, O Gilgamesh, let your stomach be full
  and satisfied.
Make merry day and night,
and make every day a celebration feast, with
  dancing and play.
Let your clothes be sparkling fresh,
and your head washed in sweet, refreshing
  waters.
Cherish the little ones who hold your hand.
Rejoice in the love of your wife.
This is the best we humans can hope for.

[1]Adapted from the Old Babylonian version of tablet 10, column 3, *ANET*, 90.

not necessarily make life meaningful, because it goes unnoticed (9:13–18). Chapter 10 contains practical sayings about the futility of human endeavors. Yet the teacher calls us to take action, even though our understanding is limited: "Cast your bread upon the waters . . ." (11:1). Ignorance or confusion is no excuse for standing still (11:1–6).

This unit ends with a moving poem about old age (12:1–8). Youth is wonderful, but "the days of trouble come" for us all (v. 1). No matter how invincible we feel when we are young, age and death await us all. The light grows dim, clouds fill the sky, sorrow arrives, and birdsongs grow faint. Each of us must go to our "eternal home" (v. 5), while "the dust returns to the ground it came from" (v. 7, referring to the curse of Gn 3:19). We should all take note that God's word contains graphic reminders of our mortality.

CONCLUSION (12:9–14)

The teacher arrives at his conclusion in this brief epilogue. After disparaging the condition of humankind throughout the book, he declares that the whole of humanity is dependent on God: "Here is the conclusion of the matter: Fear God and keep his commandments" (12:13). Meaningfulness and significance in life are fleeting, and may even seem impossible. But we are placed here to live in relationship with God, regardless of our circumstances. This is our only goal in life, and if we miss it, we miss meaning.

The "fear of God" is defined as keeping his commandments. Walking in his ways and obeying his will are the only human endeavors with meaning. Many translations take the last phrase of 12:13 as "for that is the whole duty of everyone" (NRSV; see also NIV and NLT). But the Hebrew literally means "for this is the whole of humankind." To obey him is to be truly human and to reach our greatest potential as part of his creation.[3]

Authorship

The question of authorship of Ecclesiastes usually centers around the book's unique language. The Hebrew of Qohelet is unlike any other of the Old Testament. Scholars have long believed the book's language was affected by later Aramaic influences, and that this, along with other linguistic peculiarities, gives evidence of a very late date.[4] Most scholars date the work to the third century B.C.

However, recent research on Qohelet's language has thrown this analysis into question. The grammar and vocabulary of Ecclesiastes do not appear to be postexilic, but in fact completely consonant with preexilic Hebrew.[5] Though the precise question of authorship must be left open, it is no longer possible to hold to a late, postexilic date for the Book of Ecclesiastes on the basis of linguistic evidence.

The phrase "son of David, king in Jerusalem" and certain passages like 1:16–17 are clearly meant to remind the reader of Solomon: "I thought to myself, 'Look, I have grown and increased in wisdom more than anyone who has ruled

An artist's impression of an Eastern wedding party, with the bride and groom seated beneath a special canopy.

over Jerusalem before me; I have experienced much of wisdom and knowledge.' Then I applied myself to the understanding of wisdom." Yet the boast that he had surpassed all who preceded him on the throne is rather weak if his father David was his only predecessor. Since the book nowhere claims Solomon is its author, it is better to leave the matter unsettled.

Yet the book clearly has some connections with Solomon. He was the human stimulus for much of the wisdom literature according to the Bible, and it is certainly possible to see some kind of historical connection between King Solomon and the Book of Ecclesiastes. He was in fact, the author of some of the wisdom literature (Prv 1:1; 10:1), and as such he became the fountainhead, the model for all Israel's wisdom writings.[6]

The Song of Songs

Just as Qohelet's motto "vanity of vanities" is a Hebrew superlative meaning "everything is utterly meaningless," so with the expression "song of songs." This is the most beautiful of all songs, the best or number one song. This song tops the charts!

Contents

The structure of the book has been hotly debated among Old Testament scholars. The obvious lack of unity has led many scholars to conclude the book is not a single song, but a collection or anthology of many different poems woven together. Though the Song appears to be an anthology, it is not totally without unity. It is highly repetitive, and its consistent char-

Excerpts Adapted from Egyptian Love Songs

Ancient Egyptian love songs contain lists of beautiful bodily features, much like the Song of Songs (4:1–7; 5:9–16; 7:1–5). Notice how the beloved is called "sister" as in the Song of Songs.

One alone is (my) sister, having no peer:
more gracious than all other women.
Behold her, like the star rising
at the beginning of a good year:
shining, precious, white of skin,
lovely of eyes when gazing.
Sweet her lips when speaking:
she has no excess of words.
Long of neck, white of breast,
her hair true lapis lazuli.
Her arms surpass gold,
her fingers are like lotuses.[1]

Some of the Egyptian love songs exhibit the same pattern as the individual poems in the Song of Songs: description of beauty followed by a wish.

Your love is mixed throughout my body
like honey mixed with water,
like medicine in which gum is mixed,
like the blending of dough and water.
So hasten to see your sister,
like a stallion dashing onto a battlefield.[2]

[1]Papyrus Chester Beatty I, group A, no. 31. Michael V. Fox, *The Song of Songs and the Ancient Egyptian Love Songs* (Madison: University of Wisconsin Press, 1985), 52.
[2]Papyrus Harris 500, group A, no.2. Fox, 8.

ways throughout the centuries, too often in an attempt to suppress the obviously sexual nature of the poems.[8]

Song of Songs is a simply stated celebration of love shared between young lovers created in God's image. They bask in each other's beauty and in their ability to satisfy their need for physical love. Song of Songs pays homage to the wonder and majesty of monogamous sexual love, when that love is intensely pursued with honor and faithfulness.

Many interpreters throughout history have been uncomfortable with such explicit material. Some, both Jewish and Christian, have taken either a typological or allegorical approach. In the typological model, the Old Testament events described are thought to be historical, but a corresponding New Testament parallel is primary in meaning. So this book is said to illustrate God's intimate, covenant bond with his people. In the allegorical model the text relates a hidden meaning. It assumes the book is also about God's intimate relationship with his people, though it does not accept a historical basis for the book. Many Jewish interpreters have taken the Song as an **allegory** of the love between Yahweh and Israel, while Christian scholars have often accepted the book as praising the love between Christ and the church. But it is doubtful whether this is the intended message of Song of Songs. It seems best to take the book at face value, inasmuch as no evidence indicates the book is symbolic. The book celebrates sexual love between husband and wife.

Outline

I. **Love's Strong Desire** (1:1–2:7)

II. **Love Lost and Found** (2:8–3:5)

III. **Celebration and Consummation** (3:6–5:1)

IV. **Love's Anxiety and Consummation** (5:2–8:4)

V. **Love's Affirmation and Consummation** (8:5–14)

Overview

The use of the personal pronouns in Song of Songs ("you," "I," "me," "he," "his," . . .) often makes it difficult to know who is

allegory

acter portrayal and common themes indicate a certain unity, though not a consistent narrative plot.[7]

The powerful ancient Near Eastern metaphors used in the song seem distasteful or confusing to some modern readers (e.g., "your teeth are like a flock of sheep," 4:2). But these are part of the cultural heritage of the ancient Oriental world and should not detract from the amorous nature of the material. Nor should we overspiritualize the song. Song of Songs has been interpreted in radically different

Part of the Garden of Gethsemane, Jerusalem. The writer of the Song of Songs employs the imagery of the garden in his song of longing.

speaking. Some scholars who have taken the Song as a drama see three parties in a sort of love triangle. In this interpretation, Solomon was trying to seduce a simple but beautiful girl away from her shepherd boyfriend. Others have assumed a two-character drama, taking the shepherd and the king as the same character. However, no indications in the text suggest that the Song was intended as a drama, and we have no evidence such literature was produced in ancient Syria-Palestine. Rather than a drama, it is better to take the Song as a collection of love songs with no particular plot or story line. The pronouns switch back and forth because the individual units were originally independent.

In order to account for unity in the Song, some scholars have attempted to find a chiastic structure for the whole.[9] But these attempts have not successfully demonstrated an overall formal structure. Instead, the Song of Songs appears to have been preceded by smaller collections of love poetry, just as the Books of Psalms and Proverbs were preceded by smaller collections of praise hymns and wisdom sayings. The collector or editor of the Song appears to have drawn together poems with similar themes and arranged them on the basis of catchwords and content.[10]

The book is a song about awakening love, written (or sung) in two parts, the

man's and the woman's, with choral responses sprinkled throughout. The individual poems of the Song appear to have shared a similar structure, with several variations. The woman (or occasionally the man) is described as beautiful and desirable. Then the speaker expresses a wish to be with her (or him).[11] For example, Song 4:1–5 is a descriptive section followed by the expression of will and determination in 4:6.

4:1 How beautiful you are, my darling!
    Oh, how beautiful!
    Your eyes behind your veil are doves.
    Your hair is like a flock of goats
        descending from Mount Gilead.
4:2 Your teeth are like a flock of sheep
        just shorn,
        coming up from the washing.
    Each has its twin;
        not one of them is alone.
4:3 Your lips are like a scarlet ribbon;
        your mouth is lovely.
    Your temples behind your veil
        are like the halves of a pomegranate.
4:4 Your neck is like the tower of David,
        built with elegance;
    on it hang a thousand shields,
        all of them shields of warriors.
4:5 Your two breasts are like two fawns,
        like twin fawns of a gazelle
        that browse among the lilies.
4:6 Until the day breaks
        and the shadows flee,

I will go to the mountain of myrrh
and to the hill of incense.

Sometimes the descriptive section of a unit stands alone and the wish for love is only suggested.

4:9 You have stolen my heart, my sister, my bride;
you have stolen my heart
with one glance of your eyes,
with one jewel of your necklace.
4:10 How delightful is your love, my sister, my bride!
How much more pleasing is your love than wine,
and the fragrance of your perfume than any spice!
4:11 Your lips drop sweetness as the honeycomb, my bride;
milk and honey are under your tongue.
The fragrance of your garments is like that of Lebanon.

Occasionally the order is reversed altogether. In 1:2, the desire is expressed first, followed by the descriptive statement. Notice in this example that the pronouns switch from the third person in the expressed wish (1:2a) to the second person in the descriptive statement (1:2b).[12]

Authorship

The opening reference of the book is to "Solomon's Song of Songs" (1:1). But the language here is not necessarily referring to authorship. The words themselves may indicate the song was written about Solomon, was dedicated to Solomon, or was placed in a collection of Solomon-like songs.[13] Many of the references to Solomon are in the third person, and it is more likely that the compiler of the Song was an admirer of the great king's successes and supporter of the wisdom literary traditions.

The most logical conclusion is that the Song is an expression of two young lovers rejoicing in the splendor of their own "royal" occasion. Part of this expression may have been written originally in honor of one of King Solomon's weddings, and later became part of the standard musical celebration of every wedding.[14]

Theological Themes

Ecclesiastes

Christian faith never attempts to suppress the questioning mind. Genuine faith in God is not afraid to bring the rising doubt into the light of his revelation for examination. The very presence of a book like Ecclesiastes in the biblical canon is evidence that our faith welcomes closer scrutiny. This book acknowledges the fact that the circumstances of life sometimes make faith difficult. But its inclusion among the wisdom books of the Old Testament teaches that questions, or even

Summary

1. The central idea in Ecclesiastes is that humankind's only hope of surviving the trials of this life is to fear and obey God.

2. The term "ecclesiastes" may mean leader or speaker of an assembly, preacher, or teacher.

3. The author of the Book of Ecclesiastes is anonymous.

4. The Song of Songs means that this is the best of all songs.

5. Song of Songs is a song about the sexual love of a husband and wife.

6. Ancient Near Eastern metaphors like "your hair is descending like a flock of goats" abound in the Song of Songs.

Key Terms

Vulgate
Septuagint
allegory

Key People

Qohelet
Gilgamesh

dant living (Proverbs). But things do not always work out so well. Bad things can and sometimes do happen to good people! Should we abandon our faith in God when bad things happen to us? Certainly not, according to Qohelet. Life without trust in God becomes truly meaningless. Our task is to enjoy life as he grants it and to continue trusting in him who gives meaning to our existence.

Song of Songs

Our world today is enamored with sexual pleasure. Modern culture tends to compartmentalize such pleasure and disassociate our sexuality from our faith in God. But this best of songs provides a point of contact between human sexuality and biblical faith.[15] The Israelites recognized the sensual side of human nature as part of God's wonderful creation. God created us "male and female," and most of us are quite happy

doubts, need to be grappled with honestly. Over time, such honest grapplings stretch our faith and lead to deeper faith commitments.

Together with the other wisdom books (Job and Proverbs), Ecclesiastes balances the wisdom view of life. Yes, there are certain discernible principles of life that, when closely followed, will lead one into abun-

Study Questions

Ecclesiastes

1. What type of outlook on life does Ecclesiastes reflect?

2. How did the book get the name Ecclesiastes? What other names does the book have?

3. What is the purpose of the author in writing this book?

4. How is this purpose accomplished?

5. According to the author, what is the whole duty of humanity? What practical meaning does this have?

6. Discuss the date and authorship issues of the book of Ecclesiastes. What is the only sure conclusion concerning authorship?

7. What theological themes are found in the book?

Song of Songs

1. What is the meaning of the title "Song of Songs"?

2. With what subject does Song of Songs deal?

3. What is the book's intended message?

4. What is the overall structure of Song of Songs?

5. Discuss the authorship issues of the book.

6. What does Song of Songs teach about erotic, heterosexual love within the bonds of marriage?

Further Reading

Bullock, C. Hassell. *An Introduction to the Old Testament Poetic Books.* Rev. ed. Chicago: Moody, 1988. Helpful introduction to all the poetical books.

Carr, G. Lloyd. *The Song of Solomon: An Introduction and Commentary.* Tyndale Old Testament Commentary. Downers Grove/Leicester: InterVarsity, 1984.

Garrett, Duane A. *Proverbs, Ecclesiastes, Song of Songs.* New American Commentary 14. Nashville: Broadman, 1993. Best comprehensive commentary available. Contains thorough scholarly presentation, yet sensitive to theological issues as well.

Keel, Othmar. *The Song of Songs: A Continental Commentary.* Trans. Frederick J. Gaiser. Minneapolis: Fortress, 1994. Excellent exposition and richly illustrated with ancient Near Eastern sources.

Kidner, Derek. *A Time to Mourn, and a Time to Dance: Ecclesiastes and the Way of the World.* The Bible Speaks Today. Downers Grove: InterVarsity, 1976.

Murphy, Roland E. *Ecclesiastes.* Word Biblical Commentary 23A. Dallas: Word, 1992.

Scott, R. B. Y. *Proverbs, Ecclesiastes: Introduction, Translation, and Notes.* Anchor Bible 18; Garden City, N.Y.: Doubleday, 1965.

about that! In this most intimate of human relationships we somehow reflect God's image (Gn 1:27). Furthermore, the marriage bond provides the closest possible unity in human relations (Gn 2:24), and one in which there need be no shame or disgrace (Gn 2:25). In this sense, Song of Songs transports the marital relationship to the pre-fall Garden of Eden, where husband and wife enjoy each other with no inhibitions.

This book testifies to the mutual complementarity of man and woman. It affirms the sanctity of marriage and approves erotic, heterosexual love within the marital bonds.

Part

4

Encountering
the Prophets

24 The Prophets
Voices of God's Servants

Objectives

**After reading this chapter,
you should be able to**

- Explain the circumstances surrounding
  the dividing of Israel into northern
  and southern kingdoms
- Trace the development of the Hebrew
  nation from Egyptian captivity
  to the age of the prophets
- Summarize the basic content of the
  message of the classical prophets
- Tell what the prophets were
  and what they weren't
- Compare the Hebrew prophets' work
  with similar activities in other
  Near Eastern nations
- Explain how the messages
  of the prophets were recorded
- Relate the common themes
  of the prophets
- Identify the prophets who prophesied
  during the Assyrian domination
- Identify the prophets who prophesied
  during the Babylonian domination
- Identify the prophets who prophesied
  during the Persian domination

What comes to mind when you think of prophets? Do you picture wild fanatics dressed in strange clothes? Do you envision them gazing into their crystal balls and describing the future? Do you view the prophets as a somewhat bizarre group of individuals, who somehow served God in very strange ways we don't understand very well?

None of these understandings really fits the biblical evidence. The Bible asserts that God prepared his prophets for a very special ministry. They brought the divine word to a people who desperately needed to hear it. The prophets' voices rang with an authority that still rings today if we will only listen.

Prophecy's Biblical Heritage

How Do the Prophets Fit into God's Unfolding Purpose?

Before we discuss the prophets and their contribution to biblical history, we will briefly review Israel's history. Doing so will provide us a framework for studying the prophet's lives and words. The Pentateuch describes how God began to carve out a people for his name, a people who would become the nation of Israel. God established his covenant with Abraham, brought him to the land of Canaan, and gave him Isaac, through whom the blessings of the covenant continued. Isaac fathered Esau and Jacob, and God chose Jacob to carry on his covenant purposes. Jacob fathered twelve sons who became the ancestors of the twelve tribes of Israel.

The patriarchal family eventually settled in Egypt and became a numerous people. The Egyptians enslaved them, but after the people spent 430 years in bondage, God sent Moses to deliver the Hebrews from the Egyptians. The Lord led his people out of Egypt to the foot of Mount Sinai, where he gave them his laws and instructions for holy living.

The Hebrews' persistent rebellion against God led to forty years of wandering in the wilderness, but God protected them every step of the way. Finally, after Moses died and Joshua assumed control, the people conquered the land God had promised to their ancestors.

But despite the fact that Israel controlled the land, the trouble was far from over. Israel's neighbors often attacked her borders. Within Israel, pockets of foreign peoples still struggled for independence. After many years of battling such enemies, the Israelites decided they wanted a king.

Under Saul, Israel's first king, Israel won a few battles and strengthened her position in the land. But Saul did not fully follow the Lord, and finally, he met his death in battle with the Philistines. David, Saul's successor and one of Israel's greatest kings, conquered the neighboring peoples and secured Israel's borders. What David conquered his son and successor Solomon exploited economically.

After Solomon's death, the kingdom divided into north and south—Israel and Judah, respectively. Both Israel and Judah faced serious spiritual challenges. Idolatry and other foreign religious practices crept into the people's faith. Many of these temptations had appeared earlier in the Hebrews' history, during the wilderness and the judges periods, and now God's people were paying the spiritual price of their failures.

Religious compromise increased as ungodly religious practices began enjoying royal sanction. Solomon accommodated his foreign wives' desires to worship their own gods, and gradually, he began to follow other gods. Jeroboam, the first king of the northern kingdom, took deliberate steps to ensure Israel would remain distinct from Judah. He altered the dates of the Hebrew festivals, appointed his own priests, and established other worship sites in place of Jerusalem. Under Ahab a few generations later, Israel sank to her lowest spiritual depths. Although Judah generally fared better, the south also suffered spiritually during the reigns of many of her rulers.

By 750 B.C., major foreign powers began to arise in the ancient Near East. These powers formed a threat to smaller nations such as Israel, Judah, and their neighbors. During the following two centuries, Assyria, Babylon, and Egypt would all take their turns pushing into Syria and Palestine. Ultimately, they would bring about the downfall of Israel and Judah.

In the midst of all these factors, a crucial question appeared on the horizon: Would Israel and Judah return to their God and their spiritual heritage, or would they continue to embrace false religious faith? At this key turning point in Israel's and Judah's history, God sent his servants the prophets.

Who Were Prophecy's "Founding Fathers"?

When we say "The Prophets," we usually mean those individuals who lived from about 800 to 450 B.C. and served as God's special messengers to his people by the power of the Holy Spirit. Bible scholars often refer to these prophets as the **classical prophets** and their writings as **classical prophecy** because their messages tend to have certain similar features. As a general rule, the classical prophets address all the people, inform them of God's wrath against their sin, warn them of approaching judgment, call them to repentance, and proclaim God's salvation for those who will turn to him. The Old Testament books Isaiah–Malachi fit the category of classical prophecy.

Long before classical prophecy appeared in Israel and Judah, however, God had called others to prophetic ministries. Three men especially helped lay classical prophecy's foundation: Moses, Samuel, and Elijah.

As we have already seen, Moses, the son of Hebrew slaves, grew to manhood in the royal court of Egypt, but later fled Egypt after he killed an Egyptian. With Moses as his instrument, God brought the Hebrews out of Egypt to the land he had promised to their ancestors. God spoke with Moses face to face (Ex 33:11; Nm 12:8), and on Mount Sinai, Moses received God's Law, the foundational revelation on which the prophets would later build.

Moses realized that God would send other prophets after him (Dt 18:15). The classical prophets built on the foundation Moses had laid, appealing constantly to the Mosaic law and calling the people to heed its commands.

About 1100 B.C., Samuel began his prophetic-priestly ministry in Israel. He traveled from town to town, proclaiming God's word to the people and judging their important cases. When Israel's king violated God's commands, Samuel confronted him, for the king was not above the law (1 Sm 13:8–14; 15:10–31). Samuel's life was a life of godliness; at the end of his life, all Israel acknowledged his personal integrity (1 Sm 12:1–5).

About 870–860 B.C., the prophet Elijah appeared in Israel and began his ministry (1 Kgs 17:1). He challenged Israel to forsake Baal worship and turn back to the Lord. Elijah's biggest opposition came from Israel's royal house—Ahab and his queen Jezebel. When Elijah tried to block Jezebel's plans to exalt Baal worship in Israel, she took steps to kill him. First Kings 18 records Elijah's dramatic contest with the prophets of Baal on MOUNT CARMEL, a contest in which God demonstrated that he, not Baal, was Lord in Israel.

Moses, Samuel, and Elijah thus helped set the stage for the classical prophets. As these three faithfully served the Lord in what he had called them to do, the Lord used them to lay the foundation for his future prophetic work.[1]

The Nature of Prophecy

The Hebrew Terms for "Prophet"

The Hebrew language used three different words to refer to a prophet: ḥōzeh, rō'eh, and nābî'. Although the biblical writers clearly used these terms interchangeably,[2] the words do seem to connote different aspects of the prophetic office. The first two terms come from verbal roots that mean "to see, gaze, or look at." These words thus suggest that the ḥōzeh or rō'eh was someone who saw the very things of God; he had special insight (and usually a special message) that God gave him directly. The various English translations often translate these two terms as "seer."

The term nābî' occurs most frequently in the Hebrew Old Testament—over three hundred times! One common interpretation of the word relates it to the Akkadian verb nābû, "to call." The term nābî', then, might refer to a "called one," someone whom God had especially called to bring his divine message to his people. Indeed, the prophets certainly possessed a strong

True Prophet or False Prophet?

When the prophets prophesied, they did so on God's authority—*"Thus says the Lord."* But what if someone claimed to speak in God's Name, but really didn't? How would the people know a true prophet from a false one?

Deuteronomy 13:1–5 and 18:21–22 provided the people with two tests to discern true prophets from false prophets. First, a prophet's message had to be consistent with earlier revelation. For example, if a prophet counseled the people to worship other gods, he was a false prophet, for the Law of Moses had already commanded worship of God alone (Ex 20:3). God would not contradict himself.

Second, a prophet's predictions must always come true. If a prophet prophesied some sign or wonder, and the sign or wonder did not occur, the people were not to listen to him.

God ordered the death penalty for false prophets. This punishment might sound severe, but we must remember the incredible spiritual harm a false prophet could do. If the people believed a false prophet's words, the whole nation could suffer God's wrath. The prophetic office was something that God took very seriously.

sense of calling. God had personally chosen them to proclaim his message to a people who desperately needed to hear it.

What Are Some Common Wrong Ideas about the Prophets?

Before we explain who the prophets were, we should explain who they were not. Many Bible readers have come to false understandings of the prophetic office because they have studied only part of the biblical evidence.

First, the prophets were not hysterical babblers. Some scholars have portrayed the prophets (especially earlier prophets) as men who often went into frenzied trances and babbled uncontrollably until the Spirit of God left them. These writers cite two instances from Saul's life (1 Sm 10:10; 19:23–24) to support this theory. However, 1 Samuel 10:10 does not say the men were babbling out of control, and 1 Samuel 19:23–24 refers only to a special judgment against Saul to prevent him from catching David.

Second, the prophets were not fortune tellers. They did not tell people their personal futures, as a psychic, palm reader, or horoscope might claim to do today. As God revealed his future plans to the prophets, they revealed them to the people to motivate their hearers to holiness and godliness. The prophets had no interest in entertaining people with fanciful notions about the future.

Third, the prophets were not "religious fanatics." They were not cantankerous individuals who were always looking for the opportunity to have a spiritual argument with someone. To portray them in such a way would seriously misrepresent the prophets. The prophets were servants of God who saw God's will for his people and grieved deeply that his people fell so far short of it. They possessed strong convictions about religious truth, and longed for the day when their hearers would possess them, too.

How Are All the Prophets Alike?

The prophets came from many different backgrounds. The prophet Amos, for example, tended flocks and cared for sycamore trees before the Lord called him to the prophetic ministry (Am 7:14). Isaiah often spoke directly to Judah's royal house (Is 7:3–9; 37:6–7, 21–35; 38:1–8; 39:3–8); Jewish tradition suggests he may even have been a relative of King Uzziah, though this is uncertain.[3] Jeremiah grew up among the priests of the village of Anathoth (Jer 1:1). In each case, God used the prophet's prior experiences to shape the prophet's ministry.

But despite the vast differences in their backgrounds, the prophets shared many characteristics. First, the prophets possessed hearts devoted to God. They loved the Lord, and therefore, they loved his word and ways. They placed their commitment to him above all else, even when doing so brought trouble and persecution. The prophets knew that if God's people could somehow come to realize what he expected of them, they might repent of their sins and turn back to him.

Second, the prophets possessed a strong

Relief of the Assyrian camp. The background to many of the prophets was invasion and war.

forthtellers

foretellers

sense of calling. They had not chosen the prophetic role for themselves; rather, God had called them to this ministry and commissioned them for his service. The knowledge that God had called them and empowered them for their tasks gave them strength to continue, even in the face of the most serious opposition. Sometimes God's calling came early in the prophet's life (Jer 1:4–5). At other times, the Lord took his servant from an established profession (Am 7:14–15). But each prophet knew that his ministry was not his own. He must live the life God had called him to live.

Third, the prophets were messengers. The expression "This is what the Lord says" or "thus says the Lord" occurs over 350 times in the prophetic books. The prophets were not trying to sell their own ideas. Rather, they were delivering messages—urgent messages—that God had revealed to them. Sometimes Israel or Judah persecuted the prophets because the prophets declared stern words of judgment against the people and the nation. The people failed to understand that their real argument was with God, for it was *his* word the prophets spoke.

Fourth, the prophets were **forthtellers**,

telling forth God's truth to their own generation. They pointed out the evils of their day and called the people to repent. They warned them that while the covenant brought many privileges, it also brought many responsibilities, including justice, righteousness, and holiness. They focused primarily on their own generations, though their messages contain many timeless principles. Since God never changes, the prophets' words continue to challenge his people and our society today.

Fifth, the prophets were **foretellers**. God revealed to them the future—sometimes the near future, sometimes the distant future—and the prophets declared it to their own generations. They spoke of judgment and of restoration, of bad news and good news. They did so primarily to motivate God's people to faithful living in the present.

Sixth, the prophets were creative individuals who used a variety of literary and oral techniques to communicate their messages. Some employed parables, while others sang songs or chanted laments in which they denounced the people's sad spiritual state. They sometimes used sarcasm to make their points. They employed rhetorical questions to challenge their lis-

omen texts

Mari prophecy

Akkadian
prophecies

teners to reflect, and they appealed to history and God's covenant. Through all these devices, the prophets called the people to return to their spiritual heritage.

Did Other Nations Have Prophets?

As we have already noted, the Hebrews had many neighbors in the ancient world, and these nations and peoples had much in common with the Hebrews. Many of these peoples shared a common linguistic background with the Hebrews and thus spoke languages related to Hebrew. Most countries had a king to rule them. Many countries had similar laws regarding how people should treat each other.

In our study of Genesis, we saw how other ancient peoples had their own ideas about creation. We also compared the Hebrew flood story with other ancient flood stories. In each case, we saw how the bib-

lical accounts, while similar in some respects, display a very different theological perspective.

What about prophecy? Did other civilizations of the biblical world have prophets who claimed to speak in the name of a god? Did they have people who predicted the future? If so, what is their relationship to the biblical prophets? Did the Hebrews obtain the whole idea of prophecy from their neighbors? In order to answer these questions, we must look at the ancient Near Eastern evidence. Three basic categories of evidence exist: **omen texts**, **Mari prophecy**, and **Akkadian prophecies**.

During the early second millennium B.C., during what historians call the Old BABYLONIAN PERIOD (2000–1595 B.C.) , the Babylonians began to compile what we now call omen texts. The Babylonians probably would have thought of these texts as science, though the texts would not seem very scientific to us. According to these ancient people, the world was a complex web of cause-and-effect relationships. Certain events happened because other events caused them. In addition, a supernatural intention often lay behind an event. The people believed the gods used unusual or unnatural occurrences to reveal their will. People familiar with these unusual occurrences could interpret them and predict the future. Thus, the omen texts preserved a written record of these events and their consequences; if certain events happened again, that meant the gods were about to do the same thing they had done before.

The Babylonians examined all types of events and recorded their observations in the omen texts. For example, if a certain bird appeared during a certain month, that might indicate a famine was coming. If a sacrificial animal had a red spot on its liver, that might indicate a military victory for the king. Some of the omen texts dealt with medicine, while others dealt with the economy, war, or everyday life.

Even a casual reading of the omen texts reveals they have little in common with biblical prophecy. The omen texts lack any sort of moral basis. The gods simply revealed their will through interrelated events in nature. The prophets, on the other hand, took their stand on God, his

Jesus Christ and The Prophets

As we study the characteristics of Old Testament prophets, we can understand why the New Testament refers to Jesus Christ as a prophet, for he displayed these same qualities.

- Jesus possessed a heart devoted to God, and always sought his Father's will (Jn 5:30).
- Jesus displayed a strong sense of calling; God had sent him for a specific purpose (Mt 16:21–23).
- Jesus was a messenger, bringing God's ultimate will to the earth (Heb 1:1–2).
- Jesus was a "forthteller," challenging his contemporaries to repent and by faith to live the lives God expected of them, instead of trusting in dead traditions (Mt 15:1–7; 23:16–28).
- Jesus was a foreteller, and predicted the future on several occasions (Mk 13:3–27; Lk 23:34, 54–62).
- Jesus used a variety of techniques to communicate his message, including parables (Lk 15:3– 16:31), quotes from the Old Testament (Mt 5:17–19; 12:7; 26:31–32), illustrations (Mk 9:36–37), and other significant prophetic acts (Mt 21:1–5; Mk 11:15–17).

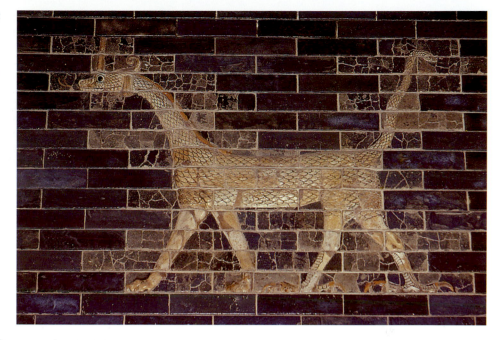

A mythical beast depicted on glazed tiles, Babylon. The Babylonians examined many events and recorded their observations in omen texts.

ecstatics

vaticinium ex eventu

word, and the covenant he had made with his people. They called people to surrender their lives to God and his ways. They placed moral demands on their hearers because such qualities as holiness, righteousness, and justice reflected God's nature, and God expected his children's lives to display the same qualities.

The ancient city of MARI, located on the Euphrates River, was an important city in Old Babylonian times, and presents us with a second possible parallel to biblical prophecy. Under its king ZIMRI-LIM, Mari became a leading city that controlled much of upper Mesopotamia until the Babylonian king Hammurapi (1792–1750 B.C.) conquered Mari and added its territory to his own. People known as **ecstatics** (Akkadian *muḫḫû*) resided in and around Mari, and many scholars have noted parallels between the *muḫḫû* and the biblical prophets. The *muḫḫû* delivered messages they received through dreams, visions, or trances. The *muḫḫû* could be male or female, and each served a particular god or goddess. In their utterances, the *muḫḫû* might warn the king of rebellion, counsel him regarding expeditions, promise him victory over his enemies, or encourage him to serve the deity more faithfully.

Although similarities between Mari prophecy and biblical prophecy do exist, striking differences appear when we look closely at the texts. The Old Testament prophets asserted that God's covenant with his people had implications for daily living. A proper relationship with God should result in just and ethical treatment of other people. Certain actions and beliefs were true and right because God had so ordained them. Furthermore, the prophets spoke to all society, not just the royal household. These differences sharply distinguish the biblical prophets from the *muḫḫû* at Mari.

Certain Akkadian texts of the first millennium B.C. furnish us with a third possible parallel to biblical prophecy. These texts simply list various political events of a particular historical period. The following is an excerpt from one of these texts:

A ruler will arise, he will rule for thirteen years. There will be an attack of Elam against Akkad, and the booty of Akkad will be carried off. The temples of the great gods will be destroyed, the defeat of Akkad will be decreed (by the gods). . . . A ruler will arise, his days will be few, and he will not rule the land.[4]

The texts are somewhat vague as to their intention, and scholars do not agree exactly what they are. Some have argued that they are examples of *vaticinium ex eventu*, or "prophecy written after the event." The scholars have suggested the writers wrote the texts to make them look like prophecy. This view seems likely, although other scholars have suggested the texts are more closely related to **apocalyptic literature** or omen texts. Clearly, the Akkadian prophecies differ significantly from classic biblical prophecy.

In conclusion, although biblical prophecy shares a few features with other types of ancient Near Eastern literature, it remains unique in at least four respects. First, biblical prophecy distinguishes itself by addressing the whole nation, not just the rulers. The prophets speak to young and old, rich and poor, common people and priests, kings and princes. Every person has a responsibility to yield to God's word.

Second, biblical prophecy focuses on people's attitudes, not just their rituals. If the people's hearts did not change, God counted all their sacrifices as worthless. The prophets sought an inner moral change of the heart, not simple adherence to a sacrificial system. Sacrifices had their value only in connection with genuine repentance and faith.

Third, biblical prophecy contains a moral imperative. The prophets did not call people to offer sacrifices; rather, they called them to be holy, for God was holy (Mi 6:6–8). God's people must live in a manner that reflects their Father.

Fourth, biblical prophecy looks at the far-reaching implications of people's actions, not just the immediate. The prophets looked to the present, but they also looked to the future. God was guiding history, and the prophets knew the deeds of the present generation would affect coming generations. They therefore called people to live lives pleasing to God, not only for themselves, but for the sake of all who would come after them.[5]

Did All Prophets Write Down Their Messages?

When we study the prophets, we are dealing with material that has come to us in written form. But not all the prophets of the Old Testament committed their words to writing. The Old Testament mentions many prophets whom God called to prophesy, but who never wrote down their messages. We know about their ministries only through the accounts of them in the Old Testament historical books. We call these prophets "**nonliterary prophets**."

We have already noted the prophet Elijah's significant role as a predecessor of classical prophecy. Elijah's successor Elisha carried on the prophetic ministry his master had begun (2 Kgs 1:1–13:21). He performed many miracles on the people's behalf as God used him to strengthen the faith of many Israelites. Elisha, by God's power, purified poisonous stew, caused an axe head to float, healed a leper, and even raised a widow's son from the dead.

Elijah and Elisha both had very significant callings, yet neither apparently ever committed his words to writing. In addition to these two men, many other prophets did not write down their words. Unnamed prophets appeared in Saul's day (1 Sm 10:10–12; 19:20–21) and later during the divided kingdom (1 Kgs 13). Ahijah prophesied that God would tear the kingdom from Solomon (1 Kgs 11:29–39). Micaiah prophesied to Ahab and Jehoshaphat before Ahab died at the hand of the Syrians (1 Kgs 22:7–28). A man designated only as "a man of God" spoke words of judgment to Jeroboam I when the king began to turn Israel away from the Lord (1 Kgs 13:1–10). And a woman named Huldah prophesied for Josiah, aiding his religious reforms (2 Kgs 22:14–20).

As a general observation, we may say that the nonliterary prophets tended to focus on the king and his court. They advised the king on various matters and sometimes warned him about the consequences of his sin. They displayed the same courage and convictions the writing prophets did, though they left to others the task of recording their words and deeds.

How Was Prophecy Passed Down to Us?

The prophets first communicated their messages orally, not in written form. Isaiah and Jeremiah, for example, sometimes spoke directly with the kings of Judah (Is 7:1–14; Jer 37:17–20). At other times, prophets spoke to the general population (Jon 3:4; Jer 7:1–15). These facts raise an important question. What is the relationship between the spoken word and the written word? In other words, who wrote down the prophets' words, and when?

eschatological

Three answers are possible, and probably all have some truth to them. First, some prophets wrote down their own words. A prophet may have spoken them first in public before recording them, or perhaps he wrote them down first and then proclaimed them to the people as a herald would. Sometimes God instructed a prophet to write down his message as a testimony, so when the day of judgment came, people would see that God had warned them through his prophet (e.g., Is 8:16; Jer 36:2; Dn 12:4).

Second, some prophets used scribes to record their words. Baruch, Jeremiah's scribe, recorded Jeremiah's words and sometimes even passed along the prophet's words for him (Jer 36:4–6). Other prophets may also have used assistants who carefully copied down their words. The practice of using a scribe also appears in the New Testament (Rom 16:22; 1 Pt 5:12).

Third, some prophets may have had disciples who collected their words and organized them into the books we have today. This suggestion is really a combination of the first two. A prophet may have written down his words by himself or through a scribe, but never arranged them into a book. Toward the end of his life or shortly after his death, his disciples or close followers put them into writing and/or collected them. In this way, the prophet's ministry could continue even after his death.

What Are Some Common Themes of the Prophets' Writings?

As we have already mentioned, the prophets varied greatly in their backgrounds, audiences, and styles. Nevertheless, the prophetic writings possess a common thrust and push toward a common goal. The prophets emphasize certain themes again and again.

One common prophetic theme is covenant obligations. The prophets called the Hebrews to remember that something very significant had happened at Mount Sinai. God had revealed his Torah, his manual for faithful living. He had confirmed his covenant, a covenant with far-reaching implications. True worship of God affected every aspect of life. Whatever roles people might have—father, mother, son, daughter, employee, employer, neighbor—they were to live them in light of their relationship to God.

This theme of covenant obligations contained several facets. First, covenant obligations included a call to return to God and his word. Israel and Judah's world contained many temptations to compromise spiritually and morally, just as our world does today. At Sinai, the people had affirmed God's covenant, but later generations had changed their attitude. They slowly drifted away from the God who had made them what they were, and as they did, they became less and less like what God wanted them to be. The prophets called God's people to return to their heritage, a heritage rooted in God and his word.

Second, covenant obligations contained a call to personal holiness. God had acted in history to redeem his people, but he wanted more than redemption for them. God wanted his people to experience holiness—not just the absence of sin, but a positive goodness and righteousness that would shine as a light to those in spiritual darkness around them. In the Garden of Eden, man and woman had lost the holiness God gave them. Now, through his law and his prophets, God showed his people their sin and continued his work to restore his holiness in humankind.

Third, covenant obligations called God's people to be at peace with each other. The Hebrew word shalom (šālôm, often translated "peace") literally means "completeness" or "wholeness." God desired that his divine qualities such as love, mercy, compassion, holiness, and justice also express themselves through the lives of his people. As the Hebrews by faith conformed to the teachings of Torah, every aspect of their society would come into line with God's highest will. The people would then experience true shalom in their nation.

A second common prophetic theme is the Day of the Lord. Often this concept refers to a time of immediate judgment, whereas in other passages it refers to God's **eschatological** judgment at the end of the age. The Day of the Lord includes three aspects: God's judgment on unbelievers, the cleansing and purging of God's people, and the salvation of God's people. The prophets warned that God would judge all sin wherever he found it, in the lives of unbelievers as well as in the lives of believers. But he also desired that his people would conform to his image, and he promised to refine their lives even if he had to use extreme measures. As for those who were following the Lord faithfully, the Lord assured them he would not forget them. The Day of the Lord would come, but for the faithful, it would be a blessed day indeed.

A third important prophetic theme is the concept of Messiah. The term "Messiah" comes from the Hebrew word *māšîaḥ*, which means "anointed one." (In the New Testament, the Greek parallel is the word *Christos*, "Christ.") Anointing someone with oil symbolized God's setting him apart for special service to Him and placing His Spirit upon him to empower him for that service.

The Scriptures testify that kings, priests, and prophets might receive this anointing. In the Old Testament, the term *māšîaḥ* usually refers to kings, who were "the Lord's *anointed*" (e.g., 1 Sm 24:6; 2 Sm 1:14). But by the time of the New Testament, the term had gained a new sense. The Messiah was God's chosen instrument who would come one day to establish God's kingdom and to rule in power and glory. The Lord had anointed others to his service, but this one would surpass them all. The prophets do not always use the term "Messiah" when they speak of this coming one, but they do speak of him and point with anticipation to his coming. The New Testament proclaims that we have seen his coming in the person of Jesus Christ, and we will one day see his coming again in power and glory.

The Historical Setting of the Classical Prophets

The prophetic books of the Old Testament reflect the ministries of individuals who prophesied some time during the period of 800–450 B.C. This period witnessed great shifts of power in the ancient Near East. When major kingdoms and powers began to appear on the scene, many smaller nations faced the choice of submission or destruction.

The prophets saw God's hand at work in these historical events. They explained that he was raising up and bringing down the earth's kingdoms in accordance with his higher purpose. He could and would judge one nation—even Israel or Judah!—by means of another nation. The prophets proclaimed that Israel and Judah's only hope lay in their willingness to stand firm on their spiritual heritage. They called God's people to repent of their sin and to live faithfully under God's covenant.

Three major powers most directly affected Israel and Judah's history: Assyria, Babylon, and Persia. Briefly sketching the history of these empires will help us understand what the prophets faced as they preached their messages to their people.

The Assyrians

Archaeologists have discovered evidence that the Assyrians were present in the ancient Near East as early as about 2000 B.C.[6] Most of the early evidence comes from Asia Minor, though an early king, Shamshi-Addu (1815–1782 B.C.), pushed eastward and controlled most of upper Mesopotamia, including Mari, the city of which we spoke earlier.

For the rest of the second millennium, the Assyrians remained a separate people in upper Mesopotamia, struggling against other powers of the ancient world. With the beginning of the first millennium, however, Assyrian kings began pushing westward into Syria. One of the most noted kings was Shalmaneser III (859–824 B.C.), who in 853 B.C. at the city of Qarqar battled a coalition of small nations whose leaders included Ben-Hadad II of Damascus and Ahab of Israel. Although Shalmaneser was unsuccessful at Qarqar, later battles won him control of many of these western nations, including Israel, whose King Jehu paid him homage.

The rise of Tiglath-Pileser III (745–727 B.C.) to the throne of Assyria marked the beginning of a period of Assyrian expansion. In the west, Israel and Judah were at the end of a long period of prosperity under the reigns of Jeroboam II (793–753 B.C.) and Azariah/Uzziah (792–740 B.C.), respectively. Spiritual decay had crept in as the people increasingly blended

Relief of Tiglath-Pileser III (745–727 B.C.). This monarch's rise to the throne marked the start of a period of Assyrian expansion.

Canaanite religious practices with the worship patterns Moses had given them in the law. Revolts and unrest in Syria and Palestine led to Tiglath-Pileser's western campaigns; Damascus eventually fell in 732 B.C., while Israel and Judah became vassal states. When Hoshea, Israel's last king, revolted, Shalmaneser V (726–722 B.C.) and his successor SARGON II (722–705 B.C.) conquered Samaria and led Israel into exile. A later king, Sennacherib (705–681 B.C.), came against Hezekiah, king of Judah, but God's special intervention prevented Assyria from enjoying victory.

Constant warfare in the seventh century, especially with Babylon, led to Assyria's decline. In 626 B.C., Nabopolassar assumed control in Babylon, and in 612 B.C., with the help of the Medes and others, he defeated Nineveh, Assyria's capital. Within a few years all Assyrian resistance was gone.[7]

The prophets who prophesied during the period of Assyrian domination include Isaiah, Hosea, Amos, Jonah, Micah, Nahum, and Zephaniah. Jonah, Hosea, and Amos spoke to a generation that was beginning to feel Assyria's renewed strength. Isaiah and Micah addressed a people that had seen Assyria expand westward and begin to dominate political events in Palestine. And Zephaniah and Nahum prophesied at a time when As-

Key Terms

classical prophets
classical prophecy
forthtellers
foretellers
omen texts
Mari prophecy
Akkadian prophecies
Babylonian period
ecstatics
vaticinium ex eventu
apocalyptic literature
nonliterary prophets
eschatological

Key People/Places

Zimri-Lim
Shalmaneser III
Shamshi-Addu
Tiglath-Pileser III
Sargon II
Merodach-baladan II
Nabopolassar
Nebuchadnezzar II
Astyages
Artaxerxes
Cambyses
Darius
Xerxes
Alexander the Great
Mount Carmel
Mari
Qarqar
Armenia
Cappadocia

Summary

1. The classical prophets addressed all people, informed them of God's wrath against their sin, warned of approaching judgment, called people to repentance, and proclaimed God's salvation to all who would turn to him.

2. Prophets were not hysterical babblers, fortune tellers, or religious extremists.

3. Prophets were alike in that their hearts were devoted to God, they had a strong sense of calling, they were God's messengers, they proclaimed God's truth, they revealed the future, and they used a variety of literary and oral methods to communicate their messages.

4. Babylonian omen texts have little in common with biblical prophecy; they have no moral basis.

5. The ecstatics of Mari spoke only to the royal household, while the Hebrew prophets spoke to all the people.

6. Biblical prophecy differed from other prophetic types of activity in the Near East because it addressed the whole nation, it focused on people's attitudes, it contained a moral imperative, and it looked at far-reaching implications of people's actions.

7. Nonliterary prophets—those who did not write down their messages—focused on the king and his court.

8. Prophets' messages were recorded by themselves, scribes, or disciples.

9. Common prophetic themes included covenant obligation, the day of the Lord, and the Messiah.

10. The prophets Isaiah, Hosea, Amos, Jonah, Micah, Nahum, and Zephaniah all prophesied during the period of Assyrian domination.

11. Hammurapi of Babylon is best known for his law code.

12. The prophets who prophesied during the domination by the Babylonians were Jeremiah, Ezekiel, Daniel, Obadiah, Nahum, Habakkuk, and Zephaniah.

13. Joel, Haggai, Zechariah, and Malachi ministered during the period of Persian domination.

syria's empire was crumbling before the onslaught of Babylon and her allies.

The Babylonians

The Babylonians, like the Assyrians, first appear in ancient Near Eastern records around 2000 B.C. Babylon became the center of an empire when Hammurapi (1792–1750 B.C.), best known for his famous law code, took control and extended his influence from the Persian Gulf to Syria. Later Babylonian kings could not maintain the territory Hammurapi had won, and in 1595 B.C. Babylon fell to invaders.

In the eleventh and tenth centuries, new peoples entered Mesopotamia. Some moved to the south, organized themselves into strict tribal groupings called "houses," and settled along the lower Tigris and Euphrates Rivers. The Babylonians called these people the "Chaldeans," and by the eighth century the Chaldeans were contending for the kingship of Babylonia. One Chaldean, MERODACH-BALADAN II (see Is 39:1), challenged Assyrian power from 721 to 710 B.C. and briefly in 703 B.C. before meeting defeat. In 626 B.C., with Assyria declining, NABOPOLASSAR (626–605 B.C.) established a Chaldean dynasty at Babylon, and with the help of the Medes and others, defeated Nineveh in 612 B.C.. His son, NEBUCHADNEZZAR II (605–562 B.C.), firmly established Babylon as the dominant empire in the ancient Near East.

Meanwhile in Judah, spiritual trouble was brewing. Although the Judeans had seen God use the Assyrians to judge Israel, most persisted in their evil ways. Manasseh (697–642 B.C.), one of Judah's most wicked kings, led the nation into spiritual decline. The people added Canaanite religious practices to their own faith and believed that no matter what their lifestyles, God had bound himself to bless Judah and Jerusalem forever. Although Josiah's reign (640–609 B.C.) brought revival and renewal, after his death the kingdom quickly faded. Jehoiakim (609–597 B.C.) rebelled against Nebuchadnezzar and Jehoiakim's son Jehoiachin paid the price of exile. Nebuchadnezzar placed Zedekiah (597–586 B.C.) on the throne and gave Judah one more chance, but when Zedekiah revolted, the king of Babylon returned, defeated Judah, destroyed Jerusalem and its temple, and led the people into exile.

The four Babylonian kings who followed Nebuchadnezzar could not control the empire he had established. Finally, in 539 B.C., less than twenty-five years after Nebuchadnezzar's death, Babylon fell to Cyrus, king of Persia.[8]

The prophets whose prophecy reflects the period of Babylonian domination include Jeremiah, Ezekiel, Daniel, Obadiah, Nahum, Habakkuk, and Zephaniah. Jeremiah received his call about the same time Nabopolassar rose to power, and Habakkuk soon followed. Daniel and Ezekiel ministered as exiles in Babylon, while Obadiah prophesied right after Jerusalem's fall. Nahum and Zephaniah also prophesied in the late seventh century, though their books speak of Assyria and mention nothing of Babylon.

The Persians

By the middle of the sixth century, Babylon and Media existed as the two great powers in Mesopotamia. In 550 B.C., ASTYAGES was king of Media. Cyrus, his son-in-law, led a revolt against him and defeated him, thus inheriting northern Mesopotamia, Syria, ARMENIA, and CAPPADOCIA. In 539 B.C., Cyrus marched on Babylon and took the city without a fight.

In contrast to the Assyrians, the Persians maintained very tolerant policies toward cooperative subject peoples. Cyrus showed favor to the various people's social and religious customs, and issued a decree in the first year of his reign that all Jews who wished to return to Judah could go. Almost fifty thousand Jews accepted Cyrus's offer!

The Jewish people returned home and laid the foundation of the temple, but opposition from neighboring peoples quickly brought the work to a halt until the reign of Darius I (522–486 B.C.). Under Haggai and Zechariah's influence, the people fin-

Study Questions

1. Describe the historical and spiritual circumstances that led to the rise of classical prophecy. Why were the prophets an essential part of God's plan for his people?

2. What are some characteristics that all prophets shared?

3. What parallels to biblical prophecy did other nations have? How is biblical prophecy unique?

4. What are some common themes of biblical prophecy?

5. What three major empires formed the historical backdrop for the classical prophets?

Further Reading

Bullock, C. Hassell. *An Introduction to the Old Testament Prophetic Books.* Chicago: Moody, 1986. Graduate-level survey of the prophetic books. Provides good discussion of pertinent issues, good documentation, and rich bibliography.

Smith, Gary V. *The Prophets as Preachers: An Introduction to the Hebrew Prophets.* Nashville: Broadman & Holman, 1994. An advanced study of the prophets, their approaches to preaching, and their value for today's Christian expositor.

VanGemeren, Willem A. *Interpreting the Prophetic Word.* Grand Rapids: Zondervan, 1990. A rich volume with excellent insights for the more serious student.

Walton, John H. *Ancient Israelite Literature in Its Cultural Context: A Survey of Parallels between Biblical and Ancient Near Eastern Texts.* Grand Rapids: Zondervan, 1989. Surveys and provides analysis of Ancient Near Eastern literary parallels to Old Testament texts. Valuable for students and teachers alike.

ished the temple in 516 B.C. Ezra and Nehemiah came to Judah later during the reign of ARTAXERXES (464–423 B.C.), rebuilding the walls and establishing further religious reforms. Many Jews, however, stayed behind in Babylon, remaining part of Babylonian society.

Under CAMBYSES (530–522 B.C.), Persia's second ruler, Persia extended its influence into Egypt, and DARIUS and XERXES (486–464 B.C.—the "Ahasuerus" of the Book of Esther) fought extensively with Greece. Persian victory over Greece, however, did not last, for ALEXANDER THE GREAT defeated Darius III (335–331 B.C.) in 331 B.C., bringing an end to the Persian Empire.[9]

The prophets who ministered during the period of Persian domination include Joel, Haggai, Zechariah, and Malachi. Haggai and Zechariah urged the people to complete the temple and look ahead to what God would do with his people. Malachi challenged the people to give God their best in everything, and Joel used a locust plague of his day to warn people of the Day of the Lord.

25 Isaiah 1–39
Prophet of Judah's Royal Court

Outline

Objectives

After reading this chapter, you should be able to

- Outline the content of chapters 1–39 of Isaiah
- Explain the themes of chapters 1–39 of Isaiah
- List the key features of the kingdom of God
- Present the elements of Isaiah's call
- Discuss possible interpretation of the sign Isaiah offered to Ahaz
- Demonstrate the fulfillment of Isaiah's prophecy in the messianic era
- Show how Isaiah's prophecies illustrate that God is Lord of all

Isaiah is one of the most famous Old Testament prophets. Even many people who know little about the Bible recognize his name. More than one interpreter has called the Book of Isaiah "the Gospel of the Old Testament" because of the prophet's emphasis on God's grace and love. As we study Isaiah, we'll see God's love displayed in dramatic fashion.

Outline

Background
of the Book of Isaiah

Isaiah the Man

Isaiah's name means "The Lord has saved," and is related to the names "Joshua" and "Jesus" in their Hebrew forms. Isaiah 1:1

A watchman's hut in fields near Shechem. Isaiah said that God's people had rebelled, and Jerusalem was to be left as defenseless as a watchman's hut in a vineyard (1:8).

remnant

states that Isaiah was the son of Amoz. Unfortunately, we know nothing about Amoz except that he was Isaiah's father!

Isaiah had two sons—Shear-jashub (7:3), whose name means "a **remnant** shall return," and Maher-shalal-hash-baz (8:3), whose name means "swift is the booty and speedy is the prey." By giving his sons these names, Isaiah showed his faith in God's plan for Israel's future. The name "Shear-jashub" pointed to God's preserving a faithful remnant. The name "Maher-shalal-hash-baz" announced God's swift judgment against Judah's enemies.

Isaiah served as a prophet in Judah's royal court. He thus prophesied mainly to Judah, though he also had words for Israel and other nations. The Book of Isaiah recounts several contacts he had with Judah's kings, particularly Ahaz and Hezekiah. Ahaz showed little regard for Isaiah's word (7:3–13), but Hezekiah placed great faith in him (37:2–7, 21–35; 38:1–8; 39:3–8). As we study Isaiah's words, we will see he also has much to teach us.

Isaiah's Times

Most scholars date Isaiah's prophetic ministry around 740–690 B.C. When Isaiah responded to God's call, the northern kingdom of Israel had less than twenty years left before it would fall to Assyria. Meanwhile, the southern kingdom of Judah

faced an important test. Would Judah learn from Israel's tragic example, or would Judah follow in Israel's evil footsteps?

As Isaiah began his ministry, Assyria was beginning to flex its muscles under the leadership of Tiglath-Pileser III (745–727 B.C.). Smaller kingdoms such as Judah certainly must have seen this potential danger on the horizon. Nevertheless, God had promised his people he would protect them from anything and anyone if they stood strong in their faith. The Lord sent the prophet Isaiah to encourage them to do so.

Authorship and Date

The book itself names Isaiah as the prophet behind its message (1:1; 2:1; 7:3; 20:2; 37:2, 21; 38:1, 4; 39:3). We may assume Isaiah either recorded his own words or committed them to others—perhaps his disciples. Many evangelical scholars date the Book of Isaiah to the early seventh century B.C.

Other scholars (including some evangelicals) believe the prophet Isaiah was basically responsible only for the material in Isaiah 1–39. They cite certain differences between chapters 1–39 and chapters 40–66 that suggest someone besides Isaiah wrote the last part of the book. We will deal with this question in our discussion of Isaiah 40–66.

Themes of the Book of Isaiah

Remnant

Isaiah described a remnant whom God had preserved (1:9). In fact, he even named one of his sons "a remnant shall return" (Shear-jashub, 7:3). Exile might come, but God one day would lead his remnant home (10:20–21). This people had a deep faith relationship with the Lord that distinguished them from other Israelites. Many people descended from Jacob's twelve sons, but the remnant lived faithful to the covenant God established with Jacob and the other patriarchs.

The sovereignty of God

Isaiah's view of God's sovereignty dramatically shaped his ministry. He knew God controlled the nations, and therefore he prophesied boldly that God would deal with those nations (chapters 13–23). God had a right to rule his creation and he did. Isaiah 40–66 especially develops the idea that God has proven his sovereignty, first through sending his people into exile and then by delivering them from it.

Servant

The servant theme appears in several places in Isaiah, and the servant carries a number of identities. The word "servant" may denote an individual Israelite (22:20), the nation of Israel (41:8), the remnant (49:3), or the Messiah (52:13). The servant works diligently to accomplish God's purpose despite numerous challenges and difficulties.

Holy One of Israel

Isaiah used the expression "Holy One of Israel" twenty-nine times to describe the Lord; only seven other occurrences are found in the rest of the Old Testament. Isaiah faced God's holiness when the Lord called him into prophetic service (6:1–8), and he never forgot it. The people had forsaken the Holy One of Israel who had struck them (1:4). But the Holy One of Israel might strike any enemy nation who challenged his people (37:23)! He would act in holiness to judge sin wherever he found it.

Messiah

Isaiah described the Messiah, God's anointed one, who would come to redeem his people. His glorious reign would bring blessing to all the earth (11:1–16) and light to those who lived in spiritual darkness (9:1–2). Cyrus might receive the title "messiah" (45:1), but he would never accomplish God's purpose in the way Jesus, God's Son, would. Messiah one day would come to reign in glory, but he first would show himself worthy through suffering (53:10–12).

Message of the Book of Isaiah

Opening Words to Judah (1:1–31)

Isaiah's opening words to Judah introduce many ideas the prophet develops in the rest of the book. Chapter 1 thus lays a firm foundation for the next sixty-five chapters.

God brought a scathing indictment against his people (vv. 2–15). They acted like rebellious children! God's initial judgment against them had little effect; in fact, their behavior reminded him of Sodom and Gomorrah (v. 10)! Their sacrifices came from impure motives, and their hands committed deeds of social injustice. The Lord would honor their prayers no longer (v. 15).

Isaiah called the people to repentance, forgiveness, and blessing (vv. 16–20). God could and would cleanse the people's sin. But wickedness pervaded the society, beginning with the leadership and working its way on down (vv. 21–23). Isaiah laid the choice squarely at Judah's feet: God would redeem those who repented, but the persistently rebellious would die (vv. 27–31).

God's Judgment Revealed (2:1–5:30)

The coming blessing (2:1–4)

God's future kingdom would include three features—God's people, God's temple, and God's peace. God's people would include people from all nations. They would stream in from everywhere to Jerusalem, the site of the temple and centerpiece of God's purpose. The instruction people would receive from God's word

Today's Twisted Morals

Isaiah pronounced woe against those who substituted evil for good. Many in our society have done the same thing by giving more attractive names to practices the Bible calls evil. Consider the following examples; the more accurate descriptions follow in parentheses.

Affair (fornication, adultery, illicit sex)
Alternate lifestyle (homosexuality)
Abortion (killing of unborn babies)
Becoming a man or becoming a woman
  (giving away one's virginity)
Sexually active (promiscuous, sexually immoral)
Pro-choice (pro-abortion)
Adult entertainment (pornography, strip joints)
Adult videos (pornographic videos)
New Age philosophy (old lies of Eastern
  philosophy)

Many also have tried to put down Christians while justifying their own sinful behavior by giving less attractive names to practices the Bible calls good. Again, the more accurate expression follows in parentheses.

Chicken (afraid; usually used to challenge
  someone who is unwilling to go along with the
  group's sin)
Old-fashioned (adhering to traditional standards
  of morality)
Prude (adhering to traditional standards
  of sexual morality)
Rigid, inflexible, intolerant (sticking to one's
  opinion, especially on moral issues)

---

chy would result as the people looked in vain for leaders to replace them.

Third, Isaiah declared God's judgment against Judah's women, who proudly displayed themselves with elaborate ornamentation (3:16–4:1). God promised to remove the dignity in which they so firmly trusted. Isaiah's words foreshadow those of Paul, who reminded women that godliness and good works are much more important than fancy external adornment (1 Tm 2:9–10).

Isaiah closed this section with a word about God's coming Branch (4:2–6). The branch, part of David's line, serves as God's instrument to bring in his kingdom. We will see this concept again in Isaiah 11, as well as in Jeremiah and Zechariah.

Parable of the vineyard (5:1–7)

Isaiah portrayed God's people as a vineyard. God had cared for his vineyard diligently, but it produced worthless grapes! God called to Judah to bear witness—he had done everything he should to care for his vineyard. The problem lay in them and their unwillingness to respond to his care.

Six woes against the nation (5:8–30)

Isaiah pronounced six **woe oracles** against various segments of Judah's population. A woe oracle is a judgment speech that typically begins with the word "woe."

First, Isaiah denounced oppressors who selfishly increased their estates at the expense of others (vv. 8–10). God would judge them by reducing their crop yields, thus rendering the increased land meaningless.

Second, Isaiah condemned drunkards who lived only to pursue strong drink and merrymaking (vv. 11–17). They often partied late into the night, unaware that spiritual ruin lay all around them. God's people would suffer exile for their lack of knowledge.

Third, Isaiah rebuked those who put God to the test (vv. 18–19). They assumed God was doing nothing only because they could not discern his purpose. Meanwhile, they persisted in their evil.

Fourth, Isaiah reprimanded the morally twisted, who called good evil and evil good (v. 20). They did so in order to justify their sin. They could continue in it without feeling guilty.

---

woe oracles

would bring lasting peace everywhere. Most interpreters believe Jesus Christ will fulfill this prophecy when he returns.

Judgment speeches (2:5–4:6)

Isaiah presented three judgment speeches. First, he called the people to recognize God's ways (2:5–21). False religion, riches, and pride had corrupted the nation. Isaiah warned that a terrible day of reckoning was coming soon.

Second, Isaiah announced God's judgment against Judah's leaders (2:22–3:15). He would cut off the leaders who used their positions for dishonest gain. Anar-

sign

Fifth, Isaiah pronounced woe against the self-exalted (v. 21). They believed themselves wise, but others held quite a different opinion! God was sure to humble them.

Sixth, Isaiah admonished immoral opportunists (vv. 22–23). These people caroused together and took away the rights of the defenseless. They took bribes and rejected God's standards.

These six groups thought they had gotten away with their behavior, but God had seen it all. In his anger, he would call another nation to consume them and carry them away.

Isaiah's Call (6:1–13)

The vision (6:1–8)

Isaiah's reference to King Uzziah's death places his prophetic call in the year 739 B.C. Isaiah saw a vision of God that absolutely overwhelmed him. Most of all, he saw two things: God's utter majesty and his own sinfulness.

The seraph's touching of Isaiah's mouth symbolically represented God cleansing him from sin. Isaiah now stood clean before his holy God, so when God issued his call, he responded quickly (v. 8)—"Here am I. Send me!"

The prophecy (6:9–13)

God's initial message through Isaiah proclaimed the people's lack of understanding. They would persist in their sin, not really seeing, hearing, or understanding God's purpose for them. The proclamation of God's word would only make the people harder against him. Yet, God promised to raise up a righteous remnant after his judgment. His purposes for his people would continue.

The Sign of Immanuel (7:1–17)

The historical setting (7:1–9)

The years 735–732 B.C. witnessed what historians call the Syro-Ephraimite War. The major issue was how small countries like Syria, Israel, and Judah would deal with Assyria's impending westward expansion under Tiglath-Pileser III.

The major players included Rezin, king of Syria, Pekah, king of Israel, and Ahaz, king of Judah. Rezin and Pekah wanted to join forces with Ahaz to stop Assyria, but when Ahaz refused to join the alliance, Rezin and Pekah marched against him (7:1–2). Isaiah encouraged Ahaz to trust in the Lord (7:4–9), for God would protect David's line if David's descendant would place his trust in God.

The sign offered, refused, and given (7:10–17)

Isaiah offered Ahaz a **sign** from God to strengthen the king's faith. Ahaz masked his lack of faith with false piety (7:10–12), for he already was thinking of trusting Assyria instead (2 Kgs 16:7–8). Isaiah condemned him for his lack of faith and said God himself would provide a sign. A virgin would conceive, bear a son, and name him Immanuel, which means "God is with us" (7:14). Before the child could choose between good and evil, the kings of Syria and Israel would be gone.

Possible interpretations

As we deal with this prophecy, we need to determine the relationship of Isaiah 7:14 to Matthew 1:23, which says Jesus' virgin birth fulfilled Isaiah's words. Below are two common interpretations scholars have given:

• The sign Isaiah offered was the virgin birth of Christ. The prophet understood he was making such a prophecy, and it came true. By the time Jesus could distinguish right from wrong, the kings of Syria and Israel were gone. Isaiah 8 records an unrelated incident.[1] Many Christians over the centuries have understood the prophecy in this way. Some, however, have suggested the long time gap between Isaiah's words and Jesus' birth weakens the meaning of the sign.[2]

• The prophecies of Immanuel and Maher-shalal-hash-baz describe the same birth. The woman, Isaiah's wife (the "prophetess," 8:3), was a virgin at the time, but he then married her and she conceived the child in the usual way. The sign in Isaiah's day was that she named the child "God is with us" when all events suggested God was far from his people. Jesus' birth then fulfilled Isaiah's words on an even higher level. The text records that

Campaigns of the Syro-Ephraimite War

Damascus

Tyre

MEDITERRANEAN SEA

ISRAEL

Samaria

Jordan R.

AMMON

Rabbath-bene-ammon

Ashdod
Ekron

Ashkelon

PHILISTIA

Gaza

JUDAH

Arad

MOAB

Beer-sheba

Jerusalem

Sela

EDOM

Scale

0   10   20 mi

0   10   20 km

Philistines

Rezin, king of Aram

Pekah, son of Remaliah,
king of Israel

Edomites

Mary remained a virgin until Jesus' birth (Mt 1:24–25).[3] But some scholars have difficulty with this interpretation because the sons have different names and different criteria exist for when the kings will disappear.[4]

Both interpretations have tried to do justice to the text of Isaiah, and both maintain the deity of Jesus. The virgin birth of Jesus continues to point to his supernatural origin and divine sonship in either case.[5]

The Coming Assyrian Invasion (7:18–8:22)

Ahaz chose instead to trust in Assyria. He sent a large gift to Tiglath-pileser and enlisted his help (2 Kgs 16:7–8). The Assyrian king responded swiftly, moving westward, conquering Damascus in 732 B.C., and killing Rezin (2 Kgs 16:9). He also overran Israel and allowed Hoshea, who had killed Pekah, to rule as a **vassal** (2 Kgs 15:29–30). The people of the land paid an incredible price for Ahaz's lack of trust in God.

Isaiah warned the people about Assyria's incredible power (7:18–25). The land would experience devastation, and fertile areas would become desolate, fit only for thorns and briars.

The Syro-Ephraimite war also provided the context for the prophecy of 8:1–4. In this prophecy, Isaiah fathered a son named Maher-shalal-hash-baz. Isaiah predicted the boy's birth in the presence of witnesses. He said that before the child could cry out, "Mommy! Daddy!" Syria and Israel would no longer comprise a threat to Judah. (We already have discussed this prophecy's possible connection with 7:14; see above.)

Isaiah further described Judah's coming judgment (8:5–22). The people had rejected God's continual, gentle protection, instead turning to the king of Assyria, who would overflow the land with his fury. Their lack of spiritual light led them to forsake the law and trust in mediums and spiritists. Many in today's world also seek substitutes for God's word, but only in the Bible do we find the answers to life's deepest questions.

Description of the Messianic Era (9:1–7)

Isaiah provided his audience another glimpse into the messianic age. These prophetic words also find their fulfillment in Jesus Christ.

Isaiah described how the northern tribal territories of Zebulun and Naphtali, formerly a place of great spiritual darkness, would see great light. Jesus provided these regions great spiritual light because he carried out much of his earthly ministry there (Mt 4:15–16).

Isaiah also described the Messiah's great names—"Wonderful Counselor," "Mighty God," "Father of Eternity," and "Prince of Peace." Such names can only describe one who is more than human! The prophet further described Messiah's ministry. He would assume his father David's throne and rule righteously forever. Notice how Isaiah brought together Jesus' first and second comings in two adjacent verses. Verse 6 describes Jesus' first coming, whereas verse 7 describes his second coming. Prophets sometimes wrote in this way as they spoke of God's plans for the distant future.[6]

Judgment Against Israel and Assyria (9:8–10:34)

Israel hardened itself to God's judgments (9:8–10:4). The people ignored God's discipline and continued their evil ways. The expression "His anger does not turn away, and his hand is still stretched out" (9:12, 17, 21; 10:4) reveals how God repeatedly punished his people without seeing any repentance. Israel's bad leadership and pride angered the Lord the most.

Assyria would also receive judgment (10:5–34). God used Assyria as an instrument of correction against his ungodly people (10:5). But the Assyrians never realized the role they played in his grand purpose. Instead, they became proud and arrogant. God promised to judge Assyria and to restore a faithful remnant of his people to Israel (10:12–23).

Further Description of the Messianic Era (11:1–12:6)

Isaiah described a branch (see 4:2) who would come from the line of Jesse, David's father. The Spirit of the Lord would em-

An orthodox Jew with a ram's horn trumpet, or *shofar*, at the Western Wall, Jerusalem. Isaiah said a trumpet would summon God's people from exile (ch. 27).

oracles against the nations

power him to lead the nations. He would bring peace to all people. Even wild animals would experience harmony again! God's people would sing for joy and celebrate God's goodness and salvation. Those who have placed their faith in the Lord Jesus Christ anticipate that day with great excitement!

Oracles Against the Nations (13:1–23:18)

Isaiah's "**oracles against the nations**" described God's plans to deal with the other nations of the ancient world. These prophecies illustrate an important truth for us to remember: God is Lord of all nations and peoples.

Babylon (13:1–14:23)

Babylon topped Isaiah's list of kingdoms God would judge. This fact should surprise us somewhat because Assyria, not Babylon, ruled the world during Isaiah's day. But Isaiah looked ahead to a day Babylon *would* rule the world, and he announced her condemnation.

God often used human instruments to accomplish his purposes. He would use the Medes to judge Babylon (13:17). Indeed, many Medes formed part of the forces that King Cyrus of Persia led against Babylon in 539 B.C. Isaiah compared Babylon's destruction to the destruction of Sodom and Gomorrah (13:19–20).

Isaiah described the taunt God's people would sing in the day of Babylon's defeat (14:3–21). Babylon's ruler had made godlike claims (14:13–14), but God would humble him. Some Bible interpreters have seen in 14:12–15 a secondary description of Satan's fall from heaven, though the text only specifically identifies the king (14:4). God would destroy Babylon's pride and arrogance.

Assyria (14:24–27)

God soon would use Assyria to humble the northern kingdom of Israel (2 Kgs 17:1–6). But even the mighty Assyrians could not frustrate God's plans. His purpose would overtake them.

Philistia (14:28–32)

The Philistines rejoiced when King Ahaz died, presumably because they thought they could shake off Judah's domination. But Isaiah assured the Philistines God would still protect his people.

Moab (15:1–16:14)

The Moabites, Judah's southeastern neighbors, descended from Lot, Abraham's nephew (Gn 19:37). Isaiah described how God's judgment affected all Moab's major cities (15:1–9). He warned that within three years God would greatly reduce Moab's status (16:14). Unfortunately we do not know precisely when the Lord fulfilled this prophecy. Both Assyrian kings Sargon II (721–705 B.C.) and SENNACHERIB (704–681 B.C.) claim victories over Moab.[7]

Damascus and Israel (17:1–14)

Isaiah probably described Damascus and Israel together because his words dated from the time of the Syro-Ephraimite coalition (735–734 B.C.). He warned that God would level Damascus, and God did through Tiglath-Pileser III in 732 B.C. He also promised to judge Israel, though he said he would provide a remnant who would follow him (vv. 6–8).

Cush and Egypt (18:1–20:6)

The Lord also promised to humble CUSH (Ethiopia) and Egypt. Cushites would one day bring gifts to Zion (18:7). Moreover, God would judge Egypt and her idols. Centuries earlier, Egypt had enslaved God's people, but now he would turn the tables and enslave her (19:4). He would dry up the Nile, Egypt's source of water, thus devastating the country (19:5–8). Isaiah even walked around naked and barefoot for three years as a sign of Egypt's and Cush's coming destruction by Assyria (20:1–6).

But Isaiah also announced exciting news for Egypt. One day Egypt would swear allegiance to the Lord! The Lord would bring healing to Egypt, and even bring peace between them and the Assyrians. In that day, Egypt, Assyria, and Israel would become a united blessing to all the world. As we look at today's world, such words seem impossible, but we must remember that nothing lies beyond the reach of our all-powerful God.

Babylon, Edom, and Arabia (21:1–17)

Isaiah announced further words of judgment against Babylon (vv. 1–10). Elam and Media would work together to bring Babylon down. The prophet also included a brief word concerning EDOM and ARABIA. Judgment would sweep them away within a year.

Jerusalem (22:1–25)

Isaiah then declared the day of Jerusalem's judgment. The people had lived there in security for many years, and had come to believe God would protect them forever, no matter how they lived. The day of judgment would dash those beliefs (vv. 1–14).

Isaiah presented two pictures of leadership—Shebna (vv. 15–19) and Eliakim (vv. 20–25). Shebna used his office for dishonest gain; God would bring him to noth-

The Nations in Isaiah 13–23

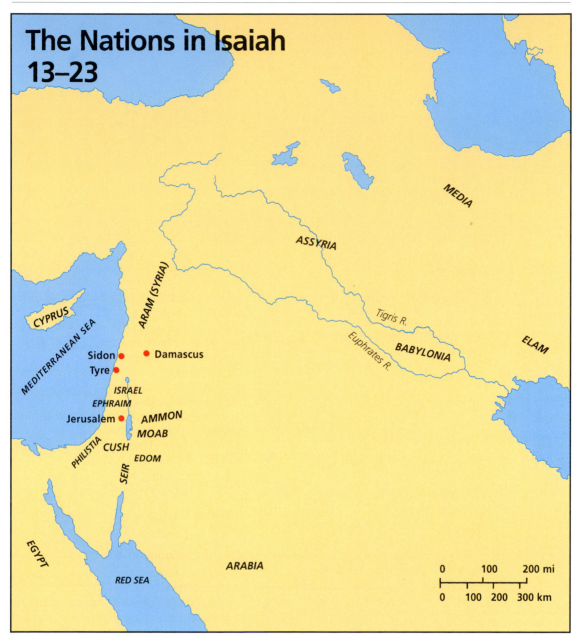

Little Apocalypse

apocalyptic literature

ing. But Eliakim would serve his people as a father. Unfortunately, Eliakim provided one of only a few examples of quality leadership in his generation.

Tyre (23:1–18)

TYRE, a Phoenician port city, had used its strategic location to accumulate great riches. But Tyre soon would experience the heartache of bankruptcy. God would destroy the city's pride and give her possessions to another. Tyre would at last submit to God's sovereign purposes.

The "Little Apocalypse" (24:1–27:13)

Many interpreters have named Isaiah 24–27 "the **Little Apocalypse**" because these chapters read like a miniature Book of Revelation. (See the discussion of **"apocalyptic literature"** in chapter 31.) They serve as a grand conclusion to Isaiah's oracles of chapters 13–23. In the previous section, the prophet showed how God was Lord over many different kingdoms. And if he ruled all those nations and peoples, he also controlled the entire world. Isaiah 24–27 announces God's final judgment of the world and the ultimate salvation of his people.

The earth's destruction (24:1–23)

Isaiah announced the earth's destruction with strong language (vv. 1–6). The Lord would show no partiality in judgment. One's status in society did not matter.

But in the midst of the violent upheaval that would bring the end of history, God's people praised him anyway! They gave him glory, for the time of salvation was drawing near (vv. 14–16). His people would see him in all his splendor (v. 23).

God's victory over his enemies (25:1–12)

God's people sang to him—he had brought them victory! Isaiah foretold a lavish banquet the Lord would prepare (vv. 6–9). He would abolish death forever and establish personal, intimate fellowship with those he loved. Today, God offers to all of us a personal relationship with him through faith in Jesus Christ (Rom 3:21–22). Those who trust in him have the promise that one day they will see him face to face (1 Jn 3:1–3).

Judah's song of deliverance (26:1–21)

God's people would sing another song celebrating God's deliverance. God had brought the victory, and he deserved their trust (vv. 1–6). As Isaiah pondered this great day, he offered the Lord a prayer (vv. 11–18). God's people stood defenseless before their enemies. Did they really have any hope? God answered with a resounding *yes*! He promised to deliver them and to destroy their enemies in his perfect timing.

Israel's coming salvation (27:1–13)

Bible interpreters have wrestled with the identity of Leviathan (v. 1). Some have attempted to connect Leviathan with a particular Canaanite deity. But all such attempts have their problems. Probably we should understand Isaiah as using the image of Leviathan to describe God's ultimate destruction of evil.[8]

God intended his judgment as a means of turning people back to him. He anticipated the tender care of his own (vv. 2–6) as they realized their helplessness apart

from him and asked for forgiveness (v. 9). He vowed to gather them for a grand reunion one day (vv. 12–13).

Oracles of Woe (28:1–33:24)

Isaiah 28–33 contains five woe oracles. These oracles pronounced doom on various peoples and nations. Isaiah 34–35 provides a climax to chapters 28–33, much as chapters 24–27 (the "Little Apocalypse") do for chapters 13–23 ("Oracles against the Nations").

Woe against Ephraim (28:1–29)

Isaiah denounced Ephraim's pride and arrogance. The people thought they had found a way to cheat death and escape God's judgment (v. 15). Instead, their immature leadership rendered them unable to understand God's teaching (vv. 9–13). They did not realize what a desperate situation they faced!

God vowed to bring justice and righteousness to the land (vv. 16–22). His "tested cornerstone" would provide a key part of Zion's new foundation. The New Testament revealed that Jesus Christ is this cornerstone (Rom 9:33). Jesus is the foundation of the church, a structure he is building with believers, who are "living stones" (1 Pt 2:6).

Woe against Ariel (29:1–24)

The term "Ariel" refers to Jerusalem (v. 1). Many scholars suggest it means "hearth of God," a description that would fit the context.[9] The people of Jerusalem thought they were the center of worship of the one true God. But God was not pleased. Isaiah proclaimed judgment against the city and its people. He vowed to lay them low like the dust (v. 4).

Isaiah described the spiritual stupor that gripped the people (vv. 9–16). They spoke as though they knew the Lord, but had closed their hearts to following him. They thought no one knew about their sin, but God had seen it all. Yet the Lord promised restoration (vv. 17–24). The people eventually would return to him.

Woe against foreign alliances (30:1–31:9)

Isaiah condemned Judah's attempt at foreign alliances (30:1–5; 31:1–3). Treaties with foreign powers courted disaster. How could other kingdoms provide more se-

would hear, and stammering tongues would speak clearly (vv. 3–4)! God's Spirit would bring this day, an everlasting day of peace and security. Christians look for Jesus Christ to fulfill these words when he returns. The Bible calls people everywhere to prepare for that day by yielding their lives to him.

Woe against Assyria (33:1–24)

Isaiah pronounced Assyria's coming destruction. The Assyrians thought they ruled the world, but they merely served as God's instruments. After they had completed God's purpose for them, he would bring them down (vv. 1–2).

How could God's people prepare for that day? By turning back to him! Who could escape God's holy wrath? Only those whose lives reflected their faithfulness to him (vv. 14–16). They would see a new Jerusalem in all its splendor, but most of all, they would see their God in all his splendor. The New Testament also speaks of a day when believers will see him face to face (1 Jn 3:2–3).

Eschatological Summation (34:1–35:10)

Isaiah brought his pronouncements concerning God's coming judgment and kingdom to a climax in chapters 34–35. Chapter 34 describes God's ultimate vengeance against the nations. Chapter 35 announces the joy that will come to those who know him.

God's vengeance against the nations (34:1–17)

The prophet described God as a powerful Warrior who executed vengeance on his foes. But the judgment went far beyond earthly nations. Even heaven itself felt the impact (v. 4). The Lord singled out Edom for special attention, perhaps because of its persistent enmity against God's people (cf. Obadiah). He would bring ruin on Edom forever. All God's enemies would suffer the same fate. God had decreed it and it would be so (vv. 16–17).

The salvation of the redeemed (35:1–10)

The wilderness and desert normally became dry and parched during the summer months, and did not flourish even at other times of the year. But the day Isaiah

curity than the Lord God?[10] Furthermore, concluding foreign treaties often included formally recognizing the other nation's gods. No king devoted to the Lord could ever participate in such a ceremony.

Isaiah also heralded the folly of trusting in Egypt. Egypt had developed a reputation for promising its allies assistance and then failing to provide it (36:6). God vowed to judge Egypt and those who trusted in her.

Woe mixed with hope (32:1–20)

Isaiah announced hope in the midst of woe. The Lord would one day raise up a righteous king whose coming would renew society! Other leaders would follow his example and bring blessing to all the land. Isaiah also promised other wonders—blind eyes would see, deaf ears

Summary

1. Isaiah was the prophet who served in the royal court of Judah, but he did have some words for Israel as well as other nations.

2. The major themes of chapters 1–39 include the remnant, the sovereignty of God, the servant, the Holy One of Israel, and the Messiah.

3. Isaiah's prophetic call came in 739 B.C. when he had a vision in which he saw the majesty of God as well as his own sinfulness.

4. Isaiah offered Ahaz a sign from God but Ahaz declined it because he trusted more in the power of Assyria than he did in God.

5. Isaiah's prophecies about the messianic era told how the northern tribes would be influenced by the Messiah, describes the Messiah by different names, tells about the Messiah's ministry, and describes Messiah's first and second comings.

6. In Isaiah's "Oracles Against All Nations" God's judgment was declared on Babylon, Assyria, Philistia, Moab, Damascus, Israel, Cush, Edom, Arabia, Jerusalem, and Tyre.

7. Chapters 24–27 have been designated by many scholars as the "Little Apocalypse."

8. The woe oracles of chapters 28–33 included woes against foreign alliances.

9. Hezekiah demonstrated his foolishness in showing the delegation from Babylon all of his nation's treasures.

Key Terms

remnant
woe oracles
sign
vassal
oracles against the nations
Little Apocalypse
apocalyptic literature

Key People/ Places

Tiglath-Pileser III
Sennacherib
Merodach-baladan II
Cush
Edom
Arabia
Tyre
Babylon
Assyria
Syria
Israel
Judah
Moab
Egypt

heralded would witness lush growth comparable to that of Carmel and Sharon, two of Israel's richest areas. The Lord would bring this wonderful blessing.

Society also would experience great rejuvenation. God would prepare his people in three ways to receive his blessing. First, he would heal their infirmities (vv. 4–6). Second, he would make water abundant in dry areas (v. 7). Third, he would prepare a highway of holiness, a special road on which his people could return to worship him (vv. 8–10). They would come safe and secure, and with great joy.

Historical Interlude: Highlights and Lowlights from Hezekiah's Reign (36:1–39:8)

Four chapters link the first part of the Book of Isaiah (chapters 1–39) with the second part (chapters 40–66). Scholars have noted that the events of chapters 38–39 chronologically precede the events of chapters 36–37. But Isaiah was not giving a chronological account. Chapters 36–37 deal with Assyria and serve to "tie off" the first part of the book, during which Assyria appeared as the dominant force in the ancient world. Chapters 38–39 focus on Babylon, whose empire formed the backdrop for Isaiah 40–66.[11]

Sennacherib's threat and God's deliverance (36:1–37:38)

Sennacherib (704–681 B.C.), king of Assyria, came against Hezekiah (727–698 B.C.), king of Judah, when Hezekiah refused to pay tribute (2 Kgs 18:7). Scholars debate whether Sennacherib invaded Judah in 701 B.C. or 714 B.C. because we do not know exactly when Hezekiah reigned.[12] After Sennacherib defeated Judah's fortified cities, Hezekiah offered to surrender and pay whatever penalty Sennacherib imposed (2 Kgs 18:13–16). But Sennacherib decided he would push to take Jerusalem itself.

With mocking scorn Sennacherib's representative taunted Jerusalem's populace and urged them to surrender (Is 36:4–20; 37:8–13). But Hezekiah sought the face of his God, who sent Isaiah with a message of deliverance (37:14–29). And God fulfilled his word, sending his angel to decimate the Assyrian army.

From a human perspective, the battle ended and Sennacherib returned home with what he already had taken from Hezekiah. But from a theological perspective, the Lord brought dramatic deliverance, saving Jerusalem from destruction and his people from exile! He had defended his city for David's sake (37:35).

Interestingly, archaeologists discovered Sennacherib's royal annals when they excavated Nineveh. The annals proudly describe his siege of Jerusalem, but mention no conquest.

Hezekiah's illness and recovery (38:1–22)

Around 711 B.C.[13] Hezekiah became mortally ill. When Isaiah warned him he would not recover, Hezekiah wept bitterly and prayed for God's mercy. God responded by giving the king another fifteen years of life. He even provided Hezekiah a sign to bolster the king's faith—the shadow on the king's stairway receded!

Three years later, the king had a son—Manasseh—who eventually succeeded him as king (2 Kgs 21:1). Manasseh's birth proved to be a mixed blessing. On the one hand, the king now had an heir. On the other hand, Manasseh (698–642 B.C.) became one of Judah's most wicked kings, and effectually undid all the reforms his father had established. His evil led to a spiritual decline from which Judah never recovered (Jer 15:4).

Hezekiah's visit with Merodach-baladan (39:1–8)

Merodach-baladan II ruled as Babylon's king from 721 B.C. to 710 B.C. and again briefly in 703 B.C. He seized the opportunity that Assyria's decline provided. When the Assyrians became stronger, they removed him from power.[14]

Study Questions

1. What do we know about Isaiah from the details in his book? What themes were most important to him?

2. If you only had Isaiah 1–12, what could you learn about God's Messiah?

3. Against which nations did Isaiah pronounce judgment in chapters 13–23?

Why did he take the time to deal with each one?

4. Identify the main details of chapters 36–39. What function do these chapters serve in the Book of Isaiah?

Further Reading

Machen, J. Gresham. *The Virgin Birth of Christ*. 2nd ed. New York: Harper, 1932. The classic treatment of the Virgin birth and its implications for the Christian faith.

Motyer, J. Alec. *The Prophecy of Isaiah: An Introduction and Commentary*. Downers Grove: InterVarsity, 1993. A thorough commentary for the advanced student.

Oswalt, John N. *The Book of Isaiah: Chapters 1–39*. New International Commentary on the Old Testament. Grand Rapids: Eerdmans, 1986. A commentary for the student who desires thorough research, with abundant footnotes and documentation.

Webb, Barry G. *The Message of Isaiah: On Eagle's Wings*. Downers Grove: InterVarsity, 1996. A shorter survey, but rich in application.

Wolf, Herbert M. *Interpreting Isaiah: The Suffering and Glory of the Messiah*. Grand Rapids: Zondervan, 1985. A college-level textbook that combines good scholarship and readability.

Youngblood, Ronald F. *The Book of Isaiah: An Introductory Commentary*. 2nd ed. Grand Rapids: Baker, 1993. A shorter survey.

Merodach-baladan sent a delegation to Hezekiah to congratulate him on his recovery. He also probably hoped to try to establish an ally to the west against Assyria. At any rate, Hezekiah proudly gave the Babylonian delegation a thorough tour and showed them all his splendor and treasures.

Later, Isaiah confronted Hezekiah over the foolishness of showing the Babylonians everything. He assured him the Babylonians would remember the treasures they had seen, and one day they would return to take it. In 587 B.C., Isaiah's words proved true. Nebuchadnezzar II (605–562 B.C.), king of Babylon, defeated Jerusalem and led the people into exile.

26 Isaiah 40–66
Great Days Are Coming!

Outline

Objectives

**After reading this chapter,
you should be able to**

- Describe the contents and major themes
  of Isaiah 40–66
- Evaluate the multiple-author view
  of Isaiah
- Compare the three interpretations
  of the Suffering Servant passages
  in chapters 52 and 53
- Summarize what Isaiah prophesies about
  Judah's return from Babylonian exile

Deutero-Isaiah

Do you know people who speak negatively almost all the time? They adopt a pessimistic view toward life and assume circumstances will turn out for the worst. I have known people like that and find it hard to stay around them for long. If I do, *I* start to get depressed!

Isaiah proclaimed many strong words to Judah. He called the people to confess their sin, humble themselves before God, and turn back to God. Most probably did not want to hear those words, but they *needed* to hear them.

But not all Isaiah's words were negative. Isaiah prophesied God's judgment against his people, but he also proclaimed a day when God would restore his people and bless them again. Isaiah 40–66 especially focuses on these days of blessing.

Outline

XV. **Comfort, Comfort My People** (40:1–31)

XVI. **The Coming Deliverance** (41:1–29)

XVII. **The Role of the Lord's Servant** (42:1–25)

XVIII. **Israel's Redemption from Babylon** (43:1–45:25)

XIX. **Judgment against Babylon** (46:1–47:15)

XX. **Israel's Release and Exaltation** (48:1–52:12)
- A. Israel's Stubbornness and God's Even More Stubborn Grace (48:1–22)
- B. The Lord's Servant (49:1–7)
- C. Israel's Return (49:8–26)
- D. God and His Servant (50:1–11)
- E. Encouragement to the Righteous (51:1–16)
- F. Good News for Jerusalem (51:17–52:12)

XXI. **The Suffering Servant** (52:13–53:12)

XXII. **Celebrating the Return** (54:1–59:21)
- A. Jerusalem's Rebirth (54:1–17)
- B. Call to Trust in God (55:1–13)
- C. Foreigners Join God's Family (56:1–8)
- D. Summary of Israel's Sin (56:9–57:21)
- E. Call to True Righteousness (58:1–14)
- F. Israel's Sin and God's Deliverance (59:1–21)

XXIII. **The Climax of God's Restoration** (60:1–66:24)
- A. Zion's Glorification (60:1–22)
- B. God's Further Restoration (61:1–11)
- C. Zion's Marriage to God (62:1–12)
- D. Judgment of the Nations (63:1–6)
- E. Prayer for God's Intervention (63:7–64:12)
- F. Blessing for God's Servants (65:1–25)
- G. The Ultimate Conclusion (66:1–24)

Who Wrote Isaiah 40–66?

Over the centuries most Jews and Christians have believed the prophet Isaiah wrote the entire book that bears his name. However, some Bible scholars have suggested other writers—perhaps Isaiah's disciples—wrote chapters 40–66. In recent years even many evangelicals have adopted this position. The evidence for the multiple-author view and one-author view appears below.

Multiple-Author View

The multiple-author view has taken numerous forms over the years.[1] Basically, this view suggests the prophet Isaiah more or less produced the material in chapters 1–39 while another author or authors produced chapters 40–66. Proponents of this view refer to the author of chapters 40–66 as "**Deutero-Isaiah**," which simply means "second Isaiah."[2]

Other scholars have suggested yet another division within chapters 40–66. They believe Deutero-Isaiah wrote Isaiah 40–55,

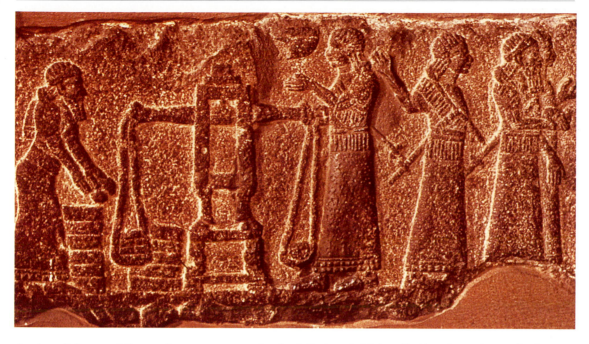

Assyrian relief showing officials weighing tribute in the balance.

Trito-Isaiah

while another person or school of disciples (**Trito-Isaiah**, "Third Isaiah") wrote Isaiah 56–66 somewhat later. Some have argued the section came from many hands, perhaps a school of Isaiah's disciples.[3]

Those who hold that more than one person wrote the Book of Isaiah generally have argued along four lines: time span of the book, different subject matter of 1–39 and 40–66, different vocabulary and style of 1–39 and 40–66, and the mention of King Cyrus by name.

The time span of the book

Some who hold a multiple-author view suggest the time span of the book rules out a single author. They see no way Isaiah could have known about the circumstances in chapters 40–66. Isaiah prophesied from about 740 to 690 B.C., but much of Isaiah 40–66 describes the period of return from Babylonian exile that began about 538 B.C.

The different subject matter of 1–39 and 40–66

Multiple-author proponents highlight the different subject matter of Isaiah 1–39 and Isaiah 40–66. Chapters 1–39 focus on Assyria, whereas chapters 40–66 focus on Babylon. Chapters 1–39 deal primarily with Isaiah's generation, whereas chapters 40–66 look to the future. God's judgment forms a major theme of chapters

1–39, but God's redemption and salvation lead the way in chapters 40–66. Such sharp differences suggest the involvement of more than one author.

The different vocabulary and style of 1–39 and 40–66

This point follows naturally on the previous one, since different subject matter normally requires different vocabulary. But multiple-author advocates also stress how the different poetic style of chapters 40–66 suggests it came from a hand other than Isaiah's. They cite this poetry as among the best in all the Old Testament while contrasting it with the poetic style of chapters 1–39.

The mention of King Cyrus by name

Isaiah 44:28 and 45:1 mention Cyrus, the Persian Empire's first king, by name. Multiple-author supporters cite these verses as examples of specific information only someone living at that time could know. Since Isaiah's ministry concluded long before the time of Cyrus, they argue that someone else must have written the references to Cyrus as well as the surrounding material.

One-Author View

In spite of the above evidence, many Bible scholars continue to support the view that Isaiah wrote the entire book that bears his name.[4] Some of their arguments counter the assumptions of multiple-author proponents, while others present positive reasons why we should consider this view.

The time span of the book

The Bible says God knows the future and sometimes reveals it to his servants the prophets (Am 3:7; Rv 1:1–2, 19). If God informed Isaiah about the future, then Isaiah could have described events without actually seeing them himself. The one-author view thus accounts for the book's time span according to the guidelines the Bible establishes for itself regarding predictive prophecy.

The different subject matter of 1–39 and 40–66

One-author advocates simply argue that an author may write on many different subjects, just as many do today. Different subject matter does not form an adequate basis for discerning the work of a distinct author.

At the same time, many common themes do occur in both parts of Isaiah. Passages about Messiah appear in both parts (9:6–7; 11:1–16; 42:1–4; 52:13–53:12). So also do terms like servant, remnant, the nations, and the Holy One of Israel. These common themes do not necessarily prove the one-author view, but they do show the two parts of the book may not be as radically different as multiple-author proponents sometimes suggest.

The different vocabulary and style of 1–39 and 40–66

Again, one-author proponents assert that human writers have the capability to use different vocabulary and styles in accordance with their topics and purposes. For example, a college student today may write a research paper according to a set of detailed specifications and then write a letter to loved ones at home. Each document has a unique style and vocabulary, yet each one clearly comes from the same author. Ancient biblical writers certainly had the same gifts and abilities!

The mention of King Cyrus by name

One-author supporters generally have responded in one of two ways to this issue. First, some suggest we should assume God revealed the name to Isaiah. One

other biblical example of such a prophecy does seem to occur (1 Kgs 13:2). Second, some suggest Isaiah originally gave the prophecy without specifically mentioning Cyrus, and a scribe later filled in the name when the fulfillment became clear. Either explanation removes the necessity of seeing a distinct author for chapters 40–66.

Textual evidence for single authorship

Old Testament manuscripts are not as plentiful as New Testament manuscripts. Nevertheless, no textual evidence suggests Isaiah 1–39 and Isaiah 40–66 ever existed as separate documents. For example, the Isaiah text from Qumran, part of the Dead Sea Scrolls and the earliest known copy of Isaiah, has no break between chapters 39 and 40. Those who hold to a multiple-author view do so against the existing textual evidence.

Evidence from the New Testament

Evidence from the New Testament also suggests the Book of Isaiah came entirely from Isaiah. New Testament writers appear to attribute both sections of Isaiah to the prophet (Mt 3:3; Acts 28:25; Rom 9:27–29; 10:16, 20). This fact suggests they understood the entire work as coming from him.

Summary of the authorship issue

The cumulative evidence suggests the one-author view has much to commend it. The time span of the book and issues of subject matter, vocabulary, and style do not present difficulties if we allow God to reveal the future to his prophets and if we grant that one author can write in more than one style. Textual evidence and the witness of the New Testament writers also appear to support the one-author view. Bible scholars no doubt will continue to study and debate this issue.

The Servant Passages in Isaiah 40–66

The servant theme appears in several places in Isaiah and the servant carries a number of identities. The word "servant" may denote an individual Israelite (22:20),

unifying focus. The servant is God's instrument, fully yielded to his purpose. He accomplishes the Lord's will because he gives himself totally into his hands. Are you willing to make such a complete surrender? Just think of how the Lord might use you!

Isaiah's Message Continues

Comfort, O Comfort My People (40:1–31)

Verses 1–11 serve as a prologue to chapters 40–66, laying a foundation for the rest of the book. Isaiah announced God's coming glory and contrasted it with the people's helplessness. But the prophet encouraged the disheartened—they could count on God's promise! The Lord would comfort and care for them as a shepherd cared for his sheep.

The rest of chapter 40 answers the question, "Can God really do all he says?" The Lord marked off the heavens with his hands and stretched them out like a curtain. He raised rulers to glory and reduced them to nothing. He even called all the stars by name! In light of his majesty, how could God's people think he would forget them? He would certainly accomplish his purpose for them and renew their strength day by day. Isaiah's words also provide us with comfort and assurance when we face difficult challenges.

The Coming Deliverance (41:1–29)

Isaiah 41 introduces a threefold theme or motif that runs throughout chapters 40–66. First, God's people are in captivity for their sins. Second, this captivity proves God is God, for he alone predicted it. Third, he now will restore and redeem them.

The prophet stated God's case against false gods. The Lord had called a ruler (Cyrus) to fulfill his purposes. But idols had no power to do such a work. God challenged the idols directly. Had *they* predicted the future? In fact, had they said anything at all? No! All stood speechless and powerless before him. Isaiah told Israel not to fear, for Israel was God's chosen servant.

Part of the Isaiah Scroll, the longest and oldest of the Dead Sea Scrolls from Qumran. There is no break between chapters 39 and 40 in the scroll.

the nation of Israel (41:8), the remnant (49:3), and even the Messiah (52:13). The servant works diligently to accomplish God's purpose despite numerous challenges and difficulties. Isaiah 40–66 features four passages in which the servant theme receives special attention (42:1–9; 49:1–7; 50:4–11; 52:13–53:12).

The servant's identity in the Book of Isaiah remains somewhat fluid: the servant is alternately Israel, the remnant, the Messiah, and perhaps even Isaiah himself. But in every passage, and particularly in the servant songs, we see a

The Role of the Lord's Servant (42:1–25)

The first servant passage presented a servant whom God chose for a special purpose. God's Spirit rested on him as he fulfilled God's plan. The servant brought in God's kingdom in a quiet, unexpected way. He drew little attention to himself but achieved powerful results.

Matthew 12:18–21 quotes Isaiah 42:1–4 and applies the Old Testament's words to Jesus Christ. Jesus quietly fulfilled God's purpose and brought in God's spiritual kingdom. He did powerful works such as healing many kinds of diseases, but did so in a humble way, and told people to give glory to God, not to him.

Christ's example stands in stark contrast to Israel's role as God's blind, deaf, and unfaithful servant (Is 42:18–25). Israel spurned God's ways, ignored God's prophets, and in the end, paid the high price of exile.

Israel's Redemption from Babylon (43:1–45:25)

Isaiah described God's power and blessing (43:1–44:8). God was Savior and Redeemer. God was his people's leader, and he would lead them home from exile. He would display his grace. In contrast, Israel had displayed a rebellious attitude from the start of her relationship with God.

God proclaimed his superiority to idols (44:9–23). He described how carefully workers prepared the materials that later became objects of worship. How could the people bow before an image they themselves had crafted? It made little sense, but neither do many of the false religious faiths that have appeared in today's world. The Bible says spiritual blindness presents a powerful obstacle to accepting the truth of the gospel (1 Cor 2:14; 2 Cor 4:4).

Isaiah declared that God ruled as absolute sovereign over creation (44:24–45:25). The Lord controlled mighty King Cyrus; in fact, he even referred to him as his shepherd and anointed one (44:28; 45:1)! One day, every knee would bow to this almighty God (45:23).

Judgment Against Babylon (46:1–47:15)

Isaiah predicted Babylon's fall to Persia. He described the contest between God and the gods of Babylon (46:1–13). Every year, the Babylonians celebrated an annual festival (the **Akitu festival**) at which they paraded the statues of their gods through Babylon. But this time, the idols cowered in shame. They could not save Babylon, but God assured his people he would save them. He would protect them and lead them from womb to glory.

Babylon also received God's taunt (47:1–15). The Lord would expose Babylon's shame, dethrone her from world dominion, and bring terrible judgment on her. Babylon had applied words to herself that applied only to God—"I am, and there is no one besides me" (47:8; cf. 45:5–6). God would teach the Babylonians the meaning of humility.

Israel's Release and Exaltation (48:1–52:12)

Israel's stubbornness and God's even more stubborn grace (48:1–22)

Isaiah contrasted Israel's stubbornness with God's even more stubborn grace (48:1–22). God's people had received God's grace and wasted it, delighting instead in their sin and rebellion. They had no excuse before a righteous, holy God. But God chose to love them anyway, just as he chooses to love us anyway. He vowed to redeem them, restore them to their land, and teach them to love and serve him again.

The Lord's servant (49:1–7)

The servant of Isaiah 49:1–7 received God's call from the womb. He experienced a frustrating ministry and worried that perhaps his work was in vain. Surely God was with him, but how? God replied by giving his servant an even greater mission. He would not only be God's servant to Israel, but also to all the nations, that God's salvation might reach the ends of the earth.

Isaiah 49:3 identifies the servant as Israel, but Israel cannot have a mission to himself (49:5). Probably we should understand Isaiah as referring to the remnant, the righteous faithful within the community of Israel. This interpretation seems likely in light of the apostle Paul's words (Acts 13:47). Paul quoted Isaiah 49:6 and told his audience in Asia Minor that those who faithfully proclaimed the gospel fulfilled God's command through Isaiah.

Israel's return (49:8–26)

God promised to re-establish his covenant with his people. He would feed them, shelter them, care for them, and bring joy to their hearts once again. But Zion struggled with some serious doubts; could God really love her again? God assured them he could. In fact, all the mothers in Israel would abandon their children before the Lord would ever abandon his people (49:14–16)! God vowed to establish a new generation of those who loved him, a generation that would overflow Israel's borders!

God and his servant (50:1–11)

The Lord assured Israel he had the power to save them. They had not slipped from his sovereign control; rather, he had punished them for their sins! Verses 4–11 described an obedient servant humiliated for God's cause. But as in other servant passages, the servant received God's grace to strengthen him for his task. As a result, he stood resolute in his purpose. No one could defeat him because God stood on his side!

Commentators differ as to who fulfilled Isaiah's words. Some have suggested Isaiah prophesied about Jesus Christ, since some of his words might aptly describe Jesus' trial (50:6; cf. Mt 26:67–68; 27:26). Others have proposed that Isaiah spoke about his own suffering. Interestingly, the New Testament does not cite this passage anywhere.

Encouragement to the righteous (51:1–16)

God encouraged the righteous to look to the past, future, and present. They should look to the past to remember their spiritual roots. They should look to the future to appreciate God's great coming works. And they should look to the present to see their salvation and deliverance.

Good news for Jerusalem (51:17–52:12)

Isaiah announced exciting news for Jerusalem. He portrayed the city as a drunkard inebriated with the wine of God's judgment. But she would be set free from her bondage to sin so she could serve God. She would rejoice in the knowledge that her God reigned over all.

The Suffering Servant (52:13–53:12)

Isaiah 52:13–53:12 comprises the most famous of the servant passages. Isaiah described a servant whom God exalted, before whom kings of the earth shut their mouths (52:13–15). Yet he suffered rejection from the people and experienced sorrow and grief (53:1–3). He suffered on behalf of God's people who truly merited the punishment he received. All this came through God's hand (53:4–6).

The servant accepted his fate without protest, with silent resignation. Despite his innocence, he went to his death on behalf of God's people (53:7–9). But God who crushed him also would reward him. The servant achieved victory through a life of suffering, for that suffering fulfilled God's plan.

Bible scholars have typically offered three possible interpretations of this servant passage. First, some identify the servant with the prophet Isaiah (or another prophet if they hold the multiple-author view). But no concept of a prophet suffering for the nation's sins appears elsewhere in the Bible, and silent submission does not seem to fit the prophets.

Second, some scholars suggest the servant represents Israel. In this view, the nations express their surprise that Israel suffered in their place. Other interpreters have modified this position by arguing that the servant represents the faithful remnant of Israel who suffered for the nation's sins. But again difficulties arise. The Bible clearly states that Israel and Judah paid for their own sins (2 Kgs 17:7–23; Is 42:23–25). Perhaps the remnant suffered unjustly because of evil people's sins, but the remnant did not suffer *in place of* the evildoers.

Third, some interpreters argue that the servant represents Jesus Christ. They suggest the New Testament evidence demands the messianic interpretation. Jesus quietly grew to manhood in Israel and then began proclaiming God's kingdom. Many despised and rejected him and finally put him to death. In his death, Jesus suffered for the sins of others. He experienced crucifixion between two robbers and burial in an official's tomb. And God planned it all to bring eternal life to all who respond in faith to his offer of forgiveness and salvation.

Isaiah 52:13–53:12 portrays a beautiful picture of the depth of Christ's sacrifice for sinful humanity. Read it again. Ask God to sear the images into your heart. Are you beginning to understand God's love for you?

Celebrating the Return (54:1–59:21)

Judah's return from exile was definitely something worth celebrating. As we examine this section of Isaiah 40–66, we find Isaiah's words accenting various aspects of that celebration.

Jerusalem's rebirth (54:1–17)

Jerusalem's rebirth would boast two aspects—fertile land and numerous people.

Barren wasteland would sprout vegetation. Desert regions would become lush. And the nation's population would stretch its borders. People would have to scramble to make room for one another. God would put his people's shame behind them. He had struck them in anger for their sin, but now he planned to gather them with compassion.

Isaiah also described Jerusalem's gates. Many interpreters have argued that his beautiful depiction denotes a time yet future, for Judah's return from exile never featured such splendor.

Call to trust in God (55:1–13)

Isaiah called the people to trust in God in light of his abundant blessings. They should quit spending their money for things that could not bring lasting satisfaction and invest their lives in a relationship with God. He called them to repent while they had time, and urged them to trust in God's

---

Jesus and Isaiah 52:13–53:12

Isaiah 52:13–53:12 (often simply called "Isaiah 53") forms one of the Old Testament's most remarkable prophecies concerning Jesus Christ. The chart below summarizes Isaiah's words and how Jesus fulfilled them:

Verse	The Servant's Description	Fulfillment in Christ
52:13	Raised, lifted up, exalted	God exalted him and will exalt him fully at the second coming (Phil 2:9–11)
52:14	Appearance disfigured	Received beating at his trial (Mt 26:67)
52:15	Sprinkled many nations	Sprinkling of his blood brings forgiveness (1 Pt 2:9)
53:3	Despised and rejected	Many rejected him, especially the leaders (Jn 11:47–50)
53:4–6	Suffered for our sin; stricken by God	Died for our sin according to God's plan (1 Cor 15:3)
53:7	Silent before oppressors	Silent before accusers at his trial (Mk 14:60–61)
53:8	Killed for the people's sin	Died for our sin (2 Cor 5:14–15)
53:9	Assigned a grave with the wicked and rich, but did no wrong	Crucified between two robbers, buried in a rich council member's tomb (Mk 15:27–28, 43–46)
53:10	Lord's will to crush him; he will see his offspring	God prepared him as an offering for sin (Rom 5:9)
53:12	Receives great reward because he poured out his life	Receives great reward because he poured out his life (Phil 2:9–11; Heb 1:3–4)

The busy approach to the Damascus Gate into the old city of Jerusalem. Isaiah described Jerusalem's gates; many interpreters have argued that his beautiful depiction denotes a time yet future, for Judah's return from exile never featured such splendor.

eunuchs

Torah

ways. God's word would accomplish its purpose in their lives and bring them great joy if they only embraced it.

Foreigners join God's family (56:1–8)

Foreigners and **eunuchs** worried that they would not receive a share of God's coming blessing. Indeed, certain passages of the **Torah** appeared to give preference to native Israelites (Dt 23:3–4). But God promised rich blessings for both groups. He would grant the eunuchs a name better than that of sons and daughters. And he also would bring the foreigners into his family. Faithfulness to God counted more than bloodline.

This passage anticipated the apostle Paul's announcement that believers of all nations and types would become one family in Jesus Christ (Gal 3:28–29). Perhaps the Ethiopian eunuch served as a foreshadowing of the fulfillment of this prophecy (Acts 8:26–40).

Summary of Israel's sins (56:9–57:21)

Isaiah summarized Israel's past sin. Spiritual blindness, injustice, and idolatry all characterized the people's lives. But again, the prophet held out hope. No sin lay beyond the cleansing power of God's grace. But those who persisted in wickedness would never experience that grace.

Call to true righteousness (58:1–14)

The people wondered why God didn't seem to notice their fasting. God responded that they fasted from impure motives. They forced their workers to work just as hard and thought that mere fasting would earn God's approval. But the Lord desired a fast that touched the people's hearts, not merely their stomachs. He wanted them to humble themselves before him and show their repentance by acts of kindness and grace to their fellow citizens. Then he would respond to their fasting.

Isaiah also called the people to honor the Sabbath. They treated the day the same as any other, but God called them to turn aside from the pursuits of their livelihood and to rest and meditate on him. Even today, God asks us to set aside a day to cease from our normal routine to give honor and worship to him.

Israel's sin and God's deliverance (59:1–21)

Isaiah described Israel's predicament. The Lord was more than capable to save them, but their sins had separated them from him. They defiled their hands with bloodshed and spoke lies while their feet quickly pursued new paths of evil. As a result, justice and righteousness departed from the land.

God responded to this description of the people's hopeless condition. *He* would bring salvation! He vowed to bring his Spirit and revive the people. Those who feared his Name would receive his blessing, but His enemies would face swift judgment. Paul applied Isaiah 59:20–21 to Christ's second coming, when the Lord will restore godliness and holiness forever (Rom 11:26–27).

The Climax of God's Restoration (60:1–66:24)

In the remaining chapters the prophet's words become more and more exciting. He looked ahead to a day when God would climax redemptive history and bring ultimate victory for his people and glory to himself.

Zion's glorification (60:1–22)

Isaiah called a redeemed Zion to arise and prepare to serve as God's instrument of blessing. Nations enveloped in spiritual darkness would see their great spiritual light and stream to it in great numbers, bringing their wealth with them. The Lord would provide his people lasting security; they would never need to close their gates. The prophet was at least partly looking ahead to God's coming kingdom (v. 20). His description of the nations joining in worship of the true God foreshadows Revelation 7:9–14, where people from every nation and tribe gather around God's throne to praise him.

God's further restoration (61:1–11)

Verses 1–3 present another picture of a servant whom God had anointed and on whom God's Spirit rested. The servant had a ministry of announcing good news and comfort to the oppressed. He proclaimed the year of the Lord's favor was at hand.

Luke 4:16–30 records Jesus' fulfillment of these words. As he stood in the synagogue at Nazareth, Jesus took the scroll of Isaiah and read the words we now call Isaiah 61:1–3. He then announced, "Today this scripture is fulfilled in your hearing" (Lk 4:21). Many became confused over what Jesus had said and others became quite angry at him. But indeed, the words were fulfilled; the time of God's visitation had come The world lay in bondage to sin, and Jesus came to proclaim liberty and freedom from its power (Jn 10:10).

Isaiah also promised God's people would see their ancient ruins restored (61:4–11). Again, foreigners would participate in the restoration project. Isaiah described Israel's special blessing among the nations. Praise and righteousness would spring up before all nations.

Zion's marriage to God (62:1–12)

Isaiah foresaw a grand marriage between the Lord God and Zion, his bride. His prophecy provides a beautiful picture of God's love for his people and a foreshadowing of Christ's marriage to the church (Rv 19:7–9).

Today, a bride generally assumes her husband's name. The name change signifies the beginning of a new special relationship. God also had new names chosen for his bride (Is 62:4). Hephzibah means "my delight is in her" and Beulah means "married." These names may or may not sound beautiful to us, but the

Should Christians fast today?

Both Old and New Testaments mention fasting. People sometimes abstained from food to seek God's favor (2 Sm 12:21), mourn the dead (1 Sm 31:13), or commemorate some tragic time (Zec 7:5). They might fast as individuals (1 Kgs 21:27) or in groups (Jon 3:5). Jesus spoke about fasting (Mt 6:16–18), and the early church sometimes practiced it (Acts 13:3).

Should Christians fast today? And if so, when and how? Here are some suggested guidelines:

- The Scriptures do not command Christians to fast. However, Christians may sometimes choose to fast in order to focus more

completely on the Lord in prayer and worship.
- Fasting is more than going without food. Fasting involves a humble heart attitude that results in holy living (Is 58:5–7).
- Fasting does not guarantee God will answer our prayers the way we want. Rather, fasting helps us concentrate more fully on him.
- Fasting does not make someone spiritually mature. We should not make fasting a test of spiritual maturity or think less of someone who chooses not to fast.
- Christians who fast should practice their fasting privately, not to impress others (Mt 6:16–18).

premillennialism

meanings they convey certainly are. The Lord rejoiced in his people as a bridegroom rejoiced in his bride. What a picture of God's love!

Judgment of the nations (63:1–6)

God's judgment would precede his final salvation. He would deal with sin wherever he found it. His coming from Edom may indicate that Edom posed a special problem for God's people at that time. The people would hear Isaiah's prophecy and know God would deal with every enemy.

Prayer for God's intervention (63:7–64:12)

Isaiah's prayer for God's intervention emphasized the people's absolute dependence on God. When we pray, we confess our need for God to reach into our lives and touch them in some way. The prophet knew God's people had failed him in many ways. Yet he also knew hope of forgiveness lay within their reach if they only would repent. He pleaded for God to restore them. Do you regularly pray for God's people?

Blessing for God's servants (65:1–25)

Isaiah 65 described further blessing God's servants would receive in God's coming kingdom. Many had offended the Lord with their sin, and he would see that they received their just punishment. But God was going to create a new heavens and a new earth for his faithful ones (vv. 17–25). Joy, long life, and security would prevail in this new world.

Some interpreters suggest this passage refers to an earthly reign of Christ after he returns (**premillennialism**). Others believe we should understand it as denoting eternal life in heaven. However way we interpret these verses, we can see God has planned an incredible future for his children (1 Cor 2:9).

The ultimate conclusion (66:1–24)

Chapter 66 draws Isaiah's prophecies together into a grand conclusion. The

eunuchs
Torah
premillennialism

Key Terms

Deutero-Isaiah
Trito-Isaiah
Akitu festival

Summary

1. The proponents of the theory that Isaiah was written by more than one author give as support the time span of the material in Isaiah, the differences in subject matter and vocabulary in 1–39 and 40–66, and the mention of King Cyrus by name.

2. Proponents of the one-author view cite Jewish and Christian tradition, the possibility of predictive prophecy, and the use of Isaiah in the New Testament.

3. The themes found in Isaiah 40–66 are: God's people are in captivity for their sins, the captivity proves that God is God, and God will restore and redeem his people.

4. The suffering servant has been interpreted as Isaiah, Israel, or Jesus.

5. Isaiah's celebration of Judah's return included mention of Jerusalem's rebirth, the need for the people to trust in God, the sins of Israel, the call to true righteousness, and how God would deliver Israel.

6. Isaiah, like other prophets, predicted that one day, foreigners would become part of God's people.

7. Isaiah presented the climax of God's restoration by stating that it would include Zion's glorification, Zion's marriage to God, and the judgment of the nations. Isaiah's presentation included his prayer for God's intervention, a blessing for God's servant, and the conclusion that the restoration would be complete.

prophet began by describing God as a sovereign servant seeker (vv. 1–2). Even though he created the universe, he reached down in love to those who humbled themselves before him.

Isaiah described Jerusalem's amazing coming rebirth. The Lord would bring salvation in an instant! Again, the restoration would include people from all nations submitting themselves to God. The idea of

Study Questions

1. What are the arguments some interpreters have given to support the multiple-author view of the Book of Isaiah? What evidence have others used to support the single-author view?

2. How do the concepts of chapters 40 and 41 lay a foundation for the rest of the book? What key ideas occur there?

3. How does Isaiah 40–66 develop the motif of the Lord's servant? What characteristics best describe the servant?

4. Isaiah's words concerning Gentiles joining God's family suggest God intended Israel to bring spiritual light to them. What responsibility do you have personally in God's plan to reach the world?

Further Reading

Oswalt, John N. *The Book of Isaiah: Chapters 1–39.* New International Commentary on the Old Testament. Grand Rapids: Eerdmans, 1986. A solid thorough evangelical commentary for the advanced student.

———. *The Book of Isaiah: Chapters 40–66.* New International Commentary on the Old Testament. Grand Rapids: Eerdmans, 1998. A solid, thorough evangelical commentary for the advanced student.

Motyer, J. Alec. *The Prophecy of Isaiah: An Introduction and Commentary.* Downers Grove: InterVarsity, 1993. For the advanced student.

Webb, Barry G. *The Message of Isaiah: On Eagles' Wings.* Downers Grove: InterVarsity, 1996. Rich in application.

Wolf, Herbert M. *Interpreting Isaiah: The Suffering and Glory of the Messiah.* Grand Rapids: Zondervan, 1985. A college-level textbook that combines good scholarship and readability.

Youngblood, Ronald F. *The Book of Isaiah: An Introductory Commentary.* 2nd ed. Grand Rapids: Baker, 1993. A shorter survey.

Gentiles becoming part of God's people probably seemed odd to many Jews, but God fulfilled his words as the gospel of Christ reached the Gentiles (Eph 2:11–18).

The Book of Isaiah ends with a sobering warning. God has prepared a wonderful conclusion to history, but only those who belong to Christ through faith will enjoy it. The rest will experience God's wrath. Isaiah's warning reminds us that the Holy One of Israel calls each of us to holy living. Such a lifestyle comes only through the Lord's work in our lives.

27 Jeremiah 1–20
Struggling with God's Call

Outline

- **Outline**
- **Jeremiah's Background**
- **Jeremiah's Message**
  God Calls Jeremiah to Service (1:1–19)
  Jeremiah Describes Judah's Sad Condition (2:1–10:25)
  Jeremiah Wrestles with People and with God (11:1–20:18)

Objectives

After reading this chapter, you should be able to

- Outline the contents of Jeremiah 1–20
- Discuss Jeremiah's background
- Summarize the detail of Jeremiah's call to prophetic service
- Describe the situation in which Jeremiah found Jerusalem
- Compare idols with God as Jeremiah compared them

Do you ever face struggles in your Christian life? If you have not, you probably will at some point. Perhaps you will not understand why God allows you to experience a particularly difficult situation. Or maybe you will serve the Lord faithfully for many years, but suffer heartache because people do not want to listen to you. At times, you may feel resentment toward God for giving you such a task. You might even question whether God has called you at all.

The prophet Jeremiah's life illustrates how costly serving the Lord can be. As you study his life and message, try to discover what drove this prophet of Judah to continue God's work whatever the cost. Doing so will help you face whatever challenges the Lord sends your way.

Outline

Jeremiah's Background

Jeremiah 1:1 calls Jeremiah "the son of Hilkiah, one of the priests at Anathoth in the territory of Benjamin." Probably Jeremiah's father was not the Hilkiah who served as high priest and discovered the Book of the Law in the temple (2 Kgs 22:8). The high priest would almost certainly have lived in Jerusalem.

Jeremiah lived in Anathoth, three miles northeast of Jerusalem. Anathoth was one of forty-eight cities Joshua had given to the Levites (Jos 21:18). Some scholars suggest Jeremiah may have descended from Abiathar, from the line of Eli (1 Kgs 2:26–27). The prophet lived within sight of Jerusalem, and could walk there in about an hour.

As far as we know, Jeremiah never served as a priest. Priests began their service at age thirty (Nm 4:3), but Jeremiah was still a young man when the Lord called him to prophesy (Jer 1:6). In fact, some suggest Jeremiah may still have been a teenager! But Jeremiah's youth did not hinder God's purposes. God gave Jeremiah the strength to serve him. God also commanded Jeremiah not to marry and have children, for Judah's future contained only suffering (16:1–4).

As he took a stand for the Lord, Jeremiah experienced incredible opposition. He suffered beatings and public humiliation (20:1–6), and battled many false prophets (6:13–14; 28:1–17; 29:8–9). King Jehoiakim scorned his words, and even sought to kill him (36:21–23, 26). Zedekiah, Judah's last king, often sought Jeremiah's counsel, but then refused to obey it (37:17; 38:14–23). After Jerusalem's fall, a group of Judeans took Jeremiah to Egypt against his will (43:4–7).

At times, Jeremiah wondered why the Lord let him suffer so much. The prophet's complaints to God reveal how deeply Jeremiah struggled with the task God had given him (15:10, 15–18; 20:7–10, 14–18). They also show a man with a deep relationship to God, a man who knew he could trust God with his innermost thoughts and feelings. In spite of all the opposition, Jeremiah faithfully pursued his prophetic calling. By God's strength, he determined to complete all the Lord gave him to do.

Jeremiah prophesied during Judah's last forty years (627–587 B.C.). During Josiah's reign (640–609 B.C.), Judah experienced some religious renewal. But the kingdom suffered rapid spiritual decay after Josiah's death. Many people continued to trust in empty religious rituals, and believed God would bless Jerusalem no matter how they lived. God sent Jeremiah to warn the people to repent, but unfortunately, most did not listen.

In 626 B.C.—about the same time God called Jeremiah—NABOPOLASSAR established himself as king of Babylon. During his reign and the reign of his son Nebuchadnezzar, Babylon became the dominant power in the ancient Near East. Ultimately, God would use Babylon to judge Judah.

The Book of Jeremiah provides an account of Jeremiah's message and ministry. It describes Judah's last days, and shows why God finally judged his people as he did. It powerfully presents Jeremiah's message so later generations might avoid the same sins.

Baruch, son of Neriah, worked closely with Jeremiah, sometimes serving as his scribe (Jer 36:4–21). Many scholars believe Baruch helped to collect Jeremiah's prophecies into what we now know as the Book of Jeremiah.[2] Perhaps others also helped collect Jeremiah's words.

The Book of Jeremiah has much to teach us. Jeremiah's words faithfully proclaim God's message, and his life illustrates the deep commitment God expects and deserves from each of us.

Jeremiah's Message

God Calls Jeremiah to Service (1:1–19)

Jeremiah 1:1–3 reminds us that God called Jeremiah at a particular place and time. However, because Jeremiah brought God's message, the prophetic words continue to speak to us today.

The Lord called Jeremiah clearly and directly—"Before I formed you in the womb I knew you, before you were born I set you apart; I appointed you as a prophet to the nations" (v. 5). The verbs stress how God sovereignly prepared Jeremiah for prophetic service. First, God *knew* Jeremiah before Jeremiah's conception. Second, God *set apart* Jeremiah before Jeremiah's birth. Third, God *appointed* Jeremiah a prophet. God had

planned Jeremiah's ministry long before the prophet was even born!

Most Bible scholars believe Jeremiah was only sixteen to twenty-five years old when he received God's call. He therefore was astonished that God would choose him, and protested he was too young for the job! But God promised to be with him and protect him. He would equip Jeremiah to perform this great task. As believers today, we also might feel overwhelmed by God's call, but he has promised to provide the strength for us to do whatever he asks.

The Lord confirmed Jeremiah's call in three ways (vv. 9–19). First, the Lord touched Jeremiah's mouth, symbolically placing the divine word there. Second, God showed Jeremiah the branch of an almond tree. The almond tree's early blooming announced the coming of spring. The sign was also a play on words. The almond tree (Hebrew *šāqēd*) indicated God's watching (Hebrew *šōqēd*) over the fulfillment of his word. God's second promise thus assured Jeremiah God also would accomplish the rest of his word. Third, the Lord showed Jeremiah a boiling pot, symbolizing the disaster God would pour onto the land. Again, God confirmed he would protect and defend his prophet.

Jeremiah Describes Judah's Sad Condition (2:1–10:25)

A failing marriage (2:1–3:5)

Jeremiah called on the people of Jerusalem to remember the days of old when God had blessed them. How far they had strayed from their early devotion to him! Their ancestors soon forgot the Lord and followed other gods. Israel's leaders—priests, prophets, and rulers—all participated in the spiritual rebellion and ignored God's grace.

Jeremiah's generation had followed the bad example their ancestors set. They had committed two great evils (2:13). First, they had turned away from God, the source of all they had, "the spring of living water." Second, they had substituted idol worship for their relationship with God. Jeremiah compared their idols to broken cisterns that could hold no water. The Lord had freed his people to serve him, but they persisted in worshiping other nations' gods.

Jeremiah also likened the people's idolatry to harlotry. Judah was God's unfaithful wife, who defiled herself with other lovers. She strayed from the Lord—her true husband—to follow Baal. She had as many gods as she had cities (2:28)!

The people wanted the freedom to sin and still enjoy God's blessing. They ignored God's discipline and continued to chase after other gods. God withheld rain and brought other nations against Judah, but they persisted in their rebellion. The people rejected God's Law and oppressed the poor and innocent.

A story of two sisters (3:6–4:4)

Jeremiah likened Israel and Judah to two sisters. Israel acted wickedly, so the Lord judged her and sent her into exile. But Judah, Israel's sister, learned nothing at all from this, proving to be even more faithless than her unfortunate sister!

In spite of these severe words, God promised blessing would still come if his people repented. He commanded them to abandon their idols and to commit themselves totally to him. Repentance must come from deep within their hearts. Today, God still expects sincere commitments from his children. Half-hearted repentance and faith have no place in God's service.

Trouble from the north (4:5–6:30)

Jeremiah intensified his words of judgment. Judah's rulers would panic, unable to stop the disaster. The nation's sin had corrupted its heart. Its rebellion would bring God's judgment.

As Jeremiah described Judah's judgment, he felt God's anguish (4:19–22). The prophet loved his people and his country, and did not wish to see calamity. Yet, he admitted his people had no spiritual understanding. He shuddered as he pondered the extent of God's anger.

God challenged Jeremiah to find a single righteous person in Jerusalem (5:1). The people professed faith in the Lord, but they did not live according to his ways. Leaders and common people alike transgressed his laws and worshiped idols. Their stubborn hearts convinced them God would never judge them. God warned the people he would bring a foreign nation to judge their sin (5:18–19). They had worshiped the gods of other nations; soon, they would serve those gods *in a foreign land!*

Jeremiah expressed his frustration—no one would listen to his warnings (6:9–15)! Corruption pervaded the society. The leaders assured the people everything was fine, but everything was not fine. The people refused to follow God's commandments or listen to God's prophets. Judah stood at a spiritual crossroads. Would they choose the way of life, or the way of death?

Worthless public worship (7:1–8:3)

Bible scholars generally believe Jeremiah preached this message in 609 B.C. because of its close connections with 26:1–24.[3] As Jeremiah stood at the temple gate, he saw many worshipers pass by. They trusted in empty words to save them—"This is the temple of the Lord, the temple of the Lord, the temple of the Lord!" (7:4).

In 2 Samuel 7, God had established a covenant with David and promised to establish David's throne forever. David understood that God still demanded faithfulness from him and his sons (1 Kgs 2:3–4), but later generations did not. The people assumed David's descendants would rule forever, and God's blessing would rest on Jerusalem and the temple no matter how Judah lived. They overemphasized the Davidic covenant, and totally neglected the demands of the Mosaic covenant. God *had* to bless them, didn't he? After all, they were in *Jerusalem*, worshiping at the *temple!*

Jeremiah confronted the people's false hopes. How could they steal, murder, commit adultery, swear false oaths, and practice idolatry, and then come to the Lord's temple, say a few "magic words," and expect his blessing? They could not! Empty words would not save Jerusalem! Jeremiah challenged the people to show their faith by obeying God's commandments. When God saw changed hearts, he would bless the nation again.

Jeremiah challenged the people to consider the fate of Shiloh, the city that had once contained the tabernacle. The Lord brought judgment on Shiloh because of its wickedness (7:12), and he could and would do the same to Jerusalem. God did not have to have his house of worship in any particular city.

God instructed Jeremiah to stop pray-

The ruins of Shiloh. Jeremiah challenged the people to consider the fate of Shiloh, the city that had once contained the tabernacle.

ing for the people. Their evil had become unthinkable—they were even sacrificing their children to pagan gods! The Lord promised to bring judgment as terrible as their sin. He would turn their pagan shrines into places of slaughter, and feed their carcasses to the beasts of the field.

Many people today trust in their rituals for security. They think God will accept them because of their baptism, church attendance, faithful giving, or service to their church. But Jeremiah warns us that apart from faith, even important church activities are empty rituals. We must place our ultimate trust in the Lord, never in people or things.

Treachery, trouble, and tears (8:4–10:25)

The Lord marveled at Judah's wickedness. Common animals observed the laws God had given them, but God's people did not. Rather, they acted as if they had never even *heard* of God's laws! Prophets and priests pursued their own gain while telling the common people peace and prosperity would last forever.

Jeremiah shared God's agony over the people's lack of understanding. What more could the Lord do? What would it take to heal Zion? Did anyone realize the reason for Judah's calamity? Again, the prophet drove home the truth—the people had transgressed God's Law, and thus were experiencing adversity in the form of famine and drought. If they did not turn back to God, he would scatter them among the nations. Jeremiah called on Judah to embrace God's wisdom, for only then would the nation have reason to boast.

Jeremiah powerfully contrasted Judah's idols with the Lord God. Idols were the work of people's hands. Workers cut down trees and carved them into the proper shape. They secured the idols so they stood upright. Metalworkers decorated the idols with silver, gold, and precious stones. But idols had no power to do anything. In contrast, the Lord God ruled as King of the nations. He created the world and sustained it by his wisdom and power. One day, idols would perish, but God would rule forever.

Jeremiah mourned Judah's sad spiritual state (10:17–25). No one could heal Judah's wounds. An enemy would soon turn the nation into desolate wasteland.

Jeremiah Wrestles with People and with God (11:1–20:18)

Jeremiah 11–20 contains what many interpreters call "Jeremiah's confessions." Many of the prophet's personal prayers and complaints to God occur within these chapters (11:18–20; 12:1–6; 15:10–21; 17:14–18; 18:18–23; 20:7–18). Jeremiah often struggled with people who did not want to hear his words, and he received a lot of mocking and persecution. But sometimes

Jeremiah struggled with God. Did not the Lord see his pain? Why did Jeremiah have to suffer so much and see so few positive results? Jeremiah 11–20 highlights many of Jeremiah's struggles as he sought to understand his place in God's purpose.

Coping with conspiracies (11:1–12:17)

God had confirmed his covenant with Israel when he led the people out of Egypt, through the wilderness, and into the land he had promised to their ancestors. But God's people often rebelled against his authority. The Lord had endured many generations of disobedience. He warned that he would not tolerate much more, but Judah continued the sins of earlier generations. Again, God instructed Jeremiah not to pray for the people. He would forgive them only if they truly repented.

Jeremiah then learned his enemies were plotting against him (11:18–23). People from Anathoth, his hometown, had commanded him not to prophesy any longer. Now, they were trying to silence him permanently! But the Lord assured Jeremiah he would deal with the situation. The prophet's enemies would not prevail.

Jeremiah also pondered God's justice—why did the wicked prosper? They did not honor God at all, yet they lived lives of relative ease. Jeremiah asked God to punish them severely, but God warned him not to get tired and discouraged yet. Jeremiah's ministry was just beginning!

Three signs of judgment (13:1–27)

God often commanded his prophets to perform symbolic actions that had spiritual applications for his people. He instructed Jeremiah to purchase a linen waistband and hide it in some rocks by the River. The Hebrew may refer to the Euphrates hundreds of miles away or perhaps to FARAH, a place a few miles from Anathoth (Jos 18:23).[4] After some time, God commanded Jeremiah to retrieve the waistband. When the prophet did so, he found the waistband ruined from prolonged exposure to nature's elements.

The Lord said his people were just like the waistband. He had stayed close to them, but they strayed from him and followed other gods. They exposed their lives to pagan influences, and those influences soon made them spiritually worthless.

Many people today profess to know Christ, but their lives reflect many ideas or practices that oppose Christianity. If we allow unchristian attitudes and behaviors into our lives, our Christian faith will suffer. The Lord calls us to submit our entire lives to him and focus on things that please him (Phil 4:8; Col 3:1–3).

Jeremiah then commanded the people to fill their jugs with wine. Just as wine could lead to drunkenness, so the Lord was bringing spiritual drunkenness on Judah. God would show his people no compassion as they suffered sin's consequences.

Jeremiah pleaded with the people to heed God's warning. Everyone would experience humiliation—even the rulers. But sin had hardened the people's hearts. They could not and would not change their sinful condition.

Judah's desperate situation (14:1–17:27)

The Lord sent a drought to turn the people back to him. The ground cracked, and water became so scarce that animals deserted their young. Jeremiah prayed for the people, but God told him not to do so. The Lord needed to deal severely with them so they would understand how seriously he took their sin. Indeed, Jeremiah himself began to wonder if God had rejected Judah forever (14:17–22).

False prophets formed a large part of Judah's problem (14:13–16). They went about telling the people the Lord would bring lasting peace, so no one needed to fear famine or war. The Lord promised to punish these false prophets. They would die by famine and sword—the very judgments they told the people would never come!

God told Jeremiah interceding for the people was pointless. He would not forgive Judah even if Moses and Samuel stood before him in prayer (15:1)! The Lord spelled out the people's only choices—death, sword, famine, or captivity. King Manasseh (697–642 B.C.), Hezekiah's son, had filled Judah with idolatry and social injustice. The evil influences he established lasted long into the reigns of his successors. The Lord declared the time had come to deal with Judah's sins.

Jeremiah lamented his situation—every-

our standards, but should point others to Christ's standards by our words and examples.

God instructed Jeremiah not to marry and raise a family, for terrible times were coming (16:1–9). God also told him not to mourn the dead, for they died as punishment for their sin. The Lord would send Judah's survivors into exile. He promised to regather them someday, but punishment had to come first.

Meanwhile, Judah's sin continued (17:1–18). The people trusted in themselves instead of God. Jeremiah warned them only God could give their lives meaning and purpose. Their healing needed to come from the God they had forsaken.

The Lord called his people to honor the Sabbath with rest and worship, and promised blessing if they did (17:19–27). David's descendants would rule forever, and temple worship would prosper. Today, God has given us one day out of seven to set aside especially for worship and rest. Does the way you spend the Lord's day honor him?

A lesson from the potter's house (18:1–19:15)

The Lord sent Jeremiah to the potter's house and gave his prophet a message to preach there (18:1–12). As the potter worked, he could easily refashion a clay vessel that developed a defect. He simply pressed the clay back into a lump and refashioned it according to his purpose.

The potter's work illustrated a valuable spiritual principle. As the potter fashioned clay, so the Lord shaped the nations according to his sovereign purpose. If God decreed judgment against an evil nation but the nation repented, God might cancel the judgment. But if God promised blessing to a nation and the nation turned against him, he might cancel the blessing. The people should never presume God would bless them in spite of their sinful lives. On the other hand, they would receive God's forgiveness if they truly repented.

The people rejected Jeremiah because they rejected God. Jeremiah knew his enemies planned evil against him. He asked God to protect him and to judge them for their sin. Sometimes people will shun us, too, when we share God's message with them. We should remember they are re-

An eastern potter. The Lord sent Jeremiah to the potter's house and gave him a message to preach there (18:1–12).

one cursed him for speaking God's word (15:10)! He also asked God to remember his faithful service (15:15–18). The prophet followed God's commandments and faithfully shared the messages God gave him. Now, he bluntly challenged God's character. Had the Lord forgotten him? Jeremiah had not understood how difficult serving the Lord might be!

The Lord reassured his struggling servant by repeating words from Jeremiah's call (15:19–21; see 1:17–19). He would strengthen Jeremiah to continue prophesying, and Jeremiah's enemies would not prevail. God also reminded Jeremiah to maintain a godly example. The prophet must not sink to the people's spiritual level, but strive to raise theirs to his.

Peer pressure often tempts us to compromise our Christian principles in some way. When we face such challenges, we need to remember God has called us to holiness (1 Pt 1:15). We dare not lower

Pluralism and the Christian

Judah's borders touched several other kingdoms, each with its own religious ideas. Judah soon adopted many practices from those kingdoms and began to worship their gods. Judah became a pluralistic society, holding conflicting religious views side by side.

Today's world displays many similarities with ancient Judah. Numerous non-Christian faiths exist, and some groups encourage us to join them. What should our response be to such pluralism?

First, Christians should try to impact society for Jesus Christ. Jesus said we should light our world as we shine forth with the truth (Mt 5:14–16). We should try to win others to faith in Christ and help them grow in their faith. We also should try to promote Christian principles of social justice so our society reflects a Christian perspective as much as possible.

Second, Christians should avoid spiritual compromise with other faiths. We must respect other people's right to believe as they wish, but we dare not dilute our Christian faith.

Israel began by accommodating idolatry, and soon, the people were practicing it themselves. Believers must strive to impact the world for Christ, and at the same time avoid compromising the truth of the gospel.

jecting God more than they are rejecting us (Mt 5:11–12). Jesus commanded us to love our enemies and pray for them (Mt 5:43–47), leaving their judgment in God's hands.

Jeremiah took an earthenware jar from the potter's house to the HINNOM VALLEY south of Jerusalem (19:1–2). He warned Judah calamity would come, for the people had abandoned the Lord to worship idols. They shed innocent blood, and even sacrificed some of their children to Baal!

Jeremiah described the terrible things that would occur when invading armies besieged Jerusalem. People would run out of food and turn to cannibalism. Corpses

Summary

1. Jeremiah of Anathoth was the son of a priest, Hilkiah. He was quite young when he began his service as a prophet during the last forty years of Judah.

2. The people of Jerusalem had fallen into a sinful condition because they had turned away from God and had substituted idol worship for their relationship with God.

3. God expects his people to serve him faithfully.

4. Because the people of Judah had turned from God, they were experiencing adversity and faced being scattered among the nations.

5. When Judah's situation was desperate, God showed no sympathy and told Jeremiah not to pray for Judah because it would not be effective.

6. Jeremiah suffered personally as he tried to do what God commanded amidst pressure from the people.

Study Questions

1. What does the Book of Jeremiah reveal about the prophet Jeremiah himself? Even when Jeremiah suffered opposition, was he still in the center of God's will for his life? Does God sometimes call his people to suffer today for his cause?

2. How did the people defend their actions during Judah's last days? Why did Jeremiah have such a hard time convincing them of their sin?

3. Do you think Jeremiah had a right to complain to God so much? How do you think God used Jeremiah's complaints in the prophet's life?

4. What lessons did Jeremiah learn from the potter's house?

5. Jeremiah complained, but he also trusted. When you pour out your heart to God, will you trust him as well when he answers?

Key Person/Places

Nabopolassar
Farah
Hinnom Valley

would lie everywhere and become food for wild animals. At the end of his message, Jeremiah smashed the jar, thus symbolizing Jerusalem's complete and irreversible destruction. The Hinnom Valley would become the valley of slaughter for all who placed their trust in idols.

Persecution leads to despair (20:1–18)

Pashhur the priest reacted angrily to Jeremiah's words against Judah and Jerusalem. He had the prophet beaten, and locked him in the public stocks until the next day. But after Jeremiah was released, he pronounced judgment against Pashhur. God would give the priest a new name—Magor-Missabib, which means "terror on every side"! Pashhur, along with his family and friends, would experience the horror of Jerusalem's siege. The city would fall, and Pashhur would die in captivity.

Such experiences forced Jeremiah into a deep personal struggle (vv. 7–13). If he spoke God's word, people persecuted him. If he remained silent, God's word became

Further Reading

Brueggemann, Walter. *To Pluck Up, To Tear Down: A Commentary on the Book of Jeremiah 1–25.* International Theological Commentary. Grand Rapids/Edinburgh: Eerdmans/Handsel, 1988. Rich in theological exposition and application.

Harrison, R. K. *Jeremiah and Lamentations: An Introduction and Commentary.* Tyndale Old Testament Commentary. Downers Grove: InterVarsity, 1973. Standard college-level commentary.

Thompson, J. A. *The Book of Jeremiah.* New International Commentary on the Old Testament. Grand Rapids: Eerdmans, 1980. For the more serious student.

a fire in his bones that he simply could not stifle. He *had* to preach it, whatever the cost.

Jeremiah's suffering sometimes drove him to despair (vv. 14–18). Why did the Lord make him endure so much? Every day brought more trouble and sorrow. Jeremiah cursed the day of his birth and wished he had died in his mother's womb.

Maybe at some point in your life, you have felt as discouraged as Jeremiah. Maybe you even feel this way now. Jeremiah's life demonstrates that biblical faith offers no guarantees of easy living. The Lord may call us to serve him in ways that stretch us to the limit, where life's struggles sometimes seem overwhelming and where God seems to ignore our prayers. But Jeremiah pressed on, and so must we. He did not understand God's ways, but he knew that somehow he could keep trusting the Lord in every situation. The Lord has not promised to show us the reason for everything we encounter, but he has promised to equip us for whatever he calls us to do and to give us the strength to complete it (Phil 1:6).

28 Jeremiah 21–52 and Lamentations

Dealing with Disaster

Objectives

After reading this chapter, you should be able to

- Outline chapters 21–52 of Jeremiah
- Describe how Jeremiah challenged the rulers and prophets
- Explain why Jeremiah 30–33 is often called "The Book of Comfort"
- Compare God's covenant with Moses with the new covenant with his people
- List the incidents of disobedience leading to the fall of Jerusalem
- Name the nations to which Jeremiah spoke oracles in chapters 46–51
- Outline the Book of Lamentations
- Give examples of how acrostics are used in Lamentations
- Describe the results of the destruction of Jerusalem

In the previous chapter, we saw how Jeremiah faced many difficult challenges. He battled enemies who did not want to hear God's message and often suffered because he obeyed God's call. Jeremiah also struggled with God, wondering why God had given him such a frustrating task.

Jeremiah's struggles continued as Judah's sin brought God's judgment ever closer. The people firmly resisted the truth Jeremiah proclaimed, and eventually they paid a terrible price for their sin. Jeremiah, too, mourned Jerusalem's fall, because he had warned the people for forty years to no avail.

Outline

Jeremiah's Message Continues (21:1–52:34)

Jeremiah Challenges Rulers and Prophets (21:1–29:32)

Jeremiah rebukes rulers and governments (21:1–23:8)

As King Nebuchadnezzar of Babylon attacked Jerusalem, Zedekiah, Judah's last king, sent messengers to ask Jeremiah for guidance (21:1–2). Jeremiah replied that God himself was fighting against Judah! Those who surrendered to the Babylonians would live, but whoever remained in Jerusalem would die (21:8–9).

God promised to spare the city if the king and his leaders truly repented, but if they persisted in unbelief, God would destroy Jerusalem (22:2–5). The city would become a frightening object lesson to all who might consider opposing God.

Jeremiah told the people to mourn for Shallum (Jehoahaz), King Josiah's son (22:10–12). Jehoahaz ruled only three months before Pharaoh Necho deposed him and took him captive to Egypt (2 Kgs 23:31–34). The prophet then denounced Jehoiakim, Shallum's successor and another of Josiah's sons (22:13–23). Josiah had served the Lord faithfully, but Jehoiakim had not followed his father's righteous example! Jeremiah declared Jehoiakim would die a disgraceful death and receive a donkey's burial (22:19)!

Jehoiachin (Coniah), Jehoiakim's son, soon would suffer for his father's wickedness (22:24–30). Nebuchadnezzar took him to Babylon, where he spent thirty-seven years in prison (2 Kgs 24:10–15; 25:27–30).

Judah's other leaders also cared only for themselves, but God promised he would one day raise up a righteous leader who would establish justice in the land (23:5–6). Jesus Christ began to establish this kingdom at his first coming, and will complete the task when he comes again.

Jeremiah rebukes prophets and their audiences (23:9–40)

Jeremiah often battled false prophets. These men assured the people God would bless Judah forever, but their words did not come from the Lord. Some even spoke in the name of Baal and encouraged evildoers to continue their sin (vv. 13–14)! Even today, many people tolerate all kinds of evil rather than change their lifestyles.

Priests also acted corruptly and disgraced the temple. They claimed to speak God's truth, but really spoke lies. Jeremiah urged the people not to listen to the false priests and prophets who perverted God's word. The Lord would punish those who dared to speak falsely in his Name!

Jeremiah describes God's anger (24:1–25:38)

In 605 B.C., Nebuchadnezzar became king of Babylon. That same year, Jeremiah again warned the people trouble was coming (25:1–14). The Lord had prepared his instrument—Nebuchadnezzar! The Judeans would experience seventy years of exile, and only then could they hope for deliverance. God revealed for the first time how long his people would have to suffer in exile for their sin.

God had not forgotten the other nations either (25:15–38). He would deal with sin wherever he found it! Drinking God's cup symbolized receiving God's wrath (Ob 16;

Mt 26:39, 42). The nations would receive full punishment for their evil.

Eight years after this prophecy—in 597 B.C—Nebuchadnezzar took King Jehoiachin (Jeconiah) and many Judean officials prisoner to Babylon. He also placed Zedekiah, another of Josiah's sons, on Judah's throne, and gave Judah one more chance to submit to Babylon's rule. The Lord used that occasion to bring Jeremiah another prophetic message.

God showed Jeremiah two baskets of figs—one good, one bad (24:1–3). The good figs represented the exiles in Babylon, whom God would protect, bless, and one day restore. But the bad figs symbolized Zedekiah and those who remained in Jerusalem. This faithless group would die by sword, famine, and disease.

Jeremiah confronts the people (26:1–24)

As Jeremiah stood outside the temple, he challenged the worshipers to change their ways. How much more clearly could God state his concern? The Lord had destroyed Shiloh, a former tabernacle site, in judgment for Israel's evil. Jeremiah warned that Jerusalem would soon suffer the same fate.

Jeremiah's harsh words angered his hearers, and many screamed for his death. How *dare* he speak against Jerusalem and the temple? But Jeremiah stood firm, warning the people that if they killed him, they would have innocent blood on their hands.

Other people defended Jeremiah. He was only speaking God's message—just as a prophet was supposed to do! They recalled how Micah the prophet had spoken strong words against Jerusalem a century earlier, but no one had punished him. In fact, his words brought King Hezekiah and the people to repentance! If Micah had committed no crime, how could the people accuse Jeremiah?

Jeremiah wears a yoke (27:1–28:17)

At the beginning of Zedekiah's reign, God instructed Jeremiah to wear a yoke to symbolize Judah's future submission to Babylon. God would place all nations under Nebuchadnezzar's yoke; any nation that resisted would perish.

Jeremiah continued to confront false prophets, who insisted no disaster would come. He urged the king and his officials not to listen to them. Submission to Babylon would save lives, but if the people resisted, Nebuchadnezzar would destroy Jerusalem.

The prophet Hananiah was one such false prophet. In 594 B.C., he declared God would soon free the nations from Babylon's yoke (28:1–4). Jehoiachin and all the exiles would return within two years! In dramatic fashion, Hananiah seized Jeremiah's yoke and broke it, symbolizing God's breaking of Babylon's power.

But Hananiah spoke only his own wishes, not God's truth. He convinced many people to trust in a lie, a very serious lie, and for that he would pay with his life. Two months later, this false prophet was dead.

Jeremiah writes to the exiles (29:1–32)

Shortly after Jehoiachin's exile, Jeremiah sent a letter to the Judeans in Babylon. False prophets there were actually assuring the people exile would soon be over! But Jeremiah told the people to build homes, plant gardens, raise families, and pray for Babylon's welfare, for they were not leaving anytime soon. He restated God's timetable for exile (25:12)—seventy years!

Jeremiah named several false prophets who had led the people astray by claiming to speak for God. The Lord's death sentence on them would prove they were false prophets.

The Book of Comfort (30:1–33:26)

Bible scholars refer to Jeremiah 30–33 as "The Book of Comfort" or "The Book of Consolation."[1] Jeremiah's prophecies often contained strong words against God's sinful people; it seemed that God had given up on Judah. But the Book of Comfort proclaimed an exciting message—God had *not* cast aside his people! A glorious future would follow their judgment.

Israel's return to the land and to God (30:1–31:40)

God promised to restore his people from captivity. He told Jeremiah to write down the prophecy as a testimony. Other prophets also wrote down God's words so later generations could see his faithfulness (Hb 2:2–3).

Terrible times lay ahead for God's people. Apart from his intervention, they could not recover from their sin. The foreign gods in whom they trusted had proven worthless. Treaties with other nations also gained them nothing but problems.

Nevertheless, God loved his people and promised to save them. He would plunder the nations who plundered them, and raise his people to new heights of blessing. He also promised to restore David's line (30:9), a promise that awaits its ultimate fulfillment in Jesus Christ (Lk 1:32–33). God judged Assyria, Babylon, and other nations who oppressed his people, but the Bible also warns of a coming day when God will judge his enemies forever (Rv 20:11–15).

God was determined to honor his covenant with his people (31:3). He would turn their mourning and suffering into joy and celebration. As we face difficult circumstances—times that drive us to despair or grief—we need to remember God knows our pain. We should take our concerns to him in prayer, for he has promised to work in his children's lives according to his great purpose (Rom 8:28; Phil 2:13).

The nation felt the agony of exile—it had lost its children to enemy conquest (31:15). But God's stubborn love for his people would triumph over their tragedy! The Lord had appointed Jeremiah to proclaim words of judgment *and* blessing (1:10), but so far, the prophet had spoken mostly judgment. Now he declared that one day the Lord would pour out great blessing and revitalize the nation (31:28).

Jeremiah also reported God was making a new covenant with His people (31:31–34). After God led his people out of Egypt to Sinai, he confirmed his covenant with them, vowing to bless and guide them as they lived in faithful obedience to him. But in the centuries that followed, Israel broke the covenant many times despite God's faithfulness. Jeremiah promised this new covenant would be different.

Moses wrote the old covenant on scrolls and stone tablets (Dt 4:13; 29:20). As the people read it, they knew what God expected. But in the new covenant, God

A small field near Jerusalem. During the siege of Jerusalem, the Lord instructed Jeremiah to buy a field that Hanamel, the prophet's cousin, was selling.

would place his law in his people's hearts in a way he had not done in earlier times. God's Spirit would guide their lives from within them in a deep, new way.

Jeremiah was not saying teaching would be unnecessary under the new covenant (31:34), for God's people would still need to grow spiritually. But each person would know the Lord personally and enjoy direct access to him. Furthermore, God would forgive his people's sin—sin that formed a barrier between him and them. The Lord guaranteed his words by appealing to nature (31:35–37). The sun, moon, and stars all would change their courses before his promises would fail!

The New Testament declares Christ is the mediator of the new covenant (Heb 8:7–13), a covenant he established with his own blood (Lk 22:20). Through his death on the cross, Christ paid for sin once and for all (Heb 9:12), and his sacrifice brings God's forgiveness to all who place their faith in him (Rom 3:21–24). The Holy Spirit helps believers live according to God's will, and we enjoy direct access to God the Father through Christ (Rom 5:1–2; 8:3–4). Many people today think Christianity is a list of rules or a set of teachings, but the heart of our faith is a personal relationship with Jesus Christ (Jn 14:6).

Jeremiah's symbolic land purchase (32:1–44)

During Nebuchadnezzar's siege of Jerusalem, Jeremiah received an unusual request. Hanamel, the prophet's cousin, was selling a field, and the Lord instructed Jeremiah to buy it.

Jeremiah obeyed, but wondered what the Lord could possibly have in mind! For forty years, Jeremiah had proclaimed Jerusalem's downfall at the hands of Babylon. Why, then, was God telling him to buy Hanamel's field? Buying it was wasting money, for soon the Babylonians would own all of Judah! Had the Lord changed his mind about the calamity?

The Lord assured his bewildered spokesman all was going according to plan. In fact, he challenged Jeremiah to listen to his own prayer (vv. 17, 27)! The people *had* angered God, and he *would* judge them for all their wickedness. Nevertheless, the Lord intended Jeremiah's land purchase as a sign of hope. One day, Judean land would again have value! God's people would return and claim it again.

God's great future works (33:1–26)

The Lord had just given Jeremiah a command he did not understand (32:7). Now, he promised to show the people marvelous things they would not understand (33:2–3)! Judgment would come first, of course, but voices of joy and celebration would one day resound in the land again. Jeremiah reinforced his prophecy by repeating his earlier words (33:15–16; see 23:5–6). God would give his people a king—the Branch of David's line. Furthermore, the Lord promised to bless the priesthood. Corrupt kings and priests were to blame for much of the nation's depravity, but one day, these two offices would serve the Lord faithfully (33:17–18).

The New Testament declares that Jesus Christ fulfills both aspects of Jeremiah's prophecy. He currently intercedes for believers as our great High Priest (Heb 7:24–28), and one day will sit on David's throne (Lk 1:32–33) when he returns as King of kings (Rv 19:11–16).

The Failure of Jerusalem's Leadership (34:1–39:18)

God's people had often suffered from their leaders' bad examples. This trend continued during Jerusalem's last, desperate years, as the rulers led the nation into utter ruin.

The leadership does not keep its word (34:1–22)

As Nebuchadnezzar's siege began, Zedekiah faced desperate circumstances and initiated a half-hearted attempt to win God's favor. The king proclaimed the release of all Hebrew slaves in accordance with the Mosaic Law (Ex 21:2), but the people soon reversed the king's decree and took back their slaves.

Jeremiah proclaimed God's displeasure. The Lord would "release" his people to sword, pestilence, and famine! If they would not live in faithful obedience to the covenant, they would suffer the curses of the covenant.

The leadership has not learned obedience (35:1–19)

During Jehoiakim's days, Jeremiah gave his people an object lesson. He brought the Rechabites—one of Judah's clans—into the temple area, and commanded them to drink wine. But the Rechabites refused, for Jonadab, their ancestor, had instructed them to abstain from wine and live a nomadic lifestyle forever.

Jeremiah urged the people of Judah to learn from the Rechabites' example. These men faithfully obeyed their earthly father; why could not God's people obey their heavenly Father?

The leadership refuses to respect God's word (36:1–32)

God instructed Jeremiah to prepare a scroll that contained all the prophetic words Je-

remiah had received. Jeremiah dictated the words to Baruch, his scribe, who carefully copied them.

Baruch read the scroll to many of Judah's officials, who insisted Jehoiakim hear the words. But the king showed his utter contempt for God's words by cutting the scroll into pieces and casting them into the fire. Jehoiakim also ordered the arrest of Jeremiah and Baruch, but they had hidden before the officials took the scroll to the king.

Jehoiakim's defiance did not erase the truth of God's words. The king had dishonored God, and would die a dishonorable death (see also 22:18–19). Jeremiah prepared another scroll as a testimony to that generation and to future generations.

The leadership refuses to listen to God's prophet (37:1–38:28)

When Egypt's army entered the land to stop the Babylonians' advance, the Babylonian army temporarily lifted the siege from Jerusalem. Zedekiah sent messengers to Jeremiah requesting prayer for the city, but Jeremiah assured the king no mercy was coming. Egypt's army would return home, and Nebuchadnezzar would return to Jerusalem!

When Jeremiah tried to go to Benjamin on business, he was accused of desertion and arrested. Zedekiah summoned him and asked for a message from the Lord. Jeremiah replied that the Lord had spoken—Zedekiah would soon face captivity in Babylon! The prophet also complained to the king—why had the king put him in prison? Many false prophets had announced Babylon would never come against Jerusalem. Now, only the true prophet remained; the rest had scattered!

Jeremiah's dialogues with Zedekiah reveal the king's lack of courage. Zedekiah seemed to believe the prophet's words, but would not follow them. He met secretly with Jeremiah and asked his counsel, but Jeremiah expressed only frustration—the king was not going to listen anyway! The prophet insisted Zedekiah's only hope was surrender, but the king feared reprisal from his own citizens. Consequently, Zedekiah took no action, and Jeremiah remained a prisoner of the king until Jerusalem fell.

As we share our faith, we will also find

The Assyrian forces advance on Lachish; from an Assyrian relief.

those who, like Zedekiah, are willing to listen, but hesitate to act on our words. Others, like Jehoiakim, may oppose us directly. In such situations, we cannot compromise the truth, but must remain patient. Instead of arguing and fighting, we should pray the Lord will lead these people to repentance (2 Tm 2:24–26).

Jerusalem pays a tragic price (39:1–18)

The terrible hour Jeremiah had prophesied finally came. The Babylonians breached Jerusalem's walls and captured the city. Zedekiah and his officials tried to flee, but Babylonian forces captured them and brought Judah's king to face his conqueror.

Nebuchadnezzar showed no mercy, blinding Zedekiah and leading him in chains to Babylon. The last thing Zedekiah ever saw was the death of his sons. Nebuzaradan, captain of the guard, oversaw Jerusalem's destruction. Everything in which God's people had trusted lay in smoldering ruins.

Nebuchadnezzar allowed Judah's poor people to remain in the land, since the poor offered little threat of revolt. Jeremiah received his freedom, and chose to stay in Judah among the poor. Imagine how the prophet felt when he saw all his prophetic words come true! He had warned God's people for forty years; now it was too late.

Jerusalem after Its Fall (40:1–45:5)

Trouble from within (40:1–41:18)

Nebuchadnezzar appointed Gedaliah, the son of a Judean official (26:24; 40:5), governor of Judah. Gedaliah urged the people to stay in the land and serve Babylon faithfully.

Judean officials warned Gedaliah that enemies threatened his life, but Gedaliah did not believe their warnings. Soon, he paid with his life. Ishmael, a member of the royal house, struck him down, and he and his men fled to Ammon, taking many captives with them. Judean forces rescued the captives, but Ishmael escaped.

Trouble in Egypt (42:1–43:13)

Facing the prospect of real trouble from Babylon, the people sought Jeremiah's advice. They even promised to do whatever the Lord commanded. But when Jeremiah told them God wanted them to stay in the land, they rejected his counsel! Despite Jeremiah's warnings that God would judge them for doing so, a large group fled to Egypt, taking Jeremiah and Baruch with them.

Even in Egypt, Jeremiah continued prophesying. God would use Babylon to judge Egypt, too, and when he did, the Jews living in Egypt would experience conquest's horrors again.

Failure to learn from history (44:1–45:5)

Jeremiah challenged the Judeans to learn from the past. For generations, God had endured their idolatry and rebellion, and finally had cast them into exile. Jeremiah warned his hearers idolatry in Egypt would bring the same bitter consequences. Nebuchadnezzar would visit Egypt just as surely as he had visited Judah!

But Jeremiah's audience interpreted the historical evidence differently. They believed listening to Jeremiah had brought their trouble, and vowed to continue sacrificing to their idols in Egypt. Even today, many people deny God's truth and continue in their rebellion.

Oracles about the Nations (46:1–51:64)

Like many other prophets, Jeremiah spoke prophecies about other nations. God's power did not end at Judah's borders. He controlled all nations, and would also judge their sin.

Egypt (46:1–28)

In 605 B.C., as Babylon's army pushed west, Egypt moved northward into Syria in an effort to stop the invader. At Carchemish, Nebuchadnezzar's forces won a decisive victory and established Babylon as the dominant power in the ancient world. Jeremiah used that occasion to announce Egypt's judgment. Egypt would survive, but only after feeling God's wrath.

God vowed to use Nebuchadnezzar to strike Egypt. For centuries, Egypt's location had provided it a certain amount of natural security. Mesopotamian armies had to travel a long way and fight many battles before arriving there. But this time, Egypt would not escape. The Lord would dash the hopes of those who trusted in Pharaoh and Egypt's gods.

The Babylonian Chronicle, an ancient historical record, reports that Nebuchadnezzar invaded Egypt in 601 B.C.[2] Both sides suffered heavy losses.

Philistia (47:1–7)

The Philistines also suffered God's wrath. Jeremiah's words about Gaza may refer to Necho's campaign into Judah in 609 B.C.

when he killed Josiah (2 Kgs 23:29–30), his campaign in 601 B.C. on the way to meet Nebuchadnezzar, or perhaps to a later attack by Hophra (588–568 B.C.) around the time of Jerusalem's fall (Jer 37:5).[3] Perhaps God used both Babylonian and Egyptian forces to judge Philistia.

Moab (48:1–47)

The Moabites descended from Lot, Abraham's nephew (Gn 19:36–37), and lived east of the Dead Sea. Pride lay at the heart of Moab's problems, perhaps because the country had faced little serious hostility from major powers (48:7, 11, 29–30). Nebuchadnezzar conquered Moab and its neighbor Ammon sometime after Jerusalem fell. Josephus, the Jewish historian, suggests the year 582 B.C.[4]

Jeremiah's detailed listing of Moab's cities suggests the judgment was extensive. Even Chemosh, chief god of the Moabites, went into exile with those who worshiped him! Nevertheless, the Lord held out some hope for Moab's restoration (48:47), perhaps during the messianic age.

Ammon (49:1–6)

The Ammonites also descended from Lot (Gn 19:36, 38) and lived east of the Jordan. They often fought with God's people and treated them cruelly (1 Sm 11:1–2; 2 Sm 10:1–4; Am 1:13). God announced he would humble their pride, too, though Jeremiah also expressed some hope for their restoration.

Edom (49:7–22)

The Edomites descended from Esau, Jacob's brother (Gn 36:1), and became a bitter enemy (Am 1:11–12; Ob 10–14). Using words similar to the prophet Obadiah's (cf. Jer 49:9, 14–16 and Ob 1:1–5),[5] Jeremiah denounced Edom's pride and promised complete destruction, comparable to that of Sodom and Gomorrah.

Edom probably fell to Babylon shortly after Judah (Jer 25:9, 21; Mal 1:3). Edom's western territory became the province of Idumea during Roman times, and the Edomites soon lost their national identity.

Damascus (49:23–27)

Damascus and the surrounding Aramean city-states had suffered under the As-

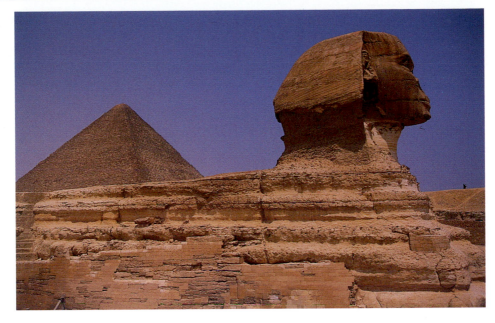

The sphinx, Cairo. Like many other prophets, Jeremiah spoke prophecies about other nations, including Egypt.

syrian conquests in the late eighth century. Nebuchadnezzar also subdued them around 605 B.C.[6] Days of joy and celebration became days of panic, death, and destruction.

Kedar and Hazor (49:28–33)

Jeremiah also mentioned these two Arab tribes from east of the Jordan.[7] Perhaps their raids on Judah's territory made a special prophecy about them necessary! God promised to overthrow them, and wild animals would take over their land.

Elam (49:34–39)

Elam lay east of Babylon, and rarely figured in biblical events, though it occasionally became a significant power in Mesopotamia. Nevertheless, Elam did not lie outside of God's control. The Lord's fierce anger would devour the nation, though he also promised to restore them one day.

Babylon (50:1–51:64)

Jeremiah saved Babylon's judgment for last. A northern nation would utterly vanquish this rebellious kingdom. Bel (or Marduk), Babylon's chief god, would be shown powerless. God wanted all the world to see who *really* controlled the nations!

God warned his people to flee Babylon. Terrible times were coming and the city would become plunder. Babylon rejoiced because it had conquered the world, but the Lord would show the temporary nature of humanity's power. He called the nations to attack Babylon and retrieve their share of the spoils.

Jeremiah described the Lord as "the Holy One of Israel" (50:29) and "the LORD of hosts" (50:34), stressing God's awesome power. The Lord despised human arrogance, and humbled those who thought themselves wise and powerful. Political leaders, warriors, and priests would all perish from the land. Jeremiah compared Babylon's destruction to the destruction of Sodom and Gomorrah (50:40). Only wild animals would live near its ruins!

Babylon thought itself great, but it was only fulfilling God's purpose. The Lord had used Babylon to judge his people and the other nations, but now, it was Babylon's turn to face God's judgment (cf. 6:22–23 and 50:41–42). They would drink the cup of God's wrath, and the Lord had a *large* cup for them! Jeremiah mentioned the Medes (51:11), who, along with the Persians, would soon bring Babylon's dominion to an end.

Jeremiah commissioned Seriah, a Judean official, to take these prophetic words to Babylon and read them there. Throwing the scroll into the Euphrates graphically portrayed Babylon's ultimate

Ancient Near Eastern Laments

Other ancient peoples also composed laments to mourn disasters. One example is the Lamentation over the Destruction of Ur, composed during the early second millennium B.C.:

To Anu the water of my eye verily I poured; to Enlil I in person verily made supplication. "Let not my city be destroyed," verily I said unto them; "Let not Ur be destroyed," verily I said unto them. . . . The utter destruction of Ur verily they directed; that its people be killed, as its fate verily they decreed. . . . Enlil brings Gibil to his aid. The great storm of heaven he called; the people groan. The great storm howls above; the people groan. The land-annihilating storm roars below; the people groan. The evil wind, like the rushing torrent, cannot be restrained. (ANET, 458)

In general, laments from the ancient world parallel Lamentations in that the peoples mourn the destruction of their cities and ascribe the destruction to a god or group of gods. However, the strong moral tone of Lamentations makes it unique. The writer describes God as bringing judgment because of the people's covenant violation, and calls the nation to repentance. Other ancient laments lack such a theme.

fate—it would sink and not rise again. In 539 B.C., the Lord used Cyrus the Persian to end Babylon's world domination. No nation could thwart God's ultimate purposes.

Jerusalem's Fall Revisited (52:1–34)

Jeremiah closed his book with a final reminder of the horrors of Jerusalem's fall. The chapter closely parallels Jeremiah 39, but gives a bit more detail regarding the aftermath of Jerusalem's destruction. Nevertheless, the book closes on a note of hope. When Evil-merodach, Nebuchadnezzar's successor, came to power, he released King Jehoiachin from prison (2 Kgs 25:27–30), and Jehoiachin ate at the king's table regularly. Babylonian cuneiform records have even confirmed Jehoiachin's regular ra-

tion.[8] Someday, God would bring all his people home.

The Book of Jeremiah stands as a great monument to God's work through one man's faithful life. The prophet Jeremiah bravely faced terrible and horrifying circumstances, even though he saw little positive response to anything he said or did. He knew that somehow, God was using him, and his life displayed the faith God desires his children to have.

The Lord also calls us to submit to his purposes, even when we do not fully understand them and even when they bring us great heartache. In such times, we may cling to his promise—God has a great future in store for His people (Jer 29:11).

Lamentations: A Cry of Agony

The Book of Lamentations is not an easy book to read. In it we hear the tragic cries of a people experiencing the horrors of war, humiliation, and exile. On a spiritual level, the author ponders God's relationship with his exiled people. He even wonders aloud whether God has finally cast his people aside.

Outline

    I. **Jerusalem's Lament** (1:1–22)

    II. **Jerusalem's Angry God** (2:1–22)

    III. **Judah's Lament** (3:1–66)

    IV. **Judah's Utter Ruin** (4:1–22)

    V. **Judah's Plea** (5:1–22)

The Background of Lamentations

Scholars differ over the authorship of Lamentations.[9] The title "The Lamentations of Jeremiah" appears in many Bibles, reflecting early Jewish and Christian tradition. Furthermore, we know Jeremiah wrote other laments (2 Chr 35:25) and that he witnessed Jerusalem's fall. Lamentations and Jeremiah also contain many similar themes, and these facts together point to Jeremiah as the author.

Some scholars, however, have suggested

Summary

1. Jeremiah challenged the rulers and false prophets by rebuking the rulers and the government, by rebuking the false prophets and their audiences, by describing God's anger, by confronting the people about their behavior, by wearing a yoke, and by writing to the Judeans in exile in Babylon.

2. God promised to spare Jerusalem if the king and his leaders truly repented.

3. The yoke God instructed Jeremiah to wear symbolized Judah's submission to Nebuchadnezzar.

4. God had not forgotten his people, in spite of their sin.

5. God promised that he would make a new covenant with his people.

6. Jeremiah's land purchase pointed to God's coming restoration of the land.

7. Jesus will one day fulfill Jeremiah's prophecy by ruling as a good king and a faithful high priest.

8. The Judeans in Egypt placed blame for their captivity on Jeremiah rather than on their own sin and continued to worship idols.

9. The nations to which Jeremiah spoke oracles included Egypt, Philistia, Moab, Ammon, Edom, Damascus, Kedar, Hazar, Elam, and Babylon.

10. The author of the Book of Lamentations used acrostics as a literary device.

11. The author of Lamentations is in great sorrow because of the total devastation of Jerusalem.

---

acrostics

Jeremiah did not write the book. They believe the writing styles of Lamentations and Jeremiah are too different. Furthermore, the book does not specifically name Jeremiah as its author.

The Book of Lamentations contains a series of **acrostics**, or alphabetic poems. The Hebrew alphabet has twenty-two letters, and each letter begins a verse. Lamentations 1:1 begins with *aleph*, the first letter of the Hebrew alphabet. Lamentations 1:2 begins with *beth,* the second letter, and so on throughout the chapter. Chapters 1, 2, and 4 follow this pattern. Chapter 3 has sixty-six verses—twenty-two groups of three. There, each letter begins three verses. Chapter 5 is not an acrostic, though it, too, has twenty-two verses.

Whoever wrote Lamentations probably wrote it shortly after 587 B.C. The book reflects the heartache of someone who still anguished over the vivid scenes surrounding Jerusalem's fall.

The Message of Lamentations

Jerusalem's lament (1:1–22)

Three contrasts describe Jerusalem's sorrow. First, the city that once stood full of people now sat alone. Second, the community that had enjoyed greatness now experienced the grief of a widow. Third, the princess of cities had become a lowly slave. Jerusalem wept bitterly, but no one comforted her.

God had finally dealt with the city's uncleanness, and she called to others to see her pain. God had laid a trap for his people and judged their wicked leaders. Zion's neighbors gave her no comfort, but rather, rejoiced at her fall! But despite her distress, Jerusalem did not blame God. Rather, she asked God to see her sorrow and punish those who mocked her.

Jerusalem's angry God (2:1–22)

God showed his people no mercy, demolishing everything in which Judah had trusted—fortresses and palace, temple

? Study Questions

1. Describe King Zedekiah's relationship with Jeremiah. Do you think Zedekiah really believed Jeremiah? Why or why not?

2. Identify Judah's last five kings and give a brief appraisal of each one's reign.

3. Why did false prophets pose such a problem for God's people?

4. Describe the role of the Book of Comfort (chapters 30–33) in the Book of Jeremiah. How was Jeremiah's prophecy of the new covenant fulfilled in Jesus Christ?

5. Why do you think the people refused to listen to Jeremiah even after Jerusalem fell?

6. When was the Book of Lamentations written? Since God had judged his people so severely, did the people have any hope of a future?

and sacrifices. The Lord also brought judgment against the priests and prophets who had led the people astray. Religious festivals ceased, and people everywhere mourned.

The author wept as he saw Jerusalem's suffering. Little ones starved to death in their mothers' arms while enemies mocked the city's downfall. The dead became food for the living due to the extreme food shortage! Jerusalem's fall meant God had fulfilled his word, for the people had failed to heed his persistent warnings. The prophet challenged the people to pray for God's compassion.

Judah's lament (3:1–66)

The author shared the people's agony. God had cut off any path to relief and would not listen to his people's prayers. The people had become a laughingstock to the world as God's fierce judgment overtook them.

At the same time, the people's only hope for salvation and restoration lay in the God who had fiercely judged them! His discipline would strengthen them, and would not last forever. His faithfulness was great! All needed to confess their sin and return to the Lord. The author also asked the Lord to deal with Judah's enemies. They would receive the penalty for their sins, too.

Further Reading

Brueggemann, Walter. *To Build, To Plant: A Commentary on Jeremiah 26–52.* International Theological Commentary. Grand Rapids/Edinburgh: Eerdmans/Handsel, 1991. Rich in theological exposition and application.

Harrison, R. K. *Jeremiah and Lamentations: An Introduction and Commentary.* Tyndale Old Testament Commentary. Downers Grove: InterVarsity, 1973. Standard college-level commentary.

Huey, F. B., Jr. *Jeremiah, Lamentations.* New American Commentary 16. Nashville: Broadman, 1993. A solid commentary rich in biblical exegesis and exposition.

Kaiser, Walter C., Jr. *A Biblical Approach to Personal Suffering.* Chicago: Moody, 1982. A short survey with many devotional thoughts.

Thompson, J. A. *The Book of Jeremiah.* New International Commentary on the Old Testament. Grand Rapids: Eerdmans, 1980. For the more serious student.

Judah's utter ruin (4:1–22)

The siege of Jerusalem brought many horrors of war. People everywhere slowly died of starvation, then became food for others! Even the rich lost everything in a city that thought it would stand forever.

Jerusalem had tolerated social injustice too long. Even prophets and priests mistreated the righteous for their own personal gain. The people hoped their king would save them, but he could not. Judah consoled herself a little with the knowledge that one day God would judge her enemies, too.

Judah's plea (5:1–22)

The people begged God to have compassion on them. Foreigners controlled their nation, and they had to work hard just to have enough to survive. Many had died in battle or starved. The survivors had suffered physical and emotional abuse. Mount Zion, God's chosen temple site, lay in ruins.

The people asked God to restore them as he had in the past, but behind their petition loomed a frightening question. Had God abandoned them forever?

29 Ezekiel 1–24
Rough Days Are Coming!

Outline

Objectives

**After reading this chapter,
you should be able to**

- Outline the basic contents of Ezekiel 1–24
- Apply the events of Ezekiel's commission to your own life
- Describe the four symbolic acts of Ezekiel that showed how seriously God takes sin
- List the sinful acts Ezekiel was shown by God
- Describe the events preceding the destruction of Jerusalem

A human-headed winged bull from the entrance to the palace at Calah, Nineveh.

The Book of Jeremiah portrays the incredible discouragement Jeremiah often faced as he served God. He proclaimed God's message to Judah for forty years but saw little if any response. Nevertheless, he diligently pressed on to accomplish the task God gave him.

The prophet Ezekiel faced rough days, too, and like Jeremiah, he knew even worse were coming. As he spoke to Judeans already in exile in Babylon, Ezekiel warned them of God's impending judgment and urged them to repent. But tragically, the people failed to realize the depth of their depravity. Soon, their fellow Judeans who still lived in Jerusalem and Judah would join them in exile.

Outline

Background of Ezekiel

Ezekiel's name means "God has strengthened." We know little about him outside the book that bears his name. We do know he served as a prophet in Babylon (Ez 1:3;

2:5; 33:33) and could have served as a priest in Jerusalem's temple had the Babylonians not taken him into exile. He went into exile in 597 B.C. as part of Jehoiachin's deportation. (This was the second deportation of Jews to Babylon. The first took place in 605 B.C.; see Dn 1:1.) He was married, but his wife died as part of a sign to the people (Ez 24:15–27). He ministered primarily to the Jews in Babylon, but also by correspondence to those in Jerusalem.

At the time of Ezekiel's deportation, Babylon was strong under Nebuchadnezzar. Jerusalem, slow to believe prophecies of judgment, had only about ten years left before Nebuchadnezzar's final invasion would lead to the city's destruction. Ezekiel warned the Jews in Jerusalem they soon would join their brothers and sisters already in Babylon if they did not repent.

Many interpreters have argued for the unity of the Book of Ezekiel. The book's smooth flow, consistent autobiographical style, and other factors all suggest the text of Ezekiel came from one hand.[1] Prophecies in the book date to as late as 571 B.C. (29:17). Assuming the writing came from Ezekiel, we may presume he completed the book by around 550 B.C.

Message of Ezekiel

Oracles and Events Relating to Ezekiel's Call (1:1–5:17)

Setting (1:1–3)

Ezekiel had his first vision in 592 B.C. by the RIVER CHEBAR, a large irrigation canal that flowed southeast from Babylon.[2] Most interpreters believe the expression "the thirtieth year" refers to the thirtieth year of Ezekiel's life. According to the Law of Moses, Ezekiel normally would have entered the priesthood at that age.

God's glory appears (1:4–28)

Ezekiel saw four dazzling beings. The prophet described them as having certain resemblances to creatures he knew, but they also possessed characteristics unlike anything he ever had seen. These creatures moved as the Spirit of God directed them.

Ezekiel also saw four wheels far up in the air. The wheels were dazzling and moved about like the creatures. Many commentators have tried to explain what Ezekiel might have seen. We do not know exactly what the wheels represented, but one thing is certain—they really impressed Ezekiel!

As Ezekiel watched the creatures and wheels move, he heard something else—a voice. At the sound of the voice, the creatures dropped their wings as if in submission. Ezekiel then saw a throne and a radiant being on it. The prophet fell on his face as he realized he stood in the very presence of God's glory.

Ezekiel's commission (2:1–3:27)

God commissioned Ezekiel for his prophetic ministry (2:1–10). He promised to send Ezekiel to a stubborn and rebellious house. In fact, the words "stubborn and rebellious house" occur over and over again in these verses. God told his young prophet the ministry would be hard and the people unwilling to listen to him. We also may encounter difficult challenges and unresponsive people as we serve the Lord. Our task, as Ezekiel's, is to remain faithful and leave the results to him.

As the last part of the prophet's initial commission—probably as part of Ezekiel's vision—God told him to eat a scroll (3:1–15). The scroll contained a list of all the people's sins—so many that God needed both sides of the scroll to list them all! Ezekiel probably thought the scroll would taste bitter, but found as he ate it that it tasted sweet. Perhaps this experience taught Ezekiel God's word should taste sweet to him whether it brought blessing or judgment.

Ezekiel then visited the exiles at TEL ABIB, a settlement along the Chebar near Babylon. The name "Tel Abib" means "heap of ruins," apparently referring to an abandoned town site where the Babylonians settled a Jewish community.[3] Ezekiel visited the exiles for seven days, apparently only watching and observing them. His presence caused consternation among the people—what was he doing there anyway?

God called Ezekiel to serve as his messenger (3:16–21). He held the prophet accountable for accurately reporting his message to the people. He did not hold him accountable for the people's response. God also holds us responsible to faithfully complete the ministry opportunities God gives us. The response of the people is not in our hands.

God told Ezekiel he would face trouble (3:22–27). The people would bind him with ropes to keep him from proclaiming God's judgment. God also promised to restrict or silence Ezekiel at times so the people would not hear his message.

Four symbolic actions (4:1–5:17)

Ezekiel performed four symbolic actions to show the people how seriously God took their sin. The people were moving faster and faster toward the day of judgment.

First, God told Ezekiel to take a brick and write on it "Jerusalem" and then lay siege to it (4:1–3). When people asked what he was doing, he replied, "I'm laying siege to Jerusalem." Ezekiel's apparent child's game contained a much deeper meaning. God, through Nebuchadnezzar's armies, was about to lay siege to Jerusalem one last, terrible time.

Second, God told Ezekiel to lie on his left side for 390 days to bear the iniquity of Israel (4:4–8). He also was to lie on his right side for forty days to bear the iniquity of Judah. Scholars disagree over the meaning of God's instructions. Some believe God was describing the length of Israel and Judah's past iniquity. Others argue God was instructing Ezekiel about his people's future time of judgment.[4]

Ezekiel's symbolic action illustrated the depth of sin to which God's people had sunk. Only deep repentance could save them from drowning in their evil.

Third, God told Ezekiel to cook his bread making small rations and using human dung for fuel (4:9–17). Ezekiel responded in horror—he had *never* eaten anything unclean! God told Ezekiel he could use cow dung instead of human dung as fuel. That may sound like small consolation, but many peoples of the world use cattle dung as a fuel. Once the dung is dry, it is odorless and burns cleanly.

Nevertheless, Ezekiel's point remains the same. The people would have small rations in the day of their captivity. The Babylonians would surround the city and cut off the food supply.

Fourth, God told the prophet to divide his hair into three parts (5:1–17). He was

to burn a third of it in fire, chop a third of it to bits with a sword, and toss a third into the wind and let it blow away. He also was to take a few pieces and bind them into his garment.

The hair's division represented the different fates the people would suffer. Some would die in the fire as the Babylonians set fire to the city. Others would die by the sword, while still others would experience exile to a distant land. But God would protect a small remnant and keep it close to him. His purposes for his people would continue through them.

Such actions naturally appear strange to us, and Ezekiel's original audience probably thought them quite strange, too! But desperate times demanded desperate measures. God used Ezekiel's prophetic actions to warn the people how little time remained for them to repent.

The Day of the Lord (6:1–7:27)

The concept of the **Day of the Lord** occurs commonly in the prophets and in the New Testament. It includes three elements: the judgment of God against sin, the cleansing and purging of God's people, and the salvation of God's people.

Prophecy to the mountains of Israel (6:1–14)

Ezekiel called for a prophecy to the mountains of Israel. The mountains stood as silent witnesses to everything that had happened in Israel since the people entered the land and conquered it. God promised the mountains would see their idolatrous altars and high places smashed.

Second, God announced the cities would be laid waste. Famine, sword, and siege all would come against the city to destroy it. When that happened, Ezekiel vowed, "then they will know." This phrase—"they will know"—occurs again and again in Ezekiel and presents a note of irony. God warned of terrible judgment and said when it happened, "Then they will know." When calamity finally came and the people realized God was serious, it would be too late. Nevertheless, Ezekiel's warning did offer the people the opportunity to repent.

The end (7:1–27)

Ezekiel described the awful conditions that would accompany Jerusalem's fall.

Tammuz

Ishtar

All hands would hang limp and shame would cover their faces. They would fling into the streets the silver and gold they prized so greatly, for it would not save them from the Babylonians. Again, God promised—"Then they'll know."

God's Glory Departs (8:1–11:25)

Setting (8:1–6)

Ezekiel 8–11 presents one of the most tragic visions of the Book of Ezekiel. The year was 591 B.C., fourteen months after Ezekiel's initial vision. Ezekiel received the vision while sitting in a house in Babylon with some of Judah's elders.

God's Spirit gave Ezekiel a vision of Jerusalem. The first thing the prophet saw was an idol of jealousy sitting in the temple court area. This probably represented Asherah, the wife of the pagan god Baal. Ezekiel, a man of the priestly line, no doubt revolted at the presence of any idol anywhere, let alone on the temple grounds! But God told him he would see even worse things in his vision.

Elder-led idolatry (8:7–13)

God took Ezekiel to the entrance of the court to the secret chamber, closer to the holiest of the temple area. There, seventy elders were practicing idolatry, right on the temple grounds! They thought God didn't see their sin, but he saw it all.

As God took Ezekiel on this tour of Jerusalem, the prophet probably could not believe how bad things had become. Yet at each step, God told him worse abominations were yet to come.

Tammuz worship (8:14–15)

The Lord took Ezekiel to the gate of the temple at the outer court, where Ezekiel saw women weeping for **Tammuz**. Tammuz was a Mesopotamian agricultural god, husband of the goddess **Ishtar**. His followers believed that every year at harvest time, Tammuz died, and these women joined Ishtar in mourning his death.[5] Tammuz came back to life in the spring when crops rejuvenated themselves and buds appeared on the trees. Again, God warned Ezekiel greater sins lay ahead.

Sun worship (8:16–18)

Ezekiel next saw people bowing down to the sun between the temple's porch and the altar of burnt offering. The people chose a holy place to worship, but they dishonored God by choosing his temple as a place to worship false gods! God promised to cleanse the land of such idolatry. He would not tolerate this obnoxious offense to his holy character. His people must worship him alone.

Executioners summoned (9:1–11)

Ezekiel's vision continued as God summoned six executioners and a scribe to carry out his judgment on Jerusalem. First, God commanded to mark those people who truly had repented and who agonized over Jerusalem's terrible spiritual condition. He knew who followed him and he would protect them.

Second, God commanded the messengers to have no pity on the rest. The executioners began to kill everyone as the Lord shouted, "Fill the temple courts with the corpses!" (9:7). Ezekiel reacted in horror at the sight—were God's people *really* this corrupt and deserving of judgment? God assured him they were. The Lord saw their sin in all its ugliness and promised to judge it completely.

The glory prepares to depart (10:1–22)

The glory of God filled the temple court. It rose over the temple area, accompanied by the cherubim and wheels Ezekiel had seen earlier. God's presence prepared to depart Jerusalem. Did anyone care he was leaving? Apparently few did.

The elders rebuked (11:1–21)

Ezekiel rebuked the elders who sat at the east gate of the Lord's house for their fatalistic attitudes. They believed nothing they could do would make any difference to God at this point. But Ezekiel held out a sliver of hope. Perhaps it was too late to save the city and even the nation, but individuals could still turn to the Lord. They might suffer exile, but they would escape with their lives and perhaps become part of the faithful remnant with whom God would renew his purposes.

The glory departs (11:22–25)

The vision came to a sad end. The cherubim lifted up their wings with the wheels beside them and God's glory hovered over them. The Lord's glory went up from the midst of the city and stood over the Mount of Olives east of the city, the very mountain from which Jesus would describe the end of the age (Mt 24:3). God paused as if to take one more long, painful look at the rebellious city. Then, in an instant, the glory departed. God had cleared the way for his judgment to begin.

Judgment Against Jerusalem (12:1–24:27)

Ezekiel packs for exile (12:1–20)

God told Ezekiel to pack his bags as if preparing for exile. The prophet did so and began to dig by the city wall. When people asked what he was doing, he responded, "I'm preparing to go into exile." His symbolic act represented the situation soon to occur in Jerusalem. Some people, such as Ezekiel, already lived in exile. Others soon would follow.

Revelation fulfilled (12:21–28)

The people misunderstood God's patience with them. They believed prophetic visions were failing because they did not see the prophets' predictions coming true. But God assured them there would be no more delay. He would accomplish it soon, in his perfect timing.

False prophets denounced (13:1–23)

False prophets of Ezekiel's day continued to follow their own spirit. They apparently hoped God was merely going to "slap their wrists" and let them go home. But it was not to be.

The Lord promised to clean away the whitewash. A rotten wall with a nice coat of paint or whitewash on it looks fine, but it will not support anyone who tries to lean against it! Jesus described the religious leaders of his day as whitewashed tombs—beautiful on the outside, but filled with corruption and dead men's bones (Mt 23:27–28). This description also fit the prophets of Ezekiel's day. Those who promised deliverance would be the first to experience God's awful judgment.

Idolatry denounced (14:1–11)

The first commandment required that the people have no other gods as rivals to the Lord (Ex 20:3). He wanted their absolute allegiance, but their idols were everywhere. False prophets tolerated and even encouraged the people's worship of many gods. Ezekiel said both prophets and idolaters were guilty. Many people today also remain unwilling to make an absolute commitment to follow the Lord.

Righteousness inadequate to save the wicked (14:12–23)

Ezekiel described the people's degree of wickedness. Even if Noah, Daniel, and Job lived among these people and prayed for them, probably only those three would survive on the basis of their righteousness! God's grace had preserved a remnant but few people sincerely followed him.

The prophet Daniel lived as a contemporary of Ezekiel. At the time of this prophecy, he was probably no more than thirty to thirty-five years old. The Scriptures encourage us to live faithfully as examples for Christ no matter how young we are (1 Tm 4:12).

Three analogies (15:1–17:24)

In chapters 15–17 Ezekiel used three analogies to describe God's people. First, he described them as a vine (15:1–8). Second, he compared them to an unfaithful wife (16:1–63). Third, he likened them to two eagles (17:1–24).

Ezekiel described a vine that fire had charred. One might dare to put his trust in a vine to support him, but certainly not a burned vine! In similar fashion, the people were placing their trust in Jerusalem, but Jerusalem would not support them. The people thought their beloved city would sustain them forever, for God's blessing rested on it. Instead, Jerusalem had become charred with spiritual decadence.

Ezekiel next compared Israel to an unfaithful wife. God took her from infancy (the days of Abraham) and raised her. He did so according to his grace. Nothing in Israel made her worthy of God's attention and favor. When Israel reached maturity, God took her for his bride.

But Israel spurned God's love and became a harlot to all the nations. She adopted the pagan customs and worship practices of the nations around her. Many of these nations had religious rituals that included sexual promiscuity, so Ezekiel's language fit the situation quite well. His words are amazingly graphic when one considers they come from a much more

The Jews weep after the fall of Jerusalem; from a relief on a *menorah* (lampstand) in the modern city of Jerusalem.

socially and culturally conservative time than today! But again, Ezekiel used desperate language for desperate times. Probably his words shocked many, but he was determined to focus their attention on the depravity of the situation.

Ezekiel told his hearers they had become worse than Sodom and Samaria. What an awful thing that God's people would become this way! Only deep repentance and a touch of God's grace could rescue them from destruction.

Ezekiel described two eagles in chapter 17. The first eagle is Babylon and the second eagle is Egypt. He also portrayed two vines. The first vine represented the captives of Jehoiachin already in captivity (597 B.C.). The second vine represented Zedekiah, the spineless king who listened to Jeremiah but did not have the courage to obey his counsel (Jer 38:17–23).

Ezekiel related his story. The first eagle took the choice vine and transplanted it. Nebuchadnezzar, the first eagle, came and took the captives in Ezekiel's group to Babylon. Zedekiah, the second vine, remained behind in Jerusalem. But this vine quickly turned toward Egypt, the second eagle, for help when it appeared, ignoring the power Babylon had shown.

The prophecy appears to come from Jerusalem's last days. Zedekiah rebelled, counting on Egypt for support that never came. Nebuchadnezzar marched on Jerusalem, conquered the city, blinded Zedekiah, and led the people into captivity.

Individual responsibility affirmed (18:1–32)

Amid all the calamity of exile, many people began to complain. This situation was not their fault! The proverb they quoted underscored their belief that they suffered because of their ancestors' sins, not their own. Even today, many try to excuse their sin by blaming their parents, their background, or other factors.

But Ezekiel affirmed individual responsibility. God would punish people for their own sin, not for the sin of others. The Lord also affirmed that he took no pleasure in the death of the wicked (18:23, 32). His righteous holy character demanded that he punish sin, but he derived no joy from judging his people. He preferred that they turn to him in repentance and live. Today God still prefers that people turn to him rather than persist in their evil (2 Pt 3:9).

Lament for the leaders (19:1–14)

Ezekiel compared Judah to a lioness with two cubs. The first cub was Jehoahaz and the second cub Jehoiachin. Jehoahaz was Josiah's oldest son and Judah's last good king. His reign lasted only three months after his father's death. Pharaoh Necho of Egypt captured him and took him to Egypt where he died (2 Kgs 23:31–34). Nebuchadnezzar captured Jehoiachin, the second cub, and took him to Babylon.

Ezekiel lamented the fact that Judah now had no ruler—or at least, they had no *real* ruler. Zedekiah lacked the courage and conviction he needed to lead the people and soon the nation would crumble away into oblivion.

Lesson from history (20:1–44)

Had God's people learned from history? No, not really. In 591 B.C., the elders came to inquire of the Lord. But Ezekiel sensed a problem with their sincerity. They enjoyed listening to his counsel but did not intend to follow his advice. Ezekiel refused to give them an audience. The Lord would give them no more revelation until they were ready to receive it.

Ezekiel reminded the elders of the people's dismal spiritual history. Israel barely had left Egypt when the people began to complain. Despite all the miracles they had seen, they lacked the faith to trust God to provide their needs. For almost a thousand years, they maintained this rebellious attitude and learned precious little about a relationship with God. God in his grace withheld judgment but he would not do so anymore.

Judgment against Judah (20:45–21:32)

The people suggested Ezekiel was only speaking parables. They thought his messages were mere stories composed to emphasize the tragedy of their experience. But Ezekiel's message reflected more than parables. It accurately described the people's condition—racing toward judgment! Unfortunately, the prophet's warnings fell on deaf ears. The people loved to hear him preach but did not take his words seriously.

Three oracles (22:1–31)

Ezekiel uttered three oracles to get the people's attention. First, he declared Israel had become a nation of bloodshed, dross, and uncleanness. The term "bloodshed" denotes murder or injustice. Ezekiel was not describing capital punishment, but the social injustice that permeated the land. The people remained bent toward idolatry as they strayed farther and farther from the Lord. Apart from God and his laws, they adopted their own standards—of injustice and immorality.

Second, Ezekiel described Israel as a nation of dross. The term "dross" designates the refuse material that rises to the top of molten metal. The process of heating the metal separates the impurities from the pure metal. These impurities are lighter than the metal, so they rise to the top. The refiner skimmed the dross from the top of the metal and threw it away because it had no value.

Ezekiel said God's people had become like dross because of their sin. As God refined his people he found a lot of spiritual dross in their lives. He would remove it through the fires of judgment. God still wants to remove all impurities from our lives today so we can serve him more completely (Rom 13:14).

Third, Ezekiel depicted God's people as a nation of uncleanness. He condemned prophets and priests alike for leading the people astray. The nation's sin grew worse and worse. But God could find no one among the leadership who would take a stand for Israel and beg God to forgive her.

Ezekiel used the imagery of plugging a breach in the city wall to make his point. When an enemy comes against a walled city, it must find a way to penetrate the

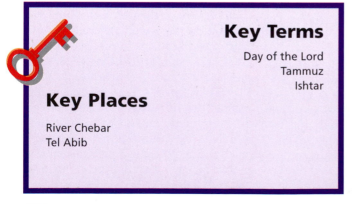

Key Terms

Day of the Lord
Tammuz
Ishtar

Key Places

River Chebar
Tel Abib

wall. If the army succeeds in doing so, those defending the city must stop the advance or the city will fall. Brave men must answer the call to stand in the gap. But God could find no one to defend Jerusalem from his judgment—prophet, priest, or prince.

Oholah and Oholibah (23:1–49)

Ezekiel described two sisters—Oholah and Oholibah. Although we know what the names literally mean ("her tent" and "my tent is in her," respectively), scholars have proposed quite different views as to precisely what significance the names had.[6] Oholah represented Samaria, the northern capital, and Oholibah represented Jerusalem, the southern capital. Both sisters were terribly wicked but God took them as his own and married them anyway.

Oholah committed great evil so God gave her into the hands of the Assyrians in 722 B.C. But Oholibah her sister—who saw this judgment—learned absolutely nothing. That is, Judah saw what hap-pened to Israel because of Israel's sin but continued her evil practices anyway. She thus would face a more severe judgment.

The rusty pot (24:1–14)

In 588 B.C., the Babylonian siege of Jerusalem began. In July of 587 B.C., the city finally fell to Nebuchadnezzar's forces. On the day the siege began, God commanded Ezekiel to prophesy.

The prophet likened Jerusalem to a rusty pot. Have you ever tried to cook something in a rusty pot? You should not—the rust comes loose from the pot and mixes in with the food. In the same way, sin pervaded the land and contaminated all Jerusalem. Just as a cook would throw out contaminated food, so God would hurl his people into captivity.

Ezekiel's wife dies (24:15–27)

Ezekiel 24:15–27 records the death of Ezekiel's wife. The Lord warned the prophet she was about to die and instructed him how to respond. Ezekiel was to mourn inwardly, but make no external display of mourning and lamentation.

Summary

1. The Book of Ezekiel is written in an autobiographical style.

2. God told Ezekiel to perform four symbolic actions to demonstrate how seriously he took the people's sin: playing a game with a brick, lying on his right and left sides for a specific number of days, cooking bread using small rations and using human dung for fuel, and dividing his hair into three parts and performing different actions with each part.

3. The concept of the Day of the Lord includes the judgment of God against sin, the cleansing and purging of God's people, and the salvation of God's people.

4. The people of God sinned greatly against him; led by the elders they practiced idolatry in the holiest part of the temple, they worshiped a pagan agricultural god, and they worshiped the sun.

5. In preparation for the judgment, Ezekiel denounced the false prophets and the idolatry of the people.

6. Ezekiel described God's people with analogies in which he compared them to a vine, an unfaithful wife, and two eagles.

7. In his lament for Judah Ezekiel analogously used cubs to represent Jehoahaz and Jehoiakim.

Study Questions

1. What was the historical setting for Ezekiel's prophetic ministry?

2. What do we know about the prophet himself from his book?

3. List the various symbolic prophetic actions Ezekiel performed for the people. In general, how do you think the people responded to those actions?

4. Describe Ezekiel's vision of chapters 8–11. What was the significance of God's glory departing Jerusalem?

5. How would you characterize the general attitude of Ezekiel's audience? What seems to have been the viewpoint of the people who stayed behind in Jerusalem after the second deportation?

Further Reading

Block, Daniel I. *The Book of Ezekiel: Chapters 1–24.* New International Commentary on the Old Testament. Grand Rapids; Eerdmans, 1997. A detailed commentary for the advanced college student or graduate student. Rich in exegesis and footnotes.

Cooper, Lamar Eugene, Sr. *Ezekiel.* New American Commentary 17. Nashville: Broadman & Holman, 1994. A thorough exegesis and exposition of the text of Ezekiel.

Craigie, Peter C. *Ezekiel.* Daily Study Bible. Philadelphia: Westminster, 1983. For the general reader.

Taylor, John B. *Ezekiel: An Introduction and Commentary.* Tyndale Old Testament Commentary. Downers Grove: InterVarsity, 1969. Good college-level commentary.

Ezekiel's apparent lack of reaction to his wife's death naturally got the people's attention, and they asked him why he did not mourn. Ezekiel responded that God intended to do the same to Jerusalem very soon. The city's destruction would mean the death of many of their loved ones. The survivors would suffer such horror they would find themselves unable even to cry or mourn. Tragically, they would finally realize the prophet Ezekiel had been right all along.

But God had not finished with his people. He planned to restore them and bless them again! In the next chapter, we see how God described the judgment of his enemies and ultimate salvation of those he loved.

30 Ezekiel 25–48
God's Planning an Exciting Future!

Outline

- **Ezekiel's Message Continues (25:1–48:35)**
  Oracles Against the Nations (25:1–32:32)
  Israel's Restoration (33:1–39:29)
  Israel's New Temple (40:1–48:35)

Objectives

After reading this chapter, you should be able to

- Name the nations to whom Ezekiel directed his oracles in chapters 25–32
- Identify the common theme of the warnings Ezekiel pronounced on the seven nations in chapters 25–29
- List the specifics of the new temple that God revealed to Ezekiel
- Present the five major approaches to interpreting Ezekiel 40–48

Have you ever known people who always seem to have a sour attitude? No matter what the circumstances, they tend to see things in the worst possible light. Such people can quickly put you in a melancholy mood and ruin your day!

Perhaps you felt a little like you were talking to one of those people as you read Ezekiel 1–24. Ezekiel's message focused on God's dissatisfaction with his people's spiritual condition. The prophet tried many different tactics, but they all basically pointed out that God would judge his people's sin.

In chapters 25–48, the tone of Ezekiel's messages begins to shift. The prophet describes how God will judge those who oppose his people, whether those people live among them or in the nations surrounding them. He also looks ahead to a glorious day in which God will defeat sin for all time, restore his people, and dwell with them forever. Ezekiel's ministry contained many difficult challenges, but he still closed his book on a positive note—God was planning an exciting future!

Ezekiel's Message Continues (25:1–48:35)

Oracles Against the Nations (25:1–32:32)

We already have seen how Isaiah and Jeremiah proclaimed oracles against the nations (Is 13–23; Jer 46–51). Ezekiel now took his prophetic turn at depicting these kingdoms' ultimate lot. God would display his sovereignty over all of them.

Ammon (25:1–7)

Ezekiel declared that Babylon would conquer Ammon. The Ammonites rejoiced in Judah's fall, but God would judge them, too. When he did, they would know he was the Lord.

Moab and Edom (25:8–14)

Moab and Edom believed Judah was just like all the rest of the nations. Only through a fluke of history had God's people risen to prominence in the land. Ezekiel warned that Nebuchadnezzar's mighty army

would crush these two kingdoms just as it had all the rest.

Ezekiel singled out Edom for special attention because the Edomites had played a significant role in Jerusalem's destruction (Ob 10–14). They cut down the Judeans as they tried to flee, turned them over to the Babylonians, or sold them into slavery. God promised to lay Edom and its cities waste. When he did, they would know he was the Lord.

Philistia (25:15–17)

The Philistines, ancient enemies of God's people, also were soon to fall. They rejoiced in Judah's fall but God would judge them, too. They also would learn the sting of his wrath.

Tyre (26:1–28:19)

Ezekiel prophesied about Tyre in the year 587 B.C., around the time of Jerusalem's fall. Tyre, a Phoenician port city, would soon come under God's wrath.

Tyre rejoiced over Jerusalem's fall because it thought it would gain financially by Jerusalem's ruin. After all, Jerusalem's destruction meant one less competitor in the world of trade! But Ezekiel vowed that Tyre also would become spoil for the nations and experience utter desolation and devastation.

Tyre had often bought its way out of trouble when enemies threatened her. Attacking kings would leave loaded with riches and Tyre would promise to send more each year.

Ezekiel mentioned such a situation regarding Tyre and Babylon. Babylon received a lot of money from Tyre but could not destroy the city. Alexander the Great finally destroyed Tyre around 332 B.C. The total desolation Ezekiel had prophesied came at last. All the nations would lament, for Tyre's fall also spelled financial trouble for many foreign merchants.

The people of Tyre also lamented their leader. Note the leader's pride in 28:2—he claimed to be a god! He possessed great riches and wisdom, but God would lay him low.

Some Bible interpreters have noted the parallels between Isaiah 14 and Ezekiel 28. Isaiah 14 described the morning star, the son of the dawn, whose pride God would humble. This proud ruler, like the ruler of

A shepherd tends his flock in the Judean hills. The shepherds of Israel did not look after their flock—God's people—so God himself promised to be their shepherd (ch. 34).

Sheol

Ezekiel 28, had also uttered pompous, arrogant boasts, lifting himself up to a level with God.

Like Isaiah 14, Ezekiel 28 is another passage many evangelicals believe describes Satan because the language goes so far beyond what we would normally expect of a human ruler. Yet verse 12 specifically refers to the king of Tyre as the object of Ezekiel's words. Also, the New Testament does not cite these verses as referring to Satan. Probably Ezekiel's lofty language symbolically described the great material blessing God had given Tyre's ruler. Other interpreters have understood Ezekiel's words to have a secondary fulfillment in Satan.[1]

Sidon (28:20–26)

Sidon was another leading Phoenician city. God said he would bring glory to himself by judging Sidon. Neither Sidon nor Tyre would provide an irritation to Israel anymore.

Egypt (29:1–32:32)

Ezekiel closed his oracles against the nations with four chapters against Egypt. Egypt at this time was one of Judah's worst enemies, mainly because of what Egypt did not do. Egypt typically encouraged smaller kingdoms in Palestine to revolt on promise of Egyptian support.[2] But when mighty kingdoms came against these kingdoms, Egypt did nothing to help, and their hapless neighbors suffered terrible con-

sequences. God promised that when the Day of the Lord came for the Egyptians, they would know that he was God.

Ezekiel began these prophecies in 587 B.C., a short time before Jerusalem's fall. The prophet used Assyria as an example of pride that led to a great fall. God had made Assyria great, but she congratulated herself instead of praising him.

Ezekiel vowed God would treat Egypt as he had treated Assyria just twenty-five years earlier. Nineveh had fallen in 612 B.C.; Egypt would fall soon. Her pride would lead to her downfall.

In 585 B.C., Ezekiel chanted a lament for Pharaoh, king of Egypt. He compared Pharaoh to a raging sea monster in the bonds of captivity. God would use Babylon to tame this monster. Egypt's fall would bring fear to many because of Egypt's high status at that time. As other kingdoms saw Egypt's defeat, they would contemplate their own futures.

In haunting language, Ezekiel described God's taking Egypt to **Sheol**. There, Egypt found a welcoming committee—Assyria, Elam, and Edom. These nations had also trusted in their own power and splendor, but God had brought their dominion to an end. Ezekiel warned the Egyptians they would become like every other nation that had challenged God's authority.

The prophet's words stand as a sober warning today for any nation faced with the temptation to pride. All of us will one day face death. How should we prepare for that? The New Testament writers tell us we need to make our peace with God through the Lord Jesus Christ. If we do that, death's power over our lives will be broken. Will our nation learn this lesson? Will *we*?

Israel's Restoration (33:1–39:29)

So far in the Book of Ezekiel we have seen a lot to get discouraged about. Ezekiel has performed many symbolic actions through which he warned the people of God's impending judgment. In chapters 33–39, he began to describe the wonderful blessings God had in store for his faithful people.

Call to repentance (33:1–33)

In chapter 33 God appointed the prophet as a watchman over the city (see also 3:17). A watchman kept watch for signs of the enemy and warned the people of any threat or attack. Ezekiel was responsible to warn the people of their sin before God judged them for it. He served as a spiritual watchman for God's people.

The people felt discouraged as they heard all these gloomy prophecies. (Perhaps *you* feel this way as you read Ezekiel!) Ezekiel presented God's message using a variety of creative techniques and methods. But the bottom line remained the same—God would judge his people for their sin if they did not repent. Many of God's people felt their situation was hopeless. Nothing could save them now!

Ezekiel assured Israel the situation was *not* hopeless. God still held out the hope of repentance, and would judge people according to their own ways. Even if the nation was headed for exile, individuals could still turn to God and receive a right relationship with him through faith. And even in Jerusalem's last days, if the whole nation repented, who knew what mercy God might extend?

The year was 587 B.C. and Jerusalem had fallen to the Babylonians. God had withheld prophetic words from Ezekiel during Jerusalem's siege, but now opened the prophet's mouth to bring the people a message.

The exiles protested that the whole situation smacked of unfairness. "It was our land," they said. "It's not fair that they took it." God's response indicated the land

belonged to him, not them. They had ignored his commandments and shown themselves unfit to possess it, and therefore, he had delivered them into exile.

But even in these desperate times, the people refused to listen to Ezekiel. They heard the words, but would not allow them to reach their hearts. "What a wonderful preacher," they probably said to one another. But they walked away from his messages without any hint of change in their lives.

People today often like to hear a good sermon. They will listen to preachers who can deliver a quality message and even enjoy their oratorical skill. But they do not apply the truth they hear to their own lives. Neither did Ezekiel's audience. God warned them that one day, they would understand that Ezekiel was indeed a prophet of God. But by the time they realized it, Jerusalem lay in ruins and they stood in captivity in Babylon.

God's flock (34:1–31)

Ezekiel compared Israel's leaders to shepherds who tended their flock (the people). He warned them to feed the flock, not themselves. They were to use their positions of authority to serve the people, but instead used their power for dishonest gain or merely to satisfy their own needs. Even today, many Christian leaders fail to understand that leading means serving.

Ezekiel told them they were responsible for God scattering the flock. Why? Because the shepherds cared only for themselves. They only cared about the sheep insofar as the sheep brought blessing to them. The church today desperately needs leaders who will give of themselves because they care deeply for the people God has given them to lead.

What solution did Ezekiel present? *God himself* would care for them! The Lord promised to regather his people, care for them personally, and even reestablish King David over them. Many interpreters understand this passage as referring to the messianic kingdom.[3] When the Lord Jesus returns, he will establish his people and care for them personally.

Judgment on Edom (35:1–15)

We mentioned earlier in the chapter how Edom sided with the Babylonians against

Gog

Magog

Great Tribulation

God's people as Nebuchadnezzar conquered Judah and Jerusalem. Perhaps that is why Ezekiel singled out Edom for more special attention at this point in the book. God would humble the Edomites for their hostility and arrogance. When he did, they would know he was the Lord.

Blessing to Israel (36:1–37:28)

God promised to restore Israel and reestablish them as his people again. This restoration included two aspects—physical restoration and spiritual restoration.

First, God promised to bring the people back to the land and rejuvenate it. He would implore nature to come alive again, and nature would respond in all its fullness. The Lord would cause vegetation to sprout and bear fruit again as it had in the days of God's blessing.

Second, God promised to awaken the people spiritually again. God had judged his people to protect his holy character. He had to punish all sin wherever he found it! God's patience was tempered by his justice, and the day of justice came. God was acting for his sake and when he brought judgment they understood at last that God was Judge.

As part of the spiritual re-creation Israel would receive a heart of flesh. God did not restore them to the land so they could lapse into idolatry and rebellion again. He would restore them to serve him faithfully. But they could do so only if his transforming power touched their hearts. The New Testament calls this experience the new birth (Jn 3:3, 5).

God then confirmed his words by giving Ezekiel the famous vision of dry bones. The vision described a two-stage resurrection. First, the dry bones received flesh on them. Second, they came to life!

The deadness of the dry bones symbolized the deadness of the people's hope. They were dried up, hopeless, powerless! But God's Spirit would breathe life into them again. He was able to take them and reunite them into one nation under his lordship.

God gave the people a second sign. He told Ezekiel to take two sticks and write "Judah" on one and "Joseph" on the other. These two sticks represented Judah and Israel, respectively. Just as the sticks became bound as one in Ezekiel's hand, so

God would bind his broken nation together again.

Gog and Magog: The ultimate triumph (38:1–39:20)

In chapters 38–39, Ezekiel looked far into the future to see some things that God would do one day. Ezekiel up to this point had focused primarily on the events of his own generation. The words he spoke now had meaning for his day in that they challenged his hearers to live faithfully in light of the great kingdom God would usher in some day.

Bible scholars disagree over the meaning of **Gog** and **Magog**.[4] The terms appear to describe the ultimate foe of God's people. Revelation 20:8 also mentions them in an equally difficult context. We can say that whoever they are, God's power will overcome them. As they gather against God's people, the Lord will bring final victory.

Ezekiel's description of this battle parallels the Book of Revelation. God's call to the birds to eat the bodies of his vanquished enemies (39:17) sounds like the call that accompanies Christ's return (Rv 19:17). Many Bible interpreters have therefore linked Ezekiel 38–39 with the time of the **Great Tribulation**, the final period of history before the Lord returns, brings victory, and establishes his kingdom.[5] Gog and Magog are defeated, and God secures absolute victory.

The triumph of God is the triumph of Israel. God's people win because God wins. Most important, a spiritual outpouring occurs. People turn to God in large numbers as they realize he alone is God. In that day, the Lord will be their God and they will be his people.

Israel's New Temple (40:1–48:35)

Evangelicals have long discussed the meaning and interpretation of Ezekiel 40–48. Indeed, these chapters present some of the greatest challenges facing Old Testament interpreters. Does the prophet speak of events that were fulfilled after the exile, or does he refer to events yet future? And if the events are yet future, is Ezekiel referring to Israel, the church, or both? Let's look at the basic details of the chapters and then try to make some general conclusions.

Setting (40:1–4)

The year was 572 B.C. Ezekiel had served as a prophet for about twenty years. God took Ezekiel to Israel to an unnamed high mountain. From there Ezekiel could see God's plans unfold in a vision.

The Lord instructed him to write down everything he saw. Much of the vision pertained to the new temple God was planning. We may find these descriptions and details quite foreign, but as a priest, Ezekiel must have been fascinated with each item God revealed. As you read Ezekiel 40–48, try to imagine the prophet eagerly taking notes on everything God described.

The courts (40:5–47)

Ezekiel described the temple's inner and outer courts. This was nothing new. He also saw special chambers for temple personnel. Priests could go there and change their garments, eat a meal, and more.

The temple and associated structures (40:48–41:26)

Ezekiel depicted the utter splendor that would characterize God's house. Again, we may find such detail hard to follow, but God's priest was enjoying himself immensely as he took it all in. Jerusalem had lost its temple in 587 B.C., but God one day would restore it again.

Chambers for the priests (42:1–14)

Ezekiel again highlighted the chambers for the priests. The priests would sometimes eat on the temple grounds because someone would bring a sacrifice and part of that sacrifice belonged to them. Priests could don their priestly robes in these rooms and change back into their ordinary clothes before they left.

Perhaps such description excited Ezekiel because he had missed out on being a priest. Nebuchadnezzar had taken him into captivity before he had a chance to serve. Maybe Ezekiel hoped to serve in the Lord's new temple.

The temple area (42:15–20)

Ezekiel depicted a huge temple area five hundred reeds (1,500 yards) on a side. Such an area would be much larger than the temple mount of Jesus' day, which probably was about five hundred yards on a side. Clearly, God had big plans for his temple!

God's glory returns (43:1–12)

In Ezekiel 11 God's glory had departed the temple. The glory had hovered over the temple, then moved to the Mount of Olives, then disappeared. But Ezekiel 43 portrayed God's glory returning to Jerusalem! The details also should remind us of Ezekiel 1, where the prophet initially saw angelic creatures, bright, dazzling wheels, and the glory of God. God promised to set his glory there forever.

The altar (43:13–27)

Ezekiel described the altar of burnt offering's dimensions. This altar stood in the temple court area. On it the priests offered up the sacrifices the people brought. The prophet carefully gave precise details concerning the altar's size and shape. He then described in similar fashion the offerings the priests would offer in that day. And, most of exciting of all, God would accept their offerings again, because he accepted his people again.

The ministers and their duties (44:1–45:8)

Ezekiel described a sealed gate on the city's east side. No one entered by it because "the LORD God of Israel has entered by it" (44:2). Interestingly, when Jesus entered Jerusalem on Palm Sunday he probably came through this eastern gate. Jerusalem's current eastern gate, located somewhere near where Ezekiel's eastern gate would have been, is sealed shut because a Muslim king heard of Ezekiel's prophecy and wanted to make sure (too late!) that no Jewish Messiah would come through the gate. It serves as an interesting commentary on Ezekiel's prophecy.

The prophet announced that God's holiness would pervade the city. A zeal for holiness lay close to Ezekiel's heart, for God had called the priests to mediate his holiness to the people. God worked through them to show people his holiness. And as the people came into right relationship with him by faith, their lives began to reflect his holy character. A holy people lives like its God, and God used the priests to help bring that about.

Offering regulations (45:9–46:24)

Prophets had often condemned the people for their use of dishonest weights and measures (Hos 12:7; Am 8:5). In the day

Salt deposits on the Dead Sea, Israel. The lake is so salty that no fish can survive. In Ezekiel's vision, water flowed from the temple in Jerusalem into the Dead Sea, making it fresh and teeming with life.

Ezekiel described, all would use honest measures. Perhaps priests like Ezekiel genuinely grieved over the way people abused the sacrificial system and cheated each other. This would not happen when the Lord brought restoration.

Ezekiel said the prince will provide for the national offerings. Some evangelicals understand the prophet's words as a reference to Jesus Christ. Unfortunately, we cannot say for sure, as the New Testament does not cite this passage.

The river (47:1–12)

Ezekiel's description of the river closely parallels Revelation 22. Most evangelicals believe Revelation 22 describes heaven, and this fact raises questions about the interpretation of Ezekiel 40–48. Does Ezekiel describe a restored temple on earth during the course of history, or something that occurs after Christ returns or in heaven?

The river flows from the temple and provides healing for the nations (47:12). This is also true in Revelation 22:2. God is concerned about the healing of his people forever.

Tribal boundaries (47:13–48:29)

The tribal boundaries appear basically similar to those from the reigns of David and Solomon. God's people will include native Israelites but also foreigners who join themselves to God's people by faith. Such prophetic words beautifully foreshadow the New Testament assertion that

peoples of all nations comprise Christ's body, the church (Eph 2:11–22).

Ezekiel listed the tribal allotments. The priests and Levites surround the sanctuary, a feature some might expect in light of their continual duties there. The prince, who also would play an important role in national worship, had territory on the east and west sides.

Jerusalem's gates (48:30–35)

Jerusalem had twelve gates—one for each tribe. The gates had tribal names written on them, a fact paralleled in the Book of Revelation's description of the new Jerusalem (21:12).

Ezekiel closes his book by affirming that after all is said and done, the name of the city will be "The Lord is there." The personal presence of the Lord with his people stands as the goal of redemptive history. He will be there—personally, visibly, face to face in intimate fellowship with his people forever. For the Christian, the promise of God's eternal presence remains most precious. He promises believers he will never desert them in this life, but he also promises that one day, a new age will dawn in which they will enjoy personal fellowship with him forever.

Possible interpretations of Ezekiel 40–48

Evangelicals have suggested various interpretations of Ezekiel 40–48.[6] One view

Key Terms

Sheol
Gog
Magog
Great Tribulation
millennium

Key Places

Ammon
Moab
Edom
Philistia
Tyre
Sidon
Egypt

end of the great tribulation period and establish his rule with Jerusalem as his capital. During this time, the priests will offer sacrifices as a memorial to Christ's atoning work. According to this view, then, the earthly reign of Christ will possess markedly Jewish characteristics.

A third view understands these chapters as prophetically referring to the church. This position's proponents may perceive the events Ezekiel describes as being fulfilled today in some spiritual sense. Others believe his words refer to life in God's heavenly kingdom. They point to Jesus words regarding his fulfilling of the Law and the Prophets (Mt 5:17–18) and suggest the church has taken Israel's place in God's redemptive program (Gal 3:28–29).

A fourth view combines the first and third views.[8] It proposes that Ezekiel's words were partially fulfilled in the second temple period. The rest will be fulfilled completely in the church age or in the millennial kingdom.

A fifth view suggests that we should understand Ezekiel's language symbolically, as apocalyptic literature.[9] Ezekiel expressed important spiritual truths about God and his kingdom through tangible terms his readers would understand.

millennium   proposes that Ezekiel's prophecy found its fulfillment in the return and rebuilding of Jerusalem under Zerubbabel, Ezra, and Nehemiah. Because the people lacked the faith to follow through completely on God's promise, the temple never achieved the dimensions Ezekiel described.

A second view argues that we should take Ezekiel's words as literally as possible, but understand them to describe God's future kingdom.[7] Those who hold this position usually believe Christ will fulfill this prophecy during a one thousand-year reign on earth called the **millennium.** The Lord Jesus will return at the

Summary

1. Ezekiel continues his message in chapters 25–32 by directing oracles of judgment against the nations of Ammon, Moab, Edom, Philistia, Tyre, Sidon, and Egypt.

2. In Ezekiel 33–39 the prophet describes the blessings of the restoration.

3. Even in the worst of times the people refused to listen to the prophet Ezekiel and apply his messages to their own situation.

4. God's restoration of Israel would be both physical and spiritual.

5. God led Ezekiel to a high mountain, where he showed him a vision that revealed the description of the new temple, and God instructed him to write down everything he saw.

6. Each one of the twelve gates of Jerusalem was designated for one of the twelve tribes.

7. Bible interpreters have many possible interpretations of Ezekiel 40–48.

Study Questions

1. What are the implications of Ezekiel's prophesying against other nations (chapters 25–32)? How does God still show his power over all nations?

2. Describe the role of the watchman in the Book of Ezekiel. In what sense do modern Christians have this role?

3. Evaluate the statement, "Ezekiel's audience listened to him, but they didn't really listen to him." What subtle warning does Ezekiel 33:30–33 give to today's Christian?

4. In the Book of Ezekiel, God promised he would judge evil and restore his people. What difference should that promise make in the lives of God's people today?

5. Describe the various ways Christians have interpreted Ezekiel 40–48. Do you lean toward a particular view yourself? If so, why?

Further Reading

Cooper, Lamar Eugene, Sr. *Ezekiel.* New American Commentary 17. Nashville: Broadman & Holman, 1994. Strong on exegesis and exposition.

Craigie, Peter C. *Ezekiel.* Daily Study Bible. Philadelphia: Westminster Press, 1983. For the general reader.

Taylor, John B. *Ezekiel: An Introduction and Commentary.* Tyndale Old Testament Commentary. Downers Grove: InterVarsity, 1969. Good college-level commentary.

Throughout chapters 40–48, he depicted God's perfect plan for his people, the lasting presence of God with his people, and the blessings and responsibilities of life in God's coming kingdom.

Whichever view of Ezekiel 40–48 we embrace, we should come away expectant. God is planning an exciting future! He will restore his people and gather them to himself. He will be their God and they will be his people. He will show them his glory and care for them forever. And he will wipe away every tear from their eyes. Perhaps believers should allow the Lord the freedom to fulfill Ezekiel's words in the way he chooses. Whatever he does is certain to be beyond description!

31 Daniel

The Kingdom of God— Now and Forever

Outline

- **Daniel as Apocalyptic Literature**
  Uniqueness of Apocalyptic Literature
  Characteristics of Apocalyptic Literature
  "Biblical" Apocalyptic
- **Contents of the Book of Daniel**
  Outline
  Overview
- **The Theological Themes of Daniel**
  The Sovereignty of God
  The Pride of Humankind
  The Ultimate Victory of God's Saints
- **Problems of Interpretation**
  Bilingualism
  Identify of the Four Kingdoms
  Vision of the "Seventy Weeks"
  Historical Questions
  Date of Composition

Objectives

After reading this chapter, you should be able to

- Describe the distinctiveness of the Book of Daniel compared to the rest of the Old Testament
- Outline the Book of Daniel
- Demonstrate how Daniel and his three friends were faithful to God
- Describe the visions of Daniel
- Identify the three dominant themes of the Book of Daniel
- Tell how Daniel's approach to the nations differs from that of the other Old Testament prophets
- Explain why there are problems of interpretation in Daniel
- Respond to the charges that the Book of Daniel is full of errors
- Evaluate the two positions taken on the date of the Book of Daniel

Daniel is one of the most disputed and debated books of the Bible. Yet its message is clear and unmistakable. While Bible scholars still wrestle with controversial issues like date and historical accuracy, the Book of Daniel consistently calls for faithfulness among God's people of every generation. The book relates the episodes and visions of Daniel, a believer trying to remain faithful while living in a foreign land hostile to his faith.

Daniel as Apocalyptic Literature

One of the reasons for the debate is the distinctiveness of Daniel when we compare it to other Old Testament books. The Christian **canon** includes Daniel among the prophets, but the Jewish canon groups it among works it calls "the Writings" (see discussion in chapter 1). Indeed, a casual reading will reveal that Daniel is different in content and style from the other Old Testament prophets. But how is it different and why?

Uniqueness of Apocalyptic Literature

Daniel is singular because it contains material modern scholars call **apocalyptic literature.** This type of literature is defined by the Book of Revelation in the New Testament, which is the oldest document actually claiming the title "apocalypse" or "revelation." The term refers to a body of documents containing a unique manner and style of communication, and having in common a basic content.[1] Apocalyptic literature was widespread in Judaism around the time of Christ and had a profound influence on early Christianity.

Characteristics of Apocalyptic Literature

The **intertestamental apocalyptic** books have several characteristics in common. They always contain some type of vision. The initial revelation is usually symbolic and mysterious, and requires interpretation by a heavenly mediator. The name of the author, if given, is assumed to be a **pseudonym** or pen name. Many of these books claim their authors are ven-

erated heroes of Israelite faith (such as Enoch, Abraham, Isaiah, or Ezra) who lived centuries before the books were actually written.

These apocalyptic writings also share a similar content. They are concerned with the future and often reveal an **eschatological** judgment. They usually divide history into distinct periods of time (for example, four kingdoms and seventy weeks of years). History culminates in final judgment, which rewards the good and punishes the wicked in a life beyond death.

This literature is sensitive to the distinction between the spiritual world and the physical world. Sometimes angels or demons represent the supernatural world. At other times, the recipient of the vision is carried into the other world for a heavenly journey. So apocalyptic literature involves both the temporal (eschatological time) and spatial (heavenly truth).

Many of these writings employ a technique whereby a well-known event of the past is cast in predictive, futuristic language. The author assumes the position of a predictive prophet and speaks of the event as though it were still in the future. Such a prophecy (known as a *vaticinium ex eventu,* "prediction after the fact") would lend credence to the whole message if its readers believed it was a real prophecy. Some scholars believe the Book of Daniel used this technique (see below).

"Biblical" Apocalyptic

The Old Testament contains a few passages that display certain, though not all, of these characteristics, and are generally apocalyptic in nature (Jl 3, Is 24–27, and parts of Ezekiel and Zechariah). Although these passages and the Book of Daniel clearly have apocalyptic features, they show significant differences from the later apocalyptic books of the **intertestamental period**. We should probably view these sections, along with the New Testament Book of Revelation, as comprising another literary category that we may call **"biblical apocalyptic."** This subcategory opens with historical material, and gradually moves to the more apocalyptic type of material (especially in Zechariah and Revelation).

Daniel has much in common with other Old Testament apocalyptic passages. Yet

An Assyrian relief showing a lion released from its cage. The Assyrian kings kept lions for hunting. Daniel was sentenced to be put into a lion pit.

when we compare the Book of Daniel with the Old Testament prophets in general, we see that this book is thoroughly unique. Other eschatological passages view the future from the perspective of Israel and the covenant promises to God's people. But Daniel's perspective is different. He considers the secular world empires in the light of God's ultimate purposes and describes the coming, final kingdom of God.[2] Daniel uses a universal panorama when he describes the future.

Also, the purpose of the Book of Daniel is unique. This book does not call its readers to repent and lead a new life, as is true of many other prophets. The Book of Daniel calls God's people to faithfulness and obedience during times of hardship. This is in line with its nature as apocalyptic literature.

Contents of the Book of Daniel

The Book of Daniel conveniently falls into two parts: the narrative stories of chapters 1–6 and the visions of chapters 7–12. The stories of the first half relate the events of Daniel and his ministry in the foreign courts of Babylonia and Persia. The visions

of the second half are the personal accounts of Daniel dated to the later part of his life.[3]

Outline

    I. **The Preparation of Daniel and His Friends** (1:1–21)

   II. **Nebuchadnezzar's Dream and Daniel's Interpretation** (2:1–49)

 III. **The Fiery Furnace** (3:1–30)

 IV. **Nebuchadnezzar's Dream and Daniel's Interpretation** (4:1–37)

  V. **The Writing on the Wall** (5:1–31)

 VI. **The Lions' Den** (6:1–28)

 VII. **Vision of the Four Beasts** (7:1–28)

VIII. **Vision of the Kingdoms** (8:1–27)

 IX. **Daniel's Prayer and Vision of the Seventy Weeks** (9:1–27)

  X. **Message of Encouragement** (10:1–11:45)

 XI. **Troubles and Victory** (12:1–13)

chiasm

Overview

Daniel 1–6

The opening chapters contain three of the most famous stories of the Bible: Nebuchadnezzar's burning fiery furnace (chapter 3), the handwriting on the wall at Belshazzar's party (chapter 5), and Darius' den of lions (chapter 6). But all the stories of chapters 1–6 have in common a single theme: Daniel and his three friends successfully bear witness to their faith before a hostile world. Though the circumstances are often unpleasant, these young men consistently stand up for righteousness against overwhelming odds. In the process they find that God is faithful.

Chapter 1 introduces the young Daniel (probably a teenager) and his three friends. Nebuchadnezzar, the conquering Babylonian king, captured them and took them into exile to serve in his royal court. The Babylonians relocated Daniel, and attempted to train him in their pagan culture. They took away his family, his home, his native Jerusalem, and anything that might give him security in life. But Daniel was determined to obey God's will for his life, even in what he ate. He refused to give up his faith in God (1:8). Daniel proved faithful in the little things first, and ultimately God honored him for his obedience and prepared him for a long life of service (1:9, 17).

In chapter 2 Nebuchadnezzar envisioned a bizarre statue in a dream. Daniel was able to avert disaster by discerning both the dream *and* its interpretation. God thus demonstrated that he was in control of earthly kingdoms (four represented in the vision) and had given Daniel a special gift of discernment (2:19).

Nebuchadnezzar attempted to compel the entire Babylonian Empire to worship his ninety-foot tall golden idol (chapter 3). The resistance of Shadrach, Meshach, and Abednego landed them in a burning, fiery furnace. But God delivered them, and their tenacious faith inspires all generations of believers. Nebuchadnezzar's dream (chapter 4) was a mystery to every wise man in Babylon except Daniel. Daniel was miraculously able to warn Nebuchadnezzar that his pride was inevitably going to be his downfall.

Pride is also a central theme in chapter

5. Belshazzar is the perfect picture of the arrogant ruler who thinks of himself as invincible. But God quickly turned his pompous rebellion into helpless terror (v. 6). In chapter 6, Daniel became the object of jealous hatred and deceit. But God honored his spiritual fortitude, even in the midst of the den of lions.[4]

Each chapter of the historical section opens with a specific problem that finds resolution as the narrative progresses. Often the problem threatens the faith or life of Daniel or his friends. But always, the problem is resolved through the faithfulness of a servant of God faced with challenging circumstances. In chapters 1, 3, and 6, the religious faithfulness of Daniel or his friends is directly attacked. In each case, loyalty to God and faith in his holy character bring deliverance. In chapters 2, 4, and 5, Babylonian kings receive mysterious messages from God that they are unable to understand (two are dreams and one is an esoteric inscription). In all three cases, the problem is resolved because God grants to Daniel the interpretation of the divine communication.

Chapters 1–6 combine with chapter 7 and are intentionally organized around a concentric structure known as **chiasm:** chapters 2 and 7 correspond, chapters 3 and 6 correspond, chapters 4 and 5 correspond. Thus we have the following pattern.

2 A vision of four kingdoms and their end (Nebuchadnezzar)
  3 Faithfulness and a miraculous rescue (the three friends)
    4 Judgment predicted and experienced (Nebuchadnezzar)
    5 Judgment predicted and experienced (Belshazzar)
  6 Faithfulness and a miraculous rescue (Daniel)
7 A vision of four kingdoms and their end (Daniel)[5]

This organization takes chapter 7 as a transitional chapter between the book's halves. Chiasm usually emphasizes the central point as the main thought of a unit. This would mean chapters 1–7 are concerned with God's punishment of proud rulers, as is clear from the midpoint at chapters 4 and 5. So the historical section

Christian Citizenship

Christians living in today's world have both a responsibility to be faithful to God and a responsibility to be productive citizens in society. Daniel, Shadrach, Meshach and Abednego serve well as examples of how to achieve such a balance.

The first priority for every Christian is to live within the will of God. Any society's laws form a practical framework conveying that society's consensus on what is mutually beneficial for every citizen. Christians should be committed to upholding and obeying that moral consensus. But in addition, Christians have a higher voice to obey.

Christians can and should contribute to society. Daniel and his friends became high officials in the government and served in the best capacity available to them. But if the society demanded allegiances or actions that interfered with their service to God and their commitments to live within his will, they quietly disobeyed the law of humankind.

So Christians listen to higher orders. The world needs Christians to express opinions and stand as correctives to the denigrating aspects of each culture. Jesus calls his church to be salt for the world, which involves acting as a purifying agent, preservative and flavor enhancer (Mt 5:13). As the light of the world, Christians are to reflect and proclaim the salvation Christ died to provide (Mt 5:14–16).

The Ancient of Days

The Son of Man

Seventy sevens

saints of the Most High

in general forms a theology of history in which God delivers those who faithfully represent him in the world and humiliates the proud who fail to acknowledge him.

Daniel 7–12

Though the visions of chapters 7–12 are in general less famous than the stories of the first half, they nonetheless contain individual passages that are well known for their theological import. The vision of chapter 7 portrays God as "**The Ancient of Days**"; another figure is called "**The Son of Man**," a designation that Jesus applied to himself (Mt 16:27; 24:30; 26:64; Mk 8:38; 13:26, etc.). Chapter 9 includes the often discussed "**Seventy sevens**" or "seventy weeks of years" passage (vv. 24–27).

The concluding vision contains the clearest Old Testament reference to the resurrection (12:1–3).

Chapters 7 and 8 are intimately related even though they are in different languages (see the discussion of bilingualism below). Daniel's vision in chapter 7 foresees four kingdoms represented as animals that are increasingly more terrible in appearance and conduct. Out of the last one emerges a pompous little horn that speaks rebellious words, defies God's authority, and persecutes God's people. As Daniel watches, he sees in his vision the "Ancient of Days" and "one like a son of man," who together establish a fifth and final kingdom, an eternal kingdom of the **saints of the Most High**. The vision of chapter 8 foresees two of the creatures in more detail. Again an earthly, human empire is responsible for inflicting suffering on the people of God.

In chapter 9 Daniel was studying the Book of Jeremiah and praying for the exile to end. His prayer for Judah's forgiveness and restoration resulted in another vision in which the angel Gabriel related the mysterious revelation of the seventy weeks. Chapters 10–12 relate Daniel's dramatic vision in which he sees an attempt to destroy Judaism in the second century B.C. by the Greek ruler ANTIOCHUS IV EPIPHANES. This king epitomizes the pompous earthly ruler. Though he is unable to annihilate the people of God, he inflicts them with unprecedented suffering. Ultimately, the supernatural forces of heaven intervene to ensure victory for God's kingdom. In chapter 12, Daniel learned that the godly are not informed about the timing of God's final victory. God's people must learn to live in faith and in the assurance of victory without requiring specific details.

The Theological Themes of Daniel

There are many secondary theological themes in the Book of Daniel that are beneficial for study, such as the role of prayer in Daniel (2:18; 9:3, 20–23) or Daniel's understanding of the Old Testament prophetic message in general (4:27). But three themes dominate this book: the sovereignty of God, the self-destructive pride of humankind, and the ultimate victory of God's kingdom.

The Sovereignty of God

Other prophets of the Old Testament knew that Yahweh, the God of Israel, was sovereign over the whole world, including the other nations (e.g., Am 1–2). But Daniel illustrated this fact in graphic new ways. Through both the stories and visions, Daniel demonstrated the lordship of God over the whole world, not just Jerusalem and the Israelites. This truth was meant to be a source of great comfort for exiled Israelites living in a foreign context.

This pervasive theme is apparent from the outset of chapter 1. The very first verse asserts that Nebuchadnezzar came to besiege Jerusalem. The reader of the book may assume the Babylonian king has come in his own awesome strength and at his own instigation. But the next verse makes it clear that Nebuchadnezzar was acting in accordance with the will of Yahweh: "The Lord gave Jehoiakim into the hand of Nebuchadnezzar . . ." (1:2—Hebrew nā-tan, "give," is a key word in this chapter).

After Daniel decided to resist the cultural pressure to compromise, God "gave" (nātan) him favor with Nebuchadnezzar's chief of staff (1:9). Later, God "gave" (nā-tan) the four young Jews surpassing knowledge and discernment, and Daniel a gift for understanding visions and dreams (1:17). So this chapter emphasizes God's sovereignty over the affairs of nations (Babylon and Israel, 1:2) as well as individuals (Daniel and his three companions, 1:17).

Specifically with regard to the nations, Daniel adds a new twist to the prophetic view of the nations. Most other prophets have oracles against Israel's enemy nations (Is 13–23, Jer 46–51, etc.). But Daniel views the key empires in a sequential order of four, followed by a fifth, eternal kingdom. Rather than preaching sermons against Israel's immediate neighbors, Daniel sees visions of future empires that oppose God and oppress his people everywhere.

Both the stories and the visions portray a struggle between the successive rulers of the world and God's kingdom. The stories relate how God's servants (Daniel and his friends) were able to overcome the strongest human forces of earth in their efforts to remain faithful to God. The first of the visions (chapter 7) portrays three frightening beasts and a grotesque monster that threatens to exterminate God's people. But the Ancient of Days prevails and establishes an eternal kingdom for his saints. Even in persecution and death, the sovereign Lord of the kingdom will provide resurrection (12:1–3). In the stories, God was sovereign over all his past enemies. The visions reveal how that sovereignty will play itself out in human history.

This emphasis on God's sovereignty leads naturally to the next two primary themes of the book. Human pride and rebellion are self-destructive because they fail to acknowledge the sovereign Lord of the universe; God's people will ultimately succeed because with him they cannot fail.

The Pride of Humankind

A further emphasis of the Book of Daniel is the pride and arrogance of humankind and God's total condemnation of egotism. In the stories of chapters 1–6, rebellious pride is the issue behind the problem that introduces each chapter. In the visions of chapters 7–12, the obstinate arrogance of future world leaders is the enemy of God and his people. Ultimately in each case God has acted, or will act, to turn human pride and arrogance into shame and disgrace.

Nebuchadnezzar (chapter 4) and Belshazzar (chapter 5) are specific examples of human pride (these chapters form the literary centerpiece of chapters 1–6, see above). In both cases, their pride reduces them to pathetic states of absolute helplessness and ridicule. After God has acted, they are hardly recognizable as kings of the great and mighty Babylon (4:33; 5:6, 20).

The pride of world empires forms a central theme in chapters 7–12. Chapters 7 and 8 portray a succession of proud world leaders, finally reaching a climax of imperial pride at the little horn with the big mouth (7:8). But a new heavenly kingdom led by the Ancient of Days and the Son of Man replaces these proud earthly reigns. In chapters 10–12, the supernatural forces of heaven will move to crush the ultimate anti-Christian ruler of earth, who has arrogantly raised himself above every god (11:36–45).

The Book of Daniel is especially relevant for every generation of believers because it confronts pride as our ultimate problem. Sin and rebellion always find root in pride and self-absorption. So salvation must involve confession, rejection of prideful self-sufficiency, and a dependence on God (Mk 8:34), all of which are so magnificently modeled by Daniel, his three companions, and later by the Saints of the Most High.

The Ultimate Victory of God's Saints

Daniel also reveals much about the kingdom of God. The fundamental message of Daniel is that through every circumstance of life, it is possible to live a life of faith and victory with God's help. God reigns supreme in heaven and earth, and those allied with him share in his triumph. No matter how severe the persecution, the enemies of God cannot bring an end to his community of believers. The unique apocalyptic nature of Daniel teaches that this has always been so (chapters 1–6) and always will be so (chapters 7–12). Even in death, God's people are victorious (12:1–3).

Prevalent in this book is the idea of four great world kingdoms followed by a fifth (chapters 2 and 7). Interpreters have traditionally taken these kingdoms to refer to Babylonia, MEDO-PERSIA, GREECE, and ROME respectively. But the accurate identity of the kingdoms is much disputed even among evangelicals.[6] Though the precise details are in doubt, the message is clear and irrefutable. All earthly kingdoms are temporary, even fleeting, no matter how impressive they may look at the moment. Ultimately the Son of Man will usher in the eternal kingdom of the Ancient of Days (7:14).

Although this promise is certain, the rest of the book describes a delay in the arrival of God's eternal kingdom. During the postponement, God's faithful people will endure severe testing and persecution at the hands of proud, unbelieving leaders of the world. The seventy weeks of years (9:24–27) and the promise of the resurrection (12:1–3) presuppose that the faithful saints of God will have to endure hardship for a limited time. But those who faithfully endure and await his timing will participate in his final victory.

Daniel is a primary source for Old Testament eschatology. Together with the New Testament Book of Revelation, it provides much of our data for various interpretations about the endtimes. Though Christians disagree on issues such as when Christ will return and the details of his reign, the most important question is whether the church is currently living a life worthy of his blessing and acceptance, whenever he comes again.

In other words, the details of eschatology are not as crucial as eschatological ethics: behaving Christ-like now in this world, and living in anticipation of his return. Daniel teaches that God's people can and should live holy, righteous lives while suffering the injustices of this life. They

A replica of the Ishtar Gate, ancient Babylon. The first half of the Book of Daniel relates the events of Daniel and his ministry in the courts of Babylonia and Persia.

are encouraged to do so because God will one day bring them ultimate victory.

Problems of Interpretation

Bilingualism

Interestingly, Daniel is one of only two books in the Bible that are bilingual (Ezra is the other).[7] The book contains both Hebrew and Aramaic, a sister language of Hebrew that slowly replaced it as the native language of exiled Jews. The most surprising aspect about the interchange of Hebrew and Aramaic is that the changes do not coincide with the unit breaks of the book. Instead of chapters 1–6 being in one language and 7–12 being in the other, the book has Hebrew in 1:1–2:4a, Aramaic in 2:4b–7:28, and Hebrew again in chapters 8–12.

Scholars have suggested many creative explanations for why the author of Daniel used two languages.[8] The most widely held position believes the entire book was originally composed in Aramaic. The beginning (1:1–2:4a) and ending (8–12) were later translated into Hebrew in order to ensure the book's acceptance into the canon.[9] All such attempts to explain the bilingual nature of Daniel are highly speculative. Perhaps the author used Aramaic deliberately as a literary device to cast the stories set in Babylonia and Persia in a much different light from the visions of chapters 8–12.[10]

Identity of the Four Kingdoms

There are many difficult issues of interpretation in the Book of Daniel. For example, in the previous section we mentioned that scholars disagree on the identity of the four kingdoms of chapters 2 and 7. Many define the debate narrowly between evangelical and nonevangelical positions. The evangelical position would assume the four kingdoms of Daniel 2 and 7 are Babylonia, Medo-Persia, Greece, and Rome. In this way, the kingdom of heaven may be clearly identified with the coming of Christ and the birth of Christianity during the Roman period.

On the other hand, the nonevangelical position, which usually dates the book to the second century, assumes the empires are Babylonia, Media, Persia, and Greece. Thus the kingdom of heaven that succeeded the Greek period would be the Jewish state set up by the **Maccabees** during the second century B.C. (we will say more on this later). This position denies the possibility of detailed and accurate predictive prophecy.

Now, however, some evangelicals have accepted the possibility that the fourth empire was Greece while maintaining a sixth-century date for the book.[11] The traditional approach, which identifies the fourth kingdom with Rome, still has much to commend it to all readers of Daniel.

Vision of the "Seventy Weeks"

Daniel's vision of the "seventy weeks" or seventy periods of time is also difficult to interpret (9:24–27). Many interpreters today assume the prophecy is *ex eventu*, or written after the supposedly predicted events that took place in the second century B.C. The disruption of the sacrificial system and the "**abomination of desolation**" are routinely dated to 167 and 166 B.C.[12] In this approach, the passage is no real predictive prophecy at all, but only a retrospective look on events that have already taken place.

But many evangelical scholars argue that these verses are indeed futuristic, predictive prophecy, and that they are most perfectly and completely fulfilled in Jesus Christ, though there is little agreement on the specifics of the interpretation. Daniel saw details of the coming of Christ vaguely, as though looking across several mountain ranges. The mountains farthest away are clear only in outline form and it is impossible for the viewer to gauge their proper distance because of the intervening mountain ranges and valleys. No doubt Jews of the second century felt this prophecy was fulfilled in their day. And so it was partially, since they stood on an intervening mountain range. "But guided by the Holy Spirit, [Daniel] was actually pointing to the coming of Jesus Christ more than a century and a half later."[13]

Historical Questions

The Book of Daniel, then, contains certain passages that are controversial and present more than one possible meaning. But in addition to this, some modern scholars assert the book is full of historical inaccuracies. Typically, they argue that the author incorrectly identified historical figures and mixed up certain dates within the book. We now discuss a few of these problems.

Nebuchadnezzar's madness

Many scholars regard Nebuchadnezzar's madness (4:32–33) with skepticism. Some even aver that it is "beyond reasonable doubt" that the author has confused a tradition about Belshazzar's father, NABONIDUS (found in the Dead Sea Scrolls), with Nebuchadnezzar.[14] But documentary evidence from the later years of Nebuchadnezzar's forty-three-year reign is meager, and ancient references mention a severe illness just before his death.[15]

"King" Belshazzar

King Belshazzar plays an important role in the Book of Daniel, and three chapters are dated to his reign (5, 7, and 8). Yet, as far as we know, he never assumed the title "king" (only "son of the king") in Babylonian records.[16] Indeed, his name was so little known to historians before the decipherment of cuneiform literature in the middle of the nineteenth century that some considered the name a pure invention of the author of Daniel.[17] Some scholars who study Daniel have often assumed the author was misinformed or confused about Neo-Babylonian history, since the book often refers to Belshazzar as "king" and as "son" of Nebuchadnezzar.

However, we now know that Belshazzar had been established as a co-regent with Nabonidus his father for ten years and exercised royal authority during that time.[18] The author of Daniel has related a situation in which Belshazzar is acting king, rather than the official state co-regent.[19] The Aramaic word "king" is broader than our English term. It was appropriate for the author of Daniel to refer to Belshazzar as king, since Nabonidus appears to have been out of the picture at this time. Actually the author was quite informed on Neo-Babylonian history, since he knew that Belshazzar himself was only the second in the kingdom and could offer

to make Daniel only third in the kingdom (5:7, 16, 29).

Many also assume the author was confused about Belshazzar's father. Chapter 5 frequently refers to Nebuchadnezzar as his father, whereas we know that Belshazzar was the son of Nabonidus, who may not have been related to Nebuchadnezzar at all. But it is widely known that the terms "father" and "son" have broader meanings in Hebrew and Aramaic than in our own languages, and may be used to designate the royal ancestor or even simply one's predecessor on the throne. In addition it may be that Nabonidus was actually a son-in-law of Nebuchadnezzar.[20]

Darius the Mede

Another historical comment in Daniel that scholars assume to be inaccurate is the reference to DARIUS THE MEDE in 5:31. Cuneiform sources from Babylonia prove that the city of Babylon fell in October 539 B.C., to the better-known and more famous Cyrus the Persian. Many scholars believe Darius the Mede is strictly unhistorical.

Rather than assume mistaken judgment on the part of the ancient author, there are several indications that the misunderstanding is on our part due to lack of detailed information. One scholar has suggested that Darius the Mede may be identified with Gubaru, a certain provincial governor of Babylon.[21] Or Darius the Mede may have been a different individual also known as Gubaru who served, not as provincial governor, but as the actual conqueror of Babylon.[22]

An entirely different explanation is that the name "Darius the Mede" is a throne name for Cyrus the Persian, and that they are in fact the same individual.[23] There is linguistic evidence for the idea that Daniel 6:28 should be translated "Daniel prospered in the reign of Darius, that is, in the reign of Cyrus the Persian." The Aramaic word "and" (translated "that is" here) sometimes clarifies what goes before it, and in this case explains that the two names belong to the same person.[24]

Whichever of these explanations seems more attractive, we should not assume the Book of Daniel contains historical inaccuracies. Before the discovery of the relevant Babylonian documents, many scholars assumed Belshazzar was completely ficti-

*vaticinium
ex eventu*

tious. But now it is clear the ancient author was much closer to historical accuracy than previously thought. Although several historical difficulties remain in the book, the author of Daniel was not confused about historical events, as modern scholars often suggest. We should give credit to the ancient author and assume any inconsistencies are due to our own lack of available data. The burden of proof continues to rest on those who wish to discredit Scripture.

Date of composition

All of these difficult questions relate in one way or another to the most controversial problem of all: When was the book composed? There are basically two options: either the book came from the late sixth century B.C. or it was written during the second century B.C.[25] The first option emphasizes the differences between Daniel and the rest of apocalyptic literature. The second option maximizes the similarities.

Our first option is to accept Daniel as a composition from the late sixth century B.C., in which case it must be genuine predictive prophecy and not merely prophecy after the event (*vaticinium ex eventu*, see above). In this case, there is no need to presume the book is pseudonymous (written

under a pen name) like other apocalyptic books. Thus the first-person account of the visions in chapters 7–12 is actually that of the historical Daniel. This option assumes the book is what it claims to be: a book about the exiled Daniel, his experiences in the Babylonian and Persian courts, and his visions.

The second option holds that the book as it stands comes from the second century B.C. Many scholars believe the Aramaic section (2:4b–7:28) was composed sometime in the third century B.C. and then incorporated into the current arrangement during the Maccabean crisis. When Antiochus IV Epiphanes threatened to destroy Judaism in the 160s B.C., an author living in Judea wrote an introduction in Hebrew and the visions of chapters 8–12 to round out the book. The author wanted to encourage the Jews to remain faithful during the crisis and trust in God for deliverance.

This second approach assumes Daniel has much in common with the rest of apocalyptic literature. It assumes the book is pseudonymous, written in the name of a mythological Daniel who is known only vaguely elsewhere.[26] It also assumes the specific prophecies of the book are prophecies made after the events had already occurred. The author has presented them in futuristic garb to encourage the readers to remain faithful to God.[27] This option assumes the book is an attack on the anti-Judaism policies of Antiochus.

One of the great difficulties with this second option is that it assumes pseudonymous works were accepted into the canon. We have no conclusive evidence that literature written under a pen name was ever admitted into the canon.[28] But if it were in this case, the community of faith would have accepted a pseudonymous document as Scripture in a startlingly brief period of time (presumably one or two centuries). Moreover, pseudonymous works normally used the name of a venerated hero of faith from the past: Enoch, Abraham, Moses, Ezra, and so on. But Daniel is mostly unknown outside the Book of Daniel.

Furthermore, the second-century date for Daniel fails to explain the book's major influence on the QUMRAN community as reflected in the Dead Sea Scrolls. The large number of fragments and copies of Daniel

Key People/ Places

Antiochus IV Epiphanes
Nabonidus
Darius the Mede
Belshazzar
Medo-Persia
Greece
Rome
Qumran

Key Terms

canon
apocalyptic literature
intertestamental apocalyptic
pseudonym
eschatological
vaticinium ex eventu
intertestamental period
biblical apocalyptic
chiasm
Ancient of Days
Son of Man
seventy sevens
Saints of the Most High
Maccabees
abomination of desolation

Summary

1. The Book of Daniel is classified as apocalyptic literature and is unique in many ways.

2. The characteristics of intertestamental apocalyptic literature are: it contains a vision and requires interpretation by a heavenly mediator, the author's name is a pseudonym, it has similar content in that it divides history into periods of time and history ends as a final judgment, it involves the temporal and the spatial, and it often takes a past event and writes it as a prediction for the future.

3. Old Testament apocalyptic literature does not have all the features of the intertestamental apocalyptic literature.

4. There are two parts to Daniel: the narrative story (1–6) and the vision (7–12).

5. The dominant themes of the Book of Daniel are the sovereignty of God, the self-destructive pride of humankind, and the ultimate victory of God's kingdom.

6. Daniel is the primary source for eschatology in the Old Testament.

7. There are problems of interpretation with the Book of Daniel as it is bilingual, the interpretation of each of the four kingdoms is difficult, and the vision of the "seventy weeks" is also difficult to interpret.

8. Evangelical and nonevangelical scholars disagree on the identity of the four kingdoms.

9. Many modern scholars point to Nebuchadnezzar's madness, and the facts about Belshazzar and Darius the Mede to conclude that the Book of Daniel is full of errors.

10. The two positions on the date of Daniel are the second century and the late sixth century B.C.

11. One of the major problems with the theory that Daniel was written in the second century is that it assumes that pseudonymous works were accepted into the canon.

Study Questions

1. Define apocalyptic literature.

2. How is Daniel unique from other Old Testament books?

3. What is the basic call the Book of Daniel puts forth to its readers?

4. How are the themes of faithfulness and loyalty to God and deliverance by God worked out in Daniel?

5. Explain the chiastic structure of the first seven chapters of Daniel. What is the central thought in this chiasm?

6. What are some of the more well-known visions contained in chapters 7–12?

7. Discuss some of the major theological themes in the Book of Daniel.

8. Discuss the problems in interpreting Daniel.

Further Reading

Baldwin, Joyce G. *Daniel: An Introduction and Commentary.* Tyndale Old Testament Commentary. Downers Grove: InterVarsity, 1978. Excellent, though brief exposition.

Collins, John J. *Daniel: A Commentary on the Book of Daniel.* Hermenia. Minneapolis: Fortress, 1993. Best and most complete presentation of mainline critical scholarship. Assumes late date.

Goldingay, John E. *Daniel.* Word Biblical Commentary 30. Dallas: Word, 1989. Informative and thorough, though limited in its usefulness due to dogmatism about the late date of composition.

Russell, D. S. *Daniel, An Active Volcano: Reflections on the Book of Daniel.* Louisville: Westminster/John Knox, 1989. Helpful theological observations with many contemporary applications.

Wenham, Gordon J. "Daniel: The Basic Issues," *Themelios* 2, no. 2 (1977):49–52.

Wiseman, Donald J., ed. *Notes on Some Problems in the Book of Daniel.* London: Tyndale, 1965. Scholarly assessment of the difficult issues in Daniel, from an evangelical position.

Young, E. J. *The Prophecy of Daniel.* Grand Rapids: Eerdmans, 1949.

among the scrolls demonstrates the book's popularity at Qumran. There would have been insufficient time for the book of Daniel—so recently composed—to have such profound influence on the Qumran community.[29]

In conclusion, we should recognize Daniel as "biblical apocalyptic," a subcategory of apocalyptic literature. It is apocalyptic in nature (especially chapters 7–12), though it differs significantly from the intertestamental apocalyptic literature. Biblical apocalyptic was thus the forerunner of later Jewish and early Christian apocalypses. Chapters 7–12 must have their origin in Daniel, and the stories of chapters 1–6 have proven to be historically reliable. The evidence that the book is genuinely predictive in nature rather than retrospective is convincing, and the sixth-century date of composition should not be dismissed lightly.[30]

32 Hosea, Joel, and Amos
A Call for Repentance
and a Promise for Blessing

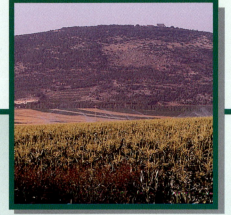

Outline

- **Hosea: Sharing God's Heartache**
  Outline
  The Man
  His Times
  Major Themes of the Book
  Content of the Book
  Hosea and the New Testament
- **Joel: The Day of the Lord**
  Outline
  Joel's Background
  Joel's Message
- **Amos: Shepherd for Social Justice**
  Outline
  Amos's Background
  Amos's Message

Objectives

**After reading this chapter,
you should be able to**

- Outline the basic content
  of the Book of Hosea
- Describe the time period
  of Hosea's ministry
- List the themes of Hosea
- Outline the basic content of Joel
- Outline the basic content of Amos
- Identify the eight nations
  Amos prophesied against
- List the five visions of judgment
  Amos prophesied

Asherah

A famous poem reads like this:

> For the want of a nail, the horseshoe
> was lost,
> For the want of a horseshoe, the horse
> was lost,
> For the want of a horse, the rider
> was lost,
> For the want of a rider, the battle
> was lost,
> For the want of a battle, the kingdom
> was lost,
> And all for the want of a horseshoe nail!

The point of the poem, of course, is to show how sometimes small and seemingly insignificant items can have a major impact on present and future events.

The prophets of the last twelve books of the Old Testament have been designated the Minor Prophets. Most of these books have only a few chapters, and at first glance, they may seem a small and somewhat insignificant part of God's word. But the minor prophets pack a powerful spiritual punch all their own. Each one is minor in size but mighty in impact.

As you study the minor prophets, try to understand what unique contribution each prophet made to the biblical revelation. The first three we will study are Hosea, Joel, and Amos.

Hosea: Sharing God's Heartache

Outline

I. **Hosea's Family/God's Family** (1:1–3:5)

II. **God Takes Israel to Court** (4:1–5:15)

III. **Hosea's Invitation Tarnished by Reality** (6:1–11:11)

IV. **God's Final Arguments against Israel** (11:12–13:16)

V. **The Possibility of Restoration** (14:1–9)

The Man

Hosea's great courage and conviction shaped his prophetic ministry. His wife Gomer committed adultery against him, and Hosea suffered the agony of jealousy, betrayal, humiliation, and shame. Yet as those around him laughed, Hosea prophesied. He told Israel that she, God's wife, was just like Gomer. As God called husbands and wives to total commitment to each other, so God expected total commitment from his bride Israel. As Hosea lived among his hearers, they saw his pain and received his message through his words and life.

We know little about Hosea's background. Hosea's name means "The Lord saves" and is related to the names "Joshua" and "Isaiah." His father, Beeri, appears only in Hosea 1:1. No other Old Testament book mentions this prophet, and New Testament references to Hosea's words give us no information about the prophet himself.

We do know that Hosea lived and prophesied in the northern kingdom. Although he had an occasional word about Judah,[1] Hosea focused on Israel. He challenged God's people to recognize their sinful ways and repent.

His Times

Hosea began his ministry during a period of prosperity. In the north, Jeroboam II (793–753 B.C.) restored Israel's border from HAMATH in Syria to the Dead Sea (2 Kgs 14:25). In Judah, Uzziah (792–739 B.C.) extended his dominion into Philistia along the coast, received tribute from the Ammonites, fortified Jerusalem, and amassed a strong army (2 Chr 26:6–15). Israel and Judah's territory expanded to what it had been in David's time.

With economic prosperity, however, came spiritual trouble. The people had already adopted many of the religious practices of those around them. They no longer worshiped the Lord alone, but also served other gods. They worshiped the god Baal, Canaanite god of agriculture and fertility, and his consort Asherah. They built shrines to these gods, and adopted the sexual fertility rites that accompanied their worship. Sacred prostitution actually became part of Israel's religion! Gradually, the people became convinced that Baal, not the Lord God, had provided them with life's blessings.

Most Bible scholars date the beginning of Hosea's ministry to late in Jeroboam's reign. At this time, Assyria was rising to power, and would soon establish itself as a world empire under TIGLATH-PILESER III. Many in Israel saw this nation as a possible ally, but Hosea warned against trusting Assyria for anything (5:13; 7:11). Tragically, history would prove the prophet's concerns well-founded. Since Hosea does not specifically describe Samaria's fall, most interpreters date the writing of his book to just before 722 B.C.

Major Themes of the Book

Spiritual adultery

God created marriage for humanity's good. He ordained that a man and a woman should make a lifelong commitment of love to each other. Adultery violated the marriage relationship and defiled the basic institution God had established for humanity's well-being.

Hosea declared that in a spiritual sense, God and Israel were husband and wife. Israel had forsaken her marriage bond with the Lord, joining herself to Baal and other lovers. She had mocked the divine love that had made her a people. She had taken God's gifts and used them to worship idols (2:8). Israel was committing nothing less than spiritual adultery.

Gomer's unfaithfulness portrayed on a human level the spiritual adultery Israel was committing. Gomer defiled herself and hurt her husband; Israel defiled herself and grieved God.

Hosea's graphic language (e.g. 2:2–3, 10) shows the depths to which Israel had plummeted, as God through his prophet called his bride back to himself.

Knowledge of God

The Christian life is a relationship with the living Lord. God calls people to know him deeply and to grow in that knowledge. Regular prayer, Bible study, and meeting with other believers are some ways God uses to help people know him better.

Hosea challenged Israel to know God. The people lived lives that totally opposed God because they did not know him (4:1–3). They rejected his Law and prophets. God lamented, "My people are destroyed for lack of knowledge" (4:6).

Hosea urged Israel to press on to know the Lord fully, for only then could she live as he expected (6:3).

God's frustrated love

As Hosea experienced Gomer's unfaithfulness, he learned more of God's pain and frustration with Israel. God's frustration surfaces again and again in Hosea's words. God deeply loved his people, and seeing their adultery truly grieved him. He knew he would have to judge their sin, and yet how could he send his own people—his own bride—into exile?

God's love would eventually prevail. Though Israel had hurt him, God expressed his special love for her in Hosea's closing chapter. If she repented and trusted in him, God would forgive her and heal her. He could make her into what he had intended her to be all along—his own beautiful bride.

Content of the Book

Hosea's family/God's family (1:1–3:5)

God commanded Hosea to marry Gomer, a woman who proved unfaithful to Hosea. Scholars have debated the nature of this command. Did God command Hosea to marry a woman who was already sexually immoral, or did Gomer become unfaithful after her marriage to Hosea?

Some scholars have found difficulty with the idea that God would command his prophet to marry a prostitute. They argue that Gomer became unfaithful after Hosea married her, and that this understanding better fits the analogy of God and Israel (2:15). In this interpretation of the text, the expression "adulterous wife" refers to what Gomer became after her marriage to Hosea.

Other scholars have focused their attention on the Hebrew expression translated "adulterous wife" (NIV). The wording literally reads "woman/wife of harlotries." The Hebrew word in question, zenûnîm ("harlotries"), occurs twice in 1:2 and a total of twelve times in the Old Testament.[2] In the ten other occurrences, the term refers to past or present harlotry, never to future harlotry. This evidence suggests that Gomer was already a prostitute when Hosea married her.

In either case, God's actions certainly

seem extreme to us, but so were the times. God determined that he would get his point across to Israel, even if he had to invite one of his prophets to share in his own experience.[3]

Hosea's three children received symbolic names that warned of God's coming judgment. Jezreel alluded to the place where Assyria would win a decisive victory over Israel. Lo-ruhamah, "not pitied," indicated that God would not pity Israel any longer. Lo-ammi, "not my people," pointed to a coming separation between God and Israel.

Nevertheless, a ray of hope shone through the darkness of God's judgment. God promised he would restore Israel for his very own, depriving her of her immoral ways and making her holy instead (1:10–11; 2:6–23). Hosea portrayed this truth by buying Gomer back after she had abandoned him and somehow become the property of another (3:1–5).[4] He had brought her home, and one day, God would do the same for Israel.

God takes Israel to court (4:1–5:15)

The language of Hosea 4:1, especially the Hebrew word rîb ("charge" in the NIV), suggests that God was bringing a legal dispute against Israel. When Israel failed to live up to her part of the covenant God had made with her, God had the right to bring charges against her. Israel stood guilty before God.

Hosea declared that the people did not really know God. This lack of knowledge led to sin, which would bring judgment. The priests used their office for dishonest gain; they pointed out the people's sin so the people would bring them more sacrifices.[5] While some in Hosea's day apparently blamed the women for harlotry, God said that since both men and women participated in sexual sin, both were guilty before him. Many in Israel held out hope that Assyria would rescue them from their troubles, but Hosea warned that Assyria would not stop God's judgment.

Hosea's invitation tarnished by reality (6:1–11:1)

Hosea invited Israel to return to the Lord, to know him more intimately, but the people largely ignored the prophet's invitation. Israel had transgressed the covenant;

her treachery was everywhere. She thought God did not see her sin, but God saw everything. The leaders failed to consult the Lord, and this failure brought tragic consequences.

Israel's harlotry included both religious and political aspects. She committed religious harlotry when she forsook God's laws and worshiped idols, adopting some of her neighbors' worship patterns. She committed political harlotry when she appealed to other nations rather than to God for help. She turned to Assyria and then to Egypt, but God said her only hope lay in him.

Hosea compared Israel to four things in 9:10–11:11. First, Israel was like a bunch of choice grapes in the wilderness that had spoiled; God said she would bear no more fruit. Second, Israel was like a vine that grew according to its own plan, choosing her own way instead of God's way. Third, Israel was a trained heifer who loved to thresh grain because she could eat as she threshed.[6] God said he would yoke Israel to work in fields where righteousness and kindness grew. Fourth, Israel was like a toddling son. God had loved him, called him out of Egypt, raised him, taught him to walk, and Israel, in ungrateful response, had turned to Baal.

God's final arguments against Israel (11:12–13:16)

Hosea tried to teach the people a lesson from history. Their forefather Jacob had wrestled with his brother in Rebekah's womb, and as a man, he had wrestled with God. He had sought God's favor and prevailed. Later, God had sent many prophets to his people. These men received numerous visions and prophecies, all calling the people back to their God who loved them. The prophets' messages, however, fell on deaf ears. Israel did not follow Jacob's example, and she did not heed the prophets' words.

God warned Israel her judgment would be swift. God would remove her king, in whom she trusted so completely. God would prove him powerless in the face of divine power and wrath. Samaria, the northern capital, would fall—and hard!

Part of the valley of Jezreel, near Mount Tabor. The valley contains the ruins of Megiddo, from which the name Armageddon is derived (Jl 2).

The possibility of restoration (14:1–9)

Despite Hosea's scathing indictment of Israel's sin, he still held out hope for the nation and its citizens. He called them to repent and to acknowledge that God alone could provide for their needs. In return, God promised them healing and blessing. Hosea used agricultural terms to describe Israel's future restoration. Israel would flourish like the vine, blossom like the lily, take root like the trees of Lebanon, become all God wanted her to be.

Hosea and the New Testament

The New Testament cites Hosea several times. When Joseph and Mary brought the infant Jesus out of Egypt, the Gospel writer Matthew affirmed in 2:15 that God had fulfilled Hosea 11:1 again—"Out of Egypt I called my son." When Jesus' enemies challenged him because he associated with sinners, Jesus challenged them to learn the meaning of Hosea 6:6—"I desire mercy and not sacrifice" (Mt 9:13). Finally, the apostle Paul cited Hosea 1:10–11 and 2:23 in Romans 9:25–26. Paul explained that God was creating for himself a people that would include Jews and Gentiles alike. Gentiles who had never known the Lord would become his children through faith in Jesus Christ.

Joel: The Day of the Lord

Outline

   I. **The Locust Plague** (1:1–20)

  II. **The Day of the Lord** (2:1–17)

 III. **The Lord's Answer** (2:18–3:21)

Joel's Background

During Joel's day, a locust plague came upon the land such as its citizens had never seen. Joel described this locust plague as "the Day of the LORD" (1:15; 2:1, 11, 31) and called the nation to repentance. He also warned that an even more terrible day of judgment was coming, one for which the people needed to prepare themselves.

We know very little about Joel's background other than that he was the son of Pethuel. The name "Joel" appears elsewhere in Scripture, but we have no evidence to connect the prophet with anyone else who had that name. His name means "The Lord is God." Scholars disagree as to when Joel prophesied, suggesting dates anywhere from 900 B.C. to 400 B.C. We propose a date of somewhere about 500–450 B.C. for three reasons. First, 3:1–3 appears to refer back to the Babylonian exile. Second, Joel mentions priests and elders (1:13–14), but no king, which may suggest that Judah did not have one at the time. Since the prophet called the entire nation to repentance, it would be odd if he omitted the royal house. Third, Joel mentions no opposition from pagan cults. This fact seems to reflect postexilic conditions.[7]

Joel's Message

The locust plague (1:1–20)

Joel depicted the locust plague as uncommonly severe. Earlier generations had not witnessed such a terrible thing, and later generations would surely remember it. Joel compared the locusts to a mighty army that ravaged the land and laid it bare. Every part of society felt the effects of the plague. Joel called the people to humble themselves and cry to the Lord, for he alone could save them.

The Day of the Lord (2:1–17)

Joel saw in the locust plague a sign of things to come. A day of darkness and gloom was coming, and only those whose hearts were right before God could endure it. The prophet challenged the people to return to God with all their hearts, not just with external signs of repentance (vv. 12–13). This call to deep repentance forms a turning point in the book. Only through repentance and faith could the people hope for God's compassion and restoration.

The Lord's answer (2:18–3:21)

The Lord's answer to his people included four parts. First, the land would experience restoration. The Lord would have compassion on his people and renew nature so the crops would grow abundantly. The Lord would remove oppressors and display his glory, and God's people would rejoice in him.

Second, the people would experience a spiritual awakening. Joel declared that one day the Lord would pour out his Spirit on people in every category of society—male and female, young and old, slave and free. Cataclysmic events would accompany this outpouring, and whoever called upon the name of the Lord would receive his salvation (2:28–32). On the day of Pentecost,

the apostle Peter announced that the Lord had fulfilled Joel's words. The Holy Spirit had come, indwelling all believers and enabling them to become like Jesus Christ their Lord (Acts 2:14–21).

Third, God would judge unrepentant nations. He would gather those who had sinned against him and his people and repay them according to their evil. All the earth would know God's sovereignty in that day!

Fourth, Judah would enjoy special blessing and prominence. Joel used figurative language to describe the people's coming agricultural, political, social, and spiritual benefits. Nature would flourish as God removed Judah's enemies, and the people would live in harmony, for their God would dwell with them.

Amos: Shepherd for Social Justice

Outline

   I. **Superscription and Introduction** (1:1–2)

  II. **Israel Is No Better Than the Other Nations** (1:3–2:16)

 III. **Various Prophecies against Israel** (3:1–6:14)

 IV. **Five Visions of Judgment** (7:1–9:10)

  V. **Promises of Restoration and Blessing** (9:11–15)

Amos's Background

Amos worked among the sheepherders of Tekoa, a small town in Judah about ten miles south of Jerusalem (1:1). The Hebrew word translated "sheepherder" (*nōqēd*) is not the usual word for "sheepherder." It occurs elsewhere only in 2 Kings 3:4, where it refers to Mesha, king of Moab. Because of this fact, some scholars have suggested that perhaps Amos was a wealthy shepherd. However, this argument rests on only two occurrences of the word *nōqēd*. Furthermore, Amos himself seems to emphasize his humble background (7:14).

Amos also earned part of his living tending sycamore trees. Certain kinds of sycamores in Palestine produce figs. Fig growers helped the figs ripen by piercing them a short time before harvest.[8]

Amos grew up in Judah, but God sent him to prophesy in Israel. Certainly many Israelites looked at Amos with suspicion (7:10–13). Nevertheless, Amos faithfully performed his prophetic ministry. He called Israel to repent of her sin and establish justice as the law of the land. God desired his people to love him and to reflect that love to their fellow citizens.

Amos, like Hosea, prophesied during the reigns of Jeroboam II of Israel (793–753 B.C.) and Uzziah (= Azariah) of Judah (792–739 B.C.).[9] Economic prosperity and political stability had led to Israel's spiritual decay. This spiritual decay displayed itself in social injustice. The rich exploited the poor; the powerful dominated the weak. Morality meant little or nothing.

The Book of Amos does not specifically mention Assyria. This omission may indicate that Assyria was not yet a major power in the ancient Near East. Furthermore, both Jeroboam and Uzziah ruled as co-regents during part of their reigns. The fact that Amos only mentions Jeroboam and Uzziah may indicate that he prophesied during the time when these kings ruled independently. If so, we may date Amos's prophecy somewhere between 767 B.C. and 753 B.C.[10] The reference to the earthquake in 1:1 does not help us pinpoint the beginning of Amos's prophecy because we do not know for sure when this disaster occurred.[11] Such a precise reference might indicate, however, that the prophet's ministry was fairly short.

Amos's Message

Israel is no better than the other nations (1:3–2:16)

Amos began by speaking against eight nations that God had singled out for judgment. Each of the eight judgment speeches contains an announcement of God's judgment, the reason for judgment, and the nature of judgment. Most of the sins Amos mentions appear only here, and we do not know exactly when each nation committed its crime.

Numerical expressions like "For three sins . . . even for four" occur elsewhere in the Old Testament (Jb 5:19–27; 33:14; Ps 62:11–12; Prv 6:16–19; 30:15b–16, 18–20, 21–23, 29–31; Mi 5:5). By using this expression, Amos was indicating that God would be gracious to these nations no longer. The time to pay for their sins had come.

Amos commenced his prophecy with Damascus and Philistia, two kingdoms against whom Israel had always struggled. Damascus had brutalized the inhabitants of Gilead, while the Philistines had deported captive Israelites to Edom to sell them as slaves. Amos then preached against Tyre, a kingdom that had enjoyed good relations with Israel during the reigns of David and Solomon (2 Sm 5:11; 1 Kgs 5:1–12). Tyre, a merchant city, had also sold Israelites into slavery in Edom.

After speaking judgment against Damascus, Philistia, and Tyre, Amos prophesied against Edom, Ammon, and Moab, three of Israel's blood relatives (Gn 19:36–38; 36:1). Edom, the closest blood relative, had continually made war against Israel and showed no compassion to his brothers. Moab had desecrated the bones of Edom's king, while Ammon had killed the unborn babies of Gilead by cutting them from their mothers' wombs.

Amos then turned to Judah, his own people. In contrast to the other nations' crimes, Judah's crime was spiritual in nature. Judah had forsaken the Mosaic law and followed after false gods. Each generation plunged deeper into sin. Amos announced that God would deal with Judah, too.

When Amos first came to the northern kingdom, many Israelites probably looked at him with suspicion. Why, they wondered, had this southern prophet come up north to preach? But as Amos began to proclaim his message, the people discovered they liked what he said. He was condemning all their enemies!

Then Amos's message suddenly took a new direction: God would now judge Israel! Amos dealt with Israel much more extensively because she had committed so many sins! The powerful oppressed the weak, caring only for their own personal

Social Justice Today

For Amos, a proper relationship with God demanded social justice. What about today? Are such issues as feeding the poor, providing shelter for the homeless, working for civil rights, and fighting abortion part of the gospel? Should Christians care about social justice?

The gospel message centers on Jesus Christ and his death, burial, and resurrection. Through repentance and faith, we can receive his offer of salvation. The Holy Spirit then begins to work in us to make us more like Jesus (Rom 8:29).

The Bible clearly teaches that social justice should be a natural product of the gospel. Consider the examples below:

- The Law of Moses insists on fair treatment of foreigners, widows, and orphans (Ex 22:21–24).
- The prophets speak of God's concern for social justice, and demand fair and compassionate treatment of underprivileged people (Is 58:6–7; Am 2:6–7).
- Jesus showed concern for those whom society rejected (Mk 7:24–30; Lk 17:11–19; Jn 4:7–26).
- The early church sent famine relief to Jerusalem (Acts 11:27–30).
- James, the Lord's brother, encourages us to put our faith into action and help those in need (Jas 2:14–26).

As the Holy Spirit makes us more like Jesus, we learn to share God's concerns. Christians today should work to bring about social justice in our society.

Key Terms

Asherah
election

Key People/Places

Tiglath-pileser III
Uzziah
Jeroboam II
Gomer
Jezreel
Lo-ruhamah
Lo-ammi

gain. Sexual sin abounded. The people enjoyed the fruit of their wickedness in pagan temples. God had redeemed Israel from Egypt and brought her into Canaan, yet Israel showed no gratitude. The people silenced God's prophets and mocked the Nazirites who had dedicated themselves to God's service (Nm 6:1–21). Israel had burdened God with her sins, and now she would bear the punishment.

Various prophecies against Israel (3:1–6:14)

Amos reminded Israel that God's **election** brought responsibility. God had indeed chosen Israel and brought her out of Egypt. He had blessed her more than other nations. God's election was a great privilege, but also made Israel more accountable for her sins. God's word told her she was wrong, but she refused to listen.

Amos used many methods to drive home his prophetic points. For example, he asked his hearers a series of rhetorical questions with obvious yes-or-no answers (3:3–6a). By doing so, he set up his audience for his last question (3:6b): "When disaster comes to a city, has not the LORD caused it?" This last question surprised Amos's hearers with its shocking truth—God had brought calamity to turn the people back to him.

Amos also challenged Israel by comparing her actions to the actions of other nations. If the Philistines and Egyptians, two of Israel's early enemies, came to Samaria and saw the city's wickedness, they would be appalled (3:9–15). The Philistines and Egyptians lived by higher moral standards than Israel did, and they didn't have God's word to follow! Therefore, God would bring an enemy against Israel who would remove Israel's strength and plunder her goods.

The rich, pampered women of Samaria were the prophet's next target (4:1–3). These women oppressed the poor, concerning themselves only with their own indulgences. Amos compared them to the well-fed cows of Bashan, a region of rich soil and good cattle (Ps 22:12; Is 2:13; Ez 39:18; Zec 11:2). The enemy would soon round them up and drag them away.

Amos sarcastically challenged the people to persist in their sacrifices (4:4–5). They knew all the rituals so well! They brought

The Eight Kingdoms of Amos 1–2

Damascus •

• Tyre

ISRAEL

Jordan R.

Samaria •

Bethel •

AMMON

Jerusalem •

• Gaza

JUDAH

MOAB

Scale

0   10   20 mi

0 10 20 30 km

EDOM

ple into facing reality. If Israel persisted in sin, she would die.

Amos called the people to embrace true values (5:4–17), but his call went unheeded. In seeking the Lord there was life, but the people preferred their own ways. They sought spiritual guidance at the false religious sites Jeroboam had established.[13] They rejected authority and mistreated the poor. Many called for the Day of the Lord, the day when God would judge his enemies. Amos warned the people, however, that the judgment would fall on them. God hated and rejected their religious rituals because those rituals did not flow from lives of faith. What God really wanted was justice and righteousness in the land (5:18–24).

Many people had become complacent or even arrogant. They trusted in Samaria for deliverance instead of grieving over Israel's spiritual ruin. Amos said these people would be the first to go into exile (6:1–14).

Five visions of judgment (7:1–9:10)

Amos had prophetic visions that helped him understand what God was going to do in Israel. The first three visions—locust, fire, and plumb line—form a unit (7:1–9). When God showed Amos a terrible locust plague, Amos begged God not to bring it, lest he utterly destroy Israel. God relented. The Lord then showed Amos a fire so hot it consumed even the Mediterranean Sea! Again, Amos interceded for the people, and again, God relented. Finally, God showed Amos a plumb line. A plumb line tested a wall's straightness. Here, it symbolized God's righteous standard. As God tested Israel, he found her crooked. He would have to tear her down and start over.

Many in Israel did not like the prophet's preaching. They responded to God's word by rejecting God's messenger. Amaziah, priest of Bethel, even accused Amos of treason and ordered him to go back to Judah where his messages against Israel would be more popular. Amos responded by affirming his own prophetic call. God had called him to prophesy and had equipped him to complete the task (7:10–17).

The fourth vision God showed Amos was a basket of summer fruit, which sig-

election

all sorts of sacrifices, but their lives were full of sin. God had sent famine, drought, and plagues to get their attention, but the people failed to repent (4:6–11). Amos warned Israel that she soon would meet her God—in judgment.

The prophet then launched another attack on the nation—he sang at her funeral (5:1–3)! The word translated "lament" in 5:1 (NIV) refers to a song or chant by which people mourned the dead.[12] By using such a statement, Amos hoped to shock the peo-

Summary

1. The prophet Hosea had great courage and prophesied in spite of the humiliation he suffered because of his wife Gomer's adultery.

2. The Book of Hosea was written shortly before 722 B.C.

3. The major themes of Hosea are: spiritual adultery, knowledge of God, and God's frustrated love.

4. Hosea compared Israel to: a bunch of choice green grapes in the wilderness that had been spoiled, a vine that grew according to his plan, a trained heifer who loved to thresh grain because she could eat as she threshed, and a toddling son.

5. The prophet Joel probably prophesied about 500–450 B.C.

6. Amos worked among the sheepherders of Tekoa and earned part of his living tending sycamore trees.

7. Amos spoke out against other nations, but especially against Israel.

8. Amos used a variety of oratory methods to make his prophetic points.

9. God showed Amos visions to help Amos understand what he was going to do to Israel.

Study Questions

1. How did Hosea's marriage and family background shape his prophetic ministry? In what sense does *your* family background affect your perception on life?

2. Hosea described the people's spiritual adultery. Why did idolatry and harlotry occur together in Israel?

3. What major event of Joel's day shaped his message? To what extent did his message apply to his generation, and to what extent did it have a future application?

4. Describe Amos's background and calling.

5. What were some examples of social injustice against which Amos prophesied? How should our faith in God relate to our actions toward other people?

nified that Israel was ripe for judgment (8:1–3). Many in Amos's day could hardly wait for the Sabbath to end so they could open their shops again and start cheating people with dishonest weights and measures (8:4–14). Amos warned the people that God would never forget their deeds.

The fifth and final vision (9:1–6) pointed to the absolute certainty of God's judgment. No one would escape the hand of the sovereign Lord. Ironically,

Further Reading

Allen, Leslie C. *The Books of Joel, Obadiah, Jonah and Micah.* New International Commentary on the Old Testament. Grand Rapids: Eerdmans, 1976. A more advanced commentary for the serious student.

Hubbard, David A. *Hosea: An Introduction and Commentary.* Tyndale Old Testament Commentary. Downers Grove/Leicester: InterVarsity, 1989. Good for college-level students.

McComiskey, Thomas E., ed. *The Minor Prophets: An Exegetical and Expository Commentary.* 3 vols. Grand Rapids: Baker, 1992–98. For the serious student seeking advanced study. Rich in textual analysis and exposition.

only those who ran to the Lord (in repentance and faith) would find forgiveness and deliverance.

Promises of restoration and blessing (9:11–15)

Amos closed his book with a message of hope. Despite all Israel's sin, God still loved her. One day, he would create a world in which David's line would again have prominence. Amos also spoke of other nations who would bear God's Name and enjoy God's blessing along with Israel. In the coming of Jesus Christ and the establishment of his church, we see at least part of the fulfillment of Amos's prophecy (Lk 1:32–33; Acts 15:13–18).

33 Obadiah, Jonah, Micah, Nahum, Habakkuk, and Zephaniah

God's Plan for the Nations

Outline

- **Obadiah: Edom Will Fall!**
  Outline
  Obadiah's Message
- **Jonah: Running away from God**
  Outline
  Jonah's Background
  Jonah's Message
- **Micah: Zealot for True Covenant Living**
  Outline
  Micah's Background
  Micah's Message
- **Nahum: Nineveh Will Fall!**
  Outline
  Nahum's Background
  Nahum's Message
- **Habakkuk: Lord, What's Going On?**
  Outline
  Habakkuk's Background
  Habakkuk's Message
- **Zephaniah: God Will Judge All the Earth!**
  Outline
  Zephaniah's Background
  Zephaniah's Message

Objectives

After reading this chapter, you should be able to

- Outline the basic content of the Book of Obadiah
- Outline the basic content of the Book of Jonah
- Compare the opinions about the date of Jonah
- Contrast God's compassion with Jonah's attitude toward Nineveh
- Outline the basic content of the Book of Micah
- Identify the themes of Micah's message
- Outline the basic content of the Book of Nahum
- Explain the cause of Nineveh's downfall
- Outline the basic content of the Book of Habakkuk
- Outline the basic content of the Book of Zephaniah

Jaffa—Yafo—modern Tel Aviv. When God told Jonah to go on a mission to Nineveh, he went instead to the port of Joppa, modern Jaffa, to take a ship in the opposite direction.

Israel and Judah had many neighbors. The Philistines and Phoenicians lived along the Mediterranean coast. Ammon and Moab lay east of the Jordan. Edom controlled the region south of the Dead Sea. Syria ruled the land north of Israel to the Euphrates River. Beyond Syria in Mesopotamia lay Assyria and Babylonia.

The prophets asserted that God was Lord of all nations. He would hold these nations accountable for their actions. In this chapter, we study several prophets who spoke about God's plans for other nations. One of these prophets personally delivered his message to his foreign audience!

Obadiah: Edom Will Fall!

Outline

Obadiah's Message

Heading (1a)

The Book of Obadiah tells us nothing about the prophet Obadiah, not even his father's name. Many Old Testament people bear the name "Obadiah," but we cannot definitely identify any of them with the prophet.

Scholars have disagreed over the date of Obadiah's ministry. Some have argued that Obadiah prophesied around 850 B.C.,[1] while others argue for a date shortly after 587 B.C., when Jerusalem fell to Babylon. The later date seems preferable in light of verses 11–14, where Obadiah describes the disaster that befell Jerusalem. Such strong language suggests Obadiah is referring to Nebuchadnezzar's conquest.[2]

The Edomites, descendants of Esau (Gn 36:1), had treated the Judeans cruelly, especially when Jerusalem fell to Babylon. Obadiah warned Edom that her day of judgment loomed just around the corner.

The Lord's message against Edom (1b–14)

The message God gave Obadiah focused on three issues: Edom's arrogance (1b–4), Edom's coming humiliation (5–9), and

Aramaisms

allegory

Edom's violence against Judah (10–14). Sela, Edom's capital city, stood on a very high rock, which made it easy to defend. The nation thus developed an arrogant confidence as expressed in verse 3—"Who will bring me down to earth?"

Obadiah warned the Edomites that God would bring utter humiliation on them. Thieves and robbers would steal only what they could use, but God would sweep everything away!

Edom had committed terrible violence against his brother Jacob (Judah). When Jerusalem fell, the Edomites had captured Judean fugitives and either killed them or turned them over to the Babylonians. They rejoiced at Jerusalem's defeat. Judah would not soon forget Edom's wickedness (Ps 137:7).

The Day of the Lord (15–21)

Obadiah prophesied that the coming Day of the Lord would bring both judgment and salvation. Edom and other nations would drink God's cup of wrath for their sins, but God would restore his people to a position of prominence. They would possess the land and live in peace forever.

Jonah: Running away from God

People today try to run from God in many ways. Some people try to avoid God and his word altogether so they will not feel guilty about the way they live. Others avoid God by filling their lives with the pursuit of power and success. Sometimes even Christians run from God if he calls them to do something they do not want to do.

Jonah ran from God because he didn't want to do God's will. Jonah convinced himself that he knew best, but in the end, God's prophet realized he had a lot to learn.

Outline

I. **Jonah Wants His Own Way**
(1:1–16)

II. **Jonah Decides on God's Way**
(1:17–2:10)

III. **Jonah Preaches to Nineveh**
(3:1–10)

IV. **Jonah Pouts over Nineveh**
(4:1–11)

Jonah's Background

Jonah 1:1 tells us only that Jonah was the son of Amittai. Second Kings 14:25 reveals that Jonah lived in GATH-HEPHER, a town in the tribal territory of Zebulun (Jos 19:13). He prophesied during the reign of Jeroboam II, king of Israel (793–753 B.C.), who gave Israel some political stability. Spiritually, however, the kingdom was suffering.

If Jonah recorded his own story, the book dates to the eighth century B.C. Some scholars have dated the book many centuries later because of alleged inaccuracies and **Aramaisms**. None of their arguments is conclusive, however, and a preexilic date seems most likely.[3] Other scholars have suggested that the book is a parable or **allegory**, and should not be taken literally. But the book itself gives no hint that its author so intended it. Furthermore, Jesus affirmed that Jonah preached to Nineveh (Mt 12:41).

Jonah's Message

Jonah wants his own way (1:1–16)

God's command to Jonah was clear—"Go to the great city of Nineveh and preach against it, because its wickedness has come up before me" (1:2). Jonah, however, decided a trip east to Nineveh made no sense (4:2), and tried to flee west by ship to Tarshish.

The rebellious prophet underestimated God's resolve to send him to Nineveh. The Lord hurled a great storm against the ship, terrifying the sailors. Meanwhile, Jonah, the person responsible for the danger, lay fast asleep in the ship's lower level!

After the captain woke him, Jonah joined the others, who were trying to determine why the storm had come upon them. When Jonah explained he was fleeing from his God, they grew more frightened than ever, and tried desperately to bring the ship under control. Finally, they accepted Jonah's solution and threw him overboard. The storm ceased immediately.

Jonah decides on God's way (1:17–2:10)

As Jonah entered the water, he thought he would drown. God's grace prevailed,

What about those who have never heard?

The Bible stresses that people can only experience God's salvation through Jesus Christ (Jn 14:6). Everlasting judgment awaits those who reject Christ (Jn 3:36). What about people who have never heard the gospel? Are they without hope? Will God judge them anyway?

Some people suggest that those who never hear the gospel might still receive salvation if they respond to God's spiritual light in nature. But the Bible gives no clear indication of any other way to salvation. We need to keep three points in mind:

1. Salvation by works is impossible. If we can earn our salvation, then Christ did not need to die (Gal 2:21).

2. God has revealed his power and being through the beauty and order of creation. However, people suppress that truth and choose sin instead (Rom 1:18–23). God has also placed his moral law (conscience) in everyone, but people do not follow that law perfectly (Rom 2:14–15). Consequently, even people without God's written word perish (Rom 2:11–12). Only the Holy Spirit can bring new life (1 Cor 12:3).

3. The Scriptures often assert that Christ is the only way to God and salvation (Jn 14:6; Acts 4:12).

Realizing that people without Christ face God's judgment should motivate us to share the gospel more urgently.

the shore; Jonah was now ready for his Master's purpose.

Jonah preaches to Nineveh (3:1–10)

Jonah obeyed God's second command and began his five-hundred–mile journey. When he arrived in Nineveh, he began preaching the message God had given him—"Forty more days and Nineveh will be overturned" (v. 4). Jonah needed three days to cover the city completely (v. 3).

Probably to Jonah's great surprise, the people believed God's message! They humbled themselves with fasting and sackcloth. Even the king of Nineveh participated, and commanded all citizens to do the same.[4] Although Jonah had conveyed no hope of deliverance, the Ninevites probably decided they had nothing to lose. Perhaps God would spare them if they truly repented. Their hopes proved true: When God saw their repentance, he relented and did not destroy Nineveh.

Jonah pouts over Nineveh (4:1–11)

Jonah, meanwhile, was anticipating Nineveh's destruction; he became very upset when God spared the city. He felt he had wasted his time coming all the way to Nineveh, and asked God to take his life.

The plant God provided for Jonah's shade furnished an important object lesson. Jonah became angry to the point of death over a mere plant, but didn't care at all for the thousands of people in Nineveh. In sharp contrast, God's compassion reached out to Nineveh, honoring her repentance. God still accepts those who admit their helplessness, repent of sin, and trust in him.

however, and a large fish swallowed Jonah. Speculation over what kind of fish this might have been misses the point— the fish was a miraculous touch of God's grace. Through this fish, the Lord preserved his prophet for the task that lay ahead.

Jonah prayed to the Lord from the fish's belly. The prophet described his desperate situation, and affirmed the Lord's deliverance. Jonah had thought his life would end, but God had intervened. Salvation had come! The fish vomited Jonah onto

Micah: Zealot for True Covenant Living

Outline

I. **First Round of Judgment and Salvation** (1:1–5:15)
   A. God's Judgment of Apostasy and Social Sin in Samaria and Judah (1:1–3:12)
   B. God's Word of Salvation to His People (4:1–5:15)

II. Second Round of Judgment and Salvation (6:1–7:20)
- A. God's Indictment of His People (6:1–16)
- B. Micah's Lament Ends with Hope (7:1–20)

Micah's Background

Micah's message centered on the themes of social injustice, true worship, and false security. The prophet lived in MORESHETH, a town usually identified as Moresheth-Gath, about twenty-five miles southwest of Jerusalem. He prophesied concerning the evils of Samaria and Jerusalem. He mentions only kings of Judah in 1:1, and this may indicate a focus on the southern kingdom. The kings Micah listed—Jotham, Ahaz, and Hezekiah—help us date his ministry to approximately 740–700 B.C.[5]

Micah's Message

First round of judgment and salvation (1:1–5:15)

Micah called the whole earth to see God's coming judgment against his people. The prophet singled out Samaria and Jerusalem because they were Israel and Judah's capital cities. The thought of judgment produced a real tension in Micah's life (1:8–16), a tension also present in other prophets. On the one hand, Micah's prophetic office united him with God's purposes, and he had to announce judgment. On the other hand, Micah loved his people, and the thought of their exile drove him to personal lament. Christ's church still needs leaders who will speak God's truth, but at the same time, love God's people.

Social injustice enraged Micah. The wicked lay awake at night because they couldn't sleep until they had calculated how to steal their neighbors' possessions! Society's leaders displayed an especially poor example. The political leaders' policies destroyed what little hope the poor had. Micah said the rulers cooked the poor like stew (3:1–3)! False prophets also abused their office by letting money influence their words. They uttered blessings to those who paid them well, but condemned those who could pay nothing.

Jerusalem also stood on her false security—"Is not the LORD among us? No disaster will come upon us" (3:11). After all,

had not God promised King David that Jerusalem would stand forever? Was not David's descendant on the throne? How could anything possibly go wrong? Micah warned that such faith would prove a very weak foundation when God dealt with Judah's sin.

Micah's message also contained encouraging words for the future of God's people (4:1–5:15). Micah spoke of God's ultimate kingdom, when Jerusalem would serve as a channel of blessing for the world. The world would experience peace under God's rule, and people would walk with him (4:1–8). Furthermore, God's ultimate King would be born in Bethlehem, a relatively minor city. God had planned for this king's coming since ancient times (5:2). Micah proclaimed these prophecies to motivate his hearers to godly living in their own generation (4:9–13).

Jesus Christ fulfilled God's word through Micah (Mt 2:4–6; Lk 2:1–7). Jesus accomplished spiritual salvation during his first coming, and one day, he will return to reign over all as King of kings.

Second round of judgment and salvation (6:1–7:20)

Micah called Israel into court (6:1–5), just as Hosea had done (Hos 4:1–5:15). The Lord called mountains and hills to testify because they had been present throughout Israel's history. They thus could serve as excellent witnesses! God questioned his people: "What have I done? How have I wearied you?" Clearly, the failure lay with Israel.

Micah also advised the proper response to God's indictment. The prophet's imagined listener asked what he might do so God would accept him (6:6–7). Micah replied that God had already said what he wanted—a life displaying justice, mercy, and a close walk with God. The Lord desired faithfulness that resulted in holy living. God still wants this from his children today.

Unfortunately, as God looked at Micah's generation, he saw few such lives. Instead, he saw crooked business practices, violence, and deceit (6:11–12). The people followed the ways of Omri and Ahab, two evil kings from Israel's past (6:16). God warned his people: He would not allow these sins to continue!

Micah ended his book with a personal

lament (7:1–20). As he searched the nation, he could find no godly people. Injustice abounded. People looked only for their own personal gain. The leadership set a bad example by accepting bribes. Micah mourned that even within the family, society's foundational institution, one could find no security—"A man's enemies are the members of his own household" (7:6).

Nevertheless, Micah found hope in the midst of tragedy. He could still experience personal salvation, and perhaps others would, too. He was willing to endure persecution from God's enemies because he knew that one day, God would vindicate him. Judgment would surely come to those who opposed the Lord.

Micah closed his lament (and book) as many psalmists ended their laments—with a prayer (7:14–20). He prayed that God would shepherd his people as he had when he first brought them into the land. He asked that the Lord would again display his miraculous power, for it would inspire his people and terrify his enemies. Micah also confessed God's utter uniqueness. No other god was compassionate enough to forgive the sin of his people forever. Micah affirmed that in days to come, God would again show his faithfulness in every way. He would confirm his everlasting relationship with his people because of his promises to Israel's forefathers over a thousand years before.

We may face difficult circumstances today and suffer for our faith in Christ. Evil may surround us, and we wonder why God allows it to continue. In such times, our hope must lie in the God who can cast our sins into the depths of the sea (7:19). We can trust him to work all things together for good in his children's lives (Rom 8:28).

Nahum: Nineveh Will Fall!

Outline

I. **The Zeal and Power of God** (1:1–2:2)

II. **The Siege and Destruction of Nineveh** (2:3–13)

III. **The Cause and Certainty of Nineveh's Downfall** (3:1–19)

Nahum's Background

We know very little about the prophet Nahum outside the book that bears his name. Nahum 1:1 calls him "the Elkoshite," but scholars do not agree on where Elkosh was.[6] Some have suggested Elkosh was in Galilee to the north, while others have proposed Judah as its location. Still others have advanced the idea that Elkosh was near Nineveh, against whom Nahum prophesied.

We can date Nahum's prophecy because of his allusions to datable events. Nahum mentions the fall of Thebes (3:8), an event that occurred in 663 B.C. The prophet also speaks of Nineveh's fall, which took place in 612, as something yet future. Consequently, we may date Nahum's prophetic ministry between 663 B.C. and 612 B.C.

The Book of Nahum, like the Book of Obadiah, deals primarily with a foreign kingdom. During the late seventh century B.C., a power struggle arose in the Near East as Assyria began to decline. In 626, Nabopolassar founded an independent Chaldean dynasty in Babylon, and soon, with the help of the Medes, destroyed the Assyrian Empire. Soon after, Nebuchadnezzar would take Babylon to heights it had not attained since the days of Hammurapi (1792–1750 B.C.). As Nahum looked at his world, he saw the hand of God moving against Assyria. The prophet announced that Nineveh, Assyria's capital, would soon fall forever.

Nahum's Message

The zeal and power of God (1:1–2:2)

Nahum began by describing God's awesome power (1:2–8). God was an avenging God and would not tolerate sin forever. God was also the almighty Sovereign. Creation trembled before him, and none could withstand his wrath. At the same time, God was the Savior of those who trusted in him. He was a stronghold in trouble, and he knew his own. These truths about God's character lay the foundation for the rest of Nahum's book.

Nahum 1:9–2:2 contains three cycles in which Nahum alternates between describing vengeance on Nineveh and compassion toward Judah. First (1:9–13), Nahum warned Nineveh her plans would fail. Nineveh had plotted evil against the Lord, ignoring his ways, and now would pay the price. Judah, however, would gain freedom from Nineveh's yoke of oppression and shackles of slavery. Second (1:14–15), Nahum announced that God would cut off Nineveh's name and prepare her grave. He would destroy the city's idols and temples. Judah would rejoice when she heard the announcement of Nineveh's fall. Third (2:1–2), Nahum warned Nineveh an attacker was coming! Meanwhile, as Nineveh finished her last

days, the Lord would restore his people's splendor.

The siege and destruction of Nineveh (2:3–13)

Nahum continued with a graphic description of Nineveh's fall. Her enemies would defeat her army and plunder the city. Nahum described the irony of the situation; Nineveh's army appeared strong, but anarchy and panic would take over. The chariots would race madly in the streets, but to no avail. And, of course, God was behind it all, for he had determined that Nineveh's day of judgment had come.

Nineveh's defeat would lead to a frantic desertion of the city. People left everything behind and ran for their lives; silver and gold weren't that important anymore! Nineveh's plundering vividly reveals the fact that material goods can bring only temporary pleasure. Jesus was right when he said, "A man's life does not consist in the abundance of his possessions" (Lk 12:15). We need to build our lives on our relationship with God, never on material things.

The cause and certainty of Nineveh's downfall (3:1–19)

Nineveh was a wicked city, a city of bloodshed. The Assyrians' ruthless political policies led other nations to fear them. Signs of their oppression were evident even within their own capital city.

Nahum described Nineveh as a prostitute and a sorceress (vv. 4–5). Nineveh contained a temple to ISHTAR, a goddess depicted as a harlot, so sexual immorality was common. Nineveh had plundered many nations and had an insatiable lust for power. Assyrian society also contained many who practiced magic and divination. Whatever Nineveh trusted in would fail, however, for God would shame her before the nations and heap disgrace on her.

Nahum instructed Nineveh to prepare for her final ruin (vv. 8–19). Thebes, the pride of Egypt, had fallen, and now, so would she. No escape would appear, only the inevitable destruction. The rest of the world, who had suffered under Assyria's oppressive yoke, would greet the news of Nineveh's fall with thunderous applause.

This tablet includes part of the Babylonian Chronicle describing the fall of Babylon.

Habakkuk: Lord, What's Going On?

Have you ever felt that what God was doing made absolutely no sense? If you have, you're not alone. The prophet Habakkuk struggled with these same questions. He could not understand why God would work the way he did. As we read Habakkuk, we'll see that Habakkuk learned an important lesson: He might not always understand God's ways, but he could always trust God, no matter what the circumstances.

Outline

I. Habakkuk Struggles with God's Purposes (1:1–2:20)
   A. Habakkuk's First Struggle (1:1–11)
   B. Habakkuk's Second Struggle (1:12–2:20)

II. Habakkuk Yields to God's Purposes (3:1–19)

Habakkuk's Background

Habakkuk's name appears only in his book (1:1). We really know little else about him.

Habakkuk lived during Judah's last days. Most scholars place the beginning of his ministry before 605 B.C., when **Babylon**, under Nebuchadnezzar, became a dominant world power (1:5).[7] Habakkuk's words against Babylon (2:5–20) imply that Babylon had already become a strong nation. Probably Habakkuk's ministry began before 605 but continued until shortly before Jerusalem's fall in 587.

Habakkuk's Message

Habakkuk struggles with God's purposes (1:1–2:20)

Habakkuk began his theological struggle with a cry of bewilderment (1:2): "How long, O LORD, must I call for help, but you do not listen?" Habakkuk knew God loved justice and hated injustice, so why did God let Judah's injustice continue? Habakkuk took his concerns straight to the sovereign God. God also invites us to take our struggles and concerns to him.

God replied (1:5–11) that he had big plans that would astound Habakkuk—he was raising up the army of Babylon! God would use this mighty nation to judge Judah.

Now Habakkuk was really confused (1:12–2:1)! How could God use a wicked people like the Babylonians to judge Judah? Certainly Judah deserved God's judgment, but certainly not at the hands of Babylon! How could God use a nation more wicked than Judah as his instrument of judgment against Judah?

But God, of course, had a reply (2:2–5). He told Habakkuk to write down the vision, for the judgment would occur very soon, exactly as God had said. In the face of such calamity, two responses were possible. One was to remain proud and arrogant like the Babylonians. The other was to live by faith, knowing God was still in control.

Habakkuk 2:4—"The righteous shall live by his faith"—occurs three times in the New Testament (Rom 1:17; Gal 3:11; Heb 10:38). Through faith in Jesus Christ, we receive God's righteousness. The Holy Spirit enables us to live lives of faith and godliness. Habakkuk's statement lies at the heart of Christian theology. God calls us to salvation through faith and calls us to live by that faith.

Habakkuk launched a series of woes against the Babylonians (2:6–20). The Babylonians had extended themselves too far, and would soon pay the price. They had gained at the expense of others, founding their empire on violence and bloodshed. They had forced other nations to drink God's cup of wrath, but the cup would soon come to them. They had followed worthless idols who faded quickly against the Lord's splendor and glory. God would bring Babylon down, too, in his perfect timing.

Habakkuk yields to God's purposes (3:1–19)

Habakkuk expressed his submission to God's ways in a prayer set to music (vv. 19). He feared the Lord's report, and asked the Lord to remember his mercy when the judgment began (v. 2). Habakkuk described the Lord's majesty and power (vv. 3–15). God was sovereign over the whole earth. He had judged the nations, but also brought about the salvation of his people.

The Temple Scroll from the Dead Sea Scrolls. Archaeologists discovered this scroll and many others at the ancient settlement of Qumran near the Dead Sea. Texts such as this help us better understand how ancient scribes passed down copies of the Scriptures over the centuries.

Because he knew of God's absolute faithfulness in the past, Habakkuk resigned himself to God's present purposes (3:16–19). The prophet's fear stirred his innermost being, for all he could do was wait for Judah's judgment. Nevertheless, Habakkuk determined to trust in the Lord despite all circumstances. No matter how hopeless his situation, he would hope in his God. God also desires this kind of "no-matter-what" faith from his children today.

Zephaniah: God Will Judge All the Earth!

Outline

I. Judgment against Judah (1:1–2:3)

II. Judgment against the Nations (2:4–15)

III. Judgment against Judah and the Nations (3:1–8)

IV. Restoration of Israel and the Nations (3:9–20)

Zephaniah's Background

Zephaniah traces his ancestry back four generations (1:1). Bible scholars have debated whether the "Hezekiah" in the genealogy is King Hezekiah of Judah (716–686 B.C.).[8] Those who doubt the connection point out that no other biblical genealogies connect these five names. Furthermore, if Zephaniah meant Hezekiah, king of Judah, he would only have had to add the words "king of Judah." On the other hand, those who favor a connection with King Hezekiah suggest that Zephaniah felt adding the words "king of Judah" was unnecessary, since everyone knew who Hezekiah was.

Zephaniah dates his ministry to the reign of Josiah (640–609 B.C.). In the eighteenth year of Josiah's reign, the Book of the Law was discovered in the temple, and this discovery ignited a period of sweeping spiritual revival in Judah (2 Kgs 22:3–23:7). In light of this, many propose that Zephaniah prophesied early in Josiah's reign, before the revival occurred.[9] Since Zephaniah 2:13 mentions Nineveh's fall as future, Zephaniah's ministry apparently ended before 612 B.C.

Zephaniah's Message

Judgment against Judah (1:1–2:3)

After a general statement about God's judgment of creation, Zephaniah focused on Judah. Many worshiped Baal, Molech, and the host of heaven (1:4–5), while others adopted a stagnant view of God—"The Lord will do nothing, either good or bad"

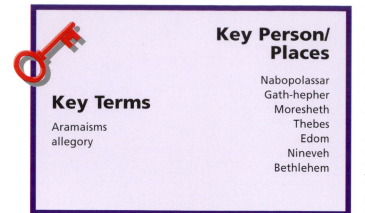

(1:12). The Day of the Lord would bring punishment to every rebellious corner of Jerusalem. Zephaniah warned Judah to prepare for that day. Those who humbled themselves before the Lord might escape the coming disaster (2:1–3).

Judgment against the nations (2:4–15)

Zephaniah, like other prophets, affirmed God's sovereignty over all nations, not just Israel and Judah. Neighboring countries such as Philistia, Moab, and Ammon

would pay a penalty for their evil (vv. 4–11). One day, they would fall, and God's faithful would dispossess them. Distant nations would fare no better. The CUSHITES (Ethiopians) would fall to the sword (v. 12), and Assyria, long-time enemy of Israel and Judah, would receive due recompense for her arrogance (vv. 13–15).

Judgment against Judah and the nations (3:1–8)

Jerusalem would not escape God's chastening. Corrupt leadership displayed itself at every level—royalty, judges, prophets, and priests. These leaders did not trust in the Lord or listen to his Word. Zephaniah promised the Lord would bring real justice to all the nations on the day of his wrath (v. 8).

Restoration of Israel and the nations (3:9–20)

Zephaniah closed his book with a message of hope. The day of God's judgment would also bring God's healing and restoration. The Lord would purify the lips of his people so they might serve him faithfully. He would remove the proud, exalt the humble, and give his people se-

Summary

1. The message God gave the prophet Obadiah focused on Edom's judgment because of its violence against Judah.

2. Jonah wanted his own way instead of God's way and because of that was swallowed by a great fish.

3. Jonah became angry at God because he did not destroy Nineveh after Jonah had traveled so far to that city.

4. Micah's prophecy centered on the themes of social injustice, true worship, and false security.

5. Micah offered encouraging words for God's people and said that God's king would be born in Bethlehem.

6. Nahum includes three cycles describing vengeance on Nineveh and compassion toward Judah.

7. The Book of Habakkuk tells us all that is known about the prophet Habakkuk.

8. Habakkuk questioned God's ways but determined to have faith no matter what.

9. Zephaniah prophesied judgment against Judah and the nations, but also prodicted future blessing for the nations.

Study Questions

1. What is the major theme of Obadiah? What had Edom done that he considered so terrible?

2. Summarize the story of Jonah. Identify the important spiritual lessons Jonah learned.

3. Describe Micah's background. How does his message parallel that of the prophet Amos? What did Micah have to say about the coming Messiah?

4. Identify Nahum's historical setting. What is the major theme of his book?

5. Summarize Habakkuk's dialogue with God in fifty words or less. What was Habakkuk's basic complaint? How did he respond (at first and finally to God's answer?

6. How did the apostle Paul use Habakkuk 2:4 in his letter to the Romans?

7. Identify the key issues surrounding Zephaniah's background. How did the prophet affirm God's sovereignty over all nations?

Further Reading

Allen, Leslie C. *The Books of Joel, Obadiah, Jonah and Micah.* New International Commentary on the Old Testament. Grand Rapids: Eerdmans, 1976. A more advanced commentary for the serious student.

Baker, David W., T. Desmond Alexander, and Bruce K. Waltke. *Obadiah, Jonah, Micah.* Tyndale Old Testament Commentary. Downers Grove/Leicester: InterVarsity, 1988. Good college-level text.

Baker, David W. *Nahum, Habakkuk, Zephaniah: An Introduction and Commentary.* Tyndale Old Testament Commentary. Downers Grove/Leicester: InterVarsity, 1988. Good for basic reading at the college level.

McComiskey, Thomas E., ed. *The Minor Prophets: An Exegetical and Expository Commentary.* 3 vols. Grand Rapids: Baker, 1992–1998. For the serious student seeking advanced study. Rich in textual analysis and exposition.

Robertson, O. Palmer. *The Books of Nahum, Habakkuk, and Zephaniah.* New International Commentary on the Old Testament. Grand Rapids: Eerdmans, 1990. For the serious student. Contains ample footnotes for further study.

curity in the midst of their land. Such blessings would normally cause God's people to rejoice over him, but Zephaniah affirmed that God would rejoice over them! The prophet gave his people this glimpse into the future to motivate them to live lives pleasing to God. We, too, should yield our lives to the Lord daily in gratitude for all he has done, is doing, and will do for us.

34 Haggai, Zechariah, and Malachi

Rebuilding a People

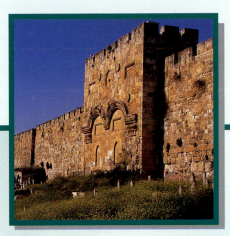

Outline

- **Haggai: Dealing with People Who Just Don't Care**
  Outline
  Haggai's Background
  Haggai's Message
- **Zechariah: Get Ready for God's Kingdom!**
  Outline
  Zechariah's Background
  Zechariah's Message
- **Malachi: Give God Your Best!**
  Outline
  Malachi's Message

Objectives

After reading this chapter, you should be able to

- Outline the basic content of the Book of Haggai
- Outline the basic content of the Book of Zechariah
- Discuss the problem of the authorship of Zechariah
- Outline the basic content of the Book of Malachi
- Identify the concerns of God found in Malachi's prophecy

Babylon's fall to Cyrus the Persian in 539 B.C. launched an exciting time for God's people. Cyrus promptly issued a decree that any Jews who wished could return to Judah and rebuild the temple (Ez 1:1–3). A group of almost fifty thousand returned to Judah and began the rebuilding process (Ez 2:64–65). Tragically, opposition soon stopped the temple work (Ez 4:1–5).

Haggai and Zechariah prophesied at a time when God's people needed a fresh challenge to finish the temple. Haggai focused on the people's spiritual apathy, while Zechariah declared the great things God would do in the future. Malachi, ministering about sixty years later, encouraged the nation to give God its best.

Haggai: Dealing with People Who Just Don't Care

Outline

I. **First Message: A Call to Action** (1:1–15)

II. **Second Message: A Word of Encouragement** (2:1–9)

III. **Third Message: Confirmation of Blessing** (2:10–19)

IV. **Fourth Message: The Restoration of the Davidic Kingdom** (2:20–23)

Haggai's Background

Haggai began prophesying in the fall of 520 B.C. (1:1).[1] Work on God's temple had ceased about fifteen years earlier because of opposition from Judah's neighbors. DARIUS I (521–486 B.C.), Persia's third king, now ruled the empire. Zerubbabel, who had helped the people establish themselves in Judah (Ez 2:2; 3:2), ruled as governor, while Joshua (Ez 2:2; 3:2) served as high priest. Some scholars have suggested Haggai was an elderly man (Hg 2:3), but we cannot say for certain. Ezra 5:1 mentions Haggai, but we know little else about him.

Haggai possessed great zeal for the Lord's temple—he wanted the people to complete it right away! But many of God's people had become apathetic. They didn't care about the temple as much as they cared about their own comfort. God used Haggai to stir the people's hearts toward God's concerns.

Haggai's Message

First message: A call to action (1:1–15)

Haggai challenged his hearers with a question—"Is it a time for you yourselves to be living in your paneled houses, while this house remains a ruin?" (v. 4). The people had plenty of time to tend to their own desires, but no time to finish God's temple!

Haggai confronted them with their current situation. Their fields produced meager crops. Their food and drink did not satisfy. Their clothes did not keep them warm, and their wages disappeared much too quickly. Why? Because the people had allowed God's house to lie in ruins while they scurried here and there in pursuit of their own ambitions!

Haggai's initial challenge moved the people to action. Within the month, work on the temple resumed, with Haggai assuring the people the Lord would help them.

Second message: A word of encouragement (2:1–9)

About a month after the temple work began, Haggai brought another challenge. He asked Judah's elders how the temple's current state compared to its appearance before the exile. Clearly, the present glory did not match the former glory. But Haggai encouraged the people to keep working. God's Spirit was with them! The Lord would make the house's latter glory greater than its former glory.[2]

Throughout history, God's temple has indeed advanced in glory. The church is God's temple, and God's Spirit dwells in her (1 Cor 3:16). Individual believers are temples of the Holy Spirit (1 Cor 6:19–20). And when the Lord establishes his everlasting kingdom, he himself will be its temple (Rv 21:22).

Third message: Confirmation of blessing (2:10–19)

Two months after his words of encouragement, Haggai questioned the priests regarding laws about clean and unclean things. If a man carried holy meat in his garment, and his garment touched any other food, would the food become holy? The priests said it would not. Haggai then asked what would happen if any one of these things touched someone unclean. Would it become unclean? The priests said it would. "So it is with this people and this nation," Haggai said. "Whatever they do and whatever they offer is defiled" (v. 14).

The people thought they would become holy if they built their homes near the temple. Instead, they profaned the temple by their unclean living. Many people today think if they merely spend time in God's house, they will receive God's blessing. Instead, their unholy lives hurt the church's ministry.

Despite Judah's sin, God determined to bless the people. He told them to mark their calendars, for blessing would begin immediately. God's favor would encourage the people to continue the temple work.

Fourth message: The restoration of the Davidic kingdom (2:20–23)

Haggai further described God's future plans. The Lord would bring down kingdoms and exalt his people. Zerubbabel, a descendant of King David, would serve as God's special servant in that day. God would establish David's kingdom again.

Perhaps Zerubbabel's connection with David's line inspired hope for Messiah's coming. Christians see the ultimate fulfillment of this prophecy in Jesus Christ (Lk 1:32–33), a descendant of David through Zerubbabel (Mt 1:1, 12).

Zechariah: Get Ready for God's Kingdom!

Outline

   I. **Call for a Return to the Lord**
     (1:1–6)

  II. **The Eight Night Visions**
     (1:7–6:8)

 III. **The Crowning of Joshua**
     (6:9–15)

 IV. **The Observance of Fasts**
     (7:1–8:23)

  V. **The Coming of the Messiah**
     (9:1–14:21)

Zechariah's Background

Zechariah 1:1 calls Zechariah the son of Berechiah and grandson of Iddo. The Book of Nehemiah lists Iddo among the priests who returned to Judah with Zerubbabel (12:4). It also mentions Zechariah as head of his father's household (12:16). Perhaps Zechariah returned from Babylonia as a young man and his father Berechiah died at an early age.

Many modern scholars have questioned whether the entire Book of Zechariah comes from the prophet himself.[3] Most generally accept Zechariah 1–8 as coming from Zechariah, but have suggested Zechariah 9–14 is later material for three reasons:

1. The subject matter in 1–8 and 9–14 is quite different. Chapters 1–8 deal primarily with rebuilding the temple and Jerusalem, whereas chapters 9–14 focus on the distant future.
2. Vocabulary and style are very different in the two sections.
3. Zechariah 9:13 mentions Greece, which was not a major power until after Zechariah's days.

But these items do not prove multiple authorship for the Book of Zechariah. We will address each point in order:

1. Prophets often wrote about a variety of topics. Moreover, the Book of Zechariah's structure resembles other biblical apocalyptic writings. The book opens with a historical frame of reference and then moves into a more universal picture of God's work in the world (cf. Dn 1–6 and 7–12; Rv 1–3 and 4–22).
2. Different topics naturally require different vocabulary and style. Moreover, prophets sometimes varied their styles for a specific purpose.
3. Greece was becoming a major power during Zechariah's lifetime, especially during Zechariah's later years. Perhaps Zechariah wrote chapters

9–14 later in his life. We also should not rule out the possibility of predictive prophecy. God knows the future and can reveal it to his prophets.

Zechariah began his ministry two months after Haggai (Hg 1:1; Zec 1:1). Like Haggai, he encouraged the people to rebuild the temple. He also spoke about God's coming kingdom. Through special visions, Zechariah learned God's plans for the present and future. God's eternal kingdom was coming, but he also called people to serve him in Zechariah's day.

Zechariah's Message

Call for a return to the Lord (1:1–6)

Zechariah called God's people to rededicate themselves to him. Their ancestors had persisted in their evil ways and refused to follow God's commandments. When God sent prophets to them, they would not listen. Finally, they paid the price of exile. Zechariah challenged Judah to make a clean break with past sin and follow the Lord.

The eight night visions (1:7–6:8)

Each of Zechariah's night visions follows a certain pattern. First, Zechariah describes what he sees. Second, he asks the heavenly messenger what the vision means. (The fourth vision does not include this item.) Third, he receives an interpretation from the heavenly messenger.

Zechariah's first vision revealed a host of horsemen who patrolled the earth (1:7–17). They reported all was quiet. The angel of the Lord asked how much longer God would withhold mercy from Jerusalem and Judah. The Lord replied that he would restore his people and judge the nations who had oppressed them.

The prophet's second vision revealed four horns and four craftsmen (1:18–21). The four horns symbolized the nations that had scattered God's people and destroyed their dignity. The four craftsmen represented God's forces against those nations. He would scatter them as they had scattered his people.

The third vision featured a man measuring Jerusalem (2:1–13). Today, when people sell property, a surveyor surveys the property and marks its boundaries so

the buyers know exactly what they are buying. Likewise, God was marking off Jerusalem as his own. He would protect the city from harm and dwell there. He warned Judah's enemies they would become slaves, but offered repentant nations the chance to join themselves to him!

The fourth vision focused on the high priest's office (3:1–10). Joshua's filthy garments represented the priesthood's failure to serve the Lord faithfully (Jer 6:13; Mi 3:11). Satan stood ready to point out Joshua's sin and the sin of Joshua's predecessors. But Satan received God's rebuke—God had chosen Jerusalem and would restore the priestly office. Joshua's new clothes signified forgiveness and cleansing. The high priest and his colleagues represented the beginning of a great work. God would raise up a servant he called "Branch," who would bring in a wonderful new age. (See comments on 6:9–15).

In Zechariah's fifth vision, he saw a lampstand and two olive trees (4:1–14). The text does not identify the lampstand, though the two olive trees appear to represent Zerubbabel and Joshua. The Lord brought a special word to Zerubbabel— the temple would soon be complete! God's Spirit, not human effort, would complete the temple (4:6). Zechariah 4:6 provides Christians with an important principle to remember. God may call us to do difficult tasks, but through his Holy Spirit working in us, we can accomplish his purpose (Phil 2:13; 4:13).

Zechariah's sixth vision featured a flying scroll (5:1–4). The scroll measured thirty feet by fifteen feet, and writing covered both sides. The scroll represented the curse, God's convicting word against the land. God's word stood as a standard against sin and would judge the guilty. People today also stand under the judgment of God's word. His word points out our sin, but it also tells us about Jesus Christ, who died to take away our sin.

The prophet's seventh vision portrayed a woman in an ephah basket (5:5–11). The woman represented wickedness. The heavenly messenger threw her into the basket and sealed it with a lead cover. Winged messengers then flew the basket to Babylonia. This action signified that God was going to remove his people's sin.

This monumental menorah was presented to Israel by the British Parliament. In Zechariah's fifth vision, he saw a menorah (lampstand).

He freed them from sin so they could serve him faithfully, just as he does for his children today (Rom 6:17–18).

In Zechariah's eighth vision, the prophet saw four chariots coming from between two bronze mountains (6:1–8). The chariots represented spirits of heaven who patrolled the earth at God's command. Some interpreters believe this passage refers to God's judgment of Egypt, Assyria, and Babylon, but the passage names no specific countries. The vision probably describes God's general sovereignty over all the nations. The spirits reported that God's Spirit now had rest in the north. God had dealt with his enemies, and could now continue to restore his people.

The crowning of Joshua (6:9–15)

The Lord gave Zechariah an unusual command. He was to make a crown and place it on the head of Joshua, the high priest. God then interpreted the action. God's servant "Branch" would build the temple, rule as a priest on his throne, and bring peace between the offices of king and priest.

Some scholars suggest the text may have originally hinted at Zerubbabel and Joshua's unity of purpose—political and spiritual leadership working together in harmony. But ultimately the text points to Christ, in whom the offices of king and priest find perfect unity. Jesus built God's temple, the church (Mt 16:18; 1 Cor 3:16), and intercedes for believers as our great High Priest (Heb 7:24–28). He is also the successor to David's throne (Lk 1:32–33), and will rule forever as King of kings (Rv 19:11–16).

The observance of fasts (7:1–8:23)

In 518 B.C., a delegation from Bethel came to ask the priests and prophets a question. During the exile, the people fasted during the fifth month to mourn the temple's destruction (2 Kgs 25:8). They also fasted in the fourth, seventh, and tenth months (Zec 8:19). The fast of the fourth month probably commemorated the breaching of Jerusalem's wall (Jer 39:2), the seventh month fast either the Day of Atonement (Lv 16) or Gedaliah's assassination (Jer 41:2), and the tenth month fast the beginning of the siege against Jerusalem (Jer 39:1). Now that exile was over and the temple was almost finished, the people wondered—should they continue fasting in the fifth month?

The Lord's reply contained two key points. First, the people should remember the past. God had warned their ancestors that he expected them to live in faithful obedience to him. Exile came as his final judgment against their persistent rebellion. The Lord encouraged the people to learn from their past sins so they would not repeat them.

Second, fasting as self-pity was worthless. God had judged his people for their sin. He had called them to repent, but they refused to listen. Therefore, when they called for help in their time of distress, he refused to listen. Fasting provided a way for God's people to humble themselves before him, but true humility and repentance should lead to righteousness. If the people only fasted to feel sorry for themselves, they were wasting their time.

Nevertheless, the Lord's reply also contained a message of grace. He would regather his people and reestablish his Name in Jerusalem. He would restore his relationship with his children. He would bring lasting peace and blessing, and Israel would become a light to other nations. Other peoples would see God's blessing and seek it for themselves. God would turn Israel's fasts into times of blessing; He was in control!

The coming of the Messiah (9:1–14:21)

Zechariah said the Lord would remove Israel's enemies from Syria, PHOENICIA, and Philistia (9:1–8). He also would form a remnant from among them! This prophecy illustrates how God was preparing the way for the gospel to spread to all the world. One day, people from all nations would become part of God's family.

The prophet then announced another reason for rejoicing—Israel's king was coming, riding on a donkey (9:9–17)! He would bring lasting peace, and his dominion would stretch to the ends of the earth.

Jesus partially fulfilled Zechariah's words when he rode triumphantly into Jerusalem on Palm Sunday (Mt 21:1–11). Great numbers of people cheered his coming. Many rejoiced because they thought Jesus would fulfill this entire prophecy, becoming King of the Jews, destroying Rome's power, and establishing God's kingdom on earth.

But the complete fulfillment of the prophecy would have to wait. Jesus rode into Jerusalem that day to prepare for his death. Within a week, God's grand redemptive purpose would reach its climax—Jesus died on a cross, but rose from his grave on the third day. He secured the salvation of all who place their faith in him. But when Jesus returns, he will fulfill the rest of Zechariah's words. His kingdom will last forever.

Part of God's restoring his people included removing their bad leaders (10:2–11:17). Zechariah described the leaders as worthless shepherds who cared little for their sheep. They were interested only in their own personal gain. At God's command, Zechariah assumed leadership, but the people rejected his good leadership. They apparently did not want their sin exposed. The prophet warned the people another evil leader would come before God's ultimate leader.

Bible scholars have tried to identify the three shepherds Zechariah mentioned (11:8), as well as the future evil shepherd (11:16). Some suggest the shepherds were priests of Zechariah's day, while others propose they were political leaders. Still others have proposed the three represent three groups—prophets, priests, and rulers. Whoever the bad leaders are, Zechariah guaranteed the Lord would remove them.

Zechariah 12–14 reveals several features of the Lord's coming kingdom. First, God will bring the victory (12:1–9). Jerusalem will be God's instrument, but the triumph will be his. He will destroy all the nations that gather against his people.

Second, the nation will embrace its Lord (12:10–13:6). As God pours out his Spirit, his people will look upon one whom they have pierced, and mourn for him as one would mourn the death of an only son. John the apostle connected this prophecy with Jesus' crucifixion (Jn 19:37; Rv 1:7). For almost two thousand years, the Jewish people as a whole have not recognized Jesus as their Messiah. Zechariah proclaimed that one day, in God's perfect timing, they will (see also Rom 11:25–27). When this happens, they will mourn bitterly over their years of unbelief. Sin and impurity will disappear, and false prophecy will cease.

Third, God's shepherd will be struck down (13:7–9). In Zechariah 13:7, God commanded, "Strike the shepherd, and the

millennium

sheep will be scattered." Through this process, the Lord would prepare a special remnant for his purposes. He would establish a personal relationship with them. At his last meal with his disciples, Jesus warned them about his coming arrest (Mt 26:31). He told them they would fulfill this prophetic word, and they did. As Jesus' enemies led him away, His disciples ran frightened into the night, unaware that the dawn of his resurrection lay just ahead (Mt 26:56).

Fourth, the Lord will return to save his people (14:1–21). Zechariah foretold a day when all nations will gather themselves against Jerusalem. At the last minute, the Lord will intervene, deliver his people and establish his everlasting kingdom. He will destroy his enemies, and all nations will worship the one true God. Some Bible interpreters believe 14:6–21 describes a personal reign of Christ on the earth **(millennium).** Others believe it denotes Christ's eternal rule in heaven. Still others suggest it refers to both earthly and heavenly kingdoms.

When Zechariah wrote about Messiah's coming, he did not distinguish sharply be-

The Golden Gate, Jerusalem. Some people believe that this gate will not be opened until Messiah comes in glory. Zechariah writes of the coming of the Messiah.

tween his first and second comings. For him, as with many other prophets, Messiah's coming kingdom was one glorious future. We who live after Jesus Christ's first coming can look back with gratitude for his victory over sin. We can also look ahead with excitement to the kingdom he will establish when he comes again.

Malachi: Give God Your Best!

Outline

I. **Introduction** (1:1)

II. **God's Love for His People** (1:2–5)

III. **God's Honor among His People** (1:6–2:9)

IV. **God's Concern about Intermarriage and Divorce** (2:10–16)

Malachi's Message

Introduction (1:1)

Malachi's name means "my messenger." Consequently, some scholars have suggested the book is anonymous and that we should translate 1:1 as "The word of the LORD to Israel through my messenger." This view, however, is not likely.[4] We have

Apathy and the Christian

Haggai's hearers had not repeated their ancestors' sins. The prophet did not preach against their idolatry, immorality, or social injustice. The people were not worshiping other gods or violating their marriage commitments. They were not cheating each other or oppressing the poor. Yet, Haggai denounced them because they had placed their own concerns above the Lord.

While the people cared for their own needs, God's house lay in ruins. They rebuilt their homes, but could not find time to rebuild the temple. Perhaps the initial opposition from neighboring peoples had discouraged them, but Haggai told them the time had come. They needed to finish the temple and give God the honor he deserved!

Today, many things compete for our attention. As we pursue our active schedules, other concerns may keep us from giving the Lord the time he deserves. As a result, our lives fail to bring him the glory they should.

Jesus said we should give God's plans for our lives our highest priority (Mt. 6:33). We dare not crowd the Lord out of our schedules, but rather, we should live our lives in light of our relationship with him. Doing so will help us avoid the sin of apathy.

no other examples of such an expression referring to an unnamed prophet.

We know little about Malachi other than that he lived in postexilic Judah. His book attacks God's people for their general disregard for the law and proper worship. Through a series of disputations, Malachi challenged his audience to give the Lord their best in everything. In these disputations, he stated the people's sin, their unbelieving response, and God's evidence of their sin.

Scholars generally date Malachi's ministry to the time of Ezra and Nehemiah or just slightly before, since Malachi speaks against many of the same problems. A date of around 470–460 B.C.—just before Ezra's arrival—seems probable.[5]

God's love for his people (1:2–5)

The people questioned the extent of God's love. In reply, Malachi reminded them of God's covenant. Jacob and Esau, ancestors of Israel and Edom, were brothers, but God chose Jacob to receive the covenant blessings. God blessed Israel, but made no covenant with Edom. In fact, he devastated Edom's land. The Edomites' pride made them think no one could stop them, but God said he would frustrate their plans. On the other hand, God's covenant with Israel demonstrated his love for his people.

God's honor among his people (1:6–2:9)

Malachi brought a charge against the priests—they were showing contempt for God's Name! They were accepting blind, lame, and sick animals for sacrifice. They led the people astray by showing them God's sacrifices were not really important.

Malachi gave three reasons why God deserved the people's honor and respect. First, God was their father. Children honored their earthly fathers; why didn't they honor their heavenly Father? Second, God was their Master. The people called him "Lord," so why didn't they treat him like one? Third, the Lord was a great King. Subjects would not bring a sickly animal as a gift to an earthly king, so why should they bring such an animal to heaven's King?

The prophet warned the priests God would curse their sacrifices. The Levites

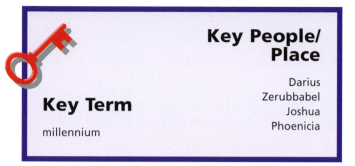

Key Term

millennium

Key People/ Place

Darius
Zerubbabel
Joshua
Phoenicia

were not taking their duties seriously. They should have been teaching the people God's ways by word and example, but they were failing miserably. Today, the Lord still expects Christian leaders to be models of godly living. They should set a high standard for others to follow.

God's concern about intermarriage and divorce (2:10–16)

God established marriage as a sacred institution. He prohibited marrying outside the faith because doing so would compromise Israel's relationship to him (Jos 23:12–13). In fact, intermarriage was one of the main reasons Israel and Judah began to practice idolatry. Ezra and Nehemiah attacked this problem a short time after Malachi (Ez 9–10; Neh 13:23–29).

God also intended marriage to be a life-long commitment. The expression "wife of your youth" (2:14) suggests many men were abandoning the vows they had made early in life. As wives grew older, their husbands divorced them, apparently to marry younger, more attractive women. God's statement "I hate divorce" (2:16) shows how seriously he takes marriage commitments. Jesus affirmed this standard when religious leaders questioned him (Mt 19:3–9). Many marriages today end in divorce, but God's word commands us to marry for life. Sometimes serious sin brings conditions where divorce seems the best solution, but God's ideal is still lasting commitment.

God's justice and patience (2:17–3:6)

Many people felt God didn't care about the nation's evil. The wicked appeared to escape unnoticed. Malachi assured his people God's perfect justice would prevail. The Lord would send his people a special messenger, and then the Lord himself would come (3:1). He would judge sin wherever he found it—even among his own people—and bring the world ultimate justice.

The Lord fulfilled his word to Malachi through John the Baptist and Jesus Christ. John came first to announce Jesus' coming (Lk 7:27). Jesus' death and resurrec-

Study Questions

1. Identify the historical circumstances out of which Haggai and Zechariah arose. How would you characterize Haggai's audience?

2. How did Haggai (and Zechariah) motivate the people to rebuild the temple?

3. Discuss the pertinent issues surrounding the authorship of Zechariah.

4. On what aspects of Judean life did Zechariah's visions touch? How many visions do you remember?

5. What did Zechariah promise about the priesthood?

6. How did Zechariah describe the messianic kingdom? How were his words fulfilled in the New Testament?

7. What's the main theme of Malachi?

8. Malachi prophesied against many types of abuses in his day. How are people—even Christians—sometimes guilty of these same abuses today?

Summary

1. Haggai's messages included: a call to action, a word of encouragement, a confirmation of blessing, and the restoration of the Davidic kingdom.

2. While Haggai had great zeal for the temple, the people were most interested in their own comfort.

3. The subject matter of Zechariah is different in chapters 1–8 from chapters 9–14 and this has caused some to maintain a multiple-authorship view of the book.

4. God often revealed his plans to Zechariah through night visions.

5. Malachi's message is a series of disputations.

6. God fulfilled his word to Malachi through Jesus Christ and John the Baptist.

7. Malachi closed his book with a command to remember the Law of Moses and a promise that God's judgment was coming.

tion defeated sin, and the Holy Spirit enables believers to live as God wants (Rom 8:3–4). And when Jesus returns, he will destroy sin forever.

God's concern for tithes and offerings (3:7–12)

Malachi brought a serious charge against the people—they were *stealing* from God! The Law of Moses required the people to tithe, to give 10 percent of their income to the Lord. Tithing reminded the people that

God had given them everything. The tithe also provided for the Levites. To neglect giving one's tithe was to steal from God. Even today, people steal from God by giving the Lord less than they should.

God challenged his people to put him to the test. If they faithfully brought their offerings, he would flood them with blessing! Other nations would recognize the Lord had abundantly blessed Israel and would also praise him.

Further Reading

Baldwin, Joyce G. *Haggai, Zechariah, Malachi: An Introduction and Commentary.* Tyndale Old Testament Commentary. Downers Grove: InterVarsity, 1972. Good, solid, college-level commentary.

Kaiser, Walter C., Jr. *Malachi: God's Unchanging Love.* Grand Rapids: Baker, 1984. Good survey with a more devotional focus.

McComiskey, Thomas E., ed. *The Minor Prophets: An Exegetical and Expository Commentary.* 3 vols. Grand Rapids: Baker, 1992–98. For the serious

student seeking advanced study. Rich in textual analysis and exposition.

Merrill, Eugene H. *Haggai, Zechariah, Malachi: An Exegetical Commentary.* Chicago: Moody, 1994. A detailed, yet readable analysis of the text with ample footnoting.

Verhoef, Pieter A. *The Books of Haggai and Malachi.* New International Commentary on the Old Testament. Grand Rapids: Eerdmans, 1987. A solid commentary for the serious student.

God's love for the remnant (3:13–4:3)

Some of God's faithful followers wondered if God really loved them. They felt they served him in vain. They saw others sin against the Lord and get away with it. But Malachi said the Lord would remember his children's faithful lives. When God judged the world, he would preserve his people for his own possession. He would celebrate with those who truly feared him.

Conclusion (4:4–6)

Malachi closed his book with a command and a promise. First, he commanded God's people to remember the Law of Moses. The Law laid a foundation for life, and those who lived by it would experience life as God intended it. People who live by God's words today also experience that blessed life.

Second, Malachi promised the people God's judgment was coming. The Lord would send Elijah before that day to call the people to repentance. Jesus affirmed that John the Baptist fulfilled Elijah's role (Mt 11:13–14; 17:10–13). John announced the coming of Messiah, who would bring the world salvation and judgment. Jesus secured eternal salvation at his first coming, and, at his second coming, he will judge the world (Heb 9:28).

Epilogue
A Final Word

Heilsgeschichte

"... when the fullness of time had come,
God sent his Son .. "

Galatians 4:4

Now we have come to the end of the matter. Or have we? The Old Testament has no clearly stated completion or resolution. Instead, the Old Testament ends in expectation, awaiting a fuller revelation to usher in a new kingdom and its Messiah. The Old Testament's many and varied prophecies about the coming Son of David and his new era point to a future time. Yet no one in the Old Testament can be said to be that Messiah, and there was certainly no period in Israel's history that ushered in a messianic era.

In this sense, every reader of the Old Testament is confronted with an important question: "Since the Old Testament claims God revealed himself in ancient Israel and that he will reveal himself further in the future, what do I make of these theological claims?" Or to put it another way, "How are the Old Testament's claims resolved in history?" The Old Testament clearly presents a history of redemption and promise, a "salvation-history" (*Heilsgeschichte*). But as one scholar has pointed out, it is a salvation-history that never actually arrives at salvation. And that history is not quite complete, since it never arrives at a terminus point.[1]

In the history of religion, there are only two possible answers to this question—the one offered by Judaism and the one offered by Christianity. Judaism believes the truth-claims of the Old Testament were preserved in the Pharisaic traditions of the Mishnah (approximately A.D. 200) and, finally, in the Talmud (commentary on the Mishnah produced in Palestine and Babylonia). In this approach the culmination of Old Testament hopes and expectations is deferred to the future. The Messiah's arrival is still a future event, and the kingdom of God is postponed.

On the other hand, Christianity has been clear from its inception that the New Testament fulfills and complements the Old. The Gospel writers' genealogies of Jesus (Mt 1:1–16; Lk 3:23–28) explicitly affirmed that the Messiah has arrived, and that he is the culmination and fulfillment of the Old Testament prophecies. Over and over again in the New Testament, the authors emphasize the intimate connections between the events of their day and the Old Testament with quotes such as "All this took place to fulfill what had been spoken by the Lord through the prophet .. " (Mt 1:22; and see also Lk 24:44–47). And the early church clearly recognized and affirmed the importance of the Old Testament to Christian faith.[2] The arrangement of Old Testament books in the Christian canon (see chapter 1) intentionally ties Old and New together. By concluding with the prophets, the Old Testament collection has left off with a final prediction of that day when one greater than David will appear (Mal 3:1).

But this raises one of the thorniest questions of reading the Bible: How do the Old and New Testaments relate to each other? Some today would say the Old Testament does not relate to modern culture; indeed, even many Christians cut it from their Bibles, either intentionally or by neglect. But with the earliest Christian believers we must assert that the Old Testament is God's word for our times! The question is not *whether* we should read both Testaments, but rather *how* we should read them together. Exactly how do they relate? We must define this relationship as more than a simple promise–fulfillment connection, since much of the Old Testament is something other than promises. Likewise, it is more than a simple chronological sequence, as the terms "old" and "new" might imply. This is not an old, outmoded covenant system now made obsolete by a

Key Term

Heilsgeschichte

newer, sleeker model. Instead, the relationship is more integrative and reciprocal. There is a codependency between the Old and New Testaments. Reading either in isolation from the other will result in misunderstanding both.

The intimate relationship between the Testaments has at least three aspects. First, the Old Testament is the literary background for the New. This can be illustrated by the sheer mass of New Testament quotations of or allusions to the Old. One scholar has counted 295 separate explicit references to the Old Testament, occupying some 352 verses of the New.[3] But the literary relationship is more than mere quotations. The rhetorical techniques, and to some degree even language and style of the New Testament authors, are shaped by the Old Testament.

Second, the Old Testament is the historical foundation of the New. It is no exaggeration to say the New Testament would be incomprehensible without the historical information of the Old. How would readers of the New Testament understand the claim that Jesus of Nazareth is the Messiah without first learning something about the history of national Israel and her Davidic dynasty? This historical interdependency could be illustrated in countless ways. But perhaps the most obvious is the New Testament's claim to historically fulfill the Old Testament's future hopes.

Third, the Old Testament is the theological centerpiece of the New. The authors of the New Testament begin by affirming the theological truths of the Old, and they assume their readers also know those truths and accept them. In fact, most of the great doctrinal truths of the church are defined first, not in the New Testament, but in the Old. Furthermore, many of these truths are not defined at all in the New Testament; they are taken for granted. So for example, the significance of creation, the consequences of human sin, the central role of covenant in redemption, the doctrine of substitutionary atonement—all are given definitive statement in the Old Testament and assumed by the authors of the New (respectively Gn 1–2, Gn 3, Gn 12, 15 and numerous places throughout the Pentateuch, Is 53). And this is only a partial list. In many ways, the New Testament contains little that is actually new, but rather describes the climactic fulfillment of the theological themes and messages from the Old Testament. In these ways, and in many others, the Old Testament is clearly the literary, historical and theological matrix of the New.

So we return to that intimately personal question the Old Testament poses for every reader: "Since God claims to reveal himself in the Old Testament and promises to reveal himself further in the future, what do I make of these theological claims?" The New Testament and two thousand years of church history have affirmed with one voice: Jesus Christ is the fulfillment of that revelation. Together the truth-claims of the Old and New Testaments give us pause to consider restating the question. Perhaps we should ask, not what do I make of the claims of the Bible, but what do they make of me? The Bible offers truth, and invites all of us to confess, receive, and believe. In so doing, these writings become the means of grace whereby God's Spirit makes us new people.

Glossary

Abomination of Desolation Term for an idolatrous action or image. Some hold that it refers to the four passages in the Book of Daniel relating to the sacrilegious desecration committed by Antiochus IV Epiphanes, the pagan king of Syria, who sacrificed a pig on the holy altar before the Jerusalem temple in 168 B.C. When referenced by Jesus (Mt 24:15; Mk 13:4) and Paul, however, the term possibly refers to that future sacrilege associated with Antichrist and the second coming of Christ.

Acrostic Alphabetic poem in which the first letter of each line is the next successive letter of the Hebrew alphabet. Hence, there are twenty-two lines or verses, one for each of the twenty-two letters of the alphabet. In some examples, more than one line opens with the same letter (see, e.g., Ps 119 and Lam 3).

Akitu Festival Annual festival celebrated by the Babylonians at which they paraded statues of their gods through Babylon. Isaiah predicted Babylon's fall to Persia, describing this contest between God and the gods of Babylon (46:1–13); this time, the idols cowered in shame, unable to save Babylon. This arrogant nation, which had applied to herself words describing God alone—"I am, and there is no one besides me" (45:5–6; 47:8)—would be shamed and humbled by God, dethroned from her world dominion, and delivered over to terrible judgment.

Akkadian Language of the Assyrians and Babylonians, which was in the same language family as Semitic Hebrew and Aramaic. The Akkadians were a Semitic group who rose to power during the last quarter of the third millennium B.C. and occupied southern Mesopotamia together with the Sumerians.

Akkadian Prophecies Akkadian texts of the first millennium B.C. that simply list various political events of a particular historical period; their intention is somewhat vague. It seems that the writers wrote these texts to make them look like prophecy, although some scholars have suggested the texts are more closely related to apocalyptic literature or are examples of prophecy written after the event. These prophecies differ significantly from classic biblical prophecy.

Allegory Story that contains hidden or symbolic meaning.

Amarna Letters Nearly four hundred letters found at El Amarna, Egypt, between Memphis and Thebes, dating from the fourteenth century B.C. Most are in Akkadian and are written by kings and vassal rulers of Syria-Palestine to Amenhotep IV (Akhenaten) and his father Amenhotep III.

Amillennialism See Millennium.

Ammonite Language of Ammon, in the same family as Hebrew and Aramaic.

Amorite Language in the same family as Hebrew and Aramaic. As the ancestor of the Aramaic language, it helps clarify our understanding of certain aspects of biblical Hebrew. The Amorites dominated the history of Mesopotamia during the second millennium B.C. and eventually established major foci of power in the south at Babylon on the Euphrates, and in the north at Assur and Nineveh along the Tigris.

Amphictyony Association of twelve members centered around a central religious shrine at Delphi, in Greece, dated to around 600 B.C. The twelve members were committed to peaceful coexistence and united defense against foreign aggression. The central sanctuary was the site of yearly religious festivals and provided an important unifying factor to otherwise disparate groups. In 1930, Martin Noth suggested Israel's twelve-tribe system was sociologically analogous to the Greek model.

Ancient of Days Title given to God in Daniel 7. Daniel foresaw four kingdoms represented as animals that were increasingly more terrible in appearance and conduct. As Daniel watched, he saw the Ancient of Days and "one like a son of man" (a title Jesus used for himself in Mt 16:27; 24:30; 26:64; Mk 8:38, 13:26; etc.) together establish a fifth and everlasting kingdom, a kingdom of the saints of the Most High.

Anthropomorphic Having human-like qualities (in this context, the term relates specifically to biblical terminology used in the presentation or description of God).

Antithetic Parallelism Common, easy-to-recognize literary characteristic of Hebrew poetry in which two lines stand in sharp contrast to each other (e.g., Ps 1:6, "For the LORD watches over the way of the righteous, but the way of the wicked will perish"). The Book of Proverbs also often employs such parallelism.

Aphorisms Short statements that embody general religious truths. Aphorisms are found in most holy books of world religions. Although aphorisms do appear in the Bible, they stand in literary contrast to the historical narratives of Israel.

Apocalyptic Literature Body of symbolic, "revelatory" documents containing a unique manner and style of communication and having in common a basic content. Apocalyptic literature was widespread in Judaism around the time of Christ and had a profound influence on early Christianity. The New Testament book of Revelation is the oldest document actually claiming the title "apocalypse" or "revelation."

Apocryphal Term specifically relating to the extra books, in addition to the sixty-six books of the traditional canon, which are included in Roman Catholic Bibles; in general, means "hidden" or "concealed" and refers to any extracanonical scripture.

Arabic Language in the same family as Hebrew and Aramaic.

Aramaic Semitic language, closely resembling Hebrew in vocabulary and basic morphology, in which a few portions of the Old Testament were written (Gn 31:47b; Ezr 4:8–6:18; 7:12–26; Jer 10:11b; Dn 2:4b–7:28). The term "Aramaic" comes from the pre-Hellenic name of Syria, Aram. Although the Arameans never enjoyed a mighty empire, their language impacted the entire Near East, partly because they used a system of alphabetic writing rather than the more tedious system of cuneiform. Aramaic eventually became the common language of postbiblical Judaism, as seen in the Mishnah, Midrash, and Talmud.

Aramaisms Words or expressions in the Hebrew text of the Old Testament which suggest that the language has been influenced by Aramaic.

Archives Places where public records or other historical documents are kept and preserved. In the ancient Near East, archives contained official state records, including lists of kings, books of annals or chronicles that presumably listed each king's political activities, royal inscriptions, historical epics, and biographical data.

Asherah Canaanite goddess of the sea and the female consort of Baal, the Canaanite god of agriculture and fertility. The Israelites began worshiping these two deities, building shrines to them and adopting the sexual fertility rites that accompanied their worship, including sacred prostitution.

Atone, Atonement Biblical terms describing the removal of sin or defilement. The Hebrew *kipper* means literally "to cover over," which usually denotes "to atone by offering a substitute." Whether the term refers to an atoning action directed toward God (propitiation) or toward the offense (expiation), it illustrates the Bible's theology of reconciliation.

Baal Most important god of the Canaanite pantheon, his name means "master." Baal was a god of fertility and was worshiped extensively in western Asia from Babylonia to Egypt.

Baal-Zebub Deity that was a form of Baal worshiped by the Philistines at Ekron. Ahaziah, who was guilty of continuing both the Canaanite fertility religion of Ahab and the idolatrous calf worship of Jeroboam I, feared that an injury he received in a fall might be fatal (2 Kgs 1) and thus sent messengers to Philistia to ask Baal-Zebub about his health— resulting in God's interception of the messengers and Elijah's warning.

Babylonian Period Early second millennium B.C. (2000–1595 B.C.), during which the Babylonians began to compile what we now call omen texts.

Behemoth In Job 40, probably refers to the hippopotamus as a picture of strength, resilience, and apparent indestructibility which God uses to contrast his mighty power with the weakness and ignorance of the human being.

Biblical Apocalyptic Subcategory of apocalyptic literature (i.e., the Book of Daniel) that opens with historical material and gradually moves to the more apocalyptic type of material (especially in Zechariah and Revelation). While the Old Testament contains a few passages that are generally apocalyptic in nature (Jl 3; Is 24–27; parts of Ezekiel and Zechariah), these passages and the Book of Daniel show significant differences from the later apocalyptic books of the intertestamental period and are thus classified, along with the New Testament Book of Revelation, as biblical apocalyptic literature.

Book of the Law During the reign of young king Josiah, this term probably referred to all or part of Deuteronomy, which had been deposited in the temple at Solomon's dedication (1 Kgs 8:1–4; Dt 31:26). This temple copy had been neglected during the reigns of Manasseh and Amon, and the discovery of the law-book by Josiah's high priest in the temple of the Lord (2 Kgs 22:8–10) greatly affected the young king. He quickly purged pagan worship from the country, reestablished Israel's covenant with the Lord, and reinstituted the Passover feast, which had been neglected since the time of the judges.

Branch Prophetic description of the coming Messiah in Isaiah 4:2 as a branch who would come from the line of Jesse, David's father, and would be empowered by the Spirit of the Lord to lead the nations and bring God's peace, goodness, and salvation to those who have placed their faith in him.

Bronze Age See Early Bronze Age, Middle Bronze Age, Late Bronze Age.

Canaanite Baalism Baal-worshiping religion of the Canaanites with which the Hebrew faith experienced significant ideological conflict during Ahab's reign, as Ahab's religious apostasy led him to confuse Baal, the Canaanite fertility god, with Yahweh and thus to desecrate the unique covenant relationship between Yahweh and Israel.

Canon Greek word *(kanon)* meaning rule. In biblical studies, it connotes an authoritative collection of books accepted as the rule of faith and practice. For discussion, see chapter 1.

Canonical Criticism Critical approach to the Old Testament developed in the second half of the twentieth century that attempted to study the received form of the Old Testament and to expose its theological message. While not totally rejecting the findings of the documentary approaches, scholars using canonical criticism seek to study the final form of the Bible, as this is what has authority for the religious community; they are less concerned with how the text arrived than with the internal message of the canon. This approach provides a helpful corrective to the atomizing tendencies of its critical predecessors.

Casuistic Law Class of case law, in contrast to apodictic law or absolute prohibitions. Such laws begin with a conditional clause (protasis, "if . . .") in which the case is described, followed by the penalty (apodosis, "then . . ."). For example, "If a thief is caught breaking in and is struck so that he dies, [then] the defender is not guilty of bloodshed" (Ex 22:2).

Chalcolithic Age Term used by archaeologists and historians for the last of the stone ages in the Middle East, about 4200–3300 B.C. During the Chalcolithic Age, stone was displaced by copper as the dominant material of tools and weapons. The Chalcolithic Age and its immediate predecessor, the Neolithic Age, were the earliest sedentary cultures of human history. Chalcolithic sites have yielded copper implements used by inhabitants who appear to have lived a nomadic village mode of existence.

Chiasm Based on the Greek letter X (chi) denoting an inverted sequence or cross-over of parallel words, phrases, or concepts in a sentence or larger literary unit. Chiasm is common in Hebrew poetry:

A Have mercy on me, O God,

B According to your unfailing love;

B' According to your great compassion

A' Blot out my transgressions (Ps 51:1).

Chronicles Annals that in the ancient Near East listed each king's political activities; they were official state records preserved in the royal archives.

City-States Sovereign states consisting of an autonomous city with its dependencies. Old Testament examples include the Canaanite city-states of Tyre and Sidon.

Classical Prophecy Prophecy that generally addresses all the people, informs them of God's wrath against their sin, warns them of approaching judgment, calls them to repentance, and proclaims God's salvation for those who will turn to him. Such prophecy was written from about 800 to 450 B.C. by those who served as God's special messengers to his people by the power of the Holy Spirit. The Old Testament books of Isaiah through Malachi are good examples of classical prophecy.

Classical Prophets See Classical Prophecy.

Cosmogony Account or theory concerning the origin of the universe.

Coup Unexpected power play, such as Absalom attempted in the overthrow of his father David's kingdom by striving to win the people's hearts and declare himself king at the strategic time (2 Sm 5:3).

Covenant Hebrew term (*berit*) describing binding relationships between human partners, or between God and humans. The concept has a legal background and describes an agreement between two parties, where no such agreement existed by nature. Such agreements had binding obligations on both parties. This is a rich theological concept in the Bible, since God commits himself to covenant relationships with humans in which he accepts obligations.

Creatio ex Nihilo Latin phrase meaning "creation out of nothing." The early church confronted certain heresies that taught God had created the world with preexistent, uncreated matter as his raw material. But the biblical evidence led to the conviction that God created the universe from nothing (Ps 33:6, 9; Heb 11:3).

Cuneiform Writing system invented by the Sumerians around 3100 B.C. Wedgelike shapes were pressed into wet clay, or inscribed on stone or metal to represent words.

Day of the Lord Concept frequently occurring in both the prophets and the New Testament. It includes three elements: the judgment of God against sin, the cleansing and purging of God's people, and the salvation of God's people.

Dead Sea Scrolls After a shepherd boy accidentally discovered the first of these scrolls in a cave at Qumran in 1947, archaeologists explored nearby caves and found additional scrolls. These scrolls date to around 100–200 B.C. and contain at least parts of every Old Testament book except Esther. They also provide much valuable information about the Essene community at Qumran. Most important, they confirm the reliability of the Masoretic Text.

Decalogue Greek name for the Ten Commandments (Ex 20; Dt 5).

Deutero-Isaiah Simply meaning the "second Isaiah," this term is used by those scholars who hold to a multiple-author view of Isaiah to refer to the author of chapters 40–66. (See also Multiple-Author View.)

Deuteronomic Theology Doctrine of retribution, which the Bible often uses to explain that faithfulness to the covenant will result in blessings in the future while disobedience will result in curses. This is the basic theology behind the historical books and is often said to be distinctive of the Deuteronomistic History.

Deuteronomistic History Name given to the unit of the Old Testament containing Deuteronomy, Joshua, Judges, 1–2 Samuel, and 1–2 Kings. One leading theory argues that an anonymous editor (called the "Deuteronomist," and abbreviated Dtr) combined several sources into a long document detailing Israel's history theologically. After Jerusalem's fall in 586 B.C., Dtr sought to interpret the tragedy as well as to explain the fall of northern Israel in 722 B.C. He attempted to answer the question, "What went wrong?" For discussion, see chapter 10.

Dialogues Literary works in the form of a conversation between two or more persons. Dialogues were often found in ancient Mesopotamian discursive wisdom literature, that is, documents produced by ancient Near Eastern sages containing lengthy discourses or essays grappling with life's most difficult problems.

Dictation Theory Theory that suggests God simply dictated the Bible to human scribes, choosing certain individuals to record his word and giving them the exact words he wanted used. This theory accounts for some of the biblical evidence, but not all.

Distichs Units of individual proverbs consisting largely of a collection of proverbial sayings in poetic verse of two lines each (couplets), usually making complete sense (e.g., Prv 10:1–22:16); the parallelism is almost always antithetical.

Documentary Hypothesis See Source Criticism.

Doxology Closing verses of the last psalm in each of the five collections or divisions of the Book of Psalms (1–41, 42–72, 73–89, 90–106, 107–50), which "tie off" that part of the Book with an ascription of praise to the Lord. The grand psalm of praise, Psalm 150, fittingly concludes the entire collection.

Early Bronze Age Term used by archaeologists and historians of the ancient Near East to refer to the third millennium B.C., also called, in Palestine, the Canaanite Age (about 3300–2000 B.C.). This was an age of major new developments across the ancient Near East. In Syria-Palestine, the Early Bronze Age witnessed a sudden flourishing of population and urbanization. There was rapid transition from life in unwalled villages to fortifications at a number of sites. In Egypt and Mesopotamia, the Early Bronze Age marked the rise and fall of humankind's first great empires: Old Kingdom Egypt and the Sumero-Akkadian Empires in Mesopotamia.

Ecstatics People who resided in and around the ancient city of Mari, of whom many scholars have noted parallels with the biblical prophets. These individuals delivered messages that they received through dreams, visions, or trances; each served a particular god or goddess. In their utterances, they might warn the king of rebellion, counsel him regarding expeditions, promise him victory over his enemies, or encourage him to serve the deity more faithfully.

Election God's unconditional choosing of Israel to be his people, as he established his covenant with Abraham, brought Israel out of Egypt, and blessed her more than all the nations as a testimony to the world. The prophet Amos reminded Israel in 3:1–6:14 that this election

brought responsibility—that this great privilege also made Israel more accountable for her sins, and that she would suffer judgment for her violation of God's statutes.

Enuma Elish Akkadian title meaning "When on high." *Enuma Elish* is the most complete Mesopotamian account of creation and it has many interesting similarities to the biblical record. The story describes a cosmic conflict between the leading deities. The young and daring Marduk kills the monstrous Tiamat, mother goddess personifying the primeval ocean. Using Tiamat's divided carcass, Marduk creates heaven and earth; and from the blood of her co-conspirator, he and his father create humankind to do the hard labor of the universe, leaving the deities free from work. Out of gratitude to Marduk for rescuing them from wicked Tiamat, the gods build for him the great capital city of Babylon.

Epic of Atrahasis Mesopotamian document drawing direct parallels with the biblical creation account. This epic is the oldest Near Eastern primeval history in nearly complete form (early second millennium), presenting in historical sequence, and a sequence similar to that in Genesis, both the creation of humanity and their near extinction in the flood. The Atrahasis epic confirms that the basic plot of Genesis 1–11 was well known throughout the ancient Orient.

Eschatological Relating to eschatology.

Eschatology Term for that part of theology that deals with the doctrine of the last things. As such, eschatology is concerned with death, judgment, heaven, hell, resurrection, Jesus' second coming, and so on.

Eunuchs Usually castrated men, especially those formerly employed as harem attendants or officers of state. The term is applied to men of Egypt (Gn 40:2), Assyria (2 Kgs 20:18), Babylonia (Daniel), Persia (Esther), and Israel.

Evangelicalism Theological position which holds to the inspiration and infallibility of God's revelation as the authoritative guide for faith

and practice. More specifically, it is a movement in modern Christianity, transcending denominational and confessional boundaries, that emphasizes conformity to the basic tenets of Christian faith and a missionary outreach of compassion and urgency.

Expiation Result of divinely appointed sacrifices intended to free the sinner from the punishment of sin.

Fertile Crescent Area of rich soil joining the three geographical sub-regions of the ancient Near East (Mesopotamia, Syria-Palestine, and Egypt). Most of the terrain of the ancient world was rugged and inhospitable to human life, and even the fertile lands were bordered by nearly impassable mountain ranges to the north and vast deserts to the south. The Crescent's flat lands and an abundance of water made this location the birthplace of human civilization.

Fiat Latin term, meaning "let it be done" that refers to God's method of creation by decree in Gn 1. On the six successive days of creation, God created by divine order or command: "Let there be light," "Let there be an expanse between the waters," and so on.

Foretellers Prophets to whom God revealed the future—sometimes the near future and sometimes the distant future—and who then declared it to their own generations; the prophets spoke of judgment and of restoration, of bad news and good news, primarily to motivate God's people to faithful living in the present.

Form Criticism Popular approach to critical study of the Pentateuch, pioneered by Hermann Gunkel around the turn of the century and emerging shortly after Wellhausen's development of the source theory. It analyzes the various literary types, or genres, found in the Bible and isolates these smaller units. By emphasizing the "situation in life" of the smaller units, form criticism attempts to uncover the "historical kernel" for each literary genre. According to Gunkel and others, these smaller units were later joined into the four sources of the Pentateuch.

"Former Prophets" In the Jewish canon, the designation of Joshua, Judges, Samuel, and Kings; such a designation is appropriate because of the way in which these books relate the early history of prophecy and present the national history in light of theological and prophetic interests.

Forthtellers Prophets who told forth God's truth to their own generation; the prophets pointed out the evils of their day and called the people to repent, warning them that while the covenant brought many privileges, so it also brought many responsibilities, including justice, righteousness, and holiness.

Generations Literary structural device in the Book of Genesis that refers to offspring or history (Gn 2:4). It is also used to introduce either a genealogy or personal history (e.g., Adam, Gn 5:1; Noah, Gn 6:9; etc.). The phrase occurs eleven times in Genesis—in each occurrence probably introducing a new literary unit of the book. In chapter 2, because the expression is not followed by a personal name, it seems to serve as a narrative hinge, introducing 2:4b–25 and summarizing 1:1–2:3.

Genres Term used by Bible scholars to refer to literary forms or types (French "kind, sort, type"). Form critics group texts in the same genre if they share distinguishing characteristics.

Gilgamesh Epic Mesopotamian story written in poetic form on a series of twelve tablets with significant parallels to the story of Noah. In this account, Gilgamesh, probably a historical figure who was king of Uruk around 2600 B.C., rebels against death after losing his friend. Gilgamesh meets Utnapishtim (the "Babylonian Noah"), who relates how he achieved immortality when forewarned of a divine plan to flood the world. Utnapishtim had survived the flood in a large reed boat, accompanied by his family and pairs of all animals. Unfortunately,

however, this event is unrepeatable and gives Gilgamesh little hope for immortality. After failing three tests by which he could have received immortality, Gilgamesh defeatedly resigns himself to the inevitability of death and takes comfort in his achievements. No direct literary relationship may be traced between the biblical account of Noah's Flood and the *Gilgamesh Epic*. Another passage from the *Gilgamesh Epic* parallels Ecclesiastes 9:7–9, as the disparaging words of Siduri remind Gilgamesh that we all must face death, and that he must learn to enjoy this fleeting life as much as possible.

Gog One of the ultimate foes of God's people, Gog is the ruler of Magog and prince of Meshech and Tubal. Gog and Magog symbolically represent the godless nations of the world who will come from the vast ends of the earth to do battle against Israel.

Grammatical-Historical Method Method of biblical interpretation that seeks to find the basic "plain sense" meaning of a Bible passage by applying standard rules of grammar and syntax, seeking to determine what the text says grammatically and what it meant historically. It strives to discover the author's original intention by careful use of the rules of context, genre, language, and biblical consistency.

Great Tribulation Perilous period of history before the Lord returns, brings victory, and establishes his kingdom.

Hebrews Term the Bible uses to describe Abraham and his descendants through Isaac and Jacob. The origin of the term is not known. One possibility is that the Hebrews of the Old Testament may be identified at least in part with the Habiru of Middle and Late Bronze Age texts from the ancient Near East. This was probably a social designation for seminomadic Semites. The Hebrews could have been intended by some of the ancient references to Habiru. But the latter term does not have an ethnic significance and has a much wider range of meaning.

Heilsgeschichte Compound German word (from the words for "salvation" and "history") with several English equivalents: redemptive history, salvation history, sacred history, and the like. It denotes a theological principle that interprets the Bible as describing God's actions of salvation in history. The events of salvation history are supernatural divine revelations in time and space, and are recorded in Scripture to promote faith.

Herem In relation to the "holy wars" of Israel, as in the conquest of Canaan, *herem* referred to the spoil of war, including people, animals, or goods—all of which belonged to the Lord to do with as he pleased.

Hermeneutics Science of interpreting the Bible. Hermeneutics involves the application of time-tested principles to draw out the biblical text's intended message.

Hexateuch Name (meaning "six scrolls") given to the first six books of the Bible—Genesis, Exodus, Leviticus, Numbers, Deuteronomy, and Joshua—as a literary unit. Some scholars have argued that this unit was edited as a single work.

Hieroglyphs, Hieroglyphic Term for the earliest Egyptian writing system (Greek *hieros*, "sacred," and *glyphe*, "carving"). It was pictographic, relying on representations of common objects and geometric symbols.

Historical Epics Official records and documents preserved and found in royal or temple archives of ancient Near Eastern nations, as were apparently referenced by the author of Kings in his writings from the archives of ancient Israel and Judah.

Historical Narrative Predominant content of 1 and 2 Kings, which is arguably the earliest genuine historiography in world literature, as for the first time in human history a nation produced a continuous narrative organizing documents in an orderly presentation with a single overarching purpose. The author of Kings tied the historical narratives together with grand religious convictions, presenting Israel's past from a prophetic and theological point of view—rehearsing the list of Israel's kings carefully and systematically, with the goal of critiquing each one's faithfulness to God's covenant, and tracing the consequences of sin as opposed to the benefits of obedience.

Holiness Code Name given to Leviticus 17–27, a section of the Law devoted to right living outside the tabernacle.

Hymn Psalm, or song, of praise in which writers praised the Lord and offered him thanksgiving for who he was and what he had done (e.g., Pss 8, 136, 150). Such hymns featured either individual or corporate praise.

Idyll Short description of a simple and charming scene or event, especially one of country or rustic life, as in the Book of Ruth.

Imago Dei Latin expression for "image of God," referring particularly to the climax of God's creation when he made humankind in his "image" and in his "likeness" (Gn 1:26–27).

Imprecatory Psalms Psalms, or songs, which call for God's judgment on the psalmist's enemies (e.g., Pss 35, 69, 137); they may be individual or corporate in nature. Although these psalms have provoked much theological discussion because of their angry content, we must realize that the psalmists in these verses help us see the human side of Scripture, as they cried out in anger and frustration, and in their pain, realized their own weakness—that they were incapable of changing their terrible circumstances. The psalmists also left judgment in the hands of God, calling on God to judge but recognizing that only God held that absolute right.

Incarnation Christian doctrine that God took on human form in Jesus Christ. Through an act of grace, the Son of God assumed a human body and human nature. The doctrine teaches that Jesus is the eternal Son of God and the earthly Messiah, one person with two natures, who was both fully human and fully divine. Revelation in the Old Testament hints at this Christian doctrine

because God always reveals himself "incarnationally," that is, in real time and space.

Intertestamental Apocalyptic Literature written during the intertestamental period and characterized by some type of vision, the initial revelation of which is usually symbolic and mysterious and requires interpretation by a heavenly mediator. The author's name, if given, is assumed to be a pseudonym or pen name, and many of these books claim that their authors are venerated heroes of Israelite faith who lived centuries before the books were actually written (Enoch, Abraham, Isaiah, Ezra). Such writings also share a similar content. Concerned with the future and often revealing an eschatological judgment, they usually divide history into distinct periods of time, with history culminating in a final judgment that rewards the good and punishes the wicked in an afterlife. This literature is sensitive to the distinction between the spiritual and physical worlds, as sometimes angels or demons represent the supernatural world, or the recipient of the vision is carried into the other world for a heavenly journey. Many of these writings employ a technique, as was possibly used by Daniel, whereby a well-known event of the past is cast in predictive, futuristic language. The Book of Daniel and other Old Testament prophetic passages, while sharing many apocalyptic features, show significant differences from those books of the intertestamental period and are thus classified in a subcategory referred to as biblical apocalyptic literature.

Intertestamental Period Period of history between the close of Old Testament times (about 400 B.C.) and the birth of Christ.

Iron Age Term used by archaeologists and historians of the ancient Near East for the period in which iron displaced bronze as the metal used for tools and weaponry (about 1200–332 B.C.). This period is marked by the rise of the first genuinely world empires, all from a Mesopotamian base: Assyria, Babylonia, and Persia. The Iron Age

is commonly subdivided into three periods: Iron Age I (1200–930 B.C.), Iron Age II (930–539 B.C.), and Iron Age III (539–332 B.C.). This was the period of Israel's monarchy, exile, and restoration.

Ishtar Mesopotamian "goddess of love and the heroine of war" depicted as a harlot, part of the Babylonian pantheon, Ishtar was the wife of Tammuz, a Mesopotamian agricultural god, whose followers believed that every year at harvest time, Tammuz died (Ez 8:14–15).

JEDP Literary sources believed by many scholars to have been used to compile the Pentateuch, as well as the Book of Joshua, thus forming a Hexateuch.

Kassite Period Period of Mesopotamian history from the fourteenth to twelfth centuries B.C., during which we find examples of Mesopotamian dialogue literature such as the text *Ludlul bel nemequi* ("I will praise the Lord of wisdom"), a lengthy monologue in which a noble Babylonian recounts how he met with every sort of disaster before the god Marduk eventually restored him to his position. The Kassites were a people "from the eastern hills" who gradually took over Babylon and ruled for a time.

Lament Psalms Psalms, or songs, typically containing three elements, which may or may not occur in the following order: (1) the bemoaning of one's condition, (2) stating of the psalmist's trust in God, that God will somehow bring him through his trials, and (3) some kind of praise that God has heard his prayer and will eventually intervene for him (e.g., Pss 3, 4, and 6).

Late Bronze Age Term used by archaeologists and historians for the period of internationalism and communication in the ancient Near East, about 1550–1200 B.C. The Late Bronze Age is marked by Egypt's powerful New Kingdom, which exerted considerable influence on the coastal areas of Syria-Palestine. This was the period of Israel's exodus from Egypt, wilderness wanderings, and conquest of Canaan.

Levant Eastern coast of the Mediterranean Sea, which forms the western boundary of Syria-Palestine. The Levant extends for four hundred miles, and became the crossroads for all trade and travel in the ancient world.

Leviathan In Job 40, probably refers to the crocodile as a picture of strength, resilience, and apparent indestructibility which God uses to contrast his mighty power with the weakness and ignorance of the human being.

Levirate Marriage Law of the Old Testament providing children for a deceased family member (Dt 25:5–6). When an Israelite died without having fathered sons, his nearest relative was to marry the widow and continue the family of the deceased through the firstborn son of the new marriage, who was to carry the name and inheritance of the first husband.

Levites Descendants of Levi, one of the twelve sons of Jacob (Gn 29:34), after whom the Book of Leviticus was named. Aaron and his family were chosen from this tribe to serve as priests and to offer the sacrifices, while God appointed the rest of the Levites to the service of the tabernacle, to assist the priests in the worship at the sanctuary (Nm 3:5–10). Portions of the Book of Leviticus served as an instruction manual for the Old Testament priesthood.

Lingua Franca Any language used as a trade or communication medium by people of different language groups. In the Late Bronze Age, the Babylonian dialect of Akkadian was used. In the first millennium B.C. Aramaic became the international language.

Literary Criticism Critical approach to study of the Old Testament that developed in the second half of the twentieth century and, like its predecessors, addresses the larger literary issues, although its proponents are often antagonistic to the older source and form critical approaches to the Pentateuch. Literary criticism further emphasizes text-centered, or reader-centered, analysis rather than the traditional author-centered

approaches of earlier scholars. Those who use this approach have produced mixed results, but the newer literary criticism seems to hold great promise for significant new insights into biblical interpretation.

"Little Apocalypse" Name given by many interpreters to Isaiah 24–27 because these chapters read like a miniature Book of Revelation, serving as a grand conclusion to Isaiah's oracles of chapters 13–23 and announcing God's final judgment of the world and the ultimate salvation of his people (see Apocalyptic Literature).

Maccabees Hasmonean family who led the Jewish struggle for religious freedom and political independence against the Seleucid Empire in 168–160 B.C. After their victory, the priest Mattathias and his three sons ruled as monarchs in Jerusalem (the "Hasmonean dynasty") for about a century. One of the sons, Judas, was nicknamed Maccabee, "the hammer," from which the name "Maccabees" is derived.

Magog "Nation" ruled by Gog, one of the ultimate foes of God's people, and probably located between Cappadocia and Media. Gog, along with Magog, symbolically represent the godless nations of the world that will come from the vast ends of the earth to do battle against Israel in a final assault but will suffer devastating defeat by the intervention of God on the mountains of Canaan. This conflict is related in Ezekiel 38 and 39 and summarized in Revelation 20:7–9.

Mari Prophecy One of the basic categories of evidence regarding the existence of prophecy in other civilizations of the biblical world and its relationship to the biblical prophets. Although similarities between Mari prophecy and biblical prophecy do exist, striking differences appear with a closer look at the texts and sharply distinguish the biblical prophets from the ecstatics at Mari. The Old Testament prophets asserted that God's covenant with his people had implications for daily living. A proper relationship with God should result in just and ethical treatment of other people; certain

actions and beliefs were true and right because God had so ordained them. Furthermore, the prophets spoke to all of society, not just to the royal household. (See also Ecstatics.)

Masora Hebrew word meaning "bond" or "cord." In Old Testament studies, it refers to the system of vowel points and accent marks used to further clarify the Hebrew text of the Old Testament.

Masoretic Text Hebrew copy of the Old Testament that has come down to us from the Masoretes—one of the most important and accurate groups of scribes who, from A.D. 500–1000, worked to preserve the Old Testament text using a complex system of markings called the masora. The oldest copies of this text date somewhat earlier than A.D. 1000, although most scholars believe these copies reflect a text from about A.D. 100. The Masoretic Text is the most reliable Hebrew text we have.

Mesha Inscription Inscription testifying to the extension of Israel's borders by Omri of Israel (885–874 B.C.; 1 Kgs 16:21–28) eastward into Moabite territory; he forged such an impressive kingdom that Assyrian documents from a century later still referred to northern Israel as "the house of Omri." In this terse paragraph, Mesha, the king of Moab in the mid-ninth century B.C., mentions only Omri's unusual rise to power, his acquisition of Samaria as a new capital city, and his unprecedented evil. Omri's move of the capital to Samaria may have been an effort to coerce his subjects to worship other deities in addition to Yahweh; such religious apostasy was of greater concern to the author of 1 Kings than were his significant political accomplishments.

Mesolithic Age Term used by archaeologists and historians for the Middle Stone Age, about 14,000–8000 B.C. The Mesolithic Age witnessed the first cave culture. The switch from life in the open to the shelter of caves was perhaps caused by climate changes.

Messiah Literally, "anointed one." The term could denote prophets, priests, or kings, but more specifically refers to Jesus Christ, God's ultimate anointed one, who accomplished God's redemptive purpose and one day will return to establish his kingdom.

Messianic Psalms Psalms, or songs, which describe the Messiah, God's anointed one.

Meter Accent pattern in rhythmic lines or verses. Hebrew poetry relies heavily on meter, and some commentators have suggested that ancient writers used a variety of metric styles and patterns to convey certain moods or ideas.

Middle Bronze Age Term used by archaeologists and historians for the period of Amorite incursions across the ancient Near East, initiating a new era (about 2000–1550 B.C.). After an initial period of decline in Syria-Palestine, the Amorite culture brought a resurgence of sedentary life and the new development of urban centers. New Amorite kingdoms in Babylonia during this period were to play a major role in ancient Near Eastern history. This was also Israel's patriarchal period.

Millennium According to some evangelicals, a literal thousand-year reign of Christ on earth with his saints following his second coming (see Premillennialism). Others understand this term to refer to the spiritual reign of Christ in the hearts of believers now (amillennialism).

Mishnah Recorded oral conversation of the rabbis as they discussed the proper interpretation and course of action required of Jews with regard to the Mosaic law. It is a commentary, so to speak, explaining the Torah of Moses and often producing legal instruction. The Mishnah accepted Mosaic authorship of the Pentateuch. The Mishnah is an antecedent to the Talmud.

Moabite Language in the family of Hebrew and Aramaic, used by the Moabites.

Monologue Prolonged talk or discourse by a single speaker or any composition, such as a poem or drama, in which a single person or actor speaks alone. Monologues were often found in ancient

Mesopotamian discursive wisdom literature, that is, documents produced by ancient Near Eastern sages containing lengthy discourses or essays grappling with life's most difficult problems.

Monotheism Theological and philosophical position that there is only one God. Such a view was not the accepted belief of other ancient peoples, who were polytheists and henotheists.

Monotheistic Relating to the biblically grounded belief that there is only God.

Mosaic Yahwism Worship of Yahweh, the one true God, who made his covenant with Israel. Mosaic Yahwism was marked by strict adherence to the Law given to Moses at Mount Sinai. During the years of the divided monarchy, Omri of Israel and his son Ahab combined Mosaic Yahwism with Canaanite Baalism, in order to gain greater political control, as the northern kingdom was plagued by political instability.

Multiple-Author View View regarding the authorship of the Book of Isaiah which holds that the prophet Isaiah produced the material in chapters 1–39, while another author or authors (Deutero-Isaiah, or the "second Isaiah"), perhaps Isaiah's disciples, wrote the latter half of the book. This view may also include a third division within chapters 40–66, claiming that Deutero-Isaiah wrote chapters 40–55, while yet a third person or school of disciples (Trito-Isaiah, or "Third Isaiah") somewhat later wrote chapters 56–66; some argue that this third section came from many hands, perhaps a school of Isaiah's disciples. Proponents of this view generally have argued along three lines: the time span of the book; the difference in subject matter, vocabulary, and style between these two divisions; and the mention of Cyrus by name in 44:28 and 45:1.

Myth, Mythology In modern English, this term usually refers to something untrue and imaginative. But in reference to ancient Near Eastern studies, scholars use it in a

more classical sense, though there is no consensus on definition. Myth is the literary instrument by which ancient peoples ordered their world. Myths explained how the world began and provided norms for human behavior. As expressions of theological convictions, these ancient myths occurred outside time and space, and were linked to the nature religions. Ancient Israel, however, "historicized" mythology by referring not to a time distinct from world time, but to the history of Israel itself. The Israelite God, Yahweh, was Creator and established the norms for human behavior himself through divine revelation to the nation. History became the instrument for expressing theology, not myth.

Neolithic Age Term used by archaeologists and historians for the New Stone Age of the Middle East, about 8000–4200 B.C. The Neolithic Age witnessed radical changes in human culture laying the foundations of civilization, changes significant enough for scholars to refer to a Neolithic Revolution. During this period, the wandering hunters of the earlier stone ages began the transition to settled communities. Established villages appear with agriculture-based economies, made possible by the domestication of animals and the cultivation of crops. Toward the end of this period, inhabitants of Neolithic villages also began producing pottery.

Neo-Orthodoxy Philosophy born in the early twentieth century, partly as a reaction to liberalism's disregard for divine authority, significantly promoted by Karl Barth and Emil Brunner. Neo-orthodoxy holds that God is utterly transcendent—that is, absolutely different from us and far beyond our comprehension; we can only know something about him if he reveals himself to us, as he did in Jesus Christ. Neo-orthodoxy asserts that the Bible is merely a witness to the word of God or contains the word of God, as people of biblical times experienced God and recorded their encounters as best they could. As finite creatures, however, their reports sometimes contained errors or paradoxes. Still, their descriptions are valuable in helping others better understand God, and as others experience God afresh through these accounts, the accounts become God's word all over again. Although neo-orthodoxy has a high view of God, it fails to provide an adequate explanation for all the biblical evidence.

New Kingdom Term referring to Egypt during the time of Moses and the Exodus.

Nonliterary Prophets Prophets whom God called to prophesy but who never wrote down their messages, leaving to others the task of recording their words and deeds; we know of their ministries only through the accounts of them in the Old Testament historical books. The nonliterary prophets generally tended to focus on the king and his court, advising the king on various matters and sometimes warning him about the consequences of his sin. Examples of such prophets include Elijah and Elisha (2 Kgs 1:1–13:21), unnamed prophets who appeared in Saul's day (1 Sm 10:10–12; 19:20–21) and later during the divided kingdom (1 Kgs 13), Ahijah (1 Kgs 11:29–39), Micaiah (1 Kgs 22:7–28), a man designated only as "a man of God" who spoke words of judgment to Jeroboam I (1 Kgs 13:1–10), and a woman named Huldah (2 Kgs 22:14–20).

Office of Prophecy Office that began to emerge based on the ministries of Elijah and Elisha, through which prophets became God's instruments of warning to the king and the nation in light of their sin and imminent doom.

Omen Texts Collection of texts that began to be compiled during the Old Babylonian Period (2000–1595 B.C.). Probably considered scientific in their own day, these texts reflected the belief of these ancient people that the world was a complex web of cause-and-effect relationships with a supernatural intention often lying behind an event. Thus, the omen texts preserved a written record of these events and their consequences; and if certain events reoccurred, that meant the gods were about to repeat their prior

actions. For example, if a certain bird appeared during a certain month, that might indicate a coming famine; or if a sacrificial animal had a red spot on its liver, that might indicate a military victory for the king. These texts have little in common with biblical prophecy, lacking any sort of moral basis. While the gods simply revealed their will through interrelated events in nature, the prophets took their stand upon God, his word, and his covenant with his people.

Oracle Prophetic word, usually of some length, which the prophet received from God and announced to the people. Oracles could focus on a variety of topics.

Oracles against the Nations Divine communication or revelation given by God to the prophet Isaiah that described his plans to deal with the other nations of the ancient world, not just Israel. His prophecy of coming judgment began with Babylon (13:1–14:23), which, after rising to rule the world, would be destroyed by the Medes. Isaiah next spoke of God's future judgment of Assyria (14:24–27), Philistia (14:28–32), Moab (15:1–16:14), Damascus and Israel (17:1–14), Cush and Egypt (18:1–20:6), Babylon, Edom, and Arabia (21:1–17), Jerusalem (22:1–25), and Tyre (23:1–18).

Paleolithic Age Term used by archaeologists and historians for the Old Stone Age (before 14,000 B.C.). Artifacts from Paleolithic sites are primitive stone tools shaped by humans. During this period, people lived in open-air sites and the terraces of ancient river beds. The Paleolithic was a pre-cave culture.

Parallelism Feature of Hebrew poetry in which at least two parallel lines of verse complement each other in some way and typically display parallelism of thought rather than of rhyme or sound. Such parallelism may be synonymous, antithetic, or synthetic.

Patriarchal Narratives Narratives of Genesis 12–50, reflecting a new literary unit in the book and providing accounts of the patriarchs

(Abraham, Isaac, and Jacob) which are narrower in scope and unique in the ancient world. These accounts concern the members of a single family and their journey of faith, in contrast to the previous section's concern with the creation of the world. The narratives fit well into the Middle Bronze Age (2000–1550 B.C.).

Patriarchs Three individuals who stand at the fountainhead of the faith: Abraham, Isaac, and Jacob.

Penitential Psalms Psalms, or songs, which express sorrow for sin. These psalms may reflect the repentance of one person or of the community of worshipers, confessing sorrow for sin and appealing to God's grace for restoration (e.g., Pss 38 and 51).

Pentateuch Term used for the first five books of the Bible, from Greek *pentateuchos,* meaning a five-book work. The Pentateuch is also known by the Hebrew word *torah,* which is often translated "law," but really connotes "teaching" or "instruction."

Pharaoh God-king of the ancient Egyptians, to whom the people gave credit for the Nile's annual flood.

Phoenician Language in the family of Hebrew and Aramaic, used by the Phoenicians, a prosperous people who inhabited the territory on the eastern Mediterranean coast. In Old Testament times, this territory was called "Canaan" by the Hebrews.

Plenary Verbal Inspiration Theory of biblical inspiration which asserts that the Holy Spirit interacted with human writers to produce the Bible. "Plenary" means "full" or "complete" and asserts that God's inspiration extends to all of Scripture, from Genesis to Revelation, as God guided writers equally in the recording of historical details as in matters of doctrine. "Verbal" refers to the words of Scripture—that God's inspiration extends to the very words chosen by the writers. Although the writers were free to choose their own words and express their unique personalities and styles as they wrote, the Holy Spirit so guided the process that the words they chose accurately conveyed the meaning God intended. Thus, this view of inspiration holds that God inspired the entire Bible, maintaining author distinctiveness while guaranteeing a finished product that faithfully reflected his message. Plenary verbal inspiration seems to best handle all the biblical evidence—recognizing the human element in Scripture while affirming the Holy Spirit as the Bible's ultimate Author.

Polytheism Belief in many gods. Polytheism is often linked to fertility religions and nature religions of antiquity.

Premillennialism Evangelical position that holds that Jesus will return to earth to establish a literal earthly kingdom, ruling with his saints for a thousand years. After this period will come the judgment of unbelievers and the establishment of heaven.

Primeval History Prehistory, or the earliest phases of human activity, which occurred before history was recorded. A technical term used to refer to Genesis 1:1–11.

Prologue Preface or introductory part of a discourse, poem, or novel; in Job, the prose prologue helps create a literary frame for the poetic speeches.

Promise God's word to Abram in Genesis 12, where God promised him both land and descendants—to make Abram's family a great nation that would become a blessing for humankind.

Proverb Succinct and persuasive saying proven true by experience, addressing various topics that relate to God, his world, and life. Proverbs are statements of general truth, not hard-and-fast promises or commands to be applied in every situation.

Pseudonym Term used to describe the custom of attributing a writing to someone other than the real author. In intertestamental apocalyptic literature, such "pen names" were used to ascribe writings to some ancient hero of the faith.

Rationalist Individual who accepts reason as the supreme authority in matters of opinion, belief, or conduct, holding that human reason, unaided by divine revelation, is an adequate or sole guide to all attainable religious truth. Zophar, one of Job's friends, considered himself a rationalist, reasoning that Job's punishment was no less than can be reasonably expected and concluding that Job should put his iniquity and wickedness "far away" (11:14).

Redaction Criticism Critical approach to study of the Pentateuch stemming from Wellhausen's Documentary Hypothesis and attempting to explain scientifically how the four separate sources (JEDP) were edited together; this approach has met with little agreement among scholars.

Regnal Formula Formula used in 1 Kings 11:41–43 as a structuring device when considering each ruler of the divided kingdom in the concluding account of Solomon's life and reign.

Remnant Literally, "a remainder." A technical term that refers to a group of God's people that remains faithful to the Lord and with whom the Lord determines to continue his redemptive purposes.

Restoration Theme of 1 Chronicles, whereby the author looks toward future hope of salvation and balances his recurring emphasis and pattern of Israel's exile situation as illustrated through the archetype of Saul, who died because of his unfaithfulness to the Lord. For the chronicler, David fulfilled a savior role. Thus, he describes how David became king, his military exploits and successes, and his preparations for building the temple. Since the author views the temple as central to God's plan of salvation, these elaborate plans for its construction reveal David's true character as Israel's leader in the faith.

Retribution Doctrine which holds that goodness results in prosperity and wickedness leads to suffering; Mesopotamian dialogue material accepted the doctrine of retribution presented in Job and Ecclesiastes.

Rhyme Literary characteristic of Hebrew poetry that describes the agreement in ending sounds of poetic lines, verses, or words. Hebrew poetry relies much more on meter than on rhyme, although rhyme sometimes does occur.

Rift Large fissure in the surface of the earth. The Jordan Rift, extends from north of the Sea of Galilee through the Jordan Valley and the Dead Sea to the shores of the Red Sea, and is an important topographical feature of Syria-Palestine.

Royal Annals Official records preserved in the royal archives of ancient Near Eastern kingdoms that probably listed each king's political activities (e.g., 1 Kgs 11:41; 14:19; 15:31).

Royal Psalms Psalms, or songs, which focus on Israel's king, usually describing him as God's special representative to rule Israel. Psalms 2, 45, and 110 provide good examples of such royal psalms.

Sages Men renowned for wisdom who in the ancient Near East produced documents containing lengthy discourses or essays grappling with life's most difficult problems.

Saints of the Most High Individuals in the vision recorded in Daniel 7 that comprise the fifth and final eternal kingdom established by the Ancient of Days and "one like a son of man."

Salvation History See *Heilsgeschichte.*

Samaritan Pentateuch Old Testament text containing only Genesis through Deuteronomy, which originated with the Samaritans, who came from the intermarriage of Jews and foreigners in the territory of the northern kingdom after it fell to Assyria in 722 B.C. The oldest manuscript of this text dates to about A.D. 1100, although many scholars believe it is based on a text from 100–200 B.C. While the Jews viewed the Samaritans with contempt as half-breed compromisers who had denied their faith by intermarrying with foreigners, the Samaritans felt they preserved a more ancient and pure form of the faith, thus leading to inevitable theological differences. Because the Samaritan Pentateuch is slanted in such a way as to reflect these differences, the text provides an early witness to the way the Samaritans interpreted the Pentateuch but is not as reliable for determining the text's original reading.

Sea Peoples Newcomers to the ancient Near East around 1200 B.C. Presumably fleeing from the mainland of Greece after the fall of Troy, these peoples fled along the coasts of the Mediterranean, disrupting all the major powers of the day, notably Egypt and the Hittites. One group of these sea peoples was the Philistines, who settled on the southwestern coast of Syria-Palestine and played a major role in Old Testament times.

Septuagint Translation of the Old Testament into Greek that dates to about 300–200 B.C. and comes from the Egyptian city of Alexandria. Its name and abbreviation (LXX) come from the fact that a team of seventy-two scholars did the translation work. The Septuagint provides an important early testimony to the Old Testament text.

Seventy Sevens Refers to the prophetic, eschatological passage of Daniel 9:24–27 about "seventy weeks of years," or seventy periods of time; these seventy weeks of seven years equal 490 years, although interpreters disagree as to the relative dates and events of this period.

Shalom Hebrew word meaning "peace." More than the absence of conflict, it refers to a life where wholeness and well-being are present. Shalom-peace was perfectly portrayed in the Garden of Eden before the fall; there, humankind was at peace with God and with the surrounding creation—having ready access to God's presence and enjoying his favor, also capable of enjoying the rich and perfect fullness of creation.

Shema Name of the important passage in Dt 6:4–9, which is Israel's classic expression of the concept of monotheism and which became a central prayer in later Judaism. The name itself is the first Hebrew word of the opening imperative: "Hear, O Israel: The LORD our God, the LORD is one."

Sheol Hebrew word most often used in reference to the place where the dead were believed to dwell, a place of darkness (Jb 10:21–22; Ps 143:3), silence (Pss 94:17; 115:17), whose inhabitants are unable to praise God (Pss 6:5; 88:10–12) and know nothing (Jb 14:21; Eccl 9:5), who are merely shadows of their former selves. Sheol is within the reach of God, as communicated in Psalm 139:8 and Job 26:6. There are questions as to the actual location of Sheol and how closely it is to be associated with the literal grave; there is also disagreement whether Old Testament believers first went to this place of gloom for a time or directly to heaven. Ezekiel, in haunting prophetic language, described God's taking Egypt to Sheol, where Egypt found a welcoming committee of Assyria, Elam, and Edom—nations that had similarly trusted in their own power and splendor until God brought their dominion to an end; Ezekiel warned the Egyptians that they would become like every other nation that had challenged God's authority (29:1–32:32).

Sign Something that gives evidence of a past, present, or future event, which serves to warn of things to come or to prove legitimacy. For example, Isaiah offered Ahaz a sign from God to strengthen the king's faith. Ahaz, however, masked his lack of faith with false piety (Is 7:10–12), as he was already thinking of trusting Assyria instead of God (2 Kgs 16:7–8). Isaiah condemned Ahaz for his lack of faith, declaring that God himself would provide a sign, that is, a virgin would conceive, bear a son, and name him Immanuel, which means "God is with us" (Is 7:14); before this child could choose between good and evil, the kings of Syria and Israel would be gone.

Sitz im Leben German expression (meaning "setting in life") that denotes the historical and sociological setting in which a specific literary genre or form first took shape.

Son of Man In Ezekiel 2:1–3 and fifty-seven other times in this prophecy, a clear designation to a descendant of Adam; in Psalm 8:4, a phrase applying to both mortal man and Jesus Christ in his incarnation, in his human identification with mankind, and similarly suggesting a messianic figure in Daniel 7:13. In the New Testament, Jesus often referred to himself by this title, possibly drawing, as some scholars believe, on Ezekiel's use of the term to emphasize his humanity and his dependence on God the Father.

Source Criticism Critical approach to biblical study, frequently called the Documentary Hypothesis, which seeks to answer the question, "Who wrote the Pentateuch?" and which holds that the Pentateuch was compiled from four separate sources; its most pervasive protagonist was Julius Wellhausen, and its reconstructions were dominated by anti-supernaturalism and philosophical evolutionary thought, denying virtually any historical veracity in the Pentateuch and making no allowance for divine intervention in history, or for unique divine revelation.

Sovereignty Biblical teaching that God is in absolute control of all creation and subordinate to none. The Pentateuch begins by emphasizing God's sovereignty through an account of Creation that assumes the preexistence and eternality of God, who created the whole universe without assistance from anyone, without using preexistent matter, and without effort, solely by the power of his spoken word. Just as Genesis 1 powerfully establishes God's sovereignty over his creation, so also the subsequent stories of the flood (Gn 6–9) and Tower of Babel (Gn 11), as well as his dealings with individuals like Abraham, Isaac, Jacob, Joseph, and Moses, demonstrate God's supreme dominion. In stark contrast to the gods of the ancient Near East, whose jurisdiction had definite geographical limits, the scope of God's dominion is universal.

Suzerainty Treaty Political treaty of the ancient Near East between two parties of unequal rank, the suzerain (or overlord) and the vassal (or subject nation). The literary form of the Sinaitic covenant in Ex 20–24 and Deuteronomy is strikingly similar to these treaties, especially the Hittite suzerainty treaties from the royal archives at Boğbazköy, Turkey. These Hittite treaties date mostly from the Late Bronze Age, and seem to confirm the traditional date for the biblical texts, though some dispute this evidence.

Syncretism Attempt to unite or reconcile opposing beliefs or practices. Proponents of one religion will sometimes adapt or otherwise identify its deities or creeds with those of another religion in order to gain adherents.

Synonymous Parallelism Common literary characteristic of Hebrew poetry that involves a repetition of the same thought or a similar thought; the two parts basically reflect the same idea, as in Psalm 19:1, "The heavens declare the glory of God; the skies proclaim the work of his hands," or Proverbs 9:10, "The fear of the Lord is the beginning of wisdom, and knowledge of the Holy One is understanding." (See also Prv 16:18; 28; 18:6–7.)

Synthetic Parallelism Common literary characteristic of Hebrew poetry in which the second line normally completes a thought that the first line left incomplete; the two lines stand in relationship to each other, although that relationship is not as clearly defined as in synonymous or antithetic parallelism. Some interpreters suggest that this term merely provides a catch-all category for verses that do not display characteristics of synonymous or antithetic parallelism (see Ps 1:3 and 2:6; Eccl 11:1).

Table of Nations "Table" in Genesis 10:1–32 that classified the nations of the known world under the three sons of Noah: Shem, Ham, and Japheth. The Japhethites inhabited mostly the Mediterranean islands and Asia Minor and were most remote from Israel, while most of the Hamites were peoples with whom Israel had hostile relationships. The descendants of Shem were reserved for last because of

their importance as the line by which God would address the problem of humankind's sin—providing a glimmer of hope through the family of Terah, father of Abraham.

Talmud Collection of Jewish rabbinical laws, law decisions, and comments on the laws of Moses; refers to the first five books of the Bible as "the Books of Moses."

Tammuz Mesopotamian agricultural god, husband of the goddess Ishtar, whose followers believed that every year at harvest time, Tammuz died; the women Ezekiel saw in his vision weeping at the Jerusalem temple (Ez 8:14–15) were joining Ishtar in the mourning of Tammuz's death. Tammuz returned to life in the spring when crops rejuvenated themselves and buds appeared on the trees.

Targums Collections of Aramaic writings based on the Old Testament text that date from the early Christian era, though parts are earlier; arose during a time when many Jewish people understood Aramaic better than Hebrew, and provided common interpretations to the Hebrew text. In places, the Targums reflect a fairly literal translation of the Hebrew, while elsewhere they add commentary and stories as they elaborate on the meaning of the text; thus, they generally fail to provide a reliable witness to the Old Testament text, although they do help us understand early Jewish interpretations.

Temple Generally speaking, a place dedicated to the service or worship of a deity or deities; in the Old Testament, refers to any of the three successive buildings or groups of buildings in ancient Jerusalem that were devoted to the worship of Yahweh.

Tetrateuch Name (meaning "four scrolls") given to the first four books of the Bible—Genesis, Exodus, Leviticus, and Numbers—as a literary unit. Some scholars have argued that this unit was edited as one work consisting of the JEP sources. In this view, Deuteronomy was added much later.

Theodicy Attempt to vindicate the justice and holiness of God in light of the existence of evil in the world. If God is both all-powerful and all-loving, as the Bible everywhere claims, then how can evil continue to exist in the world? How can the wicked prosper if God is just? Why do good people suffer, and how could God let it happen? The Book of Job is one biblical response to this question.

Theology of Retribution Obedience to God's commands brings blessing while disobedience brings failure. This is the overriding concern in the Books of Kings, which is based on the Sinai covenant, especially as it is expressed in Deuteronomy, where Moses' final discourse (Dt 28) lists the blessings and curses of the covenant. For the author of Kings, history is the foundation on which this theology is proven, as he evaluates each king based on the monarch's loyalty to Yahweh as worshiped in Jerusalem and as he illustrates the two paths between which man must choose—the internal and external pursuit of God or disobedience and lack of devotion that ultimately leads to self-destruction.

Theophany Greek term for a manifestation of God. These sudden and unexpected appearances of God occur in perceptible forms (hearing and seeing) at decisive points in Israel's history: patriarchal promises (Gn 17; 18; 28), the call of Moses (Ex 3), the Sinai covenant (Ex 19), and more.

Torah Hebrew word that literally means "teaching" or "instruction," though sometimes also translated "law." The term refers to the first five books of the Old Testament—Genesis, Exodus, Leviticus, Numbers, and Deuteronomy.

Tradition Criticism Branch of form criticism developed in the first half of the twentieth century that devoted itself to oral tradition, that is, to the oral, preliterary history of the various literary types. This approach was most celebrated by Martin Noth, who believed that writing came late in the development of Old Testament literary sources and that the literary types reflect a long history of oral transmission, so that the pentateuchal sources evolved over many centuries before people wrote them down. Tradition criticism is more subjective than other approaches and fails to take into account evidence from elsewhere in the ancient Near East, which may provide control data for Old Testament scholars, regardless of their method. Such extrabiblical studies, for example, suggest that ancient Near Eastern literary traditions were often recorded in writing soon after the events they describe, not centuries later.

Transcendent Beyond comprehension, understanding, and explanation. Theologians use this term to describe the fact that God is totally beyond anything else in our human experience.

Transmission Faithful conveyance of the Scriptures as passed on and handed down from generation to generation. This was the sole responsibility of the scribes in the ancient world, as they painstakingly copied the biblical texts—believing that they were copying the very words of God and thus taking great care to preserve the copies which they had received.

Tribute Stated sum or other valuable consideration paid by one sovereign or state to another in acknowledgment of submission or as the price of peace, security, protection, or the like. David accepted such tribute from many Syrian city-states over whom he led Israel in victory.

Trito-Isaiah Simply meaning the "Third Isaiah," this term is used by those scholars who hold to a multiple-author view of Isaiah to refer to the author of chapters 56–66. (See also Multiple-Author View.)

Ugaritic Language in the same family as Hebrew and Aramaic, and the language of Ugarit—an important trade center near the Mediterranean coast. The Ugarit scribes created an alphabetic script of thirty cuneiform signs.

Vassal Subordinate party in a suzerainty treaty. The vassal pledged loyalty and regular tribute to his lord, who in return pledged to protect the vassal from enemies.

Vaticinium ex Eventu Latin phrase meaning "prophecy after the fact," or "a prophecy from an outcome." This refers to a literary technique employed in intertestamental apocalyptic writings, whereby a well-known event of the past is cast in predictive, futuristic language. The author speaks of events that have already occurred as if they had not actually taken place. The author assumes the position of a predictive prophet and speaks of the event as though it were still in the future.

Via Maris Latin term meaning "the way of the sea," which comes from Isaiah 9:1 and refers to an international road running along the Levant coast. This highway was used throughout biblical times and was located near some of the most important cities of antiquity. The Vulgate rendered Isaiah's phrase as *Via Maris,* which was used in later times to designate the whole network of roadways from Egypt through Syria-Palestine into Mesopotamia. On the southern coastal plain, the *Via Maris* moves northward and splits into two branches, the western continuing along the coast and the eastern passing through the Jezreel Valley to Megiddo, and from there to Hazor and Damascus and on into Mesopotamia; the various branches of this great international highway converge at Megiddo, at the entrance to the Jezreel Valley—a strategic location for all commerce and travel in the ancient world.

Vulgate Latin translation of the Bible written by Jerome about A.D. 400. This translation includes the Apocrypha, the collection of esteemed Jewish books not found in the Old Testament nor accepted by Jews or Protestant Christians.

Wisdom Literature Designation that modern scholars use for three books that share "wisdom" features: Job, Proverbs, and Ecclesiastes; selected Psalms are also part of the collection (Pss 1, 37, 49, 73, etc.), and Song of Songs is also similar to wisdom literature in its didactic function and literary form. Although all the books included in the "poetic" section of the canon are related to wisdom literature, wisdom ideas reach beyond the poetical books of the Bible. Several of the prophets use wisdom sayings and parables in their sermons, as did Jesus in many of his teachings. Old Testament wisdom literature had an international backdrop, for each nation apparently had wisdom teachers who reflected their own particular nationalistic wisdom traditions, and archaeologists have discovered examples of wisdom literature from all parts of the ancient Near East. While "wisdom" in the Israelite literature refers to the fear of God, it generally refers in other cultures to skill in magical practices rather than moral content. The content of these documents does, however, invite comparison with Job, Ecclesiastes, and the Book of Proverbs, which contains more direct parallels with ancient Near Eastern literature than any other book of the Bible. Thus, wisdom literature provides an example of cross-cultural communication of faith, as the ancient Israelites interacted with the literature and worldview of their neighbors and were comfortable incorporating materials from other cultures while eliminating polytheistic elements. Sometimes the Israelites adapted such material with little or no alterations, such as Proverbs and the Egyptian wisdom materials; at other times, the authors used pagan literature with theological modifications.

Wisdom Psalms Psalms, or songs, which relate general observations about life, in which the writers typically make little effort to defend the truths that they expound; rather, they simply present such truths as self-evident descriptions of the way God has intended life to be, usually describing God and our relationship with him in one or more of its facets (e.g., Pss 1, 14, 73).

Woe Oracles Judgment speeches typically beginning with the word "woe," that is, an exclamation of grief, distress, affliction, or lament. Isaiah pronounced six woe oracles against various segments of Judah's population in 5:8–30: (1) denouncing oppressors who selfishly increased their estates at the expense of others, (2) condemning drunkards who lived only to pursue strong drink and merrymaking, (3) rebuking those who put God to the test, (4) reprimanding the morally twisted who called good evil and evil good to justify their sin, (5) pronouncing woe against the self-exalted who believed themselves wise, and (6) admonishing immoral opportunists. In his anger, God would judge their sin and call another nation to consume them and carry them away.

Yahwism Israel's genuine worship of Yahweh, the One true God, in faithful obedience to the covenant stipulations and requirements given by God in the Mosaic covenant.

Ziggurat Stepped tower of three to seven stages that was characteristic of ancient Mesopotamian temple complexes. Near the foot of this tower stood the ancient pagan temple itself, possibly connecting the idea that gods originally lived in mountains, for which the ziggurat served as a substitute. The Tower of Babel in Genesis 11 was a ziggurat, representing the pride and arrogant rebellion of the city of Babylon and humanity in general.

Notes

Chapter 1: *What Is the Old Testament and Why Study It?*

1. R. K. Harrison, *Introduction to the Old Testament* (Grand Rapids: Eerdmans, 1969), 260–61; William H. Green, *General Introduction to the Old Testament: The Canon* (Grand Rapids: Baker, 1980 [1898]), 9–10.

2. For slightly different perspectives on Jamnia, see Harrison, *Introduction,* 277–78; Roger T. Beckwith, *The Old Testament Canon of the New Testament Church* (Grand Rapids: Eerdmans, 1985), 276–77.

3. Karl Barth, *Evangelical Theology: An Introduction,* trans. Grover Foley (Grand Rapids: Eerdmans, 1979 [1963]); Emil Brunner, *Revelation and Reason: The Christian Doctrine of Faith and Knowledge* (Philadelphia: Westminster, 1946).

4. Dewey M. Beegle, *The Inspiration of Scripture* (Philadelphia: Westminster, 1963); Daniel P. Fuller, "Benjamin B. Warfield's View of Faith and History: A Critique in the Light of the New Testament," *Bulletin of the Evangelical Theological Society* 11 (1968): 75–83.

5. For a classic discussion of plenary verbal inspiration, see R. Laird Harris, *Inspiration and Canonicity of the Bible: An Historical and Exegetical Study* (Grand Rapids: Zondervan, 1957).

6. A. R. Millard, "In Praise of Ancient Scribes," *Biblical Archaeologist* 45 (1982): 143–53.

7. Ellis R. Brotzman, *Old Testament Textual Criticism: A Practical Introduction* (Grand Rapids: Baker, 1994), 49–53, gives a good summary of the Masoretes and their contribution to preserving the Old Testament text.

8. Ernst Würthwein, *The Text of the Old Testament: An Introduction to the Biblia Hebraica,* trans. Erroll F. Rhodes (Grand Rapids: Eerdmans, 1979), gives a good summary of the ancient manuscripts pertaining to the Old Testament. See also Emanuel Tov, *Textual Criticism of the Hebrew Bible* (Minneapolis/Assen, Netherlands: Fortress/Van Gorcum, 1992).

9. Würthwein, *Text of the Old Testament,* 12–41, provides a detailed discussion of the Masoretic text.

10. Brotzman, *Textual Criticism,* 64–69; Würthwein, *Text of the Old Testament,* 42–44.

11. Brotzman, *Textual Criticism,* 87–96, gives a good summary of the scrolls and their significance. For a more complete account, see Frank Moore Cross, *The Ancient Library of Qumran,* 3rd ed. (Minneapolis: Fortress, 1995).

12. For a thorough discussion of the Septuagint, see Sidney Jellicoe, *The Septuagint and Modern Study* (Winona Lake, Ind.: Eisenbrauns, 1978 [1968]); see also Würthwein, *Text of the Old Testament,* 49–74; Brotzman, *Textual Criticism,* 72–79; and Tov, *Textual Criticism,* 134–48.

13. Brotzman, *Textual Criticism,* 69–72, provides a good summary of the Targums; see also Würthwein, *Text of the Old Testament,* 75–79; and Tov, *Textual Criticism,* 134–48. For a complete discussion, see Alexander Sperber, ed., *The Bible in Aramaic,* 4 vols. (Leiden: E. J. Brill, 1959–1973).

14. These principles are drawn from a comparison of several basic works on hermeneutics. See J. Robertson McQuilkin, *Understanding and Applying the Bible,* rev. ed. (Chicago: Moody, 1992); Gordon Fee and Douglas Stuart, *How to Read the Bible for All Its Worth,* rev. ed. (Grand Rapids: Zondervan, 1993); A. Berkeley Mickelsen, *Interpreting the Bible* (Grand Rapids: Eerdmans, 1963).

Chapter 2: *Where and When Did the Events of the Old Testament Take Place?*

1. Yohanan Aharoni, *The Land of the Bible: A Historical Geography,* trans. Anson F. Rainey, 2nd ed. (London: Burns & Oates, 1979), 3–6.

2. For more on the geography of Mesopotamia in general, see Georges Roux, *Ancient Iraq,* 2nd ed. (Baltimore: Penguin, 1980), 19–33; H. W. F. Saggs, *The Greatness That Was Babylon: A Sketch of the Ancient Civilization of the Tigris-Euphrates Valley* (New York: Hawthorn, 1962), 27; and Wolfram von Soden, *The Ancient Orient: An Introduction to the Study of the Ancient Near East,* trans. Donald G. Schley (Grand Rapids: Eerdmans, 1994), 6–11.

3. On the geography of Egypt in general, see John A. Wilson, *The Culture of Ancient Egypt* (Chicago: University of Chicago Press, 1951), 8–17; William C. Hayes, *Most Ancient Egypt,* ed. Keith C. Seele (Chicago: University of Chicago Press, 1964), 1–41; and Hermann Kees, *Ancient Egypt: A Cultural Topography,* ed. T. G. H. James, trans. Ian F. D. Morrow (Chicago: University of Chicago Press, 1961), 47–95.

4. Donald B. Redford, *Egypt, Canaan, and Israel in Ancient Times* (Princeton, N.J.: Princeton University Press, 1992), 3–28.

5. Herodotus 2.5.

6. Wilson, *Culture of Ancient Egypt,* 8–17; and William W. Hallo and William Kelly Simpson, *The Ancient Near East: A History,* ed. John Morton Blum (New York: Harcourt Brace Jovanovich, 1971), 188.

7. Kees, *Ancient Egypt,* 9–10. This helps explain how devastating the plagues described in the Book of Exodus were to the Egyptians.

8. Wilson, *Culture of Ancient Egypt,* 15.

9. Aharoni, *Land of the Bible,* 21.

10. For more details on this section, see Aharoni, *Land of the Bible,* 21–42; and Denis Baly, *The Geography of the Bible: A Study in Historical Geography* (New York: Harper & Row, 1957), 125–27.

11. Baly, *Geography,* 194.

12. Aharoni, *Land of the Bible,* 31.

13. Baly, *Geography,* 109–14; Aharoni, *Land of the Bible,* 43–63.

14. For more on the history of Israel, see John Bright, *A History of Israel,* 3rd ed. (Philadelphia: Westminster, 1981); and Eugene H. Merrill, *Kingdom of Priests: A History of Old Testament Israel* (Grand Rapids: Baker, 1987).

15. Roux, *Ancient Iraq,* 140–53; and Walter R. Bodine, "Sumerians," in *Peoples of the Old Testament World,* ed. Alfred J. Hoerth, Gerald L. Mattingly, and Edwin M. Yamauchi (Grand Rapids: Baker, 1994), 27–36.

16. Wilson, *Culture of Ancient Egypt,* 69–103; and James K. Hoffmeier, "Egyptians," in *Peoples of the Old Testament World,* ed. Alfred J. Hoerth, Gerald L. Mattingly, and Edwin M. Yamauchi (Grand Rapids: Baker, 1994), 255–64.

17. Bright, *History,* 83–87. Some prefer a slightly earlier date; see Merrill, *Kingdom of Priests,* 78–79.

18. Roux, *Ancient Iraq,* 184–207; and Bill T. Arnold, "Babylonians," in *Peoples of the Old Testament World,* ed. Alfred J. Hoerth, Gerald L. Mattingly, and Edwin M. Yamauchi (Grand Rapids: Baker, 1994), 47–50.

19. Keith N. Schoville, "Canaanites and Amorites," in *Peoples of the Old Testament World,* ed. Alfred J. Hoerth, Gerald L. Mattingly, and Edwin M. Yamauchi (Grand Rapids: Baker, 1994), 162–67.

20. The precise timing between the genealogy of Gn 11:27–32 and Abram's call in 12:1–3 is not certain. See Victor P. Hamilton, *The Book of Genesis, Chapters 1–17* (NICOT; Grand Rapids: Eerdmans, 1990), 366–68, and Allen P. Ross, *Creation and Blessing* (Grand Rapids: Baker, 1988), 258.

21. Hoffmeier, "Egyptians," 273.

22. Harry A. Hoffner Jr., "Hittites," in *Peoples of the Old Testament World,* ed. Alfred J. Hoerth, Gerald L. Mattingly, and Edwin M. Yamauchi (Grand Rapids: Baker, 1994), 130.

23. Hoffmeier, "Egyptians," 287–88.

24. David M. Howard Jr., "Philistines," in *Peoples of the Old Testament World,* ed. Alfred J. Hoerth, Gerald L. Mattingly, and Edwin M. Yamauchi (Grand Rapids: Baker, 1994), 233–36.

25. Edwin M. Yamauchi, "Persians," in *Peoples of the Old Testament World,* ed. Alfred J. Hoerth, Gerald L. Mattingly, and Edwin M. Yamauchi (Grand Rapids: Baker, 1994), 107–24.

26. Merrill, *Kingdom of Priests,* 491–515.

Chapter 3: *Introduction to the Pentateuch: The Birth of God's People*

1. Besides these explicit references, there are others connecting the Pentateuch to Moses in a less direct fashion: Ex 25:16, 21–22; Dt 28:58; 29:20, 21, 27, 29; 30:10, 11. In addition, scholars have looked outside the Pentateuch for evidence of its author-ship: Jos 8:32; 1 Kgs 2:3; 2 Kgs 14:6; 21:8; Ezr 6:18; Neh 13:1; Dn 9:11–13; Mal 4:4; Mt 19:8; Mk 12:26; Jn 5:46–47; 7:19; Acts 3:22; Rom 10:5; etc.

2. *Sanhedrin* 21b–22a; and also see *Baba Bathra* 14b.

3. *Aboth* 1.1 and *Antiquities* 4.8.48, respectively.

4. For a survey of early Jewish and Christian doubts regarding Mosaic authorship, see R. K. Harrison, *Introduction to the Old Testament* (Grand Rapids: Eerdmans, 1969), 497–98.

5. His most important book was *Die Composition des Hexateuchs* (1877).

6. Kenneth A. Kitchen, *Ancient Orient and the Old Testament* (Downers Grove: InterVarsity, 1966), 15–34.

7. James A. Sanders, *Canon and Community: A Guide to Canonical Criticism* (Philadelphia: Fortress, 1984).

8. Tremper Longman III, *Literary Approaches to Biblical Interpretation* (Grand Rapids: Zondervan, 1987).

9. Carl E. Armerding, *The Old Testament and Criticism* (Grand Rapids: Eerdmans, 1983).

10. For this assessment, see Eugene Carpenter, "Pentateuch," in *International Standard Bible Encyclopedia,* ed. Geoffrey W. Bromiley, 4 vols. (Grand Rapids: Eerdmans, 1979–1988), 3:752–53.

Chapter 4: *Genesis 1–11: The Prelude to Israel*

1. W. G. Lambert and A. R. Millard, *Atra-hasis The Babylonian Story of the Flood* (Oxford: Clarendon, 1969); and Isaac M. Kikawada and Arthur Quinn, *Before Abraham Was: The Unity of Genesis 1–11* (Nashville: Abingdon, 1985), 41–48. This basic plot is also present in the Sumerian version (Thorkild Jacobsen, "The Eridu Genesis," *Journal of Biblical Literature* 100 [1981]: 513–29).

2. For an excellent survey of the parallels, see Gordon J. Wenham, *Genesis 1–15,* Word Biblical Commentary 1 (Waco, Tex.: Word, 1987), xlvi-l, and throughout the commentary. See also John H. Walton, *Ancient Israelite Literature in Its Cultural Context: A Survey of Parallels between Biblical and Ancient Near Eastern Texts* (Grand Rapids: Zondervan, 1989), 19–42.

3. Allen P. Ross, *Creation and Blessing: A Guide to the Study and Exposition of the Book of Genesis* (Grand Rapids: Baker, 1988), 718–23.

4. For linguistic details and further discussion, see Bill T. Arnold, "ראשׁית," in *New International Dictionary of Old Testament Theology and Exegesis,* ed. Willem A. VanGemeren, 5 vols. (Grand Rapids: Zondervan, 1997), 3:1025–26.

5. Wenham, *Genesis,* 6–7; and Ross, *Creation and Blessing,* 104.

6. Gerald Bray, "The Significance of God's Image in Man," *Tyndale Bulletin* 42, no. 2 (1991): 224–25.

7. The phrase usually translated "without form and void" is literary hendiadys, meaning it expresses a single notion through two words (*tōhû wābōhû*). But what is the single notion here intended? The phrase is often said to denote a chaotic universe at this stage of creation. But recent comparative and linguistic study has revealed that the expression describes a "bare" or "empty" earth, an uninhabited place that now is to be populated and inhabited by humankind. See David Toshio Tsumura, *The Earth and the Waters in Genesis 1 and 2: A Linguistic Investigation,* Journal for the Study of the Old Testament—Supplement Series 83 (Sheffield: JSOT, 1989), 17–43.

8. Victor P. Hamilton, *The Book of Genesis: Chapters 1–17,* New International Commentary on the Old Testament (Grand Rapids: Eerdmans, 1990), 2–11; and David W. Baker, "Diversity and Unity in the Literary Structure of Genesis," in *Essays on the Patriarchal Narratives,* ed. A. R. Millard and Donald J. Wiseman (Winona Lake, Ind.: Eisenbrauns, 1983), 208.

9. F. B. Huey Jr. and John H. Walton, "Are the 'Sons of God' in Genesis 6 Angels?" in *The Genesis Debate,* ed. Ronald F. Youngblood (Nashville: Thomas Nelson, 1986), 184–209. Some (such as Huey) have argued the passage refers literally to angels cohabiting with humans.

10. Victor P. Hamilton, "Genesis," in *Evangelical Commentary on the Bible,* ed. Walter A. Elwell (Grand Rapids: Baker, 1989), 18–19.

11. Bill T. Arnold, "Babylonians," in *Peoples of the Old Testament World,* ed. Alfred J. Hoerth, Gerald L. Mattingly, and Edwin M. Yamauchi (Grand Rapids: Baker, 1994), 43–45.

12. Derek Kidner, *Genesis: An Introduction and Commentary,* Tyndale Old Testament Commentary (Downers Grove: InterVarsity, 1967), 110.

Chapter 5: *Genesis 12–50: The Patriarchs: Ancestors of Israel's Faith*

1. See, for example, P. Kyle McCarter Jr., "The Patriarchal Age: Abraham, Issac, and Jacob," in *Ancient Israel: A Short History from Abraham to the Roman Destruction of the Temple,* ed. Hershel Shanks (Englewood Cliffs, N.J./Washington, D. C.: Prentice Hall/Biblical Archaeology Society, 1988), 20–29.

2. A. R. Millard, "Methods of Studying the Patriarchal Narratives as Ancient Texts," in *Essays on the Patriarchal Narratives,* ed. A. R. Millard and Donald J. Wiseman (Winona Lake, Ind.: Eisenbrauns, 1983), 35–51. See also the other articles in this excellent volume on the patriarchal narratives.

3. It is sometimes suggested that it could also have been another Ur located closer to Haran, the traditional homeland for the patriarchal family. Barry J. Beitzel, *The Moody Atlas of Bible Lands* (Chicago: Moody, 1985), 80.

4. Stephen's speech in Acts 7:2–4 contradicts this chronological sequence. For possible solutions, see Victor P. Hamilton, *The Book of Genesis, Chapters 1–17* (NICOT; Grand Rapids: Eerdmans, 1990), 366–68, and Allen P. Ross, *Creation and Blessing* (Grand Rapids: Baker, 1988), 258.

5. Martin J. Selman, "Comparative Customs and the Patriarchal Age," in *Essays on the Patriarchal Narratives,* ed. A. R. Millard and Donald J. Wiseman (Winona Lake, Ind.: Eisenbrauns, 1983), 114, 136.

6. Though Gn 15 may not actually contain a substitutionary element. See Richard S. Hess, "The Slaughter of the Animals in Genesis 15: Genesis 15:8–21 and Its Ancient Near Eastern Context," in *He Swore an Oath: Biblical Themes from Genesis 12–50,* ed. Richard S. Hess, Philip E. Satterthwaite, and Gordon J. Wenham, 2nd ed. (Grand Rapids/Carlisle, England: Baker/Paternoster, 1994), 55–65.

7. Selman, "Comparative Customs," 119, 137, and see the sidebar. Though the parallels are not exact, they are clear enough to provide background on a custom that would otherwise be unclear to the Western reader (John H. Walton, *Ancient Israelite Literature in Its Cultural Context: A Survey of Parallels between Biblical and Ancient Near Eastern Texts* [Grand Rapids: Zondervan, 1989], 54–55).

8. Gary A. Rendsburg, *The Redaction of Genesis* (Winona Lake, Ind.: Eisenbrauns, 1986), 46–47.

9. Gn 25:26, though the exact meaning of his name is uncertain.

10. David J. A. Clines describes the theme of the Pentateuch as the *partial* fulfillment of the promises to the patriarchs (*The Theme of the Pentateuch,* Journal for the Study of the Old Testament—Supplement Series 10 [Sheffield: JSOT, 1978]).

11. Thomas E. McComiskey, *The Covenants of Promise: A Theology of the Old Testament Covenants* (Grand Rapids: Baker, 1985), 10.

Chapter 6: *Exodus: A Miraculous Escape*

1. "Exodus" is from the Greek translation of 19:1, meaning "departure."

2. James K. Hoffmeier, "Egypt, Plagues in," in *Anchor Bible Dictionary,* ed. David Noel Freedman, 6 vols. (New York: Doubleday, 1992), 2:374–78.

3. R. Alan Cole, *Exodus: An Introduction and Commentary,* Tyndale Old Testament Commentary (Downers Grove: InterVarsity, 1973), 122.

4. John J. Bimson, *Redating the Exodus and Conquest,* Journal for the Study of the Old Testament—Supplement Series 5 (Sheffield: JSOT, 1981).

5. Kenneth A. Kitchen, "Exodus, The," in *Anchor Bible Dictionary,* ed. David Noel Freedman, 6 vols. (New York: Doubleday, 1992), 2:703.

6. For details of the various lakes in the eastern Delta, see John R. Huddlestun, "Red Sea," in *Anchor Bible Dictionary,* ed. David Noel Freedman, 6 vols. (New York: Doubleday, 1992), 5: 639.

7. Yet a wider geographical meaning is possible for the Hebrew name, *yam sûp* ("Sea of Reeds") as in 1 Kgs 9:26, where it refers to the Gulf of Aqaba. See Kenneth A. Kitchen, "Red Sea," in *The Illustrated Bible Dictionary,* ed. N. Hillyer, 3 vols. (Wheaton, Ill./Leicester: Tyndale/InterVarsity, 1980), 3:1324.

8. Barry J. Beitzel, *The Moody Atlas of Bible Lands* (Chicago: Moody, 1985), 90–91.

Chapter 7: *Leviticus: Instructions for Holy Living*

1. Helmer Ringgren, *Religions of the Ancient Near East,* trans. John Sturdy (Philadelphia: Westminster, 1973), 161.

2. Ibid., 82; and A. Leo Oppenheim, *Ancient Mesopotamia: Portrait of a Dead Civilization* (Chicago: University of Chicago Press, 1964), 192.

3. R. K. Harrison, *Introduction to the Old Testament* (Grand Rapids: Eerdmans, 1969), 601.

4. Victor P. Hamilton, *Handbook on the Pentateuch: Genesis, Exodus, Leviticus, Numbers, Deuteronomy* (Grand Rapids: Baker, 1982), 246.

5. Gordon J. Wenham, *The Book of Leviticus,* New International Commentary on the Old Testament (Grand Rapids: Eerdmans, 1979), 161.

6. John E. Hartley, *Leviticus,* Word Biblical Commentary 4 (Dallas: Word, 1992), 247–60.

7. John Bright, *The Authority of the Old Testament* (Nashville: Abingdon, 1967), 53–55, 148–49.

8. Christopher J. H. Wright, *God's People in God's Land: Family, Land, and Property in the Old Testament* (Grand Rapids/Exeter, England: Eerdmans/Paternoster, 1990), 260–65.

9. Hartley, *Leviticus,* lxviii–lxix.

Chapter 8: *Numbers: Failure in the Desert*

1. Brevard S. Childs, *Introduction to the Old Testament as Scripture* (Philadelphia: Fortress, 1979), 199.

2. R. K. Harrison, *Introduction to the Old Testament* (Grand Rapids: Eerdmans, 1969), 618–22.

3. Ibid., 621–22.

4. For more on these and additional problems with the numbers, see Timothy R. Ashley, *The Book of Numbers,* New International Commentary on the Old Testament (Grand Rapids: Eerdmans, 1993), 60–61.

5. John Bright, *A History of Israel,* 3rd ed. (Philadelphia: Westminster, 1981), 134.

6. John W. Wenham, "Large Numbers in the Old Testament," *Tyndale Bulletin* 18 (1967): 30–32. On the other hand, perhaps we should view the Old Testament's use of numbers as hyperbole, on which see David M. Fouts, "A Defense of the Hyperbolic Interpretation of Large Numbers in the Old Testament," *JETS* 40 (1997): 377–87.

7. Gordon J. Wenham, *Numbers: An Introduction and Commentary,* Tyndale Old Testament Commentary (Downers Grove/Leicester: InterVarsity, 1981), 126–27.

8. Wenham, *Numbers,* 150.

9. Ibid., 164.

Chapter 9: *Deuteronomy: Restoring the Covenant*

1. The Septuagint incorrectly translated the phrase "copy of this law" in Dt 17:18 as *tò deuteronómion toûto,* "this second law."

2. Duane L. Christensen, *Deuteronomy 1–11,* Word Biblical Commentary 6A (Dallas: Word, 1991), xli.

3. Victor P. Hamilton, *Handbook on the Pentateuch: Genesis, Exodus, Leviticus, Numbers, Deuteronomy* (Grand Rapids: Baker, 1982), 406–8.

4. These words occur in one form or another in 5:29; 6:2, 5, 13, 24; 7:9; 8:6; 10:12, 20; 11:1, 13, 22.

5. In covenant contexts, love always has to do with covenant commitment, or obedience. William L. Moran, "The Ancient Near Eastern Background of the Love of God in Deuteronomy," *Catholic Biblical Quarterly* 25 (1963): 77–87.

6. Stephen A. Kaufman, "The Structure of the Deuteronomic Law," *Maarav* 1, no. 2 (1978–79): 147.

7. For this development of Kaufman's observation, see John H. Walton, "Deuteronomy: An Exposition of the Spirit of the Law," *Grace Theological Journal* 8, no. 2 (1987): 213–25.

8. For the several ways that Dt 27–34 may be outlined, see J. A. Thompson, *Deuteronomy: An Introduction and Commentary,* Tyndale Old Testament Commentary (Downers Grove/ Leicester: InterVarsity, 1974), 14–21.

9. George E. Mendenhall, "Samuel's 'Broken *Rîb*': Deuteronomy 32," in *No Famine in the Land: Studies in Honor of John L. McKenzie,* ed. James W. Flanagan and Anita Weisbrod Robinson (Missoula, Mont.: Scholars, 1975), 64–65.

10. Cecil Frances Alexander, "The Burial of Moses," in *Poems with Power to Strengthen the Soul,* ed. James Mudge (Abingdon, 1907), 36.

11. For this discussion, see George E. Mendenhall, *Law and Covenant in Israel and the Ancient Near East* (Pittsburgh: Biblical Colloquium, 1955), 32–34.

12. Ex 20–25, Dt, and Jos 24. For discussion and introduction to the extensive bibliography on this topic, see John H. Walton, *Ancient Israelite Literature in Its Cultural Context: A Survey of Parallels between Biblical and Ancient Near Eastern Texts* (Grand Rapids: Zondervan, 1989), 95–109.

13. That is, the first nine books of the Hebrew canon, omitting Ruth and counting Samuel and Kings as one book each (Genesis, Exodus, Leviticus, Numbers, Deuteronomy, Joshua, Judges, Samuel, Kings). David Noel Freedman, *The Unity of The Hebrew Bible* (Ann Arbor: University of Michigan Press, 1991), 15.

Chapter 10: *Introduction to the Historical Books: The History of Israel's Nationhood*

1. Talmud, *Baba Bathra* 14b and 15a.

2. Gordon J. Wenham, "History and the Old Testament," in *History, Criticism, and Faith: Four Exploratory Studies,* ed. Colin Brown (Downers Grove/Leicester: InterVarsity, 1976), 13–75; V. Philips Long, *The Art of Biblical History* (Grand Rapids: Zondervan, 1994), 88–119.

3. Elmer A. Martens, "The Oscillating Fortunes of 'History' within Old Testament Theology," in *Faith, Tradition, and History: Old Testament Historiography in Its Near Eastern Context,* ed. A. R. Millard, James K. Hoffmeier, and David W. Baker (Winona Lake, Ind.: Eisenbrauns, 1994), 313–40.

4. The Talmud attributes the authorship of Judges and Samuel to Samuel (*Baba Bathra* 14b).

5. Brevard S. Childs, *Introduction to the Old Testament as Scripture* (Philadelphia: Fortress, 1979), 230–31.

6. Martin Noth, *The Deuteronomistic History,* 2nd ed., Journal for the Study of the Old Testament—Supplement Series 15 (Sheffield: JSOT, 1991). For a convenient summary, see David M. Howard Jr., *An Introduction to the Old Testament Historical Books* (Chicago: Moody, 1993), 179–82.

7. Frank Moore Cross, *Canaanite Myth and Hebrew Epic: Essays in the History of the Religion of Israel* (Cambridge, Mass.: Harvard University Press, 1973), 274–89.

8. Duane L. Christensen, "Deuteronomy in Modern Research: Approaches and Issues," in *A Song of Power and the Power of Song: Essays on the Book of Deuteronomy,* ed. Duane L. Christensen, Sources for Biblical and Theological Study 3 (Winona Lake, Ind.: Eisenbrauns, 1993), 16.

9. Childs, *Introduction,* 231–33.

10. Talmud, *Baba Bathra* 15a.

11. Sara Japhet, *I and II Chronicles: A Commentary,* Old Testament Library (Louisville: Westminster/John Knox, 1993), 3–5; H. G. M. Williamson, *1 and 2 Chronicles,* New Century Bible Commentary (Grand Rapids/London: Eerdmans/Marshall, Morgan & Scott, 1982), 5–11.

12. Talmud, *Baba Bathra,* 14b.

13. Talmud, *Baba Bathra,* 15a; Josephus, *Antiquities,* 6.6.1.

Chapter 11: *Joshua: Conquest and Division*

1. Marten H. Woudstra, *The Book of Joshua,* New International Commentary on the Old Testament (Grand Rapids: Eerdmans, 1981), 5–13, presents a complete summary of authorship and date issues.

2. William F. Albright, "Archaeology and the Date of the Hebrew Conquest of Palestine," *Bulletin of the American Schools of Oriental Research* 58 (1935): 10–18; Kenneth A. Kitchen, *Ancient Orient and Old Testament* (Downers Grove: InterVarsity, 1966), 57–75.

3. See, e.g., Eugene H. Merrill, *Kingdom of Priests: A History of Old Testament Israel* (Grand Rapids: Baker, 1987), 66–75; David M. Howard Jr., *An Introduction to the Old Testament Historical Books* (Chicago: Moody, 1993), 64–65.

4. Caleb's words to Joshua (Jos 14:7, 10) indicate a forty-five-year period between Moses' sending of the spies into Canaan (Nm 13–14) and Caleb's current situation. Israel spent forty years in the wilderness, but one to two of those were at Mount Sinai receiving God's Law (Nm 10:11–12).

Chapter 12: *Judges and Ruth: Israel's Moral Crisis*

1. R. K. Harrison, *Introduction to the Old Testament* (Grand Rapids: Eerdmans, 1969), 680–81.

2. Brevard S. Childs, *Introduction to the Old Testament as Scripture* (Philadelphia: Fortress, 1979), 258–59.

3. Arthur E. Cundall and Leon Morris, *Judges and Ruth: An Introduction and Commentary,* Tyndale Old Testament Commentary (Downers Grove: InterVarsity, 1968), 30.

4. For more on this problem, see Cundall and Morris, *Judges and Ruth,* 30–33.

5. Martin Noth, *The History of Israel,* trans. Stanley Godman, 2nd ed. (New York: Harper & Row, 1960), 85–97; and see David M. Howard Jr., *An*

Introduction to the Old Testament Historical Books (Chicago: Moody, 1993), 108–9.

6. Recently, scholars have questioned whether this is really a case of levirate marriage. Our legal understanding of this passage is far from complete. For discussion of the problems, see Robert L. Hubbard Jr., *The Book of Ruth*, New International Commentary on the Old Testament (Grand Rapids: Eerdmans, 1988), 48–62.

Chapter 13: *1 Samuel: God Grants a King*

1. For a good discussion of these people, see David M. Howard Jr., "The Philistines," in *Peoples of the Old Testament World*, ed. Alfred J. Hoerth, Gerald L. Mattingly, and Edwin M. Yamauchi (Grand Rapids: Baker, 1994), 231–20.

2. Carl Friedrich Keil and Franz Delitzsch, *Commentary on the Old Testament*, 10 vols. (Grand Rapids: Eerdmans, 1978), 3:1. Ralph W. Klein, *1 Samuel*, Word Biblical Commentary 10 (Waco, Tex.: Word, 1983), xxv, suggests some explanations as to why the books are divided the way they are.

3. 1 Chr 6:33–34 establishes the levitical connection.

4. Eugene H. Merrill, *Kingdom of Priests: A History of Old Testament Israel* (Grand Rapids: Baker, 1987), 181.

5. Dt 17:14–20 had anticipated the day a king would rule Israel; see Merrill, *Kingdom of Priests*, 189–90.

6. Leon J. Wood, *Israel's United Monarchy* (Grand Rapids: Baker, 1979), 167; Joyce G. Baldwin, *1 and 2 Samuel: An Introduction and Commentary*, Tyndale Old Testament Commentary (Downers Grove/Leicester: InterVarsity, 1988), 159–60; Ben F. Philbeck Jr., "1–2 Samuel," in *Broadman Bible Commentary*, ed. Clifton J. Allen, 11 vols. (Nashville: Broadman, 1970), 3:81–82.

7. Archaeological evidence shows Beth-shan was an important city long before Bible times; see "Beth-Shean," in *Holman Bible Dictionary*, ed. Trent C. Butler (Nashville: Holman, 1991), 174–75.

Chapter 14: *2 Samuel: David's Reign*

1. For a good suggested chronology of David's reign, see Eugene H. Merrill, *Kingdom of Priests: A History of*

Old Testament Israel (Grand Rapids: Baker, 1987), 243–48.

2. Bill T. Arnold, "The Amalekite's Report of Saul's Death: Political Intrigue or Incompatible Sources?" *Journal of the Evangelical Theological Society* 32 (1989): 289–98.

3. Merrill, *Kingdom of Priests*, 237.

4. Leon J. Wood, *Israel's United Monarchy* (Grand Rapids: Baker, 1979), 229–30, discusses David's potential strategy in such a move; see also Merrill, *Kingdom of Priests*, 234.

5. Many believe Kileab, David's second son (2 Sm 3:3), died in youth, for we hear no more of him as the narrative unfolds.

6. Merrill, *Kingdom of Priests*, 253, suggests the event took place in the mid–990s B.C.

7. Ibid., 254.

Chapter 15: *1 Kings: The Glory of Solomon and the Beginning of the End*

1. Talmud, *Baba Bathra* 15a.

2. John H. Walton, *Ancient Israelite Literature in Its Cultural Context: A Survey of Parallels between Biblical and Ancient Near Eastern Texts* (Grand Rapids: Zondervan, 1989), 119; and Simon J. DeVries, *1 Kings*, Word Biblical Commentary 12 (Waco, Tex.: Word, 1985), xxix-xxxiii.

3. Mordechai Cogan and Hayim Tadmor, *II Kings: A New Translation with Introduction and Commentary*, Anchor Bible 11 (Garden City, N.Y.: Doubleday, 1988), 3.

4. See Donald J. Wiseman, *1 and 2 Kings: An Introduction and Commentary*, Tyndale Old Testament Commentary (Downers Grove/Leicester: InterVarsity, 1993), 40–43.

5. A. R. Millard, "Israelite and Aramean History in the Light of Inscriptions," *Tyndale Bulletin* 41, no. 2 (1990): 261–75.

6. Eugene H. Merrill, *Kingdom of Priests: A History of Old Testament Israel* (Grand Rapids: Baker, 1987), 294.

7. "Man of God" is this author's favorite synonym for "prophet." It stressed the divine authority of the prophet, whose words were known to have been true. This author frequently used it for Elijah and Elisha (Wiseman, *Kings*, 142–43).

8. Herbert Donner, "The Separate States of Israel and Judah," in *Israelite and Judaean History*, ed. John H. Hayes

and J. Maxwell Miller (Philadelphia: Westminster, 1977), 401–5.

9. John Gray, *I & II Kings: A Commentary*, 2nd ed., Old Testament Library (Philadelphia: Westminster, 1970), 395–96.

Chapter 16: *2 Kings: The End of National Israel*

1. Donald J. Wiseman, *1 and 2 Kings: An Introduction and Commentary*, Tyndale Old Testament Commentary (Downers Grove/Leicester: InterVarsity, 1993), 193–94.

2. R. K. Harrison, *Introduction to the Old Testament* (Grand Rapids: Eerdmans, 1969), 727–28.

3. James B. Pritchard, ed., *Ancient Near Eastern Texts Relating to the Old Testament*, 3rd ed. (Princeton, N.J.: Princeton University Press, 1969), 281.

4. Sargon boasts of actually finishing them off and deporting the population (Pritchard, 284).

5. For more, see Wiseman, *Kings*, 18–26; and David M. Howard Jr., *An Introduction to the Old Testament Historical Books* (Chicago: Moody, 1993), 197–203.

6. Brevard S. Childs, *Introduction to the Old Testament as Scripture* (Philadelphia: Fortress, 1979), 291–92.

7. Gerhard von Rad, *Old Testament Theology*, trans. D. M. G. Stalker, 2 vols. (New York: Harper & Row, 1962–1965), 1:340–43.

Chapter 17: *1 and 2 Chronicles: A Look Back*

1. Talmud, *Baba Bathra*, 15a.

2. For summary and review of this traditional position, see J. Barton Payne, "1, 2 Chronicles," in *Expositor's Bible Commentary*, ed. Frank E. Gaebelein, 12 vols. (Grand Rapids: Zondervan, 1979–1992), 4:304–6.

3. David Noel Freedman, "The Chronicler's Purpose," *Catholic Biblical Quarterly* 23 (1961): 436–42; Sara Japhet, "The Supposed Common Authorship of Chronicles and Ezra-Nehemiah Investigated Anew," *Vetus Testamentum* 18 (1968): 330–71, and *I & II Chronicles*, Old Testament Library (Louisville: Westminster/John Knox, 1993), 3–5; Frank Moore Cross, "A Reconstruction of the Judean Restoration," *Journal of Biblical Literature* 94 (1974): 4–18; H. G. M. Williamson, *Israel in the Books of Chronicles* (New York/Cambridge:

Cambridge University Press, 1977), 5–70, and *1 and 2 Chronicles*, New Century Bible Commentary (Grand Rapids/London: Eerdmans/ Marshall, Morgan & Scott, 1982), 5–11.

4. Raymond B. Dillard and Tremper Longman III, *An Introduction to the Old Testament* (Grand Rapids: Zondervan, 1994), 171–72.

5. David M. Howard Jr., *An Introduction to the Old Testament Historical Books* (Chicago: Moody, 1993), 234.

6. Williamson, *1 and 2 Chronicles*, 23.

7. Ibid., 92–95.

8. Ibid., 225–26.

9. This verse is a sort of "charter" for the rest of Israel's history (Raymond B. Dillard, *2 Chronicles*, Word Biblical Commentary 15 [Waco, Tex.: Word, 1987], 77–78).

10. Gerhard von Rad, *Old Testament Theology*, trans. D. M. G. Stalker, 2 vols. (New York: Harper & Row, 1962–1965), 1:349; see also Dillard, *2 Chronicles*, 76–81; Williamson, *1 and 2 Chronicles*, 31–33.

11. Howard, *Introduction*, 256–60.

12. Williamson, *1 and 2 Chronicles*, 132–34.

13. Ibid., 26–27.

14. Roddy Braun, *1 Chronicles*, Word Biblical Commentary 14 (Waco, Tex.: Word, 1986), xxix–xxxi; and Howard, *Introduction*, 261–63.

Chapter 18: *Ezra, Nehemiah, and Esther: A Time to Rebuild*

1. David J. A. Clines, *Ezra, Nehemiah, Esther*, New Century Bible Commentary (Grand Rapids/London: Eerdmans/Marshall, Morgan & Scott, 1984), vii.

2. Bryan E. Beyer, "Zerubbabel," in *Anchor Bible Dictionary*, ed. David Noel Freedman, 6 vols. (New York: Doubleday, 1992), 6:1085; and H. G. M. Williamson, *Ezra, Nehemiah*, Word Biblical Commentary 16 (Waco, Tex.: Word, 1985), 17, 32–33.

3. Williamson, *Ezra, Nehemiah*, 49–50.

4. A literary device known as "repetitive resumption," which returns to the narrative flow broken off by the insertion of a digression, in this case 4:6–23. Williamson, *Ezra, Nehemiah*, 57; and F. Charles Fensham, *The Books of Ezra and Nehemiah*, New International Commentary on the Old

Testament (Grand Rapids: Eerdmans, 1982), 69–70.

5. Clines, *Ezra, Nehemiah, Esther*, 116–18.

6. Williamson, *Ezra, Nehemiah*, 172; and Joseph Blenkinsopp, *Ezra-Nehemiah: A Commentary*, Old Testament Library (Philadelphia: Westminster, 1988), 204–7.

7. Fensham, *Ezra and Nehemiah*, 171–72.

8. Mark A. Throntveit, *Ezra-Nehemiah*, Interpretation (Louisville: Westminster/John Knox, 1992), 92.

9. Sara Japhet, "The Supposed Common Authorship of Chronicles and Ezra-Nehemiah Investigated Anew," *Vetus Testamentum* 18 (1968): 330–71; and Williamson, *Ezra, Nehemiah*, xxxiii–xxxvi. However, this new position is far from universally accepted. See Clines, *Ezra, Nehemiah, Esther*, 9–10; and Fensham, *Ezra and Nehemiah*, 1–4.

10. Williamson, *Ezra, Nehemiah*, xxxv.

11. For summary of the arguments, see Eugene H. Merrill, *Kingdom of Priests: A History of Old Testament Israel* (Grand Rapids: Baker, 1987), 503–6; and David M. Howard Jr., *An Introduction to the Old Testament Historical Books* (Chicago: Moody, 1993), 281–83.

12. H. G. M. Williamson, *Ezra and Nehemiah*, Old Testament Guides (Sheffield: JSOT, 1987), 81.

Chapter 19: *Introduction to the Poetical Books: The Literature of God's People*

1. David L. Petersen and Kent Harold Richards, *Interpreting Hebrew Poetry*, Guides to Biblical Scholarship (Minneapolis: Fortress, 1992), 2–6; R. K. Harrison, "Hebrew Poetry," in *Zondervan Pictorial Encyclopedia of the Bible*, ed. Merrill C. Tenney, 5 vols. (Grand Rapids: Zondervan, 1976), 3:76–87.

2. For a concise summary of the issues, see Harrison, "Hebrew Poetry," 80–81.

3. Robert Alter, *The Art of Biblical Poetry* (New York: Basic, 1985), 3–26; Robert Lowth, *Lectures on the Sacred Poetry of the Hebrews*, trans. G. Gregory (Boston/New York: Crocker & Brewster/J. Leavitt, 1829 [1787]).

4. C. Hassell Bullock, *An Introduction to the Old Testament Poetic

Books*, rev. ed. (Chicago: Moody, 1988), 45–46.

5. Robert L. Alden, *Psalms: Songs of Devotion* (Chicago: Moody, 1974), 24.

6. For a good survey of Ugarit and Ugaritic studies, see Peter C. Craigie, *Ugarit and the Old Testament* (Grand Rapids: Eerdmans, 1983).

Chapter 20: *Job: One Man's Search for Justice*

1. For extensive bibliography and discussion, see John H. Walton, *Ancient Israelite Literature in Its Cultural Context: A Survey of Parallels between Biblical and Ancient Near Eastern Texts* (Grand Rapids: Zondervan, 1989), 169–97.

2. Ibid., 178.

3. W. G. Lambert, *Babylonian Wisdom Literature* (Oxford: Clarendon, 1960), 1.

4. Walton, *Israelite Literature*, 183–85.

5. Lambert, *Babylonian Wisdom Literature*, 21–91.

6. For discussion of the parallels, see Walton, *Israelite Literature*, 175–97.

7. John E. Goldingay and Christopher J. H. Wright, "'Yahweh Our God Yahweh One': The Oneness of God in the Old Testament," in *One God, One Lord: Christianity in a World of Religious Pluralism*, ed. Andrew D. Clark and Bruce W. Winter, 2nd ed. (Grand Rapids/Carlisle, England: Baker/Paternoster, 1992), 44–45.

8. Glendon E. Bryce, *A Legacy of Wisdom: The Egyptian Contribution to the Wisdom of Israel* (Lewisburg, Pa./London: Bucknell University Press/Associated University Presses, 1979).

9. Francis I. Andersen, *Job: An Introduction and Commentary*, Tyndale Old Testament Commentary (Downers Grove/Leicester: InterVarsity, 1976), 64.

10. John E. Hartley, *The Book of Job*, New International Commentary on the Old Testament (Grand Rapids: Eerdmans, 1988), 85.

11. R. K. Harrison, *Introduction to the Old Testament* (Grand Rapids: Eerdmans, 1969), 1027.

12. Hartley, *Job*, 15–20.

13. Andersen, *Job*, 67.

14. Matitiahu Tsevat, "The Meaning of the Book of Job," in *The Meaning of the Book of Job and Other Biblical Studies: Essays on the Literature and Religion of

the Hebrew Bible (New York/Dallas: Ktav/Institute for Jewish Studies, 1980), 36–37.

15. Andersen, *Job*, 71.

Chapter 21: *Psalms: The Songbook of Ancient Israel*

1. Those who believe the term refers to the Korah of Nm 16–17 include Derek Kidner, *Psalms 1–72: An Introduction and Commentary*, Tyndale Old Testament Commentary (Downers Grove: InterVarsity, 1973), 35; other views include Hans-Joachim Kraus, *Psalms 1–59: A Commentary*, trans. Hilton C. Oswald (Minneapolis: Augsburg, 1988), 438–39; and Artur Weiser, *The Psalms: A Commentary*, trans. Herbert Hartwell, Old Testament Library (Philadelphia: Westminster, 1962), 97–98.

2. Kidner, *Psalms*, 4–7; John Durham, "Psalms," in *Broadman Bible Commentary*, ed. Clifton J. Allen, 11 vols. (Nashville: Broadman, 1970), 4:153–54; Carl Friedrich Keil and Franz Delitzsch, *Commentary on the Old Testament*, 10 vols. (Grand Rapids: Eerdmans, 1978), 5:14–19.

3. Kidner, *Psalms*, 36–43; Kraus, *Psalms*, 21–32.

4. Hermann Gunkel, *The Psalms: A Form-Critical Introduction*, trans. Thomas M. Horner (Philadelphia: Fortress, 1967).

5. For a brief overview, see Gene M. Tucker, *Form Criticism of the Old Testament*, Guides to Biblical Scholarship (Philadelphia: Fortress, 1971). The commentary series Forms of the Old Testament Literature (Grand Rapids: Eerdmans) applies this approach to the Old Testament.

Chapter 22: *Proverbs: Advice on Living in God's World*

1. Gordon Fee and Douglas Stuart, *How to Read the Bible for All Its Worth*, rev. ed. (Grand Rapids: Zondervan, 1993), 218.

2. There are five Hebrew verbs in the infinitive, often translated "to" in the older translations. Example, "To know wisdom and instruction; to perceive the words of understanding . . ." (KJV).

3. Derek Kidner, *The Proverbs: An Introduction and Commentary*, Tyndale Old Testament Commentary (Downers Grove/Leicester: InterVarsity, 1964), 59.

4. It is possible to isolate as many as fifteen separate discourses in 1:8–9:18; C. Hassell Bullock, *An Introduction to the Old Testament Poetic Books*, rev. ed. (Chicago: Moody, 1988), 165–71.

5. Duane A. Garrett, *Proverbs, Ecclesiastes, Song of Songs*, New American Commentary 14 (Nashville: Broadman, 1993), 88.

6. Hebrew has only two genders, masculine and feminine (there are no neuters, as in English "it"). Nouns for abstract concepts such as righteousness, love, and law, are feminine. Wisdom is a feminine noun (*ḥokmâ*), so it is personified here as a woman.

7. For classification by topics, see R. B. Y. Scott, *Proverbs, Ecclesiastes: Introduction, Translation, and Notes*, Anchor Bible 18 (Garden City, N.Y.: Doubleday, 1965), 130–31.

8. Robert L. Alden, *Proverbs: A Commentary on an Ancient Book of Timeless Advice* (Grand Rapids: Baker, 1983), 10; and Garrett, *Proverbs*, 46–48.

9. Kidner, *Proverbs*, 23, 149–50.

10. J. Ruffle, "The Teaching of Amenemope and Its Connection with the Book of Proverbs," *Tyndale Bulletin* 28 (1977): 33–34.

11. Garrett, *Proverbs*, 46.

12. Kenneth A. Kitchen, "Proverbs and Wisdom Books of the Ancient Near East: The Factual History of a Literary Form," *Tyndale Bulletin* 28 (1977): 69–114; and Garrett, *Proverbs*, 39–46, 52.

13. Gerhard von Rad, *Wisdom in Israel*, trans. James D. Martin (Valley Forge, Pa.: Trinity Press International, 1993 [1972]), 61–64.

Chapter 23: *Ecclesiastes and Song of Songs: Israelite Faith in Everyday Life*

1. R. K. Harrison, *Introduction to the Old Testament* (Grand Rapids: Eerdmans, 1969), 1072; R. B. Y. Scott, *Proverbs, Ecclesiastes: Introduction, Translation, and Notes*, Anchor Bible 18 (Garden City, N.Y.: Doubleday, 1965), 196.

2. Duane A. Garrett, *Proverbs, Ecclesiastes, Song of Songs*, New American Commentary 14 (Nashville: Broadman, 1993), 282–83.

3. Ibid., 344.

4. It has been suggested the book was originally in Aramaic and later translated, or that it was written under heavy Phoenician-Canaanite

linguistic influences (ibid., 254–55, 258–61; and Scott, *Proverbs, Ecclesiastes*, 192).

5. Daniel C. Fredericks, *Qoheleth's Language: Re-evaluating Its Nature and Date* (Lewiston, N.Y.: Mellen, 1988), see especially 266–78.

6. Garrett believes the book displays a gradual development of Solomon distancing himself from his role as monarch and assuming the mantle of sage. The title "Qohelet" allows him to speak, not as absolute monarch, but as teacher who "has been" king (Garrett, *Proverbs*, 264).

7. Ibid., 374–76; and Othmar Keel, *The Song of Songs: A Continental Commentary*, trans. Frederick J. Gaiser (Minneapolis: Fortress, 1994), 15–17.

8. See Garrett, *Proverbs*, 352–66, for a summary of the approaches.

9. Ibid., 376; and William H. Shea, "The Chiastic Structure of the Song of Songs," *Zeitschrift für die alttestamentliche Wissenschaft* 92 (1980): 378–96.

10. Keel, *Song of Songs*, 17.

11. Ibid., 19.

12. Such pronoun shifting is not uncommon in the Egyptian love songs; see Papyrus Chester Beatty I, group A, no. 32: "He does not know my desires to embrace him. . . . O brother, I am decreed for you by the Golden One, come to me that I may see your beauty!" (Michael V. Fox, *The Song of Songs and the Ancient Egyptian Love Songs* [Madison: University of Wisconsin Press, 1985], 52–53).

13. Tom Gledhill, *The Message of the Song of Songs: The Lyrics of Love*, The Bible Speaks Today (Downers Grove/Leicester: InterVarsity, 1994), 91–92.

14. Ibid., 23

15. C. Hassell Bullock, *An Introduction to the Old Testament Poetic Books*, rev. ed. (Chicago: Moody, 1988), 207; and Raymond B. Dillard and Tremper Longman III, *An Introduction to the Old Testament* (Grand Rapids: Zondervan, 1994), 264–65.

Chapter 24: *Introduction to the Prophets: Voices of God's Servants*

1. For a detailed discussion of the roles of Moses, Samuel, and Elijah in developing the prophetic office, see Willem A. VanGemeren, *Interpreting the Prophetic Word* (Grand Rapids: Zondervan, 1990), 27–40.

2. See e.g. 1 Sm 9:9; Am 7:12, 14.

3. The medieval Jewish scholars Rashi and David Kimchi suggested this in their Hebrew commentaries on Isaiah, but the tradition has no other support.

4. James B. Pritchard, ed., *Ancient Near Eastern Texts Relating to the Old Testament*, 3rd ed. (Princeton, N.J.: Princeton University Press, 1969), 608.

5. For a fuller comparison of biblical and ancient Near Eastern prophetic material, see John H. Walton, *Ancient Israelite Literature in Its Cultural Context: A Survey of Parallels between Biblical and Ancient Near Eastern Texts* (Grand Rapids: Zondervan, 1989), 201–16.

6. The Assyrians, like the Hebrews, were Semites; Gn 10:10–12 places the Assyrians in Abraham's genealogy.

7. For good discussions of the Assyrians, see William C. Gwaltney Jr., "Assyrians," in *Peoples of the Old Testament World*, ed. Alfred J. Hoerth, Gerald L. Mattingly, and Edwin M. Yamauchi (Grand Rapids: Baker, 1994), 77–106; and William W. Hallo, "From Qarqar to Carchemish: Assyria and Israel in the Light of New Discoveries," *Biblical Archaeologist* 23 (1960): 34–61.

8. For further reading on the Babylonians, see Joan Oates, *Babylon*, rev. ed. (London: Thames & Hudson, 1986); and Bill T. Arnold, "Babylonians," in *Peoples of the Old Testament World*, ed. Alfred J. Hoerth, Gerald L. Mattingly, and Edwin M. Yamauchi (Grand Rapids: Baker, 1994), 43–75.

9. For a discussion of the Persians, see Edwin M. Yamauchi, "Persians," in *Peoples of the Old Testament World*, ed. Alfred J. Hoerth, Gerald L. Mattingly, and Edwin M. Yamauchi (Grand Rapids: Baker, 1994), 107–24; or Yamauchi's more thorough treatment, *Persia and the Bible* (Grand Rapids: Baker, 1990).

Chapter 25: *Isaiah 1–39: Prophet of Judah's Royal Court*

1. Alfred Martin and John A. Martin, *Isaiah: The Glory of the Messiah* (Chicago: Moody, 1983), 56–57; Carl Friedrich Keil and Franz Delitzsch, *Commentary on the Old Testament*, 10 vols. (Grand Rapids: Eerdmans, 1978), 7:226–28.

2. John N. Oswalt, *The Book of Isaiah: Chapters 1–39*, New International Commentary on the Old Testament (Grand Rapids: Eerdmans, 1986), 208; Herbert M. Wolf, *Interpreting Isaiah: The Suffering and Glory of the Messiah* (Grand Rapids: Zondervan, 1985), 91–92.

3. Wolf, *Interpreting Isaiah*, 90–92; Ronald F. Youngblood, *The Book of Isaiah: An Introductory Commentary*, 2nd ed. (Grand Rapids: Baker, 1993), 47–49; Oswalt, *Isaiah*, 209–13.

4. Martin and Martin, *Isaiah*, p. 56.

5. J. Gresham Machen, *The Virgin Birth of Christ*, 2nd ed. (New York: Harper, 1932), provides a classic treatment of Christ's birth and its implications.

6. J. Robertson McQuilkin, *Understanding and Applying the Bible*, rev. ed. (Chicago: Moody, 1992), 267–70.

7. James B. Pritchard, ed., *Ancient Near Eastern Texts Relating to the Old Testament*, 3rd ed. (Princeton, N.J.: Princeton University Press, 1969), 287.

8. Oswalt, *Isaiah*, 490–91, provides a brief but thorough discussion of the issue. See also Rv 12:9 and 20:2, where Satan is described as a serpent and a dragon.

9. Oswalt, *Isaiah*, 526.

10. Dennis J. McCarthy, *Treaty and Covenant: A Study in Form in the Ancient Oriental Documents and in the Old Testament*, 2nd ed. (Rome: Biblical Institute Press, 1978), provides a great treatment of the whole issue of covenants in the ancient world.

11. Wolf, *Interpreting Isaiah*, 171; John H. Walton, "New Observations on the Date of Isaiah," *Journal of the Evangelical Theological Society* 28 (1985): 129–32.

12. Oswalt, *Isaiah*, 631, gives a brief summary of the issue; see also Edwin R. Thiele, *The Mysterious Numbers of the Hebrew Kings: A Reconstruction of the Chronology of the Kingdoms of Israel and Judah*, rev. ed. (Grand Rapids: Eerdmans, 1965), 119–23, 132–36, 182–91.

13. Oswalt, *Isaiah*, 674. The matter is related to the discussion of chapters 36–39.

14. "Merodach-baladan," in *Zondervan Pictorial Encyclopedia of the Bible*, ed. Merrill C. Tenney, 5 vols. (Grand Rapids: Zondervan, 1976), 4:191–92.

Chapter 26: *Isaiah 40–66: Great Days Are Coming!*

1. John N. Oswalt, *The Book of Isaiah: Chapters 1–39*, New International Commentary on the Old Testament (Grand Rapids: Eerdmans, 1986), 17–28, provides a detailed summary of the issue.

2. S. R. Driver, *Introduction to the Literature of the Old Testament*, 9th ed. (Edinburgh: T. & T. Clark, 1913), 238–40, provides a summary of critical issues regarding Is 40–66.

3. Claus Westermann, *Isaiah 40–66*, trans. D. M. G. Stalker (London: SCM, 1969), 296.

4. Oswalt, *Isaiah*, 25–28; Herbert M. Wolf, *Interpreting Isaiah: The Suffering and Glory of the Messiah* (Grand Rapids: Zondervan, 1985), 31–36.

Chapter 27: *Jeremiah 1–20: Struggling with God's Call*

1. J. A. Thompson, *The Book of Jeremiah*, New International Commentary on the Old Testament (Grand Rapids: Eerdmans, 1980), 51–52.

2. Thompson, 43; R. K. Harrison, *Jeremiah and Lamentations: An Introduction and Commentary*, Tyndale Old Testament Commentary (Downers Grove: InterVarsity, 1973), 31–32.

3. Harrison, *Jeremiah and Lamentations*, 85; Walter Brueggemann, *To Pluck Up, To Tear Down: A Commentary on the Book of Jeremiah 1–25*, International Theological Commentary (Grand Rapids/Edinburgh: Eerdmans/Handsel, 1988), 74.

4. Harrison, *Jeremiah and Lamentations*, 99; Thompson, *Jeremiah*, 364; Brueggemann, *To Pluck Up*, 121.

Chapter 28: *Jeremiah 21–52 and Lamentations: Dealing with Disaster*

1. J. A. Thompson, *The Book of Jeremiah*, New International Commentary on the Old Testament (Grand Rapids: Eerdmans, 1980), 551; Walter Brueggemann, *To Build, To Plant: A Commentary on Jeremiah 26–52*, International Theological Commentary (Grand Rapids/Edinburgh: Eerdmans/Handsel, 1991), 39. R. K. Harrison, *Jeremiah and Lamentations: An Introduction and Commentary*, Tyndale Old Testament Commentary (Downers Grove: InterVarsity, 1973),

133, and C. Hassell Bullock, *An Introduction to the Old Testament Prophetic Books* (Chicago: Moody, 1986), 213, limit the designation to chapters 30–31.

2. Harrison, *Jeremiah and Lamentations*, 170.

3. Thompson, *Jeremiah*, 696–97.

4. Josephus, *Antiquities* 10.9.7.

5. Scholars disagree over which prophet borrowed from whom. Some even suggest Jeremiah and Obadiah used a common prophetic source.

6. Thompson, *Jeremiah*, 723–24.

7. We should not confuse this Hazor with the Hazor in northern Galilee; Thompson, *Jeremiah*, 726–727.

8. James B. Pritchard, ed., *Ancient Near Eastern Texts Relating to the Old Testament*, 3rd ed. (Princeton, N.J.: Princeton University Press, 1969), 308.

9. See Bullock, *Prophetic Books*, 270–71 and Harrison, *Jeremiah and Lamentations*, 197–98 for a summary of the key issues.

Chapter 29: *Ezekiel 1–24: Rough Days Are Coming!*

1. John B. Taylor, *Ezekiel: An Introduction and Commentary*, Tyndale Old Testament Commentary (Downers Grove: InterVarsity, 1969), 14–16.

2. Walther Eichrodt, *Ezekiel: A Commentary*, trans. Cosslett Quin, Old Testament Library (Philadelphia: Westminster, 1970), 52.

3. Walther Zimmerli, *Ezekiel 1: A Commentary on the Book of the Prophet Ezekiel, Chapters 1–24*, trans. Ronald E. Clements, Hermeneia (Philadelphia: Fortress, 1979), 139.

4. Eichrodt, *Ezekiel*, 84–85; Taylor, *Ezekiel*, 78–81; Charles L. Feinberg, *The Prophecy of Ezekiel: The Glory of the Lord* (Chicago: Moody, 1969), 33–34.

5. Feinberg, *Ezekiel*, 51–52; Taylor, *Ezekiel*, 99.

6. Taylor, *Ezekiel*, 171; Eichrodt, *Ezekiel*, 321–22; Zimmerli, *Ezekiel*, 483–84.

Chapter 30: *Ezekiel 25–48: God's Planning an Exciting Future*

1. Charles L. Feinberg, *The Prophecy of Ezekiel: The Glory of the Lord* (Chicago: Moody, 1969), 161–64.

2. John B. Taylor, *Ezekiel: An Introduction and Commentary*, Tyndale Old Testament Commentary (Downers Grove: InterVarsity, 1969), 199; Feinberg, *Ezekiel*, 168–69.

3. Feinberg, *Ezekiel*, 197; Taylor, *Ezekiel*, 220–21; Walther Eichrodt, *Ezekiel: A Commentary*, trans. Cosslett Quin, Old Testament Library (Philadelphia: Westminster, 1970), 475–79.

4. Eichrodt, *Ezekiel*, 522–23; Taylor, *Ezekiel*, 244; Feinberg, *Ezekiel*, 219–21; Walther Zimmerli, *Ezekiel 2: A Commentary on the Book of the Prophet Ezekiel, Chapters 25–48*, trans. James D. Martin, Hermeneia (Philadelphia: Fortress, 1983), 304–5.

5. Taylor, *Ezekiel*, 242–43.

6. C. Hassell Bullock, *An Introduction to the Old Testament Prophetic Books* (Chicago: Moody, 1986), 248–49; Taylor, *Ezekiel*, 251–54.

7. Feinberg, *Ezekiel*, 233–39.

8. Willem A. Van Gemeren, *Interpreting the Prophetic Word* (Grand Rapids: Zondervan, 1990), 334–38.

9. Taylor, *Ezekiel*, 253–54.

Chapter 31: *Daniel: The Kingdom of God—Now and Forever*

1. For more on what follows here, see John J. Collins, *Daniel: With an Introduction to Apocalyptic Literature*, Forms of the Old Testament Literature 20 (Grand Rapids: Eerdmans, 1984), 1–24. There is no definitive list of the so-called apocalyptic writings. D. S. Russell listed seventeen books that fit this category, ranging from the mid-second century B.C. to the second century A.D., in addition to several more from the Dead Sea Scrolls (*The Method and Message of Jewish Apocalyptic* [Philadelphia: Westminster, 1964], 37–38).

2. Joyce G. Baldwin, *Daniel: An Introduction and Commentary*, Tyndale Old Testament Commentary (Downers Grove: InterVarsity, 1978), 53–59.

3. The approximate dates for the visions are as follows: chapter 7 in 553 B.C.; chapter 8 in 551 B.C.; chapter 9 in 539 B.C.; and chapters 10–12 in 536 B.C. These dates overlap with the events in chapters 1–6, so the book has a literary arrangement (tales and visions) rather than a chronological one.

4. Bill T. Arnold, "Wordplay and Narrative Techniques in Daniel 5 and 6," *Journal of Biblical Literature* 112 (1993): 479–85.

5. John E. Goldingay, *Daniel*, Word Biblical Commentary 30 (Dallas: Word, 1989), 158, and Baldwin, *Daniel*, 59–60.

6. Ernest C. Lucas, "The Origin of Daniel's Four Empires Scheme Re-Examined," *Tyndale Bulletin* 40, no. 2 (1989): 185–202, especially 192–94; Robert J. M. Gurney, "The Four Kingdoms of Daniel 2 and 7," *Themelios* 2, no. 2 (1977): 39–45; and John H. Walton, "Daniel's Four Kingdoms," *Journal of the Evangelical Theological Society* 29 (1986): 25–36.

7. Aramaic is found in Gn 31:47 (two words only), Ezr 4:8–6:18; 7:12–26, Jer 10:11, and Dn 2:4b–7:28.

8. Daniel C. Snell, "Why Is There Aramaic in the Bible?" *Journal for the Study of the Old Tetament* 18 (1980): 32–51.

9. H. L. Ginsberg, "The Composition of the Book of Daniel," *Vetus Testamentum* 4 (1954): 246–75.

10. Bill T. Arnold, "The Use of Aramaic in the Hebrew Bible: Another Look at Bilingualism in Ezra and Daniel," *Journal of Northwest Semitic Languages* 22, no. 2 (1996): 1–16.

11. Lucas, "Four Empires Scheme," 194; Gurney, "Four Kingdoms," 39.

12. Collins, *Daniel*, 92.

13. Robert J. M. Gurney, "The Seventy Weeks of Daniel 9:24–27," *Evangelical Quarterly* 53 (1981): 36.

14. Collins, *Daniel*, 65.

15. Baldwin, *Daniel*, 108–9.

16. Paul-Alain Beaulieu, *The Reign of Nabonidus, King of Babylon, 556–539 B.C.* (New Haven, Conn.: Yale University Press, 1989), 186–88.

17. Raymond P. Dougherty, *Nabonidus and Belshazzar: A Study of the Closing Events of the Neo-Babylonian Empire* (New Haven, Conn.: Yale University Press, 1929), 13.

18. Belshazzar may have been the real power behind the throne throughout Nabonidus's reign (Beaulieu, *Nabonidus*, 90–98).

19. E. J. Young, *The Prophecy of Daniel* (Grand Rapids: Eerdmans, 1949), 115–18.

20. A. R. Millard, "Daniel 1–6 and History," *Evangelical Quarterly* 49 (1977): 71–72.

21. John C. Whitcomb, *Darius the Mede: A Study in Historical Identification* (Grand Rapids: Eerdmans, 1959). For more detail on the discussion that follows, see Edwin M. Yamauchi, *Persia and the Bible* (Grand Rapids: Baker, 1990), 58–59.

22. This view is a slight modification of the "Gubaru" theory;

William H. Shea, "Darius the Mede: An Update," *Andrews University Seminary Studies* 20 (1982): 229–48.

23. Donald J. Wiseman, "Some Historical Problems in the Book of Daniel," in *Notes on Some Problems in the Book of Daniel*, ed. Donald J. Wiseman, et al. (London: Tyndale, 1965), 12–16.

24. David W. Baker, "Further Examples of the Waw Explicativum," *Vetus Testamentum* 30 (1980): 134.

25. For a brief summary, see Gordon J. Wenham, "Daniel: the Basic Issues," *Themelios* 2, no. 2 (1977): 49–52.

26. Ez 14:14, 20, and in mythology from the ancient city of Ugarit.

27. Especially those prophecies dealing with kingdoms (chapters 2, 7, and 8). The prophecies of the seventy weeks (9:24–27) and the king who exalts himself above God (11:36–45) are taken as references to Antiochus only, with no further fulfillment.

28. Joyce G. Baldwin has argued "there is no clear proof of pseudonymity in the Old Testament and much evidence against it" ("Is There Pseudonymity in the Old Testament?" *Themelios* 4, no. 1 [1978]: 12).

29. R. K. Harrison, *Introduction to the Old Testament* (Grand Rapids: Eerdmans, 1969), 1127.

30. There are dissenting voices in the evangelical camp. Goldingay accepts the book as late and pseudonymous (*Daniel*).

Chapter 32: *Hosea, Joel, and Amos: A Call for Repentance and a Promise for Blessing*

1. Judah appears seven times in Hosea (4:15; 5:5, 10; 6:4, 11; 10:11; 12:3).

2. The other references are Gn 38:24; 2 Kgs 9:22; Ez 23:11, 29; Hos 2:2, 4; 4:12; 5:4; Na 3:4 (2X).

3. E. J. Young, *Introduction to the Old Testament* (Grand Rapids: Eerdmans, 1949), 245–46, suggests the marriage and birth of the children were only symbolic and never really happened, but the text really gives no indication that we should understand it in this way.

4. How Gomer lost her freedom is not known. Some scholars have suggested that the woman Hosea bought in 3:1–5 was another woman, since the text does not specifically name her.

However, for Hosea to marry another woman would ruin the analogy; God was not going to marry another nation, but restore Israel.

5. According to the Law of Moses, the priests received a portion of most sacrifices to keep for themselves (Lv 6:14–7:38). The priests were apparently more concerned about their own stomachs than about the people's spiritual condition!

6. The Law of Moses said not to muzzle the ox while he was threshing; that way, the animal could share in the harvest (Dt 25:4).

7. For a complete discussion of this issue, see Leslie C. Allen, *The Books of Joel, Obadiah, Jonah and Micah*, New International Commentary on the Old Testament (Grand Rapids: Eerdmans, 1976), 19–25.

8. For an interesting discussion of this procedure and more details about the sycamore tree, see W. E. Shewell-Cooper, *Plants, Flowers and Herbs of the Bible* (New Canaan, Conn.: Keats, 1977), 156–57.

9. See the background section on Hosea for further information.

10. Edwin R. Thiele, *The Mysterious Numbers of the Hebrew Kings*, 3rd ed. (Grand Rapids: Zondervan, 1983), 107, 111, 119–20.

11. Hans Walter Wolff, *Joel and Amos: A Commentary on the Books of the Prophets Joel and Amos*, ed. S. Dean McBride Jr., trans. Waldemar Janzen, S. Dean McBride Jr., and Charles A. Muenchow, Hermenia (Philadelphia: Fortress, 1977), 124, appeals to archaeological evidence from Hazor to suggest a date of 760 B.C. This earthquake must have been quite serious; Zec 14:5 also mentions it.

12. This Hebrew expression "to take up a lament" also occurs in Jeremiah and Ezekiel (Jer 7:29; 9:10; Ez 19:1; 26:17; 27:2, 32; 28:12; 32:2).

13. Jeroboam I (931–909 B.C.) established the worship centers at Dan and Bethel (1 Kgs 12:25–29), and the people were still using them in Amos's day. Some Israelites also went to Beersheba in Judah, apparently because of its connections with Isaac (Gn 26:23–35; Am 7:9, 16).

Chapter 33: *Obadiah, Jonah, Micah, Nahum, Habakkuk, and Zephaniah: God's Plan for the Nations*

1. Jeffrey J. Niehaus, "Obadiah," in *The Minor Prophets: An Exegetical and Expository Commentary*, ed. Thomas E. McComiskey, 3 vols. (Grand Rapids: Baker, 1992–1998), 2:496–502; Carl Friedrich Keil and Franz Delitzsch, *Commentary on the Old Testament*, 10 vols. (Grand Rapids: Eerdmans, 1978), 10:339–49.

2. Robert B. Chisholm, *Interpreting the Minor Prophets* (Grand Rapids: Zondervan, 1990), 109–10; C. Hassell Bullock, *An Introduction to the Old Testament Prophetic Books* (Chicago: Moody, 1986); Carl E. Armerding, "Obadiah," in *Expositor's Bible Commentary*, ed. Frank E. Gaebelein, 12 vols. (Grand Rapids: Zondervan, 1979–1992), 7:337.

3. For an excellent discussion of the evidence for dating the Book of Jonah, see John H. Walton in Bryan E. Beyer and John H. Walton, *Obadiah and Jonah*, Bible Study Commentary (Grand Rapids: Zondervan, 1988), 65–72. Walton rightly points out that even if scholars could prove Jonah was written centuries later, that would not rule out the historical accuracy of the book.

4. The title "king of Nineveh" is somewhat strange here, since Nineveh was not the capital of Assyria at that time. Perhaps the title refers to a local governor of Nineveh.

5. Edwin R. Thiele, *The Mysterious Numbers of the Hebrew Kings*, 3rd ed. (Grand Rapids: Zondervan, 1983), 217.

6. Bullock, *Prophetic Books*, 216, and Tremper Longman III, "Nahum," in *The Minor Prophets: An Exegetical and Expository Commentary*, ed. Thomas E. McComiskey, 3 vols. (Grand Rapids: Baker, 1992–1998), 2:765–66, provide good summaries of the issue.

7. Armerding, "Obadiah," 493; Bullock, *Prophetic Books*, 181–83; J. J. M. Roberts, *Nahum, Habakkuk, and Zephaniah*, Old Testament Library (Louisville: Westminster/John Knox, 1991), 82–84.

8. Keil and Delitzsch, *Commentary*, 117; Chisholm, *Interpreting*, 201.

9. Chisholm, *Interpreting*, 201; Bullock, *Prophetic Books*, 168–69.

Chapter 34: *Haggai, Zechariah, and Malachi: Rebuilding a People*

1. Joyce G. Baldwin, *Haggai, Zechariah, Malachi: An Introduction and Commentary,* Tyndale Old Testament Commentary (Downers Grove: InterVarsity, 1972), 29; Robert L. Alden, "Haggai," in *Expositor's Bible Commentary,* ed. Frank E. Gaebelein, 12 vols. (Grand Rapids: Zondervan, 1979–1992), 7:572.

2. We could translate 2:9 either as "The glory of this latter house" (NIV) or "The latter glory of this house" (NASV). However, the second interpretation fits the context better.

3. Kenneth L. Barker, "Zechariah," in *Expositor's Bible Commentary,* ed. Frank E. Gaebelein, 12 vols. (Grand Rapids: Zondervan, 1979–1992), 7:596–97, summarizes the relevant issues, as does C. Hassell Bullock, *An Introduction to the Old Testament Prophetic Books* (Chicago: Moody, 1986), 314–17.

4. Baldwin, *Haggai, Zechariah, Malachi,* 211–12; Alden, "Haggai," 702–03; Walter C. Kaiser Jr. *Malachi: God's Unchanging Love* (Grand Rapids: Baker, 1984), 13–15.

5. Baldwin, *Haggai, Zechariah, Malachi,* 213; Bullock, *Prophetic Books,* 338–39. Kaiser, *Malachi,* 17, and Robert B. Chisholm, *Interpreting the Minor Prophets* (Grand Rapids: Zondervan, 1990), 278, place Malachi at 433 B.C. and 450 B.C., respectively.

Epilogue

1. John Bright, *A History of Israel,* 3rd ed. (Philadelphia: Westminster, 1981), 460.

2. There were dissenting voices as early as the second century A.D., but they were consistently silenced by the church. See Walter C. Kaiser Jr., *Toward Rediscovering the Old Testament* (Grand Rapids: Zondervan, 1987), 19–22.

3. Roger Nicole, "Old Testament Quotations in the New Testament," in Bernard L. Ramm, et al., *Hermeneutics* (Grand Rapids: Baker, 1971), 41–42.

Subject Index

Scripture Index

Name Index

Aaron, 97, 104, 119, 128, 130, 132, 134, 137, 177, 178, 266, 304
Abdon, 184
Abednego, 430, 431
Abel, 79
Abiathar, 384
Abigail, 204
Abihu, 130
Abijah, 223, 228, 230, 256, 259
Abimelech, 91, 183
Abiram, 134
Abishai, 204
Abishalom, 223
Abner, 212, 218, 219
Abraham/Abram, 45, 47, 65, 86, 92, 177, 178, 272, 362, 400, 412
  call of, 67, 68
  covenant with, 98, 99, 100, 107, 112, 114-15, 148, 168, 170, 226, 272, 340
  faith of, 32, 65, 66, 90, 92-97, 428, 436
Absalom, 210, 217-18, 219, 225, 304, 305, 311
Achan, 173, 182
Adam, 64, 67, 79, 80, 81, 82, 83, 84, 256
Adonijah, 225, 253
Agur, 316, 319, 321, 322
Ahab, 52, 222, 230-35, 238, 242, 240, 268, 340, 341, 346, 348, 455
Ahasuerus/Xerxes I, 272-74, 276, 349, 352
Ahaz, 222, 230, 242, 243, 244, 256, 355, 358, 360, 362, 366, 455
Ahaziah, 230, 238, 239, 256
Ahijah, 228, 346
Ahiqar, 315
Ahithophel, 218
Akhenaten. *See* Amenhotep IV.
Alexander the Great, 56–57, 349, 352, 418
Allis, Oswald, 70, 72
Amaziah, 230
Amenemope, 291, 292, 319, 320
Amenhotep
  II, 48
  IV/Akhenaten, 48, 57
Amittai, 453
Amnon, 210, 213, 217, 218, 219, 225
Amon, 230, 238, 244, 245
Amos, 53, 241, 342, 349, 350, 440, 444-49

Amoz, 355
Antiochus IV Epiphanes, 431, 436
Anu, 402
Ariel, Jerusalem as, 354, 364
Arinna, 149
Artaxerxes I, 269, 271, 349, 352
Asa, 223, 228, 230, 256, 257
Asaph, 304, 308, 311
Ashlakka, 94
Ashurbanipal, 54, 57
Ashurnirari V, 94
Astruc Jean, 71, 72
Astyages, 349, 351
Aten, 48
Athaliah, 230, 240, 256
Azariah. See Uzziah.
Azazel, 122
Baanah, 212
Baasha, 223, 228, 230
Balaam, 128, 136, 137
Balak, 136
Ballah, 108
Barak, 182
Barth, Karl, 24
Baruch, 347, 385, 398-99
Bathsheba, 210, 211, 216, 218, 219, 253, 304, 308
Beeri, 440
Belshazzar, 430, 432, 435, 437
Ben-Hadad II, 228, 232, 348
Bezalel, 104
Bildad, 294-96, 300
Boaz, 187-92
Brunner, Emil, 24
Cain, 79, 84
Caleb, 132, 168, 169, 176, 177
Cambyses, 268, 349, 352
Chemosh, 232, 400
Childs, Brevard, 128, 136
Christ. *See* Jesus Christ.
Cross, Frank Moore, 162, 164
Cyrus, 57, 257, 356, 371-73, 380
  defeat of Babylon, 46, 56–58, 265, 351, 362, 402, 435, 464
  reconstruction of temple, 265, 266, 351-52
  restoration of Israel, 56–58, 224, 234, 254, 258, 265, 274
Dagon, 199
Daniel, 269, 350, 351, 412, 429-35, 436

Darius
  I/Darius the Mede, 349, 351, 352, 430, 435, 436, 437, 464, 471
  III, 352
Dathan, 134
David, 50, 228, 242, 247, 260, 342
  conquests of, 169, 210-14, 340
  covenant with, 94, 97, 226, 252, 255, 257, 258-59, 358, 367, 386, 455
  kingdom of, 46, 52, 158, 185, 197, 200-06, 215, 218-20, 254, 423, 440, 445
  line of, 56, 192, 225, 246, 256, 326, 330, 357, 360, 396-98, 449, 465, 467, 472, 475-76
  psalms of, 30, 304, 305, 307-12
  sin of, 162, 216-17, 253, 308
De Wette, W. M. L., 71, 72
Deborah, 184
Delitzsch, Franz, 71, 72
Dinah, 91
Driver, S. R., 71, 72
Duppi-Tessub, 149
Ebal, 153, 161, 176
Ehud, 184
El, 285
Eleazar, 178
Eli, 196, 198, 199, 200, 384
Eliakim, 362-63
Eliezer of Damascus, 93, 96, 177
Elihu, 296-97
Elijah, 162, 231-34, 237-39, 242, 247, 341, 346, 473
Elimelech, 186
Eliphaz, 294-96
Elisha, 231, 232, 237, 239-41, 249, 346
Elkanah, 198
Elkosh, 456
Elon, 184
Enlil, 402
Enoch, 239, 428, 436
Esarhaddon, 54, 57
Esau, 47, 91, 97, 340, 400, 470
Esther, 158, 159, 269, 272–75, 277
Eve, 64, 67, 79, 80, 81, 82, 83, 84
Evil-merodach, 402
Ewald, H., 71, 72
Ezekiel, 55, 350, 351, 408-25
Ezra, 58, 94, 274, 352, 428, 436, 470, 471
  temple restoration, 46, 264–66, 267, 424
  writings of, 71, 161, 252, 263, 270–71
Gedaliah, 246, 399, 467
Gibil, 402
Gideon, 184, 186
Gilgamesh, 334
Gilimninu, 95
Gog/Magog, 421, 424